University of London Historical Studies

II

THEOBALD, ARCHBISHOP
OF CANTERBURY

CHARTER 31
with the seals of Archbishop Theobald
and of Christ Church

Theobald
Archbishop of Canterbury

by
AVROM SALTMAN

UNIVERSITY OF LONDON
THE ATHLONE PRESS
1956

Published by
THE ATHLONE PRESS
UNIVERSITY OF LONDON
at 2 Gower Street, London, W.C.1

Distributed by Constable & Co. Ltd.
12 Orange Street, London W.C.2

U.S.A.
John de Graff Inc.
64 West 23rd Street,
New York, 10

Printed in Great Britain by
WESTERN PRINTING SERVICES LTD.
BRISTOL

To
My Father and Mother

PREFACE

THERE was no medieval biography of Theobald. Gervase of
Canterbury put together a few excerpts from his chronicle and
a similar, most unsatisfactory *Compendium* was made at Bec,
where Theobald spent most of his life. Within the last hundred
years, Dean Hook wrote a life of Theobald which appears in his
Lives of the Archbishops of Canterbury, and the Rev. W. Hunt compiled the article on Theobald in the *Dictionary of National Biography*. This is the first attempt, however imperfect, to write a
full-scale life of Theobald.

The printed sources are reasonably accessible in the main;
the vast majority are to be found amongst the volumes of the
Rolls Series and Migne's *Patrologia Latina*. In addition should be
mentioned W. Holtzmann's *Papsturkunden in England* and R. L.
Poole's edition of the *Historia Pontificalis*. An unprinted Ph.D.
thesis of London University (1939) by W. J. Millor gives a critical edition of John of Salisbury's letters, and has been used in con-
junction with volume 199 of Migne's *Patrologia*, the most accessible printed text. For the narrative part, the chronicles and his-
tories, although generally exiguous at this period, have provided
the necessary framework, but they are supplemented by information derived from the letters and charters of Theobald and
his contemporaries. Of the three-hundred-odd charters collected
here, about half have been printed in scattered editions, but in
nearly every case the manuscripts have been consulted and the
text is mine.

From the biographical point of view, Theobald is not without
interest as an example of remarkable tenacity and honesty which
gained him the respect of unbiassed contemporaries. Devoid of
the more flashy and sensational attributes, he soon became one
of the three ciphers between Anselm and Becket. In recent years

there has been a marked reaction in his favour. Z. N. Brooke pointed the way, and now Professor C. R. Cheney in his *English Bishops' Chanceries* devotes a good deal of attention to those aspects of his activities which find favour in the eyes of present-day scholars. It is thus as a hard-working administrator that Theobald will probably be characterised in the text-books yet to appear, but at the same time his sterling moral qualities should not be forgotten. As a faithful servant of pope and king, Theobald often found himself in an impossible position, yet at all times did his best to carry the insuperable burden of a dual loyalty. Whether he or his successor followed the right road is perhaps beyond human judgment, but all will accept the verdict ensconced within the dry formula of the Inspeximus: 'Theobald of good memory, archbishop of Canterbury'.

This book is substantially the thesis approved by the University of London for the award of the degree of Ph.D. in 1951, the preparation of which was materially assisted by the tenure of a Fellowship of the Institute of Historical Research and a grant for a short visit to Paris from the Central Research Fund of the University of London. Publication has been assisted by a grant from Birkbeck College.

I wish also to express my sincere thanks for the unstinting help and kindness I have constantly received from Professor R. R. Darlington, head of the Department of History at Birkbeck College. Sir Frank Stenton's kind encouragement has been deeply appreciated, and I am grateful to Professor J. G. Edwards for many helpful suggestions. To Professor H. A. Cronne I owe much gratitude for introducing me to the subject.

Thanks are also due to Mr. C. N. L. Brooke, Professor C. R. Cheney, Miss C. M. Collins, and Miss K. Major for drawing my attention to charters of Theobald which would otherwise have remained unknown to me. The co-operation and patience of librarians and archivists have made the task of collecting the charters of Theobald a pleasant one. In particular, I should like to thank Mr. W. G. Urry of Canterbury and Miss I. J. Churchill of Lambeth. The late Mr. W. T. Mellows of Peterborough kindly made available to me his photostat copy of the Swaffham Cartulary, and Mr. W. D. Peckham and Miss K. Major lent me photostat copies of Chichester and Maidstone documents respectively. I am greatly indebted to the officials of the Athlone Press, for helpful suggestions during proof-reading and in the preparation of the Index.

A.S.

Birkbeck College
   London
      22 May 1955

CONTENTS

LIST OF ABBREVIATIONS

Adams	G. B. Adams, *Political History of England*, ii (1905).
Anglia Sacra	*Anglia Sacra*, ed. H. Wharton (1691).
Ann. Mon.	*Annales Monastici*, ed. H. R. Luard (R.S., 1864–9).
Arch. Cant.	*Archaeologia Cantiana.*
Arnulf	*Letters of Arnulf of Lisieux*, ed. F. Barlow (Camden Series, 1939).
Bibl. Nat.	Bibliothèque Nationale.
B.M.	British Museum.
Bouquet	M. Bouquet, *Recueil des Historiens des Gaules et de la France*, ed. L. Delisle (1868–1904).
Brooke	Z. N. Brooke, *The English Church and the Papacy* (1931).
C.A.	Cartae Antiquae.
C.D.F.	J. H. Round, *Calendar of Documents preserved in France* (R.S., 1899).
Chron. Evesham	*Chronicon de Evesham*, ed. W. D. Macray (R.S., 1863).
Compendium	*Compendium Vitae Theobaldi* (*P.L.*, 150, 1854).
D. and C.	Dean and Chapter.
Diceto	Ralph de Diceto, *Opera Historica*, ed. W. Stubbs (R.S., 1876).
D.N.B.	*Dictionary of National Biography.*
Eadmer	Eadmer, *Historia Novorum*, ed. M. Rule (R.S., 1884).
E.H.R.	*English Historical Review.*
Elmham	Thomas of Elmham, *History of St. Augustine's*, ed. C. Hardwick (R.S., 1858).
E.Y.C.	*Early Yorkshire Charters*, ed. W. Farrer and C. T. Clay (1914–).
Foedera	T. Rymer, *Foedera* (1816).
Foreville	R. Foreville, *L'Eglise et la Royauté en Angleterre sous Henri II* (1942).
Gerv.	*The Historical Works of Gervase of Canterbury*, ed. W. Stubbs (R.S., 1879–80).
Gesta	*Gesta Stephani*, ed. R. Howlett (*Chronicles of the Reigns of Stephen, etc.*, iii, R.S., 1886).

Haddan and Stubbs	*Councils and Ecclesiastical Documents relating to Great Britain and Ireland*, ed. A. W. Haddan and W. Stubbs (vol. i, 1869).
Haines	C. R. Haines, *Dover Priory* (1930).
Hist. Pont.	John of Salisbury, *Historia Pontificalis*, ed. R. L. Poole (1927).
H.M.C.	Historical Manuscripts Commission.
Holtzmann	W. Holtzmann, *Papsturkunden in England*, 3 vols. (1930–53).
Hook	W. F. Hook, *Lives of the Archbishops of Canterbury* (1860–76).
Hunt.	Henry of Huntingdon, *Historia Anglorum*, ed. T. Arnold (R.S., 1879).
Jaffé	*Regesta Pontificum Romanorum ad annum 1198*, ed. P. Jaffé (2nd edn. by W. Wattenbach, 1885–8).
John Hex.	John of Hexham, *Historia Johannis prioris Hagustaldensis ecclesiae xxv annorum*, ed. T. Arnold (*Symeonis monachi opera*, ii, R.S., 1885).
K.R.	King's Remembrancer.
Knowles	M. D. Knowles, *The Monastic Order in England* (1945).
Malm.	William of Malmesbury, *De Gestis Regum*, ed. W. Stubbs (R.S., 1887–9).
Mansi	*Sacrorum Conciliorum . . . collectio*, ed. J. D. Mansi (1759–98).
Materials	*Materials for the History of Thomas Becket*, ed. J. C. Robertson (R.S., 1875–85).
Monasticon	W. Dugdale, *Monasticon Anglicanum* (ed. J. Caley, etc., 1817–30).
Newb.	William of Newburgh, *Historia Rerum Anglicarum*, ed. R. Howlett (*Chronicles of the Reigns of Stephen, etc.*, i, R.S., 1884–5).
O.A.	Office of Augmentations.
P.L.	*Patrologia Latina*, ed. J. P. Migne (1844–64).
Porée	E. Porée, *Histoire de l'Abbaye du Bec* (1913).
P.R.O.	Public Record Office.
Reg. Malm.	*Registrum Malmesburiense*, ed. J. S. Brewer (R.S., 1879–80).
Reg. Roff.	*Registrum Roffense*, ed. J. Thorpe (1769).
Ric. Hex.	Richard of Hexham, *Historia de gestis regis Stephani*, ed. R. Howlett (*Chronicles of the Reigns of Stephen, etc.*, iii, R.S., 1886).

R.S.   Rolls Series.

Sarum   *Sarum Charters and Documents*, ed. W. D. Macray (R.S., 1891).

Stubbs   W. Stubbs, *Registrum Sacrum Anglicanum* (1897).

Thorne   William Thorne, *Chronica de rebus gestis Abbatum S. Augustini Cantuariae*, ed. R. Twysden (Scriptores Decem 1652).

Tor.   *The Chronicle of Robert of Torigni*, ed. R. Howlett (*Chronicles of the Reigns of Stephen, etc.*, iv, R.S., 1889).

T.R.   Treasury of Receipt.

V.C.H.   *Victoria County History.*

PART I

I

Theobald, Monk and Archbishop

1. From Bec to Canterbury

THE date of Theobald's birth is unknown. Contemporary writers indicate that he was an old man when he died in 1161.[1] The son of a knight, he was born near Thierceville in Normandy, about three miles north of Bec Abbey.[2] Other members of his family included his brother Walter, in turn archdeacon of Canterbury and bishop of Rochester, and several nephews.[3]

Theobald became a monk at Bec under its third abbot, William (1093–1124).[4] These are very wide limits for his entry into monastic life. Of the 346 monks who were admitted under Abbot William, Theobald was the 266th.[5] If the entries were regular, the year of his admission would be 1117. This date, however, seems to be rather late.

After William's death Prior Boso was elected abbot and three or four years later Theobald became prior.[6] It is not known what offices he had previously filled. Boso's health was poor[7] and it is probable that increasing responsibilities devolved upon Theobald. At any rate when Boso died in June 1136 it seemed almost natural that Theobald should succeed him, for the monks elected him speedily and unanimously to fill the vacant headship.

The election of an abbot of such an important monastery as Bec was of great interest to the duke of Normandy and the archbishop of Rouen. In the past the archbishop had been overshadowed by the power of the duke and had to acquiesce in the

---

[1] E.g. Annals of Winchester (*Ann. Mon.*, ii, 56), 'senex et plenus dierum'.
[2] *Materials*, i, 408; iii, 15. [3] See below, Charter No. 255 witnesses.
[4] *Compendium;* Porée, i, 279. [5] Porée, i, 629 (from the Vatican Library).
[6] *Compendium.* [7] Porée, i, 297.

choice of the monks of Bec as ratified by him. Under King Stephen the ducal power was feeble, and Archbishop Hugh thought to take a leading part in the election. His chagrin was great when he discovered that the monks had already accomplished the election without even notifying him of their intentions. On the other hand, it is possible that Hugh, a loyal adherent of Stephen, was maintaining the ducal interest in the election of so important a tenant-in-chief. Because he had not been consulted, the archbishop threatened to nullify the election. Audoen, bishop of Evreux, the brother of Thurstan, archbishop of York, intervened on Theobald's behalf, and Hugh, realising that his action was unprecedented in the relationship between Rouen and Bec, consented to ratify the election. [1]

An abbot-elect, as a rule, could not fulfil his functions until he had been blessed by the bishop of his diocese. [2] Just as the bishop-elect had to make a profession of canonical obedience to his metropolitan before consecration, the abbot-elect, unless exempt, had to make a profession of obedience to his ordinary before benediction. Hugh of Rouen demanded a written profession from Theobald before he would undertake the ceremony. Theobald refused and the deadlock lasted fourteen months.

To understand the motives behind this second dispute, it is necessary to examine the circumstances surrounding the election and benediction of each of the four preceding abbots of Bec. They were Herluin, St. Anselm, William and Boso. This appears to be what the monks of Bec did in 1137. Mabillon prints a document which deals exactly with these points down to the death of Boso. There is no indication of the authorship—it is based on the contemporary lives of the first four abbots by the two Crispins— but it seems to have been written for the purposes of this conflict, perhaps by order of Theobald. Had it been written at a later date, there seems no reason why Theobald's not unsuccessful conflict with Hugh should not have been included. [3] The following is a summary of the tract.

The see of Rouen was vacant when both Herluin and Anselm

---

[1] *Compendium.*   [2] Cf. *Elmham*, p. 401 (bull of Eugenius III).
[3] Mabillon, *Annales Ordinis Sancti Benedicti* (Lucca edn.), v, 601. The MS. (Bibl. Nat. Latin 2342) is written in a mid-twelfth-century hand.

became abbots of Bec. This necessitated benediction by bishops of other sees to whom it was not customary to make profession. The question of a profession to the see of Rouen and to its future archbishop was not apparently raised and is certainly not mentioned. When Anselm became archbishop of Canterbury he nominated his successor William by agreement with Robert, then duke of Normandy. Robert himself frustrated an attempt by the archbishop of Rouen to secure a profession of obedience from William during the ceremony of benediction. Although Henry I forbade the exaction of a profession at the next vacancy, Boso was prepared, entirely out of grace, to make a kind of verbal submission. In answer to the question 'Do you wish to be subject and obedient to this church of Rouen and to those who are at its head?' he replied 'I wish', but was careful not to say 'I profess'.[1]

The tract closes with a lengthy eulogy of the late Boso, another indication that his death was recent. Relations with the duke were also touched upon. Herluin and Anselm did no homage. Boso resisted the formidable Henry I, and he too succeeded in avoiding doing homage. In dealing with the lesser nobility, however, reliance was put on the ducal overlordship. The count of Meulan was told by Anselm that the abbey belonged to the duke of Normandy.[2] The question came before Duke Robert who confirmed Anselm's standpoint. There is no mention of any papal sovereignty or privileges, nor are any charters adduced in support.

The case against Archbishop Hugh was strong although somewhat fortuitous in the beginning. The intervention of Peter, abbot of Cluny, brought about a compromise and Theobald was allowed to make a verbal profession. After this it is said the two men became close friends.[3] Was this a real compromise or merely a device to save Theobald's face? For an upright man, as Theobald proved to be, a verbal profession would be no less valid than if it were written down, and in any case there were numerous witnesses. It may be suggested, however, that Theobald was acting with an eye to the future. His successors might not feel themselves bound by a personal and verbal agreement, nor could they be confronted with a document. In that sense his

[1] Cf. *P.L.*, 150, col. 729.   [2] Porée, i, 194.   [3] *Compendium.*

position was little worse than Boso's. Possible effects of Theobald's verbal profession must remain in the region of surmise, as no further reference is found during the remainder of the twelfth century to what had been a live issue ever since 1093.

This apparent absence of disputes where one would have expected them, compels a recognition of what lies behind a profession of canonical obedience. If the relations between a monastery and its diocesan bishop were undefined, it constituted a real measure of subjection. Bec was not in this defenceless position. A letter from William, archbishop of Rouen, to Anselm, written about 1092, sets forward an agreement about these questions.[1] The abbey was declared free from episcopal control with a few exceptions. Thus the question of profession would seem to be of prestige value. That Archbishop Hugh had failed hitherto to confirm these concessions, might have caused uneasiness to Theobald, but he did so in 1141.[2] Theobald and Hugh were representatives of opposing principles and when the former became archbishop, he took up exactly the same attitude towards monastic claims as did Hugh. The office was important: the man counted for little.[3]

After these early struggles the short period of Theobald's undisputed rule at Bec is of little interest. Of the thirty months from the death of Boso to Theobald's election to Canterbury, a considerable part must have been occupied by these disputes. Towards the end of his administration he went to England on some business in connection with the extensive properties owned by his monastery there.[4] Forty-seven new monks were admitted into Bec by Theobald.[5] Nothing else is known of his short administration at Bec and none of his charters from this period would appear to have survived. Nor is he mentioned in the charters of the numerous contemporary benefactors of Bec.

How far did life at Bec fit him for the position of archbishop of Canterbury during an unusually critical period, under the weakest and strongest of England's twelfth-century kings? No biographer of Theobald has denied that he faced his difficulties

[1] *Gallia Christiana*, xi, Instruments, col. 17.
[2] Porée, i, 323. There are also confirmations by Alexander III (1171) and Celestine III (1196).   [3] Cf. Brooke, pp. 192 ff.
[4] MS. Bibl. Nat. Latin 12884, f.194b (Chron. of Bec).   [5] Ibid., f.194a.

during the twenty-two years of his primacy with considerable skill. While his years at Bec may have been filled with study, his offices must have involved him in considerable administrative and judicial business in view of the wide-flung possessions of the abbey in England and France, apart from such leading cases as the disputes with Rouen. On the secular side Henry I had, in 1134, given the abbey judicial immunity and jurisdiction over all the pleas of the Crown in the parish of Bec except rape. Theobald must have been concerned in the working out of these new relationships.[1]

The library at Bec was adequate to meet demands of this nature. Although the great age of Lanfranc and Anselm had passed, their pupils such as Boso remained to give instruction, and of course the books were still there. On the legal side there were books entitled *Decreta Pontificum, Canones, Excerpta Decretorum, Corpus Canonum, Collectiones Burcardi Wormatiensis Episcopi* and *Abbreviatio Totius Corporis Canonum*.[2] Theologians included Tertullian, Jerome, Origen, Ambrose, Augustine, Gregory, Isidore, Bede, Alcuin, Rabanus Maurus and their own Anselm. Of the historians they possessed Josephus and Orosius. Secular works were also prominent, including Macrobius, Martianus Capella, and the more classical Cicero, Ovid, Seneca, Suetonius and Quintilian.[3]

As prior and abbot, Theobald must have come into contact with the great men and women of the day. Peter the Venerable has already been mentioned. Stephen was in Normandy in 1137 but Orderic, who gives the fullest account of his visit, does not mention him in connection with Bec. On the other hand the Empress Matilda was a generous benefactress and had expressed a wish to be buried at Bec.[4]

With all this taken into consideration, the election of Theobald to fill the vacant see of Canterbury has a flavour of the mysterious which cannot easily, if at all, be explained. 'There was evidently, in the whole of these transactions,' remarked Dean Hook, 'an amount of intrigue which, with our present sources of information, we are unable to penetrate.'[5] The brief

---

[1] *C.D.F.*, no. 375. [2] Cf. Brooke, pp. 57–8. [3] *P.L.*, 150, col. 771.
[4] William of Jumièges in *P.L.*, 149, col. 897. [5] Hook, ii, 330.

and contradictory statements of the chroniclers certainly leave this impression. Shortly after the unlamented[1] death of Archbishop William in November 1136, it is said that the powerful bishop of Winchester, Henry, the king's brother, was elected to succeed him.[2] Knowing that papal permission was required for his translation, he crossed over to Normandy where he wintered and applied to Innocent II, then in Italy. Orderic does not mention the result of this alleged application and notes the election and consecration of Theobald two years later without further comment.[3] It is difficult to assess the value of this uncorroborated evidence. Furthermore, if the pope rejected Henry, as must be presumed from Orderic, his open anger at the election of Theobald[4] would have been rather belated. Nevertheless, the statement of Orderic cannot be ignored. There is evidence that Henry was vicar of Canterbury during the vacancy. He is seen carrying out the late archbishop's policy with regard to a proposed new religious house at Dover.[5] The monks of St. Augustine's, Canterbury, were recipients of his favour.[6] It is therefore possible that in this strong position, he inquired from Innocent whether in the event of his election to Canterbury he could be translated from Winchester. A favourable precedent was the translation of Archbishop Ralph from Rochester, which was ultimately agreed to by Paschal II.

It did not need the penetration of an Orderic to discover that Henry of Winchester was the most likely choice to succeed William of Corbeuil. That two years elapsed and in the end he failed suggests secret diplomacy of which the chroniclers were ignorant. Alternatively they were too occupied with the civil dissensions to concern themselves with this point. It is, however, certain that Henry could not be expected to obtain the archbishopric by a free and canonical election, as the monks of Christ Church, Canterbury, were indignant after his treatment of their proposed Dover priory. Heavy pressure from Stephen

---

[1] *Hunt.*, p. 314, and *D.N.B.* iv, 1123.
[2] Ordericus Vitalis in *P.L.*, 188, col. 954.   [3] Ibid., col. 973.
[4] *Gerv.*, i, 109, see below p. 13.
[5] Ibid., i, 100–1; for similar powers of Henry at London cf. J. H. Round, *The Commune of London* (1899), p. 117; and at Salisbury cf. L. Voss, *Heinrich von Blois* (1932), p. 45.   [6] *Thorne*, cols. 1800–1.

would be required, against the terms of his recent charter to the Church. There is no evidence, however, that Stephen approved of his brother's ambitions. His quiescence suggests disapproval. He could thus take up a righteous position as defender of the liberties of the Church at no cost to himself. It is less easy to explain the passivity of the electors. They were busy for some time electing a new prior, Jeremiah, and possibly he was in no hurry to receive a superior. [1]

The pope intervened in the summer of 1138 by dispatching a legate, Alberic bishop of Ostia. [2] It was intolerable that Stephen should follow the policy of his powerful predecessors and keep Canterbury vacant indefinitely, especially in view of his earlier promises. Stephen, in the Anglo-Norman tradition, was reluctant to have any dealings with this legate, but later accorded him full recognition. [3] This reversal of policy may have been due to the king's desire to win papal favour. In a few months his claims to the throne would be investigated by the Curia. [4]

After dealing with political and ecclesiastical affairs in Scotland and the north of England, Alberic returned to the south towards the end of September 1138. [5] He turned his attention to the long overdue Canterbury election.

Alberic by the grace of God bishop of Ostia, papal legate, to his beloved brethren in Christ Prior Jeremiah and the whole convent, Helewise the archdeacon, the clergy, nobility and people of Canterbury, greetings and benediction. . . . We wish to make known to you by this instrument, that we have summoned by papal authority the bishops, abbots and all other religious persons of this kingdom to a Council which we have arranged to be held in London at Westminster on 11 December. There, God willing, we shall consecrate the bishop-elect of Exeter and discuss the appointment to Canterbury and other ecclesiastical and papal matters, with divine assistance. Wherefore we order you to have this letter read out before all the clergy and people of Canterbury on 27 November, and after invoking the grace of the Holy Spirit, prayers, proclaiming a fast and almsgiving, to provide such a person to be set over you whose appointment the authority of canon law cannot resist, to which the bishops of

[1] *Gerv.* i, 100; for the character of Jeremiah cf. pp. 97–8.   [2] *Ric. Hex.*, p. 167.
[3] *John of Worcester*, ed. J. R. Weaver (1908), p. 49.
[4] *Hist. Pont.*, pp. 108–9.   [5] *Ric. Hex.*, p. 171.

the province ought likewise to assent, to which the king could not, nay ought not, rightly refuse his assent. We therefore order you by papal authority to bring with you thither, in place of the general body, such persons as can speak for all of you and carry in themselves the assent of all. Be sure, moreover, that we shall not fail, in answer to your just demand, to give advice and help as far as we can agreeably to God. We order you furthermore to come to London on the Thursday or Friday before the aforesaid term [Sunday, 11 Dec.] so that we shall be able to discuss something of this matter and of others. Farewell.[1]

There is no account of proceedings in Canterbury on the receipt of Alberic's mandate. The form of election was to be by 'commission'. We know from Gervase that a commission did arrive at Westminster,[2] but whether it was given *carte blanche* or one name or several names by the electors cannot be determined. Alberic recognised that the provincial bishops had rights in the election, but leaves them vague. It was not till 1206 that they were eliminated from Canterbury elections.[3] Nor was the king neglected. It is clear that some consultation between the parties was envisaged. The last word rested with the chapter, and Alberic, a monk, was prepared to support the convent's choice. The stage was set for a genuinely free election, the first at Canterbury since the Conquest.

The choice of Theobald, an obscure abbot of a famous monastery, is one more mystery to add to the rest. William of Malmesbury and the author of *Gesta Stephani* do not even allude to the election. Theobald was not an outstanding European figure like Lanfranc or Anselm who had established the 'Bec tradition' at Canterbury. Robert, abbot of Torigny, the chronicler, had known Theobald at Bec and of all the chroniclers knew him best. When Theobald became abbot, he referred to him as 'vir magnae probitatis et scientiae', hardly an enthusiastic eulogy.[4] Worse was to follow. The Canterbury-elect was described by Torigny as 'vir admodum venerandus', faint praise with a vengeance.[5] Torigny was not of the laconic school as his eulogies on Boso, and on Letard, Theobald's successor at Bec, show and it

[1] *Gerv.*, i, 106.   [2] Ibid., i, 109.
[3] F. M. Powicke, *Stephen Langton* (1928), p. 80.
[4] *Tor.*, p. 133.   [5] Ibid., p. 135.

may be that he had suffered under Theobald's régime. Gervase describes the new archbishop as 'natura simplex et aliquantulum litteratus'[1] which may be ascribed to the prejudice of a Canterbury monk. The impression left, however, is that the archbishop was a man of capability, not of genius or sanctity.

Therefore one is thrown back to account for Theobald's election in a negative way. This is unsatisfactory: it is easy to be wise after the event. Henry of Winchester has already been dealt with. The prejudice against translating bishops might have ruined the chances of Robert of Hereford, the only other outstanding member of the English episcopate. The monks, if left to themselves, would not be in favour of electing a bishop. They might have hankered after electing one of their own number according to the Rule of St. Benedict, but the see of Canterbury was not the preserve of a few monks. The position of Bec, however, was different, almost traditional. It had already provided two excellent archbishops and benefactors of the cathedral priory at Canterbury.[2] The present abbot Theobald was known to be a supporter of the rights of monks against episcopal control. He was a Norman, of mature years. The Bec tradition was not an empty one. Thomas Becket probably owed his position in Theobald's household to the accident of his father's birth in the same village as Theobald. After his murder the archbishopric was once more offered to an abbot of Bec who refused it.[3] This abbot, Roger, was no better known than Theobald.

The attitude of the king as a party to the election may have been coloured by his anxiety to placate the pope, as mentioned before. It is generally assumed that he was opposed to the candidature of his brother, and having nothing against Theobald, would rather welcome him than otherwise. Stephen was always solicitous for the preferment of his nephews and under more favourable circumstances, something might have been heard of them, as at York in 1143.

Theobald was in England late in the year 1138 on the business of his monastery.[4] Hook claims that the king and queen

---

[1] *Gerv.*, i, 44.

[2] *Chronicles and Memorials of Richard I*, ed. W. Stubbs (R.S. 1884–5), ii, xxix–xxx.

[3] *Tor.*, p. 256.   [4] See above, p. 6.

brought him to England before the election but cites no authority.[1] He may well have been present at the Council as a representative of the English interests of Bec. Theobald appears as a
witness to a charter of Stephen to Westminster Abbey dated
13 December 1138 at the Council.[2] He is described as archbishop and so the charter may have been drawn up later than
its alleged date, but it cannot be completely rejected as evidence
in favour of Theobald's presence at the Council.

The authorities for the proceedings at the election of Theobald are Diceto and Gervase, neither strictly contemporary.
They both agree that the election did not take place until Henry
of Winchester was safely out of the way.[3] Henry was administering the vacant diocese of London at the time, and at the end of
the Council, on 24 December, went over to St. Paul's to ordain
to the diaconate Richard de Belmeis, a future bishop of London.
It is clear, from both sources, that matters then moved with
rapidity. The Lambeth MS. of Diceto, Stubbs' basic text, states
that the bishops elected Theobald and that the bishop of Lincoln
announced the result. The British Museum MS. adds that
Jeremiah and his associates were excluded during the episcopal
deliberations. Diceto must be referring to some ceremony of
assent by the bishops to the already accomplished election, or at
the highest a ratification. Apart from any consideration of the
rights of the monks, such an election might have been uncanonical in the absence, completely unintentional, of Winchester. The latter would not have failed to urge this point if the
alleged election by bishops had any validity.

Gervase seems to have given the correct description of the
election. The king summoned Jeremiah and some of the monks
into his presence. There were also present the legate and several
of the nobles and bishops. Jeremiah then announced the election
of Theobald. Apart from the presence of the legate this procedure resembles, in form at least, that of the Constitutions of
Clarendon, which gives the account of the monk Gervase an
authentic ring.

The Anglo-Saxon Chronicle and Henry of Huntingdon em-

---

[1] Hook, ii, 329.
[2] Westminster Abbey Muniments Charter 33.   [3] *Diceto*, i, 252; *Gerv.*, i, 109.

phasise the royal support for Theobald. 'Te king makede Teod-bald aercebishop'[1] and 'adnitente rege Stephano'. Henry of Huntingdon does not allude to any special part played by his patron the bishop of Lincoln.[2]

Meanwhile, as the bishop of Winchester was conducting the ordination, the news of the election was brought from West-minster to the City. He abandoned the ceremony in disgust. Whatever his plans had been, they were clearly frustrated. The whole episode reflects little credit on all concerned and Henry's resentment was justified. In due course he had his revenge on Stephen and Theobald.

After his election, if he had followed the precedent set by Anselm, Theobald would first have obtained permission from the monks of Bec to desert them.[3] As he had no time to settle his affairs, he arranged that no abbot should be elected until his return from the forthcoming Lateran Council of 1139.[4] Whether he remained abbot until then or whether he resigned immedi-ately is not clear. He came to Canterbury where he was conse-crated on 8 January 1139 by the papal legate Alberic bishop of Ostia, assisted by nearly all the English bishops.[5] This no doubt gave him an opportunity to become better acquainted with his future colleagues, if he had not already met them at the Council of Westminster.

They appear to have been an able collection of men by no means noted for their piety. The administrative element was strong and reflected the uninspiring ecclesiastical policy of Henry I. Roger of Salisbury and his nephews Nigel of Ely and Alexander of Lincoln were primarily servants of King Henry who had 'raised them out of the dust' to serve him and inciden-tally the Church. Similarly Everard of Norwich had been attached to Henry's chapel. Bernard of St. David's had been chancellor to Queen Matilda, first wife of Henry I; Simon of Worcester had been chaplain to his second wife Queen Adela. Their bishoprics came as a reward for loyal service to the Crown. Roger of Coventry represents the sporting type. He played an enthusiastic part in the civil wars and turned his experience to

---

[1] E. A. Freeman, *History of the Norman Conquest* (1867–79), v, 289.
[2] *Hunt.*, p. 265.   [3] Porée, i, 235.   [4] *Tor.*, p. 135.   [5] *Gerv.*, i, 109.

account in the second Crusade. Henry of Winchester could also
do his share of fighting if necessary, but his character was of far
greater complexity. The Middle Ages were not given overmuch
to psychoanalysis, but Henry of Huntingdon, in a famous epi-
gram, hinted tentatively at schizophrenia. This royal monk far
more deserved the title Magnificent than mediocre Lincoln.
Courtier, abbot, bishop (but still abbot), his progress seemed
irresistible. His failure is the yardstick of Theobald's ability.
A different character is presented by the pious Robert of Hereford, anxious for the welfare of his diocese and the liberty of the
Church which he defended with success. He can be regarded as
the model bishop of his time. The other bishops have received
little attention in the sources. Seffrid of Chichester was described
as a timeserver. London, Bangor, Llandaff and St. Asaph were
vacant.[1]

The two suffragan dioceses of the province of York were in
Scottish hands. Archbishop Thurstan, whose right it normally
was to consecrate the archbishop of Canterbury,[2] was at the
point of death. His strength of character had maintained the
independence of the weaker northern province against the en-
croachments of two archbishops of Canterbury. His undoubted
piety expressed itself in the encouragement of the Cistercian
monks.

Theobald was expected to visit Rome to obtain the archiepiscopal pallium, thus completing the final formalities atten-
dant upon his election. This visit coincided with the convocation
of the second Lateran Council by Innocent II, which was held
in April 1139. He was accompanied by four of his suffragans and
by four abbots.[3] Henry of Huntingdon, perhaps representing the
bishop of Lincoln, was also of the party.[4] This reflects sadly on
his chronicle, which does not even mention this Council. Little
is known of the arduous journey to and from Rome, which may
well have been Theobald's first visit. Before he left England,
Theobald found time to settle the Dover dispute[5] and to attend

---

[1] *D.N.B.* s.v.; *Hunt.*, pp. 314–17; *Gesta*, pp. 61–2 and 100–1, W. R. W. Stephens,
The English Church from the Norman Conquest to the Accession of Edward I (1909) cap. viii.
[2] *Gerv.*, i, 170.   [3] *Ric. Hex.*, pp. 176–7.
[4] *Tor.*, p. 65; Lincoln received a papal privilege, Jaffé, 8024.
[5] See below, pp. 75 ff.

the dedication of Godstow church.[1] On the way to Rome the party called at Bec.[2] On his return from the Council he visited Bec for the last time at Whitsun.[3]

Theobald was back in England with his pallium by August.[4] There was an unpleasant surprise awaiting him. He was now subject to Henry of Winchester who had been appointed papal legate. Legates sent from Rome to England for a specific purpose were not uncommon and their influence was transitory. In 1126 William, archbishop of Canterbury, was made legate over England by Honorius II and he retained the office until his death. This ensured his supremacy over York, although it involved the tacit abandonment of claims by Canterbury to innate primacy. Apart from having the prestige value of being a special papal representative, the legate was empowered to call councils of the Church in the area of his jurisdiction.

In view of this solitary precedent, Theobald might have thought that if anyone was entitled to be legate, he was the obvious choice. Papal logic and canon law did not support this view. By 29 April Henry was exercising his new functions;[5] William of Malmesbury thought his legation dated from 1 March.[6] It may have been a consolation to Henry for his failure to become archbishop. The English Church was not strengthened by this action of Innocent. Henry was primarily interested in developing his own power which did not necessarily accord with the interests of the Church. Any apparent successes by the Church in the years 1139–1143 merely reflect the almost complete collapse of secular government. The only gainer was the pope. He could dispose freely of the headship of the English Church, which would tend to make its focal point Rome and not Canterbury or the Curia Regis.

Some of the implications of Henry's legation are revealed in this account:

Relying on this power, Henry appropriated the totality of archiepiscopal authority. He confirmed [the election of] bishops and consecrated them, presided over councils, adjudicated on leading cases

---

[1] *Monasticon*, iv, 362.
[2] *Tor.*, p. 65.
[3] MS. Bibl. Nat. Latin 12884, f.194b (Chron. of Bec).
[4] *Malm.*, ii, 550.
[5] Jaffé, 8025; cf. *P.L.*, 190, ep. 475, cols. 1041–2.
[6] *Malm.*, ii, 550.

and cited the archbishop himself and subjected him to his jurisdiction.[1]

It was not long before Henry had a chance to use his new
powers. The long-suffering Stephen at last turned against
Bishop Roger of Salisbury and his nephews. They were arrested
and their castles were confiscated. On this Henry summoned his
first legatine council which met two months later on 29 August
1139. Theobald was present[2] but played a very minor part in
the deliberations. Nothing was accomplished by the Council,
but the opposition of Henry to Stephen was now apparent.

Overshadowed as he was by the personality and position of
the legate, the name of Theobald appears but fitfully amidst the
welter of battles and pourparlers of the next four years. After the
landing of the Empress Matilda in October 1139 he was deputed
to assist Henry on the king's side in some particularly fruitless
negotiations for a settlement.[3]

The first stage of the civil war ended with the capture of
Stephen at Lincoln in February 1141. Henry gave his approval
to the new régime, providing he was to control the appointment
of bishops and abbots.[4] Matilda entered Winchester on 3 March
1141 and was welcomed by the legate. The bishops of Bath,
Hereford and Lincoln joined her. Theobald was requested by
the legate to swear fealty to Matilda. For the first time he took
up an independent position. He declared that he would have to
obtain the king's permission first. The consciences of many were
stirred by Theobald's stand for good faith, and several bishops
and laymen went with him to Bristol where Stephen was incar-
cerated. The king good-naturedly gave his assent and Theobald
once more fell into line with the legate. John of Salisbury, recall-
ing this incident, points out that Theobald was demonstrating
his loyalty to the recent papal decision at the Lateran Council
in favour of Stephen,[5] an attitude which a papal legate might
have been expected to adopt.

Henry's second legatine council was opened on 7 April 1141.
Theobald, the bishops and many abbots attended.[6] The agenda
was to elect the Empress Matilda 'domina Angliae Norman-

[1] *Anglia Sacra*, i, 792.   [2] *Malm.*, ii, 550.   [3] Ibid., p. 564.
[4] Ibid., p. 573.   [5] *Hist. Pont.*, p. 42.   [6] *Malm.*, ii, 574.

niaeque'. This was duly accomplished. Critics of the Church complain of its action during this council and its successor. The Church is accused of arrogant pretensions in electing secular rulers. On the other hand the power of the Church here is extolled by those who approve of its exercise. In fact the Church was merely putting its seal on a *fait accompli* in both councils, as the only stable body amidst the collapse of government. The reversal of the Church's recognition of the empress at the second of these councils is more a testimony of weakness and ignominy than of strength.

In May 1141 the empress arrived at Reading. Theobald was there.[1] His own diocese was the centre of a royalist revival and for the time being was closed to him. In June she reached London and at Midsummer was ejected by the royalists. After a precipitate flight to Gloucester she rallied at Oxford where Theobald is again found in attendance.[2]

The mercurial Henry of Winchester once more changed sides being dissatisfied with the ecclesiastical policy of the empress.[3] The hostilities which ensued settled the issue of the civil war. The imperialists with Theobald as their leading ecclesiastic entered Winchester. They were defeated and fled on 14 September 1141. The unfortunate situation of Theobald in this disaster is vividly described. In the general confusion he and the bishops with him had to make their escape as best as they could, robbed of horses and vestments alike.[4] Robert, earl of Gloucester, natural son of Henry I and bulwark of the Angevin cause, was captured by the royalists. The negotiations for the exchange of the two leaders in captivity bring Theobald into the picture once more. The elaborate scheme for the exchange is described by William of Malmesbury.[5] Robert agreed to an equal exchange on the proposal of the legate and the archbishop.[6] It was also agreed that Stephen should be released first. To safeguard the release of the earl, Henry and Theobald offered themselves as sureties or hostages, prepared to go into captivity should

---

[1] H. W. C. Davis in *Essays in History presented to R. L. Poole*, p. 183.

[2] *Foedera*, i, 14; *Cartulary of St. Frideswide's*, ed. S. R. Wigram (Oxford Hist. Soc., 1895–6), i, 23–4 and ii, 115–16; *Sarum*, p. 11.

[3] J. H. Round, *Geoffrey de Mandeville* (1892), p. 85.

[4] *Gesta*, p. 83.   [5] *Malm.*, ii, 587.   [6] Ibid., ii, 589.

C

Robert be betrayed. Thereupon the earl suggested that the king would not be overmuch distressed if this occurred and it was agreed that they should inform the pope of their action. He would, no doubt, threaten to excommunicate Stephen, if he broke faith and allowed the legate and archbishop to remain imprisoned. The exchange was then successfully accomplished. It seems, therefore, that Theobald had returned to the royalist allegiance.

A month later on 7 December 1141 the third legatine Council was held at Westminster and Stephen was reinstated. The Church had again recognised the shift in the balance of power.[1] Henry once more played the principal role, and if Theobald was present he maintained an embarrassed silence.

Stephen went to Canterbury for Christmas and was crowned by Theobald. This set the seal on Stephen's rehabilitation. The right of the archbishop of Canterbury to crown the king had also been reaffirmed, despite the superior standing of the legate.[2]

The disorders continued during 1142 and 1143 with Stephen gradually gaining the upper hand. The imperialists were pushed to the west, and even the insufferable Geoffrey de Mandeville found out that the worm was turning. It was not surprising that during these campaigns the property and rights of the Church were violated and its ministers assaulted. It was left to individual bishops to combat the menace; sometimes they displayed resolution; more often they were feeble or behaved as badly as the lay persecutors. At last the legate bestirred himself and a council was held at London in the spring of 1143. The importance of this council need not necessarily be judged by its canon against those who assaulted clerks, a restatement of the fifteenth canon of the second Lateran Council and the ninth canon of the legatine council of Westminster of 1138.[3] If the council was in this sense a failure, it foreshadowed the far more effective legatine council of 1151 which, under Theobald, defined the rights of the Church. Incidentally it showed the comparative incapacity of Henry of Winchester in the domestic affairs of the Church. In 1139, when he was antagonistic to the king, he had used the arrest of the bishops to the full degree, but now that he was closely allied to the king he remained comparatively indifferent.

[1] Ibid., ii, 583.   [2] *Gerv.*, i, 123.   [3] *Hunt.*, p. 276; *Gerv.*, i, 122, cf. p. 108.

2. PRIMATE OF ALL ENGLAND

The death of Innocent II on 25 September 1143 put an end to the legation of Henry of Winchester and to the anomalous and humiliating position of Theobald. Latterly, he had even been cited before the legate by the monks of his own cathedral,[1] and by the monks of St. Augustine's, Canterbury.[2] A noted imperialist, Brian Fitzcount, wrote to Henry of Winchester, referring to Theobald 'whom they call archbishop of Canterbury'.[3] This appears to be an allusion to his powerlessness and not, as Davis suggested, to his having deserted the empress, in which he behaved no differently from the other bishops.

For Theobald, the interest of the next two years lay in whether Henry of Winchester could recover his dominant position in the English Church. The news of the election of Pope Celestine II must have reached England at the same time as that of the death of Innocent, as it took place one day later, on 25 September 1143. Celestine was a strong opponent of the cause of Stephen, with which the erstwhile legate was now completely identified.[4] The last legatine councils were held in London on 10 and 30 November.[5] At the earlier council Henry continued his efforts towards restoring the position of the Church. Two of the worst offenders amongst the bishops, Nigel of Ely and Roger of Coventry, were ordered to go to Rome to clear themselves.[6] The last council was concerned with the dispute between Theobald and the monks of St. Augustine's, Canterbury.[7]

Theobald's newly-found importance was emphasised by a mandate of Celestine to him declaring his 'foreign policy'. The attitude of Innocent was to be maintained and 'there was to be no innovation in the kingdom of England with respect to the Crown'.[8] If not pleasing to the Angevin party, this statement was consistent and dignified. It could also be twisted to suit the Angevin book as Eugenius III was to show in 1152.

Whether the archbishop was in England to receive this missive is unknown. He had made up his mind to visit Celestine in

[1] *Gerv.*, i, 127.
[2] *Thorne*, col. 1803.
[3] H. W. C. Davis in *E.H.R.*, 1910, p. 302.
[4] *John Hex.*, p. 315.
[5] *Handbook of British Chronology* (Royal Hist. Soc.), p. 356.
[6] *Ann. Mon.*, ii, 229. [7] *Thorne*, col. 1804. [8] *Hist. Pont.*, p. 88.

an attempt to secure the coveted legation or at least have it denied to any one else. He left England about Christmas-time,[1] and would thus have arrived at Rome shortly before the death of Celestine on 8 March 1144. Theobald asked Gilbert Foliot, abbot of Gloucester, to accompany him. The abbot replied with a polite refusal. While he was pleased that the Church of Canterbury was now freed from the grasp of the strangler—presumably a reference to Henry of Winchester—difficulties with the earl of Hereford and other oppressors of his monastery prevented him from leaving Gloucester. Consequently, although Theobald had offered to pay his expenses, he could only be with him in spirit.[2] Theobald would appear to have insisted on his accompanying him and to have told him to be ready to set out before Christmas 1143, for another letter of Gilbert's offers apologies and excuses for his inability to go. It is, however, possible that this second letter was an official answer to Theobald's original mandate accompanying the more intimate and personal reply. It could then be filed in the archbishop's 'chancery'. It is certainly couched in more formal language.[3]

It is probable that Theobald was accompanied by the bishops of Ely and Coventry.[4] Thomas Becket was supposed to have advised Theobald to go to Rome, but there is no direct evidence that he accompanied him, although it is not improbable.[5] It would appear that there was no royal opposition to the departure of the bishops.

Henry of Winchester had no intention of letting his case go by default. He too had set out for Rome to obtain a renewal of his legation. Hearing of the strong Angevin sympathies of the new pope, he changed his mind and wintered at Cluny, his old monastery.[6]

The death of Celestine was unfortunate for Theobald, if timely for Henry. Gervase claims that Celestine awarded the legation to Theobald,[7] but if this was correct the *status quo* was speedily restored. Lucius II followed precedent in reversing the

---

[1] *Hunt.*, p. 277.

[2] Foliot's Letters, *P.L.*, 190, ep. 6, col. 750. Cf. R. L. Poole in *E.H.R.* 1927, p. 572, n. 2.

[3] Foliot's Letters, *P.L.*, 190, ep. 7, cols. 750–1.

[4] *Ann. Mon.*, ii, 229.   [5] *Gerv.*, ii, 384.   [6] *John Hex.*, p. 315.   [7] *Gerv.*, ii, 384.

chosen by the king to attend the Council of Rheims are all found in this list.

Nine years after he had been to Rome for the Lateran Council, Theobald, together with the bishops and abbots of England was summoned by Pope Eugenius III to the Council of Rheims, which was to open on 21 March 1148. Eugenius III was a Cistercian monk and his election in 1145 consummated the triumph of the new movement. Eugenius proved himself a strong defender of the Cistercians and of the Papacy. Theobald, of course, was not a Cistercian, but Eugenius' dislike of Henry of Winchester engendered by the York dispute gave him an advantage in his dealings with the pope. Should he refuse to attend the Council, this advantage would be lost. On the other hand, continued personal contact with Eugenius, an opportunity that might not recur, would reinforce the favour of the pope and might even lead to the grant of legatine powers. The idea of disobeying the papal mandate was remote from the mind of Theobald, but no doubt he did not neglect these considerations. He may not have reckoned with the intervention of the king. Stephen expelled the papal legates who brought the summonses[1] and nominated the bishops of Chichester, Hereford and Norwich to attend the Council as representatives of the English Church. Gervase suggests that Stephen excluded Theobald in order to oblige his brother and weaken Theobald's standing with Eugenius,[2] but if this is true, it is only part of the truth. Stephen at last felt himself strong enough to return to the policy of restricting contacts between the English Church and the Papacy. Once the Church had been isolated, it would be more amenable to his control. Stephen pursued this policy for the next five years with a measure of success, but Theobald proved a worthy and resourceful antagonist.

It was expected that Theobald would attempt to disobey the royal edict and Stephen had the ports watched while he himself remained in Canterbury.[3] The archbishop obtained permission to send several members of his household to Rheims ostensibly to excuse his absence, but in fact to form the nucleus of a house-

---

[1] H. Boehmer, *Kirche und Staat in England* (1899), p. 350, n. 4.
[2] *Gerv.*, i, 134.   [3] Ibid.; *Hist. Pont.*, p. 7.

hold in exile.[1] One night he slipped away accompanied by his clerk Thomas Becket. They reached the Kentish coast and embarked on an unseaworthy vessel. Braving the March winds they arrived at the French coast and were subsequently welcomed by a surprised and touched Eugenius. Several accounts, all in substantial agreement, survive of this most romantic episode in the life of Theobald.[2] Stephen immediately confiscated the property of the see.[3]

Apart from Theobald and the three bishops deputed by the king, the other bishops in England ignored the papal summons. Roger of Coventry was on crusade. It is possible that Jocelin of Salisbury came to Rheims: he was in Normandy in June 1148.[4] At the end of the Council it was decided to punish the recalcitrant or terrorised prelates. They were suspended and Theobald was given the right of absolution.[5] Henry of Winchester alone was suspended by name and only the pope could release him.[6] Theobald used his powers moderately and most of those suspended were absolved within a short time. Writing later in the year to the archdeacon of Lincoln, Foliot mentions the bishops of Winchester, Durham, Worcester, Bath and Exeter as suspended.[7] These must have been the hardened core of offenders. They could not plead duress as they were practically outside the area of Stephen's effective rule. Henry of Winchester was regarded as Stephen's chief ecclesiastical adviser and treated accordingly. Theobald and many others pleaded for his reinstatement but Eugenius remained adamant. This contradicts the assertion of Poole[8] that Theobald refused to relax the sentence on the bishop of Winchester. The passage in John of Salisbury[9] 'Theobald archbishop of Canterbury released the English bishops and abbots from their suspension except Henry of Winchester', simply means that it was not within Theobald's power to absolve Henry of Winchester. In the end Henry's brother, Theobald of Blois, succeeded where the archbishop and

---

[1] *Hist. Pont.*, p. 8. Possibly including John of Salisbury himself.
[2] *Gerv.* and *Hist. Pont.* as before; *Materials*, iii, 356 and vi, 57.
[3] *Diceto*, i, 262.   [4] *Sarum*, pp. 14–15.
[5] *Hist. Pont.*, pp. 12 and 41; Foliot's Letters, *P.L.*, 190, ep. 77, col. 795.
[6] Foliot's Letters, *P.L.*, 190, ep. 76, col. 795.
[7] Ibid., cols. 794–5.   [8] *Hist. Pont.*, pp. lii–lv.   [9] Ibid., p. 80.

the others had failed: he was in favour with the Cistercians.
Henry was given a term of six months in which to seek personal
absolution from the pope.[1]

The other bishops were absolved by Theobald. In a letter to
the bishop of Bath and through him to the bishop of Exeter,[2]
Foliot confirms the absolving power of Theobald and the news
that the bishops could be absolved in England. Gervase notes
the absolution of the bishops of Bath, Exeter, Worcester and
Chichester on 11 November 1148.[3] This list tallies with that
given by Foliot in his letter to the archdeacon of Lincoln except
that the bishop of Chichester is substituted for the bishop of
Durham. In view of the attendance of Hilary of Chichester at
the Council, it is probable that Gervase is in error. It is, however, possible that he too was suspended by Eugenius. The pope
had been instrumental in securing the election of Hilary but he
turned out to be a supporter of the king. 'Hilary . . . excusing
Stephen, was told by the pope: "We thought we had created
you a son of the Roman Church, but in you we have created an
arrow and a sword".'[4] In this case the absence of the name of
the bishop of Durham could be accounted for by the commission of his absolution to the archbishop of York, who was present
at the Council.[5] Theobald was not yet papal legate and could
not absolve the bishop of Durham without a special papal commission.

Stephen's turn came in due course,[6] and the moderation of
Theobald was once more displayed. On the last day of the
Council the candles were lit and the pope was about to excommunicate Stephen for his behaviour towards both archbishops,
for the archbishop of York had suffered more than Theobald.
Since his consecration by the pope the year before, Stephen had
refused him admission into England. At this point Theobald
begged Eugenius to spare Stephen, much to the surprise of the
pope. Pointing at Theobald, he exclaimed

Regard him, O brethren, who exemplifies the character of the Man
of the Gospels, loving his enemies and praying for his persecutors. So
although the king by his temerity has earned our wrath and that of

[1] Ibid., p. 11.　　　　　[2] Foliot's Letters, *P.L.*, 190, ep. 77, col. 795.
[3] *Gerv.*, i, 138.　　[4] *Diceto*, i, 263.　　[5] *Hist. Pont.*, p. 5.　　[6] Ibid., p. 8.

the Church of God, we cannot disapprove of the prayers of charity, to which, indeed, we are bound to hearken. At his prayer we do now suspend sentence, awarding the king three months delay for satisfaction. Should he fail to make satisfaction in the meanwhile, he shall be cast back with an increase of yet heavier damnation on his head and on his land.

If Theobald's conduct had been designed to mollify Stephen, it was for the moment of little avail. In the third week of April 1148 the pope left Rheims[1] and the archbishop returned to England. Significantly he had obtained permission from the pope to return. He arrived at Canterbury and was welcomed by the townsfolk and the monks of the cathedral.[2] Stephen came to Canterbury to demand the reasons for Theobald's disobedience. His intermediaries were Richard de Luci and William Martel.[3] Theobald was ordered to leave the country and his property remained confiscated. Sailing from Dover,[4] he reached Flanders, accompanied by the abbot of Gloucester, who wrote to the pope describing their situation:

For we have remained with your son and our father and dearest lord of Canterbury during the days of his exile. We have no fixed residence or place of our own, but in the course of affairs have wandered from place to place. In the month of July we arrived at Arras.[5]

They finally abode at the monastery of St. Bertin at St. Omer.[6] There Gilbert Foliot was consecrated bishop of Hereford on 5 September. Theobald created a good impression at St. Bertin and became endeared to all. During his exile Theobald was in contact with his partisans in England who were allowed free access to him by the king.[7] Perhaps John of Salisbury mentioned this as a contrast with the more uncompromising conduct of Henry II in similar circumstances.

Meanwhile Theobald had informed Eugenius of Stephen's obstinacy.[8] The pope arrived at Brescia on 9 July 1148[9] and there received the envoys of the archbishop. Eugenius was now separated from the Council and St. Bernard, and several of the cardinals favoured Stephen. Nevertheless he ordered the English

---

[1] Jaffé, 9247.   [2] Gerv., i, 135.   [3] Hist. Pont., p. 42.   [4] Gerv., i, 135.
[5] Foliot's Letters, P.L., 190, ep. 73, col. 793.
[6] Gerv., i, 135.   [7] Hist. Pont., p. 42.   [8] Ibid., pp. 44–5.   [9] Jaffé, before 9281.

bishops to bring pressure on the king to recall Theobald and restore the possessions of the see of Canterbury. If the king remained contumacious, the country was to be laid under an interdict and, at Michaelmas, Stephen himself was to be excommunicated. Theobald was to be obeyed by the province of Canterbury without any appeal as if he was in his own see. To safeguard the archbishop's position in France, he ordered the bishops and secular powers there to afford him all assistance.

The English bishops again refused to co-operate with the pope. Stephen remained adamant. Accordingly the interdict was promulgated by Theobald to come into effect on 12 September.[1] In London the archdeacon and his party lodged an appeal against it although that had been expressly forbidden. The interdict was an almost complete fiasco. The diocese of Canterbury alone obeyed it and in the city itself it was ignored by the monks of St. Augustine's who claimed to be exempt.[2] Clearly there was not a great desire for 'freedom' in the English Church.

Further setbacks were suffered by Theobald in connection with the consecration of Gilbert Foliot, abbot of Gloucester, to the bishopric of Hereford. The bishops of London, Salisbury and Chichester refused to go abroad to assist at the consecration.[3] The monks of Gloucester flouted an agreement between the archbishop and the new bishop of Hereford whereby he was to retain the abbey in plurality. They elected their subprior Hamelin to fill the vacant abbacy.[4] Despite all this and the lack of continued support from Rome, the placing of an adherent in the see of Hereford was an undoubted success for Theobald.[5]

Stephen had shown that he could control the English Church. There were considerations which prevented him from attempting to push his advantage too far. The question of the disputed succession had been reopened by Geoffrey of Anjou[6] and he could not hope to rely on his supporters amongst the cardinals to prevent a possible decision against him. Continued resistance might prove fatal to the aspirations of his brother of Winchester, even to his retention of the bishopric. The queen and his loyal

---

[1] *Gerv.*, i, 135–6.   [2] *Hist. Pont.*, p. 46.   [3] Ibid., p. 47.
[4] Ibid., p. 48.   [5] See below, pp. 107 ff.   [6] *Hist. Pont.*, p. 44.

adherent William of Ypres thought it was best to strive for
peace, and opened negotiations with Theobald for his return.[1]
The archbishop, for his part, displayed anxiety as to the fate of
the possessions of the see of Canterbury.[2] He felt he could now
return with dignity and safety and arrived in England probably
in October. He did not feel sufficiently sure of himself to land in
Kent, Stephen's stronghold, but made his way from Gravelines
to Gosford in Suffolk, the territory of Earl Hugh Bigod.[3] Thence
he proceeded to the earl's castle at Framlingham. Here he once
more assumed authority over the English Church, received
bishops and decided ecclesiastical causes which had been held
over. Contact with Stephen was renewed. The king agreed to
close the dispute and Theobald was restored to his own. Much
was forgiven on either side.

It must have been at this time that Theobald instructed
Gilbert Foliot to swear fealty to Stephen. As Hereford was in the
Angevin sphere, the archbishop's relations with that party were
temporarily worsened.

In 1149 Stephen successfully met a challenge from Henry of
Anjou and David of Scotland.[4] His main concern was henceforth to be the securing of the succession of his elder son
Eustace. It was the archbishop of York and not Theobald who
was concerned in the preliminary negotiations about the coronation of Eustace,[5] although Stephen must have realised that
ultimately Theobald would have to be consulted in view of the
coronation rights of Canterbury.

In 1150 Theobald was appointed legate by Eugenius III. The
evidence for the date of the appointment is unsatisfactory. The
chronicle of Bec[6] says that Innocent II conferred a perpetual
legation on Theobald, who thus became the first English
'legatus natus'. This is absurd. Thorne, the chronicler of St.
Augustine's, claims that Theobald was legate in 1148.[7] This has
generally been interpreted as a device by Thorne to save the
faces of the monks of St. Augustine's, who would only recognise
an interdict promulgated by direct papal authority, and so

---

[1] *Gerv.*, i, 135.   [2] Ibid., i, 136.   [3] Ibid.; *Hist. Pont.*, p. 49.
[4] Adams, p. 244.   [5] *John Hex.*, p. 325.
[6] MS. Bibl. Nat. Latin 12884, f.195a.   [7] See below, p. 70.

Thorne falsely ascribed the title to Theobald. There is also an original charter of Theobald ascribing to him the legatine title which cannot be dated later than 1148, but it was not written by Theobald's clerks.[1] The earliest surviving papal bulls addressed to Theobald with the title of legate are dated 22 December 1150.[2] Endorsements on the episcopal professions of obedience from March 1151 onwards include the legatine title, but the earlier endorsements down to October 1149 omit it.[3] A large number of Theobald's charters contain the legatine style. Apart from the unique document mentioned above, the earliest appears to be a confirmation addressed to Bishop Simon of Worcester who died on 20 March 1150. Unfortunately it only exists in Dugdale's transcript.[4] From the above evidence it may be suggested that Theobald was made legate probably early in 1150 and the grant was renewed by successive popes down to Theobald's death in 1161. He might have held the office for short periods before 1150, possibly to carry out specific papal mandates. The lack of exact evidence may be ascribed to the reduced significance of the grant as compared with that made to Henry of Winchester. Theobald had been the most important ecclesiastic in England since 1144. The title did not give him much more than he had already achieved by his own efforts.

The bull which Eugenius sent Theobald announcing the grant does not appear to have survived, but it must have read similarly to the bull of Adrian IV to the archbishop of York and the English Church notifying them of his reappointment of Theobald to the office of legate.

Since, by the will of God although unworthy, we have undertaken to rule the Church Universal, we are bound to consider the welfare of the entire Church, and in the words of the prophet[5] to uproot, destroy and (with God's help) to plant. We cannot always perform these duties in person because of the increase of business, the inaccessibility of distant lands and for other reasons. Therefore we have, where necessary, summoned prudent men filled with the spirit of God, as our predecessors are known to have done, and have dele-

---

[1] No. 281.　　　　　　　　　　　　　　　[2] Holtzmann, ii, 229, 231.
[3] C. E. Woodruff, 'Some Professions of Obedience', *St. Paul's Ecclesiological Soc.*, vii, 170.　　　　　　　　　　　　　　　　　　　　　[4] No. 254.
[5] Jeremiah, i, 10. This was the standard text used in appointing legates.

gated our functions to them so that we can never be reproached with the words of the prophet: 'The children begged for bread but there was none to break it for them',[1] because we, either directly or through our legates, shall moisten as much of the earth of the Lord as God's grace may give us with gentle aspostolic rain, and shall break bread on the Lord's table to restore the souls of the hungry. Rightly did Popes Eugenius and Anastasius of happy memory delegate their functions in your land to our reverend brother T. archbishop of Canterbury, lest at any time you should lack papal care and protection, and through him exercised their apostolic duties. This was done for the common good of your kingdom on account of our brother's prudence, whose steadfastness and uprightness were so well established that they deemed him worthy of performing apostolic functions by reason of his knowledge and virtue. Following their example we have also thought fit to grant him the delegation of our functions throughout your kingdom, and so highly do we rate his prudence, uprightness and steadfastness that we have given him full powers to convene Councils should he think fit, to correct your errors in our name and to make ordinances. We therefore order you, as set out in this letter, to pay honour and obedience to him humbly and reverently as our legate, to come to his presence should he summon you, and observe inviolably whatever he should command for your good, so that by his efforts and care and by your obedience, vice shall be rooted out, virtue implanted, and the position of the Churches improved. Given at Rome, St. Peter's, 22 February [1155].[2]

The reasons for the granting of the legatine commission to Theobald at that time can only be conjectured. Possibly it was an expression of the somewhat overdue gratitude of Eugenius for the loyalty of the archbishop in 1148. There may have been a desire on the part of the pope and his mentor St. Bernard to depress the standing of Henry of Winchester. The negotiations leading up to the grant are unrecorded. It has already been shown that Theobald had been making efforts in this direction since 1143. The medium for these negotiations may have been his confidential clerk Thomas Becket.[3] One of his biographers, William Fitzstephen, says: 'The archbishop sent him to Rome several times to treat of the affairs of the English Church'.[4]

---

[1] Lamentations, iv, 4.
[2] R. L. Poole in *E.H.R.*, 1902, p. 706; Holtzman, ii, 258.
[3] *Gerv.*, ii, 384.   [4] *Materials*, iii, 16.

Theobald was now given the effective authority over the province of York which his predecessor had held. For the life-time of Eugenius at least, he could not be overreached by the bishop of Winchester. Of course the pope was not prevented from delegating jurisdiction *ad hoc* to anyone—at one time Theobald himself was threatened with trial by his suffragans or before the bishop of London[1]—but in the absence of such arrangements the archbishop was the normal channel for the exercise of papal jurisdiction. The appointment of Theobald, who recognised the canonical view of papal powers, went a long way to strengthen the Roman position in England.

There had not been a legatine council in England since 1145. Armed with his new powers, Theobald arranged for one to be held in March 1151. The only chronicler who comments on this council is Henry of Huntingdon who was no doubt present in his capacity of archdeacon.

Theobald archbishop of Canterbury and legate of the apostolic see held a general Council at London in Mid-Lent. King Stephen, his son Eustace and the nobles of England were present. The proceedings of the Council were disturbed by new appeals. For in England appeals were not in use until Henry of Winchester, when legate, wickedly introduced them, to his own injury. In this Council there were three appeals to the audience of the pope.[2]

Henry of Huntingdon probably expressed the distrust of the average English clergyman when confronted with the papalist innovations of the last few years. The presence of Stephen, Eustace and the nobles is an interesting feature. It has been said that the Council probably legislated for Canterbury province only,[3] but it is difficult to see why. Theobald had only just been granted legatine authority over the province of York. The presence of Stephen and the barons suggests that the Council embraced the whole kingdom.

Many councils of this period seemed content to reiterate most of the canons of their predecessors, but here there seems to be a good deal of originality and a genuine attempt by Theobald and his advisers to meet the difficulties of the English

[1] John of Salisbury's Letters, *P.L.*, 199, ep. 105, col. 95.
[2] *Hunt.*, p. 282.   [3] C. R. Cheney in *E.H.R.*, 1935, p. 196.

D

Church.[1] The keynote of the canons is the phrase in the preamble 'to seek out new remedies'. Many benefits had accrued
to the Church during the reign of Stephen: some were to prove
of permanent value. The disorder and prevalent insecurity had
done much to nullify these advantages. Baronial depredations
had no superior attraction over royal exactions and administration. The canons of the Council consequently show a definite
trend towards the re-establishment of royal authority and the
old co-operation between Church and State. Although the pope
could do a great deal to safeguard control of the Church by the
Church, he could accomplish little in the way of protecting its
property and lives. Significantly there is no mention of the pope
or his authority throughout the text of the canons.

In pursuance of this policy the first canon distinguished between the illegal baronial exactions from ecclesiastical possessions and royal taxation. The tenseries, execrated by the Anglo-
Saxon Chronicle, and the tallages were condemned. 'Operationes regi debitas' duly authorised by writ were to be paid by
the Church. Similarly, in the second canon the usurpation of the
jurisdiction of the Curia Regis by the barons was not to be
tolerated by the Church. Churchmen were forbidden to answer
to the barons in respect of pleas of the Crown in view of the grave
losses incurred. The wording of this canon is obscure, but a
charter of Stephen to the abbey of Abingdon may help to clarify
the position.

Stephen king of England to the justices and sheriffs and barons and
ministers and all his faithful men French and English of Oxford and
Berkshire greeting. Know that I warrant to the abbot of Abingdon
that neither he nor his men shall plead in respect of any plea which
may pertain to my crown, unless it be in my presence and whenever
I shall be at Oxford. Witness William of Ypres at London.[2]

This was an exceptional privilege, but no doubt ecclesiastical
bodies had the normal right to have pleas of the Crown tried by
the king's court or its accredited representatives. The greater
barons always had their franchises and liberties but when the

---

[1] See below pp. 547.
[2] *Chronicon Monasterii de Abingdon*, ed. J. Stevenson (R.S., 1858), ii, 181–2.

royal power weakened, they were illegally extended, thus infringing the rights of the Church. The extent of jurisdiction covered by the pleas of the Crown in the reign of Stephen cannot easily be determined. There is a case involving St. Albans abbey where the famous Assize Utrum[1] was employed, authorised by a writ of King Stephen.[2]

The sanctions to enforce the decisions of the Church were set out in the third, fourth and fifth canons. Offenders were to be excommunicated until they had restored the value of the damage caused. Provision was made for the penitents who were unable to pay immediately. Co-operation with the king is again in evidence. If anyone excommunicated were to remain contumacious for a whole year, he was to lose all legal rights and be disinherited by the king. As the Church discovered in later years, it was essential to have the support of the secular arm in dealing with the obdurate. The seventh canon gives details of the enforcement of an interdict where robbery of Church property had occurred. Officiants in chapels were to cease performing the divine offices at the same time as the mother church within whose walls they sheltered.

The prevalent disorder had affected discipline in the Church and the sixth canon was designed to restore order, although it is hard to see what it means. It was complained that a vicious, uncanonical custom had grown up, 'that in the churches of England clerks are taken in indiscriminately and with no selection'. This practice was prohibited. The meaning is probably that the credentials of priests and others in holy orders migrating from one diocese to another ought to be checked. In the reign of Henry II, Theobald, writing to the pope, said that Maurice, bishop of Bangor, when expelled from his diocese, had excommunicated a number of the contumacious, clergy and laity. Many of the clerks 'were making their way to the neighbouring bishops of Wales, England, Ireland and Scotland, and received from them ordination, chrism and other sacraments of the Church in a fraudulent manner'.[3] If this abuse is the one

---

[1] F. W. Maitland, *Collected Papers* (1911), ii, 214, n. 2.
[2] *Gesta Abbatum Monasterii S. Albani*, ed. H. T. Riley (R.S., 1867–9), i, 114.
[3] John of Salisbury's Letters, *P.L.*, 199, ep. 53, cols. 33–4.

condemned by the sixth canon, there was no doubt ample scope for its practice in the reign of Stephen.

The last canon once more condemns baronial rapacity. Illegal tolls were being levied, casting a heavy burden on cities, boroughs and villages alike. This abuse was condemned on pain of excommunication. Some may regard this canon as an example of the arrogance of clerical pretensions to intervene in the business of government, but this view seems to be extreme. The king and his adherents were present at the Council. It would be natural for them to call in the assistance of the Church in an attempt to curb a prevalent abuse which was ruinous to government and Church alike.

Apart from the work of drawing up the canons, some judicial business was also transacted at the Council. The monks of Belvoir were disputing the right of a clerk to hold a church. The matter was discussed at the Council and Theobald together with the bishops of Chichester and Lincoln adjudicated. A charter of Theobald notified the terms of settlement.[1]

Relations between Stephen and Theobald had thus returned to their old cordiality, but were soon bedevilled by the succession question. Towards the end of 1150 the king had become reconciled with the archbishop of York, who had previously supplanted his nominee and relative. In return, Murdac promised to obtain papal permission for the coronation of Eustace. He left England early in 1151 and thus had no opportunity of attending the legatine council.[2] It was no doubt hoped by Stephen that, as both Murdac and Eugenius were Cistercians, the negotiations would proceed smoothly. In fact the request of the king was summarily rejected. Thomas Becket wrote a letter during his troubles with Henry II which recalled many of the events of the reign of Stephen in which he played some part. He seems, however, to have confused his enemy Roger of Pont l'Evêque who became archbishop of York in 1154 with Henry Murdac.

Do you not recall how that man, who is now archbishop of York, set out for Rome commissioned by the king and the nobles, who, as they could not persuade the archbishop of Canterbury, tried to obtain the removal of the apostolic prohibition from the lord Pope Eugenius?[3]

[1] No. 14.   [2] *John Hex.*, p. 325; *Hist. Pont.*, p. 85.   [3] *Materials*, vi, 58.

What was the 'apostolic prohibition'? According to John of Salisbury,[1] after the death of Innocent II who had granted to Stephen what might be termed a *de facto* recognition, the Angevin party recognised in his successor Celestine II a partisan, and appealed to him to reverse the decision. This the pope did not feel himself able to do. Instead he issued a probihition against any innovation concerning the English throne. While on the surface this prohibition seemed to be innocuous or even in favour of Stephen, John of Salisbury was of the opinion that it favoured the empress. Any move on Stephen's part was to be regarded as an 'innovation'. This would not have held good under Lucius II, but his successor Eugenius III was no lover of the English king. Consequently the proposed coronation of the king's elder son was regarded by Eugenius as an innovation. Stephen could have expected little else after his conduct over the great York election dispute and over the Council of Rheims. He himself had been crowned without any reference to the pope, but by bringing his case to the Curia he had made the Papacy the arbiter of the Crown. Eugenius sent a mandate to Theobald prohibiting the coronation of Eustace.[2]

Stephen persisted. In the spring of 1152 he called a council at London and once more the bishops and barons came together.[3] This time the atmosphere was different. It was known that Theobald had a mandate from the pope against the coronation of Eustace, yet precisely that was the business before the Council. As in 1148, obedience to the pope took precedence over obligations to the king. The right of coronation, as Gervase was careful to point out,[4] belonged solely to the archbishop of Canterbury, and Theobald's refusal was a blow to Stephen. It appears that the king then applied to the other bishops but none was willing to usurp the prerogative of Theobald. Instead they supported their primate thus reversing their conduct of four years before. The bishops were imprisoned, but in the confusion Theobald succeeded in escaping to Dover and ultimately to the Continent. Once more his possessions were confiscated. After Stephen's first annoyance had passed the bishops were released.[5]

[1] *Hist. Pont.*, p. 88.   [2] *Hunt.*, pp. 283–4.   [3] Ibid., *Gerv.*, i, 150.
[4] Ibid.; for Becket's views on this cf. *Materials*, vi, 57, vii, 330.   [5] *Hunt.*, p. 284.

Apart from Gervase and Henry of Huntingdon a third and highly-coloured account is provided by the *Compendium Vitae Theobaldi*.[1] The king, queen and Henry of Winchester, many of the nobles and especially the knights, wished Theobald to crown Eustace. The archbishop refused because Henry of Anjou was about to descend on England to assert his hereditary rights. Nothing is said about a papal mandate. Stephen's anger was aroused and although he personally would not lay a finger on Theobald, he was not prepared to object if anyone else did. Hearing this the archbishop took to flight down the river Thames. About a dozen armed knights pursued him with intent to kill or mutilate him, but with divine help he evaded them. These events took place on 6 April 1152. The accusation against the bishop of Winchester in this account doubtless had some basis, but in fact he was in Italy at the time on a visit to the pope[2] and intriguing against Theobald. He had revived his old plan of erecting Winchester into a metropolitan see, but would have been content with a legation or personal exemption from subjection to Theobald. Eugenius, however, paid no attention to a favourable party among the cardinals and rejected all of Henry's proposals. Henry was still at the Curia when the news of the attempted coronation was brought to Eugenius, and although he had an obvious alibi, the pope suspected him of stirring up trouble before he left. There is therefore no essential conflict between the sources.[3]

Theobald's exile in Flanders was not of long duration. According to Thorne[4] he blessed the new abbot of St. Augustine's, Silvester, on 28 August 1152. He was at Otford on 20 September and there ordained priest the bishop-elect of London, Richard de Belmeis.[5] As Professor Knowles points out[6] there was never any personal animosity between Stephen and Theobald, and having failed to make his point, the king was ready for a reconciliation as soon as his anger had died down.

It is seen that on this occasion the English bishops supported the pope and his legate. Davis said that this was the fourth time

---

[1] *Compendium*; the same account is in the Bec Chronicle MS. Bibl. Nat. 12884, f.208a.

[2] *Hist. Pont.*, pp. 80–1.   [3] *Gerv.*, ii, 76.   [4] *Thorne*, cols. 1813–14.
[5] C. E. Woodruff in *St. Paul's Ecclesiological Society*, vii, 170.   [6] Knowles, p. 291.

Stephen and virtual ruler of Kent.[1] The diocese of Canterbury had apparently suffered much from his Flemish adherents. In a letter to Adrian IV, Theobald referred to him as 'that most notorious tyrant and most severe persecutor of our Church'.[2] Another letter written on the same topic by the archbishop complained to the pope that William of Ypres had extorted a charter of confirmation from him by threats of violence.[3] On the other hand it ought to be mentioned that on more than one occasion William used his influence with Stephen in favour of Theobald.[4]

In January 1156, Henry crossed the Channel to conduct a campaign against his brother Geoffrey who, not without justice, claimed Anjou. As far as Theobald was concerned this campaign was noteworthy for his complaints against the exaction of scutage. Henry, while protesting his desire to do everything for the honour and benefit of the Church, conveyed his polite refusal to remit scutage or indeed certain other unspecified forms of taxation.[5] Round remarked that Theobald's 'opposition' in 1156 was directed against the necessity for scutage in that instance, but not against the principle of scutage.[6] This explanation seems reasonable, especially when the first canon of the Legatine Council of 1151 is recalled. Although scutage is not mentioned, the principle of royal taxation of the Church is admitted. The scutage of 1156 was levied at the rate of £1 on each knight's fee and something under £600 was realised from ecclesiastical tenants-in-chief.[7] Theobald does not appear on the roll as a contributor. If he was indeed exempted, Theobald's complaints were made for the benefit of the Church as a whole and not for his own diocese. The other exactions to which the king referred are difficult to trace. The towns and counties paid various imposts which totalled a greater sum than that paid by the Church, but it is not likely that the Church would have been occasioned any concern on this score. There is also recorded[8] a

---

[1] *Gerv.*, i, 161; L. B. Radford, *Thomas of London* (1894), p. 97. He continued to draw his revenues from Kent until Easter 1157 (*Pipe Rolls*, 2 and 3, Henry II).

[2] *P.L.*, 199, ep. 126, col. 106.   [3] Ibid., ep. 127, col. 106. This is no. 240.

[4] *Chronicon Monasterii de Bello*, Anglia Christiana Soc., p. 66. See above, p. 30. He was a benefactor of Holy Trinity, Aldgate.

[5] John of Salisbury's Letters, *P.L.*, 199, ep. 128, col. 108

[6] J. H. Round, *Feudal England* (1895), pp. 273-4.

[7] *Pipe Roll*, 2 Henry II.   [8] Ibid., p. 11.

payment of a comparatively small 'assisa' by the bishop of Chichester. The absence from the Pipe Roll of these somewhat irregular taxes need not be taken as conclusive evidence for their non-occurrence.

After the successful conclusion of his war against his brother, Henry returned to England in April 1157.[1] In August 1158 he left England again, for the last time so far as Theobald was concerned. At a royal council the abbot of St. Augustine's, Canterbury, was forced to make a profession of obedience to the archbishop,[2] but in the famous Battle Abbey case Theobald suffered a decisive reverse at the hands of the king.[3] Henry was crowned by Theobald at Lincoln at the end of 1157 despite the opposition of Roger of York, and on the following Easter the same ceremony was performed at Worcester.[4] Although the charters of Henry II are not dated and thus an accurate itinerary cannot be plotted, it is clear from the frequent attestations of Theobald that he was very often with the king during his widespread peregrinations in England.[5]

The war of Toulouse of 1159 brought on the Church heavy financial burdens from which, since 1156, it had been comparatively free. Not only was a scutage raised at the heavier rate of two marks for every knight's fee, but also a 'donum' on a much larger scale. The bishop of Durham, for instance, paid a scutage of twenty marks, but was assessed for a 'donum' of five hundred marks.[6] According to Round's calculations[7] the scutage produced 1,101 marks from the Church and the further impositions amounted to 4,700 marks, including contributions from religious houses not liable to scutage. Thus the Church had to pay more than six times as much as in 1156. Curiously enough there was not, at the time, even the solitary protest made three years before, or if there was, it has not survived. The cordial tone of Theobald's letters to Henry in 1159 and 1160 does not contain a hint of an objection to his exactions. Yet it is known how deep an impression Henry had really made. In 1166 John of Salisbury

---

[1] *Tor.*, p. 192.   [2] *Gerv.*, i, 164.   [3] See below, pp. 156 ff.
[4] H. G. Richardson in *E.H.R.*, 1939, p. 471; Foreville, p. 120, n. 2.
[5] L. Delisle and E. Berger, *Recueil des actes de Henri II*, etc. (1909–27).
[6] *Pipe Roll*, 5 Henry II, p. 31.
[7] J. H. Round, *Feudal England* (1895), pp. 275–81.

wrote to the bishop of Exeter pointing out that the year 1159, marked by these unjust exactions, was a turning point in Henry's life. Hitherto the king's actions could be regarded as excusable, but this flagrant violation of the rights of the Church was the beginning of the decline of his fortunes.[1] Gilbert Foliot, when abbot of Gloucester, had grudged paying fifteen marks towards some campaign of Stephen's[2] and his feelings against the taxes of Henry II were naturally stronger. In a letter to Archbishop Becket he stigmatised the taxes as a 'sword plunged in the vitals of holy mother Church'[3] and blamed him as the chief cause of the disaster. As Becket was very close to Henry in 1159, his personal relationship with the king outweighing the relative unimportance of his office, there was probably some truth in Foliot's accusation. Theobald's hope that the appointment of Becket as chancellor would benefit the Church[4] was proved delusory. It may have been that the Church maintained silence during these years for fear of antagonising Henry during the crucial period of the papal schism.

On the death of Adrian IV, on 1 September 1159, the cardinals were divided into supporters and antagonists of the Emperor Frederick Barbarossa. The imperialist minority, including the former legate Ymar, elected Cardinal Octavian who took the title of Victor IV, while the Hildebrandines elected the chancellor Roland, under the name of Alexander III.[5] Henry II had now the opportunity of exercising the prerogative of recognising the pope of his choice in a disputed election. This right had remained unquestioned. Thirty years before, on the occasion of the last schism, it had been exercised by Henry I. Accordingly, the king sent a writ to Theobald and the English Church forbidding the recognition of either claimant to the Papacy, until he should give his decision after taking appropriate counsel. Henry claimed to be following the practice of his grandfather. Bishops and others were forbidden to leave England for any purpose connected with the schism or for prosecuting appeals.[6]

---

[1] John of Salisbury's Letters, *P.L.*, 199, ep. 145, col. 134.
[2] Foliot's Letters, *P.L.*, 190, ep. 54, col. 783.   [3] Ibid., ep. 194, col. 894.
[4] *Gerv.*, i, 160.   [5] *Tor.*, pp. 204-5.   [6] See below, p. 543.

The English Church was confused by this uncertainty. The Papacy had come to play a far more important rôle in English ecclesiastical affairs than it had thirty years before. The difficulties of Theobald are expressed in one of his letters to Henry written shortly after the opening of the schism.[1] He insisted on the value of co-operation between Church and State which would be endangered by a divided English Church. That indeed was the present position in England. Some had come out in favour of Alexander, others of Victor. It is significant that the archbishop himself was undecided, as is shown by his awarding both claimants their papal titles. Subsequently in Theobald's correspondence Victor becomes Octavian. At the time, however, Theobald remained impartial, although Octavian was an old opponent of his.[2] In this letter Theobald goes on to admit the right of the king to recognise the pope and to hope that the decision would be expedited.

Nor is it profitable in any way that the English Church should be split after the manner of the Roman, and provide grounds for dispute in both lay and ecclesiastical spheres. When, therefore, some of the bishops and abbots send to Rome or go there, what am I to do, who more than any one else depend on your judgment, and more than anyone else am connected with the Roman Church? For whatever others may do, I am bound 'ex professione' to visit Rome at fixed times. Moreover it will be dangerous for me if others who have received less honour from Rome should anticipate my devotion to the one—at present unknown—who will triumph. It is also said that your majesty has given a licence to leave the country to certain individuals who rejoice in the death of Pope Adrian, who cherished you as a mother loves her only son; and as is well known several of them are plotting against me and my Church.

The letter ends with an appeal for advice and a warning that the fate of the Crown was bound up with that of the Church. The bearer of the letter had further information which was to be delivered verbally to the king.

It soon became clear that the French Church favoured Alexander and rejected Octavian. Indications of this development are provided by the issue of papal bulls. As early as 2 January

---

[1] John of Salisbury's Letters, *P.L.*, 199, ep. 44, col. 27.   [2] *Hist. Pont.*, p. 45.

1160, Alexander wrote to the bishop of Châlons-sur-Marne in the province of Rheims settling a point of canon law.[1] In the same month he intervened in the affairs of the diocese of Térouanne and of the archbishopric of Rheims.[2] In February there is to be found a confirmation to the monastery of Pontigny[3] and a letter to 'the barons and all the people of Dol commending Archbishop Hugh'.[4] This inspired Theobald's next letter to Henry on the subject.[5] The situation was becoming clearer to the archbishop and it was obvious that he would disapprove of any recognition of Octavian. 'The Gallican Church', wrote Theobald, 'as I have heard from a reliable source, has received Alexander and abandoned Octavian.' Alexander was a far better choice and superior in every way to Octavian and

although I have received neither a messenger nor a letter from either of them, I know that if you gave your consent we would all favour Alexander. I have heard that the emperor is trying to bring you over to the faction of Octavian, but may it never be that you would do any thing for the love or honour of man, when the Church is in such great peril, unless you thought it would be pleasing to God. Nor does it befit your majesty to place a man at the head of the Church of your kingdom without consulting it, a man who was not elected and is commonly said not to have the grace of God. He dared to seize this position only because of the favour and decrees of the emperor, for the Roman Church is almost entirely in favour of Alexander. It would be incredible that a party could gain the day with the help of human support, that is unjust and opposed by God. In fact I recall the numerous instances of how in similar circumstances the claimants recognised and supported by the Gallican Church have prevailed, whereas those who have been intruded by Teutonic aggression have come to an unhappy end. Thus in my own days Innocent gained the day against Peter, Calixtus against Burdinus, Urban against Wibert, Paschal against his three opponents Albert, Maginulf and Theodoric, and there are similar instances in former times.

Finally he advised Henry to come to no decision without consulting the Church.

Still Henry made no move. It is possible to gain some know-

[1] Jaffé, 10612.   [2] Ibid., 10613, 10618–19.   [3] Ibid., 10624.
[4] Ibid., 10625.   [5] John of Salisbury's Letters, *P.L.*, 199, ep. 48, col. 30.

ledge of his policy from the correspondence of Arnulf of Lisieux.
He had been a supporter of Stephen at the second Lateran
Council and was rewarded with the bishopric of Lisieux in 1141.
After his diocese fell into the hands of the Angevins he changed
his allegiance and subsequently became a prominent figure at
Henry's court, frequently attesting his charters. Although not so
close to Henry as Becket was, he must have known the mind of
the king fairly accurately. Shortly after the outbreak of the
schism, he wrote a letter to some of the cardinals expressing his
allegiance to the cause of Alexander.[1] As the letter mentioned
that King Henry was still fighting, it seems to have been written
before the truce of November 1159 between Henry and Louis
of France. Arnulf proceeded to say, possibly too optimistically,
that he had confirmed Henry's resolve to support Alexander.
This did not yet mean an official recognition. Again in a letter
written about the same time to Alexander himself,[2] he claimed
that he had changed Henry's attitude of impartiality into a
distinct leaning towards Alexander's claims. On the other hand
no recognition of Alexander would as yet be promulgated as
Henry did not want to rebuff the emperor, who had sent him a
letter and an embassy asking him to put off the recognition. It is
probable that the embassy referred to by Arnulf announced the
holding of the Council of Pavia which Barbarossa intended to
hold in January 1160 to decide on recognising Victor. Arnulf
expressed his intention of watching Henry in case some of his
advisers should seek to win him over to the imperialist faction.
It seems reasonable to assume from Arnulf's correspondence
that the king, on the whole, was inclined to support Alexander,
but was awaiting the right moment for an official recognition.

Theobald, away from the centre of events and badly informed, could not take such a hopeful view as Arnulf did. At one
stage, when it appeared to him that Henry was moving in the
direction of Octavian, he begged the king to hold back rather
than make a premature decision.[3] On another occasion he
hoped that the emperor would not secure the allegiance of
Henry to his schismatic projects.[4] Later, when Henry appeared

---

[1] *Arnulf*, ep. 23, pp. 29 f.   [2] Ibid., ep. 24, pp. 30–3.
[3] John of Salisbury's Letters, *P.L.*, 199, ep. 63, col. 47.   [4] Ibid., ep. 62, col. 46.

to be throwing in his lot with Alexander he expressed his disapproval of the king's temporising which was sapping the morale of the English Church. The bishops of Winchester and Durham, distant connections of Octavian,[1] were suspected of supporting the anti-pope, and their following might increase if the position were not clarified. It appeared also that Becket had betrayed Theobald's trust and had not provided him with information.[2]

The normal processes of litigation were adversely affected by the schism. The abbess of Barking was charged by a priest with the illegal seizure of his tithes.[3] The priest ultimately appealed to Rome but, as there was no pope officially recognised, the case was brought to a standstill. At the beginning of 1160 the king ordered the case to be heard by Theobald and the priest renounced his appeal. The abbess had to be cited thrice and by the time she had put in an appearance Alexander had been recognised and so she appealed to Rome. From a different source, similar evidence is also available.[4] During the course of a dispute Theobald received a mandate from Henry ordering him to settle the dispute—clearly without allowing the option of appeal—'lest with the continuance of the schism in the Roman Church it might be necessary for anyone to go out of our realm to seek justice'. This might refer to the general writ of the king to the Church already discussed. Theobald remitted the case to the diocesan and described the procedure to be adopted.

The imperial Council at Pavia was held in the second week of February 1160 and decided for Octavian, as was expected. English and French representatives were not present. Theobald's opinions of the Council are not written down, but the views of the Canterbury Curia were no doubt expressed in a private letter of John of Salisbury[5] written a few months later. It consisted of a vigorous diatribe against the emperor, against Germans in general, against the Council of Pavia, and above all against the election of Octavian.

In May 1160 the truce between Henry and Louis was con-

---

[1] Ibid., ep. 59, col. 43; cf. *Hist. Pont.*, p. 100.
[2] Ibid., ep. 71, col. 57; ep. 78, col. 64. [3] Ibid., ep. 87, col. 74.
[4] No. 131.   [5] John of Salisbury's Letters, *P.L.*, 199, ep. 59, cols. 38–43.

E

verted into a definite peace and the two kings then decided to
clear up the question of the schism. The formality of consulting
the English Church was the next step. This was an advance,
from the ecclesiastical point of view, on the conduct of Henry I
in the schism of 1130. It seems evident from the chroniclers
Orderic, Malmesbury and Huntingdon that the recognition of
Innocent II was an entirely unilateral act of the king. In January 1131, Henry went to Chartres, met Innocent, and recognised
him as pope. His grandson felt he had to consult Theobald and
the bishops, however perfunctorily. The English Church was
summoned to a Council at London. The date of its meeting is
by no means certain, but the opinion that it took place in June
1160 seems to fit the evidence better than any other.[1]

The preliminaries to the Council were mentioned by Arnulf
in a letter to a cardinal.[2] Henry, after agreeing with Louis that
the recognition of Alexander was expedient, sent to the Council
the documents he had received from the rival claimants. They
were to form the basis of the Council's decision. Arnulf himself
could not be present at the Council but he sent on a letter to be
read out to the assembled dignitaries.[3] In it he went over the old
ground of the disputed election and the Council of Pavia. The
argument of Theobald that it was better to follow the French
rather than the Germans was re-echoed. This was proved by the
freedom of France from all portents and monsters which
abounded in other lands—'sola Gallia monstra non habuit'.
Referring to the attitude of Henry, he pointed out that his sympathies were evident because he had refused to read the rescripts
of Octavian. Any delay on Henry's part could be accounted for
by the king's desire to emphasise his power and to increase his
influence. He concluded by an attack on those in the English
Church who continued to favour the schismatic party, a reference to the bishops of Winchester and Durham. When Gilbert
Foliot wrote an account of the London Council to Pope Alexander, he singled out this letter of Arnulf for special mention.
He said that when it was read out it influenced the minds of
many listeners.[4]

[1] F. Barlow in *E.H.R.*, 1936, pp. 264–8.   [2] *Arnulf*, ep. 27, pp. 36–7.
[3] Ibid., ep. 28, pp. 38–43.   [4] Foliot's Letters, *P.L.*, 190, ep. 148, cols. 852–4.

In a letter which has already been cited, John of Salisbury deals with this Council.[1] He does not throw very much light on what actually happened, but indicated the determination of Theobald to see the matter carried to a successful conclusion. The support of Roger of York and his treasurer John of Canterbury for Alexander was contrasted with the opposition of the bishops of Winchester and Durham. Those supporting Alexander outnumbered the opposition. Theobald himself wrote to Henry giving him an account of what took place.[2] The letters of both parties were read out and as a result the 'truth shone forth'. Nothing, he hastened to add, was decided to the prejudice of the royal power. The archbishop's caution was so extreme that the letter did not say which pope the Council favoured, but possibly this was too well known to need specifying. This letter told only a small part of the story, as Theobald's messengers, Bartholomew, archdeacon of Exeter, and William de Ver, chaplain to the archbishop, had verbal instructions amplifying the bare account of the letter. Bartholomew had been present throughout the Council and whatever he was to tell Henry had Theobald's authorisation. The decision of the Council was kept secret for the time being.

The decision of the Council did not of course mean the automatic recognition of Alexander. The Council was the jury, Henry was the judge. The Norman Church was then consulted at the Council of Neufmarché, Alexander again being successful. His envoys were heard.[3] Unlike Theobald, the archbishop of Rouen, followed by the bishop of Le Mans, was rash enough to recognise Alexander forthwith, and the property of the archdeacon of Rouen and the bishop was saved from Henry's violence by the intervention of Becket. By his careful timing of the recognition of Alexander, Henry was able to secure some castles in the Vexin.[4]

When everything at Neufmarché had been concluded satisfactorily and the decision transmitted to Theobald, the archbishop, in his legatine capacity, addressed a mandate to the

[1] John of Salisbury's Letters, *P.L.*, 199, ep. 59, cols. 42–3.
[2] Ibid., ep. 64 (1), col. 47.
[3] *Materials*, iii, 27.   [4] F. Barlow in *E.H.R.*, 1936, p. 268.

English bishops ordering obedience to Alexander and condemning Octavian as a schismatic and heretic.[1] He announced that the 'Anglican and Gallican Churches had received Alexander as Father and Pastor by the assent of our princes', duly acknowledging the power of Henry II and Louis VII. As Theobald and Henry were in agreement on this issue the question of the unfettered rights of the king of England to recognise the pope of his choice was not raised in an acute form.

A final event in Theobald's lifetime of some importance in ecclesiastical history was the marriage in 1160 of King Stephen's daughter Mary, the abbess of Romsey, to Matthew, son of the count of Flanders. The question was dealt with by Miss Norgate and Round. Miss Norgate claimed[2] that they were married by papal dispensation and cited in support Torigny and Lambert of Waterloo. She went on to say that

the scheme devised by King Henry was strongly opposed by the bridegroom's father and by Henry's own chancellor. Thomas, somewhat unexpectedly perhaps, started up as a vindicator of monastic discipline and used all his influence at Rome to hinder the dispensation.

The authority cited for Becket's conduct was Bosham. Round, following this account, said that

the sole surviving child of Stephen was Maud [sic], abbess of Romsey, but ... the great heiress was restored to the world by special permission of the Pope and married to Mathew, a younger son of the count of Flanders. Becket, like Anselm in the previous instance protested vigorously, but in vain.[3]

No references are given.

Two points arise from this—the question of the alleged papal dispensation and the attitude of Theobald. Referring to the authorities cited, Robert of Torigny mentions nothing about a dispensation and in fact describes the marriage as an unheard-of precedent.[4] Herbert of Bosham is the authority for the unex-

---

[1] John of Salisbury's Letters, P.L., 199, ep. 65, col. 50.
[2] K. Norgate, England under the Angevin Kings (1887), i, 469.
[3] J. H. Round, Studies in Peerage and Family History (1901), pp. 171–2.
[4] Tor., p. 207.

pected opposition of Becket. He describes the marriage as 'profanum et omnibus post futuris saeculis detestandum'. Becket opposed it on the grounds of 'enormitatem facti'.[1] Lambert of Waterloo explains the opposition of the count of Flanders on the grounds of the marriage being 'execrable'.[2] A chronicler of Afflighem in Flanders dilates on the immorality of this transaction which, in his opinion, was equivalent to adultery.[3] The Anchin recension of this chronicle claims that 'by reason of this he [Matthew] was excommunicated by Samson archbishop of Rheims and his suffragans'.[4] The language employed by all these accounts hardly characterises a marriage procured by dispensation of the pope, and no text of the alleged dispensation has been found. The difficulty is increased when it is remembered that there was probably no recognised pope to apply to for a dispensation. Presumably, with larger issues at stake, Alexander III was prepared to acquiesce informally in what had taken place. This seems to be indicated by Round in another place[5] where he quotes from an 'unpublished MS. of John's reign'. According to this MS., the castellan of Dover who was related to Mary persuaded King Henry to write to Alexander to obtain his permission for the marriage.

There appears to be no account of the reaction of Theobald to this irregular marriage. His earlier relations with Stephen's daughter are alluded to in one of his charters issued between 1150 and 1152.[6] It recites an agreement arrived at in his presence. Queen Matilda, Hilary of Chichester and Clarembald abbot of Faversham were also present. Mary, in the company of nuns from St. Sulpice of Bourges, had been a nun at Stratford and her father and mother had given her the manor of Lillechurch in Kent for her support. Mary, together with the nuns of St. Sulpice, left Stratford after some disagreement and withdrew to Lillechurch. By the mediation of Theobald and the others, the nuns of Stratford resigned Lillechurch and Mary became

---

[1] *Materials*, iii, 328.   [2] Bouquet, xiii, 517.
[3] Ibid., p. 277. This of course must normally have been the attitude of the Church to such a transaction.   [4] Ibid., n. (b).
[5] *Genealogist* (New Series), xii, 148. But according to Lambert of Ardres (Bouquet, xiii, 438), the interdict was not lifted until 1169 when she entered a nunnery.
[6] No. 155.

prioress there. An exchange with the abbot of Colchester by which a church in the vicinity of Lillechurch was made over to the nuns was witnessed by Theobald.[1] Mary, who was apparently of a restless character, later removed to Romsey whence she became the wife of Matthew of Flanders.

Theobald died on 18 April 1161.[2] Gervase under the year 1160 records that the archbishop fell ill, took to his bed and awaited his end. His letters to Henry II and Becket during the schism period frequently allude to his sufferings from illness. Despite his grave condition he insisted on attending the Council of London in June 1160, as John of Salisbury admiringly records.[3] He was carried thither on a litter and contrary to the expectations of his secretary survived the ordeal. As can be seen from Richard of Anesty's diary, Theobald was at Lambeth and Wingham as well as Canterbury in the later part of 1160.[4] As Theobald was dying in the spring of 1161 there remained two bishops-elect unconsecrated, Richard of Coventry and Bartholomew of Exeter. They came to Canterbury in order to be consecrated at least in the presence of the archbishop.[5] Richard had already done homage to Henry and could therefore be consecrated directly. Theobald was carried into the chapel and Richard made a profession of obedience to him. Walter of Rochester acting as vicar of the archbishop then consecrated him. Bartholomew had to cross the Channel to pay homage to the king and by then Theobald was dead. His last hours were spent with the faithful John of Salisbury to whom he gave a parting blessing and exhortation.[6]

His will was characteristically pious and practical.[7] All personal movables were to be distributed as alms, under the supervision of his chancellor Philip and others. Anyone interfering with the distribution was to be anathematised. This included the royal officials who, as administrators of the vacant see, would be particularly open to temptation. Those helping in the distri-

---

[1] *Monasticon*, iv, 382.
[2] *Gerv.*, i, 168; MS. Bibl. Nat. Latin 13905, f.74b (obit. of Bec).
[3] John of Salisbury's Letters, *P.L.*, 199, ep. 59, cols. 42–3.
[4] F. Palgrave, *Commonwealth* (1832), ii, p. xiv.
[5] *Gerv.*, i, 168; *Diceto*, i, 304.
[6] John of Salisbury's Letters, *P.L.*, 199, ep. 256, cols. 298–9.   [7] No. 28.

bution were to be granted an indulgence of forty days. The officials were also warned against touching any of the monastic properties. These had been separated from the archbishop's possessions as early as the days of Anselm to provide for this very contingency. Similarly he guaranteed all the religious houses of the diocese the free use and disposal of their property during the vacancy. With regard to the archiepiscopal possessions themselves there was little he could do to secure their protection during the vacancy, but he directed that there should be no depreciation in their value unless by direct command of the king or to relieve extreme cases of poverty. He instanced excessive timber cutting as a particularly serious abuse. The diocesan clergy were not to be afflicted by grievous exactions.

Farewell in the Lord, O my dearest brethren and sons, and I pray you forgive me for whatever I have wronged you so that the Most High shall have mercy on your sins, and pray for me so that God in His mercy shall help you when you need Him.

Gervase's interpretation of Theobald's last appeal is that he 'did penance for having done so little good and so much evil to the Church of Canterbury',[1] an opinion which can only be described as a piece of monastic misrepresentation. The good name of Theobald was highly esteemed by the people of Canterbury. In 1180, during the course of repairs to the damaged Canterbury Cathedral, Theobald's body was found uncorrupted and a popular outcry arose in favour of his canonisation.[2] Nothing came of this and his memory was allowed to sink into obscurity.

[1] *Gerv.*, ii, 389.   [2] Ibid., i, 25 f.

Relations with the English Monasteries

1. The Cathedral Priory

THE cathedral church of Canterbury, like others in England, was a monastery and the archbishop was its abbot. Under him were the prior and the other obedientiaries. By virtue of his office, the archbishop of Canterbury was removed from local interests to a great extent. There was also a tendency in the twelfth century for abbots in general to cease to live a common life with their monks and to set up their own establishments:[1] this movement was necessarily accentuated in monastic chapters where the bishop himself might very well not be a monk, as in the case of Archbishop William, Theobald's predecessor. It was not unreasonable, therefore, for the monks of Christ Church to regard the prior and not the archbishop as their natural head. On the other hand, the archbishops knew their rights, and thus the elements of conflict between the archbishop and the monks were generated. The struggle of the monks for autonomy began in a fitful way under Theobald who was yet the last archbishop to bear something of an abbatial relation towards them.

It can be seen from the *Domesday Monachorum*[2] that the estates of the monks were regarded as distinct from those of the archbishop. Anselm had given the prior and convent the right of administering their estates and conducting transactions in respect of them without consulting the archbishop.[3] He also settled other revenues on the monks. His purpose was to prevent the monastic estates falling into royal hands during vacancies. At the time of Theobald's election there were about 140 monks

[1] Knowles, p. 404.
[2] *V.C.H.*, *Kent*, iii, 261–4; D. C. Douglas, *The Domesday Monachorum of Christ Church Canterbury* (1944). [3] *Eadmer*, pp. 219–20.

in the Cathedral priory.[1] No doubt they expected Theobald to follow in the footsteps of his great predecessor at Bec and Canterbury and favour them, even at his own expense. At first they were not disillusioned. Immediately after his consecration in January 1139, he sent a dozen monks to Dover to occupy the priory of St. Martin's[2] thus reversing the policy of Archbishop William and latterly of Henry of Winchester, who were in favour of canons regular. Jeremiah, the prior, had opposed the establishment of canons at Dover[3] and Theobald as a Benedictine monk found himself in entire sympathy with his viewpoint.

In December 1141 a solemn ceremony took place in Canterbury Cathedral. King Stephen, having returned from imprisonment was crowned there by Theobald.[4] During the ceremony the secular clergy who were present demonstrated their rivalry with the Canterbury monks by finishing a hymn before them in order to be blessed first by the archbishop. Little did their haste avail them for Theobald promptly excommunicated them. They were only absolved on the intervention of Stephen. Meanwhile the monks finished at the proper speed—'tam devote quam morose'—and received the blessing of the archbishop and the praise of the king.

Relations between Theobald and his prior were at first amicable. Together they fought in the uphill battle against clerical marriage and attempted to stamp it out in the diocese.[5] Jeremiah was supported by Theobald in his efforts to maintain the jurisdiction of the priory over some of its London tenants.[6] Unfortunately 'the envy of the devil and the insinuations of the malicious' put an end to the concord and 'for just or unjust causes' their mutual esteem was terminated.[7] It may be suggested that the root of the matter lay in the election of Jeremiah by the convent in 1137 sede vacante.[8] The monks had no right to do this and they were not granted the privilege of electing a prior sede vacante until the bull of Alexander III in 1174.[9] No doubt also Theobald became acquainted with the antecedents of Jeremiah and the reasons for his election. That he had

---

[1] Knowles, p. 714.   [2] Gerv., i, 109.   [3] Ibid., i, 97–8.   [4] Ibid., i, 123, 527.
[5] Ibid., i, 126.   [6] No. 32.   [7] Gerv., i, 127.
[8] Ibid., i, 100; cf. Theobald's dying request to Henry II in P.L., 199, ep. 54, col. 34, not to allow changes during the vacancy.   [9] Holtzmann, ii, 323.

opposed the dying wishes of Archbishop William as a simple monk could hardly endear him to William's successor.[1] Presumably after working three or four years with the redoubtable Jeremiah any gratitude which Theobald owed him for his election must have evaporated.

Theobald made it clear that he intended to depose the prior, who thereupon appealed to Innocent II. This should have entailed the suspension of all measures by Theobald until the case had been settled. Notwithstanding this, he declared Jeremiah deposed and appointed his own nominee, Walter Durdent.[2] Although Theobald was noted for his obedience to the apostolic see, he never appeared to recognise the right of the Christ Church monks to appeal to the pope against him. The idea of monks appealing against their abbot was no doubt unheard of at Bec. Abbot and monks formed one united body, so how could one part of the body appeal against another? Nevertheless, the pope delegated his jurisdiction over the case to his legate Henry of Winchester. Theobald was tried by his suffragan and found wanting. Jeremiah was reinstated.

Theobald, as ever, was not cast down by humiliating defeat but proceeded inexorably towards his objective. The monks, who no doubt supported the appeal, were to be made to suffer until they cast out Jeremiah like another Jonah. Theobald refused to perform any sacraments in the Cathedral until Jeremiah was removed. The consecration of Bishop Gilbert of St. Asaph at Lambeth in 1143 probably had some connection with this situation. The prestige of the priory and its finances must have suffered from the new archiepiscopal policy. The appeal had already cost them one hundred marks. Gervase hints that the attitude of the monks towards Jeremiah altered sensibly. Jeremiah, no doubt, had the interests of the monastery at heart, and not wishing to be the cause of further trouble, resigned the priorate. He left Christ Church and was admitted into the rival monastery of St. Augustine's. His subsequent career is not known.

The ultimate success of Theobald seems to show that as yet an archbishop who knew his mind could enforce his will, but the

[1] *Gerv.*, i, 96–8.   [2] Ibid., i, 127.

success of the appeal to Rome pointed out the future path for the monks to take.

Theobald's choice for the now vacant priorate had remained at Dover during the second part of the struggle. He returned to Canterbury to take up office. Gervase commends his piety and learning so it would appear that Walter was not a bad choice of the archbishop.[1] No disputes marred the priorate of Walter Durdent who was consecrated bishop of Coventry in October 1149. There are, however, two documents which show how Theobald assisted the monks to recover property which had slipped out of their hands.[2] A fresh acquisition by the monks was confirmed[3] and Theobald himself granted tithes to their almonry.[4]

After the departure of Durdent, Theobald appointed his chaplain, Walter Parvus, as prior in his place.[5] Gervase points out that he made the appointment on the advice of the convent—if so he had cause to regret the advice. The verdict of Gervase on Walter was that he was a man of learning but not at all practical.[6] Under his administration the estates of the convent suffered and the monks ran into debt. Gervase blames the anarchy, but as has been seen, admits Walter was a bad manager. Southeast England, where the bulk of the Canterbury estates were situated, suffered least from the anarchy. There were, of course, William of Ypres and his Flemings, but it is noteworthy that Gervase accuses nobody by name. The mention of a famine seems more reasonable, but the inefficiency of the prior should be given prominence.

Whatever the causes, the sufferings of the monks impelled them to advise the prior to ask Theobald to manage their estates for them until the crisis was over. They must have been in grave difficulties to take this step for independence was almost as dear to them as life itself. The estates were taken over at Easter 1151.[7] Theobald knew his monks and needed a good deal of persuading by his clerks before he would undertake the management of the estates. Having reluctantly undertaken this new responsibility, he set to work conscientiously, trying to limit

[1] Ibid., i, 141.   [2] No. 44 and Supp. B.   [3] Nos. 42, 43.   [4] No. 38.
[5] Gerv., i, 141.   [6] Ibid., i, 143.   [7] Ibid., i, 146.

monastic expenditure and restore the finances. Gervase, writing some forty years after,[1] blamed the monks for setting a bad precedent. No doubt that was the feeling at the time after the first enthusiasm had disappeared. Theobald was watched carefully. Soon the monks accused him of cheating them by recouping his own losses—his household was not inconsiderable—at the expense of the already ravaged monastic estates. Those same household advisers, alleged the monks, who had urged the archbishop to take over the administration, were now foremost in plundering the poor remnants. At last the monks began to realise what the vow of poverty meant. Coarse bread and vegetables formed their staple diet. The prior and the other obedientiaries came to Theobald and protested against his theory and practice of estate management. At first Theobald listened quietly but later lost his temper. The prior then asked for the restoration of the estates. Theobald refused the request and also threatened to depose the prior.

The monks decided to appeal to the pope. On 24 August 1151 envoys were sent out with the appeal, but were intercepted by the archiepiscopal guard and imprisoned. The appeal together with supporting charters was confiscated. Theobald was clearly maintaining his determination not to allow his own monks to appeal against him. Further steps were taken to punish the monks. They were imprisoned and not allowed to celebrate divine service. The prior's horses were removed in order to forestall any attempt at escape. These measures proved so successful that the pope heard nothing of them for two years.

After the interdict had lasted eighteen days Theobald decided to abandon his hostility towards the monks and they likewise were anxious for a reconciliation. The interdict was raised and the monks took back their estates. Theobald promised to cherish the convent, the convent to pay due respect to their archbishop and abandon their appeal. According to Gervase, Theobald retained the churches on the conventual estates, but Stubbs doubted whether the right of presenting to these churches had ever been surrendered by the earlier archbishops.[2] He also

---

[1] According to the editor, Stubbs, p. 142, n. 5.
[2] Epp. Cant., *Mems. of Richard I* (R.S., 1865), ii, xxxi.

retained the 'exennia'—the Christmas and Easter offerings from the manors. He let it be known, however, that there would be no full restitution until the prior made a formal resignation, it being understood that Theobald would immediately reappoint him. Theobald's chief counsellors explained this move on the ground that he wished to prove his supremacy after he had been held in contempt by the appeal.

The prior believed in these lying words and in the presence of the convent, in chapter and with the archbishop presiding, resigned the priorate. When the prior in the middle of his speech said 'I resign the priorate on account of your reverence,' it was thought that the archbishop would say: 'And I restore the priorate to you'; but he hastily said: 'And I depose you.' Moreover he commanded him to follow him to London where he [promised he] would restore everything to him. Although the convent, expecting his betrayal, attempted to dissuade him from going, he rejected the advice of his brethren and came to the archbishop at Lambeth with certain of the older monks. While these were called away on the pretence of discussing the restitution with the archbishop, the servants of the archbishop seized Walter and conveyed him as far as Gloucester, ordering the abbot on behalf of the archbishop at no time to let him out. From that time the deposed prior remained there practically a prisoner as long as the archbishop lived.

The date of Walter's imprisonment can be fixed from Thorne's chronicle.[1] It was between 23 March 1152 and Theobald's exile early in April. The dispute had thus lasted a year. Its repercussions were not serious. The monks learned a new respect for Theobald and the last nine years of his primacy were untroubled by dissensions at home. A sequel was a letter of Pope Anastasius IV to Theobald dated 28 February 1154. It was addressed to Theobald but contained no direct accusation of the archbishop. Anastasius had heard by verbal report that Walter, formerly prior of Christ Church, his chaplain John, and two monks who had been going to appeal to the pope had been prevented from doing so. He ordered Theobald to see to their release and send Walter and his chaplain as well as the two monks who had appealed, to Rome with an explanatory letter.

[1] *Thorne*, col. 1812.

Those guilty of the outrage were to be excommunicated until they should appear at Rome with letters from Theobald. The effect of this bull is unknown. Perhaps after the death of Anastasius in the same year the matter was dropped.[1]

Possibly as a result of the bull, Walter was allowed to return to Canterbury. A letter of Theobald to Walter warns him that he could never hope to occupy again the office of prior or even of subprior, although other offices were not closed to him.[2] Any attempt to recover the priorate would result in the excommunication of himself and his supporters. He also informed him that during the years that had passed since his deposition the monastic estates had been administered 'in a more praiseworthy manner than it had been wont. . . . Do not therefore, brother, fall into error: do not—for God is not mocked, but remain in peace with your brethren, and may God forgive you for your actions against us, who did not deserve them.' The context suggests that Walter was no longer in Gloucester as Gervase claimed.

The new prior chosen by Theobald was Wibert, who had previously been subprior.[3] This choice met with general approval. A rumour was put about that the monks, disappointed in their attempt to appeal to the pope, were conspiring to assassinate Theobald. To avoid any misunderstanding, the archbishop made a public statement rejecting the rumour as a malicious lie. Anyone who henceforth spread this tale was to be excommunicated.[4]

The silence of Gervase on Theobald's relations with his monks from the appointment of Wibert till his own death, suggests that they were happy. Evidence for this period is restricted to charters which show Theobald's genuine interest in the welfare of the priory. Three important ordinances relating to the administration of the priory were laid down by Theobald during this period.

The first[5] related to the appointment of the obedientiaries and their financial commitments. The archbishop reserved to him-

---

[1] Holtzmann, i, 304.

[2] John of Salisbury's Letters, *P.L.*, 199, ep. 55, cols. 35–6 (wrongly addressed to Walter bishop of Rochester).

[3] *Gerv.*, i, 146.   [4] No. 37.   [5] No. 47.

self the appointment of the prior, the subprior and the precentor, the steward of the court and two doorkeepers. The rest of the officials were to be elected by the monks. Specifically mentioned were the chamberlain, the sacrist and the cellarer who were to be in charge of the estates and revenues. The monks were confirmed in their right of freely disposing of their property. This arrangement was confirmed by Adrian IV and Alexander III.[1] In his will Theobald made it clear that by allowing the revenues to be apportioned amongst the three specified offices, he had no intention of breaking the essential unity of the convent.[2] In fact it was found necessary to appoint a treasurer to co-ordinate their activities: this was done shortly after Theobald's death.[3] The financial system, as ultimately perfected, became one of the most effective in medieval England.

A solution to some of the questions raised by the jurisdiction of the monks was attempted by Theobald. A conflict between the monks and the archdeacon of Canterbury over the right of the latter to have a seat in chapter was settled by an ordinance of Theobald.[4] The archbishop discovered that, in former times, the archdeacon had no right to sit in chapter but could only come when specifically summoned by the monks. He was then to occupy the archbishop's footstool. This was to be established as a permanent regulation and no archdeacon or other secular was henceforth to defy it. Theobald also established the exclusive jurisdiction of the archbishop and the monks over crimes committed in the cathedral precincts.[5] Again the archdeacon was forbidden to intervene, as well as any secular authority.

Theobald's interest in the internal welfare of the priory is evinced by an ordinance directed to Wibert and the convent regulating the terms of readmission of fugitive or expelled monks.[6] Whatever position they had occupied before absconding they were never to rise above the level of a simple monk. This charter bears the seal of the convent as well as that of the archbishop which may indicate that the monks themselves had instigated this reform.

---

[1] Holtzmann, ii, 288, 298. He did not know of Theobald's charter.   [2] No. 28.
[3] R. A. L. Smith, *Canterbury Cathedral Priory* (1943), p. 14.   [4] No. 30.
[5] No. 50.   [6] No. 31. Cf. Rule of St. Benedict, c. 29.

Certain minor points of privilege were cleared up at the same time. Theobald abolished the obligation 'begun only in our time' of the monks to roof the archbishop's palace. It had begun as a gesture on the part of the monks and Theobald did not wish it to grow into a duty. So far from the monks having to build for the archbishops, added Theobald, the archbishops should do it for the monks, as well as conferring other benefits on them 'as good fathers for the love of their sons have been accustomed to do in former times'. This is an echo of the ideal days under Lanfranc and Anselm, and it was not Theobald's fault if standards had degenerated.[1] The archbishop did, however, retain the right of being clothed at the expense of the monks.[2]

The rights of the monks against the parish priests of the diocese were asserted with regard to burials. They could receive any corpse into their cemetery whatever the claims of the parish priests.[3] Similarly, the prior was entitled to collect the synodal pennies from the parish priests. On one occasion Theobald threatened to interdict the churches of recalcitrant payers.[4]

The right of admitting novices into the priory belonged to the archbishop as well as to the convent and there is one recorded case of Theobald vindicating this right.[5] In this case, however, the monks could hardly complain as the recruit brought with him a house and an area of land adjoining the almonry. The custom of men arranging to become monks when practically on their deathbed was also not unknown in Theobald's time.[6]

Finally mention may be made of a useful gift of Theobald to the priory which consisted of an area of marshland to be used to ensure a water supply.[7] The system was put into operation by Wibert.

2. THEOBALD AND ST. AUGUSTINE'S, CANTERBURY

The existence of two large monasteries in the same city gave rise to jealousy and dispute which were exacerbated by the presence of the archbishop. The desire of the abbey of St. Augustine to gain complete exemption from the jurisdiction of the archbishop

[1] No. 30.   [2] No. 47.   [3] No. 50.   [4] No. 49.   [5] No. 35; cf. *Gerv.*, i, 231.
[6] See below, p. 538.   [7] No. 46; the Chapter library is in Wibert's water-tower.

furnishes the keynote for the conflict between the abbey and Theobald which continued almost without intermission. The monks wished to place themselves under the direct control of the Papacy which thus found itself a party to the dispute as well as a judge of its merits.

In support of their claim to exemption from any English ecclesiastical jurisdiction, the monks of St. Augustine's possessed a series of bulls going back for five hundred years. That many of these bulls were forged is not disputed, but it is possible that the forgeries were intended to provide documentary proof for the practical exemption which the monks may have enjoyed. There is evidence that St. Augustine's was the scene of some systematic forgery early in the twelfth century.[1] The attitude of the pre-Conquest archbishops of Canterbury to the alleged exemption is by no means clear. One of the papal privileges provided for the burial of the archbishops at St. Augustine's. One can imagine the prestige and money which would have accrued to St. Augustine's if Becket had been buried there, and the corresponding losses to Christ Church. The earlier archbishops, however, abandoned this dubious privilege.[2] Lanfranc disregarded their exemption. He deprived the monastery of the right of summoning priests attached to its churches to its own synod and made them attend the diocesan synod. He also forbade the monks to ring their bells unless they had previously been rung in Christ Church.[3] Subsequent archbishops had to deal with the problem of the benediction of the abbot and his profession of obedience. The monks claimed that the abbot-elect ought to be blessed by the archbishop at St. Augustine's itself without making any profession of obedience. This claim was resisted by Lanfranc's successors down to Theobald.[4]

A new phase opened with the confirmation by Calixtus II, in 1120, of the forged bulls.[5] The Augustinian chronicler described this instrument not without reason as an 'autenticum privilegium'.[6] It asserted the freedom of the monastery from all kinds of ecclesiastical and lay interference and *inter alia* allowed bell-

---

[1] *Literae Cantuarienses*, ed. J. B. Shepherd (R.S., 1887–9), iii, 365–7, cf. W. Levison, *England and the Continent in the Eighth Century* (1946), pp. 174 ff.

[2] *Thorne*, cols. 1772–3.　　[3] Ibid., cols. 1791–2.　　[4] Ibid., col. 1798.

[5] Holtzmann, i, 231–3.　　[6] *Thorne*, col. 1797.

F

ringing at all times. This bull was confirmed by Innocent II in
1139.[1] The bull of Calixtus put the archbishops of Canterbury
on the defensive. They were in the almost impossible position of
encouraging papal authority on the one hand and defying it on
the other. Already Calixtus II had written to Archbishop Ralph
complaining about his infringements of the liberties of St.
Augustine's:

for it is unworthy that a church endowed with so great liberty by the
Roman Pontiffs should be subjected to exactions of this nature.[2]

The 'exactions' complained of were certain customary payments from St. Augustine's to the archbishop. According to
Gervase they were connected with synodal payments[3] but the
bulls of Calixtus and Innocent associated the payments with the
supply of chrism which the monks could obtain only from the
archbishop. If they did not pay the dues they were deprived of
the chrism. This was, of course, simoniacal. It seems, however,
to have been a general practice.[4] If Gervase's contention is
correct, it may well have been that the archbishop associated
the payment of synodals with the delivery of chrism in order to
make sure of receiving his dues as the question of attendance at
the archiepiscopal synods was by no means dead. The customary annual payments were firstly one of £2 10s. 7d. and secondly
'rams, bread and drink'. This consisted of two rams, thirty small
loaves, two amphorae of mead and one of beer, to the value of
three shillings. It must have been very humiliating for a monastery which claimed to be exempt to have to give annual evidence to the contrary.

The bull of Calixtus had some effect, for when Theobald
began to enforce what he considered to be his rights, there was
a great outcry from the monks. Although at first he apparently
refrained from exacting the payment of the rams, etc., he insisted on the other far more lucrative tax. He also insisted on
appointing priests to the churches in possession of St. Augustine's, thus continuing the policy of Lanfranc.[5] The monks
appealed to Innocent II who was sympathetic to their cause.

[1] *Elmham*, pp. 369–72.   [2] *Holtzmann*, i, 234.   [3] *Gerv.*, i, 74.
[4] R. H. Moorman, *Church Life in England in the Thirteenth Century* (1945), p. 120.
[5] *Thorne*, col. 1800.

It had already been laid down at the Council of Westminster in 1138, and at the second Lateran Council, that no payment was to be made for chrism.[1] Accordingly the pope sent a mandate to Theobald dated 20 November. The year is not given, but it was probably 1140. He ordered Theobald to desist from exacting the £2 10s. 7d. and if not, to appear before him or before his legate, Henry of Winchester, within three months to justify his conduct.[2] Clearly he would have to prove that the payment was not for chrism, otherwise it would be uncanonical. Innocent also notified Stephen and Henry of Winchester of the action he was taking, ordering them to protect the monks as best as they could.[3] He advised Abbot Hugh and the monks always to appeal to Rome if in trouble and told them of the steps he was taking. In reply, Theobald claimed a delay on the grounds of the disturbed state of the country.[4] This claim was by no means the meaningless formality usual in such cases and Innocent recognised its justice. On 14 December 1141 he notified Hugh that the hearing before him would be postponed to 18 November 1142.[5] Meanwhile Theobald, undeterred, continued to claim his annual dues.[6]

At the appointed time the proctors of Theobald and the monks arrived at the Curia to conduct their case. After a preliminary hearing the pope decided that as the principals were not present it would be better if he delegated his jurisdiction to judges in England. Henry of Winchester and Robert of Hereford were appointed.[7] Innocent gave them a history of the case, detailing the steps by which it had finally come into the cognisance of Theobald's suffragans and judges.

The case was decided at the Council of Winchester in the summer of 1143. Fourteen bishops were present.[8] The decision was favourable to Theobald who received the substance of his claims. Thorne naturally attempted to make of the decision a moral victory for St. Augustine's. The bishop of Winchester was made to say that the archbishop had no honest case, but out of reverence to the see of Canterbury he had advised and even

---

[1] *Gerv.*, i, 107; Mansi, xxi, 532. [2] *Thorne*, col. 1800. [3] Ibid., col. 1801.
[4] Ibid., col. 1802, line 57. [5] Holtzmann, i, 248.
[6] *Thorne*, col. 1802, line 25. [7] Ibid., line 43. [8] Ibid., col. 1803.

compelled the monks to surrender to Theobald and his church, land to the value of £3 in commutation of the annual payment. This consisted of a prebend in St. Martin's (Dover) worth twenty shillings and two mills near Dover. In return Theobald renounced all rights in connection with the annual payment. The monks, however, did not regard the judgment as altogether unsatisfactory. Although Theobald had secured his income and more besides, the exemption of St. Augustine's was rendered even more complete. Among the reasons which had induced the monks to assent to this compromise were the archiepiscopal functions with which they could not dispense—the giving of chrism, the dedication of churches and the granting of orders.[1]

A sequel to this dispute took place in 1144. The monks sent their prior and a few of the brethren to Rome to obtain confirmation of their privileges from Lucius II. It happened that Theobald and Henry of Winchester were also there, both hoping to secure the headship of the English Church. Theobald took the opportunity to raise the question of the 'rams, bread and drink' which had hitherto been left in abeyance. Apparently, since the prohibition of Calixtus, a payment of three shillings had been substituted. The monks claimed that the prohibition of Calixtus covered this commutation and had refused to pay. The question was argued before Lucius and a compromise similar to that on the main question was reached. A piece of land worth three shillings was surrendered by the monks. With some knowledge of proceedings at Rome, Thorne remarked that many are the friends of the rich. Thorne's business instincts were also outraged when he discovered that the two mills that Theobald obtained were alone worth £3, and thus the archbishop had made a handsome profit out of the whole transaction.[2] At first sight, it seems ludicrous that a Church Council including fourteen bishops should solemnly debate a matter involving fifty shillings,[3] but apart from the great importance attached to the principle of exemption, the financial issue was by no means contemptible. Today, it would

---

[1] Ibid., col. 1804.
[2] Ibid., cols. 1805–6.
[3] *Chronicle of St. Augustine's*, ed. A. H. Davis (1934), p. lvi.

require a capital of several thousand pounds to bring in annually an equivalent sum of money.

Thus when the monks finally obtained their bull from Lucius, it defined all the points at issue between Theobald and St. Augustine's in this first phase of conflict.[1] All sacraments were to be given free of charge and the new arrangements to secure payment of the customary dues to the archbishop were sanctioned. The bull also dealt with the question of the presentation of priests to churches on the land of St. Augustine's. They were to be appointed by the advice of the archbishop and with the consent of the monks. This bull was confirmed by Pope Eugenius.

From 1144 to 1148 there was a period of truce between Theobald and St. Augustine's and, as might be expected, the chroniclers lost interest. There is, however, a charter of Theobald to the abbot of St. Augustine's which can be assigned to this period.[2] The archbishop confirmed the appropriation of a church and its dependent chapels to the monastery.

When Theobald pronounced his interdict on England in September 1148 at the behest of Eugenius III[3] it was for the most part ignored. In the diocese of Canterbury alone was it taken seriously. When the news of the interdict reached St. Augustine's there was some conflict amongst the monks as to the course of action they should take. They considered themselves exempt from the normal diocesan jurisdiction, therefore a local interdict pronounced by the diocesan could not affect them. They could continue to celebrate divine service normally, if discreetly. On the other hand they would have to obey a papal order for the observance of an interdict. Thus the question before them was not 'Ought we to observe the archbishop's interdict?' but rather 'Is this a papal interdict which must be observed?' This interpretation of the issues of the conflict makes it easier to follow the very complicated series of events which ensued.

Abbot Hugh thought it was a papal interdict and decided to observe it. Two of the leading obedientiaries disagreed with him and were supported by the monks. They decided to ignore the

---

[1] *Thorne*, cols. 1805–6; Holtzmann, ii, 179–81.
[2] No. 55.   [3] See above, p. 29.

interdict. These were Silvester the prior and William the sacrist.[1] William was the abbot's nephew and Gervase associated him with the earlier conflict between Theobald and the monks. He was known to that chronicler as 'Willelmus cognomento Diabolus' and Gervase probably regretted that this redoubtable adversary was not at Christ Church. He was alleged to be the originator of the policy of total exemption and took advantage of the weakness of Theobald during the legation of Henry of Winchester to forward this claim. The monks 'aroused by the sting of this devilish gadfly' were only too ready to follow his example.[2] Thorne admits that on this occasion they miscalculated as they did not realise Theobald was acting in his legatine capacity.[3] This is not strictly true, but Theobald was acting at any rate as a papal delegate. Probably Theobald himself was to some extent responsible for their misapprehension.

They appealed to the pope against the interdict although all appeals had been forbidden. The notice of the interdict must have reached them in good time as their emissaries, Nigel and Absalom, were able to set out before the actual commencement of the interdict on 12 September 1148. Had the monks observed the interdict pending the hearing of the appeal all would, no doubt, have been well, but they took the issue to be prejudged and celebrated divine service as usual. The result of the appeal was that Eugenius ordered the proctors to return and the monks to obey their archbishop.[4]

Meanwhile Theobald had returned to Canterbury. While he was disappointed at the failure of most of England to observe the interdict, he was outraged at this defiance on his own doorstep. He pronounced a general excommunication both on those who did not observe the interdict in the monastery itself and on laymen who received sacraments. He singled out Silvester and the diabolical William for personal excommunication.[5] Hugh was spared, but he was ordered to remove himself from the body of the excommunicate and accordingly retired to Thanet.[6]

The monks once more appealed, this time against the sen-

[1] *Hist. Pont.*, p. 46; *Thorne*, col. 1807; *Gerv.*, i, 136.   [2] *Gerv.*, i, 74–5.
[3] *Thorne*, col. 1807.   [4] *Thorne*, col. 1808; *Gerv.*, i, 136.
[5] *Hist. Pont.*, p. 46; *Gerv.* and *Thorne* as before.   [6] *Hist. Pont.*, pp. 46–7.

tence of excommunication.[1] They now appeared to be on firmer ground as they might well claim that they should be punished by the pope and not by the archbishop. The abbot lent his support to the appeal.[2] Theobald also felt his action needed justification for he sent emissaries to the pope to inform him of the excommunication.[3] These must have arrived before the appellants, for Eugenius refused to see them, being excommunicate.[4] Later he relented, absolved them in the name of Theobald and allowed them to state a case.[5] Finally he sent them back with written instructions to Abbot Hugh. The abbot was given the power of absolving all the monks except the ringleaders Silvester and William. In their case, as well as that of the laymen implicated, Theobald alone was given the power of absolution. The deposition of Silvester by Theobald was confirmed by the pope but he reserved to himself the right of reinstating him. The punishment for their non-observance of the interdict was to fit the crime. Beginning from the date of their receipt of this bull, they were to refrain from celebrating divine service for as long a time as they had ignored the interdict. The bull was dated 18 January 1149 and was received by the monks on 12 March.[6]

The humiliation of the monks of St. Augustine's was not relieved at all by the presence at their monastery of Queen Matilda who was staying there during the building of Faversham abbey in which she took an interest. During the interdict she summoned monks from the cathedral to celebrate services at St. Augustine's.[7] This was the cruellest blow. The pope mercifully abridged their term, and instead of the 181 days they were supposed to be bound by the interdict, they were set free on 1 August which was 142 days.[8]

As soon as the bull was received, Silvester and William came to Theobald to receive absolution but the archbishop was not as yet prepared to grant it to them. The monks thought that by the terms of the bull they were entitled to immediate absolution. Another ground of complaint against Theobald was that he was exacting a payment for absolution from laymen serving in the

[1] Ibid., p. 47; *Gerv.* and *Thorne* as before.   [2] *Thorne*, col. 1808.
[3] Ibid.; *Hist. Pont.*, p. 47.   [4] *Gerv.*, i, 137.   [5] Ibid.; *Hist. Pont.*, p. 47.
[6] *Thorne*, col. 1808.   [7] *Gerv.*, i, 139.   [8] *Hist. Pont.*, pp. xlix–l.

monastery who had been excommunicated with the others.
Accordingly they appealed once more to the pope. This elicited
a bull to Theobald ordering the absolution of Silvester and
William. He was also ordered to return the money wrongfully
exacted from the laymen who had been excommunicated. This
had been done, alleged the pope, in violation of the canonical
principle that no one was to be punished twice for the same
crime.[1] Silvester and William therefore presented themselves
for a second time to the archbishop with the papal rescript
authorising their absolution. They confessed their crime and
promised to behave themselves in future. They were scourged
at the door of Northfleet church and duly absolved.[2] The pope
had shown both parties who was the real master. After Theobald's death the position was clarified by a bull of Alexander III
which gave the monastery the privilege of celebrating divine
service even if the rest of the land should be under interdict.[3]

When an abbot of St. Augustine's died in the twelfth century
there was invariably a struggle between the monastery and the
archbishop with regard to the new abbot's benediction and profession of obedience. Abbot Hugh died on 25 June 1151.[4] Before
his death the monks were alleged to have paid King Stephen
five hundred marks so that they should be allowed to administer
the monastery during the vacancy and to have a free election.[5]
This is yet another indication of Stephen's power over the Church.
The money was paid over by Silvester—Silvester was elected
abbot. He thus lay under strong suspicion of simony and Theobald was reluctant to confirm the election, both on account of
the alleged simony and on account of Silvester's part in the
events of 1148–9.[6] The power of the king, however, was sufficient to quell any opposition, and Theobald grudgingly confirmed the election. He refused to bless Silvester until he had
cleared himself of the suspicious circumstances surrounding the
election.

Silvester went to the pope at the end of 1151 and purged himself. The pope, in his bull of 20 January 1152, remitted Silvester

---

[1] *Thorne*, cols. 1808–9, 'non enim bis in id ipsum aliqui sunt puniendi'.
[2] *Hist. Pont.*, p. 52.   [3] *Elmham*, p. 425.   [4] *Thorne*, col. 1810.
[5] *Hist. Pont.*, p. 89.   [6] *Thorne*, col. 1811; *Elmham*, p. 405.

to Theobald to receive his blessing at St. Augustine's,[1] despite the claim of the archbishops of Canterbury to bless abbots of St. Augustine's at Christ Church. Silvester had an interview with Theobald at Teynham on 6 March and after some procrastination the archbishop agreed to bless him at St. Augustine's on 23 March. Arriving there on the appointed day with the abbots of Faversham and Boxley, and having opened his address, he was interrupted by his own prior Walter Parvus who had come to protest against the infringement of the rights of Christ Church. He had come with some of the monks and a band of armed men and although the doors had been closed against him, he had 'prudently entered'.[2] Walter made a speech denying the right of Theobald to bless Silvester at any other place than Christ Church and appealed to the pope. Subsequently he was deposed and exiled to Gloucester and the appeal fell through. Nevertheless Silvester remained unblessed, partly owing to Theobald's own exile in the same year. The abbot-elect procured another bull from Eugenius ordering Theobald to bless him, which he did on 28 August 1152, in the presence of Bishop William of Norwich and Roger archdeacon of Canterbury. He did not exact a profession of obedience from Silvester, but this was without prejudice to his rights.[3] John of Salisbury considered that the ancient bulls which authorised the blessing of Silvester at St. Augustine's were suspect, but his influence at the papal chancery was apparently too weak to secure their rejection by Eugenius who was no doubt only too willing to be deceived in such a good cause.[4]

As far as Theobald was concerned the question of the profession of obedience was not closed. In the past a profession had been made and precedent was in his favour. After the death of Eugenius in July 1153 Theobald took up the question with Anastasius IV who ruled that if it was customary for the abbot of St. Augustine's to make a profession of obedience to the archbishop of Canterbury, then Silvester should follow this precedent.[5] Unfortunately for Theobald, Anastasius died before he

[1] Cf. *Hist. Pont.*, preface, p. l.   [2] *Gerv.*, i, 148; *Thorne*, col. 1811.
[3] *Thorne*, cols. 1813–14.
[4] *Hist. Pont.*, p. 89. The handwriting and the seals did not correspond.
[5] *Gerv.*, i, 76; *Thorne*, col. 1814.

could take advantage of this ruling and he felt he could take no further steps in the matter until he had consulted his successor, Adrian IV.[1] Meanwhile the monks of St. Augustine's were not idle. They had found a party amongst the cardinals who bore ill-will against Theobald and the cardinals succeeded in prejudicing the mind of Adrian against the archbishop.[2] Consequently when Theobald renewed his application he received a bull couched in a most accusing and truculent tone.[3] The pope complained of the ingratitude of Theobald, who, after being loaded with favours at the hands of the apostolic see, had attempted to diminish its powers by joining with the king in 'burying appeals'. He was grudgingly prepared to allow the dictum of Anastasius to stand but threatened Theobald with dire penalties if he failed to prove his case. Thorne adds a punning aside of the pope: 'You are rightly and deservedly called Theobaldus, i.e. *Turbaldus*, because you disturb and persecute all whom you can.' He adds that on receipt of this commination, Theobald was so astonished and terrified that he abandoned all his efforts to extort the profession from Silvester and left the monastery in peace.[4]

Theobald, however, was made of sterner metal than this. He received the bull in the spring of 1156 and it certainly upset him. In a letter written towards the end of the year to Boso, the papal chamberlain, he remarked that the bull was a dishonour to the pope and a disgrace to himself. Even if he attempted to prove that he was in the right, the monks would be encouraged to appeal against him and thus the whole sorry business would drag on interminably.[5] His only course was to win over the pope to a fairer appraisal of the situation and to secure the support of some of the cardinals. Before he had time to embark on this policy he fell seriously ill[6] and thus passed the summer of 1156. Later in the year he wrote once more to the pope and the other cardinals[7] and his efforts bore fruit. Adrian addressed two bulls

---

[1] *Gerv.* and *Thorne.*
[2] John of Salisbury's Letters, *P.L.*, 199, ep. 103–5.
[3] *Elmham*, pp. 411–13; John of Salisbury's Letters, *P.L.*, 199, ep. 102.
[4] *Thorne*, col. 1814. Pope Urban VI was called 'Turbanus'.
[5] John of Salisbury's Letters, *P.L.*, 199, ep. 105.
[6] Ibid., ep. 102.   [7] To the pope, ep. 106; to the cardinals epp. 103, 104.

to Silvester[1] in the second of which he ordered the abbot to make a profession of obedience to Theobald within thirty days if it could be proved that he ought to do so. Thus there was no longer any opportunity for the monks to appeal. Silvester continued to deny his liability. Accordingly, at the Council of Northampton in July 1157, witnesses of the profession of obedience of Abbot Hugh II to Archbishop William were brought forward and seven bishops who were present decided that Silvester ought to make a profession.[2] He made his profession in the traditional form:[3]

I, Silvester, abbot of the church of the apostles Peter and Paul and of the blessed Augustine, apostle of the English, do promise to the holy church of CANTERBURY and to you O reverend father Theobald, archbishop of the same church and to your successors, canonical obedience in all things.[4]

3. THEOBALD AND ST. MARTIN'S, DOVER

A different problem was presented to Theobald by Dover priory. In the first place he had to establish and secure the monastic order there. He also had to make it clear that the subjection of the priory to 'the church of Canterbury' meant subjection to the archbishop and not to the cathedral monks. It was further necessary to give the new priory endowment and encouragement in order to secure its future stability.

Originally St. Martin's had been a house of secular canons.[5] Archbishop William, who was an Augustinian canon, had been awarded the possessions of the ancient church by Henry I, in order to found there a monastery of canons regular. This was thwarted by the monks of his own cathedral who succeeded in installing Benedictine monks while the archbishop was on his deathbed. During the vacancy, Henry of Winchester, the vicar,

---

[1] *Gerv.*, i, 163–4.   [2] Ibid., i, 164–5.
[3] Cf. almost identical profession of Abbot Hugh I in 1099 printed H.M.C., Fifth Report, App., p. 431.
[4] Facsimile in New Palaeographical Soc., 1st series, vol. 2. The profession had little practical significance.
[5] Haines deals with these events but shows strong prejudice against Theobald and Innocent II.

removed the monks, but practically the first act of Theobald when elected archbishop was to restore them.[1] He regularised the position by obtaining a confirmation of his action from Innocent II as well as from Stephen.[2] Innocent's bull of 14 January 1140 reversed his earlier grant to William. Dover was to be established according to the Benedictine rule and was to be subject to Theobald and the Church of Canterbury. Subsequently Theobald obtained further confirmations from Eugenius III, Anastasius IV and Adrian IV.[3] Adrian's confirmation added a prohibition against the prior of Canterbury having any authority at Dover, *sede vacante*. The monks could certainly claim no authority at any other time. A confirmation of Henry II specified that the administration of Dover priory should be 'in the hands and lordship of Archbishop Theobald and his successors, and that nobody save the archbishop of Canterbury should ever have the right to dispose of or ordain its external or internal affairs'.[4] Thus, as far as in him lay, Theobald attained his first two objectives.

In the last years of his life[5] he issued a regulation governing the relationship between himself, the cathedral monks and the new priory.[6] Canterbury was the mother-church and Dover its cell. The monks of Dover ought to make their profession at Canterbury and their prior must be a monk of Canterbury. The appointment and removal of the prior of Dover was reserved for Theobald and his successors. Later generations of Dover monks who aspired to independence regarded this regulation in an unfavourable light, as can be seen from the heading in the fourteenth-century Dover Cartulary:

Ordinance of Theobald against the tenor of the charter and will of the founder to the prejudice of the church of Dover, on account of which arose the lawsuit between the monks of Canterbury and Dover.

Theobald appointed four priors of Dover.[7] Ascelin was appointed in 1139 and resigned in 1142 on his election to the see of

---

[1] See above, p. 57.   [2] *Monasticon*, iv, 536; Holtzmann, ii, 170.
[3] Eugenius: Holtzmann, ii, 214; Anastasius: *Monasticon*, iv, 536; Adrian: Holtzmann, ii, 269.
[4] *Monasticon*, iv, 538–9.   [5] Haines, p. 72, dates it before 1143.
[6] Nos. 83, 84, duplicates with variations in the witness lists.
[7] *V.C.H.*, *Kent*, ii, 136.

Rochester. His successor William became abbot of Evesham in
1149. Theobald then appointed Hugh, who died in office in
1157. He was succeeded by Richard who became archbishop of
Canterbury in 1174—a unique feat for a Canterbury monk. The
method of the appointment of the other officials is not recorded.
A precentor, Arnulf, attests one of Theobald's charters.[1]

The priory, as established by Theobald, succeeded to the
possessions and rights of the former occupants.[2] It has been seen[3]
that the abbot of St. Augustine's was in possession of one of the
prebends which he made over to Theobald in part commutation
of the annual tax. Of the other twenty-one prebends the monks
of Dover held twenty and Theobald the remaining one.[4]

Theobald augmented the income of the monks from his own
resources. He awarded them the right to levy toll as far as that
right belonged to him.[5] He also encouraged others to support
the new priory. The burgesses of Dover had been accustomed to
give a tithe of the herrings caught during October and November to their religious house. Theobald wrote to them congratulating them on their faithful payment of this tithe, but remarked
that he would be even more delighted if they gave a tithe of all
fish caught all the year round to the new priory.[6] He offered an
indulgence of fifteen days if they would do so. The burgesses
responded generously. They forwarded their reply to the archbishop under cover of a letter of Faramus, the castellan.[7] He
informed the archbishop that the burgesses had augmented the
old tithe and were now prepared to grant a tithe of all the fish
which they caught throughout the whole year, and that he himself had confirmed the gift. The enclosed letter of the burgesses
shows that they offered to pay the tithe in cash or kind which-
ever was preferable to the monks. They had also exempted the
monks from their share in the repairing of the town wall. In
return the monks had given the burgesses the right of burial in
their cemetery. Theobald wrote in reply to say how pleased he
was with their action. He offered 'to multiply prayers to God
specially for you in our church of Canterbury'.[8] A formal
charter to Prior Hugh and the men of Dover officially confirmed

---

[1] No. 86.   [2] Nos. 85, 86.   [3] See above, p. 68; cf. no. 58.
[4] *Monasticon*, iv, 533–4.   [5] No. 86.   [6] No. 87.   [7] Supp. C.2.   [8] No. 88.

the grant and anathematised anyone contravening it.[1] A similar notice was sent to Bishop Walter of Rochester and the clergy and people of Kent.[2]

Since their early intervention, the monks of Canterbury had apparently shown little interest in Dover, but about this time a charter was issued in the names of the archbishop and the convent congratulating the burgesses on their munificence and promising to pray for them.[3] As might have been expected, once the gift had been ratified, relations cooled a little on both sides, and the Church did its best to keep the burgesses to their word. This is made clear in a rare archidiaconal writ of Becket.[4] After ordering the payment of the tithes, he reminded the burgesses that payment could be enforced in the royal courts. A writ of Henry II to the same effect, witnessed by Theobald at Canterbury, completes the series.[5]

During most of Theobald's primacy the work of building and enlarging the priory went on. Theobald granted an indulgence of forty days—his maximum allowance—for those contributing to St. Martin's during this period.[6] The new priory was dedicated on 19 October 1159.[7] Theobald may have been too ill to dedicate it in person, but he issued an indulgence of twenty days to those contributing to the priory on the anniversary of the dedication and for seven days afterwards.[8] About the same time or a little earlier, an altar was dedicated to St. Giles in the monastic church and Theobald offered an indulgence of fifteen days to contributors on that occasion.[9]

Other documents are extant to show Theobald's interest in the welfare of St. Martin's. A gift of Henry of Essex, Stephen's constable, was witnessed by Theobald, 'by whose holy advice and opinion we established these and other alms'.[10] An exchange of land between Hugh of Dover and the monks there was effected by the hand of Theobald and was confirmed by him.[11] He also secured to the monks an annual rent of twenty shillings from a Dover church, to be paid by the priest he had installed there.[12]

---

[1] No. 90.   [2] No. 91.   [3] No. 89.   [4] Supp. C.1.
[5] Supp. C.3.   [6] No. 92.   [7] Supp. C.5, cf. Haines, p. 189.
[8] No. 94.   [9] No. 93.   [10] Supp. C.4.   [11] No. 95.   [12] No. 97.

In 1141, two monks of Dover founded St. Bartholomew's hospital at Buckland, near Dover. They did this 'by the authority of Archbishop Theobald and by the consent of the prior and monks of Dover'.[1] The hospital was to be entirely subject to the priory. In due course Theobald issued an indulgence of twenty days to those supporting the hospital and to those contributing to the collection for it which was being organised.[2]

4. St. Gregory's Priory, Canterbury

As this Augustinian priory was an archiepiscopal foundation,[3] one would expect that there would be some evidence connecting it with Theobald. The chroniclers refer only once to the priory. Its church was burnt in 1145.[4] The cartulary contains five charters of Theobald; there were probably more as several folios are missing just after Theobald's charters begin. The first three charters are confirmations by Theobald to the priory of three chapels and various purchases of land made by the prior Alfred.[5] A fourth charter is addressed to the bishop of Rochester, the archdeacon of Canterbury, the abbot of St. Augustine's, the prior of Christ Church and all faithful.

Be it known to you that I have granted the church of St. Gregory, founded outside Northgate to the regular canons whom Archbishop William brought there. I keep them under my own control and forbid that they should be subject to the rule of anyone else.

He then went on to confirm the possessions of St. Gregory's.[6] One of the witnesses was Miles Crispin, presumably identical with the precentor of Bec and reputed author of the *Compendium Vitae Theobaldi*.[7] A fifth charter related to a church subsequently appropriated to St. Gregory's.[8]

What degree of control Theobald exercised over the priory cannot be determined. The prior Alfred was an occasional

---

[1] MS. note on first page of Bodleian MS. Rawl. B 335.
[2] No. 82.   [3] *V.C.H., Kent*, ii, 157; cf. No. 59.
[4] *Gerv.*, i, 130; Annals of Dover (MS., B.M., Cott. Jul. D.v.).   [5] Nos. 60–2.
[6] No. 59. The address may indicate the order of ecclesiastical precedence.
[7] Porée, i, 105, 532.   [8] No. 63.

witness of Theobald's charters. In Theobald's will the canons received special mention and their possessions were confirmed.[1]

5. The College of South Malling

It seems appropriate to give an account of Theobald's relations with this collegiate church here. The college of South Malling was founded on land belonging to the archbishops of Canterbury. It later became one of the peculiar deaneries of the archbishop in the bishopric of Chichester. The foundation of the church probably goes back to the eighth century and at the time of Domesday it was a house of secular canons.[2]

It appears that by the time of Theobald their collegiate church had fallen into decay and little is known of the position of the canons. Their organisation was still functioning before Theobald's new measures, as can be seen from a charter of Theobald which can be dated 1139–48.[3] A subsequent confirmation of this charter cannot be later than 1148.[4] In the charter the dean and two canons are specifically mentioned. One of the canons had made over his church of Glynde to the monks of Bec through the good offices of Theobald, who transferred it to the representative of the monks. The church of Glynde had attached to it a pension of two shillings payable annually to the collegiate church of St. Michael, South Malling. The monks were to continue to pay the pension when they received the church. The charter was given 'at Malling' and Theobald was attended by several members of his household, including his clerk Alan of Wells, two chamberlains and his steward.

Theobald was concerned to put the college on a sound basis as appears from two of his charters relating to St. Michael's. The first is addressed to the men of the hundred of Malling and announced that he had consecrated and dedicated the church of St. Michael. This is regarded as the re-erection of the collegiate church. Furthermore he endowed the canons with all the tithes of his demesne. The charter is dated 'at Malling' and

[1] No. 28.   [2] *Sussex Archaeological Collections*, v, 128; *V.C.H.*, *Sussex*, ii, 117–19.
[3] No. 177. Cf. *Sussex Arch. Coll.*, xxvi, 46–7.   [4] No. 178.

is of the years 1150–4.[1] The second charter is addressed to the dean, reeve, and all the officials of Malling. He awarded the canons the tithe of pannage in his forest and also the right of free pannage for twenty-four pigs. This forest was the forest of Broyle, which covered an extensive area of East Sussex. Curiously enough Theobald's forester, Daniel, does not attest this charter, but the other one. This charter is also of the years 1150–4.[2]

His dedication and consecration of the church and his other endowments secured for Theobald a permanent place in the affections of the canons of South Malling and in their statutes they were directed to pray for the soul of 'the venerable father Theobald, archbishop of Canterbury, who built and endowed the church of the said College'.[3]

6. ABBATIAL ELECTIONS AND PROFESSIONS OF OBEDIENCE

Although by canon law the election of an abbot was supposed to be the free choice of the monks of the religious house concerned, in practice the monks, especially of the larger houses, were subject to a great deal of external influence. The king, the pope, the archbishop and the diocesan bishop or a local magnate might all have good grounds for intervening in what ought to have been a private affair of the monks concerned. In general there is very little evidence to show intervention by Theobald in abbatial elections.

In Kent, the archbishop's relations with the larger monasteries have already been dealt with. There are, however, some professions of obedience extant from the other houses. An almost contemporary Canterbury manuscript gives the professions of Alexander prior of Leeds (Augustinian canons), Lambert abbot of Boxley (Cistercian) and Clarembald abbot of Faversham (Benedictine).[4]

No details appear to be available with regard to the election of Prior Alexander of Leeds. A charter of Theobald[5] addressed

---

[1] No. 179.   [2] No. 180.   [3] *Sussex Arch. Coll.*, v, 130.
[4] Supp. J.; the original of Clarembald's profession has survived and is printed by C. E. Woodruff in *Arch. Cant.*, xxxvii (1925), 65.   [5] No. 148.

G

to him can be dated 1150–61. Boxley was founded by William of Ypres for the Cistercian Order in 1146.[1] Lambert was the first abbot. The second abbot, Thomas, made his profession to Theobald on 2 March 1153.[2] His profession differs radically from Lambert's and approximates to Clarembald's or any episcopal profession. It would appear that Theobald's chancery had a common form of profession but individual monasteries could submit professions of their own composition providing they were approved by the archbishop. Clarembald would appear to have adopted the normal form of profession but to have prefaced it with a preamble of his own choosing. A third abbot of Boxley, Walter, is claimed by Gervase to have been blessed by Theobald.[3] This is conceivable, but he made a profession of obedience to Becket.[4]

The abbey of Faversham was founded by King Stephen and Queen Matilda in 1147. They chose as abbot Clarembald, who was prior of the Cluniac monastery of Bermondsey. Permission was sought and obtained from the heads of the Cluniac Order for Clarembald to take up his new appointment and the letters of permission from Peter of Cluny and the prior of La Charité-sur-Loire, addressed to Theobald, were read out.

To T., by the grace of God, archbishop of Canterbury, brother P., unworthy servant of the Cluniac brethren greeting and love in the Lord. We wish it to be known to you that we have given and conceded to Stephen, king of the English, and to Queen Matilda, his wife, Clarembald, who was the prior of the monks of Bermondsey and with him twelve monks of the same monastery so that they shall build their abbey which they have already begun to found at Faversham. Moreover, I absolve the same Prior Clarembald and the aforesaid monks from all obedience and subjection which they had formerly promised to me or to the Cluniac Church or to the church of La Charité, so that they may serve God at Faversham so freely, that neither the abbot of Cluny nor the prior of La Charité shall dare to have any claims on the abbey of Faversham.[5]

This letter to Theobald with its strange feudalistic overtones had the effect of disaffiliating the new foundation. Bermondsey was

---

[1] *Arch. Cant.*, ibid., p. 55.   [2] Ibid.   [3] *Gerv.*, ii, 385.
[4] *Arch. Cant.*, ibid., p. 56.   [5] MS. Canterbury D. and C., C.A., F 87.

the daughter house of La Charité, and although Faversham was to be formed in exactly the same way as Bermondsey, it was to be set up, in accordance with the wishes of the king and queen, as an independent Benedictine abbey. This was not a difficult transition for the monks of Cluny, as they followed the Benedictine Rule with modifications. The foundation of Reading abbey under Henry I was analogous. This was of course not the first contact between Theobald and Peter the Venerable, who had been of great service to him when he was elected abbot of Bec. The letter of the prior of La Charité to Theobald was in similar terms.[1]

Normally the bishop of the diocese in which the religious house was situated received the profession of obedience. Certain monasteries which had privileges of exemption from episcopal control preferred to make their profession to the archbishop of Canterbury in order to avoid giving any semblance of control to the diocesan bishop. Thus Hugh of Bury St. Edmund's, the predecessor of the famous Samson, followed the tradition of his house in going to Theobald to be blessed and making his profession to him.[2] This took place in 1157 at Colchester. The abbey of Malmesbury, like St. Augustine's, began to obtain papal privileges in the twelfth century after a long interval. They contained the following clause:

You shall receive the abbatial blessing from the diocesan bishop, if indeed he should be catholic and should be in communion with the apostolic see and have its favour. He shall afford you the blessing freely and without any perversity; otherwise you have permission to go to any catholic bishop you prefer, who may grant what is asked of him, relying on our authority.[3]

Apparently Gregory, the abbot-elect of Malmesbury, had some trouble with Bishop Jocelin of Salisbury, for he was blessed by Theobald and made profession to him in the usual form.[4]

As Adrian IV's privilege of 1156 was addressed to Abbot Peter[5] the blessing of Gregory must be of a later date.

With regard to the actual elections, the failure of Theobald to prevent the election of Hamelin to Gloucester has already been

---

[1] Ibid., F 81.   [2] *Gerv.*, i, 163.   [3] *Reg. Malm.*, i, 350, etc.
[4] *Arch. Cant.*, ibid., p. 72.   [5] *Reg. Malm.*, i, 355.

noted. Despite the fact that he wanted Gilbert Foliot to retain control of the abbey after his promotion to Hereford, the monks held an election and displaced Gilbert.[1] Theobald's position was weak at the time, as he was abroad in exile. In the same diocese, on the other hand, it would appear that Theobald used his influence to procure the election of William at Evesham in 1149. William had been a monk of Christ Church, Canterbury, and at the time of his election was the prior of Dover.[2] On the death of Reginald, abbot of Evesham, which occurred on 25 August 1149,[3] there was a disputed election. Theobald had written to Foliot to find out the prospects of his candidate's success. In reply[4] the bishop claimed that William had been elected by 'the larger and saner part'. The dissidents had appealed to the pope and Gilbert advised Theobald to procure testimony from the ecclesiastical authorities of the neighbourhood as to the canonical election of William. In this case, the policy of Theobald and Gilbert proved successful. Abbot William died in January 1159[5] and once more Theobald intervened in the affairs of Evesham. This time the danger came from the king, who was showing more interest in abbatial elections than had Stephen. Theobald, however, succeeded in persuading Henry to allow a free election in this most important monastery. He wrote to the monks and told them of his success, but warned them not to delay. Theobald's penchant for fatherly discipline is exemplified in this letter where he dilates, in all sincerity, on the sad case of a monastery bereft of its abbot. He sketches a picture of chaos within and rapine without and no one for the unhappy monks to turn to in the day of wrath. He ordered them to hold their election on 28 June 1159. He himself would not be present, but had delegated Bishops Walter of Coventry and Alfred of Worcester as well as the abbots of Pershore and Winchcombe to supervise the election. If any of these were to be absent, they were, nevertheless, to proceed to elect a worthy abbot. It would be futile for any dissatisfied party to complain to the king—the emphasis had

---

[1] See above, p. 29.   [2] *Gerv.*, i, 141; *Chron. Evesham*, p. 99.
[3] *Chron. Evesham*, p. 99, n. 3. Reginald accompanied Theobald to the second Lateran Council.
[4] Foliot's Letters, *P.L.*, 190, ep. 107, col. 818; cf. ep. 103 to Godfrey, archdeacon of Worcester.   [5] *Chron. Evesham*, p. 100.

changed since 1149—as he was opposed to any delay in the election.[1] A certain Roger was elected who died shortly afterwards; a letter of Gilbert Foliot, which has been cited in connection with Theobald's letter, refers to the next election.[2]

There is also recorded an intervention by Theobald in the affairs of the Augustinian priory of Plympton during the Exeter vacancy in 1160. He had been informed by the earl of Devon, Richard de Redvers, that the late prior, almost at his dying breath, was asked by the canons to suggest a successor. He had chosen one of the canons, Richard. Theobald had heard that an opposition party had been set up and wrote to the canons condemning this 'diabolical manifestation'. They were to obey Richard as their prior until the election of a new bishop of Exeter, whose rights Theobald did not wish to infringe. In the meantime Richard was empowered to punish the ringleaders of the opposition. Richard was in fact subsequently elected.[3]

At Alcester there was a vacancy at some time during the years 1158–60 when Alfred was bishop of Worcester. In accordance with the foundation charter of the monastery, the bishop and the cathedral priory of Worcester claimed a share in the election and that it should be held at Worcester. The monks of Alcester had meanwhile elected their prior as abbot and appealed to Theobald. After consulting other bishops Theobald decided that that monks were in the right and that the conditions laid down by the bishop of Worcester and his chapter were uncanonical and contrary to the Benedictine Rule. He accordingly confirmed their right of free election by charter.[4]

These few cases cited may not represent the full extent of Theobald's intervention in abbatial elections. On the meagre evidence available in general on the practice of abbatial elections during the primacy of Theobald, the normal conclusion would appear to be acceptable, namely that the conduct of the elections was freer than it ever was before or after.

---

[1] John of Salisbury's Letters, *P.L.*, 199, ep. 37, col. 24.
[2] Ep. 254; cf. Prof. Knowles in *Downside Review* (1931), p. 263, n. 3.
[3] John of Salisbury's Letters, *P.L.*, 199, ep. 79, col. 65; cf. F. Liebermann, *Ungedruckte anglo-normannische Geschichtsquellen* (1879), p. 30.
[4] No. 1. This action of Theobald has been wrongly attributed to Becket, *Downside Review* (1931), p. 273.

7. THEOBALD AND MONASTIC DISCIPLINE

Although, as has already been pointed out, religious houses came under the supervision of the diocesan bishop unless exempted, there are a few cases of direct interference by Theobald in the internal affairs of certain monasteries. Generally this can be attributed to the failure of the diocesan to discharge his duties in this respect.

There is a brief entry in the Tewkesbury annals relating to the year 1145, recording the deposition of David, prior of Worcester cathedral, and the appointment of Osbern his successor.[1] A letter of Gilbert Foliot to Theobald most probably refers to this occurrence, although the names of the priors are not mentioned.[2] The abbot of Gloucester was pleading on behalf of his diocesan, Simon of Worcester, who had fallen under Theobald's grave displeasure. It appears that, hearing of the deposition of the prior—the circumstances are not disclosed—Theobald summoned the bishop to his presence and pointed out that it had not been carried out canonically. He ordered Simon to restore the deposed prior for the time being and find a successor for him within a reasonable time. According to Foliot, Simon returned to Worcester and carried out his instructions. The monks were sorely displeased at the restitution of their prior and grave discord arose between them and the bishop. Some of them realised part of the assets of the cathedral and absconded with the proceeds, presumably in order to prosecute an appeal. The bishop succeeded in detaining the runaway monks and this was the cause of Theobald's displeasure. Foliot pointed out that Simon had always adhered to the letter and spirit of Theobald's instructions and that he should put more faith in the probity of one true bishop than in an angry and disobedient horde of monks. The reaction of Theobald to this impassioned appeal is uncertain but one would like to think that his forgiveness and possible apology were conveyed to Simon in a letter which began: 'My dearest son, let not your heart be disturbed nor your modesty confounded, but rather let it rejoice. . . .'[3]

The monastery of Cernel was notorious for its internal dissen-

---

[1] *Ann. Mon.*, i, 46.   [2] Foliot's Letters, *P.L.*, 190, ep. 28, col. 765.   [3] No. 284.

sions during the primacy of Theobald, and the archbishop was constrained to take action there owing to the default of Bishop Jocelin of Salisbury. Abbot Bernard, a protégé of Foliot, had been expelled by the disobedient monks, and not unnaturally this dispute was very much to the fore in Foliot's voluminous correspondence. Between 1145 and 1147 Theobald intervened in the dispute by sending a mandate to the bishop, no doubt ordering the restoration of Bernard. Jocelin received the mandate with proper respect, but refused to take any action. Foliot therefore advised Theobald to put the monastery under an interdict and excommunicate the ringleader. In addition he advised the archbishop to order the earl of Gloucester, ruler of the west country, to see that the excommunicated ringleader was expelled from the abbey. This, he averred, would put Jocelin to shame and cause him to obey Theobald's mandates with more alacrity.[1]

Accordingly, Theobald carried out the suggestions of Foliot and commissioned a loyal monk of Cernel to take his mandate to the earl. The unfortunate monk was waylaid by the dissidents, thrown off his horse and beaten unconscious. Gilbert therefore suggested that Theobald should take further drastic action.[2] Bernard, who by this time had despaired of any assistance from the English Church and secular power, appealed to Eugenius III, as Foliot hastened to inform Theobald in his next letter.[3] Consequently for the time being the case had been taken out of Theobald's hands.[4] It will be noted that the chronological order of the letters as set out here differs from that of Böhmer, followed by Knowles.[5] This case incidentally illustrates the extent of Theobald's authority in the Angevin area, although he was an adherent of Stephen.

There is more evidence from the later period. Even the Cistercian Order, with its as yet unabated zeal for maintaining the true spirit of monasticism, came under the unfavourable notice of the archbishop. The abbot of L'Aumône, the motherhouse of Waverley, had been fomenting discord there by supporting a group of monks who had revolted from the authority

---

[1] Foliot's Letters, *P.L.*, 190, ep. 38, col. 773.   [2] Ibid., ep. 44, col. 777.
[3] Ibid., ep. 39, col. 774.   [4] Ibid., ep. 43, col. 777.   [5] Knowles, p. 654 n. 1.

of their abbot. Theobald wrote to the daughter-houses of Waverley asking them to see if they could compose the differences between the parties and to protest to the abbot of L'Aumône to refrain from his unnatural actions.[1] If this were to prove unsuccessful, the archbishop threatened to endorse the sentence of excommunication which the abbot of Waverley had launched against the contumacious monks and publish it all over England.

Similar discords were prevalent in the abbey of Lilleshall in Shropshire, a house of Arroasian canons regular. A letter of Theobald to the head of the order complained of the lack of harmony prevailing between the abbot and the canons.[2] It would appear that the abbot was in the wrong. It is normally characteristic to find Theobald supporting authority, but here he cannot find a good word to say for the abbot.

As has already been seen in connection with St. Augustine's, Theobald was reluctant to admit the right of religious houses to be exempt from diocesan control. That this was a matter of principle with him can be seen in a letter of his to Jocelin of Salisbury about the conduct of the Knights Hospitallers. They too claimed exemption, and whenever they appropriated a church, it was, in effect, subtracted from the bishop's jurisdiction. Theobald therefore advised Jocelin not to sanction any further appropriations by the Hospitallers, 'for every church you grant them, you remove from yourself and your successors'. Despite his monastic antecedents, Theobald regarded the bishop as the cornerstone of the Church.[3]

Theobald disapproved of the attempts of the cell of Malvern to gain independence from Westminster abbey. Malvern had obtained a papal privilege which Gervase, abbot of Westminster, had refused to recognise. Adrian IV delegated the case to Theobald, who cited Gervase before him to explain his actions. Gervase received support from the great ecclesiastics in the neighbourhood of Malvern—Bishop Foliot of Hereford and the abbots of Gloucester and Pershore—who testified to the disobedience of the monks of Malvern, who had deserved any

---

[1] John of Salisbury's Letters, *P.L.*, 199, ep. 45, col. 28.
[2] Ibid., ep. 43, col. 27.   [3] Ibid., ep. 95, col. 86.

suffering they might have been occasioned. He brought pressure to bear on the monks of Malvern who finally abandoned their privilege. With the help of Walter of Rochester and Silvester of St. Augustine's, peace was re-established between Westminster and its dependent house. Theobald in reporting this to the pope, told him that papal policy in this respect was likely to damage the stability of the English Church.[1]

The practice of monks absconding from their monasteries was not unknown in this period and the regulation of Theobald for the monks of his own cathedral monastery has already been discussed. A letter of the archbishop to Henry II early in 1160 warned him not to pay any attention to a monk of St. Mary's, York, who had left his monastery and was spreading evil tales about it.[2] A letter of John of Salisbury[3] contains the information that Theobald had excommunicated an apostate monk. A letter of Theobald to Becket mentions a monk who claimed to be abbot of Boxley, but whether he was referring to a wandering monk or to an internal election dispute is not easy to say.[4]

Scandal occasioned by sexual immorality seems to have been comparatively rare in this period in monastic life. There is, however, a stern letter from Theobald to the abbess of Barking warning her to mend her ways. She was ordered to cease her 'notorious familiarity and cohabitation' with her official, Hugo. The scandal was so widespread that it had reached the ears of the pope.[5] The offending official was to be removed within seven days.

The safeguarding of monastic possessions from illegal alienations by heads of the houses is illustrated by two charters of Theobald.[6] The abbots of Fécamp and Tavistock received strong admonitions to recover possessions alienated or otherwise lost by them or by their predecessors.

---

[1] Ibid., ep. 100, col. 91.   [2] Ibid., ep. 62, col. 46.   [3] Ibid., ep. 75, col. 60.
[4] Ibid., ep. 71, col. 58.   [5] Ibid., ep. 130, col. 109.
[6] No. 109 and No. 260. Fécamp had English possessions.

III

The English Episcopate during his Primacy

1. EPISCOPAL ELECTIONS, 1139–43

THE metropolitan see of *York* was the last of nine to be filled during this period. St. William was consecrated on 26 September 1143, two days after the death of Pope Innocent II which terminated Henry's legation.[1] The trouble began almost immediately after the death of Thurstan, archbishop of York, in 1140, and dragged its weary length throughout the reign of Stephen into that of Henry II. The consecration of William Fitzherbert marked the end of the first stage in the dispute.

Two modern writers have discussed this episode,[2] and a detailed account here would be superfluous. The question of filling the see of York was of vital importance to everybody. In particular the issue of the long Canterbury-York dispute, now moving in favour of York, and its prospects under a new archbishop, must have engaged the attention of Theobald and his advisers.

An early attempt to fill the see of York, which apparently fell outside the scope of Knowles's article, was that of Archbishop Thurstan himself, who had attempted to resign his see in favour of his brother Audoen, bishop of Evreux.[3] He had sent the abbot of the Cistercian abbey of Fountains to the second Lateran Council to obtain permission from Innocent to accomplish the resignation and translation. Unfortunately, Richard died at Rome and so did Audoen at the Augustinian priory of Merton. Thurstan himself followed them in February 1140. This series of fatalities provides a remarkable parallel to the better-known events of 1153–4.

---

[1] Stubbs, p. 46.
[2] R. L. Poole in *E.H.R.*, 1930, p. 273. Prof. Knowles in *Cambridge Hist. Journal* (1936), pp. 162 and 212.　　　　　　　　　　　　　　　[3] *Ric. Hex.*, p. 177.

The recorded part that Theobald played in the York election is limited to a solitary passage in Gervase.[1] It was said by this chronicler that Stephen gave the see of York to 'a certain clerk' called William but the electors were divided in their opinions. In view of this, Theobald refused to assent to an election conducted in such a manner. Henry of Winchester, therefore, and not Theobald, performed the consecration. The question of the authenticity of this passage of Gervase was discussed by Prof. Knowles, who considered that the use of the words 'a certain clerk' shows that Gervase was relying here on contemporary authorities.[2] Basing himself on this passage Knowles wrote 'it appears certain that Theobald of Canterbury designedly held himself aloof'.[3] In the same article, however, he suggests[4] that Gervase may have made this statement in order to safeguard any possible claims of Canterbury. Knowles might have added in support of this opinion that in 1191 the question of the right person to consecrate the archbishop of York did arise.[5] When writing up his chronicle Gervase followed up certain topics of interest to himself and the monks of Christ Church. Thus throughout the whole chronicle particular attention was paid to relations with St. Augustine's, York and Rochester. On arriving at the events of 1143, Gervase must have seen that Theobald did nothing. This would be tantamount to showing that Theobald had allowed the case of Canterbury to go by default, unless he could point out that the archbishop disapproved of the form of the election.

Whatever the motives behind Theobald's inactivity, the results were not without significance for him. It is true he had given up the chance of being the first archbishop of Canterbury to consecrate an archbishop of York since 1070, but had he taken the chance he would have become an abomination in the eyes of St. Bernard and his Cistercians, who contained in their ranks the man who as pope awarded him the legation in 1150. Even in the matter of consecration Theobald ultimately lost little, for he consecrated Roger of York in 1154.

Thus the election to York was a temporary triumph for the

---

[1] *Gerv.*, i, 123.   [2] Op. cit., note 20.
[3] Ibid., p. 167.   [4] Ibid., note 35.   [5] *Gerv.*, i, 496.

king and his brother, with Theobald scarcely in the picture at all.

Durham. Henry of Winchester performed one other consecration in his legatine capacity. On 20 June 1143, William of St. Barbara, dean of York, was consecrated at Winchester to the see of Durham.[1] In contrast with the succeeding Durham election of 1152–3, Theobald appears to have played no part whatsoever in the protracted dispute which took place after the death of Bishop Geoffrey in 1141. Henry of Winchester is seen here in a far better light than is usual at this period. Despite the efforts of the Empress Matilda and the king of Scotland, Henry for once justified his legatine position and saw that a free and canonical election was held.[2] It is interesting to note that the defeated usurper William Cumin, later found a place in Theobald's household.

Bangor. One of the most successful and permanent achievements of Theobald was his subjection of the Welsh episcopate to the authority of Canterbury. This began with his consecration of Maurice to the see of Bangor in 1140. He was assisted by the bishops of Hereford and Exeter.[3] There were strong elements in the Welsh Church, supported by the independent princes and chieftains, which favoured a movement of independence from Canterbury. Ancient traditions of a separate Welsh Church were an important factor. The anarchy in England greatly reduced Norman influence in Wales, and the weakness of Canterbury from 1139 to 1143 would have worked in favour of the independence movement. The bishop of St. David's was looked upon as the natural head of the Welsh Church. Instead of utilising this opportunity which fortune had presented him, he preferred to play a part in the politics of the civil war. It was only in 1144 that he seriously turned his attention to this problem and by then it was too late. He thus failed the Welsh Church in its hour of need.

According to John of Worcester, Maurice was elected in

---

[1] Stubbs, p. 46.
[2] *John Hex.*, pp. 313–14.
[3] Stubbs, p. 45.

December 1139 by the clergy and people of Bangor.[1] He came to Worcester to meet Stephen, but at first refused to pay homage, alleging a local tradition against this practice. The bishops of Chichester and Hereford were in attendance at Court and persuaded the new bishop-elect to pay homage. 'Seeing that we have done so, reason demands that you should as well.' Maurice was duly impressed and paid homage to the king in the customary form. If this pronouncement had come merely from a time-server like Seffrid of Chichester, it would not have had any great significance, but the support given to this view by Robert of Hereford was a different matter and would tend to show the attitude of the best elements of the English episcopate towards this question. An equally valid reason for the diffidence of Maurice on the question of homage may have been his fear of offending the powerful Owen Gwynedd and his brother Cadwallader in whose territories lay the diocese of Bangor. The brothers wrote to Bernard of St. David's complaining about what they considered to be the underhand installation of Maurice as bishop of Bangor. They also arranged for a meeting to be held on 1 November 1140 to discuss the situation.[2] It is clear from this that they regarded the bishop of St. David's as metropolitan of Wales.

Maurice made a profession of obedience to Theobald in the same form as that of any suffragan of Canterbury province.[3] Thus his subjection to archbishop and king was complete.

Llandaff. Uchtred of Llandaff was consecrated by Theobald at the same time as Maurice of Bangor,[4] and made a similar profession of obedience to Theobald and the see of Canterbury. Llandaff was far more under Norman political influence and control than any other of the Welsh dioceses. Uchtred had been archdeacon under his predecessor, Bishop Urban[5] and was consecrated after a vacancy of six years. He was married and his daughter subsequently married one of the more prominent Welsh chieftains.[6] As he was amenable to the supremacy of

[1] *John of Worcester*, p. 58, and his consecration on p. 60.
[2] Haddan and Stubbs, p. 345.   [3] Ibid.   [4] Stubbs, p. 45.
[5] *Liber Landavensis*, ed. W. J. Rees (Welsh MSS. Soc. 1840), p. 604.
[6] *Brut Y Tywysogion*, ed. J. Williams ab Ithel (R.S., 1860), p. 213.

Canterbury, this impediment does not seem to have stood in his way, although it became an additional ground of complaint for the Welsh nationalists.

St. Asaph. Of the election and consecration of Gilbert of St. Asaph in 1143, little more than the bare record of Gervase is forthcoming.[1] He also made a profession of canonical obedience to Theobald. The consecration of Gilbert took place at Lambeth, a manor belonging to the see of Rochester, which did not form part of the Canterbury possessions till 1197.[2] Consecrations of bishops, however, were not infrequent at Lambeth after 1121.[3] His name appears to indicate that Gilbert was a Norman. He was the first bishop of St. Asaph for about seventy years and Gilbert's consecration points to a further effort on the part of secular and ecclesiastical forces in England to gain a stronger footing in Wales.

A letter found in the works of Giraldus Cambrensis throws some light on the views of the nationalist elements of the Welsh clergy.[4] It was written by the chapter of St. David's to Eugenius III in support of the claims of St. David's. Complaining of the unjust attitude of Theobald, the writers allude to his consecration of these three bishops, which they claimed was accomplished illicitly. The bishop of Llandaff was accused of illiteracy and matrimony and the bishop of Bangor of the theft of the ring and staff from his church for his consecration. They claimed that Stephen and Ranulf, earl of Chester, had agreed that the bishop of St. Asaph should be consecrated by Bernard of St. David's. Owing to the delay caused by the capture of the king, Theobald succeeded in arrogating the consecration of that bishop as well. If this account is correct, the consecration should be put at an earlier date than 1143. In any case, however, the account is of value as showing the influence of the powerful earl of Chester in North Wales.[5] It will be remembered that Ranulf brought Welsh troops to the battle of Lincoln in 1141.

[1] *Gerv.*, i, 126; Stubbs, p. 46.

[2] I. J. Churchill, *Canterbury Administration* (1933), i, 6.

[3] Stubbs, pp. 43–5. Between 1121 and 1133 there were four consecrations at Lambeth. [4] Haddan and Stubbs, pp. 348–50.

[5] Cf. J. E. Lloyd, *History of Wales* (ed. 1939), ii, 483–5, and in *E.H.R.*, 1942, p. 465.

The absence of any recorded participation by Henry of Winchester in these events is noticeable, although it cannot be said that the terms of his legation excluded Wales. For instance, on the complaint of Gilbert Foliot, abbot of Gloucester, he forbade services to be held in new chapels in the diocese of Llandaff. They were encroaching on the privileges and income of churches belonging to Gloucester.[1] After Henry had lost his legation, Theobald sent a mandate to Uchtred in identical terms.[2]

Limerick. Patrick, elected bishop of Limerick, was consecrated by Theobald in 1140 and made his profession of canonical obedience in due form.[3] At the time Limerick was one of the chief Norse settlements in Ireland, the others being Dublin, Waterford, Wexford and Cork. To maintain their ecclesiastical independence of the Irish, the Scandinavians approved of Lanfranc's claim of supremacy over the Irish Church and several of their bishops came over to England for consecration.[4] These were the first territorial bishoprics in Ireland. Hitherto, episcopacy there had been an adjunct to monasticism. By consecrating Patrick, therefore, Theobald was maintaining the shadowy claims of Canterbury in Ireland, but Patrick was the last bishop so to be consecrated. Patrick himself was again at Canterbury in 1148 for the consecration of the bishop of St. David's.[5]

London. Robert de Sigillo was consecrated to the see of London by Theobald in 1141, having been appointed by the Empress Matilda shortly after the battle of Lincoln.[6]

There had been a vacancy of seven years. Bishop Gilbert had died in 1134 and Henry I had done nothing about appointing a successor. An electoral dispute characteristic of the times developed after the accession of Stephen. The king called on the

---

[1] *Historia et Cartularium Monasterii Sancti Petri Gloucestriae*, ed. W. H. Hart (R.S., 1863–7), ii, 14. [2] No. 113.

[3] Stubbs, p. 45; Lynch, *De praesulibus Hiberniae*, ed. O'Doherty (1944), ii, 74; MS. B. M. Cotton Cleopatra E.1 f.35.

[4] E. Curtis, *History of Medieval Ireland* (1938), pp. 6–12.

[5] *Gerv.*, i, 138, cf. *St. Paul's Ecclesiological Soc.*, vii, 169.

[6] Stubbs, p. 45; J. H. Round, *Geoffrey de Mandeville* (1892), pp. 67–8.

dean and chapter to elect a bishop in 1136.[1] Against the wishes of the dean of St. Paul's, many of the canons elected Anselm, the abbot of Bury St. Edmund's.[2] The king also disapproved of the election. At first the party of Anselm prevailed. The dean, however, appealed to the pope, supported by the archbishop of York—Canterbury was vacant at the time. The appeal was successful and elicited a papal decree of some importance annulling the election. It was delivered by the legate Alberic of Ostia, who declared that no episcopal election was valid without the assent of the dean.[3] Anselm returned to Bury, where he died ten years later.

By papal request or assent Henry of Winchester, who was not yet legate, administered the see of London after the departure of Anselm. No further effort was made to fill the see, the death of the dean in 1138 being a contributory cause. This was no doubt agreeable to Henry. It was in his capacity of vicar that he began to ordain Richard de Belmeis on that fateful day during the Council of Westminster in December 1138.[4] He also presided over diocesan synods.[5]

It was said[6] that the empress appointed Robert after taking advice. This would suggest that Henry of Winchester approved. Henry was a Cluniac and Robert was, at the time, a monk of Reading, a monastery which had strong Cluniac associations.

John of Hexham was incorrect when he stated that Robert was Henry I's Chancellor.[7] His official post in the Chancery was *Magister Scriptorii* or head of the office staff.[8] It was the next highest paid post to that of Chancellor and so Robert was no doubt unofficially regarded as vice-Chancellor. He was also described as 'keeper of the King's seal'[9]—hence 'de Sigillo', on the death of Henry I he retired to Reading until he received his reward for his many years of service at the hands of the empress.

[1] *Diceto*, i, 248.
[2] *Memorials of St. Edmunds*, ed. T. Arnold (R.S., 1890–6), iii, 5. He was the nephew of St. Anselm.   [3] *Diceto*, i, 250–1.   [4] Ibid., i, 252.
[5] John of Salisbury's Letters, *P.L.*, 199, ep. 89, cols. 77–8.
[6] *Florence of Worcester*, ed. B. Thorpe (English Hist. Soc., 1848–9), ii, 131.
[7] *John Hex.*, p. 309.
[8] *Red Book of the Exchequer*, ed. H. Hall (R.S., 1896), iii, 807; *Dialogus de Scaccario*, ed. C. Johnson (1950), p. 129.   [9] J. H. Round in *E.H.R.*, 1899, p. 428.

The mechanics of the election are not recorded. Probably the formal election was of little importance as Matilda had old-fashioned ideas about relations between Church and State and, in combination with Henry of Winchester, was irresistible. Nor was the validity of the election and the consecration by Theobald challenged by Stephen when he was restored at the end of 1141. At Easter 1142, Robert was in London unmolested.[1] It was true, however, that his see had become impoverished, both on account of the long vacancy and the misrule of Anselm.[2] He was again in London early in 1145[3] but in 1147 Stephen, who was now in a far more powerful position than hitherto, refused him admittance to his diocese.[4] This Angevin appointment in his most important stronghold must have been a thorn in Stephen's flesh.

Salisbury. Another obscure election during the worst period of the anarchy seems to show yet again that the Church was not yet master of its own destinies in England. The story of the election of Jocelin of Salisbury follows similar lines to the London election.

Roger of Salisbury died in December 1139: his death was attributed to the harsh treatment of Stephen.[5] The king and Henry of Winchester differed over the appointment of a successor. Meanwhile the vacant see was being administered by Henry.[6] The legate was in favour of the election of his nephew and the king's, Henry de Solley, who was the son of their eldest brother.[7] Stephen, however, rejected him and gave him the abbey of Fécamp instead. The king's candidate was Philip, his chancellor, and he appointed him bishop at the mid-Lent council of 1140.[8] Henry retaliated by quashing the appointment. An appeal to Rome failed and Philip, too, was consoled in Normandy with the bishopric of Bayeux. The deadlock continued until the capture of Stephen and the triumph of the empress. The king, however, had succeeded in detaching the

---

[1] M. M. Bigelow, *Placita Anglo-Normannica* (1879), p. 147.
[2] Cf. St. Bernard's Letters, *P.L.*, 182, ep. 211, col. 376.
[3] *Reg. Roff.*, pp. 41 f.
[4] Jaffé, 9088–9.   [5] *Malm.*, ii, 557.   [6] Knowles, p. 288.
[7] Ordericus Vitalis in *P.L.*, 188, col. 976.   [8] *Ann. Mon.*, ii, 228 (Waverley).

H

monasteries of Malmesbury and Abbotsbury annexed to the bishopric by Roger, and in restoring their independence.[1]

On the election and consecration of Jocelin, the sources are meagre.[2] He had been the archdeacon of Winchester and thus it is more than likely that Henry had taken advantage of the defeat of Stephen to press forward the candidature of one of his adherents. The reactions of Stephen when he regained his liberty are unknown, but he does not appear to have opposed Theobald's consecration of Jocelin in 1142. The new bishop made the usual profession of obedience to the archbishop and the see of Canterbury.

A letter of Gilbert Foliot written to Lucius II in 1144 or 1145 discloses that the chapter of Salisbury were not unanimous in their approval of Jocelin.[3] The diocese had also suffered severely from the fighting of 1141–3. Gilbert expressed his high opinion of the character of Jocelin, who had shown his fitness for high office prior to his election. Jocelin had soon come up against the opposition of the dean, Azo, and Gilbert was writing to the pope on his behalf.

Jocelin was ecclesiastically well-connected. His brother Richard became bishop of Coutances and his son Reginald, after a distinguished career, was elected archbishop of Canterbury in 1191 but died before consecration.

Rochester. The inadequacy of the sources for this period is shown by the uncertainty of historians as to whether there was a bishop of Rochester from 1137 when Bishop John died, till 1142 when Bishop Ascelin was consecrated.[4] It seems that there are strong probabilities in favour of the existence of a second Bishop John of Rochester in and around the year 1139.

With the election and consecration of Ascelin we are on somewhat firmer ground. Rochester came under the special influence and tutelage of Canterbury, and one would expect to find the influence of the archbishop to be more noticeable here than

---

[1] *Malm.*, ii, 559–60.
[2] Stubbs, p. 45; *John Hex.*, p. 302; *Ann. Mon.*, i, 14 (Margan).
[3] *P.L.*, 190, ep. 11, col. 755.
[4] *John Hex.*, p. 300; a full discussion of this question is in my article, (John II, bishop of Rochester). *E.H.R.*, 1951.

anywhere else.[1] Unfortunately nothing is recorded of the events leading up to the election. The career of Ascelin does, however, provide sufficient indication. He was a monk of Canterbury cathedral and became sacrist,[2] and in 1139 Theobald made him prior of Dover.[3]

He was consecrated in 1142[4] by Theobald. There were certain peculiar ceremonies attached to the consecration of a bishop of Rochester, designed to emphasise the special subjection of the see to Canterbury, and they were not dispensed with on this occasion,[5] but as they are described in connection with the consecration of Ascelin's successor, it would seem expedient to deal with them below.

Summary. Although the evidence is somewhat scanty, it is obvious that the principle of free election, as laid down in Stephen's charter to the Church, was not put into effective practice during the years 1139–43. It is possible that at Bangor and Llandaff there were free elections, as members of the respective Churches were elected. These sees, however, are unimportant except in so far as they played a part in the struggle for the independence of the Welsh Church. An exception must also be made for Durham. Every other election, where there is sufficient evidence, shows the rights of the nominal electors brushed aside amidst the welter of political considerations. Admittedly the times were abnormal, but that was supposed to be the great opportunity for the Church to increase its powers. Instead the depressing story of the legatine councils of 1141–3 is reflected in the course of these elections. It was not until Theobald came into his own that a change for the better was to be discerned, in this field as well as in all others.

Only one of the new bishops (London) belonged to the 'official' class which had been a prominent feature of the appointments of Henry I. Two were monks (London and Rochester), two were archdeacons (Salisbury and Llandaff), two were Cathedral dignitaries (York and Durham) and one a

---

[1] Cf. I. J. Churchill, *Canterbury Administration*, i, 279; R. A. L. Smith in *E.H.R.*, 1943, p. 262.

[2] *Gerv.*, i, 109.   [3] Ibid.; cf. *Monasticon*, iv, 536.

[4] Stubbs, p. 46; *Gerv.*, i, 132 shows it was after 24 January.   [5] *Gerv.*, i, 306.

simple clerk (Bangor). The status of two is unknown (St. Asaph and Limerick).

The influence of Theobald was only clearly perceptible at Rochester although it may possibly have been felt at Bangor and Llandaff.

2. EPISCOPAL ELECTIONS, 1143–54

York. The second phase of the great York election dispute culminated in the deposition of Archbishop William and the election of the Cistercian abbot of Fountains, Henry Murdac. He was consecrated by Pope Eugenius III at Trèves on 7 December 1147.[1] Henry's consecration might have been thought to have infringed the rights of the see of Canterbury,[2] but the papal power was considered to override all privileges, for Gervase mentions the consecration without a word of complaint.[3]

The chief architects of the downfall of St. William were St. Bernard and Eugenius. St. Bernard, in a letter to the pope, clearly showed that he considered the conduct of Theobald in this matter to be satisfactory. 'The bishop of Winchester and the archbishop of York are not in harmony with the archbishop of Canterbury. . . . Moreover the archbishop of Canterbury, whom they oppose, is a pious man of the highest reputation. For him do I beseech that his righteous conduct should be rewarded.'[4] It would not be unfair to say that in the matter of the York election, Theobald was allied to St. Bernard on the principle of 'the enemy of my enemy is my friend', as we know far more of Theobald's opposition to Henry of Winchester than of any intervention of Theobald in the York dispute.

Chichester. One of the candidates for the see of York, when it was left vacant by the deposition of St. William, was Hilary, who was subsequently consecrated to the see of Chichester by Theobald at Canterbury, assisted by the bishops of Ely, Bath

---

[1] Stubbs, p. 46; *John Hex.*, p. 321. *Hist. Pont.*, p. 6 wrongly makes the consecration take place at Auxerre; the pope was there when the election took place on 24 July (Jaffé, 9102–3). This point has not hitherto been clarified (cf. *Cambridge Historical Journal*, v, 174, n. 52).   [2] Cf. *Gerv.*, i, 496.

[3] Ibid., p. 135; cf. A. Fliche and V. Martin, *Histoire de l'Église*, ix (1946), 71–4, for similar consecrations on the Continent.   [4] *P.L.*, 182, ep. 238, cols. 429–30.

and Norwich on 3 August 1147.[1] He had previously made a profession of canonical obedience to Theobald and the see of Canterbury.

The deposition of Bishop Seffrid of Chichester in 1145 took place in mysterious circumstances, which a vague remark of Henry of Huntingdon does little to clarify.[2] Only conjecture can associate his deposition with the disappearance of Everard of Norwich and the visit of the legate Ymar in the same year. Seffrid was the brother of Ralph, a former archbishop of Canterbury, and had been abbot of Glastonbury before his elevation to the see of Chichester.[3] During the vacancy at Canterbury, before the election of Theobald, he usurped the archiepiscopal rights in certain churches situated within the geographic bounds of his diocese.[4] These later were formed into the Canterbury 'peculiar deaneries' of Pagham, Tarring and South Malling. Seffrid lived on for a few years after his deposition and died in 1150.[5]

Hilary's earlier career was elucidated by Round,[6] who pointed out that his election ought to be added to the growing number of those directly influenced by the pope. Hilary had been in the service of Henry of Winchester[7] and was adopted as the candidate of the Winchester party after the deposition of St. William. In the election of July 1147 the chapter of York was divided, Hilary receiving the influential support of the dean and treasurer.[8] Murdac, however, was favoured by the suffragan bishops of Carlisle and Durham and, as has been seen, the pope decided in his favour. Eugenius consoled Hilary with the vacant bishopric of Chichester, hoping to bind the bishop to him by ties of gratitude and presumably to free Murdac from one at least of his many embarrassments.[9] Stephen and Henry could not be altogether dissatisfied at the papal move, as Hilary's chances in a renewed York election dispute would not have been strong.

[1] Stubbs, p. 46; *Gerv.*, i, 132.

[2] *Hunt.*, p. 316 ('vir Gnatonicus et ob hoc jam depositus').

[3] William of Malmesbury's *De Antiquitatibus Glaston. Ecclesiae*, ed. T. Gale, *Historiae Scriptores XV* (1691), p. 334.

[4] John of Salisbury's Letters, *P.L.*, 199, ep. 138, col. 118.

[5] *Ann. Mon.*, i, 47 (Tewkesbury).

[6] *Athenaeum*, 23 January 1897.

[7] *John Hex.*, p. 321.

[8] Prof. Knowles in *Cambridge Hist. Journal*, v, 173.

[9] Cf. *Diceto*, i, 263.

Henry, indeed, who had designs on the see of Chichester, could have wished for no one better than his old clerk to be elected.[1] The united front of king and pope must have been sufficient to secure election by the Chichester chapter. The attitude of Theobald is not recorded.

Hilary represented a new type of English bishop. He was a competent canon lawyer and his name appears very frequently as a judge-delegate during the primacy of Theobald.[2] His skill as a canonist had been derived from his service in the papal court where he had acquired a reputation.[3] He was thus in a position to disseminate the principles of canon law, lately codified by Gratian, among the more conservative and isolationist elements in the English Church. He then became dean of the college of secular canons at Twynham about 1140, a post which he retained for some years in plurality.[4]

Norwich. William Turbe, the prior of Norwich Cathedral was consecrated by Theobald at Canterbury in 1146.[5] There is no evidence to contradict the statement of the continuator of the Annals of St. Augustine's, who claimed he was consecrated in that monastery.[6]

Henry of Huntingdon is alone in his claim that Everard of Norwich was deposed on account of his cruelty[7] and the other sources speak of his retirement.[8] It was suggested that his retirement was due to his allegiance to the empress or to his disapproval of the capitalisation of the new cult of St. William of Norwich by the monks, but these reasons are purely conjectural. He took up residence at the Cistercian monastery of Fontenay, where he died shortly afterwards. Before his death he wrote a letter to the pope, which may possibly throw some light on the causes of his retirement.[9] Because of the civil troubles he had made over two villages belonging to the see to two knights, in

---

[1] *Ann. Mon.*, ii, 53 (Winchester).
[2] John of Salisbury's Letters, *P.L.*, 199, epp. 11, 13, 21, 22, 35, 67, 119, 122, show Hilary in various judicial spheres.
[3] *John Hex.*, p. 321.   [4] Round, op. cit.   [5] Stubbs, p. 46; *Gerv.*, i, 130.
[6] F. Liebermann, *Ungedruckte anglo-normannische Geschichtsquellen* (1879), p. 81.
[7] *Hunt.*, p. 316.   [8] Cf. *Norfolk Archaeology*, v, 41–9; *V.C.H.*, *Norfolk*, ii, 222 f.
[9] Holtzmann, ii, 197.

order to save greater depredations. He had not, however, secured the consent of the convent or the archdeacons and begged Eugenius for absolution. The alleged ritual murder of a Norwich boy by the Jews in 1144—the earliest of its kind in Europe—brought Prior Turbe into prominence. Everard was but a lukewarm supporter of the sanctity of St. William, but Turbe 'was doing his utmost to induce the monks to accept the tale with unquestioning credulity, and to turn it to account'.[1]

The election of a monk of Norwich would appear to be a sound indication of the free choice of the monks. In default of any evidence to the contrary, this election may be regarded as one of the few genuinely free and canonical elections held during the reign of Stephen.[2]

Rochester. Ascelin of Rochester died on 24 January 1148.[3] The account of Gervase continues:

Walter the archdeacon of Canterbury, brother of Theobald archbishop of Canterbury, succeeded him. According to ancient custom, he was elected in the Canterbury chapter by the monks of Rochester. Hugh abbot of St. Augustine's had the first voice in this election, because he had taken the monastic habit in the church of Rochester —he had later been translated to the aforesaid abbacy—and together with the monks of Rochester, he elected the same Walter, as mentioned before, in the presence of Archbishop Theobald of Canterbury, to whom pertains of ancient right the gift of the same bishopric, in the chapter of Canterbury, and in the presence of the whole convent of Canterbury, amidst a multitude of clergy and people. After the manner of his predecessors, Walter swore on the four gospels that he would faithfully maintain the privileged position of the church of Canterbury in the church of Rochester. There is a custom of the church of Canterbury going back to ancient times and secured by the holy Fathers, namely that the bishop of Rochester ought to be elected in the chapter of Canterbury by gift of the archbishop and by election of the convent of the church of Rochester. After the election, the elect ought to swear on the four gospels, his fealty to the church of Christ, Canterbury, and to the archbishop, that the bishop of Rochester ought not to help in or consent to the deprivation of the

[1] A. Jessopp and M. R. James, *St. William of Norwich* (1896), p. xxi.
[2] Cf. Bartholomew Cotton, *Historia Anglicana*, ed. H. R. Luard (R.S., 1859), p. 393.   [3] *Gerv.*, i, 132.

honour and rights which the church of Canterbury holds in the church of Rochester, that the pastoral staff of a deceased bishop of Rochester ought to be brought to the altar of Christ Church by the monks of Rochester, that when the see of Canterbury should be vacant or the archbishop absent the bishop of Rochester ought to carry out the episcopal duties as the private chaplain of the church of Canterbury, but only if he should be summoned thereto by the convent of Canterbury. After he had made this oath of fealty, Walter was consecrated by his own brother Theobald archbishop of Canterbury.

The source of this ample account would appear to be the endorsement on Walter's profession of obedience, which is still extant.[1] It reads as follows:

In the year of the incarnation of Our Lord 1148, Theobald archbishop of Canterbury consecrated Walter bishop of Rochester on 14 March at Canterbury in front of the altar of Christ with the assistance of three of his bishops-suffragan, Nigel of Ely, Robert of Exeter and Maurice of Bangor in Wales. He had been elected several days before, on 27 January in the customary form in the chapter of Canterbury in the presence of Archbishop Theobald and of the monastic convent and of an innumerable multitude of the clergy and laity of the city. Forthwith, in the same chapter before all who were present, he did homage to the same archbishop and swore an oath of fealty on a book of the gospels to Christ Church Canterbury in all things as long as he should live and that he would neither attempt nor agree to any attempt to cause the church of Canterbury to lose in any way the power and dominion which it had hitherto been accustomed to exercise over the church of Rochester. He had been the archdeacon of Canterbury.

It is interesting to note how Gervase managed to give the greatest prominence to the part played and occupied by the monks of Canterbury. He omitted Walter's homage to Theobald and the part played by the bishops in the ceremony of consecration. The 'church of Canterbury' for Gervase meant the monks, just as today for many people 'Parliament' means the Commons. The same process of thought is evident here as in the case of the subjection of Dover Priory to Canterbury which has already been discussed.

[1] C. E. Woodruff in *St. Paul's Ecclesiological Soc.*, vii, 168.

It is clear from the foregoing that practically as soon as Ascelin died, Theobald exercised his rights and appointed his brother to the vacant see. The monks of Rochester do not appear to have had any voice in the matter, especially as the election took place three days after the death of Ascelin. The act of homage represented the knight service which the see of Rochester owed to the archbishop of Canterbury and not to the king as was usual with the other bishoprics.[1]

Walter first comes into prominence as archdeacon of Canterbury. He was appointed by Theobald some time after his accession to Canterbury but the date when he succeeded Helewise is not known. As a member of the archbishop's household he is known to have befriended the young Becket when he first came there and to have defended him against the machinations of Roger of Pont l'Evêque, who had temporarily prejudiced the archbishop against Becket.[2]

Llandaff. On the same day as Bishop Walter of Rochester was consecrated, Theobald also consecrated Nicholas ap Gwrgant to the see of Llandaff.[3] The same bishops officiated and the presence of Bishop Maurice of Bangor was perhaps more than a happy coincidence.

Uchtred had died earlier in the year.[4] His ill-health had been alluded to by Gilbert Foliot. Among the fairly numerous letters of Foliot to and about Uchtred, there is one where the abbot claimed to have restored Uchtred to the archbishop's favour, but the cause of the disagreement is unknown.[5] Nicholas was a Welshman, the son of a certain Gwrgant. In some texts of the Welsh Chronicle, Gwrgant is described as a bishop[6] and an attempt has been made to identify him with Bishop Urban of Llandaff, Uchtred's predecessor,[7] but it is more probable that the insertion of the word 'bishop' was an error of the copyist.[8]

---

[1] H. M. Chew, *Ecclesiastical Tenants-in-chief* (1932), p. 7.
[2] *Materials*, iii, 16 (William Fitzstephen).　　　[3] Stubbs, p. 46.
[4] Haddan and Stubbs, pp. 351–2.
[5] Foliot's Letters, *P.L.*, 190, ep. 56, col. 784.
[6] Haddan and Stubbs, p. 351.
[7] E. J. Newell, *History of the Welsh Church* (1895), p. 197.
[8] Lloyd, op. cit., p. 484, n. 108.

Nicholas had been a monk for thirty years at St. Peter's, Gloucester, Foliot's abbey.[1] There is some evidence that he was the special choice of Archbishop Theobald. In a letter to the archbishop, Foliot wrote 'For he is the work of your hands and your plantation.'[2]

Lincoln. After visiting Pope Eugenius at Auxerre in the summer of 1147, Alexander of Lincoln caught a fever which proved fatal, and his death occurred on 20 February 1148. It was not until 19 December that Robert de Chesney, the archdeacon of Leicester,[3] was consecrated by Theobald, the election having taken place a few days before.

On the election of Robert, the correspondence of Gilbert Foliot provides some information. Gilbert was interested in his election, amongst other reasons, because Robert was his uncle.[4] Stephen and Henry of Winchester, as usual, were anxious to provide for one of their nephews: the names of the abbots of Fécamp, Westminster and Holme were mentioned.[5] The summer of 1148 was particularly unfortunate for their designs as Stephen's resistance to papal policy had caused the suspension of Bishop Henry. In this invidious position there was little they could do when the pope unceremoniously rejected all three nephews. The way was thus left clear for the free election of the archdeacon of Leicester by the dean and chapter. The election is referred to by Foliot in two of his letters to Eugenius.[6] He speaks of the unanimous election of Robert who met with the approval of the clergy and laity of the diocese. The electors came to London where, before an assembly of bishops, including Theobald and Gilbert, now bishop of Hereford, the dean, precentor and archdeacon of Lincoln, supported by a fair number of canons and monks of the diocese, insistently put forward the name of Robert, the archdeacon of Leicester. This was agreed to by Theobald and the bishops.

[1] Ibid., pp. 484–5.
[2] *P.L.*, 190, ep. 91, col. 809.
[3] Not archdeacon of Lincoln as *D.N.B.*, iv, 198. Cf. *Lincoln Rec. Soc.*, 27, p. 262.
[4] *Eynsham Cartulary*, ed. H. E. Salter (Oxford Hist. Soc., 1906), i, 411.
[5] Foliot's Letters, *P.L.*, 190, ep. 76, col. 794.
[6] Ibid., epp. 87–8, cols. 807–8.

A slightly different picture is given in the endorsement to Robert's profession of obedience.[1]

In the year of the incarnation of the Lord 1148 on 13 December there was elected to the bishopric of Lincoln Robert, canon and archdeacon of the same church, at Westminster in the monastic chapter in the presence of King Stephen and Queen Matilda and the lord Archbishop Theobald, Nigel of Ely, Robert of London, William of Norwich, Hilary of Chichester, Walter of Rochester, Gilbert of Hereford and Patrick of Limerick in Ireland . . . Then on the next Saturday following the two bishops-elect [Lincoln and St. David's] were raised to the order of priesthood by the lord Archbishop Theobald at Canterbury, and on the next day, that is 19 December, the same archbishop consecrated them in the same place. . . .

The election would appear to have taken place at the royal court at Westminster, of which Foliot gives no hint. The consecration took place at Canterbury. Of the other sources, Henry of Huntingdon, a brother-archdeacon of Robert, personally approved of the election[2] and mentioned that his views were shared by the king, clergy and laity. Diceto also stresses the unanimity which characterised the election.[3] On his return to Lincoln after the election Robert received an enthusiastic welcome from the citizens in January 1149.

Hereford. Robert de Bethune, bishop of Hereford, was one of the English bishops authorised by Stephen to attend the Council of Rheims in March 1148. He fell ill there and died on 16 April.[4] The annalist of Oseney reflects the general opinion of Robert in characterising him as 'the good bishop'.[5]

He was succeeded by Gilbert Foliot, the abbot of Gloucester.[6] The seventy-odd letters of Gilbert when he was abbot which are extant, throw some light on his promotion. He was a man of wide contacts, writing to popes, cardinals, bishops, abbots and lay dignitaries. His correspondence with Theobald in particular was conducted on a friendly level. He was on good terms with the late bishop of Hereford,[7] and with Ralph the dean of Here-

---

[1] *St. Paul's Ecclesiological Soc.*, vii, 169.   [2] *Hunt.*, p. 281.   [3] *Diceto*, i, 258.
[4] *Anglia Sacra*, ii, 314; *John Hex.*, p. 321.   [5] *Ann. Mon.*, iv, 26.
[6] Stubbs, p. 47.   [7] Cf. Foliot's Letters, *P.L.*, 190, ep. 9, col. 751.

ford,[1] who nursed real or imaginary grievances against his bishop. Gilbert's sympathies with his troubles would no doubt create a good impression on an important elector.

Of the actual events leading up to his election, the letters of Foliot do not give any sort of a picture. Even his movements during the year 1148 are not determined. It is contended[2] that 'Theobald pressed him to attend the Council of Rheims; he declined at first [epp. 6, 7] but yielded later'. This is entirely erroneous as the letters in question refer to Theobald's earlier visit to the Curia at the end of 1143. There is, however, a letter which might be construed to refer to a summons by Theobald to Gilbert to join him in exile in the summer of 1148.[3] He was sending a messenger to Theobald to ascertain his position and went on to say that he was prepared to undertake the journey, notwithstanding the troubled state of affairs in the West Country. The mention of the bishop of Hereford as still alive shows that the letter must refer to Theobald's visit to Paris in 1147 where Gilbert did eventually join him.[4]

Shortly after the death of Robert, the pope would appear to have made Gilbert vicar of Hereford, which would obviously strengthen his position in the diocese. One of his letters begins 'G. by the grace of God abbot, and by the mandate of the lord pope vicar of the church of Hereford. . . .' He ordered an interdict in the diocese on account of the misbehaviour of the earl of Hereford. It was promulgated by the authority of the pope and the archbishop of Canterbury—a somewhat unfortunate beginning of Gilbert's rule at Hereford.[5]

His first definite appearance on the Continent was at Arras with the archbishop.[6] Later he was with Theobald at St. Omer for his consecration.[7]

There were many interests at stake in the Hereford election. The diocese lay in the Angevin area and thus the question was of vital importance to the empress Matilda, Geoffrey of Anjou and his son Henry, who would wish to preserve their influence. Eugenius and St. Bernard were near at hand. There are six

[1] Z. N. Brooke and C. N. L. Brooke in *Cambridge Hist. Journal*, viii, 7.
[2] *Hist. Pont.*, p. 116.   [3] Foliot's Letters, *P.L.*, 190, ep. 69, col. 791.
[4] See above, p. 24.   [5] Foliot's Letters, *P.L.*, 190, ep. 78, col. 795.
[6] Ibid., ep. 73, col. 793; cf. ep. 75, col. 794.   [7] *Hist. Pont.*, p. 48.

letters extant from Foliot to Eugenius written when he was abbot, and no doubt more were written.[1] There is a letter to St. Bernard, of a cordial nature, which was written in reply to a question concerning the complicated relations between two Cistercian monasteries in the neighbourhood of Gloucester.[2] A letter to the empress showed Gilbert's acquaintance with a brother of St. Bernard.[3] The same letter proved him to be a loyal supporter of papal absolutism. This followed naturally from his proficiency in canon law. It was also obvious that Stephen could not be indifferent to the outcome of the election. The English Church, even in the Angevin-controlled areas, was bound to recognise him as the rightful ruler by the papal decision of 1139.

Above all Gilbert was Theobald's nominee. 'Meanwhile, Gilbert, abbot of Gloucester, was elected to the bishopric of Hereford by the advice and will of the archbishop of Canterbury.'[4]

Theobald obtained the assent of the duke of Normandy to the election of Gilbert. The duke made it a condition of his assent that Gilbert should swear an oath of fealty to him within a month after his consecration and not to Stephen—'and that he should not make an oath of fealty to King Stephen, whom the whole English Church followed by order of the Roman Church'.[5] Thereupon Theobald, armed with papal authority, called upon the bishops of London, ·Salisbury and Chichester to leave England and to assist at the consecration. They refused to obey the summons, claiming that it was against the terms of their oath to Stephen and that it contravened the 'ancient customs' of the Church for anyone to be consecrated outside England. They made the further point that Stephen had not consented to the election, nor had Gilbert made an oath of fealty to him. The consistent support given by the bishops to the king rather than to Theobald and the pope is significant.

Undaunted, Theobald obtained permission from Eugenius to override the rights of the English episcopate in the consecration. He secured the assistance of the local bishops, including Nicholas

---

[1] Epp. 17, 18, 25, 36, 41, 73. [2] Ep. 68, col. 791.
[3] Ep. 52, col. 782. [4] *Hist. Pont.*, p. 47. [5] Ibid.

of Cambrai, Miles of Térouanne and Thierry of Amiens.[1] The endorsement to the profession gives the date of the consecration as 5 September 1148. This was the second consecration to take place abroad during the primacy of Theobald, the first being that of Henry Murdac, archbishop of York, in the preceding year.

It soon became clear that Gilbert had deceived the Angevins, for he went back to England and swore fealty to Stephen.[2] This could be justified by the terms of the papal award of 1139 and Theobald did his best to console an angry duke on these lines. 'For although the nobles were divided and paid allegiance to different princes, the Church, however, had one ruler.'[3] Stephen must have been pleased at the neutralisation of one of his opponents and an inciter to his enemies.[4] As late as 1150, Henry of Anjou continued to regard Gilbert with some suspicion.[5]

According to John of Salisbury, Theobald gave Gilbert permission to hold the abbey of Gloucester in plurality, in the same way as Henry of Winchester was holding Glastonbury.[6] The monks of Gloucester disapproved of this arrangement and elected their subprior Hamelin as abbot three weeks after the consecration of Gilbert. Simon of Worcester gave him his episcopal blessing on 5 December.[7]

St. David's. To understand the forces behind the election to the see of St. David's in 1148, it is necessary to review the attempts of Bishop Bernard to secure the independence of the Welsh Church from Canterbury and its subjection to St. David's.

While it may have been true that the Welsh sees had been more or less independent until the Norman Conquest, there was no evidence that an archbishopric of St. David's had ever existed.[8] The traditions of independence had persisted and the weakness of the Norman monarchy as a result of the accession of

---

[1] Ibid., p. 48; *Gerv.*, i, 135; *St. Paul's Ecclesiological Soc.*, vii, 168.
[2] *Hist. Pont.*, pp. 48–9.   [3] Ibid., p. 47.
[4] Cf. Foliot's Letters, *P.L.*, 190, ep. 79, col. 796 to Brian Fitzcount.
[5] Ibid., ep. 106, col. 817, 'Si qui vero sunt aemuli, etc.'   [6] *Hist. Pont.*, p. 48.
[7] *Hist. Mon.*, *S. Petri Glouc.* ed. W. H. Hart (R.S., 1863), i, 19.
[8] Lloyd, op. cit., p. 486, 'The alleged archbishopric of St. David's'.

Stephen gave Bernard an opportunity of opening the question. He wrote to Innocent II asking for his see to be accorded its rightful status of metropolitan and for a pallium, the badge of office.[1] It is possible that Innocent granted his request but for some reason changed his mind almost immediately.[2] The question was allowed to rest for some time, but on the accession of Lucius II in March 1144, Bernard wrote to him restating his claim. Lucius replied not unfavourably. He thought, however, that the position was obscure and promised to send legates to ascertain the true position.[3] The only legate whom Lucius sent to England was Ymar, and it is unknown whether he made any inquiries as to the status of St. David's. Shortly after he arrived in England his legation was terminated by the death of the pope and he probably did not have time to investigate the matter.

After the accession of Eugenius III in 1145, the chapter of St. David's wrote to him in support of the claims of their bishop. The ancient rights of the see were asserted. Theobald was accused of consecrating three Welsh bishops to the detriment of these rights, two of whom were manifestly unsuitable.[4] About the same time Bernard made a formal appeal to the pope that his rights and those of his see should be established. The hearing came on in 1147 when Eugenius was in France. Bernard conducted his case personally and Theobald joined him later. On 28 June 1147 Eugenius issued the following bull:

Our venerable brother, Bernard, bishop of St. David's, coming into our presence, asserted verbally that the church of St. David's was of old a metropolitan see and humbly requested that the same dignity should be restored to him by us. Moreover after he had remained in attendance at our court for a long time in connection with that petition, at last, brother archbishop, arising against him in

---

[1] Haddan and Stubbs, p. 344.

[2] *Hunt.*, p. 10, 'Moreover in our time the bishop of St. David's received a pallium from the pope . . . but, however, he immediately lost it.'

[3] Haddan and Stubbs, p. 348 (14 May 1144).

[4] The remaining documents in this collection relating to Bernard are in a confused chronological order as the editors place the trial at the Council of Rheims in 1148 in stead of in 1147, see above, pp. 23f. The latest account of these transactions by J. Conway Davies in *Episcopal Acts and Cognate Documents relating to Welsh Dioceses 1066–1272* (Hist. Soc. of the Church of Wales Publications, 1) appeared after this was written, but does not substantially differ from my account.

his presence, you put forward a complaint against him before us, that he withdrew the obedience he owed to his own metropolitan and became disobedient and rebellious towards you, alleging that he was consecrated by your predecessor, as by his own metropolitan and made verbal and written profession of obedience to the church of Canterbury, and obeyed and assisted you in many things just like the other suffragans. [In reply Bernard] did not deny the consecration, but altogether denied that he had made a profession or offered any canonical obedience. When you heard this, you brought two witnesses to court giving evidence that they saw and heard that after his consecration, he made both a verbal and a written profession to the church of Canterbury.

We, therefore, having heard and diligently examined the arguments of both parties, and after examining the witnesses and hearing the advice of our brethren, have accepted the testimony of the witnesses. The bishop personally should be obedient and reverent to you as to his own metropolitan, according to the dictates of justice. Since, however, we wish to conserve to the several churches and ecclesiastics their dignity and rights, we have appointed 18 October of next year [1148] for both of you, in order to find out then, in the presence of both parties, the truth about the dignity of the church of St. David's and its liberty, and to ordain thence by divine intercession what shall be just. Given at Meaux, 29 June.[1]

Unlike Bernard, Theobald was not content with a mere statement of support from the cathedral chapter of his own see. He circularised all his suffragan bishops and obtained letters of support from them. These survive from the dioceses of Bath, Ely, Exeter, Hereford and Winchester.[2] The bishop of Bath wrote that hearing that his mother church was in danger of being 'abridged', it was impossible for him to remain silent. He claimed that Bernard's predecessors had admitted the primacy of Canterbury. Bernard, by his profession of obedience to Archbishop Ralph and his later acts as a suffragan bishop in the times of Archbishops William and Theobald, had put himself out of court. The bishop concluded his statement with a sarcastic reference to the 'fabulous antiquity or antique fabulosity' of Bernard's claim.

The witnesses of Theobald were most probably old monks of

---

[1] Haddan and Stubbs, p. 354.
[2] H.M.C., 5th Report App., p. 453b; Bath in Haddan and Stubbs, p. 353.

Canterbury or Westminster, who had been present at the consecration of Bernard thirty-one years before. An anonymous life
of Bishop David of St. David's claims that these were false witnesses suborned by Theobald, who had paid Eugenius forty
marks to receive their testimony. One was a 'false monk', the
other a layman. When Bernard protested, he was overruled by
the pope.[1]

Thus Theobald, by his superior energy and the intrinsic
justice of his cause, as he saw it, had secured the personal subjection of Bernard to the see of Canterbury. It was, however, far
more important to establish the permanent subjection of St.
David's, and the battle was by no means decided. Bernard was
not disposed to allow his case to go by default. He wrote to
Archdeacon Simeon of Bangor to give evidence at the Council
of Rheims to be held in March 1148 as to the metropolitan
status of St. David's.[2] This was presumably a gesture to be made
at the preliminary session of the Council where the claims of
contending dioceses to primacy were thrashed out.[3] If this was
the case, the putting forward of this claim at the Council was not
recorded. It might therefore refer to a private discussion with
the pope or the cardinals to prepare the ground for October.

These preparations were nullified by the death of Bernard
which took place in March 1148 after a long episcopate of
thirty-two years and six months.[4] His claim lapsed for the time
being. It was obviously of crucial importance that Theobald
should secure the election of a bishop who would not be prepared to press this issue. Another bishop like Bernard might well
succeed in robbing Canterbury of four subject dioceses. He
found a complaisant nominee, taking advantage of an oppor-
tune dispute in the cathedral chapter.[5] The accounts of the
election are from the Welsh side. The unnamed candidate of the
independence group was rejected, and David, archdeacon of
Cardigan, only half-Welsh, and supported by 'the French and
English' was accepted by Theobald, on condition that he would

---

[1] *Giraldus Cambrensis*, ed. J. S. Brewer (R.S.,1863),iii, 431; Lloyd, op. cit., p. 481,
n. 85, suggests one of the witnesses was the bishop of Bath who was a monk, but he
apparently was not aware of the similar written statements by the other bishops.
[2] Haddan and Stubbs, p. 352.   [3] *Hist. Pont.*, p. xxxi.
[4] *Giraldus*, iii, 431.   [5] Haddan and Stubbs, p. 355.

I

not raise the question of the liberty of St. David's during his lifetime.

To safeguard the rights of Canterbury, his profession took a long and unusual form.

Whereas by the sin of disobedience we are exiled from the joys of paradise, it is incumbent on us to return to the same joys by the merit and virtue of obedience. And so I, David, elected to the rule of the Church of Menevia, and to be consecrated bishop in the customary manner by you, O reverend father Theobald, archbishop of the holy Church of Canterbury and Primate of all Britain, do desire that whatever obedience ought to be shown to me by those of my subjects, in the same way I should profess the reverence of subjection and obedience in all things and through all things, canonically, to you and to your successors who will take your place canonically, and to our mother church of Canterbury, and this I confirm with the sign of my own hand.

David was the uncle of Giraldus Cambrensis. His election and consecration sealed the complete victory of Theobald over the separatist elements in the Welsh Church, one of his most successful achievements. It must, however, be remembered that the other Celtic churches were harder to reduce and during the course of the twelfth century the Scottish and Irish churches succeeded in emancipating themselves from York and Canterbury respectively.

The consecration of David took place on the same day as that of Robert of Lincoln and Theobald was assisted by the same bishops. The formal election had taken place on Monday, 14 December 1148 at Lambeth, on the following Saturday at Canterbury Theobald ordained him priest, and on Sunday the 19th, the consecration took place at Canterbury.[1]

Coventry. The see of Coventry underwent numerous vicissitudes after the Norman Conquest. Like other contemporary bishops, the first bishop of Lichfield, after the Norman Conquest, removed to a larger town. He fixed his residence at Chester and established canons there.[2] Lichfield, once the home of an arch-

---

[1] Stubbs, p. 47; *St. Paul's Ecclesiological Soc.*, vii, 169.
[2] William of Malmesbury's *Gesta Pontificum*, ed. N. E. S. A. Hamilton (R.S., 1870), pp. 308-9.

bishopric, showed more vitality than the other deserted episcopal villages. The second bishop after the Conquest removed
once more to Coventry where he became head of the monastery.[1] Succeeding bishops remained at Coventry, but Roger de
Clinton (1129–48) revived the waning fortunes of Lichfield by
reconstituting the chapter on Norman lines.[2] Thus on his death
there were three bodies claiming capitular rights of election: the
monks of Coventry and the canons of Lichfield and Chester.
The monks of Coventry had suffered severely during the civil
war; in 1144 they were expelled by Robert Marmion.[3] Roger de
Clinton was the only English bishop to take part in the Second
Crusade[4] and died at Antioch on 16 April 1148. He had already
shown himself to be at home in the earlier fighting of Stephen's
reign.[5]

The vacancy of eighteen months was caused by disputes between the monks and the canons. There are two main accounts.
The protracted dispute which ended in the election of William
de Cornhill in 1215 led to some research into the respective
rights of Coventry and Lichfield as well as into the rights of the
bishop over Coventry priory.[6] According to the monastic
account, when Roger had died and had been buried at Antioch,
Theobald summoned the monks to Leicester, where they elected
Walter, prior of Christ Church, Canterbury. The canons of
Lichfield and Chester appealed to Eugenius, complaining of
their exclusion from the election. As a result of the appeal Theobald suspended judgment on the validity of the election. The
prior of Coventry, Laurence, paid a personal visit to the pope
and obtained the quashing of the canons' appeal, as well as the
confirmation of their own election. The pope ordered Theobald
to consecrate Walter. The new bishop, having been enthroned
at Coventry, proceeded to Lichfield, where he found the church
closed against him. Accordingly, he excommunicated the canons.
If this account is accepted, it is clear that the election could
not have taken place before the end of 1148 as Theobald only

---

[1] Ibid., pp. 309–11.
[2] *Magnum Registrum Album of Lichfield*, ed. H. E. Savage (William Salt Archaeological Soc., 1924), p. xxvi.
[3] *Newb.*, i, 47.   [4] *Anglia Sacra*, i, 434 (Thos. Chesterfield).
[5] *Gesta*, p. 101.   [6] *Monasticon*, vi, 1242b ('Ex vet. membr. in Bibl. Cotton.').

then returned from his long absence on the Continent. The appeals to the pope would take up most of the year 1149 and thus the consecration of Walter, in October 1149, is satisfactorily explained. Further confirmation of the account is contained in a bull of Eugenius III confirming the episcopal seat at Coventry, and mentioning the agreement made in his presence about this.[1]

A rival Lichfield tradition is preserved in the writings of the fifteenth-century historian Thomas Chesterfield.[2] He also alludes to the differences over the election between the monks and the canons. As they could arrive at no sort of an agreement, Stephen intervened and gave the bishopric to Walter Durdent, prior of Christ Church, Canterbury. On the whole, the earlier account seems preferable. Gervase claimed the election was canonical and conducted by the monks of Coventry. The elect was a man of uncommon piety and learning—a change from the valorous Clinton.[3]

Walter had been appointed prior of Canterbury by Theobald, and their relations were uniformly excellent. The election at Leicester was held under the supervision of the archbishop and there is a case for assuming that Theobald's influence was responsible for the choice of the monks of Coventry.

The consecration took place at Canterbury on 2 October 1149.[4] Theobald was assisted by Robert of London, Walter of Rochester and Nicholas of Llandaff. His profession of obedience followed the usual lines and was the last before Theobald became legate. In his charters Walter usually styled himself bishop of Coventry, but there are charters of the period which call him bishop of Chester and bishop of Lichfield.[5]

Worcester. Simon of Worcester died on 20 March 1150.[6] He was a bishop of the 'official' type, having been a member of the queen's household under Henry I and was thus rewarded for his services.

Little is known about the election of his successor John of Pagham. Pagham was an old possession of the archbishops of

[1] *Registrum Album* as before, no. 262.   [2] *Anglia Sacra*, i, 434.
[3] *Gerv.*, i, 141.   [4] Stubbs, p. 47.
[5] *Registrum Album* as before; cf. nos. 66, 167 and 275.
[6] *Anglia Sacra*, i, 475 ('Annales Menevenses').

Canterbury and is mentioned in Domesday Book as such. Richard de Belmeis was consecrated bishop of London there by St. Anselm in 1108.[1] It remained a 'peculiar' of the see of Canterbury down to the last century. Theobald must have visited Pagham on occasions, and there is one charter of his dated there.[2] John of Pagham no doubt showed himself a youth of promise and was taken into the household of Theobald. He appears on several occasions in the company of the archbishop as a witness to charters.[3] He had the title of Master and it can be assumed he was proficient in Canon Law. Thus at Worcester a new type of bishop was substituted for the old and the influence of Theobald can be seen.

The consecration of John of Pagham took place on 4 March 1151, nearly a year after the death of Bishop Simon. Theobald was assisted by Hilary of Chichester and Walter of Rochester.[4] John was ordained priest by Theobald on the day before. The profession of obedience mentions specifically that Theobald was legate: John was the first bishop to be consecrated since Theobald had received his legatine commission.[5]

London. The death of Robert de Sigillo, bishop of London, occurred on 29 September 1151.[6] John of Hexham claimed that he and many others died of eating poisoned grapes.[7] The vacancy lasted exactly one year.

John of Salisbury gives a fairly full account of the election.[8] On the death of Robert, Pope Eugenius III dispatched a bull to the chapter ordering them to elect, within three months, subject to the usual ecclesiastical sanctions, 'a man honest, literate and adorned with the habit of religion'. The text of the bull has survived and it corroborates the account of John of Salisbury

---

[1] Stubbs, p. 41.   [2] No. 245.

[3] Also Lewes Chartulary ed. L. F. Salzman, *Sussex Rec. Soc.*, 40, p. xxiii (note to vol. 38), and Chichester Chartulary, ed. W. D. Peckham, ibid., 46, p. 82, n. 1.

[4] Stubbs, p. 47; cf. *Gerv.*, i, 142. John was presented to Theobald by Ralph, prior of Worcester (*Diceto*, ii, 42).

[5] Facsimile of registered profession in *New Palaeographical Soc.*, ed. E. Maunde Thompson, etc. (1903–12), 1st series, vol. 2, plate 61, also *St. Paul's Ecclesiological Soc.*, vii, 170.

[6] Holtzmann, i, 291.

[7] *John Hex.*, p. 324. Cf. *Hist. Pont.*, p. 90.   [8] Ibid., pp. 90-1.

except that the time limit was two months and not three. The bull was issued at Segni on 14 January 1152.[1]

It might well be imagined that the dean and chapter were shocked and perturbed at the terms of this mandate which appeared to limit their choice to a monk or a regular canon. They sent a delegation to make a protest to the pope, who thereupon so far modified his terms as to allow anyone in Holy Orders to be described as 'religionis habitu decoratus', on account of the tonsure. On this *volte face*, which completely nullified the original papal intention, there was a theory at the Curia that Eugenius really wanted to exclude the possibility of the election of a layman, which he thought was not unlikely. If there was any suggestion of electing a layman, it must have come from the London magnates. In two letters to Eugenius, Foliot described how, after the death of Robert, the electors were subject to considerable pressure and threats of violence. Foliot claimed that the pope had foiled the conspiracy against the freedom of the electors.[2]

A candidate whom the pope may have had in mind was Walter abbot of Battle,[3] but since the chapter had obtained permission for a free choice they would naturally look to their own ranks to fill the vacant see. The archdeacon of Middlesex, Richard de Belmeis, was unanimously approved as bishop-elect by the chapter.[4] His family had already provided a bishop of London forty years before. Stephen was powerful in London and refused to allow a free election unless he was paid £500. This enormous sum was paid by Richard de Belmeis and it hampered him all his life.[5] The friends of the abbot of Battle claimed that his candidature failed because he refused to enter on such a simoniacal transaction. John of Salisbury expressed his disgust at these proceedings, but pointed out that many were inclined to palliate the offence of simony involved for the sake of securing a free election. About the same time, the new abbot-elect of St. Augustine's, Canterbury, had obtained confirmation of his election by paying the king 500 marks. Thus Stephen, in 1151 and

---

[1] Holtzmann, i, 291.
[2] Foliot's Letters, *P.L.*, 190, ep. 95 and ep. 94 (in that order), cols. 811–13.
[3] *Chron. de Bello*, p. 94.
[4] Foliot's Letters, *P.L.*, 190, ep. 95, col. 812.   [5] *Diceto*, i, p. xxv.

1152, was strong enough to make money out of the Church in spite of his early charter of liberties. This view is supported by a letter of Gilbert Foliot which most probably refers to this election.[1] Writing to William archdeacon of London and Master Henry at the time when the election had been held but the king had not yet given his assent, he warned them against falling away from the decision at which they had already arrived.

The newly-elected bishop and his earlier history are dealt with by Stubbs.[2] On 20 September 1152, Theobald ordained him priest and consecrated him on the 28th. The bishops named as assisting Theobald were Nigel of Ely, Hilary of Chichester, Gilbert of Hereford and Walter of Rochester.[3] Nearly all the bishops were present at the consecration. Henry of Winchester, who may have still been abroad, sent a written apology to Theobald. He excused his absence on the grounds of short notice and ill-health. He had fears for his personal safety. It may be doubted whether his assent to the election was needed but nevertheless he wrote 'we grant our kind assent to the election and consecration out of affection'. The letter concludes with a panegyric of Belmeis which may have been common form in a letter of this type.[4] The profession of obedience mentions Theobald's legatine capacity.

Theobald is not mentioned in the accounts of the election and it can be assumed he took little part in the proceedings, especially as he was in exile for part of the year 1152. It was otherwise with Eugenius who felt Richard was sufficiently indebted to him to allow him to give the vacant archdeaconry of Middlesex to John of Canterbury, a member of Theobald's household. This 'provision' failed because Richard had appointed Ralph de Diceto to the post before he heard of the pope's wishes. Foliot wrote to Eugenius on behalf of the new bishop and succeeded in persuading him not to overrule the appointment.[5]

St. Asaph. After his consecration in 1143, nothing more is heard of Bishop Gilbert and his death or removal some time

[1] *P.L.*, 190, ep. 140, col. 847.   [2] *Diceto*, i, p. xxv.
[3] *St. Paul's Ecclesiological Soc.*, vii, 170.   [4] *Diceto*, i, 295.   [5] Ibid., pp. xxix–xxx.

before 1152 must be presumed. His successor was the famous Geoffrey of Monmouth. The earlier history of Geoffrey has been dealt with comprehensively.[1] He was a secular canon of St. George's in Oxford Castle and probably taught in the schools there, whose reputation was increasing. He, too, had the title of Master and his election furnishes yet another indication of the change in the character of the episcopate.

As the diocese of St. Asaph was completely under the control of the redoubtable Owen Gwynedd, it is unlikely that its clergy had anything to do with the appointment and Geoffrey himself never went there. It cannot be said who was instrumental in securing his election. He was ordained priest by Theobald on 16 February 1152 and was consecrated by the archbishop on the 24th. The bishops of Norwich and Rochester assisted Theobald. The form of his profession of obedience is perhaps not without significance, in view of Theobald's earlier conflict with St. David's. The title of legate was omitted as if to emphasise the subjection of the see to Theobald in his normal capacity. The usual form of profession at this time was to the church of Canterbury and to the archbishop, but the reference to Canterbury is here omitted. Too much emphasis should not be laid on these points as the later profession of Richard of Coventry also omits reference to Theobald as legate.[2] The consecration took place at Lambeth, like that of his predecessor.

Durham. The events of 1153, leading to the consecration of Hugh du Puiset, bishop of Durham, illustrate the exercise by Theobald of legatine powers over the province of York, which he had been unable to do during the earlier Durham and York disputes.

There are several accounts of the election which do not differ materially. On the death of Bishop William in November 1152[3] there were troubles in the diocese, but finally the prior of the cathedral, the two archdeacons, and the clergy of the bishopric elected Hugh du Puiset, treasurer of York cathedral and a rela-

[1] H. E. Salter in *E.H.R.*, 1919, p. 384, and J. E. Lloyd in *E.H.R.*, 1942, p. 460.
[2] Stubbs, p. 47; Haddan and Stubbs, p. 360; *Gerv.*, i, 142, n. 2; *New Palaeographical Society*, as before.   [3] *John Hex.*, pp. 328–9.

tion of the king. The election was not unnaturally approved by the king.[1] The archbishop of York, Henry Murdac, was possibly hoping for the election of a Cistercian or at least a monk and was scandalised at the election of an enemy of his and a relative of Henry of Winchester. He rejected the election and excommunicated the prior and the archdeacons. This was a high-handed action, especially as there appeared nothing wrong with the conduct of the election, but Murdac had never been noted for his tact. He alleged, as grounds for quashing the election[2] the uncanonical age of Hugh—he was twenty-five years old—his worldly character, his ignorance, and the form of the election, which had been accomplished without the assent of the metropolitan. The citizens of York, who had always been loyal to Stephen, were incensed at what they considered to be an affront to the king, and for the last time Murdac was obliged to flee the city.

The election took place on 22 January 1153 and the excommunications must have come into effect shortly afterwards. The prior and the archdeacons appealed to Theobald in his legatine capacity against their excommunication. He found their complaint to be justified and he ordered Murdac to absolve them, which he did. It seems that Theobald asked Murdac to reconsider his decision on the validity of the election, but Murdac remained adamant.[3] The action of Theobald was not without courage as Murdac was a protégé of Eugenius and St. Bernard.

Hugh had remained in the south of England and decided to make a personal appeal to the pope to confirm his election. He obtained a recommendation from Theobald among others.[4] Meanwhile events were moving in his favour. The sun was setting for the Cistercians. Eugenius died in July, St. Bernard in August and Murdac himself in October. The new pope, Anastasius IV, as might have been expected, did not follow the

---

[1] *Fragmentum de electione Hugonis Puteacensis* ap. *Sim. Dun*, i, 169, and Continuation of Simeon of Durham, ibid., p. 167.

[2] *Geoffrey of Coldingham*, ed. J. Raine (Surtees Soc., 1839), pp. 4–5.

[3] *Fragmentum, etc.*, as before; '. . . eos absolvit sed Hugonem consecrare nullatenus voluit'.

[4] *John Hex.*, pp. 329–30; Hugh the Chantor ap. *Historians of the Church of York*, ed. J. Raine (R.S., 1879–94), ii, 226.

policy of his predecessor and himself consecrated Hugh on 20 December 1153.[1] He returned in triumph to Durham and was enthroned on 2 May 1154. He was succeeded as treasurer of York by a member of Theobald's household, John of Canterbury, who had previously failed to become archdeacon of Middlesex, as has already been seen.[2] The prior of Durham subsequently became abbot of Westminster in succession to Stephen's nephew Gervase.

The conduct of Theobald shows his moderate use of the legatine powers committed to him. Unlike Henry of Winchester, who was in a similar position in 1143, he made no attempt to consecrate Hugh, but only secured the redress of an unjust excommunication. In his support of Hugh's appeal, Theobald showed clearly where his sympathies lay. Strangely enough, Gervase, in his account of the election, did not mention the activities of Theobald.[3]

York. The death of Murdac in October 1153 was followed by the restoration of the long-suffering St. William by Anastasius IV and the eclipse of Cistercianism in York province as a ruling force. As Theobald is not concerned, little more need be said. William's return was not a happy one; he was opposed by the chapter although welcomed by the city. On 8 June 1154 he died under mysterious circumstances. Archdeacon Osbert was generally suspected of having poisoned him in a peculiarly horrible manner, and the case subsequently came under the cognisance of Theobald. The two great enemies Bernard of Clairvaux and William of York were both canonised.

The main source of information for the ensuing York election is William of Newburgh. He wrote about forty years after these events and is not always reliable for this period, but his account is circumstantial and seems not unreasonable.[4] When Stephen had returned from the North in the autumn of 1154, he held a council at London and on the agenda was the question of filling the vacant see of York. Stephen summoned the York dignitaries

[1] Stubbs, p. 47; *Fragmentum.*

[2] Cf. C. T. Clay, *Yorks. Arch. Journ.*, 1943, pp. 11–20; for charters showing him treasurer, 1153–4. MS. Lambeth 241 f.171a (Dover Carty.), and No. 182.

[3] *Gerv.*, i, 157.   [4] *Newb.*, i, 82, 95.

as well as the diocesan abbots and priors. It is clear from Newburgh's account that there was the usual amount of intrigue.
Supported by Stephen,[1] Theobald was attempting to force his
friend and archdeacon Roger of Pont L'Evêque on the chapter.
The task of forcing them to submit devolved on Robert dean of
York and Osbert the archdeacon. The complaisance of these
dignitaries might be attributed to the grave suspicion of com-
plicity in the poisoning of St. William which hung over their
heads and their consequent desire to win over Theobald.

Having elected Roger, the chapter dignitaries made a pretence of asking Theobald to release Roger from his office and
assent to the election. The astuteness of the archbishop in making it appear that the initiative came from the chapter itself is
commented upon by Newburgh. After this formality, Roger
asked for something which was less of a formality, that Theobald
should consecrate him in his capacity as legate and not as archbishop. Theobald agreed to this—the Canterbury-York dispute
meant little to him—and he consecrated Roger at Westminster
on 10 October.[2] He was assisted by eight bishops, London,
Lincoln, Hereford, Rochester, Bath, Ely, Norwich and Worcester. It will be noted that there were no bishops from the
Northern province. The council then broke up. Diceto points
out that Roger made no profession of obedience to Theobald[3]
and Gervase admits as much by his silence. Theobald gave the
vacant archdeaconry, the most valuable in England, to Becket,[4]
according to Gervase with the consent of the monks of Canterbury Cathedral.[5]

Theobald's refusal to reopen the York dispute because of, or
in spite of, his friendship with Roger is yet another instance of
his moderate temperament and statesmanship. His policy towards York, and it must be assumed he had one, was rather of
peaceful penetration and the extension of the influence of
Canterbury in a diplomatic manner. The election of Roger can
be viewed in this light and Theobald can hardly be blamed for
the disgraceful disputes between Roger and Archbishops Becket
and Richard, who had all grown up together under Theobald's

[1] Roger of Hoveden, *Chronica*, ed. W. Stubbs (R.S., 1868–71), i, 213.
[2] Stubbs, pp. 47–8.   [3] *Diceto*, i, 298.   [4] *Gerv.*, i, 158–9.   [5] Ibid., ii, 385.

shadow. The election of Roger could so easily have marked the opening of a new era of friendly relations between Canterbury and York.

Theobald's resoluteness in this respect is illustrated in a letter of his to Henry II.[1] It disclosed an attempt to sow discord between him, Roger and the king. Theobald anathematised an unknown forger who wrote in his name to Henry expressing Theobald's regret at the election of Roger and desiring Henry to punish the archbishop.

I neither wrote this letter nor desired it to be written, nor am I aware it was written by any of my household. It is false and the forger—whoever he is—did this for your delusion and for his own damnation.

The last repercussions of the great York election dispute of 1140–53 took the form of judicial proceedings against the archdeacon of York, Osbert, for the alleged poisoning of William Fitzherbert. Shortly after the death of William and in the lifetime of Stephen, a member of the late archbishop's household ('familia') called Symphorian, accused Osbert of having administered poison to the archbishop in the communion cup.[2] It is most probable that he made this accusation at the very council at which Roger was elected archbishop. At all events it was at a council in the presence of Stephen, the bishops and the barons of England. Symphorian offered to submit himself to any ordeal to prove his case, such as the red-hot iron, boiling water or trial by battle. Osbert, while denying the charge, claimed to be tried before the ecclesiastical courts as a clerk. Stephen, however, was determined to have the case tried by the Curia Regis and not all the arguments and complaints of Theobald and his suffragans could move him. The enormity of the crime and the presence of Stephen in York when it occurred, thus making it a flagrant breach of the peace, were given as Stephen's reasons. As Theobald was forced to admit in his letter to the pope, and not for the only time, this attitude of Stephen's was 'according to the custom of our nation'. The trial was fixed for 13 January 1155, but Stephen was dead by then.

Strangely enough, Henry II was more compliant than Stephen.

[1] John of Salisbury's Letters, *P.L.*, 199, ep. 61, col. 45.
[2] Ibid., ep. 122, col. 103.

It was after great difficulty and at the cost of the goodwill of the king and barons that Theobald succeeded in withdrawing the case to the ecclesiastical forum. The usual delays characteristic of the Canon Law ensued but finally it became clear that Symphorian could not substantiate his accusation 'according to the subtlety of the laws and canons'. There were present in court, amongst other eminent canonists, the bishops of Chichester, London, Salisbury and Exeter, who advised Theobald to award Osbert the proof of compurgation. Theobald accordingly ordered Osbert to purge himself with the help of three archdeacons and four other clerks of the order of deacon. John of Salisbury, in a private letter to Adrian IV in 1156 informed him that Osbert had failed in his purgation, and warned him not to believe anyone who said anything to the contrary.[1] Osbert thereupon appealed to the pope thus withdrawing the trial from the jurisdiction of Theobald and incidentally proving the justice of Henry II's strictures on ecclesiastical criminal jurisdiction. He received support from Foliot who wrote a letter to the pope on his behalf.[2]

Summary. The principle of freedom of election was put into practice during this second period of Theobald's primacy to a far greater extent than ever before. The removal of Henry of Winchester from his supreme position, the more settled state of the country and the increase of the influence of the Papacy and of Theobald can be held responsible for this development. The spread of the knowledge of Canon Law encouraged by the recent compilation of Gratian made the capitular bodies aware of their rights, and they were prepared to fight for them. Consequently out of the fourteen elections held during this period no less than six appear to be the result of the free choice of the chapter. These were at Norwich where the monks took the natural course of electing their prior, at Lincoln and London where archdeacons belonging to their respective sees were elected, and at Coventry, Worcester and Durham. It is true that a price was paid to the king for freedom of election at London and thus the election there was not, strictly speaking, free, but the chapter

[1] Ibid., ep. 108, col. 96. [2] Foliot's Letters, *P.L.*, 190, ep. 114, cols. 828–9.

elected the candidate of its own choice. At two places, York (1147) and Chichester, definite papal pressure seems to have been put on the electors. At York (1154), Rochester, St. David's, and probably Hereford and Llandaff, the influence of Theobald was paramount. Nothing is known of St. Asaph, except that the bishop was obviously not the free choice of the chapter.

The status of the newly-elected bishops shows the effect of the vastly increased influence of monasticism and Canon Law. The comparatively large number of five monks were elected at York (1147), Norwich, Llandaff, Hereford and Coventry. The beginnings of the recession of the monastic wave can be seen at Durham and York in 1153 and 1154. Five archdeacons were elected, at Lincoln, Rochester, St. David's, London and York (1154). Three bishops can be described as canonists, those of Chichester, Worcester and St. Asaph. At Durham, a cathedral dignitary and a relative of the king was elected.

The growing influence of Canterbury and Theobald's household is also apparent as can be seen at York (1154), Rochester, Coventry and Worcester.

3. Episcopal Elections, 1155–61

St. Asaph. Geoffrey of Monmouth died in 1155[1] and was succeeded by a certain Richard who made a profession of obedience in identical terms.[2] The profession described him as 'frater Ricardus' and Wharton deduced from this that he was a monk.[3] Nothing else is known about Richard or his election. His name would appear to indicate that he was not a Welshman, and he, too, probably never visited his diocese.

Exeter. Little is known about the first of the two Exeter elections held during this third period of Theobald's primacy. Robert Chichester died on 28 March 1155 and was succeeded by Robert Warelwast who was consecrated bishop by Theobald on 5 June of the same year.[4]

---

[1] J. E. Lloyd in *E.H.R.*, 1942, p. 466.
[2] Stubbs, p. 47; *Gerv.*, ii, 385; *New Palaeographical Soc.*, as before.
[3] H. Wharton: *De Episcopis et Decanis Assavensibus* (1695), p. 309.
[4] Stubbs, p. 48; *Gerv.*, i, 162; *St. Paul's Ecclesiological Soc.*, vii, 170.

Robert Warelwast was the nephew of a former bishop of Exeter, William Warelwast, who was consecrated in 1107 and died in 1137. During his uncle's lifetime he had been archdeacon of Exeter and later became dean of Salisbury.[1] The extremely short interval between the death of his predecessor and Robert's consecration—let alone his election—would appear to signify that intrigue was at a minimum and the new bishop approved by all. His close connections with the diocese of Exeter might well indicate that he was the unfettered choice of the chapter. Unfortunately there is no real evidence to support these conjectures.

He was consecrated at Canterbury, made the usual profession of obedience and Theobald was assisted by Bishops Hilary of Chichester, Jocelin of Salisbury, Nigel of Ely and Walter of Rochester. The endorsement to the profession adds that Henry II was laying siege to Bridgnorth Castle at the time. The significance of this may be that the election took place there.

Worcester. Even less is known about the Worcester election of 1158. John of Pagham went to Rome and died there in 1157. Le Neve ought to be upheld here against Stubbs and the *Handbook of British Chronology* when he gives the death of John as falling on 31 March 1157. If he died in March 1158 as the others assert, there would be no time for the news to reach England before Alfred's consecration which took place before 13 April 1158.[2]

A letter of Gilbert Foliot provides evidence that he was probably the vicar of Worcester during this vacancy of about a year. It was written to a certain R. of Worcester who had complained that the earl of Hereford had captured his soldiers in Evesham church, or possibly in the monastery. Because of the sacrilege and breach of the right of sanctuary involved, the case came within the scope of ecclesiastical jurisdiction, and Gilbert, as vicar, expected to be judge. The archdeacon of Worcester, however, claimed that his only superior was Theobald. He asserted that the bishop, on his departure, had given him charge of all judicial business. This contention was supported by many wit-

[1] *D.N.B.*, xx, 819.　　　　　[2] *Ann. Mon.*, i, 48 (Tewkesbury).

nesses. 'You speak of your losses,' remarked Gilbert pathetically, 'but if the aforesaid archdeacon spits in my face, it does not worry you at all!' Further remarks of Gilbert in this letter illustrate the hard lot of a vicar, unless Worcester was an exception. 'But perhaps you might object, "Whatever that archdeacon claimed, you after all were vicar of the church of Worcester, and if he had made any irregular pronouncement, you ought to have brought him to book".' In reply to this Gilbert replied that the position of vicar was to be regarded rather as a burden than as an honour, and that only his sense of obedience impelled him to accept the position. Whatever others might have done, he intended to intervene as little as possible. This might explain Gilbert's reluctance to undertake the administration of London in 1161.[1] It may be assumed that Theobald had appointed him vicar of Worcester.

Alfred was enthroned at Worcester on Palm Sunday 1158, which was 13 April, and therefore his consecration must have taken place some time before that date. There are few details available of the election and the consecration,[2] nor does the profession appear to be extant.

He was a chaplain of Henry II.[3] A 'magister Alveredus' who attested some of Henry's earlier charters might be identical with this bishop.[4] This would suggest that there was royal influence at work to secure his election, and thus we see the first beginnings of a reversion to the 'ancient customs' of Henry I in connection with episcopal elections.

St. Asaph. Godfrey of St. Asaph was the third bishop of that see to be consecrated by Theobald in seventeen years.

He has been described as a nominee of Henry II.[5] From his later behaviour this would appear to be very probable as he absolved Becket's enemies, including Richard de Luci, in 1167. Two years earlier, Henry had given him the abbey of Abingdon

---

[1] *P.L.*, 190, ep. 135, col. 842.
[2] He was presented to Theobald for **consecration by Ralph, prior of Worcester** (*Diceto*, ii, 42).
[3] *Anglia Sacra*, i, 476.
[4] L. Delisle, *Recueil*, introduction, p. 354.
[5] D. R. Thomas, *History of the Diocese of St. Asaph* (1907–12), i, 214.

which he held in plurality. Wharton, in his biographies of the bishops of St. Asaph had a very low opinion of him.[1] Some light on the earlier career of Godfrey which has apparently not been noticed before, is provided by the Register of Kenilworth priory;[2] 'Know etc. that I, Godfrey, by the grace of God called bishop of St. Asaph, while I was a monk of Coventry, was present at a certain synod in the time of King Henry the elder, which Roger, bishop of the same place celebrated in the same church . . .'. This puts a more favourable construction on his tenure of Abingdon, as Professor Knowles wrongly assumed he was a secular.[3]

Coventry. The death of Walter of Coventry in 1159 was a loss to Theobald of an old friend. In a letter to Becket written in 1160, John of Salisbury said: 'It is commonly said amongst us that the lord king has conceded the income of three vacant bishoprics to be paid to you'.[4] These three sees were Coventry, Exeter and Worcester. Thus, yet another royal prerogative, which had been abrogated by Stephen's charter of liberties to the Church, had been restored.

The man chosen to replace Walter was Richard Peche, archdeacon of Coventry. His father, Robert Peche, was bishop of the same see from 1121 to 1127. As Richard was the son of a priest, it would not be surprising if some objections had been raised against his election. These objections were countered by an excursus of Diceto, who cited several famous prelates labouring under the same disability, culminating in Pope Adrian IV.[5]

Contemporary writers say little about his election, but the fifteenth-century historian of the diocese, Thomas Chesterfield, claimed that he was elected with the consent of the monks of Coventry and the canons of Lichfield, 'voluntate regis Henrici mediante'.[6] If Richard was the king's choice, he was certainly acceptable to the chapters on account of his local affinities.

With regard to his consecration, the last of Theobald's primacy, there is some difference of opinion amongst the sources.

[1] *De Episcopis Assavensibus,* p. 311.   [2] MS. B. M. Harleian, 3650, f.43b.
[3] Knowles, p. 614.   [4] *P.L.,* 199, ep. 78, col. 65.
[5] *Diceto,* i, 305.   [6] *Anglia Sacra,* i, 435.

K

The date is not known, but it took place some weeks before Theobald's death. Gervase said that Richard first made a profession of obedience to Theobald and was then consecrated by Walter of Rochester in the archbishop's presence, as Theobald was too ill to perform the consecration himself.[1] Diceto said that Theobald himself consecrated Richard.[2] There is no essential conflict between the chroniclers as Walter would in any case have been acting as chaplain of the archbishop, this being part of his duties as bishop of Rochester. The profession of obedience is printed in facsimile by the New Palaeographical Society.[3]

Exeter. Robert Warelwast was bishop for less than five years and died on 22 March 1160. The last year of Theobald's life was taken up in a successful effort to secure the election of Bartholomew, the archdeacon of Exeter.

Some of the events which led to the election of Bartholomew can be followed in Theobald's correspondence, as well as in the private letters of John of Salisbury. The letters of Theobald do not mention any name, and the archbishop, writing to the king and Becket, urged them not to waste any more time in filling the vacant see.[4] John of Salisbury was apparently given the task by Theobald, who was confined to his bed, of negotiating the election of Bartholomew. He wrote to Becket recommending the archdeacon to the king's notice.[5] Henry was interested in the candidature of a member of the important Gloucestershire family of Harding and had written to Theobald in his favour. He was, however, illiterate and not fit to be a bishop. The supporters of this worthless candidate had importuned Theobald, even on his bed of sickness, but the Exeter chapter was unwavering in its support of Bartholomew. John advised Becket not to wait for the king to return to England before proceeding with the election, as the archbishop would think, not without justification, that they were waiting for his death, in order to put forward their own policy. The resolution of Theobald was bearing fruit, and he now felt himself in a position of being able to

---

[1] *Gerv.*, i, 168.   [2] *Diceto*, i, 304 f.   [3] First Series, vol. 2, plate 62.
[4] John of Salisbury's Letters, *P.L.*, 199, ep. 64 (3), col. 50; ep. 70, col. 57; ep. 71, col. 58; cf. Dom. A. Morey, *Bartholomew of Exeter* (1937).
[5] Ibid., ep. 78, col. 65.

write to the Exeter chapter to make arrangements for the election.[1] He ordered them to ask the king for permission to hold a canonical election. The election of Bartholomew was a foregone conclusion and John of Salisbury wrote to him to apprise him of the good news. The attempt of the Harding family had failed ingloriously and even their simony was of no avail. Even if Bartholomew were to die, there would be no hope for the rival party. He warned Bartholomew not to give his rival the vacant archdeaconry of Exeter before his election, and in any case to do nothing without Theobald's advice.[2]

Thus was obtained the last triumph of Theobald, but it was not destined to be complete. Theobald gave orders for the consecration. It was early in 1161, and the archbishop himself was incapable of carrying out the ceremony, but he at least wished to be present. This, however, was denied to him as Bartholomew had first to go to Henry to pay homage for the temporalities. In the interval Theobald died, and it would normally have devolved upon Richard of London to perform the consecration. He was incapable, being paralysed, nor was Henry of Winchester available. It was, therefore, Walter of Rochester who consecrated him early in 1162, as he would have done had Theobald remained alive. He made a profession to the Church of Canterbury and the future archbishop.[3]

Bartholomew was for a time a member of Theobald's household[4] and Theobald used him as a confidential messenger to the king during the schism.[5] He was a theologian and an accomplished canon lawyer, and was thus of the new type of educated bishop that Theobald was always anxious to have elected. The election illustrates the growing royal power in ecclesiastical matters, but at the same time shows that when Theobald saw fit to take up a stand it was hard to dislodge him. Nowhere in the course of his correspondence did Theobald assert the power of the Church in the matter of elections: indeed he treated Henry as the supreme arbiter. Henry for his part was not pre-

[1] Ibid., ep. 52, col. 32.
[2] Ibid., ep. 90, col. 81; cf. Morey, op. cit.
[3] *Gerv.*, i, 168–9; *Diceto*, i, 304 and footnote; *St. Paul's Eccl. Soc.*, vii, 171.
[4] Cf. No. 83 and 84.
[5] John of Salisbury's Letters, *P.L.*, 199, ep. 64 (1), col. 48.

pared to press the candidature of a man of whom the Church clearly disapproved.

Summary. It is unfortunate that, during this period of the first seven years of the reign of Henry II, the information we possess about the episcopal elections should be so inadequate. Of the second Exeter election alone is there any detailed account and it is difficult to say how far that election was typical of the others. At both Exeter elections, and at Coventry, local men were elected, which might give some indication as to the freedom of choice of the electing bodies. Intervention by Theobald is only recorded in connection with the election of Bartholomew of Exeter. Royal influence seems to have been definitely at work in the Worcester election and the second St. Asaph election, but nothing is known of the first election at St. Asaph.

One monk, one royal official, one cathedral dignitary and two archdeacons were elected. The status of the first bishop of St. Asaph is unknown, but he too may have been a monk. There appears to have been some tightening-up of royal control, but no sharp transition from the elections as held under Stephen.

In the Western Church, towards the end of the eleventh century, 'the control and judgment of elections began to pass from the metropolitans to the pope'.[1] In England during the primacy of Theobald, a favourable period for the assertion of papal supremacy, the position seems rather more complicated. Power was divided fairly equally if not harmoniously between king, pope and archbishop, and this position put the diocesan chapters in a uniquely favourable situation. Owing to the lack of evidence in many elections about the preliminary stages it is difficult to evaluate the influence of the capitular bodies but one has the impression that it was considerably more important than at earlier or later periods.

4. THEOBALD AND THE ENGLISH EPISCOPATE

'Theobald, by the grace of God, archbishop of Canterbury and primate of all England . . .' is a common opening form of many

[1] Brooke, p. 30.

of Theobald's charters. Yet the primatial power of Theobald was practically non-existent and his ordinary metropolitan power seriously limited. The declining importance of both these functions of the see of Canterbury since the days of Lanfranc can be attributed largely to papal policy. The centralising Hildebrandine movement, assisted by the development and spread of Canon Law, tended to depress the status of primates and metropolitans, and to reduce archbishops and bishops alike to complete dependence on the apostolic see.[1] Thus the Papacy actively encouraged the efforts of Archbishop Thurstan of York to emancipate himself from all subjection to Ralph and William of Canterbury in their primatial capacities. The only right which Theobald seems to have claimed for himself as primate was that of crowning the king, and even that was not allowed to pass unchallenged.[2] One of the commonest centralising devices of the Papacy was the employment of legates, who took precedence over archbishops and bishops while on their assignments. This aspect of John of Crema's legation in 1125 particularly impressed Henry I and Archbishop William, and the latter avoided a recurrence of this situation by obtaining the legation for himself which he held till his death in 1136. Thus a temporary inconvenience had been avoided at a price. The intrinsic powers of the archbishopric were absorbed by the legatine powers which were derived directly from the Papacy. Theobald, in many ways, had more direct power over his suffragans than Lanfranc or Anselm, but it was as a papal servant that he exercised them, thus aiding the centralising policy of the Papacy.

Innocent II gave a new direction to the idea of a permanent legation which Archbishop William had probably never contemplated by appointing the bishop of Winchester to that post, thus reducing Theobald's authority in his province to a nullity.[3] The death of Innocent in 1143 restored the position to what it had been before 1126 and the prospect of an occasional legatine visit must have seemed trifling to Theobald compared with what he had to undergo from 1139 to 1143.

---

[1] A. Fliche, *La Réforme Grégorienne* (1924–37), ii, 227–39.
[2] John of Salisbury's Letters, *P.L.*, 199, ep. 34, col. 22.
[3] See above, pp. 15–19.

The legation of Cardinal Ymar lasted for about six weeks in February and March 1145, being terminated by the untimely death of Lucius II. It is surprising how much work he succeeded in accomplishing in this short time, but for Theobald it was just as well that his legation was so abruptly ended. The question of raising the sees of St. David's and Winchester to metropolitan status was not settled[1] and subsequently Eugenius III upheld the prerogatives of Canterbury. The remissness of St. William of York prevented Ymar from bestowing the archiepiscopal pallium upon him and thus irrevocably confirming his election.[2] As William belonged to the Winchester party, Ymar's failure was to Theobald's advantage.

References to the work of Ymar are scattered in various sources. It has been suggested that he held a legatine council in London,[3] which seems to be correct, but no canons are recorded to have been passed. The nature of the council and the number of those attending is not known, but five bishops, apart from Theobald, and seven abbots or priors are named as having been present at a judicial hearing which formed part of the proceedings.[4] The bishop of Rochester and his cathedral priory were disputing the possession of two manors and Ymar gave his decision in favour of the monks. One would have expected that, in view of the exceptionally close relations between Canterbury and Rochester, a case like this would have been left to the judgment of Theobald who was, no doubt, acquainted with the facts. In the event, after Ymar had returned to Rome, Theobald persuaded the monks to pay the bishop fifty marks as a thinly-veiled compensation.

A boundary dispute between the bishops of Hereford and Coventry was settled by Ymar and this decision was subsequently confirmed by Eugenius III.[5]

The correspondence of Foliot reflects some of the activities caused by the presence of a legate in England. As abbot of Gloucester, Foliot was defending the burial rights of his dependent priory of Ewenny against the diocesan, Uchtred of Llan-

---

[1] See above, p. 111 and pp. 21 f.   [2] *John Hex.*, p. 317.
[3] J. H. Round in *Athenaeum*, 23 January 1897.
[4] No. 223 and Holtzmann, ii, 193.   [5] Ibid., p. 208.

daff. He wrote to Ymar asking for his arbitration and fixing 23 March 1145 for the hearing.[1] He also wrote to the prior informing him of the steps he had taken.[2]

In another letter to the legate concerned with the affairs of Cernel abbey, Foliot apologised for not obeying his mandate to come to London.[3] The monks of Cernel headed by their prior had visited Ymar in a body and begged of him to confirm their choice of an abbot, Bernard prior of Gloucester. He granted their request[4] and sent a mandate to the bishop of Salisbury to bless the new abbot-elect. This is perhaps not a complete catalogue of the acts of Ymar as legate in England, but serves to show the wide activities of a legation of even such a short period, and its inevitable repercussions on archiepiscopal power.

The name of another legate, Cardinal Paparo, is also associated with the diminution in the primatial status of Canterbury. His mission was the reorganisation of the Irish Church. In 1150 he came to England on his way to Ireland.[5] He visited Stephen who now felt himself secure enough to enforce the half-forgotten rules of his uncle with regard to the reception of legates. The king refused to give Paparo permission to pass through England unless he promised to do no injury to the kingdom. This reassertion of ancient custom accorded ill with papal pretensions and Paparo returned to Italy. Eugenius was even more displeased with the unregenerate Stephen, who had perhaps unintentionally saved Theobald from further humiliation as Paparo was only in deacon's orders.

On the plea of the cardinals, who were generally a restraining influence on Eugenius, Paparo was ordained priest.[6] After the completion of this formality, he returned to the British Isles in 1151, this time passing through Northumberland and Cumberland which were occupied by the king of Scotland. After dealing for some time with Scottish affairs, he reached Ireland at the end of the year. Early in 1152 he held a council at Kells. The new archbishoprics of Dublin and Tuam were created and added to Armagh and Cashel. The four archbishops were pre-

[1] *P.L.*, 190, ep. 16, col. 759.
[2] Ibid., ep. 19, col. 761.
[3] Ibid., ep. 37, col. 773.
[4] Ibid., ep. 92, col. 810.
[5] *John Hex.*, p. 326.
[6] *Hist. Pont.*, pp. 72 f.

sented with their pallia by the legate. Various canons were passed, and John of Salisbury selects for special notice the one abolishing the precedence over bishops at synods given to the abbess of St. Bridget's. They had to sit at her feet.

The reorganisation of the Irish Church was by no means a papal inspiration although it needed papal authority for its consummation. St. Malachy, who became archbishop of Armagh in 1132 and died in 1148 was a most ardent exponent of the scheme ultimately carried out by Paparo, and had convinced the Papacy of its necessity. The last flicker of the authority of Canterbury over Ireland, the consecration by Theobald of Patrick of Limerick in 1140, was ignored. Robert de Torigny writing of the effects of the synod of Kells, regarded it as a blow directed against the see of Canterbury which had anciently claimed the primacy over Ireland.[1] In practice, however, only the Scandinavian settlements had recognised the supremacy of Canterbury, as a means of dissociating themselves from the Irish. It can, however, be said that the Irish Church, as a whole, might well have come under Canterbury during the Anglo-Norman invasions, had it not been reorganised and placed on an independent footing at the Council of Kells. There is no record of any protest by Theobald, who was in exile on the Continent while the council was being held.

No further legates came to England while Theobald was archbishop. Legatine powers were exercised by Theobald himself from 1150 till his death, the grant being renewed to him by successive popes. In accordance with these powers he held a council in 1151.[2] It seemed to be generally believed that no council could be held except under a legate, but this had not always been so. In many of Theobald's charters during this period, simple confirmations or mandates to bishops, his legatine authority is invoked where one would have thought his normal metropolitan power would have been sufficient to carry the day. Thus England was familiarised with the growth of papal power.

Papal councils were another means of strengthening the unity of the Western Church under Roman headship and

---

[1] *Tor.*, p. 166   [2] See above, pp. 33 ff.

weakening the independence of the constituent units. The anti-pope Victor IV abandoned his pretensions in May 1138. The ending of the schism called for a reaffirmation of the unity of the Catholic Church, which was the function admirably fulfilled by the second Lateran Council of April 1139 at which more than five hundred bishops were present.[1]

During the Council of Westminster in 1138, the legate Alberic of Ostia had invited all the bishops and most of the abbots of England to the forthcoming council. In view of the disturbed state of the country, Stephen drastically limited the number of bishops and abbots he would allow to leave the country.[2] This limitation does not seem to have been opposed by Alberic or Innocent II and contrasts with the attitude of Eugenius III at Rheims in 1148.

The composition of the English delegation gives rise to many problems which have been largely elucidated (although in the process complicated) by Round, Poole and Hunt.[3] With regard to the bishops who attended, it is undisputed that Theobald was accompanied by Roger of Coventry, Robert of Exeter and Simon of Worcester.[4] Roger was to be Stephen's representative at the trial of his claim to the throne of England. Simon and the newly-elected Robert were probably considered by Stephen as 'safe men'. They had been with the king at Oxford in January 1139.[5] The Hexham chroniclers claim that a bishop of Rochester attended the Council, and this question has already been discussed.[6] Nigel of Ely is also involved. A letter of Theobald ostensibly addressed to him reminds him that 'we and you, O brother bishop, were present at the Lateran Council under the presidency of the lord Innocent'.[7] The presence of Nigel at the council is disproved by a bull of Innocent II of 29 April 1139.[8] In it the pope mentioned that he had received Nigel's personal representatives at the council and had accepted the bishop's

---

[1] See above, pp. 14 f.   [2] Ric. Hex., p. 177.
[3] Round in Geoffrey de Mandeville (1892), p. 250, and E.H.R., 1893, p. 515; Poole in E.H.R., 1923, p. 61, and Hist. Pont., p. 107; Hunt in E.H.R., 1923, p. 557.
[4] Hexham Chroniclers.
[5] H. E. Salter in E.H.R., 1910, p. 115; C. W. Foster in Linc. Rec. Soc., 27, p. 58.
[6] See above, pp. 98 f.
[7] John of Salisbury's Letters, P.L., 199, ep. 56, col. 36.
[8] Holtzmann, ii, 168.

excuses (as well as the abbot of Thorney's) for not attending. There remains the letter of Theobald to explain away. Poole claimed it was really not addressed to Nigel. The address only appears in the late Cambridge manuscript of John of Salisbury's correspondence. He and Hunt[1] therefore agreed that the letter was written to[2] Gilbert Foliot who was present at the council. This, if correct, would solve the difficulty. Yet the tone of the letter and its subject matter would make it extremely improbable that Theobald wrote it to Foliot. It can be reconciled neither with Theobald's friendship for Foliot, nor with the latter's justified reputation as a canonist.[3] Poole made an earlier suggestion that the letter might have been addressed to Robert of Exeter or one of the three unnamed abbots who went to the Lateran Council. Robert of Exeter died in March 1155 and the collection of John of Salisbury's letters does not seem to begin until after this date, but this possibility cannot altogether be discounted.[4] No one who was an abbot at the time of the council was a bishop between 1154 and 1161 and this rules out the latter possibility. Round's suggestion that Theobald or John of Salisbury made a slip after twenty years would appear more probable.[5] After all Nigel's representatives were present and business relating to Ely was transacted at the council and the letter would be entirely in keeping with what is known of Nigel's activities as a bishop. Furthermore, the address as given in the manuscript ought at least to be taken as a presumption in favour of Nigel.

With regard to the English abbots who attended the Lateran Council, the Hexham chroniclers agree that four abbots went to Rome, representing their colleagues. One of them was Reginald of Evesham,[6] a brother of Gilbert Foliot.[7] The others remain anonymous. The significance of the attendance of monastic elements at Roman Councils lies in the desire of many religious houses to free themselves from diocesan control and to put themselves directly under papal rule. To attend a council might bring with it the reward of a bull giving the monastery extensive

[1] *E.H.R.*, 1923.   [2] 'by' on p. 560 in *E.H.R.* above is obviously an error.
[3] 'Nos super re non ambigua consuluistis' further 'in fraudem canonum . . . nimium proni estis'.   [4] Cf. H. G. Richardson in *E.H.R.*, 1939, p. 471.
[5] *E.H.R.*, 1893, p. 517.   [6] *John of Worcester*, p. 55.   [7] Knowles, p. 284.

privileges or even exempting it altogether from any English ecclesiastical authority. It was therefore to be expected that Evesham should receive a privilege.[1] Other privileges were granted at the same time to Westminster and St. Augustine's, Canterbury,[2] and so it is conceivable that Gervase of Westminster and Hugh of St. Augustine's attended the council.

From the province of York, Richard abbot of Fountains attended, representing Archbishop Thurstan. He was not included in the enumeration of the other four abbots.[3] Among others at the council were Henry of Huntingdon,[4] Arnulf of Lisieux, then archdeacon of Séez,[5] and Lupellus, a clerk of the late Archbishop William.[6] Gilbert Foliot, a Cluniac prior, was there with his superior Peter the Venerable, who was an old friend of Theobald.[7]

The council passed thirty canons. Many of them merely renewed canons passed in former councils. Among them several would be of especial interest to England in the years to come.[8] The fifth canon provided that the goods of dying and dead bishops should remain inviolate. The eleventh decreed that priests, monks, strangers, merchants and peasants should be left in peace. The twelfth laid down the rules for the Truce of God. There are no traces of this institution to be found in England,[9] but in view of the council it is strange the Church made no effort to introduce it during the anarchy. The fifteenth ordered the excommunication of anyone laying violent hands on a clerk and, unless the offender was at the point of death, the pope alone could absolve him. The sixteenth forbade ecclesiastical benefices to be claimed by hereditary right. The eighteenth excommunicated those guilty of arson, who could only gain absolution by going on crusade. If they were released by their bishop against the provisions of this canon, the nineteenth canon suspended the bishop for a year and ordered him to pay the

---

[1] Jaffé, 7999.   [2] Holtzmann, i, 245; Jaffé, 8004.
[3] *Ric. Hex.*, p. 177. 'Praeterea' introduces the sentence about Richard. See above, p. 90.   [4] See above, pp. 14 f.
[5] *Hist. Pont.*, p. 85; Arnulf was at Stephen's court in 1137, cf. J. H. Round, *Commune of London* (1899), pp. 98–9.   [6] *Hist. Pont.*, p. 85.
[7] Foliot's Letters, *P.L.*, 190, ep. 79, col. 799; see above, p. 5.
[8] Mansi, xxi, 525.
[9] F. Pollock and F. W. Maitland, *History of English Law* (2nd edn., 1923), i, 75.

damage. The twenty-first forbade the sons of priests to minister. The twenty-eighth invalidated an episcopal election if the chapter refused to allow the 'religious men' of the diocese (i.e. the monks and canons regular) to take part in it.

The effect of these canons on the English Church is not easy to assess. Orderic was pessimistic about their influence for good in England. The poor and oppressed did not benefit from them as the secular powers regarded them as being of little or no importance.[1] The only canon that Theobald ever quoted in his subsequent correspondence was the sixteenth in the letter to Nigel of Ely, already alluded to. The twenty-eighth canon had an important bearing on the York election dispute. No English manuscript contains a copy of the canons, but their tone is to some extent reflected in Henry of Winchester's Legatine Council of 1143.[2]

The only other relevant aspect of the council was the trial of the rival claims of Stephen and the empress to the English throne. The vagaries of this trial in English historical writing constitute a history in itself. Freeman dated it in 1152, Miss Norgate in 1151 and later in 1148, and Round, refuting all who had gone before, fixed it in 1136.[3] Adams preferred 1139 at the Lateran Council[4] and was confirmed by Poole, whose arguments seem irrefutable.[5] There are two accounts of the trial, one by John of Salisbury in his *Historia Pontificalis*, and the other by Gilbert Foliot in a letter to Brian Fitzcount, a fellow-supporter of the Angevin cause.[6] The empress was represented by bishop Ulger of Angers, who charged Stephen with perjury (which gave the case its ecclesiastical character) and usurpation. Stephen's advocates were Roger of Coventry, Lupellus and Arnulf. Arnulf was their spokesman and he countercharged with the claim that the empress was illegitimate. Henry I had married a nun of Romsey in violation of Canon Law. He admitted that Stephen had sworn an oath in favour of the empress, but claimed that it was extorted under duress, and that Henry finally changed his mind and designated Stephen as his heir.

---

[1] *P.L.*, 188, col. 974.   [2] Brooke, p. 104.
[3] J. H. Round, *Geoffrey de Mandeville* (1892), p. 250.   [4] Adams, p. 223.
[5] *Hist. Pont.*, p. 107.   [6] Ibid., p. 85; *P.L.*, 190, ep. 79, col. 796.

Ulger replied to this by denying the alleged illegitimacy of the empress and that Henry had ever changed his mind. The assertions of Arnulf, however, had successfully confused the issue and Innocent refused either to pronounce judgment or to adjourn the trial. In effect, Stephen had won his case. Several of the cardinals, including the future Pope Celestine II, disapproved of the verdict and Innocent was suspected of having been corrupted by Stephen's bribes. The effect of the verdict on Theobald can be seen in his consistent loyalty to Stephen personally throughout his reign. Strictly speaking the decision, if it can be called one, was not in favour of Stephen, but in favour of the *de facto* ruler and this governed the attitude of the English Church during the upheavals of 1141.[1]

An important function of papal councils was to promote papal contacts with all members of the ecclesiastical hierarchy. This was realised by Stephen and Eugenius III and led to their quarrel in 1148 over the Council of Rheims.[2] As in 1139 all the higher dignitaries of the English Church were summoned to the council, but this time Stephen's efforts to restrict the delegation to three bishops were opposed by the pope. Theobald alone succeeded in defying the royal edict. Thus the attendance of the English episcopate was limited to Theobald, Henry of York, Robert of Hereford, Hilary of Chichester and William of Norwich. The defiance of Theobald's authority by the other bishops and its consequences have already been dealt with.[3]

Robert of Hereford fell ill at the council and died in less than a month on 16 April.[4] Hilary of Chichester justified the royal confidence placed in him by his behaviour at Rheims and equally falsified the hopes of Eugenius, who had been instrumental in securing his election.[5] Of the conduct of William of Norwich at the council, nothing is reported. The new archbishop of York, Henry Murdac, who at the time was in exile, was present, and Theobald took the opportunity of claiming the primacy of Canterbury over York, at the preliminary session of the council.[6] Had William still been archbishop of York, Theo-

---

[1] See above, p. 37, for Eugenius III's attitude to the verdict.
[2] See above, pp. 25 ff.   [3] See above, pp. 26–9.
[4] *Anglia Sacra*, ii, 314; cf. *John Hex.*, p. 321.   [5] *Diceto*, i, 263.   [6] *Hist. Pont.*, p. 5.

bald might have had some hope of carrying his point, but it was chimerical to hope to make any headway against the Cistercian nominee of the pope. In fact Eugenius refused even to entertain the claim until Henry should be settled in England, which was not for nearly three years. In fairness to Theobald it ought to be said that, by this claim, he was keeping alive the Canterbury pretensions which might otherwise have gone by default. The policy of reducing the status of Canterbury was thus continued. The Papacy was to replace Canterbury as the bond uniting the two English provinces.

The canons passed by the council are little more than repetitions of those of previous councils.[1] After the official ending of the council, the more important prelates were retained for the extra-conciliar business.[2] One of the most important items was the charge brought against Gilbert, bishop of Poitiers, of having published erroneous Trinitarian doctrines. The chief opponent of Gilbert was St. Bernard, and Theobald figures as one of his satellites.[3] At a separate meeting of Bernard's supporters, the two English archbishops were present, as well as their successors Becket and Roger, who were there as part of Theobald's staff. The cardinals noted the strong influence of St. Bernard over the English Church, which was now at its height. They felt that Bernard, supported by the French and English bishops would be in an unassailable position.[4] Theobald might have had more than merely personal motives at stake in his support of Bernard. A passage in one of his books relating to the efficacy of baptism was admitted by Gilbert to have been copied by misguided disciples and to be extant in England.[5] This book was ordered by the pope to be destroyed. The outcome of the proceedings was inconclusive, as the cardinals were favourably inclined towards Gilbert and opposed to Bernard, and whatever the personal predilections of Eugenius, Gilbert left the council with his reputation only slightly tarnished.

After Rheims there were no more councils of this nature till Alexander's Council of Tours in 1163. On the whole it cannot be said that the Lateran Council or Rheims altered the position

[1] Mansi, xxi, 715.   [2] *Hist. Pont.*, p. 12.
[3] Ibid., p. 18.   [4] Ibid., p. 21.   [5] Ibid., p. 23.

of Theobald in relation to the English episcopate to any extent.

A factor of far greater significance than either legates or councils was the great increase in appeals to the pope, which had the effect of diminishing the judicial power of the archbishop of Canterbury. It was only under Theobald that appeals to the pope became a normal part of the procedure in English ecclesiastical causes in accordance with Canon Law. Hitherto, if litigants were dissatisfied, they could appeal from the archdeacon to the bishop and then to the archbishop, as outlined in the Constitutions of Clarendon.[1] This was all changed and now an appeal could be made to the pope at any stage in the proceedings. Clearly this reduced the status of the archbishop's court. Further, the pope could delegate the settlement of these appeal cases to English judges, not necessarily the archbishop, thus reducing archbishops and bishops to a common level.

Numerous illustrations of this procedure can be found in Theobald's letters to the pope where the archbishop is seen loyally co-operating in the development of the new system. These letters deal with select cases of appeals to the pope which passed through Theobald's hands at one time or another and necessarily exclude cases which passed him by altogether. Many of them illustrate the course of appeal from bishop to archbishop and then to the pope. Other letters show the complications of the system and the infinite possibilities of delaying a final decision. A Dorset case may be taken as an example.[2] It was between Robert Winegot and William of Sturminster over parishioners and their tithes. Robert came before the archdeacon of Dorset and claimed that they had already been restored to him *by a previous judgment*, but William was still in possession. He was prepared to bring witnesses to prove his contention. The reply of William was to appeal to Theobald. They both came before Theobald, but as William, although he appealed, had not prepared his case, the archbishop remitted the question to the diocesan bishop, Jocelin of Salisbury. As the bishop was about to come to a decision, William once more appealed to Theobald. On this second occasion the archbishop

---

[1] Clause 8. Down to 1135 appeals to the pope were exceptional.
[2] John of Salisbury's Letters, *P.L.*, 199, ep. 21, col. 14.

was assisted by the bishops of Chichester, Hereford and London. Robert produced his witnesses and their evidence was taken. Seeing the case was going againt him, William appealed to the pope without alleging any ground of complaint. Although Theobald considered this appeal to be unjustified, even from the point of view of Canon Law, he felt obliged to pass it on to the Curia.

Delegation of jurisdiction by the pope did not always bring an end to litigation. Adrian IV committed a case to Walter of Coventry as judge-delegate. One of the parties was a canon of Lichfield, and his opponent, suspecting the bishop of partiality towards him, appealed to Theobald on this ground. The canon refused to recognise the jurisdiction of Theobald over the case, pointing out that appeal could only be made from delegated jurisdiction to the delegator himself. He therefore appealed to the pope, and Theobald, in passing on the appeal, stressed the impartiality of Walter and the baselessness of the charge against him.[1] Theobald's equanimity in dealing with this type of case is remarkable. He must have been the first English archbishop to be denied jurisdiction over a variety of causes in his own province, but this was the law of the Church and Theobald was loyal to its principles.

If he chose, the pope could delegate jurisdiction *appellatione remota*, that is, prohibiting any further appeals and empowering the delegate to give a final decision. There are a few examples of this in Theobald's time,[2] but even here the door was not altogether shut against further appeals.[3] In connection with this point, the difficulties of Theobald as an executor of papal instructions is clearly brought out. William Cumin had been a firm supporter of the Angevin and Scottish cause in the North of England and, as has been seen, was for a time intruded into the bishopric of Durham. Subsequent to his ejection, he appears

---

[1] Ep. 20, col. 14.

[2] Cf. No. 212, ep. 13, col. 9, ep. 107, col. 96—this privilege had been obtained by a clerk of Theobald against Baldwin archdeacon of Norwich to be decided in the court of the bishop of Norwich and the archdeacon was trying to evade the decision —ep. 120, col. 102.

[3] There were five or possibly six grounds of appeal against the terms of a mandate *appellatione remota*, cf. *Dictionnaire du Droit Canonique* (1935–), i, 828.

to have rejoined the partisans of the Angevins in the West. Theobald was anxious to do something for him and appears to have obtained some vague expressions of sympathy from Eugenius III in or before 1152. Acting on this, Theobald ordered the bishop of Exeter to remove a certain William Giffard from the church of Budleigh and install William Cumin. This order was given under the colour of a papal mandate. It would appear that Giffard then appealed to Eugenius who thereupon delivered the following rebuke to Theobald:

We are exceedingly astonished that whenever on many occasions we write to you about complaints which are brought to us, you deal with these cases dissemblingly or negligently—you try to interpret our letters according to your own will and when we put forward only a request, you declare you have received a mandate and recognise our will. For, lo, in our letter which we sent to you on behalf of William Cumin, as we remember, we delivered no mandate but merely preferred a request that for the reverence of the blessed Peter and us you should hold him in high regard and if anyone should presume with rash daring to inflict injury on his goods or possessions you should execute due justice on them. But on receipt of this letter you restored to him the churches and prebends which he had illicitly possessed and justly lost, and compelled the bishops in whose parishes the churches and prebends were situated to make restitution. . . .[1]

Probably at the same time, on 3 November 1152, he wrote to the bishop of Exeter, ordering him to restore the church of Budleigh to Giffard, which the bishop had given to Cumin on the orders of Theobald. No appeal was to be allowed.[2] Never accepting a defeat as the last word, Theobald reopened the case of William Cumin with Pope Adrian IV, and obtained a mandate from him to the bishop of Bath restoring Cumin to the church of Chard (Somerset) which he had lost as a result of his Durham escapade. If it could be shown that Cumin had given satisfaction to the see of Durham in respect of the damage he had caused there, then the bishop of Bath was to put him into the church of Chard, *appellatione remota*. The dispossessed clerk set out for Rome, hoping to upset Adrian's decision and, accordingly, Theobald wrote to the pope encouraging him to maintain the rights of

[1] Holtzmann, ii, 240. The document breaks off here.　　[2] Ibid., no. 72.

L

Cumin.[1] John of Salisbury's pleas were added to his master's, and he even made insinuations against the character of the previous incumbent.[2]

A bitterly contested case between the monks of Ely and Henry the clerk, son of a former archdeacon of Cambridge, illustrates how the normal relationship between archbishops and bishops was seriously modified by the new 'reception' of Canon Law in England.[3] Both parties claimed the manor of Stetchworth (Cambs.), but there were several side-issues which tended to complicate matters. Probably in 1148, the dispute first came into the cognisance of Nigel of Ely, who imprisoned Henry on the charges of the monks, who accused him of arson, forgery and robbery as well as the illegal possession of Stetchworth and putting the manor to secular uses. Henry appealed to Theobald, who released him, and the case was heard before the archbishop several times, at Harrow and other places. At the same time, a clerk, Joseph,[4] accused Henry of forging papal bulls to establish his claim to Stetchworth, but Theobald was dissatisfied with Joseph's witnesses and adjudged purgation to Henry. While at Bury St. Edmund's, the archbishop delegated to the bishop of Norwich and Ording, abbot of Bury, the task of finding out the true facts at Stetchworth. The monks complained bitterly of the favour shown by Theobald and his *curiales*[5] towards Henry and appealed to Eugenius. The bishop of Norwich reported the results of his investigation to the pope, favourable to the monks. Theobald also sent a full account of the progress of the case to Eugenius. In his reply, dated 22 December 1150, Eugenius ordered Theobald and Hilary of Chichester to absolve Henry from Joseph's charge of forgery and to decide the case of Stetchworth *appellatione remota*. The archbishop and his delegated co-adjutor once more heard the case, but the monks again appealed to Eugenius on the grounds that Henry, in his statement of the case, during the appeal at

---

[1] John of Salisbury's Letters, *P.L.*, 199, ep. 120, col. 102.

[2] Ibid., ep. 121, col. 103.

[3] Holtzman, ii, nos. 61, 62, 64, 67, 68, 71, 74, 79, 80.

[4] Probably identical with the Joseph in No. 100.

[5] Cf. the similar complaints against Theobald's household by the monks of Christ Church, Canterbury, in 1151–2. See above, p. 60.

Ferentino, had made false suggestions to the pope and that he had unjustly claimed long possession of Stetchworth. Thus the delegation of jurisdiction by the pope to Theobald and Hilary had been made on the basis of incorrect facts. The second hearing before Eugenius was a failure as neither side came prepared with evidence. Accordingly Eugenius once more delegated the case, this time, however, to Gilbert Foliot, bishop of Hereford, on 15 June 1152. After several hearings before Gilbert, who also consulted Theobald, the bishop decided to absolve the monks from the payment of heavy damages which Henry had claimed from them, as a result of their alleged illegal possession of Stetchworth. Against this decision, Henry appealed to Anastasius IV. On 28 September 1153 the pope confirmed Gilbert's decision and also decided that the monks of Ely should possess Stetchworth, without prejudice to the question of ownership, which Henry was at liberty to raise within the time-limit of one year.

Whether Henry ever availed himself of this permission or whether, as is more probable, his resources were completely exhausted by the protracted litigation, is unknown. At all events the monastic possession of Stetchworth remained unchallenged. It now remained for Theobald to translate the decision into action and he issued a mandate to Henry and his abettors informing them that he had invested the monks of Ely with the manor of Stetchworth and had, in consequence, removed Henry from the manor. Henry was to obey under penalty of excommunication. The support of Stephen was enlisted, either by Theobald or by the monks, and he issued a writ prohibiting the associates of Henry from interfering in Stetchworth.[1] This case shows Theobald acting as a link, and by no means an essential link, in a long and expensive chain of litigation. No doubt the monks obtained their manor, which they might otherwise have lost in the absence of papal jurisdiction, but the crippling expense which this single action cost them must have accounted for the profits of Stetchworth for years to come. Henry must have been completely ruined, while the Papacy, Stephen, Theobald, the bishops of Hereford, Chichester and Norwich and the

[1] No. 102.

abbot of Bury St. Edmund's, together with their staffs, were suitably rewarded for their labours.

Ely also provides a clear example of the subjection of the English episcopate to the Papacy, notwithstanding the rights of the archbishop of Canterbury. Nigel of Ely would appear to have possessed little of the financial ability of his famous family, although the difficulties of the see of Ely throughout Theobald's archiepiscopate were not altogether of his making. In 1140 he was expelled from his diocese by Stephen and despoiled of his possessions and Innocent II sent a mandate to Theobald and his suffragans ordering them to help him recover his see and its property.[1] Theobald's measures must have been a comparative failure for, in 1143, Nigel went or was sent to Rome to appeal to help from the pope. Lucius II ordered Theobald and his suffragans to obtain the restoration of Nigel's lost property and the abolition of the illegal tenseries levied by the various malefactors who were to be given two months to make full restitution. Any writ or licence of the king to the contrary was to be ignored. He wrote to the Norman bishops in similar terms and also sent an appeal to Stephen to treat the bishop in an honourable manner.[2] It was the task of Theobald to see that the bishops carried out these measures but in view of the civil war raging in the Ely district, there was probably little he could do. This is illustrated by a further mandate of Lucius to Theobald issued at the end of 1144.[3] Geoffrey de Mandeville was in occupation of the Isle of Ely, while the possessions of the see outside this area were held by the royalists. Together with the bishops, Theobald was ordered to warn Stephen and Geoffrey to restore the possessions they were occupying and make full compensation for the damage they had caused.

With the final defeat of Geoffrey de Mandeville in the following year, comparative peace descended on the Ely district, but little seems to have been done by Nigel, or for that matter by Theobald, to recover many possessions of the see of Ely, lost or alienated during the war. This would certainly provide a practical justification for papal intervention. From Nigel's point of view it did not seem to matter if the estates of the Church com-

---

[1] Holtzman, ii, 171. [2] Ibid., ii, 185–6. [3] Ibid., ii, 188.

mitted to his care were irrevocably dissipated and alienated. Indeed he himself aggravated the position shortly after the accession of Henry II by buying the post of treasurer for his son Richard, the future bishop of London and author of the *Dialogus de Scaccario*. This cost him £400 and meant further inroads into the diminished possessions of the see.[1] The tone of the papal mandates had already changed. Eugenius III in 1150 had denounced as invalid the alienations of Nigel and his predecessors.[2] The patience of Adrian IV had now reached breaking-point. In February 1156 he told Nigel that if he did not recover the alienated possessions within three months, he would be suspended from his episcopal functions.[3] As might have been expected, Nigel failed to accomplish the task set him and he was duly suspended. There is no record of Theobald having been consulted on the question of Nigel's suspension, and so it would seem that even his position as legate gave him no standing in the matter. What Theobald would have done, if left to his own devices, is uncertain. The third and fourth canons of Theobald's Legatine Council deal with this question. The bishop is to supervise the repayment by the culprits of his diocese. If he remits more than one-twentieth part of the losses suffered by the Church, then he is to be suspended for six months. Far from sacrificing a small part of the losses of his see in order to recover the remainder, which would have rendered him liable to suspension in accordance with the canons of 1151, he had apparently condoned the alienations and had made himself an accomplice in the spoiling of his see. No one can question the justice of Adrian's sentence, coming as it did after years of remonstrance by the Papacy and of tergiversation not only by Nigel but by the whole English episcopate.

The suspended bishop would appear to have been brought to his senses by the long-overdue papal action and set about the work of restoration, made more difficult by the passage of time. Theobald wrote an eloquent letter to Adrian on his behalf begging the pope to relax the sentence of suspension. He referred to Nigel's belated efforts and pointed out that nobody

---

[1] *Anglia Sacra*, i, 627.
[2] Holtzmann, ii, 227. [3] Ibid., ii, 272 f.

suspended his athlete in order to help him gain the victory.[1]
Moved by these remonstrances, Adrian wrote to Theobald on
17 March 1157 informing him that he had temporarily relaxed
the sentence of suspension until the following 18 October on
condition that Nigel would continue the good work. Theobald
was to persuade Henry II, due to arrive in England shortly, to
help the bishop.[2] During this period, further pleas by Theobald
and John of Salisbury were made to Adrian in order to obtain
a complete relaxation of the sentence. Nigel deposited a pledge
of good faith with Theobald, amounting to 100 marks sterling.
The intermediary at the papal court for these negotiations was
the papal chamberlain Boso, an Englishman, who received ten
marks, equivalent to one gold mark, for his pains.[3] These efforts
were rewarded for, on 16 January 1158, Adrian addressed three
bulls to England promulgating the final relaxation of the sentence of suspension passed on Nigel. One was addressed to Nigel
himself, a second to the king, and a third to Theobald, Roger
of York and all the bishops.[4] Adrian wrote that in answer to
the prayers of Henry, the archbishops and bishops, he had
decided to relax the sentence passed on Nigel, who must promise
in the presence of Theobald to recover the lost possessions. The
offenders were to be given four months to make restitution under
the penalty of excommunication, without the option of appeal.
They included the earls of Warenne, Hertford and Oxford,
which no doubt accounted for many of Nigel's difficulties.

Occasionally Theobald showed that he was under no illusions
about the policy of depressing the archiepiscopal status. In a
letter to Boso the papal chancellor, probably of 1156, he protested against his treatment by Adrian despite his unquestioned
loyalty to the Papacy.[5] At one stage of his struggle to enforce a
profession of obedience from Silvester of St. Augustine's, the
pope had ordered him to appear 'ad tribunal Londonias'. This
could either mean before the bishop of London himself or con-
ceivably before a number of his suffragans assembled at London.

---

[1] John of Salisbury's Letters, *P.L.*, 199, ep. 14, col. 10.
[2] Holtzmann, ii, 280. Cf. No. 103.
[3] John of Salisbury's Letters, *P.L.*, 199, ep. 30–2, cols. 20–1.
[4] Holtzmann, ii, 282–6.
[5] John of Salisbury's Letters, *P.L.*, 199, ep. 105, col. 94.

In either case it was a most humiliating position for an archbishop and legate, and it would seem that on this occasion Theobald's protest was successful. In a confirmation issued by Lucius II to Theobald and the see of Canterbury, the pope wrote, 'We desire to conserve, unviolated and entire, to each metropolitan see, its honour throughout its dioceses.'[1] The foregoing is a commentary on this disingenuous claim.

Despite these striking examples and others which have not been cited, it may well be that the nature of the sources used tends to overshadow the normal relationships between Theobald and the episcopate which must have subsisted during these years. It is thus difficult to estimate how far the papalist innovations modified this traditional relationship. The charters of Theobald provide a corrective to those who would take too gloomy a view of the admitted decline in the metropolitan powers of the archbishopric of Canterbury. The large numbers of confirmations to religious houses seem to show that the monks and canons of England still thought it worth while applying to Theobald, at some cost to themselves. Several of his judgments are extant, no doubt representing but a small proportion of the cases which reached him in a normal way, originally or by means of appeal from lower courts. There is also a collection of mandates to bishops, archdeacons and rural deans. If Theobald's charters were the only evidence of his activities, the reverse impression would be obtained, and papal intervention would be thought to be on a very small scale indeed. Similarly, some of Theobald's letters in John of Salisbury's correspondence provide evidence of the normal metropolitan powers being exercised. There are four letters giving legal guidance to bishops, who were uncertain how to proceed in difficult cases.[2] On several occasions Theobald called on the services of bishops to sit with him in deciding cases.[3] Hilary of Chichester, Gilbert of Hereford and Richard of London appear most frequently in this capacity. Other letters show Theobald delegating jurisdiction to bishops or sending them mandates.[4] Alfred of

---

[1] Holtzman, ii, 179.
[2] John of Salisbury's Letters, P.L., 199, epp. 56, 58, 67, 68.
[3] Epp. 13, 21, 22, 35, 100, 119, 122.   [4] Epp. 7, 11, 21, 69, 83, 88, 93.

Worcester received a rebuke for failing to grant a church to a clerk in accordance with the wishes of the king, queen and pope.[1]

It now remains to consider the repercussions on Theobald and the English Church of the marked revival in the royal power in England which developed during the earlier years of Henry II.

[1] Ep. 23, col. 15.

IV

Henry II and the English Church

THE significance of this period is clearly brought out by Brooke[1] who describes Henry's early policy towards the English Church and the papacy as follows:

His object was to rebuild the barriers again, and by excluding the papal authority, to revive the royal in its old form. But he had to act with caution. He was indebted for the ease of his accession to the pope and to Archbishop Theobald, and had to be careful not to antagonise them by too sudden a reaction. Relations with Rome remained for a time as they had been and there was no interference with appeals. But Henry began slowly to exert his influence on elections, to get a personnel amenable to him, and to insist on their doing homage to him before consecration; moreover, he also, with the aid of his chancellor, Thomas Becket, seized opportunities to employ ecclesiastical revenues to his own advantage. The archbishop of Canterbury, however, mattered most, and when Theobald died in 1161 the opportunity for which he had been waiting seemed to have arrived.

We have here a picture of Henry waiting for the old man to die and in the meanwhile encroaching as much as he dared. In another place he writes:[2]

It is a signal testimony to the importance of Theobald that in the history of the English Church the date that matters is not the death of the king, Stephen, but the death of the archbishop of Canterbury, Theobald . . . it was rather policy than gratitude that caused [Henry] to bide his time until Theobald was dead.

It is clear that Theobald himself was not unaware of these tendencies. Henry's designs, however carefully concealed, were at least suspected by Theobald and his entourage. In a letter to the king, Theobald said:

---

[1] Brooke, pp. 198–9. [2] Ibid., p. 189.

The children of this age have advised you to diminish the authority of the Church in order to enhance the dignity of your royal position. Whoever these people are, they surely attack your greatness and bring about the wrath of the Lord.[1]

The archbishop added that this conduct would be ingratitude to the Church, presumably a reference to Theobald's support of the Angevin cause from 1152 onwards. The bitter attack of Pope Eugenius on the conduct of Hilary of Chichester in 1148[2] might, with greater justice, have been applied by Theobald to Thomas Becket. From the reference in this letter of Theobald to the Exeter election, it was written in 1160, probably after the settlement of the question of the recognition of Alexander III.

Two points made by Brooke have already been dealt with. With regard to episcopal elections the evidence, on the whole, supports his contention, but it should be pointed out that Stephen's reign provides us with far more flagrant examples of interference with elections than any of the five elections of Henry's earlier years can furnish. It can only be said that Henry was continuing the policy of Stephen, without much greater success, despite his far stronger position. The attack on the wealth of the Church has already been dealt with in connection with Henry's wars[3] and the slight and ineffective protests of Theobald and others have been discussed. To this may be added the question of the disposal of the revenues of vacant sees and abbacies and the notorious pluralism of Becket.[4]

The question of appeals to the pope needs a little more attention. The relevant clause in the Constitutions of Clarendon lays down that ecclesiastical appeals can be made from the archdeacon to the bishop and thence to the archbishop. Should the archbishop fail to do justice the dissatisfied party could then apply to the king who would send a writ to the archbishop deciding the case in the archbishop's court. No appeal could be made to the pope without royal permission.[5] According to Brooke this system was an anachronism and from 1154 to 1161

---

[1] John of Salisbury's Letters, *P.L.*, 199, ep. 64, part 3, col. 49.
[2] See above, p. 27.   [3] See above, pp. 43 ff.
[4] Cf. L. B. Radford, *Thomas of London* (1894), pp. 164 ff.
[5] W. Stubbs, *Select Charters* (9th edn.), p. 165, clause 8.

there was no interference with appeals. There are, however, some indications that the system was in partial operation even during this period. In one of his letters to the pope, Theobald gives an account of the litigation between Roger the priest and the abbess of Barking.[1] At one stage of the proceedings, 'Roger came to us with a letter of the lord king and renounced the appeal [to the pope] which he had made, and out of reverence to the royal mandate, he asked that justice should be done to him'. This was at the beginning of 1161. It is true that the abbess herself appealed to Rome shortly after, without any mention of royal intervention. A *cause célèbre* of these years was that of Richard of Anesty. He appealed to the pope in 1161 and a lengthy account of the case was forwarded to the Curia by John of Salisbury.[2] In his own account of the case[3] Richard mentions that he had to go overseas to obtain from King Henry a licence to appeal to the pope, before Archbishop Theobald would authorise the appeal. On the other hand it may possibly be argued that this was a special case which had its origin in the lay courts, but a most significant point which emerges is that, if we only had John of Salisbury's account of the case written to the pope, nothing would have been known of the royal licence. In writing to the pope it may well have been thought unnecessary or inadvisable to mention this fact. The bulk of our knowledge about papal appeals during this period comes from John of Salisbury's correspondence, which cannot be regarded as reliable on this point. It may well be asked, in how many other cases, where we are not so fortunate as to have the diary of a litigant, licence of appeal had to be obtained from the king, and in how many others it was refused. Finally, in a letter of Theobald to Henry late in 1159 or early in 1160, the archbishop mentioned that permission was being obtained for going to Rome.[4] This evidence is vitiated to some extent by the peculiar conditions obtaining during the schism. Possibly the passage in question does not refer to appeals at all, but the idea that a

---

[1] John of Salisbury's Letters, *P.L.*, 199, ep. 87, col. 74; see above, p. 49.

[2] Ibid., ep. 89, cols. 75–80.

[3] F. Palgrave, *English Commonwealth* (1832), ii, p. lxxv.

[4] 'Dicitur autem quod majestas vestra quibusdam dedit illuc eundi licentiam', etc. *P.L.*, 199, ep. 44, cols. 27–8.

royal licence should be obtained for going to Rome was clearly accepted by Theobald, even if it was not acceptable to him.

Whatever may be said against the charters fabricated by the monks of Battle Abbey, the Chronicle of that monastery is a most valuable source throwing many interesting sidelights on eleventh- and twelfth-century English history. Battle Abbey, in the diocese of Chichester, can be compared to St. Augustine's at Canterbury, trying to free itself from diocesan control. Whereas St. Augustine's looked to the pope to secure this desirable end, Battle, which was a royal foundation, relied on the support of the king and the charters of his predecessors, genuine and not so genuine. Our knowledge of the dispute between Hilary of Chichester and Walter de Luci abbot of Battle is derived chiefly from the Chronicle of Battle,[1] and as the case went in favour of the monks, no doubt the account is reasonably truthful, especially as it receives independent support from the terms of Theobald's charter.[2] The result of the dispute was that Hilary of Chichester, with the personal support of Theobald,[3] and furnished with a mandate from Adrian IV, failed miserably at the king's court in 1157 to assert his claims of supremacy over Battle, which was declared exempt from his control for all practical purposes. Henry asserted the supremacy of royal charters over papal privileges and mandates in what should have been, according to Canon Law, a domestic matter of the Church.

The hearing before Henry took place towards the end of May 1157 at Colchester Abbey where the king was staying. It was preceded by a private or semi-public consultation between Henry and the Abbot's party. The abbot was fortunate in having the support of his powerful brother Richard de Luci the justiciar. Other supporters of the abbot included the chancellor, Becket, and the constable, Henry of Essex. The charters of liberties granted or allegedly granted by the Norman kings to Battle were produced and read by Becket, and Henry was very properly impressed. At this stage it was pointed out that Hilary's case might rest on the acknowledged fact that the abbot

---

[1] *Chronicon Monasterii de Bello* (ed. J. S. Brewer), Anglia Christiana Society, 1846, pp. 85–103.   [2] No. 11.

[3] In Stephen's reign Theobald had ordered Hilary to relax a sentence of excommunication passed on the abbot, but was convinced of the justice of Hilary's cause.

had made a profession of obedience, but this was brushed aside. 'Profession', said Henry, 'is not directed against the dignities of churches. For those who make profession, promise only what they ought.' After some further remarks by Richard de Luci, Henry affirmed 'that he would in no way allow himself to cause the aforesaid church to lose its liberties and dignities in his days'. The issue had been prejudged.

A few days later the formal proceedings opened at a full-dress council. Those prelates present were Theobald, Roger of York, Richard of London, Robert of Lincoln, Robert of Exeter and Hilary of Chichester, as well as the abbot of Battle and two other abbots. The barons were there in full force as well as the king and his loyal chancellor. Richard de Luci and his brother spoke first, drawing an impressive picture of William the Conqueror and his charters. Hilary, who was an eminent canon lawyer, demonstrated the absurdity of this line of argument before an almost wholly unsympathetic audience. He was frequently and rudely interrupted. After expatiating on the well-worn theme of the two swords and not failing to cite the verse 'Thou art Peter', he went on to point out that no bishop could be deposed, save by papal judgment or permission. 'True', said Henry, 'but he could be expelled.' (Laughter in court.)[1] Unperturbed, the bishop reached the climax of his argument. No layman had the right to bestow ecclesiastical liberties, unless confirmed by papal authority. It followed that no king of England could have freed Battle from its due subjection to the bishop of Chichester without papal authorisation. This had not been obtained and therefore the charters of William the Conqueror and his successors were, in that respect, void. As might have been expected, this lofty argument infuriated Henry. He accused the bishop of attempting, by artful subtlety, to combat the royal authority given to him by God and called on the archbishops and bishops to do justice. This indeed was a crucial moment. Perhaps the bishops looked to Theobald for a lead, but if so they were disappointed. Had they supported Hilary then, they might have supported Thomas seven years later, but they remained unaccountably silent. It was Becket himself who

[1] 'Arridentibus universis.'

knocked another nail in his coffin. He joined with Henry in condemning the attitude of Hilary. It must surely have been easier
to oppose Henry in 1157 than in 1164.

Hilary concluded that it was useless to continue arguing from
a purely theoretical standpoint. He tried to prove the abbot's
subjection to him by ascertainable facts, especially the profession
of obedience. At various stages of the proceedings, both Hilary
and Theobald tried to persuade Henry to allow the case to be
dealt with by the Church according to Canon Law, but the king
would not hear of it. The bitterness of Theobald's defeat must
have been greatly increased by the conduct of Becket, who made
a final speech in favour of the monks. Towards the end of this
address, he emphasised the fact that Hilary had obtained a papal
bull in support of his claims. 'Then the king's countenance
changed and, looking at the bishop, said: "Is it not true that you
obtained these letters as has just been said? I order you to tell the
truth by the oath of fealty which you owe me".' Hilary stoutly
denied the allegation and even tried to accuse the abbot of
Battle of having obtained the bull; whereat the king very properly remarked that it would be a strange thing if the abbot
were to obtain such a document to his own disadvantage. After
Becket had put in a few words in support of the king, it was seen
that Theobald, shocked at Hilary's duplicity, was making the
sign of the cross 'prae nimia admiratione'. Hilary felt that his
position was becoming too uncomfortable and made haste to
withdraw his claims while there was still a chance to regain the
royal favour. Theobald intervened on his behalf and restored
him to better relations with Henry and the abbot and his
brother. The renunciation was confirmed by a charter of Theobald 'by episcopal authority and as legate of the holy Roman
Church', a somewhat questionable use of his legatine powers.
The point to be made here is the weakness of the episcopate,
even when Henry, still young and inexperienced, was supposed
to be 'biding his time'. Hilary would go as far as to deny an
obvious fact rather than admit he had applied to the pope. The
strength of the English Church under Stephen seems to have
been largely fictitious and Henry wasted little time in proving
this.

It may be argued that, after all, Battle was a royal *Eigenkloster* and that the validity of royal charters was at stake, which might explain the extreme conduct of Henry and the feeble opposition of the bishops. The force of this argument can be weakened by a consideration of a similar case, the attempt made by the bishop of Lincoln to bring the powerful abbey of St. Albans to heel. Although occurring shortly after the death of Theobald in 1161, this case is well within the 'pre-Clarendon' era. St. Albans was not a royal foundation, yet this purely ecclesiastical question was heard and adjudged at the royal court. Here again[1] the bishop had recourse to papal aid. Alexander III sent a bull to St. Albans ordering the case to be heard before two bishops, who might be expected to approve of episcopal control of monasteries. When Henry heard of this, his anger was aroused and the papal intervention was ignored.

John of Salisbury himself mentions Henry's general opposition to appeals to the pope, or indeed to any contact between the English Church and the Papacy. Writing to his friend Peter, abbot of Celle, he says:

Alone in the kingdom, I am said to diminish the royal majesty . . . For whoever amongst us may invoke the name of Rome, they put the blame on me . . . as if I alone instruct the archbishop of Canterbury and the other bishops what they ought to do.[2]

Other letters belonging to the period before Theobald's death, illustrate the king's opposition to John, who, after all, was nothing more than Theobald's mouthpiece during these years.[3] It might be described as an attack on Theobald himself. Summing up on the question of appeals to the pope during this period, it would appear that Brooke's dictum would need some qualification. It is true that appeals continued to go to the pope except for a brief interruption after the death of Adrian IV, but there is enough evidence to show royal interference, which was probably increasing.

[1] *Gesta Abbatum Monasterii Sancti Albani*, ed. H. T. Riley (R.S., 1867), i, 144–5, 150–2. [2] *P.L.*, 199, ep. 115, cols. 99–100.
[3] Cf. ibid., ep. 116 and Theobald's plea for him, ep. 64, part 2 and also ep. 112. He was about to leave England, but Theobald's intervention on his behalf and the intercessions of his friends would appear to have been successful.

Apart from the question of appeals, Henry was interfering to an unknown extent in the workings of the ecclesiastical courts. As early as 1158, if not before, the question of the amenability of clerics to secular jurisdiction was engaging his attention. William Fitzstephen, whose prime interest was, of course, Becket, thought that an incident of 1158 was worth recording.[1] When Theobald was archbishop, Henry had harboured designs against the English clergy, being provoked by the insolence[2] of certain clerks. When he was at York at the beginning of the year,[3] a burgess of Scarborough complained to him about the extortions of a rural dean and of an archdeacon whereby he had been mulcted of 22 shillings. The dean had cited his wife many times to chapters on a trumped-up charge of adultery. These extortionate practices had been forbidden by royal decree and the rural dean was brought before the king's court in the presence of the justiciar, Richard de Luci, the archbishop of York and the bishops of Lincoln and Durham. John of Canterbury, a former member of Theobald's household and now treasurer at York, was also present. When the dean had failed to exculpate himself, the king remarked that the archdeacons and rural deans were exacting more money than he himself received. To save the clerk from a worse fate, John of Canterbury suggested that the money should be returned to the injured party and that the rural dean should be put in the mercy of the archbishop of York with respect to his office. Richard de Luci, always jealous for the rights of the king, said to the treasurer, 'What will you adjudge to the king, whose edict[4] this man has transgressed?' 'Nothing,' replied John, 'because he is a clerk.' The justiciar withdrew in disgust, but the prelates and other clergy present supported the sentence of John. Henry II was not present at this stage of the proceedings, else they might have ended differently, but when he heard what had happened, he was angry, as might have been expected. Denouncing the sentence promulgated as false, he turned to Theobald, as head of the English Church, and fixed a date for a rehearing. Fortunately for Theobald, Henry's

---

[1] *Materials*, iii, 43–5.
[2] Cf. John of Salisbury's Letters, *P.L.*, 199, ep. 107, col. 95, for the monstrous conduct of the archdeacon of Norwich.
[3] R. W. Eyton, *Itinerary of Henry II* (1878).   [4] 'Constitutionem.'

brother Geoffrey died on 27 July and the king went overseas before the appointed day. The matter was allowed to lapse. It seems clear then, that, but for Henry's continental preoccupations, the question of a clerk answering for his transgressions of secular law in a secular court would have bulked very large in Theobald's primacy.

A case of somewhat earlier date is the alleged murder of St. William of York. Despite the opposition of Theobald and the bishops, Stephen insisted that he had jurisdiction over the case, 'both on account of the atrocity of the crime and because it had taken place while he was present [at York]'. The king fixed a date for a hearing after having taken sureties from both sides 'according to the custom of our people'.[1] Stephen died before the date he had fixed (13 January 1155). Henry proved weaker than his predecessor and allowed the case to be transferred to the ecclesiastical forum, although he and his nobles did not hide their indignation.

With regard to procedure in the ecclesiastical courts themselves there are several cases of royal intervention mentioned in John of Salisbury's correspondence. A dispute between the earl of Cornwall and Ernaldus of Devizes, over the possession of a church, at length came before the archiepiscopal court. As a preliminary measure Theobald compelled the earl and his clerk to restore the church to Ernaldus, the possessor, until the end of the action. When the earl's procurators came before the archbishop, they claimed that Ernaldus had originally seized the church without the consent of the earl or of the patrons of the church and that 'he had entered with the violent hand of a plunderer against the custom of the whole Church and of the Kingdom of the English, against the edict[2] of the king and against the ancient dignity of all the nobles'. A writ of the king was then produced ordering Theobald to do justice to the earl with regard to the advowson of his church, or to restore the church to the earl's clerk, which had been lost by him after Henry's departure overseas, contrary to the royal edict. In reply, Ernaldus alleged that

[1] From its position in the sentence, 'juxta consuetudinem gentis nostrae' might be construed to refer to the taking of sureties, but it would seem more reasonable to refer it to the hearing in the king's court. John of Salisbury's Letters, *P.L.*, 199, ep. 122, cols. 103–4. See above, pp. 124 ff.   [2] 'Constitutio.'

M

the advocate, a certain knight, had really presented him, but was afraid of the earl. He also produced a charter of the bishop of Salisbury in his favour. Feeling that he had no hope of obtaining justice against such powerful opposition, he appealed to the pope.[1] No objection of Henry to this move is disclosed.

A letter of John of Salisbury to Bartholomew, then archdeacon of Exeter, mentions a royal writ to Theobald, ordering him to deal with the case of a citizen of London, who claimed to have been injured by a rural dean of Exeter diocese. Theobald thereupon took cognisance of the case, delegating it to Bartholomew, who was in possession of the requisite local knowledge.[2]

Another example illustrating the king's support of religious houses against their diocesan bishops is found amongst Theobald's letters. Writing to his old friend and prior, Walter of Coventry, he told him that he had received a letter from Henry directed against some judgment of Walter's, unfavourable to the canons of Lilleshall, who must have complained to the king. Henry had blamed the archbishop for his remissness in this matter. Theobald advised Walter to abandon his judgment, and that if he did so, the canons would similarly renounce their appeal to the king. The case could then be dealt with anew by Theobald himself. If Walter carried out these instructions, he would be readmitted into the royal favour 'qui pernecessarius est'.[3] A less important case of appeal to the king was that of a renegade monk of the great Benedictine abbey of St. Mary's, York, who wished to be released from his monastic vows. Theobald begs the king not to listen to him and says that out of reverence to his majesty, the monks would even take the renegade back into their midst.[4]

A letter of Theobald to the abbess of the Benedictine nunnery of Amesbury begins: 'Royal authority impels us to punish injuries done to the holy Roman Church and contempt of royal majesty—not to mention ourselves.' In defiance of a papal decision which had awarded a disputed church to the treasurer of Salisbury after lengthy litigation, the abbess had expelled him and was contumaciously occupying the church in defiance

[1] Ep. 6, cols. 4–5.
[2] Ep. 80, cols. 66–7.
[3] Ep. 47, cols. 29–30.
[4] Ep. 62, col. 46.

of the king's 'edict'. Theobald's letter to the abbess was enforcing a writ of Queen Eleanor, acting in the absence of Henry. Theobald goes on to say that if the queen should punish her, he would not disapprove.[1] This seems to be a case where Theobald encouraged royal intervention, in conformity with the general practice of the Church to rely on the secular arm to enforce its judgments, and no doubt Theobald would have been gratified if Henry had limited himself to this kind of intervention.

A few other examples will illustrate the interest of Henry II in the proceedings in ecclesiastical courts. In what would appear to be a comparatively minor dispute, the privilege of proof was granted at a Chester synod to one of the parties, and seven witnesses came forward with the necessary testimony. At this point, before the judgment was pronounced, the king intervened, presumably by a writ, and sentence was postponed, apparently *sine die*. The injured party appealed to Theobald, and ultimately the case was carried to the pope.[2] A *ministerialis* of the king, called Geoffrey, appealed to the pope 'because he would be able to say things there which he would not dare to say in England'. It must be admitted, however, that this example, while providing some evidence of Henry's influence in Church courts, is an indication of freedom of appeals to Rome.[3]

No doubt Henry's example was followed by the greater barons, although there is little evidence on this point. A case involving Henry's brother, William, may be of interest.[4] In a lawsuit about tithes, the patron of one of the priests concerned wanted the case postponed until his lord, William, returned from abroad, and the priest refused to plead. The case proceeded notwithstanding. Just when proof was about to be awarded to the other side, they thought better of it and appealed to the pope.

Jurisdiction over cases of advowson seems as yet to have been left to the ecclesiastical courts, although not many examples of this are available.[5] The Register of Holme provides a few ex-

---

[1] Ep. 74, cols. 59–60.   [2] Ep. 12, cols. 8–9.
[3] Ep. 16, cols. 11–12.   [4] Ep. 109, cols. 96–7.
[5] It is very difficult to be sure whether the innumerable litigations about churches in John of Salisbury refer to advowson, but it is probable the majority do not. In Theobald's charters, cf. Nos. 129–31, 135 and 276 (original).

amples of royal interest in the question of advowson. A writ of Henry sent to the bishop of Norwich in Theobald's lifetime reads as follows:

I order that without delay and justly, you cause the abbot of Holme to have that advowson in the church of Repps, which he proved in your court. And if you shall not have done this, the archbishop of Canterbury will do it. Witness Thomas the chancellor at Caen.[1]

It would seem that Henry maintained a special interest in advowsons, but was not yet prepared to abstract them from ecclesiastical jurisdiction. Similarly, in a letter to the bishop of Norwich, Theobald accuses him of having tried to despoil a certain A. of the advowson of the church of St. Andrew's, Runcton, under colour of a royal command. This did not deter Theobald from proceeding with the appeal which had been made to him.[2]

Thus it is clear that there was a certain amount of royal interference in the workings of the ecclesiastical courts, which must be described as uncanonical and against contemporary papal policy. How far Theobald was prepared to co-operate with the royal policy or even to welcome it, must be considered. However loyal he was to the main lines of papal policy, there must have been occasions on which he did not altogether regret the presence of another power in the land. There must have been, for instance, some basis for the accusation of Pope Adrian that Theobald and Henry were conspiring together to 'bury appeals'.[3] Furthermore the procedure followed by Richard of Anesty would appear to have been well-established and smooth in its working. First he obtained a writ from the king to the archbishop authorising the appeal and then he had to obtain a writ of appeal from the archbishop himself, which was not granted hastily. Finally, a strong king and a lover of law and order could not but be a blessing for the Church in comparison with the troubles of the preceding years. Perhaps Theobald felt that the price paid for this boon was not, in reality, very excessive.

---

[1] *Register of St. Benet's Holme*, ed. J. R. West (Norfolk Rec. Soc., 1932), i, 18.
[2] John of Salisbury's Letters, *P.L.*, 199, ep. 93, col. 84.   [3] See above, p. 74.

V

The Archiepiscopal Household

THE importance of Theobald's household has long been recognised and a great deal of work has also been done in collecting biographical material of its members. As early as 1886 Stubbs wrote: 'The household of archbishop Theobald in the reign of Stephen to some extent satisfied the want which was afterwards met by the university system.'[1] Hook regarded it as the precursor of the Inns of Court.[2] Certainly as a training ground for future rulers of Church and State it fulfilled the functions later taken over by these institutions. Although very little is known of the educational system of the household, its results speak for themselves. Theobald's household produced four archbishops and six bishops, some of whom, as was natural, took part in the secular government of the country.[3] Thus, together with the royal household and the other episcopal households, we find Theobald's household carrying out a most important task.

The main purpose of the episcopal household was not, of course, to serve as a prototype of the university. To take care of the bishop's bodily and spiritual needs, to manage the episcopal estates and discharge feudal obligations, to govern the diocese—these were its primary functions. But men had to be trained to

[1] W. Stubbs, *Seventeen Lectures on the Study of Medieval and Modern History* (1886), p. 142.   [2] Hook, ii, 337 ff.

[3] *Thomas*, archdeacon of Canterbury and chancellor, 1154–62; archbishop of Canterbury, 1162–70. *Richard*, chaplain of Theobald and prior of Dover; archbishop of Canterbury, 1174–84. *Roger*, archdeacon of Canterbury, 1148–54; archbishop of York, 1154–81. *John*, treasurer of York, 1153; bishop of Poitiers, 1162; archbishop of Lyons, 1182; res., 1193 and d. 1204. *Walter*, Theobald's brother, archdeacon of Canterbury; bishop of Rochester, 1148–82. *John of Pagham*, bishop of Worcester, 1151–7. *Bartholomew*, archdeacon of Exeter, 1155; bishop of Exeter, 1162–84. *John of Salisbury*, bishop of Chartres, 1176–80. *William of Northall*, archdeacon of Gloucester, 1177; bishop of Worcester, 1186–90. *William de Ver*, bishop of Hereford, 1186–98; justice under Henry II and Richard I.

perform all these tasks and others of a more confidential nature, and this apprenticeship took place to some extent within the household itself. Little is known of teachers of the rudiments of education either within Theobald's household or in the cathedral itself, less in fact than is known about several other centres of education, for example, Winchester or Norwich. Theobald's nephews had a master[1] and it is quite possible that he had other pupils as well. Vacarius, the jurist, was brought to Theobald's household to teach Roman law,[2] but this teaching, for the short time it lasted, would appear to have been on an advanced level.

The only references to Theobald's household as a living institution, which are not merely incidental notices, are to be found in the lives of Thomas Becket. Amongst the minor officials, knights and menials, were to be found a small group of ambitious young clerks, anxious to make their way in the world. Sometimes they worked together towards this goal, more often apparently there was discord and jealousy as was to be expected; but generally not serious enough to warrant Theobald's intervention. We know far more about Becket than all the others put together, and at first his experiences probably did not differ greatly from those of his contemporaries. His early life has been most thoroughly investigated and nearly all the available sources utilised.[3] He was born in London of Norman parents in 1118. His father belonged to a knightly family originating near Theobald's birthplace at Thierceville, and it is possible that he knew Theobald in his youth. Thomas's formal education took place under the auspices of the Augustinian canons of Merton in Surrey, and later in London and Paris. He was then employed in a clerical capacity by a wealthy kinsman Osbert Huit-deniers towards the end of 1140. About three years later he was introduced into Theobald's household, probably in 1143. The accounts of his biographers differ as to the circumstances of his introduction to Theobald but Radford has attempted, with

---

[1] No. 255, in the witness list.

[2] Most of the information about Vacarius' stay in England is contained in the edition of his *Liber Pauperum*, ed. Selden Soc. 44 (1927), in the Introduction, chapter 1 by F. de Zulueta.

[3] L. B. Radford, *Thomas of London before his Consecration* (1894).

success, to harmonise them.[1] His father, Gilbert, approached the archbishop through two brothers of Boulogne, Archdeacon Baldwin and Master Eustace, who were friends of Theobald. After the archbishop had granted his consent to the proposal, Thomas was brought to his court at Harrow,[2] by an *armiger*, Ralph of London. This Ralph may be identified with 'Baillehache', a name which stimulated the wit of Roger of Pont L'Evêque. The latter made a point of confusing Thomas with 'Baille-hache' who had brought him to the archbishop's court, an identification which mortified the young clerk.[3] The motives of Thomas in entering the household were commented upon favourably by his biographers, but as Radford put it: 'It is at least probable that the young layman . . . was as fully alive to the fact that the surest way to eminence for a commoner lay through the Church as he was to the difficulty of living a religious life in a secular environment.'[4]

If Becket's biographers are to be believed, he did not have too happy a time of it during his earlier years in the archiepiscopal household. He was looked upon as a dangerous rival by the senior members and suffered a certain amount of persecution and victimisation. Roger of Pont L'Evêque seems to have been the worst offender. Perhaps their notorious enmity in later years as rival archbishops began at this stage. On the other hand, the biographers may have read into their early squabbles and struggles for preferment, the prefiguration of the more serious conflicts of twenty years later. At any rate Roger, and for that matter John of Canterbury, established themselves before Thomas. After six years as archdeacon of Canterbury, with £100 a year, during which time he had acquired the provost-ship of Beverley, Roger became archbishop of York in 1154. John, after failing to secure the archdeaconry of Middlesex in 1152, became treasurer of York in the following year. The more glittering prizes as yet eluded Thomas, but he accumulated a fair collection of modest benefices although he was not even

[1] Ibid. pp. 28 ff.
[2] Theobald's charters are rarely dated but Harrow appears. Holtzmann confuses Harrow with Thierceville (ii, 224).
[3] Baylehache, the marshal, witnesses one of Theobald's charters, No. 255.
[4] Radford, p. 31.

ordained deacon till 1154. He enjoyed the revenues of St. Mary-le-Strand, London, the gift of John of Pagham, as well as of Otford in Kent, his reward from Theobald for his services at Rheims in 1148. He was also a prebendary of St. Paul's and Lincoln. At the same time he was encouraged by Theobald to continue his studies abroad, and he spent a year at Bologna and some time at Auxerre acquiring a knowledge of both Civil and Canon Law. Unfortunately the years of his studies are not known. The significance of these studies cannot be overstressed in relation to Theobald's household and the development of Thomas's character. In return for these favours bestowed upon him, there can be no doubt that he was of great assistance to Theobald, not only in the archbishop's struggles with Stephen and his brother of Winchester, but also in the ordinary diocesan and metropolitan administrative work. With the departure of John of Canterbury and Roger of Pont L'Evêque he became the undisputed head of the household staff for a short time. He was rewarded with the vacant archdeaconry of Canterbury and the provostship of Beverley, which seems, at this period, to have been annexed to the archdeaconry. With his appointment to the post of royal chancellor late in 1154 or early in 1155, his connections with the household were broken and indeed there is very little evidence of his activities as archdeacon of Canterbury. This did not of course interfere with the collection of the archidiaconal revenues, and Theobald's determination to reduce these revenues by abolishing the irregular practice of extorting 'second aids' from the churches of the archdeaconry, was unsuccessfully resisted by Thomas.[1]

He was probably given the office as Henry's reward to Theobald for his support of the Angevin cause in the last two years of Stephen's reign and Theobald must have hoped that Becket would generally act as his representative at court. As has already been seen, these expectations were completely disappointed and it is extremely doubtful whether Theobald saw in Becket, during those years, the future champion of ecclesiastical rights, ready to

---

[1] Radford, p. 161. This practice was introduced by Walter of Rochester when archdeacon. No doubt Thomas's expenses during these years were very high, and he must have been forced to utilise every source of revenue available.

face exile and to lay down his life for the Church. As Radford says: 'It is a tale of bitter disappointment, a tale of promises unfulfilled and affection unrequited . . . [Thomas] had been set to serve two masters and when the inevitable crisis came, he held to the one and despised the other.'[1] The pathetic letters of Theobald and John of Salisbury evoked no satisfactory response.[2]

Theobald, however, was not without some consolation for this loss, and it would appear that John of Salisbury supplied to some extent the void left by the departure of Thomas Becket. Unlike Becket he was not indebted to Theobald for a start in life and had already made a name for himself in the schools of France before his entry into Theobald's household. None the less he remained faithful to Theobald and was with him till the end. The early career of John of Salisbury has given rise to numerous chronological difficulties, owing to his disjointed and conflicting references to it in the course of his own writings, and to the question of how much of his *Historia Pontificalis* is an eye-witness account. These problems have exercised the ingenuity of scholars for many years, notably R. L. Poole who, in two important articles,[3] apparently succeeded in giving a coherent outline of his life down to 1164, from which date the evidence is simpler and clearer. The conclusions of Poole can be summarised as follows. John was born between 1115 and 1120 and studied in France from the death of Henry I, or shortly after, until 1146 or 1147 at the latest, at which time he entered the papal service and remained in this post under Eugenius III and Anastasius IV till 1154, when he joined Theobald's household, assisted by a letter of introduction from the late St. Bernard. His activities as Theobald's private secretary for the next seven years are illustrated by a collection of letters written in Theobald's name, as well as a few of his own. During these years he visited Adrian IV on three occasions in connection with his new ecclesiastical duties.

[1] Ibid., pp. 179, 184.
[2] Ibid., pp. 181 ff., with quotations.
[3] 'John of Salisbury at the Papal Court' and 'The early correspondence of John of Salisbury' in *Studies in Chronology and History* (1934), p. 248. The former article was first printed in *E.H.R.*, 1923, p. 321, and the latter in *Proceedings of the British Academy*, xi, 27.

In the year 1159 he brought out the *Policraticus*, his most famous work.

The evidence of Theobald's charters tends to complicate this picture, for there are two charters witnessed by John of Salisbury which must be dated well before 1154. In this connection it may be noted that very few of Theobald's charters are witnessed, nor have many charters of Theobald survived from the earlier part of his archiepiscopate, and that doubtless they represent only a minute fraction of the total number issued during these years. Consequently it is suggested that John of Salisbury was a member of Theobald's household at a much earlier date than Poole would allow. The first of these charters is Theobald's confirmation to the canons of Leeds of the church of Easling in Kent. It is addressed to Bishop Ascelin of Rochester, who died on 24 January 1148. The witnesses, in order of appearance, are Archdeacon Walter, John of Pagham, Roger of Pont L'Evêque, Thomas of London, Alan, Mauger, *John of Salisbury*, William Cumin, Hamo son of Roger. The charter was given at Maidstone. As can be seen, John of Salisbury's position in the list is modest. The second charter puts on record Theobald's consecration of a cemetery for the monks of Faversham, without prejudice to the rights of the parish church. This charter cannot be earlier than March 1148, when Roger became archdeacon of Canterbury, nor later than June 1151, when Hugh abbot of St. Augustine's died. The witnesses are Bishop Hilary of Chichester, Archdeacon Roger of Canterbury, Thomas of London, Roger Species, *John of Salisbury*, Peter Scriptor and many others.[1]

The evidence for John's early activities must therefore be re-examined in this light. The central issue is, how much of the *Historia Pontificalis* is eye-witness recording? In 1873 Giesebrecht proved that the *Historia Pontificalis* was written by John of Salisbury.[2] In 1881 Pauli printed an article[3] showing that the *Historia Pontificalis* could be used as important evidence for the

---

[1] Nos. 147 and 57. Faversham was built in 1148.

[2] *Sitzungsberichte of the Royal Academy, Munich*, 1873, p. 122, mainly on Arnold of Brescia.

[3] *Zeitschrift für Kirchenrecht*, 1881, p. 265.

biography of John of Salisbury, thus modifying the account of Schaarschmidt, the standard biography.[1] Schaarschmidt had contended that John had studied for about ten years after the death of Henry I,[2] and had spent two years with his friend Peter abbot of Celle, and had entered Theobald's household in 1147.[3] In view of the contents of the *Historia Pontificalis*, which provides so much information about papal history between the years 1148 and 1152, and seeing that in one or two places the writer claimed to be present at these transactions, Pauli held that John did not enter Theobald's household until 1153 and that at least since the Council of Rheims he had been a papal clerk under Eugenius III. It will be seen that this is essentially Poole's argument. After Pauli, there was still a defender of Schaarschmidt, the little-known Gennrich,[4] whose arguments were contemptuously brushed aside by Poole without any discussion[5] because he thought Ferentino was the same place as Florence. Nevertheless Gennrich makes some good points and in view of the charter evidence his arguments would appear to be cogent. He maintains, in short, that while John was a member of Theobald's household from 1147 onwards, he paid lengthy visits to Eugenius III, presumably in the capacity of Theobald's representative. In the first place John himself makes it quite clear that a substantial part of the *Historia Pontificalis* is based on reliable information supplied to him.[6] Occasionally, as at the Council of Rheims, John does definitely say he was present[7] but on the other hand his description of the papal return to Italy in the summer of 1148 seems to be the result of hearsay, as he himself

---

[1] Schaarschmidt, *Johannes Saresberiensis* (1862).

[2] 'paene duodecennium' (*Metalog.*, ii, c. 10). Schaarschmidt emended it to 'decennium' to make room for his stay with Peter.

[3] 'jam enim annis fere duodecim nugatum esse taedet' (*Policraticus*, i, 14, ed. C. C. J. Webb). The *Policraticus* was completed in 1159.

[4] *Zeitschrift für Kirchengeschichte*, 1892, p. 544.

[5] *Hist. Pont.*, p. lxxiv, n. 1.

[6] 'In hiis autem que dicturus sum nichil auctore deo scribam nisi quod visu et auditu verum esse cognovero vel quod probabilium virorum scriptis fuerit et auctoritate subnixum '(Prologue., *Hist. Pont.*, p. 4).

[7] Cf. Poole, *E.H.R.*, 1923, p. 322, n. 2, for Rheims, and on p. 328 for the divorce of Count Hugh of Apulia which Poole assigns to the summer of 1150 at Ceprano. It is probably on this latter occasion that John imbibed more Sicilian wine than was good for him.

admits.[1] John's famous statement in the third book of the *Metalogicus*[2] about his ten crossings of the Alps also gives rise to interesting speculations. Does 'egressus Angliam' refer to his departure from England in 1135 or 1136 and to nothing else, as Poole would have it? Or does the phrase refer to all his Italian expeditions? At any rate no one disputes that he departed from England on his last three Italian voyages from 1155 onwards. Finally the same sort of arguments which Poole used, to prove that John was with the pope from 1146 to 1154, can be equally applied to show he was in England at various times between 1148 and 1152. His account of Theobald's return to England after the Council of Rheims, of the behaviour of the monks of St. Augustine's and their punishment, is as circumstantial as any other part of the *Historia Pontificalis*. The book ends abruptly in the middle of a sentence dealing with the foundation of Faversham abbey in 1148, an event which would probably not have interested John had he not been present. Presumably the cemetery was consecrated and Theobald's charter, which he witnessed, issued, at the same time. If the remainder of the book had survived, it is quite possible John might have mentioned his presence at Faversham.

The following picture of the early life of John of Salisbury may now be proffered as an emendation of Poole's account, in the light of the evidence available at present. In 1147, after about eleven years of study at the French schools[3] and at the age of thirty or thereabouts, John found himself penniless and without any immediate prospects of a secure livelihood. He found a temporary home with Peter abbot of Celle and meanwhile obtained a letter of recommendation to Theobald from St. Bernard.[4] The

---

[1] 'Italiam ingressus est [i.e. Eugenius] et ideo *prout ab aliquibus dicebatur*, festinancius, quia jam audierat Christianorum exercitus in Oriente esse confectos.' (*Hist. Pont.*, p. 44). Had John been present he could presumably have ascertained the truth of this assertion.

[2] 'Siquidem Alpium juga transcendi decies egressus Angliam, Apuliam secundo peragravi dominorum et amicorum negotia ecclesia Romana saepius gessi et emergentibus variis causis non modo Angliam sed et Gallias multoties circumivi' (*Metalog.*, iii, prol.).

[3] This would correspond to 'paene duodecennium' which Poole and Schaarschmidt were forced to reject.

[4] In a letter to Archbishop Richard, Peter writes: 'Sanctissimae memoriae praedecessor vester archiepiscopus Theobaldus *de gremio et sinu nostro* magistrum

letter, after testifying to John's qualities and asking Theobald to provide him with a livelihood, continues: 'Do this quickly, for he has not where to turn'. The tone of this letter fits perfectly into the year 1147, but would not do at all for any other date. His application to Theobald proved successful and he was admitted into the archbishop's household. It was at this time that he attested the Leeds charter. We find him next at the Council of Rheims in March 1148, at which point the *Historia Pontificalis* begins. He returned to England with Theobald, saw the discomfiture of the monks of St. Augustine's and attested the Faversham charter. Up to this point there has been little difficulty in tracing John's movements. The problem now arises of fitting in two visits to Italy between 1149 and 1154 (his three other Italian journeys can be assigned to the years 1155 to 1159) and of determining what he did at the papal court. Poole has found four references to John's presence and activities in Italy. He was present at the divorce case of Count Hugh of Apulia, which Poole assigned to Eugenius' visit to Ceprano in the summer of 1150,[1] he was at Ferentino with the pope who resided there from November 1150 to the summer of 1151, he was present at Rome, in the pope's absence when the envoys of Barbarossa arrived in that city in the spring of 1152 announcing his imperial election, and he took part in drawing up a bull of Anastasius IV in favour of Celle dated 13 December 1153.[2] He must have left England in 1149 or early in 1150. A second visit can be fitted in between 1152 and 1153. At the Curia it must be presumed that he acted as a representative of Theobald, as Becket had done before him and as he himself was to do at intervals down to 1159. Whether in addition he had some employment at the Curia is difficult to say. Pauli had no real

Johannem Carnotensem episcopum inopem et pauperem suscepit sed deo juvante usque ad nomen magnorum qui sunt in terra fomentis suis provexit. Mortuus quidem est ille archiepiscopus corpore, sed adhuc vivit in propagine et durat in illo adhuc suavissimum memoriale' (*P.L.*, 202, col. 566), This generous tribute to the memory of Theobald would appear to contradict Poole's argument that even if John had enjoyed Peter's hospitality in that year, which was doubtful, it was of no significance (op. cit., p. 323). Poole finds St. Bernard's letter very difficult to incorporate in his thesis and tries to minimise its importance (p. 330). St. Bernard's letter is in *P.L.*, 182, ep. 361, col. 562.

[1] See above, p. 171 n. 7.   [2] Poole, op. cit., pp. 328 f.

evidence to support this theory and it was left to Poole to find, in the letters of Peter of Celle, a reference to a bull of Anastasius IV, which John had helped to draw up. As Poole might well say: 'No more welcome confirmation of a long series of plausible surmises could be desired.'[1] Even this evidence is not very satisfactory as a proof that John was a papal clerk. As has been seen already, John himself wrote that while he was at the Curia he transacted the business of his friends as well as of his employers.[2] The bull in question was issued in favour of Peter of Celle. Acting as Peter's representative or procurator John might well have had a hand in drawing up at least a preliminary draft of the bull. Thus there is no real evidence to controvert the conclusion that John of Salisbury made two visits to Italy in the capacity of Theobald's representative before 1154.

Poole's guidance seems more valuable for the period 1154 to 1161 where, in his article on John of Salisbury's early correspondence, he also gives an account of his life during these years. There is accordingly no need to cover this ground again in detail. John's life was still very much divided between England and Italy and, according to Poole, he made three further visits to the papal court, in the winters of 1155–6 and 1156–7 and the winter of 1158 to the late spring of 1159. He was mostly engaged on work for Theobald and for his own friends, but on his first visit he was instrumental in obtaining from Adrian IV the grant of Ireland to Henry II. Subsequently, as has been seen already,[3] he fell out of favour with Henry, but he was always cherished and trusted by Theobald who made him one of the executors of his will.[4] He does not appear to have held any official position in the household, not even in the secretarial department, but always remained what may best be described as a confidential secretary and agent, apparently devoted mainly to legal business rather than to the more general activities of the Chancery. No record of any special financial provision for him has been found. In 1159 he was in debt.[5] He never was in a very comfortable financial position until about 1174 when he became treasurer of Exeter.[6] Two years later he was elected bishop of

---

[1] Op. cit., p. 329.   [2] See above, p. 172 n. 2.   [3] See above, p. 159.   [4] No. 28.
[5] John of Salisbury's Letters, *P.L.*, 199, ep. 59, col. 38.   [6] *D.N.B.*, x, 881.

Chartres where he had once studied more than thirty years before. His brother Richard appears as a witness in a charter of Theobald[1] and may for a time also have been a member of the archbishop's household.

The third great luminary of Theobald's household was Master Vacarius, the author of the celebrated *Liber Pauperum* and also of a tract on the Canon Law of marriage. He lived in England for over fifty years and his life here has been thoroughly examined.[2] In the words of Professor de Zulueta . . . 'Vacarius was imported as a civilian by the "domus Theodbaldi" some time between 1139 and 1154, that he was used in the litigation with Henry of Winchester, that in 1149 he was teaching in England with remarkable success and then wrote his book, and that it was as an Oxford teacher that he was remembered at the end of the century.'[3] Stephen disapproved of his teaching and for a time silenced him. There are two charters of Theobald witnessed by Vacarius.[4] Later he went north and came under the wing of Roger of York, his old colleague, where he appears as an agent of Roger, a prebendary of Southwell Minster and a papal judge-delegate. He may have survived into the thirteenth century.

Theobald must therefore be given the main credit for the introduction of the study of Roman Law into England, although it is true there are one or two traces of Roman Law in the 'Leges Henrici' composed about 1118.[5] Furthermore Gilbert Foliot and his uncle Robert of Lincoln would appear to have had some interest in Roman Law and its application.[6] Still, by bringing

---

[1] No. 83. In 84 there is Richard, canon of Exeter.

[2] See above, p. 166 n. 2.   [3] Op. cit., p. xvii.

[4] No. 10 which can be dated 1150–4 and No. 263 which can be dated 1154–61. The latter charter only was known to Professor de Zulueta. It was edited by Miss Lees who suggested the alternative dates 28 March or 5 June 1155, but there is no real evidence to support this.

[5] Pollock and Maitland, *History of English Law* (1923 edn.), i, 100.

[6] In a letter to Robert of Lincoln (*P.L.*, 190, ep. 90, col. 809) Foliot writes that he has given instructions for a copy of the digest together with the gloss to be made for Robert. So there was at least one copy in Hereford and one in Lincoln about 1160. Foliot's letters provide a few references to Roman Law. Writing to Brian Fitzcount, he remarked that law could be divided into three departments—divine, natural and human. Human law was divisible into civil law and *jus gentium* (ep. 79, cols. 797–8). No doubt all this is axiomatic. There are, however, genuine references in ep. 144, col. 850, and in ep. 26, col. 764, both letters written before he came to London.

over a recognised teacher with a great reputation, Theobald can be said to have put the study of Roman Law in England on a firm basis, an achievement which was to have a profound, though ill-defined, effect on English Law in general. Theobald himself, or at least John of Salisbury writing in his name, made two references to Roman Law. In a letter to the bishop of Lincoln he warned him not to use ecclesiastical justice as a means of extorting money and cited the famous *Lex Julia repetundarum*, a law passed under the consulship of Julius Caesar against extortion by provincial governors.[1] In the letter to Alexander III about the case of Richard of Anesty a precedent from Roman marriage law was cited.[2] John of Salisbury makes a passing reference to Ulpian in a letter to Bartholomew of Exeter.[3]

Although Vacarius was also a canon lawyer of some repute, if a little off the main stream of the development of Canon Law, he cannot be given the credit for the great efflorescence of the study and practice of Canon Law in England during Theobald's tenure of the archbishopric of Canterbury. Theobald and his household played a leading part in this most important chapter of English history. A great deal of work has been done on this subject, notably by Brooke who wrote:

So far as I can discover, the collection introduced by Lanfranc into England was the only complete collection that existed in this country for half a century, perhaps even three-quarters; I have shown that it was widely diffused. It begins now [temp. Stephen] to be superseded by fuller, more up-to-date collections, arranged in a systematic form. For some of this Theobald must have been responsible, perhaps for the major part.[4]

A more recent writer enlarges on this cautious approach:

Aussi est-ce à juste titre que Théobald est regardé comme le véritable initiateur de la jurisprudence canonique en Angleterre.[5]

Was Theobald a canonist? Those of his contemporaries, who loved and admired him, never seem to allude to him as a learned man. It may be doubted whether Theobald consciously played

---

[1] John of Salisbury's Letters, *P.L.*, 199, ep. 68, col. 55.   [2] Ep. 89, col. 80.
[3] Ep. 90, col. 81.   [4] Brooke, p. 190.   [5] Foreville, p. 20.

any personal part in the diffusion of Canon Law. On the other hand he unquestionably succeeded in promoting Canon Law by encouraging its theoretical and practical development. His loyalty to the pope and his activities as legate, his undoubted administrative powers and above all his unselfish encouragement of talented young men, produced results which perhaps a more learned man would never have achieved. As Brooke pointed out, the earliest English quotations from Gratian's *Decretum* are to be found in two of Theobald's letters in John of Salisbury's correspondence.[1] This would seem to show that this new collection was almost immediately seized upon by Theobald's household and popularised in the country at large. The two letters in question give instruction to Robert of Lincoln and Alfred of Worcester in dealing with difficult cases and it may be surmised with confidence that Theobald and his household were looked up to as authorities in canonical jurisprudence.

---

[1] Ep. 67 and ep. 68, cols. 51–5; Brooke, p. 110. The dictum of 'beatus Eugenius' which Brooke could not trace is in Gratian and refers to Eugenius II. E. Friedberg, *Corpus Juris Canonici* (1879), i, 1069, causa xxvii, q.2, c.23.

N

PART II

I

Introduction to the Charters

THE following collection of documents contains over 300 charters of Theobald, several of these, however, being available only in summaries or references.[1] This is of course by no means an exhaustive collection as no doubt a number have been overlooked or are not accessible.

The uncertainty as to the exact number of the charters collected here which can definitely be attributed to Theobald is caused by the regrettable habit of contemporary scribes, attributable to custom, economy or laziness, of frequently contracting the archbishop's name to the initial letter T. This leads in some cases to confusion between Theobald's charters and those of his successor Thomas which cannot always be satisfactorily resolved. The confusion is increased by copyists who often wrongly expanded the T. of the original into Thomas, either in the heading or in the text itself.[2] That this practice should have worked to the detriment of Theobald is understandable. Throughout the Middle Ages, Becket was a household word, while Theobald, it must be admitted, was a shadowy figure. It was far more impressive to have in one's Cartulary 'Carta sancti Thome martyris' than merely 'Confirmatio Theobaldi quondam Cant. archiepiscopi'. Where witnesses or other evidence of dating are available, it is possible to rehabilitate Theobald, but often these are lacking.[3] Some help can also be derived from the respective styles of the archbishops. Thomas, at least before he became papal legate in 1166, affected the style 'T. dei gratia

[1] In a few cases the actual charter is in existence but not available to me.

[2] Examples of false headings are 71, 110, 184, 185, 199, 225, 238, 251, 269, 270, 271 and 286, of false expansion in the text 16, 22, 27 and 50, in an inspeximus 125 and 173, in an endorsement to an original charter 137, 170, and in a memorandum accompanying an original charter 204. The Curia Regis Rolls refer to several charters allegedly of St. Thomas.

[3] Doubtful cases are indicated in my headings.

Cantuariensis ecclesie humilis minister' while Theobald mainly adhered to 'Cantuariensis archiepiscopus Anglorum primas' (or 'totius Anglie primas' or 'totius Britannie primas'). Even this is not conclusive, as Theobald's scribes occasionally used Becket's normal style.[1] In any case where there is a doubtful document, the odds are in favour of Theobald who was archbishop for twenty-two years as against eight of Thomas. Furthermore there can be no doubt that the latter's output of charters must have been seriously affected by his exile of six years and therefore all doubtful documents have been included. It is thus impossible to give the exact number of Theobald's charters.

The number of original charters definitely accounted for comprises altogether seventy-four.[2] In addition there may be five others in existence.[3] This collection omits Theobald's letters edited in collections of John of Salisbury's correspondence.[4]

CONTENTS OF THE CHARTERS

It is possible to classify the subject matter of Theobald's charters in various ways and the following system has been adopted in this introduction:

1. Charters illustrating Theobald's relations with Canterbury Cathedral Priory.
2. Charters illustrating his relations with other religious houses dependent on him.
3. Charters illustrating his activities as a magnate.
4. Charters illustrating diocesan administration.
5. Charters illustrating his activities as metropolitan.
6. Charters illustrating his relations with the Province of York.
7. Charters illustrating his activities as papal legate or judge-delegate.

[1] Examples are 28, 32, 85, 86, with 288 remaining doubtful.
[2] 1, 3, 21, 23, 24, 28–46, 68, 72, 81, 83, 84, 98, 99, 102, 104, 107, 114, 122, 123, 137, 149–52, 154, 157, 160–5, 168, 170, 177, 182, 183, 187, 190, 194–7, 203–5, 209, 213, 241, 250, 252, 264, 268, 275, 276, 281.
[3] 2, 155, 156, 189, 254.
[4] *P.L.*, 199, cols. 1–112 except Theobald's will, 28. Another letter written by Theobald to Pope Eugenius III in 1151 is printed in Holtzmann, ii, 233, from the MSS. of the *Liber Eliensis*.

The actual texts have been arranged in the alphabetical order of the recipients or beneficiaries.[1] To arrange them chronologically would present insuperable difficulties, while any other classification, as for instance the one suggested above, would seem to be unsatisfactory for this purpose on account of overlapping and marginal documents. It is hoped that this introduction will compensate for the comparative formlessness of the alphabetic arrangement.

1. The Cathedral Priory

Under this heading there are twenty-four charters.[2] Of these there are several documents affecting the status and organisation of the Priory. The division of the revenues of the Priory between three obedientiaries[3] is confirmed and explained in a variant text of Theobald's will.[4] Another ordinance is concerned with the 'liberty' of Canterbury Cathedral.[5] Other important documents are the ordinance about the treatment of expelled and fugitive monks who might wish to return to the Priory.[6] and that about the freedom of the monastic chapter from the jurisdiction of the archdeacon of Canterbury.[7] There is also a mandate to the priests of the see ordering them to pay their synodal pennies to the Prior.[8]

Among the grants by the archbishop there is only one indulgence of forty days to those carrying out the terms of his will or helping the cathedral.[9]

Other archiepiscopal grants issued or confirmed in favour of the Priory comprise land,[10] tithes,[11] freedom from knight service and scutage[12] and a chapel.[13]

Apart from his own grants, Theobald ratified grants to the Priory by his tenants[14] and confirmed the grants of others.[15] He was also apparently called upon by the Priory to ratify tenancy agreements and transfers of land forming part of the monastic estates.[16] In the outlying estates of the Priory, such as those in London and Sussex, the authority of the prior was not always

---

[1] A few charters at the end have come in too late to be fitted in to this order.
[2] 28, 30–3, 35–50, 83, 84, 268.   [3] 47.   [4] 28.   [5] 50.   [6] 31.   [7] 30.
[8] 49.   [9] 28.   [10] 46.   [11] 38.   [12] 43.   [13] 39.   [14] 35, 42.
[15] 36, 41.   [16] 33, 44, 48, 268.

respected by the tenants and so we have mandates of Theobald admonishing the tenants accordingly.[1] Documents of a more personal nature are two in number. One is a request to the Priory to provide an income for a member of the archiepiscopal household[2] and the other is a denial of the all too true rumours of violent conflict between the archbishop and the monks.[3] Finally there is Theobald's ordinance subjecting the monks of Dover to the church of Canterbury which was of more than indirect interest to the Cathedral Priory.[4]

2. *Dependent Religious Houses*

Theobald was in rather less intimate relationship with various religious houses founded or refounded by himself or his predecessors. These are Dover Priory and its dependent hospital of St. Bartholomew; St. Gregory's Priory, Canterbury; St. Michael's College at South Malling; and the hospitals at Northgate in Canterbury and Harbledown not far away. There are altogether twenty-six charters of Theobald relating to these houses.[5] The most important charter relating to Dover is the ordinance subjecting the monks of Dover to Canterbury, greatly resented by later generations of Dover monks.[6] Grants by Theobald comprise the prebends of the former secular canons of Dover[7] excepting one prebend which remained in the hands of the monks of St. Augustine's, Canterbury,[8] the toll of Dover[9] and three indulgences.[10] Five charters demonstrate Theobald's activities in securing tithes for the monks.[11] There is also a confirmation of an exchange of land made by the monks[12] and another of a grant made to them.[13] To the hospital of St. Bartholomew, dependent on Dover Priory, founded by his authority in 1141, there is extant one grant of indulgence by the archbishop.[14] St. Gregory's Priory received a letter of protection and general confirmation of its possessions and a special confirmation[15] as well as two ratifications of purchases of land in the archbishop's fee.[16] Theobald consecrated and dedicated the church of South Malling and granted tithes and pannage to the canons there.[17] St. John's

[1] 32, 45.   [2] 40.   [3] 37.   [4] 83, 84.   [5] 28, 34, 53, 58–62, 82–96, 179, 180, 310.   [6] 83, 84.   [7] 85, 86.   [8] 58.   [9] 86.   [10] 92–4.   [11] 87–91.   [12] 95.   [13] 96.   [14] 82.   [15] 59, 62.   [16] 60, 61.   [17] 179–80.

hospital at Northgate received an indulgence[1] and Harbledown hospital a rent charge of one mark already established by St. Anselm[2] as well as the tithes of the manor of Westgate.[3] In his will, Theobald confirmed all the rights and possessions of the dependent houses as well as those of all others in the diocese.[4]

3. The Archbishop's Fee

The charters illustrating Theobald's activities as a great landlord tend to overlap with the previous sections and with the documents illustrating his diocesan activities. They are twenty-five in number.[5] The grants by Theobald or his tenants to the Cathedral Priory,[6] St. Gregory's Priory[7] and South Malling College[8] have already been dealt with. There are also grants to the religious houses of Lewes,[9] Holy Trinity, Aldgate,[10] Malling,[11] Southwark,[12] and the Templars.[13] He granted a small endowment to the church of Slindon on his estates when he dedicated it.[14] There are several grants or re-grants of land to tenants[15] including one instance of a wife being granted with the land.[16] Two charters contain judgments of Theobald in disputes amongst tenants: one is a comparatively trivial affair,[17] but the other is an important case of seisin involving the canons of St. Paul's Cathedral remitted to the archbishop by a writ of Henry II.[18] One of the provisions of Theobald's will laid down that all his chattels should be given to the poor and that the possessions of the archbishopric should be safeguarded during the vacancy.[19]

4. Diocesan Administration

The charters illustrating diocesan administration do not appear to throw much light on this aspect of Theobald's archiepiscopate. There are twenty-eight charters dealing with diocesan affairs[20] if those charters are omitted which are of exclusive

---

[1] 53.   [2] 34.   [3] 310   [4] 28.   [5] 28, 29, 34, 35, 38, 39, 42, 43, 46, 51, 52, 60, 61, 124, 125, 151, 161, 167, 176, 179, 180, 250, 252, 298, 310.
[6] 35, 38, 39, 42, 43.   [7] 60, 61.   [8] 179, 180.   [9] 151.   [10] 161.   [11] 176.
[12] 252.   [13] 298.   [14] 250.   [15] 34, 51, 52, 124, 125.   [16] 34.   [17] 29.
[18] 167.   [19] 28.
[20] 10, 30, 49, 54–8, 63, 97, 146–9, 153, 175, 177, 177a, 178, 219, 222, 224, 226, 239, 240, 294, 295, 297.

interest to the first three sections. There is only one charter dealing directly with the archdeacon of Canterbury—the one which limits his rights in the cathedral chapter.[1] Apart from this, there are several charters addressed to the archdeacon,[2] and it will be noted that in all except four cases[3] he is linked with the bishop of Rochester. This would suggest that the bishop of Rochester acted in the diocese of Canterbury in what might be described as a suffragan capacity. Furthermore it can be seen that in at least two cases the county of Kent was taken as an administrative ecclesiastical unit.[4] As charters of the archdeacons of Canterbury are very rare at this time, an example has been transcribed.[5]

The position of the rural deans of Canterbury diocese is even more obscure. There is no charter dealing with their functions, nor are there any charters addressed to them. This might suggest that they played a less important part in Canterbury diocese than elsewhere. The only dean appearing in Theobald's charters is Ralph, who was probably rural dean of Canterbury.[6] The equivalent or substitute for the rural deaneries would appear to be the local 'chapters' of the clergy of a hundred, which figure in some of Theobald's charters.[7] The outlying areas of the see, based on archiepiscopal possessions in other dioceses, later to be grouped into the eight deaneries of peculiar jurisdiction, are fairly well represented, only Tarring and Risborough are missing.[8] There is one document dealing with diocesan synods, which is a mandate of Theobald to the priests ordering them to pay their synodal pennies to the prior of

[1] 30. [2] 36, 59, 96, 146, 147, 174, 226, 239, 252.
[3] 146, 226, 239, 252. [4] 91, 219. [5] C.i.

[6] 33, 58, 63 *bis*. Other contemporary references to Canterbury rural deans: in a charter of Prior Jeremiah (1173–43) Walterus decanus de O. (Ospringe ?) is a witness (Canterbury C.A., M 223); Willelmus decanus is a witness in 1155 (Madox, *Formulare*, p. 74); 'decani et alii officiales' and 'decanus et synodus' about 1160 (John of Salisbury, ep. 66).

[7] Canterbury city 36, Dover 97, Reculver 146, Teynham 252, Malling (Rochester diocese) 176. Cf. chapter of Flegg (Norf.), 135.

[8] Shoreham 161, 219; Croydon 124–5, 167; Arches 32, 41, 48; Bocking 40, 44; Pagham 151, 250; S. Malling 177–80. According to E. H. W. Dunkin (*Sussex Archaeological Collections*, xxvi, 28), Edburton was 'the most westerly benefice in the deanery of South Malling, to which it was first attached by Archbishop Theobald n 1150'. No source is cited for this.

Canterbury Cathedral,[1] but there are others which mention Canterbury synods.[2]

Of the other charters, there is the record of the consecration of a cemetery for monks, saving parochial rights,[3] two judgments concerning tithes[4] and at least one ratification of a judgment.[5] There is one 'constitution' of a parson, on the presentation of the patrons, the monks of Rochester, guaranteeing them an annual pension.[6] Two other charters are obviously of a similar nature, but they are couched in the form of a grant-in-alms to the priest of the church.[7] There are twelve charters confirming the grants of churches to religious houses[8] and of these six deal with the position of the incumbent as affected by the grant.[9] There are also confirmations of the possessions of Leeds Priory and of the subjection of Monk's Horton Priory and its possessions to the monks of Lewes.[10] Finally there is a recognition by Theobald that his chaplain was occupying the church of Boxley by permission of the monks of Rochester to whom it belonged.[11]

5. *Province of Canterbury*

By far the largest group of documents are those which illustrate Theobald's activities as metropolitan of the province of Canterbury. This group comprises no less than 209 charters,[12] of which the majority are confirmations issued to religious houses, collegiate bodies or individuals,[13] and confirmations of judgments and compositions.[14] In addition there are fourteen indulgences.[15] Eighteen judgments, a comparatively small number, are con-

---

[1] 49.   [2] 149, 222.   [3] 57, cf. 294.   [4] 10, 149.
[5] 175 (possibly Rochester), 295.   [6] 226.   [7] 63, 97.
[8] 54–6, 146, 147, 177, 177a, 178, 224, 239, 240, 297.
[9] 146, 147, 177, 177a, 224, 240.   [10] 148, 153.   [11] 219.
[12] 1–9, 11–15, 17–27, 64–81, 98, 99, 104–8, 110–23, 126–43, 145, 150, 152, 154–60, 162–6, 168–71, 173, 174, 181–8, 190–201, 203–6, 208–11, 213–18, 220–3, 225, 229–37, 241–9, 251, 253–67, 269–84, 290–3, 296, 299–309, 311.
[13] To religious houses, etc. 2–8, 13, 17–19, 21–3, 25, 64–6, 68, 69, 72, 73, 77, 79, 98, 99, 105–8, 110–12, 122, 123, 126–8, 133, 137, 139, 150, 152, 153, 156, 158–60, 162–6, 170, 183, 184, 187, 190, 192–5, 197–203, 205, 209, 215–18, 220–3, 229, 230, 232–4, 236, 237, 244–8, 251, 253–6, 259, 262, 264, 269, 272, 273, 275, 280–2, 290, 291, 296, 299–301, 304, 306–7; to individuals 24, 81, 142, 157, 210, 283.
[14] 11, 104, 119, 121, 143, 169, 241, 292, 305.
[15] 9, 67, 76, 114, 188, 213, 214, 242, 243, 261, 266, 279, 293, 308; see also under sections 1, 2, 6. Confirmation of indulgences, 309.

cerned with churches,[1] parochial rights and tithes,[2] the disposal of a prebend[3] and land[4] and the restitution of an abbot.[5] The remaining judgment asserted the rights of the monks of Alcester to elect their abbot freely, despite the claims of the bishop and monks of Worcester and the provisions of the foundation charter.[6]

The bishopric of Rochester stood in a closer relationship to Canterbury than any of the other dioceses and its five charters might well be treated separately. Four are confirmations to the monks of Rochester Cathedral Priory[7] and the other is the settlement in Theobald's presence of the dispute between the bishop and archdeacon of Rochester over the revenues of the ecclesiastical courts of the diocese.[8]

A fairly large class of charters issued by Theobald as metropolitan is comprised under the heading of mandates to bishops,[9] archdeacons,[10] rural deans,[11] clerks,[12] abbots[13] and laymen.[14] Altogether there are thirty-nine charters of this type. Most of them, perhaps owing to the nature of the surviving sources, deal with the complaints of religious houses to Theobald, claiming they were unjustly deprived of their revenues. The recipients of the mandates were ordered to do justice to the monks or canons, or in the case of laymen to restore their seizures or usurpation of rights under penalty of excommunication. To some extent they reflect the conditions of anarchy and civil war during the reign of Stephen, but there was, no doubt, a fair number of disputes which could not be attributed to this cause. Those documents which illustrate the anarchical conditions most clearly are the mandates to the abbots to recover their lost possessions.[15] Of possibly greater interest are the delegations of cases to the

[1] 14, 27, 80, 117, 140, 145, 276, this last case being definitely one of advowson in the archbishop's court. [2] 78, 182, 211, 231, 263, 267.
[3] 70. [4] 71, 134. [5] 311. [6] 1. [7] 220–3. [8] 225.
[9] To a bishop 12, 15, 113, 115, 120, 129–32, 135, 136, 141, 271, 274, 277; to more than one bishop 20, 118, 181, 208, 238; to a bishop and his archdeacon or archdeacons 74, 185, 249; to bishops and archdeacons 265; to bishops, archdeacons and priests 196.
[10] To an archdeacon 168, 258, 270; to an archdeacon and his rural dean or deans 75, 171; to archdeacons and rural deans 26.
[11] To rural deans 257. [12] 303. [13] 109, 260. [14] 154, 186, 206, 278.
[15] And cf. nos. 103 and 249, although of course improvident abbots can be found at all times.

diocesan bishops giving them instructions how to conduct proceedings.[1] Among the other documents illustrating Theobald's metropolitan activities are two letters testifying to the truth of proceedings in his presence,[2] the notification of a dedication of a church by him[3] and three notifications of grants to religious houses made in his presence.[4]

6. *Province of York*

Theobald's charters relating to the Province of York owe their existence either to his legatine powers or to the prolonged periods when the see of York was vacant and he was the only archbishop in England. The three indulgences[5] would in any case never have been thought to have been a usurpation of the rights of York, and we are left with six confirmations, one to the archbishop of Rouen,[6] one to his chapter in almost identical terms,[7] one to a hospital at York[8] and three to monasteries.[9] This meagre list[10] seems to confirm the general opinion as to Theobald's lack of activity in the Province of York.

7. *Papal legate*

The limited number of documents inspired by papal mandate or delegation fails adequately to illustrate papal influence in the affairs of the English Church. Even in this collection there are probably more papally-inspired documents than appears on the surface, as for example No. 100 where the papal mandate is not mentioned in the body of the charter. It would, however, be absurd to include all the charters in which Theobald styles himself as legate, as most of them have nothing to do with the Papacy at all, while on the other hand Theobald was receiving papal mandates before the grant of the legation. There are altogether ten charters: five are decisions by the archbishop as judge-delegate, with or without colleagues[11] and the remainder are mandates passing on to the recipients the contents of a papal mandate.[12]

---

[1] 129–31, 135, 136, cf. 115.   [2] 116, 138.   [3] 188.   [4] 191, 204, 235.
[5] 286–8.   [6] 227.   [7] 228.   [8] 285.   [9] 189, 202, 289.
[10] But cf. 303. On the other hand 306 is not significant.
[11] 100, 201, 212; with colleagues 16, 207.   [12] 102, 103, 144, 172, 238.

The Form of Theobald's Charters

1. *The Archbishop's Name*

For a discussion of this topic it is unsafe to trust the copyist and only the surviving original charters will be taken into consideration. The abbreviation T. is most common, with fifty-five examples. Against this we have six instances of Teobaldus, five of Theobaldus, four of Teob', two of Tedbaldus and one each of Teodbaldus and Tedb'.[1] This result is somewhat inconclusive as to the degree of standardisation or efficiency in the archiepiscopal chancery. These original charters undoubtedly represent a small fraction of the total output of Theobald's chancery and furthermore it is unknown how many of them actually emanated from the chancery itself and how many were specially written by the recipients. At any rate out of this sample, three-quarters of the charters begin with T. All the charters beginning with Teobaldus except one,[2] and the charter beginning with Teodbaldus, are written in an imitation papal hand.

In only one original charter does the archbishop put his name after a general address.[3] This practice also occurs in two copies, neither of which commands much confidence for this purpose.[4] It can therefore be maintained that except in his letters to the pope or the king, it was Theobald's almost invariable practice to put his name first.

There is one case where 'Ego' precedes the archbishop's name, and it occurs in two variant cartulary copies.[5] The charter then continues in the first person plural.

2. *The style of Theobald*

A style which belongs exclusively to the earlier years of Theobald is 'dei gratia Cantuariensis archiepiscopus', which occurs

---

[1] The form Turbaldus, beloved of the historian of St. Augustine's, does not appear.

[2] 39, 45, 72, 160, 213, not 28; 'Teodbaldus' 275; two other pseudo-papal charters beginning with T. are 102 and 197.

[3] 28.

[4] 105 in an eighteenth-century transcript, and 119 in a variant copy.

[5] 55. Cf. 220, 221, 'ego Theobaldus', etc. in the body of the charter. These last two charters continue in the first person singular.

twenty-one times.[1] Several of these can be dated—1139,[2] 1139–40,[3] 1143,[4] 1145[5] and 1148.[6] It may be assumed that none of these charters is later than 1150. Several of them are originals[7] written in what may be described as an 'unprofessional' hand.

The next style which may be considered is 'dei gratia Cantuariensis archiepiscopus (et) totius Anglie primas', with or without the legatine style. Of these ninety charters, sixty are without the legatine style[8] and thirty have it.[9] Of the sixty charters, twenty-nine are certainly before 1150,[10] while ten others are probably before 1150.[11] On the other hand five charters are 1150 or later[12] and another four probably so.[13] The remaining twelve are doubtful.

Thirdly there is the very common 'dei gratia Cantuariensis archiepiscopus (et) Anglorum primas'. Of these there are twenty-one without the legatine title,[14] and 139 with it.[15] Of the charters without the legatine style, none can be shown to be before 1150, seven can definitely be dated 1150 or after[16] and four probably so,[17] while the remainder are doubtful.

From the examination of these last two styles it will be seen that the title of legate was not consistently affixed after 1150, and thus the practice of automatically dating all charters with-

---

[1] 25, 29, 38, 58 'Cantuarie', 60, 61, 76, 87, 104, 113, 151, 161, 169, 198, 205, 237, 242, 252, 268, 269, 301.

[2] 237.   [3] 161, probably 58.   [4] 104.   [5] 169.   [6] 76.

[7] 29, 104 not seen, 151, 161, 205, 268.

[8] 5, 21, 26, 41–4, 54, 55, 59, 63, 68, 73, 74, 98, 103, 111, 128, 131, 138, 144, 146, 156, 164–6, 168, 170, 171, 177, 178, 183, 184, 188, 194, 201, 208, 211, 216, 217, 219, 222, 223, 231, 234, 247, 257, 258, 264 'Cantuarie' (original), 267, 271, 273, 282–4, 299, 305, 308–9, 311.

[9] 2, 10, 11, 27, 31, 37, 39, 45, 51, 72, 77, 78, 90, 92, 95, 108, 117, 126, 160, 186, 190, 195, 196, 200, 213, 214, 221, 226, 266, 310.

[10] 5, 44, 55, 59, 63, 98, 111, 128, 138, 144, 146, 156, 164, 165, 168, 177, 188, 194, 208, 211, 219, 222, 223, 247, 271, 282–4, 299.

[11] 42, 54, 170, 248, 258, 264, 305, 308–9, 311.

[12] 103, 131, 216, 217, 273.   [13] 21, 43, 166, 234.

[14] 4, 9, 24, 30, 46–8, 52, 57, 81, 114, 123, 127, 132, 133, 158, 159, 175, 209, 224, 277.

[15] 1, 3, 6, 8, 12, 20, 22, 23, 34–6, 40, 49, 50, 56, 62, 64–7, 70, 71, 75, 79, 80, 82, 84, 88, 91, 93, 94, 96, 97, 99–102, 105–7, 109, 110, 115, 116, 118–22, 124, 125, 134, 137, 139–43, 145, 148–50, 152–5, 162, 163, 167, 172–4, 176, 177a, 179–82, 185, 187, 189, 191–3, 197, 199, 202–4, 210, 215, 225, 227–30, 232, 233, 235, 236, 238–41, 243–6, 249–51, 254–6, 259–63, 265, 270, 272, 274–6, 278–81, 285–7, 289, 300, 302–4, 306–7.

[16] 30, 46, 47, 81, 123, 132, 133.   [17] 127, 175, 209, 277.

out the legatine title before 1150 is untenable. Even a charter
issued well after 1150 as a result of a papal mandate omits the
legatine title.[1] Furthermore it is clear that 'Anglorum primas',
if it was used at all before 1150, was extremely rare, while the
use of 'totius Anglie primas' greatly declines after 1150.

Another style, which is considerably rarer, is 'dei gratia
Cantuariensis archiepiscopus et totius Britannie (Brittannie)
primas'. This occurs in five charters, one being an original. It
does not appear with the legatine style in Theobald's charters,
but does so appear in a letter addressed to Theobald.[2]

Finally there are the 'Canterbury' styles, so called because
they all seem to be associated with Canterbury Cathedral. The
first is 'Cantuariensis ecclesie humilis minister (minister humilis)'.
There are five charters containing this style[3] two of which have
'dei gratia'.[4] One charter has 'dei gratia archiepiscopus ecclesie
Christi Cantuarie et primas totius Anglie'[5] and another has
'dei gratia Cantuariensis ecclesie archiepiscopus Anglorum
primas et apostolice sedis legatus'.[6] These last two charters
are issued in the name of the archbishop and the Cathedral
Priory.

It is doubtful whether Theobald used the style 'dei gratia
Cantuariensis archiepiscopus Anglie primas' although it does
occur in two copies.[7] These may have been extended from
'Angl' primas' which does occur in seven originals,[8] but these
could be equally well rendered 'Anglorum primas'. There is no
original extant having 'Anglie primas', but it remains as a possible style.

3. The Address in the Charters

(a) *General Address*. To a student of permutations and combina-
tions this section must have a certain interest, because with
somewhat limited materials the archbishop's chancery succeeded in introducing a bewildering number of variations on

[1] 103.   [2] 7, 147, 157 original, 207, 220. C.2 addressed to Theobald.

[3] 28 original, 32 original, 85 and 86 almost duplicates, and 288. The last charter
has nothing to do with Canterbury and it is very doubtful if it is of Theobald at all,
but it has been inserted out of deference to Farrer, who had no doubt about it.

[4] 85, 86.   [5] 33 original.   [6] 89.   [7] 133 in a variant reading, 230.

[8] 30, 35, 40, 114, 123, 203, 204: cf. 'totius Angl' primas' 164, 165, 183.

what at first sight would seem an unpromising theme. There is an almost complete lack of common form, which may suggest that the benefits and evils of bureaucracy were still in the distance. The most popular form of general address was 'universis sancte ecclesie fidelibus' which with minor variations is found in forty-two charters.[1] It is interesting to note that almost all of these charters can definitely be dated after 1150. Four are probably after 1150,[2] one is doubtful[3] and only one can definitely be dated before 1150.[4] Other forms of address similar to this type are 'omnibus sancte ecclesie fidelibus'[5] to which no special period can be assigned, 'omnibus sancte matris ecclesie fidelibus',[6] 'omnibus fidelibus',[7] 'cunctis sancte ecclesie fidelibus',[8] 'universis ecclesie dei fidelibus',[9] 'universis sancte ecclesie filiis',[10] 'universis sancte matris ecclesie fidelibus',[11] 'universis sancte ecclesie ministerialibus et fidelibus',[12] 'omnibus sancte matris ecclesie filiis',[13] 'omnibus sancte matris ecclesie filiis et fidelibus',[14] 'universis sancte matris ecclesie filiis',[15] 'omnibus sancte matris ecclesie fidelibus per Angliam constitutis',[16] 'universis sancte ecclesie filiis tam clericis quam laicis per Angliam constitutis',[17] 'omnibus Christi fidelibus',[18] 'omnibus sancte Christi ecclesie filiis',[19] 'omnibus sancte ecclesie filiis per diocesim suam constitutis',[20] 'omnibus ecclesie dei fidelibus',[21] 'omnibus sancte dei ecclesie fidelibus',[22] 'universis sancte ecclesie filiis ac fidelibus',[23] 'episcopis et universo clero et populo per Angliam constitutis',[24] 'dilectis sibi in domino omnibus sancte matris ecclesie filiis',[25] and 'omnibus sancte ecclesie filiis tam clericis quam laicis per Angliam constitutis'.[26]

In the next group a formula which was to become far more

---

[1] 3, 21, 39, 56, 62, 64–7, 80, 81, 86, 92–4, 100, 114, 116, 133, 143, 149, 162, 163, 166, 175, 189, 192, 197, 199, 209, 210, 213, 229, 261, 262, 275, 279, 280, 289, 306–8; 81 and 94 add 'dei'.   [2] 21, 166, 175, 209.   [3] 114.

[4] 86. Also 308 is probably before 1150.

[5] 4, 42, 63, 68, 76, 177, 200, 202, 220, 221, 234, 242, 248, 266, 282, 285, 287, 305.

[6] 24, 28, 72, 82, 148, 173, 236 adds 'dei', 240, 273, 297, 304.

[7] 268.   [8] 156.   [9] 122, 204.

[10] 37, 85, 140, 193, 272, 276; 37 and 193 omit 'sancte'.

[11] 1, 2, 23, 107, 142, 281.

[12] 251.   [13] 77, 84, 153.   [14] 5, 79 omits 'omnibus'.

[15] 9–11, 22, 106, 108, 201, 203, 245, 288.   [16] 214, 216, 217.

[17] 184.   [18] 223.   [19] 222.   [20] 183.   [21] 232, 233.   [22] 151.

[23] 6, 110.   [24] 73 'omnibus ep.', 255, 256.   [25] 119.   [26] 127.

O

frequent in later years appears. The forms are: 'omnibus sancte matris ecclesie fidelibus ad quos presentes littere pervenerint',[1] 'omnibus sancte matris ecclesie fidelibus ad quos presens carta pervenerit',[2] 'omnibus Christi fidelibus ad quos presens scriptum pervenerit',[3] 'omnibus ad quos presens carta pervenerit',[4] 'universis sancte ecclesie fidelibus ad quoscumque presentes pervenerint littere',[5] 'universis sancte dei ecclesie fidelibus ad quoscumque presentes pervenerint apices',[6] 'universis sancte ecclesie filiis tam presentibus quam futuris ad quos presentes pervenerint litere',[7] 'universis sancte matris ecclesie filiis tam clericis quam laicis ad quoscumque presentes pervenerint apices',[8] 'universis sancte matris ecclesie filiis ad quos presens scriptura pervenerit',[9] 'omnibus sancte matris ecclesie filiis ad quos littere presentes pervenerint'.[10] Of these eighteen charters all but two doubtful ones can be dated after 1150.[11]

A few charters look ahead into the future: 'omnibus sancte matris ecclesie fidelibus presentibus et futuris',[12] 'omnibus sancte matris ecclesie fidelibus per Angliam extantibus tam presentibus quam futuris tam clericis quam laicis',[13] 'omnibus sancte matris ecclesie filiis tam clericis quam laicis tam presentibus quam futuris',[14] 'omnibus tam presentibus quam futuris sancte ecclesie fidelibus',[15] and 'omnibus sancte dei ecclesie fidelibus tam futuris quam presentibus'.[16] One charter is addressed to the clergy only —'episcopis abbatibus et ceteris sanctis ordinibus'.[17] There are several examples of more grandiose forms of address: 'episcopis abbatibus archidiaconis et omnibus sancte ecclesie ministris ac fidelibus',[18] 'episcopis abbatibus archidiaconis decanis et universis ecclesie dei filiis tam clericis quam laicis per Angliam constitutis',[19] 'venerabilibus fratribus episcopis et abbatibus et universis Christi fidelibus tam clericis quam laicis per Angliam constitutis',[20] 'omnibus episcopis per Angliam constitutis baronibus vicecomitibus justiciis et universis ministris regis cunctisque hominibus suis Anglicis et Francis et omnibus sancte ecclesie filiis',[21] 'episcopis abbatibus comitibus justiciis baronibus vice-

---

[1] 71 'littere iste', 167, 246, 267.   [2] 121 'carta ista', 227, 228.
[3] 105.   [4] 241.   [5] 123, 286.   [6] 139, 150, 215 omits 'dei'.
[7] 155.   [8] 224.   [9] 152.   [10] 235.   [11] 224, 267.   [12] 178.
[13] 194, 195.   [14] 7.   [15] 230.   [16] 198 and cf. 155 noted above.
[17] 237.   [18] 128.   [19] 137. Cf. 299–300.   [20] 170.   [21] 47.

comitibus ministris et omnibus sancte ecclesie dei filiis per Angliam constitutis',[1] and 'regi Anglie archiepiscopis episcopis abbatibus comitibus justiciis vicecomitibus ministris et omnibus sancte ecclesie fidelibus'.[2]

There are also eighteen charters which contain a general address added to a charter addressed specially to an individual or group.[3]

(*b*) *Charters addressed to individuals or groups.* There are fifty-seven chartèrs addressed to a bishop or bishops which are available for analysis. Of these there are thirty-one with the form 'venerabili fratri et amico N. . . . ensi episcopo' (or in the plural).[4] Most of these charters can be dated after 1150, only three are before that date[5] and two are doubtful.[6] The next commonest form is like the first except that it omits 'et amico'. Fourteen charters exemplify this form of address. Of these, six are before 1150,[7] five are later than 1150[8] and three are doubtful.[9] Two charters have 'venerabili fratri N. eadem gratia . . . ensi episcopo'.[10] Two others have 'N. eadem gratia . . . ensi episcopo'.[11] Two are addressed in the form 'N. . . . ensi episcopo[12] and three have merely '. . . ensi episcopo'.[13] Of the other variants we have 'venerabili et dilecto fratri',[14] 'venerabilibus fratribus et coepiscopis'[15] and 'dilecto fratri eadem gratia'.[16] As usual we see here what is apparently an effort at greater uniformity during the later years of Theobald's primacy. Where more than one bishop is addressed, there seems to be a tendency to put them in the order of their personal seniority, but if this was the intention it was never fully carried out as Robert of Lincoln precedes William of Norwich, who became a bishop two years before him.[17]

There are twenty-five charters addressed to an archdeacon or archdeacons, either exclusively or as part of a larger group of

---

[1] 187.   [2] 205.

[3] 27, 41, 59, 78, 95, 101, 117, 134, 145, 147, 157, 160, 174, 182, 188, 211, 254, 269.

[4] 12, 27, 36, 46, 78, 91, 96, 99, 115, 117, 118, 120, 126, 131, 132, 134, 138, 141, 174, 181, 182, 185, 191 'v. f. et a. suis', 249, 254, 264, 265, 271, 274, 277, 284.

[5] 138, 271, 284.   [6] 264, 277.   [7] 98, 144, 147, 207, 211, 247.

[8] 20, 101, 145, 160, 238.   [9] 74, 158, 159.   [10] 103, 169.   [11] 25, 104.

[12] 188, 301.   [13] 41, 59, 161.   [14] 263.   [15] 208.   [16] 113.

[17] 20, 118, 144, 174, 181, 191, 207, 208, 238, 247, 265.

persons addressed.[1] Of these, fourteen charters are addressed to the archdeacons in the first place[2] and in the remaining eleven they form a subsidiary part of the group addressed. In five charters the archdeacon is addressed as 'dilecto filio',[3] in one as 'venerabili filio'[4] and in one as 'venerabili fratri'.[5] In the order of precedence archdeacons come after bishops and the deans of cathedral chapters,[6] but precede abbots and priors[7] and sheriffs.[8] Charters addressed to archdeacons sometimes include the clergy or clergy and laity of the archdeaconry[9] or of a smaller area,[10] or merely include the rural deans of the archdeaconry.[11] In the charter addressed to rural deans their names and the names of their deaneries are given without any other appellation.[12]

There are twelve charters addressed in the first place to abbots and priors.[13] Four use the form 'dilecto filio',[14] one 'karissimis filiis'[15] and one 'fratri'.[16] In all but three cases the head of the house is associated with his brethren.[17] One charter is addressed to the chapter of a collegiate church[18] and two to the dean and chapter of a cathedral.[19] One is addressed merely 'conventui de Persora'.[20]

Seven charters are addressed to the clergy or the clergy and laity of a single diocese.[21] Amongst the other charters with a particular address may be singled out those to 'dilecte filie Ale comitisse Warrenne',[22] 'dilectis filiis et fidelibus parochianis suis omnibus probis hominibus de Dovorr'',[23] 'karissimis filiis suis hominibus universis de Dovorr'',[24] and 'dilectis filiis burgensibus Dovorr''.[25]

---

[1] 26, 27, 36, 41, 57, 59, 74, 75, 96, 146, 147, 168, 171, 174, 185, 219, 226, 231, 239, 243, 249, 252, 258, 265, 270.

[2] 26, 57, 75, 146, 168, 171, 219, 226, 231, 239, 252, 258, 265, 270.

[3] 185, 219, 226, 231, 270.   [4] 243.

[5] 168.   [6] 41, 243.

[7] 59, but cf. 128, 137.   [8] 174.

[9] 96, 147, 231, 239, 243, cf. 57, 219, 226.

[10] 36, 146, 252.   [11] 75, 171.   [12] 257.

[13] 30, 31, 38, 40, 54, 55, 90, 109, 111, 190, 259, 260.

[14] 31, 40, 109, 111.   [15] 38.   [16] 190.   [17] 109, 190, 260.   [18] 172.

[19] 70, 157.   [20] 311.

[21] 8 Bath, 49 Canterbury, 50 Canterbury (and Rochester), cf. 58 Kent, 164, 165 London, 225 Rochester, 283 Worcester (cf. 303). Huntingdonshire in 301.

[22] 154.   [23] 87.   [24] 88.   [25] 89.

4. *The Salutation*

The majority of the charters of Theobald available for analysis, without distinction of date, address or subject-matter, to the number of 233, have the simple form 'salutem'.[1] The next most popular form is 'salutem et benedictionem' which occurs in thirty charters.[2] Variants of this second form of salutation comprise 'salutem et paternam benedictionem',[3] 'salutem et benedictionem cum munere oracionum',[4] 'salutem et dei benedictionem',[5] 'salutem deique et suam benediccionem',[6] 'salutem deique benediccionem et suam',[7] 'salutem in domino et benedictionem',[8] 'salutem et benedictionem in domino',[9] 'salutem et benedictionem a domino',[10] 'salutem gratiam et benedictionem',[11] and 'benedictionem a domino et misericordiam a deo salutari suo'.[12] Of these variant forms of salutation six[13] may possibly be explained by Theobald's special interest in those charters.

The form 'salutem in domino' occurs in four charters, all addressed generally and dating after 1150.[14] Its variant 'in domino salutem' is found twice.[15] Finally there are the forms 'salutem et dilectionem',[16] 'salutem et gaudium',[17] and 'salutem et amorem',[18] the last being appropriately addressed to Henry of Winchester.

5. *The Harangue*

Of the documents available for analysis in this respect, 115 or approximately 40 per cent continue with a harangue ('arenga') after the salutation.[19] Of these, there are seventy-eight confirma-

[1] 1–12, 20–7, 29, 30, 34–41, 44, 46, 48–50, 52, 54–8, 60–8, 70–81, 83–6, 90, 92, 93–7, 100–4, 106–10, 114–18, 120–8, 131–4, 137, 140–3, 145, 148–52, 154–60, 162–4, 166–73, 175–82, 185, 186, 189–93, 196, 197, 199, 202–4, 207–13, 215–17, 219–31, 235, 238–41, 243–52, 255–68, 270, 271, 273–80, 283–9, 297, 300–8, 310, 311.

[2] 32, 42, 43, 45, 47, 51, 59, 82, 88, 91, 111, 113, 146, 147, 165, 174, 187, 194, 195, 200, 201, 205, 232, 233, 236, 237, 242, 254, 299, 309.

[3] 98, 99, 184.   [4] 89.   [5] 161.   [6] 188.   [7] 87, 198 'et dei'.

[8] 119.   [9] 183.   [10] 28.   [11] 281.   [12] 31.   [13] 28, 31, 87, 89, 161, 188.

[14] 105, 139, 153, 214.   [15] 269, 272.   [16] 144.   [17] 33.   [18] 138.

[19] 2, 3, 6, 8, 9, 20, 22, 23, 27, 28, 30, 31, 37, 45, 50, 54, 56, 59, 64, 65, 72, 73, 79, 82–4, 89, 91–3, 97–9, 111, 114, 119, 122, 123, 126, 128, 133, 137, 139–44, 148, 150, 152, 153, 155, 156, 158–60, 162, 163, 173, 183, 187, 189, 190, 193–5, 197, 199, 200, 202, 203, 205, 209, 212–16, 227–31, 235, 237, 242, 244–6, 248, 251, 254–6, 259–62, 265–7, 273, 279, 280, 285–9, 297, 304, 306–8; total 286.

tions (60 per cent of all the confirmations),[1] fifteen indulgences (75 per cent),[2] six mandates (13 per cent),[3] fourteen notifications of judgments, ordinances and grants made in the archbishop's presence (27 per cent),[4] and two grants (6 per cent).[5]

(a) *Confirmations*. In charters of confirmation there are three fairly distinct types of harangues. Where the confirmation is made in accordance with the charter of a bishop a form is used which generally says something to the effect that it is only appropriate for Theobald to confirm those things which his suffragans have rightly sanctioned. There are sixteen harangues of this type, most of them being extremely similar without any two being identical. They read as follows:

Que a venerabilibus fratribus nostris coepiscopis canonice fieri dinoscuntur, ea nostre auctoritatis testimonio securius confirmamus. (65.)

Que a venerabilibus fratribus nostris coepiscopis canonice fieri noscuntur, ea nostre auctoritatis munimine merito confirmantur. (123.)

Que a venerabilibus fratribus nostris episcopis rationabiliter circa statum ecclesie fieri novimus, merito ea rata habere debemus et auctoritate nostra corroborare. (259.)

Que a venerabilibus fratribus nostris episcopis ecclesiis aut locis religiosis canonice conferuntur, ut in firma stabilitate perseverent sunt nostre confirmationis munimine roboranda. (216.)

Que a venerabilibus fratibus nostris coepiscopis canonice fieri noscuntur, ea ad nostrum spectat officium confirmare et ut futuris maneant inconcussa temporibus perpetuo stabilire. (139.)

Que a venerabilibus fratribus nostris coepiscopis canonice fieri noscuntur, ea tum maxime cum in religiosorum usus transferuntur nostre auctoritatis robur merito consecuntur. (150.)

Ea que a venerabilibus fratribus nostris coepiscopis Norwicensi et Lincolnensi canonice fieri dinoscuntur, nostre auctoritatis testimonio securius confirmamus. (64.)

Quod a venerabilibus fratribus nostris coepiscopis canonice fieri

---

[1] 2, 3, 6, 8, 22, 23, 54, 56, 59, 64, 65, 72, 73, 79, 91, 98, 99, 111, 119, 122, 123, 126, 128, 133, 137, 139, 142, 143, 148, 150, 152, 153, 156, 158–60, 162, 163, 173, 183, 187, 189, 190, 193–5, 197, 199, 200, 202, 203, 205, 209, 215, 216, 227, 237, 244–6, 248, 251, 254–6, 259, 262, 273, 280, 285, 289, 297, 304, 306–7; total 132.

[2] 9, 82, 92, 93, 114, 213, 214, 242, 261, 266, 279, 286–8, 308; total 20.

[3] 20, 45, 141, 144, 260, 265; total 48.

[4] 27, 28, 30, 31, 37, 50, 83, 84, 140, 155, 212, 231, 235, 267; total 51.

[5] 89, 97; total 32.

dinoscitur, id nostri est officii auctoritate nostra conivente roborare et scripti nostri testimonio stabilire. (209.)

Quod a venerabilibus fratribus nostris coepiscopis canonice fieri dinoscitur, id nostre auctoritatis testimonio merito confirmatur. (133.)

Quod a venerabilibus fratribus nostris coepiscopis canonice statuitur, id merito nostre auctoritatis testimonio confirmatur. (143.)

Que a fratribus nostris coepiscopis statuuntur et firmantur quatenus ratio et justicia permiserit debemus et nos auctoritate nostra corroborare et perpetua stabilire. (251.)

Que a fratribus nostris coepiscopis auctoritatis sue et litterarum sunt canonice firmata testimoniis ea, adjecto nostre auctoritatis testimonio, rata et firmissima perpetuis decrevimus et volumus manere temporibus. (245.)

Ad nostram spectat dignitatem ex vice nobis commissa ea que a fratribus nostris et coepiscopis canonice facta sunt, ut firmiora permaneant, rata habere et auctoritate scripti nostri suffulcire. (142.)

Ad officii nostri sollicitudinem spectat que a fratribus nostris canonice gesta sunt rata habere, et ne futuris temporibus convelli possint aut concuti auctoritate qua fungimur confirmare. (246.)

Que caritatis intuitu religiosis locis collata esse et in divinos usus conversa noscuntur, sicut diocesani episcopi sunt auctoritate roborata, ita et metropolitani perpetua stabilitate consolidanda. (122.)

Cum ea que a venerabilibus fratribus nostris episcopis circa statum ecclesie rationabiliter ordinantur rata inmutilataque confirmare debeamus, majori diligencia et studio ea que a predecessoribus nostris Cantuar' ecclesie archiepiscopis statuta esse et de ecclesiis canonice ordinata noverimus ut inperpetuum durent confirmare et auctoritatis nostre munimine roborare debeamus. (297.)

It would seem that Theobald's chancery had produced something like a common form of harangue for confirmatory charters of this kind, although as has been seen in the case of the General Address, the chancery clerks seemed to have enjoyed trying to say the same thing in an infinite number of ways. It was either thought undesirable to have a stereotyped form, or it never occurred to them. All these charters date from a period after 1150.

A second type of harangue lays more stress on the duty of the archbishop to confirm grants made by the magnanimity of the donors, who are generally referred to in the harangue in a rather vague manner. There are thirteen charters of this type and their harangues read as follows:

Incolumitati ecclesiae et paci providentes ea quae ecclesiis ipsis bonorum principum largitione vel rationabili quorumcunque executione adquiruntur, pia ipsis benignitate concedimus, et auctoritate nostra confirmamus. (254.)

Incolumitati ecclesiarum et paci producentes ea que ecclesiis ipsis bonorum principum largitione vel rationabili quorumcumque executione adquiruntur, pia ipsis benignitate concedimus et auctoritate nostra confirmamus. (119.)

Que a sancte ecclesie filiis sive regibus sive principibus in religiosorum virorum usus racionabiliter collata esse dinoscuntur, ea nostre auctoritatis testimonio merito confirmantur. (3.)

Ea que a venerabilibus fratribus nostris episcopis seu principibus ecclesiis et locis religiosis in elemosinam misericordie intuitu conferuntur, ut eisdem locis inconvulsa et inmutilata perseverent merito sunt auctoritatis nostre munimine roboranda. (8.)

Donationes regum Anglorum et elemosinas principum ecclesiis seu religiosis locis canonice collatas et concessas, nostri est officii firmas statuere et auctoritatis nostre testimonio roborare. (56.)

Que a principibus viris tam regibus quam aliis fidelibus religiosis locis divine pietatis intuitu collata esse noscuntur, nostrum est officium in nostra jurisdictione ea confirmare et perpetuis scripti nostri auctoritate stabilire temporibus. (137.)

Que a principibus . . . et fidelibus in loca religiosa deo auctore conferuntur, nostri est officii illa stabilire et perpetuis firmare monimentis. (229.)

Que donatione regum vel principum venerabiliumve fratrum nostrorum episcoporum aut illustrium virorum ad aliquam ecclesiam canonice devoluntur, ut in perpetuum firma stabilitate inconvulsa perseverent utique nostre confirmationis firmitate sunt roboranda. (273.)

Quecumque bona a principibus viris seu a quibuscumque fidelibus auctoritate diocesani episcopi et principis interveniente assensu in divinos usus transferri noscuntur, ea nostre auctoritatis robore ad inexterminabilem et perpetuam stabilitatem merito deducuntur. (203.)

Quecumque pietatis intuitu religiosis locis largitione regum seu principum seu quorumcumque fidelium oblatione interveniente diocesani episcopi coniventia sub nostra jurisdictione in usus divinos cessisse noscuntur, nostri est officii illa roborare et nostre auctoritatis munimine perpetuo stabilire. (215.)

Que regum largicione seu principum concessione ecclesiis aliisve locis religiosis conferuntur, ut inconvulsa permaneant auctoritatis nostre munimine roborare debemus, et ne locis quibus caritatis intuitu sunt collata subtrahantur vel in alios usus cedant sedula (cedula) circumspectione providere. (227, 228.)

Que largitione principum seu collatione quorumlibet fidelium in usus divinos et religiosorum sustentationes cum precipue religiosarum domorum quilibet princeps prima jecerit fundamenta rationabiliter ac pietatis intuitu transisse noscuntur, ad nostrum spectat officium ea nostre auctoritatis testimonio roborare et litterarum nostrarum auctoritate perpetuo stabilire. (187.)

Ad nostram spectat solicitudinem religiosorum virorum quieti providere, et que suis sunt usibus a regibus sive a principibus rationabiliter collata nostra auctoritate firmare. (244.)

All these charters date after 1150. A third type of harangue is characterised by stress being laid on the importance of the religious life and the necessity of relieving its poverty, and generally includes a pious wish on the part of the archbishop to help to the utmost of his ability. These remaining harangues read as follows:

Quoniam ad nos spectat eos qui de saeculo exeuntes deo et religioni sese obligant, spontanei nostro tueri specialiter patrocinio, resque eis deditas vel per eos in perpetuam possessionem sanctae dei ecclesiae rationabilibus modis adquisitas confirmare. (2.)

Pastoralis sollicitudo officii nos compellit omnium eorum maxime quos religionis nomen commendat quieti providere et que eis in domino collata sunt beneficia nostre auctoritatis patrocinio confirmare et confirmata inviolabiliter conservare. (6.)

Pastoralis sollicitudo officii nos compellit domesticorum fidei precipue quos religionis nomen commendat quieti per omnia in quibus secundum deum possumus providere et ipsis ecclesiastice protectionis et confirmationis munimenta conferre. (152 and 153. Cf. 300.)

Ad pastoris spectat sollicitudinem omnium quieti eorum maxime quos religionis nomen commendat per omnia providere et que illis in domino collata sunt beneficia auctoritatis sue testimonio confirmare. (22.)

Ad pastoris spectat sollicitudinem omnium quieti maxime eorum qui divinis mancipantur obsequiis studiose providere et que eorum rationabiliter provisa noscuntur usibus perpetuo stabilire. (162.)

Ad pastoris spectat officium omnibus et maxime religionem professis quietem et pacem providere et que illorum juste et rationabiliter deputata sunt usibus perpetuo stabilire. (199.)

Ad pastoris spectat curam subjectorum pacem fovere et maxime quos religionis nomen commendat eorum bona studiosius tueri et ampliori sollicitudine patrocinari. (163.)

Ad pastoris spectat sollicitudinem loca religiosa protegere et confirmacionis beneficio communire. (307.)

Episcopalis officii est religionis viros ubique tueri eorumque paci et quieti semper invigilare. (59.)

Res ecclesiarum sicut sanctorum patrum testatur auctoritas sunt patrimonia pauperum et pretia precatorum; et quemadmodum sacrosancta ecclesia nostre salutis ac fidei perpetua mater est, ita nichilominus ejus patrimonium illesum debet perpetuo conservari et nulla desidia, nulla pravorum hominum perversitate, convelli; que enim sine macula et ruga utpote sponsa Christi virtutum circumdata fulgore clarescit, dignum est ut nullum rerum suarum detrimentum vel prejudicium patiatur, sed potius grata in omnibus tranquillitate ac libertate letetur. (202, and 72 as far as 'convelli'.)

Paci et utilitati fratrum religiosorum in omnibus. secundum rationem pro posse studere et providere ipsa nos injuncti nobis officii episcopalis sollicitudo et cura ortatur et compellit. (255, 256, 73 'injuncta' and omits 'et providere'.)

Que ad honorem et utilitatem ecclesie dei statuta rationabiliter esse noscuntur, in sua stabilitate conservare debemus. (79.)

Que deo auctore semel divinis prestita sunt usibus irrevocabiliter firmare et firmata inviolabiliter conservare debemus. (91.)

Que divinis sunt mancipata serviciis justum est ut ea ipsis locis quibus rationabiliter concessa sunt auctoritate qua fungimur confirmemus. (126.)

Que divinis usibus sunt mancipata ecclesiastico debent munimine roborari. (159, 158 'ecclesiastica debent tuitione muniri'.)

Ea que pietatis intuitu in religiosas personas canonice collata esse noscuntur bona, nostrum est teneri et stabilire. (262.)

Quae pietatis intuitu locis religiosis a fidelibus Christi conferuntur, ea nostrae authoritatis munimine merito confirmantur. (189.)

Majestas ecclesiastici regiminis hanc propriam obtinet sollicitudinem ut piis fratrum studiis ubique congaudeat eaque contra omnes impetus constanti auctoritate corroboret. (98, 99 'optinet propriam'.)

Injuncti nobis officii sollicitudo nos admonet ut paci et tranquillitati commissarum nobis ecclesiarum pro modulo parvitatis nostre providere studeamus. (111.)

Ex injuncto nobis cure pastoralis officio ecclesiasticis tenemur studere profectibus et generaliter universis specialiter vero singulis paternam sollicitudinem maternam exhibere pietatem. Illis etiam ampliorem nobis competit impendere benivolentiam qui cum Maria dominicos pedes studiosius amplexati meliorem sibi partem elegerunt qui abjectis mundi sarcinis soli deo militari querunt. (183.)

Religiosorum virorum quieti in omnibus pro posse juste consulere et eorum utilitatibus in posterum racionabiliter providendo studere a deo nobis commissi episcopalis officii nos cura compellit. (128.)

Religiosorum desideriis justis facilem prebere assensum ad episcopalem proculdubio spectat sollicitudinem. (248.)

Equum est ac rationabile ea que divinis sunt canonice mancipata servitiis ecclesiastico privilegio confirmari. (148, 197,)

Equum est ac rationabile ea que divinis sunt justis modis mancipata serviciis unde pauperes Christi sustentantur ecclesiastico privilegio confirmari. (285.)

Devocioni fidelium assensum prebere eorumque oblaciones quas pietatis intuitu religiosorum fratrum conventibus canonice impenderent confirmare, ad episcopalem maxime spectat solicitudinem. (156.)

Desiderium quod ad religionem pertinere dinoscitur augmentandam et conservandam, pio affectu promovere et confor . . . . attentius. . . . . (160.)

Justis peticionibus facilem debemus prebere assensum, ut fidelium devocio celerem sortiatur effectum. (190.)

Juste postulacio voluntatis effectui prosequente debet compleri. (200.)

Facile datur peticioni consensus cui justicie astipulatur assensus. (193.)

Ex commisso nobis admonemur officio peticionibus quas ad religionis incrementum dinoscimus pertinere facilem ac benignum prebere assensum. (194, 195.)

Ex officii nostri debito religiosa nos loca diligere convenit et eorum utilitati ac quieti in posterum providere. (230.)

Sicut sacerdotalis officii est pravorum quorumlibet erroneis conatibus justicie zelo contraire, sic nimirum esse convenit censura ecclesiastica proborum acta omnimodis confirmare. (205.)

Sollicitudo ministerii nostri nos admonet ecclesiarum necessitudinibus providere ac adversariorum incursibus resistere, quatinus in ea pro voluntate dei pax conformetur tranquillitatis ope fideles ad omne opus bonum obnixius excitentur. (237.)

Ad nostram spectat solicitudinem ecclesiasticis personis et maxime ancillis Christi de Wintineia quas religionis nomen commendat, que eis concessa sunt et in elemosinam perpetuam donata ita confirmare ut decetero ea eis inmutilata conserventur. (280.)

Sollicitudinis nostre debito convenit viros religiosos diligere et eorum possessiones et bona pia proteccione munire et ea a pravorum hominum nequicia tueri et nostro patrocinio refovere. (304.)

Ad officium nostrum spectat religiosorum [virorum] utilitati providere et eorum bona augere et fovere. (306.)

Cum ad omnes nostre jurediccioni subjectos sollicitudinis nostre aciem debeamus extendere, eisque jura sua inviolata conservare, specialiter quasdam tamen diligencia religionis compellimur pauperes Christi in utroque sexu arcioris vite regulam in monasteriis professos conservare ac studiose debemus confovere, et ne pravorum intrusione ullave potestatum secularium vexacione injuste perturbentur vel possessionibus sibi in solatium victus seu regum largicione seu principum et potentum donacione misericordie intuitu juste et canonice collatis destituantur, sedula nos convenit circumspectione providere nostraque auctoritate quatenus poterimus precavere. (173.)

In amplificationem honoris ecclesie dei studium et diligentiam adhibere et in usus divinos pie collata fovere et firmare pium et sanctum est et ad nostram precipue spectat sollicitudinem. (289.)

Cum salvator noster seipsum dicat in infirmis visitari in nudis cooperiri, gloria nostra esse debet infirmis compati pauperum inopias relevare. (54.)

Pravas consuetudines ab ecclesia dei penitus extirpare et utiles inducere et antiquitus habitas libertates illesas perpetuo conservare sicut nostre principaliter incumbit sollicitudini ita spectat omnium bonorum devocioni. (23.)

(b) *Indulgences.* The harangues prefacing grants of indulgence generally stress the importance of good works:

Equum est ac racionabile ecclesias sanctorum dei venerari votis et muneribus et edificare attencius in terris quos certum est coronari in celis. (92.)

Equum est ac racionabile fideles dei oracionibus atque dignis beneficiis venerari in terris quos fide deifica credimus coronari in celis. (93.)

Equum est ac rationabile illos sanctos et maxime dei apostolos devotione precipua venerari in terris de quorum societate certum est angelos gratulari in celis. (213.)

Qui ad celestem patriam pervenire desiderant, utile est eis misericordie operibus insistere et precipue sanctam ecclesiam devote venerari. (287.)

Eis debet dominice crucis maxime prodesse misterium qui sinceriori devotione ipsius venerantur honorem et in statutis solempnitatibus ad consequendam veniam peccatorum a salvatore crucifixo conveniunt. (9.)

Most of 214 dealing with the Fall of Man, the Redemption and the virtues of the Holy Cross.

Cum omnem intencionem vestram racio boni operis poscat augeri, non est aliquis vestrum sicut devote confidimus qui spe ad bonum opus non gaudeat incitari. Quoniam sicut homo potest habere quo recidat, ita elemosinis deo donante potest habere quo crescat. (82.)

Penitentibus et peccata confessis et ecclesiam dei devota mente venerantibus pietatis instinctu admonemur misericordie solatium retribuere et indulgentie remedium compensare. (114.)

Pauperibus ecclesiis subvenire et eis suas elemosinas impendere opus bonum est deoque acceptissimum. (242.)

Ad pastoris spectat solicitudinem omnibus maxime religionis cultum professis in sua providere necessitate. (261.)

Ad nostrum spectat officium vos comovere, quoniam non est aliquis vestrum sicut de vobis confidimus qui se ad bonum opus non gaudeat incitari, ut in precipuis festivitatibus ecclesias vestras votis et muneribus honoretis et in illis deum attencius studeatis venerari. (266.)

Condignum est et deo amabile sicut novit vestra discretio ut illis qui sanctam ecclesiam fideli devocione venerantur et bonis sibi a deo prestitis eam sustentant spiritualia remedia benigne conferamus. (279.)

Ad nostrum spectat officium religiosa loca tueri et viros religione et sanctitate probatos sub nostre protectionis munimine retinere et auctoritate qua fungimur adversus pravorum studia fovere. (286.)

Opus pietatis esse nemo ambigit pauperum Christi inopias sublevare, eorum maxime quibus solum relictum est mendicandi suffragium. (288.)

Religiosorum fratrum quieti providere ad episcopale specialiter pertinet officium. (308.)

(c) *Judgments.* The harangues going before the judgments convey the importance of committing them to writing in order to avoid trouble in the future:

Provide litteris commendantur que firmam debent et stabilem habere memoriam. (231.)

Provide litteris commendantur que firmam futuris temporibus sunt habitura memoriam, ne adversus veritatem malignancium calliditas quandoque possit prevalere. (267.)

Que ad multorum noticiam pervenire credimus ne processu temporum in oblivionem revocentur scripto commendare decrevimus. (27.)

Que sub nostra presencia canonice terminata sunt, ne transcursu temporis in oblivionem revocentur scripto commendare decrevimus. (140.)

Ne ea que coram nobis fine canonico terminantur processu temporis queant in dubium revocari ea quidem presentium attestatione litterarum usque ad notitiam vestram transferre curavimus. (212.)

Ad posterorum notitiam litterarum memorie que coram nobis gesta sunt comendamus. (235.)

Similarly:

Testimonium veritati duximus scripto perhibendum ne quod inter ecclesiam beati Leonardi Stretfordie et ecclesiam Lillecherchie super ipso manerio Lillecherchie immutetur inposterum. (155.)

The other harangues of the ordinances etc., read as follows:

Suppremis deficientium voluntatibus suum accomodant jura favorem et in se velud inhumanus provocat iram dei qui piis eorum desideriis obvius contradicit. (28.)

Cunctorum providentie set diligentium maxime prelatorum incumbit officio ut ex preteritorum experientia mala debeant precavere futura. (31.)

Quoniam grande conversationis monastice detrimentum esse dinoscitur contra usum ecclesiarum et contra statuta regule monachorum capitulo clericos quasi de jure admisceri; iccirco, etc. (30.)

Cum ecclesiarum jura nostre jurisdictioni subditarum sollicite debeamus conservare eademque iminuere presumentes festina et digna animadversione punire, majori tamen vigilancia ecclesiam Cantuariensem cui nos divina prefecit misericordia ejusdemque libertates et dignitates ab antiquo ei jure competentes integras et illesas nos convenit servare. (50.)

Universitati vestre scribere nos et ratio et providentia necessaria compellit, ne scilicet nostro silentio servorum dei innocentia in posterum periclitari aut contra justum et equum debeat fatigari. (37.)

Que ad honorem et utilitatem ecclesie dei et religionis pacem et quietem statuta sunt, ut stabilia et inconvulsa permaneant munienda sunt perpetuis firmamentis. (83, 84.)

(d) *Mandates*. The harangues in the mandates are generally directed to the object of the particular mandate thus prefaced:

Quando hiis qui sub habitu regulari divinis inminent famulatibus jura sua illicite subtrahuntur, tanto nobis major cura debet existere ut quod sui juris est nostra sollicitudine interveniente recuperent quanto suo inhibente proposito minus possunt operam contencionibus adhibere. (20.)

Quamvis omnibus in jure suo debitores in quantum ratio expetit et ammonet existimus, tamen attentiore sollicitudine dilecto filio nostro, etc. (45.)

Sicut vestra novit discretio in rebus secularibus suum cuique jus et proprius ordo servandus est, quanto magis in ecclesiasticis disposicionibus, ubi nulla debet induci confusio, ne ibi discordia locum inveniat unde pacis bona procedere debent. (141.)

Mandata sedis apostolice cum magna sunt sollicitudine a nobis effectui mancipanda et privilegia ejusdem cum omni vigilantia in sua sunt stabilitate conservanda. (144.)

Tue ut credimus discretioni satis innotuit possessiones in sustentationem pauperum Christi domibus ac locis religiosis collatas minime debere distrahi aut preter assensum et coniventiam fratrum loci quibus conferuntur in usus laicorum transferri. Quod si a quoquo illorum qui domibus custodiendis ac negociis ecclesiarum gerendis preficiuntur aliter actum esse constaverit, ad ejus poterit dejectionem sufficere nisi quod presumptum est ab eo cum festinatione studuerit revocare. (260.)

(e) *Grants*. The two harangues preceding grants made by Theobald have no distinctive features. The first approximates to the typical judgment harangue, while the second, which is a very spiritual grant conditional on a request, partakes of the character of a mandate:

Quoniam ea que a nobis rationabiliter facta sunt posteris nostris nota fieri volumus, ne transcursu temporis super his aliquid dubium oriatur, ea scripto reservanda commisimus. (97.)

Quoniam nostri officii interest lapsos revocare dubios et negligentes hortari bene agentibus perseveranciam persuadere, rogamus liberalitati vestre, etc. (89.)

Many of these harangues adopt papal phrases and rhythm to a large extent. Only one, however, has been found copied entirely from a contemporary papal harangue, and even here there are some slight variations.[1] In most of the charters the harangue is followed by some word or phrase, linking it to the body of the charter. The most common of these is 'Inde est quod', which occurs in twenty-nine cases.[2] Other phrases are 'Hinc est quod',[3] 'Ea igitur ratione',[4] 'Hac induti racione',[5] 'Hoc ergo rationis intuitu',[6] 'Hoc igitur intuitu',[7] 'Hoc quidem intuitu',[8] 'Tali itaque inducti racione',[9] 'Hoc nimirum intuitu',[10] 'Ea nimirum consideracione',[11] 'Ideo suggerente nobis ratione',[12] 'Sanctorum igitur antecessorum nostrorum exemplo et auctoritate provocati et corroborati',[13] 'Audientes itaque',[14] 'Nos siquidem',[15] 'Nos itaque',[16] and 'Nos ergo'.[17] The following introductory words are also used: 'Eapropter',[18] 'Ergo',[19] 'Idcirco',[20] 'Igitur',[21] 'Itaque',[22] 'Proinde',[23] 'Quare',[24] 'Quidem',[25] 'Quocirca',[26] and 'Unde'.[27] There are, however, four cases in which no connecting word or phrase appears.[28]

6. The Notification

Generally after a harangue there was no notification, but there are several exceptions. The forms of notification after a harangue comprise 'Noverit universitas vestra',[29] 'Noscat universitas vestra',[30] 'Universitatem vestram nosse volumus',[31] 'Notum sit vobis',[32] 'Notum vobis facimus',[33] 'Universitati vestre noti-

[1] Holtzmann, i, no. 69, a mandate to Theobald and Theobald's mandate in no. 20 above. The pope's mandate is dated 5 February 1152 and is about the monks of Ely; Theobald's mandate is after 1150 and is about the monks of St. Albans.

[2] 6, 22, 23, 65, 79, 83, 84, 91, 114, 122, 123, 133, 137, 139, 142, 150, 163, 187, 197, 199, 209, 215, 229, 245, 246, 262, 273, 288, 289.

[3] 31, 64.   [4] 3, 8 'inducti', 143, 189, 227, 228, 259, 286, 297.

[5] 193.   [6] 251.   [7] 205.   [8] 237.   [9] 173.

[10] 72, 308 'eo'.   [11] 248.   [12] 2.   [13] 73, 255, 256.

[14] 119, 254.   [15] 144.   [16] 160.   [17] 266, 280, 285.

[18] 9, 54, 56, 111, 128, 148, 152, 153, 158, 159, 183, 300, 304, 306–7.

[19] 27, 92, 93, 140, 200, 202, 213, 279, 287.   [20] 30, 37, 230, 244.

[21] 59, 155, 242.   [22] 212, 214, 216, 231, 235, 267.   [23] 82, 162, 190, 261.

[24] 126, 141.   [25] 28.   [26] 45, 156, 194, 195, 265.   [27] 50, 98, 99.

[28] 20, 89, 97, 260.

[29] 72, 140, 200, 202, 279.   [30] 27.   [31] 230.   [32] 59.   [33] 306.

ficetur',[1] 'Universitatem tam presentis quam futuri temporis fidelium Christi scire volumus',[2] 'Notum esse volumus tam presentibus quam futuris',[3] 'Ad vestram curavimus transferre noticiam',[4] 'Sciant tam posteri quam presentes',[5] 'Sciant presentes et post futuri',[6] 'Sciant tam presentes quam futuri',[7] and 'Universitatem vestram non lateat'.[8]

Of the documents without a harangue which have a general or collective address, there are several without a notification. These comprise eight confirmations,[9] one grant,[10] eleven judgments[11] and two indulgences.[12]

The notifications, excluding those mentioned above, comprise no less than fifty-one varieties ranging from the simple 'Sciatis'[13] and 'Noveritis'[14] to the far more elaborate 'Notum esse volumus omnibus ad quos presens carta pervenerit'[15]

Noverit universitas vestra (7, 62, 67, 95, 108, 127, 167, 174, 177, 204, 225, 241);

Noverit universitas presentium et futurorum (68);

Noverit tam presentium quam futurorum universitas (157);

Noverit universitas tam presentium quam futurorum (149, 275);

Noverit tam modernorum universitas quam futurorum posteritas (276);

Noverit dilecta fraternitas vestra (264);

Noverit fraternitatis vestre dilectio (272);

Noverit dilecta nobis et veneranda fraternitas vestra (120);

Noverit universitas fidelium ecclesie dei (94);

Noverit tam presens etas quam futura posteritas (239);

Noverit presentis temporis etas et futuri posteritas (180);

Noverit tam presens etas quam omnis secutura posteritas (39);

Noverit presens etas et secutura posteritas (166);

Noverit caritas vestra (201);

Noverint tam presentes quam futuri (5, 21, 36, 81, 134, 175, 177a, 184, 247);

Noverint omnes communitas tam presentes quam futuri (179);

Noverint universi fideles Christi (42);

Noverint universi (210);

[1] 235.   [2] 152, 153.   [3] 162.   [4] 231.   [5] 97.   [6] 155.
[7] 267.   [8] 212.   [9] 25, 55, 56, 66, 104, 121, 192, 217.   [10] 252.
[11] 1, 70, 78, 100, 101, 145, 147, 169, 182, 191, 211.   [12] 87, 243. Cf. 309.
[13] 4, 10, 24, 33–5, 38, 41, 46, 51, 52, 57, 63, 90, 125, 146, 161, 176, 301, 310, 311.
These are mainly grants.   [14] 170, 181, 283, 302.   [15] 116.

P

Noveritis fratres dilectissimi (198);   •
Notum sit omnibus tam presentibus quam futuris (305);
Notum sit presentibus et futuris (164, 165);
Notum sit universitati vestre (178, 223, 281);
Notum sit vobis (44, 207);
Notum sit devotioni omnium fidelium (76);
Notum sit tam presentibus quam futuris Christi fidelibus (188);
Notum vobis esse volumus (48, 96);
Notum esse volumus universis presentis temporis et futuri (80);
Notum esse volumus omnibus ad quos presens carta pervenerit (116);
Universitati vestre notum esse volumus (71, 234);
Notum universitati vestre esse volumus (224);
Notum esse vobis volo (220, 221);
Notum facimus universitati vestre (26, 43, 47, 299);
Notum facimus caritati vestre (151);
Notum vobis facio fratres karissimi (11);
Universitati vestre notum fieri volumus (232, 233, 236, 263);
Notum fieri volumus tam presentibus quam futuris (240);
Noscat universitas vestra (226);
Noscat universitas tam presentium quam futurorum (107);
Noscat universitas vestra tam presentium quam futurorum (106);
Noscant presentes et post futuri (60, 61, 85, 86);
Universitati vestre notificamus (58, 77);
Ad omnium noticiam volumus pervenire (222);
Ad omnium vestrum noticiam volumus pervenire (105);
Discretio vestra ignorare non debet (249);
Sciant tam presentes quam futuri (250);
Sciant presentes et post futuri (124);
Sciat karissimi dileccio vestra (269);
Volo ut sciatis (110);
Scire volumus universitatem vestram (268).

As there are comparatively so few examples of each variation there seems little point in trying to show when these forms were used. There seems, however, to be an obvious preference for 'Nosco' and its derivatives, as against those notifications deriving from 'Scio'.

7. *The Corroboration*

The clause of corroboration, which by the thirteenth century was a normal part of certain types of episcopal charters, is comparatively rare in Theobald's documents. Of the charters mentioning the use of Theobald's seal, there are twelve confirmations,[1] two ratifications of compositions[2] and one grant.[3] Three of these charters can be dated before 1150.[4] The following are the forms of these corroborations:

Ut ergo illa concessio firma et rata de cetero permaneat, presenti scripto atque sigilli nostri attestatione confirmari et corroborari fecimus. (39.)

Et ut ista concessio et confirmacio nostra firmam optineat stabilitatem presens scriptum sigilli nostri apposicione munivimus. (105.)

Hec que ecclesie vestre cartis et sigillis legitime confirmata dyocesani vestri testimonio cognovimus, nos quoque eidem tam scripto presenti quam nostri impressione sigilli confirmamus. (111.)

Set quoniam conventio ista coram nobis facta fuit et terminata illam ratam et illibatam esse statuimus et presentis scripti pagina nostro sigillo sigillata communimus. (58.)

Quam quidem ut firma et illibata permaneat memoratis fratribus nostris confirmamus et sigilli nostri testimonio communimus. (233 and similarly 232 and 236.)

. . . presentis scripti pagina et sigilli nostri attestacione communivimus . . . (173.)

. . . et sigilli nostri munimine corroboramus. . . . (127, similarly 247.)

. . . et hoc sigillo meo inperpetuum corroboro . . . (305.)

. . . eam ratam habentes et sigilli nostri munimine confirmantes . . . (121.)

. . . et nostre consignationis munimine roborasse. (108.)

. . . et presenti scripto et sigilli nostri attestatione corroboramus . . . (273.)

Et nos predicti episcopi idem sigillorum nostrorum impressione attestamur. (241. To this charter, issued in Theobald's name, were appended the seals of three bishops, apart from that of Theobald.)

There are other charters of Theobald, which although not mentioning his seal, none the less seem to convey the impression of containing a clause of corroboration.[5]

---

[1] 105, 111, 121, 127, 173, 232, 233, 236, 247, 255, 273, 305.
[2] 58, 241.   [3] 39.   [4] 58, 111, 232.
[5] 96 'et presentis scripti nostri munimine . . . corroboramus'; similarly 68, 80, 200, etc.

8. *Curses and Blessings*

It was not a matter of course for spiritual sanctions to be inserted in Theobald's confirmations, still less in other classes of documents. Eighty-six confirmations contain a threat of excommunication as against fifty with no such clause.[1] Out of the latter fifty charters of confirmation, thirteen contain an admonition against transgressors unsupported by any sanctions.[2] On the other hand twenty-six confirmations contain a benediction in favour of those who support the objects of the charter of confirmation.[3] All these charters, with or without sanctions, belong to all periods of Theobald's archiepiscopate. All the six ordinances contain a sanctions clause[4] and only three grants,[5] two judgments[6] and one indulgence.[7] The forms of the anathemas can be classed under a few main headings. In the first place there is a simple clause 'prohibentes ('prohibemus, inhibentes', etc.) sub anathemate ne quis', etc. There are thirty-one charters with this type of sanctions clause.[8] An even simpler form is 'Quod si quis presumpserit anathema sit'.[9] Another well-defined type is a short clause of anathema serving as a contrast with the blessings to descend on those who observe the terms of the charter, as for instance in Theobald's confirmation of Stephen's quitclaim to the monks of Bury St. Edmund's of forty knights' castle-guard at Norwich—'Conservantibus hec gratia eterna a deo perveniat, impedientibus vero ultio divina nisi resipuerint immineat.' There are twelve of these clauses.[10] A more numerous

---

[1] With: 2–4, 7, 8, 23–5, 54–6, 59, 62, 68, 72–3, 77, 81, 90, 91, 96, 98, 99, 106, 107, 110, 122, 123, 126, 128, 133, 137, 139, 148, 150, 162, 163, 174, 177, 177a, 178, 183, 184, 187–90, 193–5, 197, 198, 202–5, 209, 215, 216, 220–2, 227–9, 232, 236, 237, 245, 246, 255, 262, 264, 269, 273, 275, 280, 285, 289, 297, 299, 300, 301, 304, 306, 307; without: 5, 6, 21, 22, 36, 42, 64–6, 79, 104, 105, 108, 111, 119, 121, 127, 142, 143, 153, 156–9, 164, 165, 170, 173, 191, 192, 199–201, 217, 224, 230, 233, 234, 240, 244, 247, 251, 252, 254, 259, 272, 281–3, 305.

[2] 5, 36, 64, 79, 127, 164, 165, 170, 217, 230, 247, 281, 282.

[3] 3, 25, 56, 68, 72, 73, 98, 99, 110, 128, 137, 139, 162, 174, 184, 188, 190, 194, 195, 202, 205, 269, 285, 299, 300; 161 is unique in containing a blessing without a curse.

[4] 28 with an indulgence to observers, 30, 31, 37, 47, 50.

[5] 43 and a blessing, 85, 86.   [6] 175, 231.

[7] 242 against those hindering pilgrims.

[8] 2, 7, 23, 31, 59, 62, 77, 96, 106, 107, 122, 123, 126, 133, 137, 150, 175, 198, 203, 204, 209, 216, 231, 242, 245, 264, 269, 273, 289, 297, 306.   [9] 163; cf. 30, 275.

[10] 25, 43, 91, 128, 139, 162, 174, 188, 190, 194, 195, 300.

class resembles to a greater or lesser extent the comparable clause or clauses in the contemporary papal bulls, although no exact copy can be found. An example of this type may be found in Theobald's confirmation to the Templars of the church of Sompting—'Quicumque ergo contra hanc nostram confirmacionem ausu temerario venire et eos super hiis inquietare vel vexare presumpserit, nisi cito resipuerit et dampna cum integritate resarcierit, indignacionem omnipotentis dei et nostram maledictionem in extremo examine se noverit incursurum'. There are altogether forty-two charters with this form, no two being completely alike.[1] In two charters the draftsman contents himself with referring to the sanctions clauses of earlier charters on the same subject.[2] There remain nine charters with forms which do not fit in with any of the above classifications, but in no case do they reach the dramatic heights of earlier charters, as for instance the clause in Bishop Gundulf of Rochester's charter as inspected by Theobald.[3]

In Theobald's mandates to bishops and others the penalties laid down for disobedience by the parties ultimately affected was generally excommunication and sometimes interdiction of the lands of the culprit. In only two cases is a time limit fixed for obeying the terms of the mandate.[4]

9. *Charters of Theobald with Witnesses*

There are altogether sixty-two charters of Theobald which are witnessed or which show signs of having been witnessed.[5] Of these, twenty-one are grants[6] and eighteen other charters are

[1] 3, 4, 8, 24, 37, 47, 50, 54–6, 72, 81, 83–6, 90, 98, 99, 110, 148 the awe-inspiring 'maranatha' merely means 'our Lord has come' (Aramaic), 177a, 183, 184, 187, 189, 197, 202, 215, 227–9, 232, 236, 246, 248, 262, 280, 285, 299, 304, 307.   [2] 73, 220.

[3] 28 excommunication threatened six times, 177, 178, 205, 221, 222 inspeximus of Gundulf's charter, 237, 255, 301.

[4] 20 time allowed 8 days, 278 time allowed 15 days. Cf. 129, 131, for the canonical triple citation before excommunication. The duration of the excommunication was usually till the culprit finally obeyed, but in one case a visit to the pope was also enjoined, 186.

[5] 10, 11, 16, 33–5, 42, 44, 46, 52, 54, 55, 57–61, 63, 64, 77, 78, 83, 84, 86, 95, 97, 100, 108, 124, 125, 140, 145–7, 151, 153, 161, 164, 165, 167, 176–80, 182, 207, 211, 221–3, 225, 235, 236, 239, 240, 250, 252, 255, 263, 281, 306.

[6] 33–5, 46, 51, 52, 60, 61, 63, 97, 124, 125, 146, 151, 161, 176, 179, 180, 239, 250, 252.

concerned with the see of Canterbury.[1] Four charters deal with Rochester.[2] For the rest of the province there are nine judgments,[3] eight confirmations,[4] and two notifications.[5]

Apart from helping in many cases to provide narrower dating limits for a number of the charters, these witness lists provide the main evidence for the reconstruction of Theobald's household. The following is a list of its members who witness the charters together with the charters they attest:

Chancellors

(a) Philip: 34, 46, 51, 100, 124, 125, 145, 153, 176, 179, 180, 239, 240, 250, and as archdeacon of Norwich: 35, 83, 84 (also A).
(b) Elinand: 255.

Scribe

Peter: 34, 35, 46, 51, 57, 77, 100, 124, 125, 176, 179, 180, 250; described as clerk: 77 (also A and H2).

Clerks and Chaplains

Alan of Wells: 34, 51, 55, 59, 61, 86, 145–7, 161, 177, 179, 180, 225, 250, 252, 310, B.
Daniel, monk: 63.
David, master: 281.
Elias, monk: 63.
Eudo: 225.
Eudo Manefer', master: 263.
Eudo, notary: 83, 84.
Felix: 222, 310.
Gilbert of Bec, monk: 177.
Gilbert of Clare, monk: 42, 59, 63, 146, 151, 164, 165, F.
Guido de Pressenni, master: 146, 255.
Henry, master: 281.
Henry, monk: 151.
Hervey: 222, C4.
Hugh de Gant: 46, 83, 84, 125.
Hugh of Hollingbourne: 250.
John of Canterbury: 55, 61, 63, 86, 146, 151, 164, 252, 255, 310, F.
  Treasurer of York: 182.

[1] 10, 42, 44, 54, 55, 57, 58, 59, 83, 84, 86, 95, 147, 153, 167, 177, 178, 240.
[2] 221–3, 225.   [3] 16, 78, 100, 140, 145, 182, 207, 211, 263.
[4] 77, 108, 164, 165, 236, 255, 281, 306.   [5] 11, 235.

John, son of Mary: 10, C4.
John of Pagham: 42, 146, 147, B; Bishop of Worcester: 140.
John of Salisbury, master: 10, 16, 34, 35, 46, 57, 83, 84, 95, 125, 147,
    176, 182, 240, 255, 263, A.
John of Tilbury, master: 10, 16, 46, 95, 125, 140, 225, 255.
Jordan Fantôme, poet: B.
Mauger: 55, 146, 147, 179, 222.
Miles, monk: 310.
Miles Crispin: 59.
Osbern: 35.
Osbert: 176, 281.
Osbert Bonitas: 10.
Osbert of Preston, master: 83, 84, 263.
Philip de Sal': 255.
Ralph Bixon', master: 225.
Ralph of Lisieux: 58, 86, 146.
Ralph, son of Ranulf, Bishop of Durham: 34, 59, 145, 180, 250, H2.
Ralph of Wingham: 225.
Reginald Apostolicus: 10, 58.
Richard, master: 281.
Richard Castel: 55, 124, 146, 178, 182, F.
Richard of Clare, monk: 77, 78, 176, 225, 255, 306.
Richard of Salisbury, canon of Exeter: 83, 84.
Richard of Whitstable, monk: 225.
Roger: 281.
Roger of Pont L'Evêque: 58, 59, 61, 146, 147, 164, 165, 178, 252, B,
    F; Archdeacon of Canterbury: 10, 51, 57, 179, 239, 255, C4, H2;
    Archbishop-elect of York: 182; Archbishop of York: 11.
Roger Species, master: 16, 34, 35, 51, 57, 78, 124, 145, 179, 180, 255,
    263, 306, C4, H2.
Thomas of London: 42, 44, 55, 57, 77, 78, 86, 100, 124, 146, 147, 178,
    180, 182, 250, 252, 255, B, C4., F, H2; Archdeacon of Canterbury:
    153, 306; Chancellor: 11.
Vacarius, master: 10, 263.
W., medicus, master: 77, 78.
Walter, monk: 310
Walter of Gloucester, monk: 225, 255, F.
Walter de Moyri, monk: 146, 164, 165.
William: 281.
William of Clare, monk: 77, 78.
William Cumin: 147, B.

William of Northall, master: 77, 78, 83, 84, 125, 263.
William de Ver: 46, 100.
Wulfric of Wrotham: 59, 61, 151, 161, 252.

Almoners

(a) Alfred: 34, 83, 84, 125, 176.
(b) Ralph: 59, 146.

Chamberlains

(a) Gilbert: 34, 46, 161, 177, 255.
(b) Godfrey: 177, 178.
(c) William: 34.
(d) Hugh de Tirreville: 255 (perhaps of Rochester).

Crossbearer

Osbert: 255.

Treasurers [dispensator]

William: 46.
Richard: 255.

Butler [pincerna]

Robert: 34, 46, 164, 165, 255.

Constable

Ralph Picot: 161; as knight of the archbishop: 44, 51, 59, 60, 61, 86, 153; as sheriff of Kent: 55, 225 (also A and C4).

Seneschal

Odo: 255.

Stewards [dapifer]

(a) Odo: 164, 165.
(b) William of Bec: 34 also 179.
(c) William of Eynesford: 60, 161; as knight of the archbishop: 59, 86, 151.
(d) William: 61.

Marshal

Bailhache: 255.

Porters

(a) (Ostiarius) Laurence: 255.
(b) (Portarius) William: 42, 51, 255, A, B.
(c) (Portarius) Roger: 42, A, B (possibly of Christ Church).

Master Cook

William: 34, 255.

Forester

Daniel: 179.

Knights

Geoffrey de Cromille: 310.
Hugh de Munfort: 55.
Hugh Paisforiere: 252.
Nigel son of Godfrey: 34, 60, 61, 310.
Odo son of John: 59, 86; cf. Odo [seneschal] and Odo [steward] above.
Payne of Otford: 153.
Peter de Thalawrde: 55.
Richard de Maris: 86.
Walter of Wingham: 34.
William of Malling: 59, 86.
William of Pagham: 51, 59, 151.
William son of Nigel: 153.

Also in Theobald's household may be included his four nephews and their master who appear in 255.

The Cathedral Priory is also represented to some extent in lists of witnesses to Theobald's charters. Apart from individual monks, the following names appear:

Prior Walter Durdent: 86, 222, B; as bishop of Chester: 16.
Prior Walter Durdent or Walter Parvus: 42, 63.
Prior Walter Parvus: 310.
Berner the steward: 44, B.
Thierry 'de altaribus': 42.
William 'de buteillis': 42.

Other witnesses include:

Bishops

Robert of Bath: 211.
Roger of Chester: 211.
Hilary of Chichester: 57, 140, 207.
Nigel of Ely: 124.
Robert Chichester of Exeter: 55.
Robert Warelwast of Exeter: 16.
Robert of Hereford: 211.
Robert of Lincoln: 11, 16, 108.

Robert of London: 207.

Richard of London: 11, 140, 239; as archdeacon 'of London': 145; without title: 124.

Ascelin of Rochester: 59, 60, 207, 221.

Walter of Rochester: 42, 95, 239, C.4; as archdeacon of Canterbury: 55, 58, 59, 86, 147, H.

Jocelin of Salisbury: 207, 211.

Henry of Winchester: 207.

Simon of Worcester: 211.

Abbots

Anselm of Bury St. Edmund's: 281.

Hugh of St. Augustine's, Canterbury: 222.

Silvester of St. Augustine's, Canterbury: 240.

Anselm of St. Benet's Holme: 161.

William of Lilleshall: 140.

Martin of Peterborough: 161.

William of Peterborough: 16.

Gervase of Westminster: 16.

Priors

William 'the Devil' of St. Augustine's, Canterbury: 240.

Alfred of St. Gregory's, Canterbury: 55, 161.

William of St. Martin's, Dover: 60, 86, 222.

Hugh of Dover: C4.

Walter of St. Neot's: 59.

Fulk of St. Osyth's Chick: 161.

Brian of Rochester Cathedral: 222.

Archdeacons

David of Buckingham: 16, 108.

Froger of Derby: 145.

Bartholomew of Exeter: 83, 84.

Henry of Huntingdon: 16.

Ralph de Diceto 'of the Church of London': 16; and as 'archdeacon' 140.

Robert of Oxford: 108.

Paris of Rochester: 263.

Jordan of Salisbury: 16.

Walter of York: 178.

While ecclesiastical dignitaries are well represented as can be seen, the lay nobility are completely absent.

The majority of the witness lists are in the ablative case to the number of forty-three. There are, however, eleven charters, with the nominative case, five of them after 1150,[1] three in the genitive case, one after 1150,[2] and one in a mixture of the nominative and accusative.[3]

10. Dating of the Charters

The great majority of Theobald's charters are undated. A few of them, however, have a date of place like the contemporary royal charters, or a date of time or both. In three cases only are unwitnessed charters dated.[4]

(a) Place:
Canterbury: 34, 35, 42, 60, 161, 222, 239.
Lambeth: 46, 124, 207.
(South) Malling: 177, 179, 180.
Malling (Kent): 176.
Lavant: 250.
Hayes (Middlesex): 125.
Maidstone: 147.
Teynham: 100.

(b) Time:
In anno m°.c°. lvi ab incarnatione domini et xvii kal. Junii (117).
Anno m°c°l°vii^{mo} crastina die post festum sancti Luce ewangeliste (241 original).

(c) Time and place:
Anno incarnacionis dominice m°c° quinquagesimo primo apud Pageham (245).
Apud Cantuariam anno ab incarnacione domini mcliiii° (182).
Apud Cantuariam die pasche (63).

They comprise fifteen grants,[5] four judgments,[6] three confirmations[7] and one notification.[8]

Owing to the inadequacy of the dating of the charters, the evidence for their dates must be sought mainly from information

---

[1] 54, 55, 151, 177, 178 and 222 and also 176, 235, 240, 255, 263 after 1150.
[2] 33, 42 and 225 after 1150.
[3] 100 in corrupt copy.
[4] 107, 241 and an original 245.
[5] 34, 35, 42, 46, 60, 63, 124, 125, 161, 176, 177, 179, 180, 239, 250.
[6] 100, 117, 182, 207.   [7] 147, 222, 245.   [8] 241.

provided by their texts. The following list of dates[1] suggested for
Theobald's charters shows how very often the information to be
extracted is extremely meagre:

1139:	237.
c. 1139:	58, 111.
1139–43:	32.
1143:	104.
c. 1144:	168.
1139–45:	25, 188.
1144–45:	5.
1145:	169, 222, 223.
c. 1145:	206.
1139–47:	294, 295.
1143–47:	138.
1147:	147.
c. 1147:	208.
1139–48:	85, 113, 177, 219, 247, 282, 301.
1141–48:	164, 165, 211.
1142–48:	59–61, 220, 221.
1143–48:	55, 86, 146, 178, 232, 252.
1144–48:	281.
1145–48:	156.
1147–48:	207.
1148:	76.
1144–49:	268.
1147–49:	128.
1148–49:	57.
1149:	144, 299.
c. 1149:	194, 264.
1139–50:	24, 29, 33, 87, 151, 198, 205, 242, 269, 271, 283, 284, 305, 311.
1144–50:	38, 98.
1145–50:	308, 309.
1150:	17.
c. 1150:	154, 238, 254.
1139–51:	54.
1148–51:	42.
1150–51:	300.
1151:	245.

[1] The system of arrangement of documents of doubtful date used by Jaffé in his
Regesta Pontificum Romanorum has been adopted here.

c. 1151:   251.
1139–52: 170, 258.
1144–52: 63.
1150–52: 70, 124, 145, 155, 162, 163, 310.
1152:   100, 101.
1145–53: 184.
1148–53: 158, 159.
1150–53: 255.
1152–53: 239, 244.
1153:   37, 102.
c. 1153: 68.
1139–54: 73, 248.
1143–54: 44.
1148–54: 127, 277.
1150–54: 3, 10, 36, 71, 77–9, 179, 180, 192, 250, 272, 275, 285.
1151–54: 190.
1153–54: 51.
1154:   182.
1139–55: 4.
1150–55: 200.
1155:   18, 112, 143.
1150–56: 27, 115, 150.
1156:   19, 116, 117.
1150–57: 88–90.
1151–57: 191, 265, 291.
1152–57: 140.
1155–57: 129, 134.
1156–57: 16, 118.
1157:   11, 103, 241, 270.
1150–58: 50, 276, 278.
1153–58: 47.
1154–58: 153, 306.
c. 1158: 130.
1150–59: 12, 92, 126.
1152–59: 72.
1155–59: 141, 249.
1158–59: 212
1150–60: 80, 181, 274.
1151–60: 136.
1154–60: 46.
1158–60: 1, 303.

1159–60: 131.

c. 1160: 28, 94.

1139–61: 7, 9, 26, 48, 52, 53, 114, 175, 224, 257, 293, 298.

1141–61: 41, 74.

1143–61: 183.

1148–61: 21, 157, 166, 209, 234, 253, 290, 292.

1149–61: 43.

1150–61: 6, 8, 13, 15, 22, 23, 34, 45, 49, 56, 62, 64–7, 75, 82, 88, 91, 93, 95, 97, 99, 105, 107, 109, 110, 119, 122, 123, 125, 142, 148, 149, 152, 160, 172, 176, 177a, 185, 189, 195–7, 199, 202, 210, 213–5, 217, 225, 229, 230, 233, 235, 243, 246, 256, 261, 266, 279, 280, 286, 287, 289, 297, 302, 304, 307.

1151–61: 14.

1152–61: 20.

1153–61: 30, 39, 40, 69, 132, 133, 135.

1154–61: 96, 108, 227, 228, 240, 259, 260.

1155–61: 31.

1157–61: 35, 83, 84.

1158–61: 2, 137, 139, 203, 204, 216.

1159–61: 81, 273.

1160–61 or 1166–69: 121.

1139–61 or 1162–70: 288.

1141–61 or 1162–70: 201.

1143–61 or 1162–70: 171.

1150–61 or 1166–70: 106, 120.

1154–61 or 1162–70: 267.

11. *The use of 'Fiat' and 'Amen'*

Two charters, both of early date have 'Fiat' together with 'Amen'. After the anathema, one charter ends 'Amen. Fiat',[1] while the other, a copy, continues after the anathema with 'Fiat. Fiat. Amen', followed by a cross.[2] Both these charters are confirmations. A third charter of a later date has 'Fiat. Amen. Amen. Amen'.[3]

Of the twenty-three charters containing 'Amen', twenty are confirmations, two are indulgences, and the remaining charter is Theobald's will.[4] These charters do not belong to any special

---

[1] 205 original. [2] 188. [3] 304.

[4] Confirmations: 25, 56, 72, 91, 98, 110, 148, 174, 184, 188, 197, 202, 205, 215, 248, 280, 285, 299, 300, 304; indulgences 94, 279; will 28.

period of Theobald's archiepiscopate. In nine of these charters 'Amen' seems to be used as a substitute for 'Valete',[1] while in twelve others 'Valete' is added as well.[2]

12. *The use of 'Valete'*

In the case of the valediction it would seem better to deal with the original charters and the copies separately, as a small word at the end of the charter, not affecting the meaning of the document might easily be omitted by the copyist. In the case of the originals the general rule seems to be that where there are witnesses the valediction is omitted. There is one charter with witnesses and valediction[3] while on the other hand there are six charters lacking both witnesses and valediction.[4] In addition there are two unwitnessed charters with 'Amen'[5] and two incomplete charters.[6] Otherwise the rule holds. The most usual form is 'Valete' which occurs forty-nine times. Exceptional forms are 'Valete in Christo' occurring twice,[7] 'Valete in domino dilectissimi filii et fratres[8] and 'Vale'[9] With the copies the results are not quite so clear. One hundred and thirty-nine charters contain 'Valete' of which ten have a dating clause or witnesses.[10] Of the sixty charters without 'Valete', twenty-eight are witnessed and eight have 'Amen'. It does not seem possible to make any distinction between the practice in Theobald's earlier and later years. There is one exceptional form— 'Valeat in domino fraternitas vestra'.[11]

13. *The use of the Singular and Plural*

The majority of Theobald's charters keep to the plural number. There are, however, twenty-three charters in which Theobald throughout speaks of himself in the singular[12] and seven others in which the singular and plural are confused.[13] Of these char-

---

[1] 25, 56, 98 original, 188, 205, 248, 299; 285 and 304 'Amen. Amen. Amen'.
[2] 28, 72, 91, 94, 174, 184, 197, 202, 215, 279, 280, 300.
[3] 44.   [4] 104 and 190 not consulted, 183, 252, 264, 275.
[5] 98, 205.   [6] 152, 160.   [7] 32, 33.   [8] 28.   [9] 29.
[10] 52, 63, 95, 100, 117, 140, 145, 178, 211, 240.   [11] 272.
[12] 10, 11, 29, 34, 38, 44, 52, 60, 61, 63, 76, 110, 161, 169, 176, 180, 188, 220, 221, 235, 301, 305, 310.
[13] 25, 28, 57, 59, 146, 151, 178.

ters, seventeen can be dated before 1150, nine after 1150 and four are doubtful.[1] All except six of these charters relate to the Cathedral and Kent.[2]

THE APPEARANCE OF THE CHARTERS

1. *Size*

Of the surviving original charters of Theobald, the largest is his confirmation to the nuns of Littlemore, which in its unmutilated state must have been well over a foot long and ten inches broad.[3] The others are of much more modest dimensions. The majority tend to be broader than they are long. In some charters the breadth exceeds the length by several times.[4] The reverse is occasionally found,[5] although nothing like to the same degree. Where measurements of the charters are given below, the length is the first figure mentioned.

2. *Handwriting*

Three or four main types of writing appear in Theobald's charters. In the first place there is the book-hand[6] which seems to be especially popular amongst charters relating to Canterbury Cathedral.[7] Several of these charters are written in a typical 'Canterbury hand'.[8] A number of charters are written in a charter-hand similar to those employed in the contemporary English royal chanceries.[9] It is possible to show that some of these charters were written by the same person.[10] Some charters are written in hands which share the characteristics of both book-hand and charter-hand.[11] Finally there is the papal-hand,

[1] Before: 25, 29, 38, 59, 60, 61, 63, 76, 146, 151, 161, 169, 178, 188, 220, 221, 301; After: 10, 11, 28, 34, 110, 176, 180, 235, 310; Doubtful: 44, 52, 57, 305.

[2] 11, 25, 76, 110, 188, 235.   [3] 160.

[4] 21, 29, 32, 33, 38, 41, 183, 252, 268, 281.   [5] 45, 123, 150, 203.

[6] 29–33, 37, 38, 41–4, 68 'coarse', 83, 84, 98, 151 very coarse, 205, 264, 268, 281.

[7] Only 68, 98, 205, 264, 281 do not relate to the see of Canterbury.

[8] 31, 37, 38, 264, 268, cf. A in supplement.

[9] 21, 34–6, 40, 46, 81, 99, 107, 114, 122, 123, 150, 154, 157, 162–5, 194, 203, 204, 209, 250.

[10] 107, 114 and 250; 21 and 194; 164 and 165; 123, 150, 203, 204, 209 show great similarity and some may be by identical hands; also 36, 40, 46, 81, 122, 154 and 162.

[11] 1, 28, 43, 152, 161, 183, 196, 252.

copied with more or less fidelity, which appears in several charters.[1] The 'papal' charters are all after 1150. It does not seem possible to fix any date at which a change was made from book-hand to charter-hand, but it can be said that the latter type was predominant after 1150.[2]

3. *Seals and other marks of authentication*

No original charter of Theobald contained in this collection is authenticated by a cross.[3] The cross appears in two copies.[4] Theobald also witnesses a charter of Stephen in this traditional manner.[5]

The following are Birch's descriptions of the seals appended to Theobald's charters:

1. Theobald's usual seal: about $3\frac{1}{4}''$ by $2\frac{1}{4}''$. Pointed oval, the archbishop full length in vestments lifting up the right hand in benediction, in the left hand a pastoral staff curved outwards, standing on a corbel. Legend:

SIGILLŪ : TEOBALDI : DEI : GRATIA :

ARCHIEPISCOPI : CANTUARIENSIS

2. Theobald's counterseal: a small oval counterseal with mark of handle at top, $1\frac{3}{4}''$ by $1''$. A bearded bust in profile to the right, the hair filleted, from a finely engraved intaglio gem.[6] The letters of the legend:

SIGNUM SECRETUM

are arranged to read towards the outside contrary to usual method.

3. Theobald's counterseal reset: The gem in the counterseal reset in a rim to read inwards according to the usual manner:

SIGNUM SECRETUM.[7]

4. First seal of Christ Church, Canterbury: about $1\frac{7}{8}''$ diameter

---

[1] 39, 45, 72, 213; 160 is extreme; 102, 197 and 275 are more moderate.
[2] Cf. 98 and 99 almost identical charters to Ely, one before 1150 and one after. Also charters to Ramsey 205 and 209.
[3] But cf. A in supplement to which Theobald's seal is appended.
[4] 188 and E.
[5] Westminster Abbey Muniments 33.
[6] The head is said to be of Jupiter, J. H. Bloom, *English Seals* (1906), p. 11.
[7] W. Birch, *Catalogue of Seals in the British Museum* (1887), i, 158.

Q

circle, the Cathedral with porch, side turrets, tiled roof and centre tower. Legend on a raised rim:

SIGILLUM ECCLESIAE CRISTI.

The matrix of this seal may be of the eleventh century.

5. Second seal of Christ Church, Canterbury: Circular, diameter $3\frac{3}{8}''$. The Cathedral from the South carefully detailed, etc. Legend on a raised rim:

SIGILLUM . ECC'E . XP̄I . CANTUARIE .

PRIME . SEDIS . BRITTANIE:

(Used until the beginning of the fifteenth century.)[1]

In this collection there are altogether thirty-five specimens of Theobald's seal, as described above.[2] In addition sixteen charters, none of which can be dated before 1150, have the counterseal.[3] Of these three have the legend reading outwards.[4] The most normal colour of the wax is red, but brown, yellow, white and green are also found.[5] The first seal of Christ Church is found in two charters issued in the name of Theobald and the Priory.[6] It also appears together with Theobald's seal on both parts of a chirograph between the Priory and their tenant, Godfrey of Malling, embodying an agreement concluded in the archbishop's 'camera'.[7] The second seal is found together with Theobald's in a charter issued in the name of Theobald alone, but possibly the conventual seal was added to show the consent of the Priory to this ordinance.[8] A charter issued in Theobald's name had the seals of three bishops as well as his own, but they are now missing.[9]

The seals are attached to the charters by different methods. Perhaps the most interesting of these is where the seal is found on a strip projecting from the left side of the charter, a device which seems to have been popular at Canterbury at the time.[10] As might be expected these are all Canterbury charters.

[1] Ibid., i, 190.

[2] 21, 24, 28, 31, 35, 36, 38, 40–5, 72, 81, 99, 122, 137, 161, 162, 168, 170, 177, 183, 187, 190, 194–7, 209, 213, 264, and A twice.

[3] 28, 31, 35, 36, 40, 45, 72, 81, 99, 122, 137, 187, 195–7, 209; 46 had a counterseal in 1804.   [4] 45, 72, 99.

[5] Brown: 28, 35, 42, 43; yellow: 168, 177, 209; white: 213; green: 81.

[6] 33, 268.   [7] A.   [8] 31.   [9] 241.

[10] Theobald: 38, 44, 268, A; Ch. Ch.: 33, A; 32 seal missing.

The Development of the Inspeximus Charter

It can be said that by the time of Theobald the idea of the Inspeximus charter had been evolved, but it was only partially put into use, nor had its form been fixed. Very often in confirmation charters of Theobald, the confirmation of a bishop or the charter of the donor would be alluded to, and its substance incorporated. The reference was generally introduced by some such form as 'sicut carta N. testatur'.[1] More rarely appears the clause 'quam oculis nostris conspeximus'[2] and only once the formula 'Inspeximus cartam'.[3] The wording of the charters confirmed is sometimes reproduced with considerable fidelity,[4] in one case even including the harangue without acknowledgment.[5]

There are six charters which deserve further consideration. There are two cases where a charter was sent to Theobald to be confirmed and where, instead of a new confirmation charter being written out, the confirmation of Theobald was added to the original charter, which was then sent back.[6] A rather incongruous effect is produced by Theobald's long confirmation charter to Gloucester Abbey.[7] In the year 1138, Stephen issued a comprehensive charter of confirmation to Gloucester Abbey. Subsequently Gilbert Foliot, who had meanwhile become abbot of Gloucester, asked Bishop Simon of Worcester, his diocesan, to inspect the charters of the Abbey, which he did. Convinced of the accuracy of Stephen's charter, which embodied the substance of the charters he had inspected, Simon sent it to Theobald with an accompanying letter asking the archbishop to confirm it. Thereupon Stephen's charter was copied out, and an introduction and a short conclusion were added in Theobald's name, alluding to the charters of Gloucester but not mentioning Stephen's charter which was copied practically word for word. The result is that Theobald speaks of the gifts of his 'royal predecessors' and of his gelds and also seems to have acquired

---

[1] Very common, cf. 5, 7, 21, 24, 72, 81, 123, 127, etc.
[2] 7, 194, 195, 199, 245, 275. [3] 270; 126 has ' testimonium . . . inspeximus'.
[4] 123, 157 Alexander, 197 Prof. Stenton notes that Theobald's scribe altered the Danelaw 'villa' to the Southern 'manerium'.
[5] 194, 195. [6] 68, E. [7] 111.

extensive rights and properties in a somewhat remote district. On the other hand 'our venerable brother, Robert bishop of Hereford', sounds better coming from Theobald than from Stephen.

The two lengthy confirmation charters to the priory of Stoke-by-Clare, the second of which runs to well over 2,000 words, and must have been a fine sight in the original, have some points in common with the Gloucester charter.[1] Theobald must have had at his disposal fifty or sixty of the priory's charters, unless the documents were prepared by the monks themselves. The first charter gives an elaborate list of all the donors and their grants, ranging from the founder, Gilbert of Clare, to his third generation, and then cataloguing the grants of about fifty people. The second charter covers much the same ground, although there are several omissions and additions. The form of the charter is, however, significantly different. The substance of fifty charters is reproduced and in addition the witnesses to every charter are given. Except that the text of the charters is not given in full, this can be regarded as a most elaborate form of Inspeximus.

Finally there is Theobald's inspection of the charter of Gundulf, bishop of Rochester which he had 'seen, read and touched with his own hands at his full synod at Canterbury', in 1145, and 'after a diligent investigation and examination both as to the writing and as to the seal, had found it completely lacking in blemish or fault'—in fact 'in all parts sound and undamaged'. The charter of Gundulf is then recited in full. After Gundulf's charter, Theobald's confirmation follows with a provision 'that at such time when it might happen that the letter of the same bishop should perish by reason of age or for any other cause, this writing of our testimony may always suffice as if the original itself had been exhibited'.[2] Although this remarkable charter was executed so early in Theobald's career, no other examples of a genuine Inspeximus like this seem to have survived, if indeed they were ever issued. This form was probably regarded as being no better than the others cited previously, and was not to become popular till the end of the century. Its importance at the time should not be over-estimated.

[1] 255, 256.   [2] 222.

Theobald's Chancery

The general impression one seems to obtain from a study of Theobald's charters is that his chancery was a somewhat easy-going and amateurish organisation. While it may be true that bureaucracy and efficiency are not always synonymous, a little more regularity of form would inspire more confidence in Theobald's chancery, if at the same time it would detract from the intrinsic interest which the charters command. It may even be doubted whether there was an organised chancery during the first ten years or so of Theobald's archiepiscopate. The task of drafting and writing charters may well have been a sideline of the numerous clerks and chaplains in Theobald's household. Still there must have been someone in charge of the archbishop's seal. These clerks or one of them must take the responsibility for that monstrous charter to Gloucester Abbey discussed above, but at the same time they must claim the credit for the brilliant effort of the Inspeximus of 1145, a precedent which fell on stony soil. The disruption caused by the war, especially from 1141 to 1143, and possibly Theobald's misfortunes in 1148, ought to be mentioned here.

From 1149 onwards things seemed to be approaching a more settled condition and simultaneously, as has been shown above, there appears to be a definite increase in the output of charters, and a greater regularity of form. Peter Scriptor appears in 1149 and Philip the chancellor shortly afterwards. Together with John of Salisbury and other clerks, a definite chancery organisation would appear to have been built up. Philip witnesses seventeen charters, the earliest of which can be dated 1150–1152.[1] It would appear that it was not essential for the chancellor to attest Theobald's charters. Philip was given preferment probably in 1157:[2] he was made archdeacon of Norwich. This might well indicate the importance of the archiepiscopal chancellor, when it is remembered that the accomplished John of Salisbury languished in a subordinate, if confidential, position for so many years. Philip was also appointed one of the executors

---

[1] 124, 145; see also witness list.
[2] *Suffolk Inst. of Arch. and Nat. Hist.*, 1930, pp. 14–15.

of Theobald's will.[1] A certain Elinandus appears as chancellor in a charter which can be dated 1154.[2] This falls within the period of Philip's chancellorship and it is very questionable whether he was Theobald's chancellor at all. In the witness list he occupies a low position in marked contrast to Philip. Nor was he necessarily a member of Theobald's household. The corrupt witness list reads 'Elinandus cancellarius, Ricardus de Clare de Gloucestre, monachi et capellani archiepiscopi'. It should be emended to read 'Elinandus cancellarius, Ricardus de Clare, Walterus de Gloucestre monachi et capellani archiepiscopi' which makes some difference to Elinand's position. It is interesting that the name Elinand appears three times in Theobald's charters and all three are curiously linked together. In this same charter a sheriff Elinand appears, who must have been dead for several years. In another charter is found Elinand, monk of Bec, who was acting as proctor for that monastery.[3] Elinand the chancellor is a witness to the charter confirming the possessions of Stoke-by-Clare which was a priory of Bec.

There was, however, only one 'scribe' who was given that appellation. Peter Scriptor witnesses fifteen charters, two of which can be dated as early as 1149.[4] Philip witnesses six charters without Peter[5] and Peter witnesses four charters without Philip[6] so they were by no means inseparable even allowing for the excisions of the copyists. Like Philip, Peter was also provided for by Theobald, although more modestly as befitted his inferior position. The archbishop requested the monks of Canterbury to grant him an income, which they did.[7] It appears from the request of Theobald and the reply of Prior Wibert that Peter was also serving the priory in a clerical capacity, although with one exception[8] he does not appear as a witness in any of the surviving priory charters. It is unlikely that Peter wrote any of the charters himself despite his surname, as he was clearly a man of some importance. It is much more probable that he drafted the charters and supervised the copying activities of his sub-

---

[1] 28.   [2] 255.   [3] 177.   [4] 57, H2.
[5] 83 and 84 original, 145, 153, 176, 239, 240.   [6] 57, 77, 176, H2.
[7] 40, both charters appear to be written in the same hand. A Peter Scriptor witnesses a charter to Nuneaton (c. 1155–60) B.M. Additional Charters 47599.
[8] A., a special case anyway.

dat quieti providere et quę eis in domino collata sunt beneficia
nostrę auctoritatis patrocinio confirmare et confirmata inviolabiliter conservare. Inde est quod omnia beneficia ęcclesię
apostolorum Petri et Pauli Bathoniensi juste et canonice a
quibuscumque fidelibus collata sive ęcclesiastica sive mundana
et ab episcopo ejusdem loci Rodberto confirmata ipsi ęcclesię
et fratribus in ea Christo militantibus in perpetuum possidenda
confirmamus et presentis scripti nostri testimonio communimus.
Ipsas autem possessiones quas in presentiarum possident propriis dignum duximus exprimere nominibus, videlicet [p. 121] v
hidas in Westona, villam de Cumba, et plenariam decimam de
Batha et Lincumba et decima vineę de Lincumba, capellas
monachorum tam Bathon' quam alibi sitas, ęcclesiam quoque
de Forda, ęcclesiam de Estona, et terram etiam de Suđstocha,
et molendinum juxta virgultum episcopi, et salinarum episcopi
xx summas salis singulis annis, duas virgatas terre unam apud
Cerdram alteram apud Evercriz. Hęc ergo omnia cum cęteris
omnibus quę legitime adquisiverunt vel futuris adipisci temporibus rationabilibus modis poterint, in pace et summa libertate possidenda concedimus sicut venerabilis frater noster Rodbertus Bathon' episcopus eis concessit et carta sua confirmavit
sicut carta ipsius testatur. Valete.

DATE: 1150–61.
PRINTED: W. Hunt, *Somerset Record Society* (1893), p. 59.

7

Confirmation by Theobald of those possessions confirmed to Bath
Priory by Bishop Robert on the occasion of his dedication of the
altar of Holy Trinity and also of grants confirmed to them by
William, bishop of Exeter (1107–37).

MS. Corpus Christi College Cambridge, 111, p. 121 (Cartulary of
Bath).

> Carta Teodbaldi archiepiscopi: confirmacio ecclesie
> de Bantona.

TEODBALDUS dei gratia Cantuariensis archiepiscopus et totius
Brittannię primas omnibus sanctę matris ęcclesię filiis tam

clericis quam laicis tam presentibus quam futuris salutem.
Noverit universitas vestra quoniam priori et monachis Bathoniensis ęcclesię concedimus et confirmamus omnes terras et
capellarum donationes aliasque possessiones quas venerabilis
frater noster Rodbertus Bathon' episcopus in dedicatione altaris
sanctę Trinitatis eis dedit aut ab aliis prius datas confirmavit,
sicut confirmationis suę carta quam oculis nostris conspeximus
testatur. Confirmamus quoque eis ęcclesiam de Baentona cum
capellis et omnibus eis adjacentibus, videlicet de Petetona, de
Donningestona, de Deopeforda, de Lasela, et dimidium decimę
de Kari de donatione Rodberti de Baentonia, ęcclesiam quoque
de Broctona, et v virgatas terrę in Foxcumba de donatione
Girardi dapiferi Walteri patris Rodberti, sicut venerabilis frater
noster Willelmus Exoniensis episcopus eis illas concessit et carta
sua confirmavit. Iccirco volumus et precipimus ut predictę
ęcclesię monachi predictas possessiones in perpetua pace et
quiete possideant et habeant, et ne quis eas inquietare, vel eis
molestiam vel injuriam aliquam irrogare presumat sub anathemate interdicimus. Valete.

DATE: 1139–61.

PRINTED: W. Hunt, *Somerset Record Society* (1893), p. 60, and the charter of
Robert of Bath on p. 58 and of Wm. of Exeter on p. 39.

8

Confirmation by Theobald of grants made to Bath Priory by the
lords of the honour of Dunster (Somerset) and confirmed by St.
Anselm (1093–1109) and William II.

MS. Corpus Christi College Cambridge, 111, p. 122 (Cartulary of
Bath).

De Dunestorra.

TEODBALDUS dei gratia Cantuariensis archiepiscopus Anglorum
primas et apostolice sedis legatus omnibus sanctę matris ęcclesię
fidelibus per episcopatum Bathoniensem constitutis salutem.
Ea quę a venerabilibus fratribus nostris episcopis seu principibus
ęcclesiis et locis religiosis in elemosinam misericordię intuitu

conferuntur, ut eisdem locis inconvulsa et inmutilata perseverent merito sunt auctoritatis nostrę munimine roboranda. Ea
igitur ratione inducti, inspectis etiam cartis dominorum fundi
et honoris de Dunestorra et confirmatione sanctę memorię
Anselmi Cantuariensis archiepiscopi et illustris regis Anglorum
Willelmi Ruffi, quę ęcclesiam de Dunestorra cum omnibus ad
eam pertinentibus terris decimis et capellis, in liberam elemosinam monachis Bathoniensibus esse concessam et datam astrue-
bant, eisdem monachis confirmamus ęcclesiam prenominatam
cum terris et decimationibus de Karentona et Stochelanda et
Kelvetona et Avelhamme et Stantona et dimidiam decimam
Menehafe et dimidiam decimam Exeforde et cęteris eis jure
adjacentibus, et presentis scripti patrocinio corroboramus.
Auctoritate itaque qua fungimur inhibemus ne quis ęcclesiam
Bathoniensem vel monachos in ea jugem deo famulatum exhi-
bentes, super ęcclesia de Dunestorra que eis in liberam elemosinam auctoritate sancti Anselmi Cantuariensis archiepiscopi
confirmata est et regiis cartis corroborata temere presumat
inquietare vel ullam attemptet inferre molestiam. Quod si quis
attemtaverit injuste, dei omnipotentis indignationem et nostram
se noverit incursurum. Valete.

DATE: 1150–61.
PRINTED: W. Hunt, *Somerset Record Society* (1893), p. 61.

9

Grant by Theobald of twenty days indulgence to those visiting **Bath
Priory** on the occasion of 'exaltatio sancte crucis' (September 14).

MS. Corpus Christi College Cambridge, 111, p. 54 (Cartulary of
Bath).

[T]EDODBALDUS dei gratia Cantuariensis archiepiscopus et
Anglorum primas universis sancte matris ęcclesię filiis salutem.
Eis debet dominice crucis maxime prodesse misterium qui
sinceriori devotione ipsius venerantur honorem et in statutis
solempnitatibus ad consequendam veniam peccatorum a salva-

R

tore crucifixo conveniunt. Ea propter de divina confisi misericordia omnibus qui in exaltatione sancte crucis Bathoniensem
ęcclesiam fideli devotione visitaverint, peccatorum de quibus
corde contrito confessi sunt, viginti dierum indulgentiam facimus et omnium orationum et beneficiorum ecclesię Cantuariensis participes eos constituimus. Valete.

DATE: 1139–61.
PRINTED: W. Hunt, *Somerset Record Society* (1893), p. 2.

10

Notification by Theobald of his decision in the dispute between the
abbot of Battle (Walter, 1139–71) (Ben. Sussex) and William, clerk
of Hythe (Kent) over the tithes of Dengemarsh (Kent). The abbot
is to have the tithe of his demesne and the rest is to go to the parish
priest.

MS. Lincoln's Inn Hale 87 f.26a (Cartulary of Battle Abbey).

T. DEI gratia Cantuariensis archiepiscopus tocius Anglie primas
apostolice sedis legatus universis sancte matris ecclesie filiis
salutem. Sciatis quod coram me definitum est et constitutum
inter Walterum abbatem de Bello et Willelmum clericum de
Hyda, quod presbiter illius loci de terra abbatis de Bello de
Dengemareys de hominibus scilicet illius terre habebit decimam
sicut de parochianis suis. Decimam vero de dominico abbatis
ecclesia de Bello absque omni calumpnia habebit sicut semper
habuit. Quod ego episcopali auctoritate concedo et hoc presenti
scripto confirmo. Test' Rogero archidiacono Cant', Johanne
clerico filio Marie, [Johanne de Saresburia, magistro Vaccario,
Johanne de Tileburia, Reginaldo Apostolico, Osberto Bonitas]
et aliis multis.

The additional witnesses are supplied from a 15th c. notarial instrument,
   MS. P.R.O. Exchequer K.R. Ecclesiastical Documents 15/4 (E. 135 15/4).
   There are no other variations.

DATE: 1150–54.

II

Notification by Theobald of the decision in the court of Henry II at Colchester (Essex) in his presence, also of Roger archbishop of York (1154–81) and others in the dispute between Bishop Hilary of Chichester (1147–69) and Walter abbot of Battle. Battle Abbey is to be entirely exempt from episcopal control.

MS. Lincoln's Inn Hale 87 f.25a (Cartulary of Battle).

Arbitrium Theobaldi archiepiscopi inter ecclesiam de B[ello] et episcopum Cicestr' Hylarium.

THEOBALDUS Cantuariensis archiepiscopus totius Anglie primas et apostolice sedis legatus universis sancte matris ecclesie filiis salutem. Notum vobis facio fratres karissimi quod coram domino nostro H[enrico] rege me presente et archiepiscopo Ebor' Rogero et aliis quampluribus coepiscopis et abbatibus et populi multitudine apud Colecestre, discordia que erat inter venerabilem Hylarium Cic' episcopum et W[alterum] abbatem de Bello de dignitatibus et libertatibus ecclesiarum suarum ad pacis concordiam perducta sit et hoc modo: episcopus Cic' Hylarius cartarum auctoritate ecclesie de Bello simulque ratione cogente, nobis omnibus audientibus, ecclesiam de Bello et abbatem cum leuga circumjacente ab omni subjectione et exactione Cic' ecclesie et episcopi quietam proclamavit et liberam, neque hospitari quasi ex consuetudine in eadem abbatia vel in maneriis eidem ecclesie pertinentibus, nec quicquam disponere vel quelibet ibi prosequi episcopalia, neque ibidem ordines facere, nec cathedram collocare, preter licenciam abbatis et monachorum se posse vel debere, protestatus est. Quod ego etiam ut in perpetuum firmum sit et ratum auctoritate episcopali et sicut sancte Romane ecclesie lelegatus [*sic*] presenti scripto confirmo. Teste Rogero Ebor' archiepiscopo, Ricardo London', Ricardo[1] [*sic*] Lincoln', Thoma regis cancellario et aliis.

ALSO: in an abridged transcript, MS. B.M. Additional 5706 f.25b (Sussex Collections).

DATE: 1157.

PRINTED: (from this transcript) *Chron. Monast. de Bello*, Anglia Christiana Society, Appendix vi, p. 188.

[1] The bishop of Lincoln was actually named Robert.

12

Mandate of Theobald to Bishop William of Norwich (1146–74). The bishop must complete his task of restoring to Battle Abbey the churches and revenues of which it had been deprived and do justice on recalcitrants in his diocese.

MS. Bodleian Norfolk Rolls 81, no. 9 (Roll of St. Benet's Holme).

Teotb' dei gratia Cantuariensis archiepiscopus Anglorum primas apostolice sedis legatus venerabili fratri et amico W[illelmo] Norw' episcopo salutem. Meminimus vobis scripsisse ut dilecto filio nostro [Waltero][1] abbati ecclesie de Bello justiciam exhiberetis de his qui ecclesias suas cum pertinentiis suis in vestra parrochia occupare presumebant et redditus ecclesie sue assignatos persolvere contempnebant. Quia igitur quedam adhuc restant quę desideramus justicie ipsius adimpleri sicut de ecclesia de Middelhala, presentium auctoritate vobis mandamus quatinus ei justiciam ecclesiasticam ita inde exhibeatis saltem usque ad nostrum reditum ut vestro labore quę sui juris sunt in illa ecclesia se accepisse gaudeat. Alioquin quęrimoniam super illa ecclesia motam cum dei dispositione redierimus, sub nostra presentia fine canonico terminari faciemus. Valete.

Date: 1150–59.

13

Confirmation by Theobald archbishop, primate and legate of the gift of William Ursel of Crasmesnil of land in Denton and men on it, in accordance with charter of Stephen, illustrious king of the English.

MS. Duke of Rutland, Belvoir Castle, Belvoir Cartulary f.55a (not accessible).

Date: 1150–61.

Calendared: J. H. Round, *H.M.C.*, *Various Collections*, iv, Duke of Rutland, p. 134.

[1] MS. has N. for the name of the abbot.

14

Notification by T[heobald] archbishop, primate and legate that it has been thus settled concerning the church of Horningwold, between the monks of Belvoir and Gilbert the clerk, in the presence of himself and of his brethren Hilary bishop of Chichester and R[obert] bishop of Lincoln in the Council of London. Gilbert is to hold the church for life paying the monks a mark yearly, and after his death the monks are to hold the church at their own use, at the disposition of the prior.

MS. Duke of Rutland, Belvoir Castle, Belvoir Cartulary f.58b (not accessible).

DATE: 1151–61.

CALENDARED: J. H. Round, *H.M.C.*, *Various Collections*, iv, Duke of Rutland, p. 137.

15

Precept of Theobald archbishop, primate and legate addressed to R[obert] bishop of Lincoln. As Geoffrey de Normanvilla, who had appealed to him in his case against the monks of Belvoir for the church of Horningwald neither appeared on the day of [hearing] the appeal, nor sent excuse for his absence, while the monks appeared with deeds and witnesses, they are to hold that church in peace, and be no more impleaded therein.

MS. Duke of Rutland, Belvoir Castle, Belvoir Cartulary f.58b (not accessible).

DATE: 1150–61.

CALENDARED: J. H. Round, *H.M.C.*, *Various Collections*, iv, Duke of Rutland, p. 137.

16

Notification by Thomas [*sic*] archbishop and legate and Richard bishop of London concerning the dispute between the monks of Belvoir and of Thetford for the tithes of the demesnes in four parishes which has been referred to them by Pope Alexander [*sic*] IV. It has been agreed in their presence that the monks of Belvoir shall have two-thirds of the tithes from the demesnes of Bradelei and Jokesford, and the monks of Thetford the same from Melna; and they should divide equally those from Selham if they can be acquired.

Testes sunt: Robertus Lincolniensis, Robertus Excestrensis, Walterus Cestrensis } episcopi,
Gervasius Westmonasterii, Willelmus de Burgo } abbates isti,
Henricus de Huntingdon, Radulfus Londoniensis ecclesie, David de Buccingeham, Jordanus Saleberiensis } isti sunt archidiaconi

Magister Johannes Saresberiensis, magister Johannes de Tillebiria, Rogerius Species, Gwillelmus de Albenia brito, Rogerius frater ejus.

MS. Duke of Rutland, Belvoir Castle, Belvoir Cartulary f.88b (not accessible).

DATE: 1156–57.

CALENDARED: J. H. Round, *H.M.C.*, *Various Collections*, iv, Duke of Rutland, p. 159.

For Mandate of Pope Adrian IV delegating jurisdiction see Holtzmann, i, 305.

17

Confirmation by Theobald of the grant to Bermondsey Priory (Clu. Surrey) by Richard son of Osbert of tithes at Melcombe (Dorset).

MS. B.M. Harleian 231 f.17a (Annals of Bermondsey).

ET HOC anno [1150] Ricardus filius Osberti dedit monachis de Bermundeseie decimas, scilicet ii partes decimarum de pecoribus et bladis in Melcumbe, et Theobaldus Cantuariensis archiepiscopus confirmavit.

PRINTED: *Ann. Mon.*, iii, 438.

18

Confirmation by Theobald of the grant to Bermondsey Priory by William son of Henry of Eltham of tithes at (North) Woolwich (Kent).

MS. B.M. Harleian 231 f.17b (Annals of Bermondsey).

Et /[f.18a] hoc anno [1155] Willelmus filius Henrici de Eltham dedit monachis de Bermundeseye decimas de Wiklondes in parochia de Wolwich', et Theobaldus Cantuariensis archiepiscopus confirmavit.

PRINTED: *Ann. Mon.*, iii, 439.

19

Confirmation by Theobald of the grant to Bermondsey Priory by Raynold de Tannay of the church of Bengeo (Herts).

MS. B.M. Harleian 231 f.18a (Annals of Bermondsey).

ET EODEM anno [1156] Raynoldus de Tannay dedit monachis de Bermundeseye ecclesiam de Bengehoo, et Theobaldus archiepiscopus Cantuariensis ac Robertus Lincoln' episcopus confirmaverunt.

PRINTED: *Ann. Mon.*, iii, 439.

20

Mandate of Theobald to (Richard) bishop of London and William bishop of Norwich (1146–74). They should compel Richard de Calva and Geoffrey Tresgot to restore the land of Barney (Norf.) to R. the abbot and the monks of St. Albans, which they were continuing to occupy notwithstanding their agreement before Theobald to vacate it. Barney belonged to Binham Priory (Norf. dep. of St. Albans).

MS. B.M. Cott. Claud. D xiii f.51b. (Register of Binham.)

Littere Theobaldi Cantuariensis archiepiscopi de terra de Berneye.

THEOBALDUS dei gratia Cantuariensis archiepiscopus Anglorum primas apostolice sedis legatus venerabilibus fratribus Arch' [*sic*] London' et W[illelmo] Norw' episcopis salutem. Quando hiis qui sub habitu regulari divinis inminent famulatibus jura sua illicite subtrahuntur, tanto nobis major cura debet existere ut quod sui juris est nostra sollicitudine interveniente /[f.52a] recuperent quanto suo inhibente proposito minus possunt operam contencionibus adhibere. Ex parte filiorum nostrorum R. abbatis et monachorum sancti Albani adversus Ricardum de Calva et Gaufridum Tresgot querelam accepimus quod transaccionem que sub nostra presencia super terra de Bern[eye] inter eos et confirmata fuit [*sic*], stare contempnunt et ipsam terram quam ex dono Walteri de Valoniis in perpetuam elemosinam possidere deberent eis retrahunt et auferre presumunt. Quia igitur omnibus et maxime viris ecclesiasticis in sua justicia debitores existimus, presencium significacione vobis mandantes precipimus quatinus eos districte conveniatis et ideo moneatis ut transaccionem illam diligenter observent et terram predicti manerii eos in pace sicut ante nos eis pepigerunt possidere permittant. Quod si infra viii dies post presencium suscepcionem vestris admonicionibus minime obtemperaverint in eos anathematis et in omnes terras eorum que sub vestra jurisdiccione sunt interdicti sentenciam profatis. Valete.

DATE: 1152–61.

The charter of Geoffrey Tresgot recognising the agreement concluded in Theobald's presence is on f. 51a. Cf. also F. M. Stenton, *English Feudalism* (1932), pp. 37–9.

21

Confirmation by Theobald of the possessions of Biddlesden Abbey (Cist. Bucks.) under Abbot Richard, in accordance with the charter of Robert II, bishop of Lincoln (1148–66).

Original   MS. B.M. Harleian Charters 84 C41.

T. DEI gratia Cantuariensis archiepiscopus et totius Anglie primas universis sancte ecclesie fidelibus salutem. Noverint tam presentes quam futuri quoniam Ricardo abbati Sancte Marie de Bettesdena et fratribus suis monachicam vitam professis necnon et successoribus eorum regulariter victuris in perpetuum confirmamus et presentis scripti testimonio communimus ecclesiam ipsam Sancte Marie de Bettesdena cum omnibus que canonice et juste possident aut rationabiliter in futurum adipisci poterunt, sicut venerabilis frater noster R[obertus] Lincol' episcopus eis concessit et scripto suo confirmavit. Valete.

ENDORSEMENT: Confirmacio Theobaldi archiepiscopi Cantuariensis de Bitlesden.

SEAL: usual (most of legend chipped off).

SIZE: 1·6 in. × 9·2 in.

DATE: 1148–61.

22

Confirmation by Theobald of the possessions of Bruton Priory (Aug. Somerset) in accordance with the charters of Bishop Robert of Bath (1136–66) and others.

MS. P.R.O. Transcripts Record Commission ii vol.140b part iii p. 335 (Trans. 8/140b/3). From a roll in archives of Calvados containing Inspeximus of Jocelin, bishop of Bath (1206–42).

THOMAS [*sic*] dei gratia Cantuariensis archiepiscopus Anglorum primas et apostolice sedis legatus universis sancte matris ecclesie filiis salutem. Ad pastoris spectat sollicitudinem omnium quieti eorum maxime quos religionis nomen commendat per omnia providere et que illis in domino collata sunt beneficia auctoritatis sue testimonio confirmare. Inde est quod fratribus religiosis canonicis regularibus de Briweton' locum ipsum in quo divino mancipati sunt obsequio cum omnibus possessionibus suis tam ecclesiasticis quam mundanis quas juste et canonice possideant vel quas futuris temporibus rationabilibus modis poterint adipisci concedimus et litterarum nostrarum munimine confirmamus. Eas autem quas inpresentiarum possident possessiones propriis dignum exprimere nominibus, videlicet ecclesiam de Briwetona cum omnibus ei adjacentibus, terram etiam quam Willelmus de Moyon habuit in eadem villa cum hominibus et omnibus aliis rebus quas ibi habuit sicut carta donationis ejus testatur, de ejusdem dono terram de Briwenham, ecclesiam quoque de Lokesberg' a venerabili fratre nostro Roberto Bathoniensi episcopo eis confirmatam, terras etiam de parrochia Briweton' de donatione Alexandri de Cantelu et Henrici de Carevilla, virgatam quoque terre de dono Wandregisili de Curcella et Rogeri de Grantona, duas etiam partes decime de Pidecumba et Dichenescova de donatione Gaufridi de Kari et de ejusdem Gaufridi dono unam virgatam terre apud Dichenescova et aliam virgatam apud Hunewicam. Hec omnia igitur eisdem fratribus possidenda in perpetuum confirmamus sicut carte Bathoniensis episcopi et aliorum benefactorum suorum scripta testantur. Valete.

DATE: 1150–61.

CALENDARED: *C.D.F.*, p. 173. Round is almost certainly correct in ascribing this charter to Theobald, even though Thomas became legate four months before the death of Robert of Bath in August 1166.

23

Confirmation by Theobald to Burton Abbey (Ben. Staffs.) of the exemption of Burton parish church from diocesan jurisdiction in accordance with the charter of Bishop Robert of Chester (1086–1117).

Original (not consulted)   MS. Anglesey Burton Charters.

THEODBALDUS dei gratia Cantuariensis archiepiscopus Anglorum primas et apostolice sedis legatus universis sancte matris ecclesie fidelibus salutem. Pravas consuetudines ab ecclesia dei penitus extirpare et utiles inducere et antiquitus habitas libertates illesas perpetuo conservare sicut nostre principaliter incumbit sollicitudini ita spectat omnium bonorum devocioni. Inde est quod auctoritate qua fungimur confirmamus matri ecclesie Burton' libertatem omnem quam ecclesia ipsa antiquiter habuit et quam bone memorie Robertus Cestrensis episcopus carta sua ei concessit. Id est ut non reddat ullam consuetudinem pro crismate vel oleo sancto neque pro aliqua alia re parrochiali de parrochia Burton'. Nec mittat hominem nec feminam ad capitula vel ad synodos set teneat rectum in curia sua et habeat curiam suam in omni causa quamdiu justicia non defuerit. Capellanus quoque ejusdem ecclesie nullam solvat consuetudinem vel exactionem archidiacono Stafford' aut ministerialibus ejus sicut nullam solvere consuevit et sicut Rogerus Cestrensis episcopus non solvendam scripto suo constituit. Prohibemus itaque sub anathemate ne quis hanc libertatem predicte ecclesie presumat infringere aut aliquatenus diminuere. Valete.

DATE: 1150–61.

CALENDARED: the original was calendared by I. H. Jeayes, *Stafford Rec. Soc.* (1937), p. 11, and its SEAL is missing.

COPY: MS. B.M. Burton Cartulary f.23a (deposited by the Marquess of Anglesey).

PRINTED: (Inspeximus) K. Major, *Acta Stephani Langton* (1950, Canterbury and York Soc.), p. 26.

24

Confirmation by Theobald to Turstin priest of Bristol of the church of St. Owen's Bristol granted to him in alms by Robert earl of Gloucester (1122–47) and in accordance with the charter of Simon, bishop of Worcester (1125–50).

Original   MS. Bristol Library no. 173.

T. DEI gratia Cantuariensis archiepiscopus et Anglorum primas omnibus sancte matris ecclesie fidelibus salutem. Sciatis nos Turstino sacerdoti de Bristold' ecclesiam sancti Audoeni de Bristold' cum omnibus appendiciis ejus, quam R[obertus] comes

Gloec' ei in elemosinam dederat, concessisse et presentis scripti nostri munimine confirmasse, sicut venerabilis frater noster Simon Wigornensis episcopus ei illam concessit et carta sua confirmavit, precipientes ut bene et libere et quiete teneat, hoc addentes et omnimodo interdicentes ne aliquis decetero ecclesiam predictam inquietare aut ejus bona que canonice possidet minuere aut aliqua vexatione temere infestare presumat. Quod si quis presumpserit anathematis vinculo innodatus donec condigne satisfecerit firmiter teneatur. Valete.

SEAL: usual.

SIZE: 3 in. × 7 in.

DATE: 1139–50.

PRINTED: (with facsimile and translation), *Clifton Antiquarian Club*, vii, 83, also W. G. Birch in *British Arch. Assoc.* (1875), p. 290.

25

Confirmation by Theobald notified to Bishop Everard of Norwich (1121–46) of the quit-claim by King Stephen to the abbey of Bury St. Edmund's (Ben. Suff.) and Abbot Anselm (1121–48) of 40 knights' castle-guard at Norwich.

MS. Cambridge U.L. Mm.iv.19 f.106a (Reg. of Bury St. Edmund's).

T. archiepiscopus confirmat sancto Edmundo wardam a Stephano rege donatam.

TEDOALDUS dei gratia archiepiscopus Everardo eadem gratia Norwicensi episcopo et omnibus aliis Anglie episcopis et baronibus Francis et Anglis salutem. Donationem /[f.106b] illam de warda, scilicet xl militum apud castellum de Norwic quam illustris rex Stephanus quietam clamavit beato Ædmundo et abbati Anselmo omnibusque successoribus suis imperpetuum et super altare ejusdem martyris optulit pro se et regina et filiis suis quoque pro animabus omnium antecessorum suorum, auctoritate nobis a deo collata omnimodo confirmo et presentis nostri scripti pagina munio atque corroboro. Conservantibus hec gratia eterna a deo perveniat, impedientibus vero ultio divina nisi resipuerint immineat. Amen.

DATE: 1139–45.

PRINTED: D. C. Douglas, *Feudal Documents from Bury St. Edmund's* (British Academy Records of Social and Economic History, vol. viii), p. 160.

26

Mandate of Theobald to archdeacons and rural deans to carry out his sentence of excommunication on those interfering with pilgrims to Bury St. Edmund's.

MS. Cambridge U.L. Mm.iv.19 f.106b (Reg. of Bury St. Edmund's).

Quod anathematizati sunt qui violentam manum mittunt in peregrinos sancti Ædmundi.

T.[1] gratia Cantuariensis archiepiscopus et tocius Anglie primas omnibus archidiaconis et decanis ad quoscumque littere iste pervenerint salutem. Notum facimus universitati vestre quoniam omnes orationis causa ecclesiam sancti Ædmundi visitantes in protectione dei et sancte ecclesie et nostra suscipimus et omnes qui in eos euntes illuc aut inde redeuntes manum violentam extenderint anathematis sententia dampnavimus. Vobis quoque idem facere in parrochiis /[f.107a] vestris presentibus litteris precipimus et eos excommunicatos denunciare. Valete.

ALSO: MS: ibid., f.147a.

VARIATIONS: [1] *adds* dei.

DATE: 1139–61.

PRINTED: D. C. Douglas, *Feudal Documents from Bury St. Edmund's* (British Academy Records of Social and Economic History, vol. viii), p. 160.

27

Notification by Theobald to Bishop William of Norwich (1146–74) and his archdeacons of the decision in his presence in the dispute between William deacon of Brettenham (Norf.) and Ording abbot of Bury St. Edmund's (1148–56). The church of Brettenham was adjudged to the abbey and William was henceforth to hold it from the abbey.

MS. Cambridge U.L. Mm.iv.19 f.106b (Reg. of Bury St. Edmund's).

Quod ecclesia de Brethenham sit de jure sancti Ædmundi.

T.[1] gratia Cantuariensis archiepiscopus tocius Anglie primas apostolice sedis legatus venerabili fratri et amico W[illelmo] Norwicensi episcopo et omnibus archidiaconis ejusdem loci et omnibus aliis sancte ecclesie fidelibus salutem. Que[2] ad [3]multorum noticiam[3] pervenire credimus ne processu temporum in oblivionem revocentur scripto commendare decrevimus. Noscat ergo universitas vestra Willelmum diaconum de Brethenham ante [4]presentiam nostram[4] [5]esse confessum ecclesiam de Brethenham esse de jure monasterii beati Ædmundi[6] et se fidelitatem fecisse dilecto filio nostro Ordingo[7] abbati et conventui super [8]ęcclesia illa[8] quando illam ab illo abbate recepit et de illo monasterio recongnovit[9]. Valete.

ALSO: MS. ibid., ff.ii.33 f.59b (*A*) and MS. B.M. Addl. 7096 f.102b (*B*) (Registers of Bury).

VARIATIONS: [1]*A omits, adds* dei. *B* Thomas dei. [2]*A* Quod. [3-3]*A* noticiam multorum. [4-4]*B* nostram presentiam. [5]*B* f.103a. [6]*A* Eadmundi. [7]*AB* O. [8-8]*AB* illa ecclesia. [9]*B* recognovit.

DATE: 1150–56.

PRINTED: D. C. Douglas, *Feudal Documents from Bury St. Edmund's* (British Academy Records of Social and Economic History, vol. viii), p. 161.

28

Will of Theobald. He appoints as his executors Bishop Walter of Rochester (1148–82), his chancellor Philip, Ralph of Lisieux and John of Salisbury and leaves his chattels to the poor. The archbishop's fee and monastic estates and privileges are to remain intact during the vacancy. The dependent religious houses of St. Martin's Dover and St. Gregory's Canterbury are similarly safeguarded. An indulgence of 40 days to benefactors of Canterbury and those carrying out his will is granted.

Original   MS. D. and C. Canterbury C.A. A3.

OMNIBUS sancte matris ecclesie fidelibus Teobaldus sancte Cantuariensis ecclesie minister humilis salutem et benedictionem a domino. Suppremis deficientium voluntatibus suum accomodant jura favorem et in se velud inhumanus provocat iram dei qui piis eorum desideriis obvius contradicit. Nostra quidem voluntas est et que deo auctore numquam mutabitur ut residuum bonorum nostrorum mobilium que propter necessitates domesticas et diuturnitatem languoris usque ad exitum vite duximus conservanda in usus pauperum omnino cedat secundum quod nobis dominus inspiravit et sicut dedimus in mandatis venerabili fratri nostro Gauterio Roffensi episcopo et fidelibus nostris Philippo cancellario nostro, magistro Radulfo Lexoviensi et Johanni de Sar' quos elemosine nostre dispensande prefecimus. Precipimus ergo quod ab initio dispositionis nostre precepimus et omnibus ministris et fidelibus nostris per fidem quam nobis debent injunximus ut istis obtemperent et eis omnia nostra exponant et omnes amicos dei suppliciter exoramus ut pro misericordia omnipotentis dei eis ausilium [*sic*] et consilium prebeant. Omnes autem qui in prefatis pauperum rebus fraudem committent aut qui quo minus dispositio nostra procedat inpedient, anathematis sententia condempnavimus. Ipsique officiales regis si se dispositioni perturbande inmiscuerint se fidelium communione noverint esse privatos et tanquam sacrilegi et excommunicati ab introitu omnium ecclesiarum abstineant. Omnibus autem dispositionis nostre adjutoribus benedictionem dei et nostram damus et ipsos beneficiorum sancte Cant' ecclesie participes constituimus, eisque de injuncta sibi penitentia xl dierum indulgentiam facimus. Preterea ex parte omnipotentis dei et sub anathemate interdicimus ne quis [1]officialium domini regis[1] ad res que propriis monachorum Cant' ecclesie usibus dicate sunt temerariam manum presumat extendere, set habeant omnes res suas[2] in ea integritate et libertate qua easdem ipsis domini pape et nostro privilegio fecimus confirmari. [3]Ad hec sub eodem anathemate terrarum que ad archiepiscopum pertinent omnem alienationem fieri prohibemus et excidia et dampna nemorum donec nobis successor subrogetur nisi quantum nessecarius [*sic*] ecclesie exegerit usus vel dominus rex proprio ore preceperit vel misericordia discreta cum moderatione pauperum hominum necessitati indulserit. Sub eadem quoque interminatione clericos [e]piscopatus nostri prohibemus indebitis exactionibus et injustis vexationibus opprimi et eis omnes libertates et justas consuetudines quas habuerant tempores [*sic*] Willelmi bone memorie decessoris nostri precipimus conservari. Valete in domino dilectissimi fratres et filii et quod in vos deliqui queso mihi remittite peccatori penitenti ut peccatis vestris propicietur altissimus et orate pro me ut vos in necessitatibus vestris exaudiat misericors deus.

ENDORSEMENT: Carta Theob' archiepiscopi de testamento suo et de confirmatione rerum nostrarum et de multis ...

SEAL: usual, brown, fragment, counterseal.

SIZE: 4·9 in. × 6·1 in.

DATE: *c.* 1160.

COPIES: in MSS. of John of Salisbury's letters; omit last sentence.

PRINTED (partly): C. E. Woodruff, *Kent Arch. Soc. Records Branch*, iii (1914), p. 61.

PRINTED: from these copies, John of Salisbury's Letters, *P.L.*, 199, ep. 57, col. 36 (MSS. cited in col. 1178) and Gilbert Foliot's Letters, ibid., 190, col. 1002.

ALSO IN THE FOLLOWING MSS.: B.M. Addl. 6159 f.10a (Canterbury Reg.); D. and C. Canterbury Reg. E f.60a; Reg. A f.186a; Reg. I f.84a; C.A. C204 (a transcript), with the following significant variations:

[1]*omit and have* hominum ullo unquam tempore.

[2]*add* redditus et possessiones.

[3]*omit the rest and continue* [Reg. E] Ne quis autem hominum maliciose valeat interpretari quod in eisdem predictis privilegiis specialiter nominavimus et confirmavimus eis sacristariam cameram et cellarium cum omnibus rebus ad easdem tres obediencias pertinentibus quasi voluerimus unitatem Cantuariensis ecclesie in tres dividere, sciatis quod hec erat et nunc est nostra intencio quod illis confirmavimus et in presenciarum et in perpetuum confirmamus omnes res suas et possessiones que ad victum eorum et vestitum et ad omnes necessarias expensas ecclesie pertinent—id est quicquid habent vel habituri sunt cum pertinenciis omnibus et proventibus cum libera rerum omnium et hominum suorum disposicione, prohibentes sub perpetuo anathemate ne quis eis injuriam vel molestiam faciat. Quod si quis presumpserit eum a cetu fidelium et ab ingressu omnium

ecclesiarum sequestramus. Monachis et sancti Martini Dovorie et canonicis sancti Gregorii Cantuar' et aliis diocesis nostre domibus omnia jura sua
cum libera disposicione sub predicta sentencia confirmamus. Si quis [*sic*]
autem de jure suo eis subtraximus vel interventu precum nostrarum
optinuimus eis in integrum restituimus et confirmamus et ab omnibus
indulgenciam cum precum suarum instancia petimus ut deus nobis omnibus indulgenciam prestare dignetur. Amen. Prohibemus eciam sub predicta sentencia ne clerici vel homines episcopatus nostri injuste graventur
ab aliquo, terrarum quoque alienacionem et nemorum succisionem, donec
ydoneus nobis successor subrogetur nisi dominus rex ore proprio hoc pre-
cipiat. Valete filii dilectissimi et orate pro nobis.

MS. B.M. Addl. *alone ends at* Amen.

It would appear that the Canterbury Registers preserve another draft of
Theobald's will, but its original has not come to hand. It incorporates
fresh material in the will without omitting any significant details. Theobald was not the only man to change his will.

29

Mandate of Theobald to R. (a tenant). He is to restore livestock and
produce he has taken from his nephew Robert, otherwise he will
forfeit two marks that Robert owes him.

Original   MS. D. and C. Canterbury C.A. A4.

T. DEI gratia Cantuariensis archiepiscopus R. salutem. Miror
multum quod sicut tibi preceperam nepoti tuo Roberto restauramentum suum non reddidisti, quapropter nunc iterum
mando tibi et mandando precipio ut infra quintum diem ex quo
has litteras receperis, sua omnia illi restituas, hęc scilicet quinquaginta duas summas partim tritici partim ordei quas in hoc
anno de terra ejus abstulisti unde et pars terra que seminari
debuit non seminata remansit et in altero anno viginti v
summas, xv porcos bonos, tres boves et vaccam, cum vitulo et
vaccam juniorem, tres equas, v capras. Quod si magis placet
duas marcas quas tibi reddere pepigit nepos tuus pro restauramento suo quietas clamare, concedo ego et amici ejus, licet
restauramentum plus valeat, et hoc ipsum infra tercium diem
ei notifica. Si vero nolueris, scias quod ipse vel plegii ejus de

s

duabus marcis donec sua omnia illi restitueris non respondebunt. Vale.

ENDORSEMENT: [sewn to a paper and not visible].

SEAL: none.

SIZE: 2·7 in. × 11·9 in.

DATE: 1139–50, probably early.

30

Notification by Theobald to Wibert prior of Canterbury Cathedral (1153–67) that he has abolished the pretended jurisdiction of the archdeacon of Canterbury in the monastic chapter and that he has abolished the base custom of the monks being obliged to roof the archbishop's palace.

Original   MS. D. and C. Canterbury C.A. C15.

T. DEI gratia Cantuariensis archiepiscopus Angl' primas W[iberto] priori et conventui ejusdem ecclesię salutem. Quoniam grande conversationis monasticę detrimentum esse dinoscitur contra usum ęcclesiarum et contra statuta regulę monachorum capitulo clericos quasi de jure admisceri: iccirco ne quis clericorum sive Cant' archidiaconus sive alius nostrorum quoquomodo habeat capitulum prohibemus. Si vero vobis archidiaconus noster necessarius fuerit et eum vocaveritis, tunc demum non differat et ad vos venire, et vobis si opus est pro viribus auxiliari. Quotiens autem ipse a vobis accersitus vel archiepiscopum comitatus, sive in cena domini sive aliis opportunis temporibus in vestrum venerit capitulum more predecessorum suorum archidiaconorum, Asketini scilicet, Willelmi et Helewisi, qui nos precesserunt semper in suppedaneo sedis archiepiscopi sedeat, nec occasione hac vel alia in capitulo vestro juris quippiam se habere arbitretur. Si quis igitur hanc nostram sciens institutionem ei in aliquo obviare conatus fuerit, anathema sit. Servicia quoque illa nostris tantum temporibus inchoata et nobis non de jure vel consuetudine set ob amorem nostri mutui gratia beneficii a vobis exhibita, ne in consuetudinem vertantur ulterius fieri interdicimus et in perpetuum

amovemus, videlicet ne domum archiepiscopi aliquam plumbo
vel aliunde tegatis aut quicquam intromittatis. Turpe etenim
dictu et auditu etiam verecundum, quod deo dicata libertas
filiorum, servilia hujusmodi facere debeat, cum non conventus
archiepiscopis set archiepiscopi conventui et ędificia construere
et bona alia multa conferre, ut boni patres amore ducti filiorum
a priscis temporibus consueverint. Valete.

ENDORSEMENT: Theob' archiepiscopus ne archidiaconus Cant' in capitulo
nostro sibi vendicet aliquid juris et ne archiepiscopo aliquam domum
faciamus vel tegamus.

SEAL: none.

SIZE: 3·6 in. × 6·8 in.

DATE: 1153–61.

PRINTED: J. B. Sheppard, *Literae Cantuarienses* (R.S.), iii, 355. J. Battely,
Somner's Antiquities of Canterbury (1703), appendix, p. 65.

COPIES: MS. D. and C. Canterbury, Reg. A f.186b; Reg. E. f.61a; Reg. I.
f.83b.

31

Notification of Theobald to Wibert prior of Canterbury Cathedral of
his new regulation of the treatment of monks, fugitive or ejected,
should they wish to return to the Cathedral priory. They must
always remain at the lowest rank.

Original   MS. D. and C. Canterbury C.A. C163.

T. DEI gratia Cantuariensis archiepiscopus totius Anglię primas
et apostolicę sedis legatus dilectis filiis Gwiberto priori et toti
conventui ecclesię Christi Cant' benedictionem a domino et
misericordiam a deo salutari suo. Cunctorum providentie set
diligentium maxime prelatorum incumbit officio ut ex preteritorum experientia mala debeant precavere futura. Hinc est
quod scandalis illis que nostris videntur contigisse temporibus
per quosdam qui de vobis exierunt set ex vobis non erant,
vobiscum vehementer offensi adversus hujusmodi ne tam sepe
contingant, quanta possumus sollicitudine vobis inposterum
providere studemus, vestris super hoc justis et religiosis petitionibus gratanter annuentes qui zelo justicie et ignito monasticę
religionis amore succensi hoc unanimi postulatis assensu ut

ecclesię vestrę famę providentes, occasiones ex quibus predicta
scandala sepius oriuntur qua debemus et possumus auctoritate
radicitus amputemus. Nostra igitur et apostolica qua fungimur
auctoritate precipimus atque in ecclesia vestra cunctis tenendum
temporibus, et ratum fore sub anathemate constituimus ut
quotienscumque quemlibet monachum de ecclesia vestra fugi-
tivum vel meritis suis ejectum sive quolibet modo relicto religionis habitu ad seculum reversum redire tandem aliquando
et per gratiam recipi contigerit, in ultimo gradu recipiatur
ibique tota vita sua remanens ad altioris locum ordinis non
ascendat, illos tantummodo precessurus in ordine qui post
reversionem ejus in ecclesia suscipientur ut ex hoc et qui post
lapsum redierint perpetuo degradationis suę intuitu erubescant
et humilientur, et qui forte similiter temptari poterunt amissa
spe recuperandi ordinis sui si a vobis vel exeant vel eiciantur,
caveant sibi ab utroque ne vel exire audeant vel eici mereantur.
Ne quis autem hanc constitutionem nostram presumat infringere sub anathemate prohibemus. Valete.

ENDORSEMENT: Constitutio Theob' archiepiscopi de monachis si ejecti vel
   fugientes revertuntur   [later] qualiter et in quem ordinem recipientur.

SEAL: (a) Theobald's usual seal and counterseal; (b) to the right of it the
   second seal of Christ Church.

SIZE: 6·5 in. × 6·8 in.

DATE: 1155–61. The first seal was still in use in 1155.

COPIES: MS. B. M. Cott. Galba E iv f.81b. (Reg. of Henry of Eastry); D. and C.
   Canterbury Register I f.84b; C.A. C196 (15th-century paper).

PRINTED in *Literae Cantuarienses* (R.S.), iii, 354.

32

Mandate of Theobald to Æthelwine and Robert sons of Leofstan,
John son of Ralph and the other (London) tenants of the Cathedral
Priory. They must recognise the jurisdiction of Prior Jeremiah
(1137–43).

Original   MS. D. and C. Canterbury C.A. C218.

T. DEI gratia Cantuariensis ęcclesię humilis minister Eilwino
Leofstani filio et R[oberto] fratri ejus et Johanni filio Radulfi

et omnibus tenentibus de ecclesia Christi Cantuar' tam clericis quam laicis ad monachos pertinentibus salutem et benedictionem. Mandamus vobis et precipimus quod in justicia et sub tuitione domini Jeremię prioris Cantuar' sitis et ei sicut nobis diligenter obędiatis. Priori vero firmiter et per obedientiam injungimus ut pro vobis sit et vos pro posse suo in omnibus defendat et inter vos et de vobis plenam justiciam teneat et faciat. Illud etiam mandando precipimus nequis de ecclesiis vel terris vel domibus aut hominibus, clericis videlicet et laicis seu rebus aliis ad monachos Cantuar' pertinentibus nisi quem prior ęcclesię Christi Cantuar' ad hoc statuerit se in aliquo intromittat. Valete in Christo et estote obedientes per omnia.

ENDORSEMENT: Litere T. archiepiscopi . . . . nisi per Jeremiam priorem . . . .
de ecclesiis et de . . . . monachos pertin. . . .
SEAL: none. Tag at left side torn off with part of the endorsement.
SIZE: 2 in. × 6·7 in.
DATE: 1139–43.
PRINTED (partly): *H.M.C., Appendix to Fifth Report*, p. 446b.
    See J. H. Round, *Commune of London* (1899), pp. 105, 120.

33

Grant by Theobald and the Cathedral Priory notified to the citizens of Canterbury, French and English. Achemund the clerk is to hold the land, bequeathed to him by his uncle Wibert priest of St. Margaret's, from the Priory at an annual rent of sixpence.

Original   MS. D. and C. Canterbury C.A. C579a.

T. DEI gratia archiepiscopus ęcclesię Christi Cantuarie et primas totius Anglie, et totus ejusdem ęcclesię conventus omnibus civibus Cant' Francis et Anglis salutem et gaudium. Sciatis quod concedimus et volumus quod Achemundus clericus teneat tam libere et quiete in pace et sine omni calumpnia terram suam quam Wibertus sacerdos sancte Margarite avunculus suus divisit ei et dedit et concessit habendam sicut hereditatem propriam dum sanus et incolumis adhuc fuerit testimonio Radulfi decani et Geldewini sacerdotis et Rodberti Calvelli; et ita quod singulis annis reddet vi d. super magnum altare ęcclesię nostrę die dedicationis ejusdem. Valete in Christo.

ENDORSEMENT: de terra Agemundi clerici.

SEAL: first seal of Christ Church, on tag projecting from left-hand edge.

SIZE: 2·2 in. × 8·1 in.

DATE: 1139–50, probably early.

34

Grant by Theobald, notified to the hundred court of Westgate, Canterbury, to his servant Robert de Aquaticis of the land of Bishopsbourne (Kent) together with Odelina, niece of the previous tenant Wolurona, the sister of Esbern the priest, given to him by Theobald in marriage. Robert is to hold the land by hereditary tenure paying one mark annually to Harbledown hospital as established by St. Anselm, as well as all payments due to the king.

Original   MS. D. and C. Canterbury C.A. C1099.

T. DEI gratia Cantuariensis archiepiscopus Anglorum primas et apostolice sedis legatus toti hundredo de Westgata et universis fidelibus suis Francis et Anglicis salutem. Sciatis me dedisse et concessisse hereditabiliter Roberto de aquaticis servienti meo terram de Laborna quam tenuit Wolurona soror Esberni sacerdotis totam cum bosco et omnibus aliis rebus ad terram illam pertinentibus cum Odelina nepte predicte Wolurone quam ei dedimus in uxorem, reddendo singulis annis de terra illa pro omni servicio et consuetudine infirmis de Herebalduna unam marcam argenti sicut beatus Anselmus Cantuariensis archiepiscopus eandem marcam pro omni servicio dandam constituit, salvis consuetudinibus regalibus quas terra debet. Iccirco volo et firmiter precipio quod predictus Robertus et heredes sui post eum ita bene et libere et quiete teneant sicut Esbernus frater Wolurone melius et quiecius tenuit. Test' Philippo cancellario et Johanne Sal' et Radulfo Dunell' et Alano de Well' et Aluredo elemosinario et Petro scriptore et Rogero Speces et Willelmo de Becc' dapifero et Waltero de Wingeham et Nigello filio

Godefridi et Gileberto camerario et Willelmo camerario et
Roberto pincerna et Willelmo coco et multis aliis apud Cant'.

ENDORSEMENT: none.
SEAL: never sealed.
SIZE: 5·4 in. × 6·5 in.
DATE: 1150–61.

35

Grant by Theobald notified to the hundred court of Westgate,
Canterbury, of the house and land of John son of Walter de Sartrimo
forming part of the archbishop's fee of Westgate, to the Cathedral
Priory. He has made John a monk. Saving customary payments to
the archbishop.

Original   MS. D. and C. Canterbury C.A. C1109.

T. DEI gratia Cantuariensis archiepiscopus Angl' primas et
apostolice sedis legatus omnibus hominibus suis de Cantuaria
et de hundreto Westgate salutem. Sciatis nos concessisse conventui nostro Cantuariensis ecclesię domum et terram Johannis
filii Walterii de Sartrimo que est juxta novum murum elemosinarie monachorum de feodo nostro de Westgata sicut idem
Johannes eam dedit et concessit ęcclesie Cantuar' et conventui
cum corpore suo ad faciendum se monachum. Et nos ei mona-
chatum concedimus et conventui Cant' terram ejus predictam
confirmamus, salva consuetudine et censu annuo quem nobis
eadem terra debet. T. Philippo cancellario archidiacono
Norwic' et Johanne de Saresberia et Petro scriptore et Rogero
Spec[ie] et Osberno clericis archiepiscopi et multis aliis apud
Cantuariam.

ENDORSEMENT: Carta Teob' archiepiscopi de terra Walterii de Sartrino juxta
    murum elemosinarie nostre.
SEAL: usual, brown, counterseal.
SIZE: 4·4 in. × 6·5 in.
DATE: 1157–61.
COPIES: MS. D. and C. Canterbury, Reg. C f.13b; Reg. E f.91b.

36

Confirmation by Theobald, notified to Bishop Walter of Rochester (1148–82), Roger archdeacon of Canterbury (1148–54) and all the chapter of the city of Canterbury of the grant made by Eustace de Mustrel of the church of Crundale (Kent) to Canterbury Cathedral Priory and appropriated to the monastic table. In return the monks will pray annually for the soul of Eustace's wife Helewis on the anniversary of her death. Saving the rights of the archbishop.

Original   MS. D. and C. Canterbury C.A. C1258.

T. DEI gratia Cantuariensis archiepiscopus Anglorum primas et apostolice sedis legatus venerabili fratri et amico W[altero] Roffensi episcopo et Rogero Cant' archidiacono et toti capitulo Cantuar' civitatis salutem. Noverint tam presentes quam futuri quoniam Eustachius de Mosterolio per manum nostram in perpetuam contulit elenosinam [*sic*] deo et ecclesie Cantuariensi in usum monachorum ecclesiam de Crumdala cum terra et decimis et omnibus ad eam pertinentibus nominatim cum decimis gabuli et omnium reddituum ejusdem ville pro anima Helewidis uxoris sue. Et nos consequenter eandem ecclesiam ecclesie Cantuar' et monachis in cibum conventus ad propriam mensam eorum concedimus et eis in perpetuam confirmamus possessionem, salva dignitate archiepiscopali. Prohibemus igitur ex parte dei et nostra ne hec elemosina a mensa monachorum aliquatenus transferatur in posterum quia ideo data est ut singulis annis in ecclesia Cant' fiat predicte Helewidis anniversarium. Valete.

ENDORSEMENT: Theobaldi archiepiscopi de ecclesia de Crumdale quam Eustachius de Mustrel ecclesie Christi concessit.

SEAL: usual, with counterseal, on leather tag.

SIZE: 3·8 in. × 7·7 in.

DATE: 1150–54.

COPIES: MS. D. and C. Canterbury, Reg. A f.398a; Reg. I f.82b; B.M. Addl. 6159 f.285b (Canterbury priory Reg.) and B.M. Addl. 4526 f.22a (Madox's transcript).

37

Notification by Theobald that the rumours spread about of strife between him and the Cathedral Priory are unfounded.

Original   MS. D. and C. Canterbury C.A. C1292.

T. DEI gratia Cantuariensis archiepiscopus totius Angliȩ primas apostolicȩ sedis legatus universis ecclesie filiis salutem. Universitati vestrȩ scribere nos et ratio et providentia necessaria compellit, ne scilicet nostro silentio servorum dei innocentia in posterum periclitari aut contra justum et ȩquum debeat fatigari. Hec iccirco ita prosecuti sumus quia dilecti filii nostri deo dicatȩ congregationis monachi Cant' ecclesiȩ specialiter a deo nobis commissȩ appellationem quandam quasi contra nos aliquando fecisse dicuntur. Cujus appellationis occasione rei gestȩ sinistri interpretres, aut ob odium monachorum vel potius ob nostri favorem tanquam per mendacia nostram captantes gratiam, publice eos infamare conati sunt, asserentes illos in nostram necem conspirasse, manus in nos injecisse, et alia in hunc modum plura egisse. Quorum maledicorum assertiones utpote quibus nullum inest veritatis vestigium nos zelo dei refellentes, prefati conventus monachos non solum a predictis verumetiam ab omni infamiȩ nota immunes esse erga nos veritatis verbo attestamur quemadmodum et erga omnes prelatos suos semper fuisse dinoscuntur. Illi ergo cum de talibus re vera sint innocentes ne falsis criminationibus discrimen incidant in futurum, et nos puram rerum gestarum veritatem scientes ne ipsam tacendo animȩ nostrȩ periculum incurramus utrumque precavere volentes presentibus litteris nostris si forte necessitas poposcerit quandoque proferendis, memoratos dilectos filios nostros Cant' videlicet ecclesiȩ monachos omnimodo excusamus. Si quis igitur hanc nostram sciens excusationem eos super his perturbare aut molestiis vexare presumpserit sciat se anathematis subjacere sententiȩ quam omnipotentis dei auctoritate et beati Petri apostolorum principis cujus vice fungimur per apostolicȩ legationis officium confirmamus. Valete.

ENDORSEMENT: excusatio Theobaldi [later] archiepiscopi scilicet quod nos non zelamus malum suum sicut quod sibi pro favore suo et pro malo nostro narraverunt.

SEAL: none.

SIZE: 5·1 in. × 6·9 in.

DATE: *c.* 1153.

PRINTED (partly): *H.M.C., Appendix to the fifth Report*, p. 439a.

38

Grant by Theobald of the tithe of corn from the manor of Eastry (Kent) to the monks of the Cathedral Priory to be appropriated to the almonry.

Original MS. D. and C. Canterbury C.A. E167.

T. DEI gratia Cantuariensis archiepiscopus karissimis filiis suis Waltero priori et toti suę ęcclesię conventui salutem. Sciatis me concessisse totam decimam bladi de curia de Æstreia ad elemosinam vestram emendandam. Valete.

ENDORSEMENT: carta Theob' archiepiscopi confirmans ad elemosinam nostram decimam de dominio nostro de Estreia.

SEAL: usual (mounted on wax), but on a strip at the left side.

SIZE: 1·2 in. × 5·6 in.

DATE: 1144–50.

PRINTED: C. R. Cheney, *English Bishops' Chanceries* (1950), p. 48, n. 6.

39

Grant by Theobald to Wibert the prior (1153–67) and the convent of Canterbury Cathedral of the chapel of Halstow (Kent).

Original MS. D. and C. Canterbury C.A. H88.

TEOBALDUS dei gratia Cantuariensis archiepiscopus tocius Anglie primas apostolice sedis legatus universis sancte ecclesie fidelibus salutem. Noverit tam presens etas quam omnis secutura posteritas nos concessisse per manum Wiberti prioris Cant' ecclesie capellam de Halgastowa cum omnibus pertinentiis suis in elemosinam perpetuam altari ecclesie Christi Cant'. Ut ergo

illa concessio firma et rata de cetero permaneat presenti scripto
atque sigilli nostri attestatione confirmari et corroborari fecimus.
Valete.

ENDORSEMENT: carta Theob' archiepiscopi qua confirmat capellam de Hale-
    gesto ad altare Christi.

SEAL: none.

SIZE: 6·6 in. × 7·5 in.

DATE: 1153–61.

COPIES: MS. D. and C. Canterbury Reg. A f.186b; Reg. E f.61a; Reg. I f.82b.

40

Request by Theobald notified to Wibert the prior and William the
subprior that the convent should assign their demesne tithes of (Monks)
Eleigh (Suffolk) to Peter the writer for the term of his life only.

Original   MS. D. and C. Canterbury C.A. H122.

T. DEI gratia Cantuariensis archiepiscopus Angl' primas et
apostolice sedis legatus dilectis filiis suis in Christo Guiberto
priori et W[illelmo] subpriori et toti conventui ecclesie Christi
Cant' salutem. Pro dilecto filio nostro Petro scriptore devoto
vestro universitati vestre preces porrigimus rogantes quatinus
pro dei amore et nostro et ejus devoto affectu quem erga vos
eum habere cognoscimus persone sue decimam dominii vestri
de Hellega solummodo dum vixerit concedatis. Et ne ista
donatio vobis in prejuditium vel dampnum fiat in posterum,
decedente illo, decima illa in usus vestros iterum cedat et in
testimonium adversus malignantium quorumlibet usurpationes
hec cartula perpetuo apud vos remaneat. Valete.

ENDORSEMENT: carta Teob' archiepiscopi quod decime de dominio nostro de
    Helleg' Petro scriptori personaliter concesse fuerunt [later] ad vitam ipsius.

SEAL: usual and counterseal.

SIZE: 4·5 in. × 6·1 in.

DATE: 1153–61.

Following is the reply of the priory (MS. D. and C. Canterbury C.A.,
    H123):
Guibertus prior ecclesia Christi Cantuar' totusque conventus prepositis
ministris suis tam presentibus quam futuris et omnibus hominibus suis
Francis et Anglicis de Hellega salutem. Sciatis nos communi assensu et

benigno affectu concessisse et donasse pro dei amore et prece domini nostri
Theob' Cantuariensis archiepiscopi Petro scriptori clerico archiepiscopi et
nostro personaliter decimationem totius dominii nostri de Hellega tam in
segetibus quam in aliis omnibus que decimari solent quamdiu vixerit vel in
seculo remanserit plenarie possidendam. Et cum obierit vel seculo renun-
tiaverit, ipsa decima cedet in usus nostros et in pristinum statum, ita quod
nullus qui post dies ejus ecclesiam illam habiturus est in decimatione ista
poterit reclamare nec jus aliquod sibi vendicare. Set exinde habeat ecclesia
illa bladum iiii acrarum singulis annis in messe, sicut antiquitus habere
consuevit. T. Willelmo subpriore, Thoma tercio priore, Honorio cantore,
Florentio, Ernulfo cellerario, Roberto secretario, Laurentio elemosinario,
Atson' magistro infirmorum, Felice, Ailrico camerario, Ricardo de Wit-
stapla, Viviano de Sancto Albano, monachis Cant'; et Hamone preposito
Cant', et Osberto clerico de Horselega, et Willelmo camerario prioris. Apud
Cantuariam in capitulo, presentibus monachis.

[Copy MS. ibid. Reg. B f.146b.]

41

Notification by Theobald to (Robert) bishop of London (1141–51),
the dean of St. Paul's and the archdeacons that Peter priest of St.
Mary's Bothaw (near Cannon St.) has given his church, which was
of his own patrimony, to Canterbury Cathedral Priory, and will
continue to hold it paying an annual pension of 5s. to the prior.

Original   MS. D. and C. Canterbury C.A. L71.

TEOB' dei gratia Cantuariensis archiepiscopus et totius Anglie
primas episcopo Lond' et decano et archidiaconis et omnibus
sanctę ecclesię fidelibus salutem. Sciatis quod Petrus sacerdos
de Bothahe de London' dedit ecclesiam sancte Marie de
Bothahe que sui patrimonii esse dinoscitur ecclesie Christi
Cantuar' et nominatim priori ejusdem ecclesie reddendo inde
priori singulis annis v solidos ad pascha medietatem et aliam
medietatem ad festum sancti Michaelis. Valete.

ENDORSEMENT: carta Theob' archiepiscopi de ecclesia de Bothakhe quam
    Petrus sacerdos ecclesie Christi contulit et nominatim priori.

SEAL: usual (mounted).

SIZE: 1·9 in. × 6·6 in.

DATE: 1141–61.

COPIES: MS. D. and C. Canterbury, Reg. A f.187a; Reg. B f.244b; Reg.
    E f.61b.

PRINTED: *Literae Cantuarienses* (R.S.), iii, 357.

42

Confirmation by Theobald of the grant by William of Eynsford to the Cathedral Priory of the land of Ruckinge (Kent) as renewed by his son and grandson of the same name. The revenues are to be appropriated to the sacristy to provide a perpetual lamp before the great altar. Saving to the archbishop the service of one knight.

Original MS. D. and C. Canterbury C.A. R1.

T. DEI gratia Cantuariensis archiepiscopus et totius Anglie primas omnibus sancte ecclesie fidelibus salutem et benedictionem. Noverint universi fideles Christi quoniam Willelmus de Ainesford' senex cui Hadewisa uxor fuit deo et ecclesie Cantuariensi in perpetuam concessit elemosinam terram de Rochinges ut inde sacristarius ecclesie luminare provideret, quod coram magno altari et ante sacrum corpus dominicum nocte dieque continuam redderet lucem. In hunc eundem usum eam concessit Willelmus filius ejus factum patris cum magna devotione confirmans. Filius autem illius, Willelmus scilicet tercius qui nunc est, beneficio avi et patris sui tota animi voluntate adquiescens factum ipsum laudavit et assensum suum prebens ut nostri quoque assensus auctoritate factum firmaretur, in manus nostras elemosinam illam tradidit; et nos ipsam super idem sacrum altare predicti luminaris usibus optulimus et perpetualiter concessimus et auctoritate litterarum nostrarum confirmavimus. Servicium autem unius militis quod ipsa terra debet tantummodo retinuimus testimonio subscriptorum virorum: Walterii Roffensis episcopi et W[alterii] prioris Cant' et G[ilberti] de Clara monachi, et magistri Johannis de Pageham et Thome de Lond' et Therrici de altaribus et Walteri de Petreponte et Willelmi de buteillis. Apud Cantuariam.

ENDORSEMENT: carta archiepiscopi T. de manerio de Rokinges quod Willelmus de Einesford dedit ecclesie Christi.

SEAL: usual, brown (mounted).

SIZE: 6·5 in. × 6·5 in.

DATE: 1148–51.

COPIES: MS. D. and C. Canterbury Reg. C f.246a; Reg. E f.282b.

43

Grant by Theobald to Canterbury Cathedral Priory of the freedom from the service of one knight and scutage which the land of Ruckinge owed to the archbishop.

Original MS. D. and C. Canterbury C.A. R2.

T. DEI gratia Cantuariensis archiepiscopus et totius Anglie primas universis sancte ecclesie fidelibus per Cantiam existentibus tam clericis quam laicis tam presentibus quam futuris salutem et benedictionem. Notum facimus universitati vestre quoniam terram de Rocchinges quam Willelmus de Ainesford' senex et filius ejus et filius filii ejus Willelmus assensu nostro dederunt in elemosinam perpetuam ecclesie sancte Trinitatis Cantuar' et monachis in ea deo ministrantibus, concedimus eis et confirmamus et perpetualiter eidem ecclesie possidendam corroboramus, ita videlicet ut ejusdem terre fructus secretarius ecclesie semper futuris temporibus percipiat ut lucernam continuam quam diebus ac noctibus in honorem sacratissimi dominici corporis et sanctarum ejusdem ecclesie reliquiarum venerationem ante magnum altare semper ardere dignum duximus inde provideat, ut tante venerationis locus nunquam luminis assidui careat honore. Preterea ex nostra additione terram predictam ab omni seculari servitio, maxime a servitio unius militis et a scutagio quod terra illa debebat liberavimus et in capitulo Cantuar' presente predicto Willelmo de Ainesford' quietam et absolutam clamavimus, ut in omnibus futuris temporibus liberrima et absolutissima ab omni mundiali servitute ecclesie Cantuar' remaneat possidenda. Hanc itaque donationem et nostram confirmationem firmam et stabilem esse volumus et ratam habemus. Omnibus igitur eam delere, sive infirmare, sive diminuere querentibus, dei et nostram maledictionem; conservantibus autem benedictionem et gratiam preoptamus. Valete.

ENDORSEMENT: carta Teobaldi archiepiscopi de manerio de Rokinge quod Willelmus de Einesford dedit ecclesie Christi.

SEAL: usual, brown (mounted).

SIZE: 5·2 in. × 8·8 in.

DATE: 1149–61 (after No. 42).

COPIES: MS. D. and C. Canterbury, Reg. C f.245b and f.247a; Reg. E f.284a; Reg. I f.81b.

44

Notification by Theobald that during the vacancy before his accession (1136–39) the manor of Stisted (Essex) had been usurped by
John son of Ansfrid, whose father had held it by a life tenancy from
the monks of Canterbury Cathedral. John has now died and
Theobald has restored the manor to the monks. Matilda de Sancto
Sidonio now holds the life tenancy at an annual rent of ten pounds
and has a charter to that effect from the monks.

Original   MS. D. and C. Canterbury C.A. S315.

THEOBALDUS dei gratia Cantuariensis archiepiscopus et totius
Anglie primas omnibus amicis et filiis Cantuar' ecclesie salutem.
Notum sit vobis quod post obitum Johannis filii Ansfridi reddidi
priori et conventui ecclesie Christi Cant' manerium quod dicitur Stistede liberum et absolutum ab omnium calumnia sicut
proprium et dominium manerium suum. Veraciter enim com-
peri a prudentibus et fidelibus viris quod Ansfridus pater videlicet supradicti Johannis numquam habuit aliquam hereditatem
sive aliquod feudum in prefato manerio Stistede quod etiam
gesta beati patris Anselmi apertissime testantur, nisi tantummodo ad firmam. Post mortem quoque Willelmi archiepiscopi
predecessoris mei supranominatus Johannes per violentiam et
tortitudinem manerium Stistede invasit quod Willelmus archiepiscopus dum vixit sasiverat et reddiderat priori et conventui
ecclesie Christi. Unde precipio ut prior et conventus prefate
ecclesie manerium illud Stistede habeant et possideant ita libere
et bene inperpetuum sicut aliquam terram suam liberius et
melius tenent. Sciatis preterea quod permissione mea Mahalt
de sancto Sidonio tenet predictum manerium Stistede sine omni
hereditate et absque ullo feudo ad firmam tantum quam diu
vixerit et singulis annis reddiderit x libras priori et conventui
ad terminos constitutos, et manerium et homines ejusdem
manerii bene custodierit eo scilicet pacto ut statim post obitum
ejus totum manerium cum omni restauramento quod ipsa
fecerit redeat libere et quiete et sine aliqua contradictione in
manus et dominium monachorum ecclesie Christi Cant'. Hec
omnia se facturam et servaturam ipsa Mahalt super iiii evan-

gelia in capitulo Cant' coram conventu et Willelmo de Ypre juravit sicut cyrografum ejusdem Matildis testatur quod habet contra predictum conventum. T. Radulfo Picot, Willelmo Travers, Thoma capellano, Berner[io] dapifero, Willelmo portario, Rogero portario, et multis aliis. Valete.

ENDORSEMENT: Carta Teodbaldi archiepiscopi demonstrans quomodo Mahald tenet Stistede et quod rectum habent filii Ansfridi de eodem manerio et quomodo reddit Stistede conventui ęcclesie Christi.

SEAL: usual, mounted on wax, but at left side.

SIZE: 4·9 in. × 10·9 in.

DATE: 1143–54.

The following (MS. D. and C. Canterbury C.A. C 71 (i)) is of interest: H. rex Anglorum et dux Normannorum et Aquitanorum et comes Andegavorum T. archiepiscopo Cantuariensi salutem. Si ecclesia Christi Cant' est dissaisita injuste et sine judicio de manerio suo de Stiesteda post regis H. avi mei mortem, tunc precipio quod eam inde juste et sine dilatione resaisiatis et teneat ita libere et honorifice et juste sicut beatus Anselmus archiepiscopus ei illud concessit per cartam suam, ne amplius inde clamorem audiam pro penuria recti et justicię. Teste Comite Reginaldo apud Dovram.

COPIES: MS. D. and C. Canterbury, Reg. B f.160b; Reg. H f.26a.

45

Mandate of Theobald to the men of Wootton and Patching (Sussex) French and English, tenants of Canterbury Cathedral Priory. They are to recognise the jurisdiction of the prior and the monks.

Original MS. D. and C. Canterbury C.A. W49.

TEOBALDUS dei gratia Cantuariensis archiepiscopus totius Anglie primas apostolice sedis legatus omnibus hominibus de Wdetona et de Pachinges tam Franchis quam Anglis salutem et benedictionem. Quamvis omnibus in jure suo debitores in quantum ratio expetit et ammonet existimus, tamen attentiori sollicitudine dilecto filio nostro W. priori et monachis Cant' ecclesie providere debemus ut ea que sui juris sunt in predictis villis libere et quiete decetero possideant et nostro consilio ipsa honeste disponant. Quocirca per presentia scripta vobis mandamus atque precipimus quatinus prefato priori et monachis prescriptis et eorum ministris quos ibidem constituerint et nulli alii de omnibus que in illis villis possidetis respondeatis amodo. Set ad eos tantum intendatis et eorum preceptis per omnia obediatis. Illas enim villas cum omnibus pertinentiis suis predictis fratribus libere reddidimus sicut presenti scripto contestamur. Valete.

ENDORSEMENT: [contemporary] T de Wdet' et de Peccinkes [later] preceptum Theobaldi archiepiscopi quod homines et tenentes nostri de Wodetone et de Pecchinges nobis et ministris nostris intendant que loca ipse nobis reddidit.

SEAL: fragment of usual seal with counterseal attached to charter by string.

SIZE: 10·8 in. × 6·2 in.

DATE: 1150–61. Probably c. 1153 in connection with Theobald's restitution of the conventual estates, but see Supp. A.

COPIES: MS. D. and C. Canterbury Reg. A f.186a; Reg. B f.330b; Reg. E f.60b; Reg. I f.85a; Reg. O f.184b.

46

Grant by Theobald to the Cathedral Priory, notified to Bishop Walter of Rochester (1148–82) and the halimote of St. Martin's of an acre of marshland at 'Horfalde' (near Canterbury) as a reservoir for irrigation and water supply.

Original   MS. D. and C. Canterbury C.A. W224.

T. DEI gratia Cantuariensis archiepiscopus, Anglorum primas venerabili fratri et amico W[altero] Roffensi episcopo et toti hallimoto de sancto Martino salutem. Sciatis nos dedisse et concessisse in perpetuum pro salute nostra et pro animabus omnium predecessorum nostrorum dilectis filiis nostris priori et conventui ecclesie nostre in elemosinam et perpetuam possessionem paulo plus quam unam acram paludis usque ad arabilem terram in valle apud Horfalde, ubi fontes erumpunt et defluunt usque ad stagna eorum, ut melius et liberius possint fontes suos curare et stagna sua emendare et utilius custodire. Iccirco volumus et precipimus quod perpetuo permaneat ecclesie Cant' palus illa. T. Philippo cancellario et Johanne de Sar' et Willelmo de Ver et Johanne de Tileberia et Hugone de Gant et Petro scriptore et Gisleberto camerario et Roberto

T

pincerna et Willelmo dispensatore et multis aliis apud Lamhedam.

ENDORSEMENT: Theob' archiepiscopi de una acra paludis apud Horsvalde.

SEAL: none (Bunce 1804 endorsed charter 'curious counterseal').

SIZE: 3·9 in. × 8·1 in.

DATE: 1154–60.

PRINTED: *Literae Cantuarienses* (R.S.), iii, 355. R. Willis, *Arch. Cant.*, vii, 181, also 158 ff.

COPIES: MS. D. and C. Canterbury, Reg. C f.11a; Reg. E f.89a; Reg. H f.27b; Reg. I f.81b.

47

Notification by Theobald to all bishops, barons, sheriffs, justices, servants of the king and to his own men English and French of the division of the revenues of the Cathedral Priory between the chamberlain, sacrist and cellarer. Theobald asserts his right to appoint the prior, subprior, precentor, steward and two porters, and also the duty of the monks to provide him and two of his chaplains, being monks, with vestments.

MS. D. and C. Canterbury Register A f.188a.

Carta T. archiepiscopi que confirmat conventui tres obediencias, scilicet cellarium cameram et sacristariam cum suis pertinenciis.

T. DEI gratia Cantuariensis archiepiscopus[1] Anglorum primas omnibus episcopis per Angliam constitutis, baronibus, vicecomitibus, justiciis et universis ministris regis cunctisque hominibus suis Anglicis et Francis et omnibus sancte ecclesie filiis salutem et benediccionem. Notum facimus universitati vestre quod nos quieti et utilitati conventus ecclesie nostre in perpetuum prospicere volentes spontanea et benigna liberalitate pro salute nostra et tam predecessorum quam successorum nostrorum reddidimus et concedimus monachis predictis cameram suam et sacristariam et cellarium cum omnibus rebus ad easdem tres obediencias pertinentibus ipsorum usibus [2]in perpetuum[2] profuturis et libere possidendis, possessionumque ad easdem obediencias spectancium in locando vel certarum personarum custodie deputando liberam administracionem illis concedimus, nullum temporale comodum attendentes vel nobis retinentes preter quam indumenta que nobis et duobus monachis capellanis nostris ex antiqua consuetudine ecclesie debentur, reservata nobis et successoribus nostris personarum eisdem obedienciis preficiendarum ordinacione, nostro et illorum communicato consilio, secundum regulam beati Benedicti[3], sicut prioris, supprioris et cantoris, serviencium quoque trium scilicet dapiferi curie eorum et duorum janitorum curie atque ecclesie. Quicumque autem hujus nostre constitucionis paginam sciens temere perturbare vel in aliquo diminuere temptaverit, omnipotentis dei indignacionem se noverit incursurum. Valete.

ALSO: MS. D. and C. Canterbury, Reg. I f.83b.
VARIATIONS: [1]adds et. [2-2]inperpetuum. [3][f.84a].
DATE: 1153–58: confirmed by Adrian IV in 1158 (Holtzmann, ii, 288).

48

Notification by Theobald to all his men of London French and English, and of the parish of St. Vedast's (Foster Lane, Cheapside) that his clerk William of Northall (bishop of Worcester 1186–90) had bought the land and houses of Robert de Bosco in the above parish with the advice and permission of the archbishop for twelve marks of silver and 20s. Theobald confirms the land and tenements thereon to William and his successors, saving the annual payment of 6s. to the church of Canterbury which the land owes.

MS. D. and C. Canterbury Register B f.243b.

Confirmacio T. archiepiscopi de vi solidis annui redditus de terra quam W[illelmus] de Norhale emit de Roberto de Bosco in parochia sancti Vedasti in London'.

THEOBALDUS dei gratia Cantuariensis archiepiscopus Anglorum primas omnibus hominibus suis Francis et Anglis de Lond' et de parochia sancti Vedasti salutem. Notum vobis esse volumus quoniam Willelmus de Norhalla clericus noster, licencia nostra et consilio nostro emit terram Roberti de Bosco quam habebat in parochia sancti Vedasti ab ipso Roberto et heredibus ejus pro duodecim marcis argenti et pro viginti solidis quos idem Willelmus dedit ipsi Roberto pro domibus ejusdem terre, salvo servicio Cantuariensis ecclesie de cujus feodo terra ipsa est, scilicet sex solidis annuis pro omni consuetudine, ita quod sepedictus Robertus et heredes sui accepta predicta pecunia eandem terram et jus hereditarium et feodum quod in ea habebant quietum clamaverunt Willelmo et omnibus successoribus suis inperpetuum in nostra presencia et multorum audiencia. Iccirco eandem terram Willelmo et omnibus successoribus confirmamus, precipientes quod eam libere et quiete et in pace et honorifice teneant; salvo predicto annuo censu sex solidorum Cantuariensi ecclesie. Valete.

DATE: 1139–61.

49

Mandate of Theobald to all the priests of his 'parish'. At a recent synod the archbishop had ordered them to pay their synodal pennies to the prior of Canterbury Cathedral, but some priests have not as yet paid. They must consider their churches interdicted until they pay.

MS. D. and C. Canterbury Register H f.26a.

T. DEI gratia Cantuariensis archiepiscopus Anglorum primas et apostolice sedis legatus omnibus presbiteris de parrochia sua salutem. In sinodi celebratione sedentes vobis precepimus quatinus sinodales denarios dilecto filio nostro W. priori Cantuariensi persolveretis. Set quia pars quedam solvit, pars alia solvere non curavit, vobis mandamus et precipimus quatinus ad submonitionem prioris nostri, illos aut solvatis aut a divinorum celebracione cessent ecclesie vestre donec eos solveritis. Valete.

The prior in question was most probably Wibert.

DATE: 1150–61.

50

Notification by Theobald that no parish priest can deny to his parishioners the right of burial in the cemetery of Canterbury Cathedral. Crimes committed in the Cathedral precincts are to be judged by the archbishop and the monks without any lay or ecclesiastical interference.

MS. D. and C. Canterbury Register I f.82a.

Quod libere possumus recipere quemlibet ad sepeliendum in cimiterio nostro.

T.[1] DEI gratia Cantuariensis archiepiscopus Anglorum primas et apostolice sedis legatus omnibus sancte matris ecclesie fidelibus per parochiam nostram Cancie constitutis salutem. Cum ecclesiarum jura nostre jurisdictioni subditarum sollicite debeamus conservare eademque iminuere[2] presumentes[3] festina et digna animadversione punire, majori tamen vigilancia ecclesiam Cantuariensem cui nos divina prefecit misericordia ejusdemque[4] libertates et[5] dignitates ab antiquo [6]ei jure[6] competentes integras et illesas nos convenit servare. Unde universitati vestre clericis tamen specialius[7], auctoritate qua fungimur[8] inhibemus [9]ne quis[9] ullum ex parrochianis[10] suis vel alium quemlibet qui in cimiterio Cant' ecclesie se sepeliri petierit vel amici sui pro eo impedire presumat. Clericus eciam in cujus parrochia[11] defunctus erit, usque ad ecclesiam corpus defuncti commitetur.[12] Quod si noluerit monachi libere defunctum /[f.82b] ad ecclesiam obsequiis rite peractis deferant et sepeliant. Porro eadem quoque auctoritate inhibitum esse sanccimus[13] quod siquis in predicta ecclesia vel infra ambitum murorum ecclesiam et curiam [14]nostram et monachorum[14] cingentium homicidium vel furtum fecerit, sanguinem fuderit, personam quemlibet [15]dicto vel facto injuriaverit[15], vel aliquid illicitum commiserit, [9]ne quis[9] archidiaconus, decanus vel prepositus, ullave justicia ecclesiastica seu secularis se intromittere presumat. Soli enim persone archiepiscopi et monachis ecclesie nostre correctionem et satisfaccionem delictorum in memoratis locis contingencium reservanda esse constituimus. Quod siquis hanc nostram con-

stitucionem infringere presumpserit vel[16] temere contravenire
temptaverit, dei omnipotentis indignacionem et nostram proculdubio se noverit incursurum. Valete.[17]

ALSO: MSS. B.M. Addl. 6159 f.285b (A); D. and C. Canterbury Reg. B
241b (B); B.M. Cotton Galba E iv f.58b (C) and D. and C. Canterbury
Reg. A f.307b.

VARIATIONS: [1]A Theob' BC Thomas. [2]BC minuere. [3]A presumentis. [4]B
ejusque. [5]BC ac. [6-6]A jure ei. [7]B spiritualibus. [8]B frungimur. [9-9]C
nequis. [10]AC parochianis. [11]A parochia. [12]BC comitetur. [13]C sancimus.
[14-14]A omits. [15-15]B injuraverit dicto vel facto. [16]A adds ei. [17]C omits.

DATE: 1150–58. See No. 47.

51

Grant by Theobald to William his cook and his heirs, notified to all
the archbishop's men French and English of the hundred of Westgate, of the land formerly of Ralph Batnoise subject to an annual
rent of 5s. payable at the archbishop's court of Westgate (Canterbury).

MS. Lambeth 241 f.171a (Cartulary of Dover Priory).

Carta Theobaldi archiepiscopi Willelmo coco de
quadam terra apud Westgate et bosco.

THEOBALDUS dei gracia Cantuariensis archiepiscopus tocius
Anglie primas et apostolice sedis legatus omnibus hominibus
suis Francis et Anglis de hundredo de Westgate salutem et benediccionem. Sciatis nos concessisse et dedisse Willelmo coco
nostro terram que fuit Radulphi Batnoise quam Ancelmus bone
memorie archiepiscopus predecessor noster prefato Radulpho
dedit pro servicio suo. Nos quoque similiter illam prefato
Willelmo concedimus cum omnibus mansuris et bosco ad
eandem terram pertinenti, ut ita libere et quiete jure hereditario illam teneat per quinque solidos annuatim reddendos pro
omni consuetudine in curia nostra de Westgate, sicut illam
[sic] Radulphus prememoratus illam terram melius ac liberius
umquam tenuit. Hiis testibus Rogero Cant' archidiacono,
Johanne Cant' thesaurario archidiacon' Eborac', Philippo cancellario, Alano clerico de Wellis, Radulpho Picot, Willelmo de

Pagaham, Willelmo janitore, Rogero Specie, Petro scriptore et multis aliis. Valete.

DATE: 1153–54. Hugh, treasurer of York, became bishop of Durham in 1153.

52

Grant by Theobald to Adam of Charing, notified to all the archbishop's men French and English of the hundred of Teynham (Kent) of a sheepfold with land which Wolstan had held and paying the same rent.

MS. Lambeth 1212, p. 212 (Documents of Archbishop of Canterbury).

Carta Theob' archiepiscopi de bercaria de Tenham.

T. DEI gratia Cantuariensis archiepiscopus et Anglorum primas universis hominibus suis Francis et Anglis de hundredo de Tenham salutem. Sciatis me concessisse et confirmasse Ade filio Yvonis de Cerring' illam bercariam quam tenuit Wolstanus sibi et heredibus suis hereditabiliter tenendam per idem instauramentum quod Wlstanus habuit, et eundem redditum singulis annis reddendo in firmam de Tenham quem Wlstanus reddidit et ad eosdem terminos cum terra ad bercariam pertinente et cum omnibus consuetudinibus cum quibus Wlstanus melius et liberius tenuit. Valete. T. etc.

DATE: 1139–61.

53

Grant by Theobald of an indulgence of 40 days to benefactors of Northgate hospital Canterbury.

MS. Canterbury Northgate Hospital Muniments (burnt, June 1942). List of Indulgences.

ISTA vero fuerunt beneficia ab archiepiscopis omnibus benefactoribus nostris concessa . . . . Theobaldus archiepiscopus Cant' xl dies.

DATE: 1139–61.

PRINTED: J. Nichols, *Bibliotheca Topographica Britannica* (1780), i, 254.

54

Confirmation by Theobald addressed to Hugh II (1126–51), abbot of St. Augustine's Canterbury, of the appropriation of the churches of Northbourne and Chislet (Kent) to the infirmary and guest-house of the monastery.

MS. B.M. Cott. Julius D ii f.76a (Reg. of St. Augustine's Cant.).

Confirmatio Theodbaldi archiepiscopi ecclesiarum de Norb' et de Chistelet.

T. DEI gratia Cantuariensis archiepiscopus et tocius Anglie primas secundo Hugoni abbati sancti Augustini et fratribus ejusdem loci salutem. Cum salvator noster seipsum dicat in infirmis visitari in nudis cooperiri gloria nostra esse debet infirmis compati pauperum inopias relevare. Eapropter cum vos ecclesias maneriorum vestrorum de Norburn' et Cistelet cum capellis suis ad sustentationem infirmitorii vestri et sus-ceptionem pauperum et peregrinorum, communi consilio depu-taveritis et hoc factum vestrum nostra pietatis auctoritate roborari, nos piis petitionibus vestris libenter cum deo annuentes assignationem istam presenti scripto roboramus et confirmamus. Hoc autem facientes, volumus ut hec eadem actio omnibus venturis temporibus firmum robur optineat /[f.76b] illibataque permaneat. De consensu vestro nihilominus statuentes ut fructus dictarum ecclesiarum quos jam diu integre percepistis non nisi ad prefatos usus aliquo tempore convertatis. Siquis igitur hanc concessionem a nobis et vobis comuniter factum infringere temptaverit vel ei ausu temerario contraire, nostra determina-tione a consortio fidelium fiat alienus donec reatum suum con-grua satisfactione emendaverit. Hujus nostre confirmationis testes sunt hii etc. [*sic*].

ALSO: in a transcript MS. Jesus Coll. Oxford 75 f.141b (Baker collections deposited in Bodleian Library).

DATE: 1139–51.

55

Confirmation by Theobald of the appropriation to the repair and maintenance of St. Augustine's abbey of the (mother) church of Thanet (Minster) as granted by Abbot Hugh II (assigned to the Sacristy).

MS. B.M. Cott. Julius D ii f.76a (Reg. of St. Augustine's Cant.).

> Confirmatio Theodbaldi archiepiscopi super ecclesia
> de Tanet'.

Ego[1] Theobardus[2] dei gratia Cantuariensis archiepiscopus[3] tocius Anglie primas secundo Hugoni abbati sancti Augustini et [4]fratribus ejusdem loci[4] salutem. Vestris justis [5]petitionibus annuentes[5], roboramus et confirmamus presenti scripto et sigillo nostro donum illud de ecclesia de Tanet[6] quod tu dilecte filii[7] Hugo abba altari beati Augustini[8] ad reparationem et ad servitium ejusdem monasterii dedisti et carta tua confirmasti, scilicet ipsam ecclesiam cum omnibus[9] capellis oblationibus et decimis omnium hominum infra insulam ad feudum[10] beati Augustini pertinentium. Hoc autem facientes volumus ut hec eadem actio et donum omnibus venturis[11] temporibus firmum illibatumque permaneat. Quod siquis[12] temerario ausu infregerit, nostra determinatione a consortio fidelium fiat alienus nisi ad dignam satisfactionem venerit. Hujus confirmationis testes sunt hii: Robertus[13] episcopus Exoniensis, Walterus archidiaconus Cant',[14] Aluredus prior sancti Gregori[15], Rogerius de Ponte Episcopi, Thomas de Lond', Johannes de Cant', Ricardus Castel et[16] Alanus, Malgerius, clerici; Radulfus Picot vicecomes[17], Hugo de Munfort[18], Petrus de Thalawrde, Haimo[19] prepositus[14].

Also: MSS. P.R.O. Exch. Misc. Books i 27 f.37a (A); B.M. Cott. Claudius D x f.113a (B); Jesus Coll., Oxford, 75 f.140b (a transcript deposited in Bodleian).

Variations: [1]A omits. [2]AB Theobaldus. [3]A omits. [4-4]A cujusdam loci fratribus. [5-5]A postulacionibus. [6]A Thanet. [7]B fili. [8]B f.113b. [9]A illis. [10]AB feodum. [11]A futuris. [12]B si quis. [13]B Rodbertus. [14-14]A omits. [15]B Gregorii. [16]B omits. [17]B vicicomes. [18]B Mundfort. [19]B Hamo.

Date: 1143-48.

56

Confirmation by Theobald to the abbot and monks of St. Augustine's of the churches and tithes of Milton and Faversham (Kent) except the tithe of honey and of the gable pennies, granted by William I and Henry I.

MS. B.M. Cott. Julius D ii f.76a (Reg. of St. Augustine's Cant.).

Theodbaldus confirmat ecclesiam de Feversham.

T.[1] DEI gratia Cantuariensis[2] archiepiscopus Anglorum primas et apostolice sedis legatus universis sancte ecclesie fidelibus salutem. Donationes regum Anglorum et elemosinas principum ecclesiis seu religiosis locis canonice collatas et concessas, nostri est officii firmas statuere et auctoritatis nostre testimonio roborare. Eapropter[3] donum regis Anglorum celebris memorie Willelmi a glorioso rege Henrico filio suo confirmatum videlicet ecclesias et decimas de Middeltona[4] et de Favresham[5] ex omnibus redditibus qui regi reddebantur ex his[6] mansionibus et ex omnibus ibidem appendentibus, terra, silva, pratis et aqua, excepta decima mellis et gabli denariorum concedimus et confirmamus deo et sancto Augustino et abbati et fratribus ejusdem loci ut habeant et teneant et possideant ita libere et quiete, sicut predictorum regum carte quas oculis nostris vidimus attestantur eos habere et tenere debere. Siquis[7] igitur hoc violare temptaverit secundo terciove commonitus, nisi digne satisfecerit[8] anathemati subjaceat. Conservantes autem gratiam et benedictionem dei consequantur. Amen.

ALSO: MSS. B.M. Cott. Claudius D x f.256b (A); Jesus Coll., Oxford, 75 f.141a (a transcript deposited in Bodleian) and in an Inspeximus of Archbishop Hubert Walter, Cotton, Julius D ii f.76b, Claudius D x f.256b, P.R.O. Exch. Misc. Books i 27 f.37b.

VARIATIONS: [1]A Theobaldus. [2]A Cantuarie. [3]A Ea propter. [4]A Middeldona. [5]A Faveresham. [6]A hiis. [7]A Si quis. [8]MS satisferit.

DATE: 1150–61.

57

Notification by Theobald that he has consecrated a cemetery at Faversham for the use of the monks there (Ben. Abbey) only, without prejudice to the parochial rights of St. Augustine's.

MS. B.M. Cott. Claud. D x f.264a (Red Book of St. Augustine's).

Item alia littera domini Theobaldi dei gratia Cantuariensis archiepiscopi et totius Anglie primati [*sic*] pro abbate et conventu sancti Augustini Cantuarie videlicet de cimiterio monachorum de Faveresham.

[T]HEOBALDUS dei gratia Cantuariensis archiepiscopus et Anglorum primas archidiacono R[ogero] Cantuar' et omnibus tam clericis quam laycis in Kancia existentibus salutem. Sciatis quod precibus Matildis regine Anglorum domine nostre inclinatus [*sic*] et dilecti filii nostri Clarembaldi abbatis de Faversham et fratrum ibi deo servientium ad sepulturam monachorum eis ibidem cimiterium indulsimus et consecravimus salvo parochialis ecclesie jure in omnibus et per omnia, ita videlicet ut nullus omnino de parochianis pertinentibus ad ecclesiam parochialem de Faveresham aliquo modo in eo recipiatur nisi per Osbertum cui ejusdem ecclesie regimen precibus Hugonis abbatis sancti Augustini concessimus et illius Osberti successores. Et ne quis de predicte ecclesie parochianis aliter recipiatur auctoritate dei et nostra omnimodis prohibemus. Valete. Teste H[ilario] Cycestrensi episcopo, R[ogero] Cantuar' archidiacono, Thoma London', Rogero Speres [*sic*], Johanne de Sar', Petro scriptore et multis aliis.

ALSO: (heading only) MS. ibid. Jul. D ii f.97a (Reg. of St. Aug.).
DATE: 1148–49.

58

Notification by Theobald that Hugh II, abbot of St. Augustine's has given Roger Folet 100*s.* for the land of Guston (Kent) which Roger had claimed was his, and which belonged to the demesne lands of the prebend which St. Augustine's held in the church of St. Martin's Dover.

MS. B.M. Cott. Claud. D x f.273a (Red Book of St. Augustine's).

Item alia carta cyrographata Theobaldi dei gratia
Cantuariencis archiepiscopi et tocius Anglie primati
[*sic*] videlicet de prebenda quam sanctus Augustinus
habet apud Dovram et de terra de Gucestone cujus
tenor talis est:

[T]HEOBALDUS dei gratia Cantuarie archiepiscopus omnibus
sancte dei ecclesie filiis per Chent constitutis tam presentibus
quam futuris salutem. Universitati vestre notificamus quod
Hugo secundus abbas sancti Augustini cum nostro et aliarum
honestarum personarum consilio dedit Rogerio Folet centum
solidos pro terra de Guziestone que est de dominio prebende
quam habet beatus Augustinus in ecclesia sancti Martini de
Dovra quam videlicet terram Rogerius tum hereditario jure
tum donatione Jordanis canonici cognati sui sibi pertinere
dicebat. Et ipse Rogerus et uxor sua et heres suus scilicet filius
ejus primogenitus et Nicholaus frater suus et Eustacius filiaster
suus clamaverunt eam liberam et quietam beato Augustino et
abbati ad dominium prebende et hoc manibus suis in manu abbatis posuerunt ipsique [*sic*] Rogerus conventionatus est se de-
fensurum et adquietaturum terram illam contra omnem parente-
lam Jordanis et suam ad opus prebende et hoc se servaturum
bona fide prius in nostra postea in manu abbatis posuit coram
hiis testibus: Waltero archidiacono, Radulfo de Lisewys,
Raginaldo Apostolico, Radulfo elemosinario, Radulfo decano,
Andrea clerico, Willelmo de Tichesi, Willelmo de Staes,
Stephano Heregod, Haymone filio Henrici, Roberto fratre suo,
Willelmo de Horsfalde, Baldewyno Calveal[lo], Lamberto
Gargate, Rogero coco, Johanne filio suo, Symone de Hesdignel,
Thoma de Sancta Margareta, Rogero de Ponte Episcopi et
aliis pluribus. Set quoniam conventio ista coram nobis facta
fuit et terminata illam ratam et illibatam esse statuimus et
presentis scripti pagina nostro sigillo sigillata communimus.
Tradidimus eciam Rogero aliam cartam nostro sigillo sigillatam
hec eadem verba continentem — — — [*sic*].

ALSO (heading only) MS. ibid. Jul. D ii f.98b (Reg. of St. Aug.).
DATE: 1139 or a little later.

59

Confirmation by Theobald of the possessions of St. Gregory's
Canterbury (Aug. priory). He takes the canons under his protection.

MS. Cambridge U.L. LL.ii.15 f.9a (Cartulary of St. Gregory's
Canterbury).

Confirmatio generalis Theobaldi archiepiscopi.

THEOBALDUS dei gratia Cantuariensis archiepiscopus et tocius
Anglie primas episcopo Roffensi, archidiacono Cantuariensi,
abbati sancti Augustini, priori ecclesie Christi Cant' et omnibus
fidelibus per Angliam constitutis salutem et benediccionem.
Episcopalis officii est religionis viros ubique tueri eorumque paci
et quieti semper invigilare. Notum igitur sit vobis me ecclesiam
sancti Gregorii extra portam de Northgate fundatam canonicis
regularibus quos ibidem Willelmus archiepiscopus aggregavit
concessisse. Hos in mea propria potestate et successorum
meorum retineo et ne alterius persone dominio subjaceant constituo atque prohibeo. Elemosinas quoque et possessiones quas
bone memorie Lamfrancus archiepiscopus et alii predecessores
mei in decimis sive in ecclesiis sive in terris sive in molendinis
prefate ecclesie contulerunt vel alii fideles largiti sunt aut
inposterum largituri vel ego ipse adauxi, auctoritate dei omnipotentis et nostra confirmamus et presentis carte privilegio
corroboramus. Hec igitur sunt que predicta tenet ecclesia:
duodecim cotidiane prebende de hospitali ante ecclesiam,
ecclesia sancte Marie de Northgate, ecclesia Sancte Crucis de
Westgate, ecclesia sancti Dunstani extra civitatem, ecclesia
sancti Nicholai de Tanintune cum omnibus decimis tam in
terris quam in molendinis, ecclesia sancti Bartholomei de
Waltham cum terra que vocatur Joclete et decimis militum et
rusticorum, ecclesia sancte Margarete de Bederichesdenne cum
bosco et decimis, Hugifeld cum molendino de Tuniford, terra
de Jethinges, terra de Ritherle, decima vini de Tenham, terra
que fuit Humfridi cum Clopham, duo molendina ad Forwic,
terra que vocatur Pinchestegele, molendinum quod vocatur
Crienmelne cum aliis redditibus intra civitatem et extra, octo

acre ad Northflites quatuor de tritico et quatuor de ordeo, decima de Leanham, decima de Plukeleya, decima de Waedenhale et Denstede, decima de Wetechra, decima de Bereham, decima de Wedetune, decima de Gosehale, decima de Fliete, decima de Herteslonde cum ceteris omnibus que juste possident. Hoc igitur nostrum privilegium ne quis infringere vel aliqua ex parte violare presumat, ex auctoritate dei et ecclesie cui deo annuente presidemus sub anathemate prohibemus. Testibus istis Ascelino episcopo Roffensi, Waltero archidiacono Cantuariensi, Milone Crispino, Galtero priore sancti Neothi, Gileberto de Clare, monachis; Rogero de Ponte Episcopi, Alano de Welles, Wulfrico de Wroteham, Radulfo elemosinario, Radulfo filio episcopi, clericis; Willelmo de Einesford, Radulfo Picot, Ricardo de Plit///td [*sic*] Odone filio Johannis, Willelmo de Mellinges, Willelmo de Pagaham.

ALSO: in an abridged transcript MS. B.M. Harleian 7048 f.176a.

DATE: 1142–48.

60

Grant by Theobald to the canons of St. Gregory's of the land which their prior Alfred bought from Humphrey de Suniford and from Edmer, to be free from all services and payments for an annual rent of 10*s*.

MS. Cambridge U.L. LL.ii.15 f.2b (Cartulary of St. Gregory's Canterbury).

> Theobaldus archiepiscopus super terram que vocatur Northlande.

TEOBALDUS dei gratia Cantuariensis archiepiscopus omnibus ministris et hominibus suis de hundredo de Westgate salutem. Noscant presentes et post futuri me concessisse Alveredo priori sancti Gregorii et canonicis ibidem deo servientibus inperpetuum terram quam idem prior Alveredus emit ab Hunfrido de Suniford et terram quam emit ab Edmero, liberas et quietas ab omni servitio et consuetudine, singulis annis pro decem solidis. Test' Atselino episcopo Roffensi et Willelmo priore de Dovera et Willelmo dapifero de Einesford et Radulfo Picot et Nigello filio Godefridi cum multis aliis apud Cantoroburiam.

DATE: 1142–48.

61

Grant by Theobald as in 60, and also of three pieces of land free from all services and payments for an annual rent of 40d.

MS. Cambridge U.L. LL.ii.15 f.2b (Cartulary of St. Gregory's Canterbury).

Item Theobaldus archiepiscopus super idem tenementum (i.e. terram que vocatur Northlande).

TEOBALDUS dei gratia Cantuariensis archiepiscopus omnibus ministris suis et hominibus de hundredo de Westgate salutem. Noscant presentes et post[1] futuri me concessisse Alveredo[2] priori sancti Gregorii Cant' et canonicis[3] ibidem deo servientibus terram quam idem prior Alveredus[4] emit ab Hunfrido de Suliford[5] et terram quam emit ab Ædmero[6] pro quibus duabus reddent singulis annis decem solidos; terram eciam quam emit [7]ab Aisgaro cementario et quam emit ab Wluardo[7] de Tanet et[8] ab Ældiva[9] vidua pro quibus iterum reddent per annum xl[10] denarios. [End of folio and document in Cambridge MS.; Canterbury MS.:] Has terras eis confirmo imperpetuum ut teneant illas liberas ac quietas ab omni servicio et consuetudine per pretaxatum censum. Testibus Willelmo dapifero, Radulfo Picot, Wulfrico de Wroteham, Alano de Wellis, Rogero de Ponte Episcopi, Johanne de Cantuaria, Nigello filio Godefridi et multis aliis.

ALSO: copy of early 15th century on paper, found in Canterbury, June 1948, among fragmentary MSS.

VARIATIONS: [1]omits. [2]Aluredo. [3]canonisis. [4]Aluredus. [5]Suliforde. [6]Admero. [7-7]omits. [8]omits. [9]Aldiva. [10]quadraginta.

DATE: 1142–48.

62

Confirmation by Theobald to the canons of St. Gregory's of the chapels of Wadden Hall, Ashenfield and Elmsted, pertaining to their church of Waltham (Kent).

MS. Cambridge U.L. LL.ii.15 f.2b (Cartulary of St. Gregory's Canterbury).

Theobaldus archiepiscopus super ecclesiam de Waltham [later] et Elmisted.

TEOBALDUS dei gratia Cantuariensis archiepiscopus Anglorum primas et apostolice sedis legatus universis sancte ecclesie fidelibus salutem. Noverit universitas vestra quoniam ecclesie sancti Gregorii Cantuar' et priori et canonicis regularibus ibidem Christo militantibus cum ecclesia sancti Bartholomei de Waltham quam eis confirmavimus, eis similiter tres capellas ad predictam ecclesiam de Waltham pertinentes scilicet capellam de Wadehale et capellam de Æsmeresfelda et capellam de Ælmestede concedimus et donamus et ex auctoritate dei et nostra hanc donationem presentis scripti privilegio confirmamus, prohibentes sub anathemate ne quis in bona eorum manum violentam extendat nec contra presens auctoritatis nostre munimen temere venire nec eos inde decetero inquietare presumat. Valete.

ALSO: in an abridged transcript, MS. B.M. Harleian 7048 f.176a.
DATE: 1150–61.

63

Grant by Theobald to Edmund the priest of the church of Bekesbourne (Kent) in accordance with the grant of Robert de Hastinges.

MS. Cambridge U.L. LL.ii.15 f.16a (Cartulary of St. Gregory's Canterbury).

Theobaldus archiepiscopus super ecclesiam de Burnis.

THEOBALDUS dei gratia Cantuariensis archiepiscopus et tocius Anglie primas omnibus sancte ecclesie fidelibus salutem. Sciatis

me concessisse et hac carta mea confirmasse Ædmundo presbitero ecclesiam de Burnes quam Robertus de Hastinges filius
Godwini Frem ei in elemosinam concessit cum omnibus pertinenciis suis ita bene et libere et honorifice tenendam sicut ullus
antecessorum suorum eam unquam melius et honorificencius
tenuit. Testibus Waltero priore Cantuariensi, Gilberto de Clara,
Helya, Daniele, monachis; Johanne de Cantuaria, Radulfo
decano, Wlfwardo presbitero, apud Cantuariam die pasche.
Valete.

DATE: 1144–52.

The following is the charter of Robert de Hastinges, MS. ibid:

R[obertus] de Hastinges de Burnes omnibus inde probis hominibus salutem.
Sciatis quod consilio et concessione Theobaldi archiepiscopi Cantuariensis
concessi Edmundo sacerdoti ecclesiam sancti Petri de Burnes in elemosinam
ita libere et quiete et bene sicut aliquis suorum predecessorum liberius et
quietius ac melius tenuit. Unde vos exoro et exorando precipio ut predictum
Edmundum presbiterum vestrum diligatis honoretis et obediatis et ad illum
ut decet per omnia intendatis. Decimas et consuetudines illius ecclesie pertinentes de omnibus parochianis suis, si quis eorum aliquid detinuerit, per-
quiratis. Hujus donationis sunt testes: Radulfus decanus, Radulfus elemosinarius, Wlfwardus presbiter, Framelinus, Rogerus Folet, Elias monachus,
Daniel monacus et multi alii.

64

Confirmation by Theobald of the appropriation to Castle Acre
Priory (Clu. Norf.) of the churches of Castle Acre, West Newton,
South Creake, East Barsham, West Briggs, Methwold (Norfolk),
Haverhill (Suffolk), Sutton with the chapel of Lutton, and Fleet
(Lincs.), in accordance with the charters of Bishops William of
Norwich (1146–74) and Robert II of Lincoln (1148–66).

MS. B.M. Harleian 2110 f.119a (Register of Castle Acre Priory).

> Theobaldus de ecclesiis Acra, Neuton', Sudcrec, Est-
> barsham, Westbrig', Melewde, Haverill', Suttona, et
> Flet in proprios usus.

T. DEI gratia Cantuariensis archiepiscopus Anglorum primas et
apostolice sedis legatus universis sancte ecclesie fidelibus salutem. Ea que a venerabilibus fratribus nostris coepiscopis Nor-

U

wicensi et Lincolnensi canonice fieri dinoscuntur, nostre auctoritatis testimonio securius confirmamus. Hinc est quod justis postulationibus dilectorum filiorum nostrorum monachorum de Acra adquiescentes ecclesiam de Acra, ecclesiam de Neutona, ecclesiam de Sudcrec, ecclesiam de Estbarsham, ecclesiam de Westbrige, ecclesiam de Melewde, ecclesiam de Havereil, ecclesiam de Suttona cum capella de Ludtona, ecclesiam de Flet, cum omnibus pertinentiis prescriptarum ecclesiarum ad sustentationem pauperum in suos proprios usus sicut venerabiles fratres nostri W[illelmus] Norwicensis et Robertus Lincolniensis episcopi cartis suis eis confirmaverunt, nos quoque auctoritate qua fungimur confirmamus et presentis scripti nostri munimine corroboramus firmiter interdicentes ne quis aliquo modo de eisdem ecclesiis monachos vexare vel molestare presumat: salva in omnibus diocesani episcopi dignitate et justicia. Valete.

DATE: 1150–61.

65

Confirmation by Theobald of the appropriation to Castle Acre Priory of the churches of Sutton and Lutton with certain demesne tithes and the church of Fleet, in accordance with the charter of Bishop Robert II of Lincoln.

MS. B.M. Harleian 2110 f.119b (Register of Castle Acre Priory).

De ecclesiis Suttona et Flet, et decimis Bricheles-worde, Suavetone, Owestorpe.

T. DEI gratia Cantuariensis archiepiscopus Anglorum primas et apostolice sedis legatus universis sancte ecclesie fidelibus salutem. Que a venerabilibus fratribus nostris coepiscopis canonice fieri dinoscuntur, ea nostre auctoritatis testimonio securius confirmamus. Inde est quod justis postulationibus dilectorum filiorum nostrorum fratrum religiosorum monachorum de Acra adquiescentes ecclesiam de Suttona et ecclesiam de Luttona, cum omnibus earum pertinentiis, et terciam partem de dominio de Brichelesworda et duas garbas de dominio de Suavetona et duas garbas de dominio de Owestorp'; ecclesiam quoque de Flet cum suis pertinentiis in perpetuam elemosinam monasterio de Acra et fratribus ejusdem loci sicut venerabilis frater noster Robertus Lincolniensis episcopus eis sua carta confirmavit, nos quoque auctoritate qua fungimur confirmamus et presentis scripti nostri munimine corroboramus; salva in omnibus diocesani episcopi dignitate et justicia. Valete.

DATE: 1150–61.

66

Confirmation by Theobald of the creation of the parish of St. Mary Magdalene, Wiggenhall (Norf.), out of the parish of St. Peter's, Wiggenhall, in accordance with the charter of Bishop Everard of Norwich (1121–45). Should the endowments of St. Mary's be despoiled, it should once more be included in the parish of St. Peter's (as a subject chapel to its mother church).

MS. B.M. Harleian 2110 f.119a (Register of Castle Acre Priory).

Divisio parrochiarum de Wigehale.

T. DEI gratia Cantuariensis archiepiscopus Anglorum primas et apostolice sedis legatus universis sancte ecclesie fidelibus salutem. Divisionem parrochiarum sancti Petri de Wigehale et sancte Marie Magdalene ejusdem ville a bone memorie Ebrardo Norwicensi episcopo factam confirmamus et presentis scripti munimine communimus sicut predicti episcopi carta testatur. Si vero postea spoliata est aliquibus ecclesia beate Marie Magdalene reducatur in possessionem si sine judicio eam constiterit fuisse spoliatam et in pace decetero teneat. Valete.

DATE: 1150–61.

f.123b. Ebrardus dei gratia Norwicensis episcopus omnibus presentis et futuri temporis fidelibus salutem. Sciatis me concessisse et presenti carta confirmasse divisionem parrochiarum sancti Petri de Wigehale et sancte Marie Magdalene ejusdem ville et hoc rogatu Radulfi presbiteri qui eo tempore erat persona in supradicta ecclesia sancti Petri. Quare volo et precipio ut sicut supradicte parrochie meo tempore sunt divise ita firmiter et inconcusse teneantur in posterum. Valete.

See F. W. Maitland, *Domesday Book and Beyond* (1897), p. 367.

67

Grant by Theobald of twenty days indulgence to those visiting Cerne Abbey (Ben. Dorset) on the festival of SS. Peter and Ethelwold (1 August).

MS. Cambridge U.L. LL.i.10 f.1b (Cartulary of Cerne).

xx dies.

T. DEI gratia Cantuariensis archiepiscopus Anglorum primas et apostolice sedis legatus universis sancte ecclesie fidelibus salutem. Noverit universitas vestra quod omnibus qui ecclesiam Cernel' in solemnitatibus annuis beati Petri apostolorum principis et beati Edwoldi confessoris seu infra xv dies sequentes pia devotione visitaverint aut aliquod bonum transmiserint, viginti dierum indulgentiam de divina confisi misericordia concedimus. Et eos orationum ac beneficiorum Cantuariensis ecclesie participes constituimus. Valete.

DATE: probably 1150–61.

PRINTED: Dorset Nat. Hist. and Antiqu. Field Club, xxviii, 65, and translation on p. 77 alleging charter to be of Becket.

68

Confirmation by Theobald of the possessions and liberties of Chester Abbey (Ben.) as founded by Hugh, earl of Chester (1071–1101) and his wife, in accordance with the charter of St. Anselm (1093–1109).

Original (not consulted)   MS. Eaton Hall Charters 1.

TEDB' dei gratia Cantuariensis archiepiscopus et tocius Anglie primas omnibus sancte ecclesie fidelibus salutem. Noverit universitas presentium et futurorum quoniam abbatiam sancte Werburge Cestrie quam comes Hugo Cestrie et Ermentrudis comitissa uxor sua in honorem dei et sancte Werburge construxerunt et omnes possessiones quas servuli Christi monachi qui in ejusdem beate Werburge ecclesia divinis sunt obsequiis mancipati juste et canonice ex predicti comitis et comitisse donatione, sive aliorum principum largitione seu fidelium quorumcunque oblatione in presentiarum possident, sive in futuro canonice adipisci poterunt, confirmamus et presentis scripti munimine corroboramus, hoc adicientes et summopere monentes libertates quas sanctissime memorie beatus Anselmus venerabilis pater et predecessor noster prefate ecclesie scripto suo confirmavit stabiles permanere et a nullo diminutionem aut conturbationem sustinere. Si quis igitur patris nostri predicti beati Anselmi confirmationem aut nostram ausu temerario infestare aut irritare attemtaverit dei et nostre subjaceat maledictioni. Conservantibus autem et predictorum monachorum bona augentibus, dei benedictionem et nostram et vitam eternam optamus. Valete.

This original charter measures 23 in. long by 16 in. broad. The text is contained in five columns. The first 4¼ columns contain a charter of Ranulf II earl of Chester which includes earlier charters as well as Anselm's confirmation mentioned in Theobald's charter. Theobald's charter, written in a bookhand, occupies the second quarter of the fifth column, the remainder of which is blank. The charter originally had two seals. There is at present one damaged seal on the charter, but it is neither Theobald's nor the earl of Chester's. The charter is accepted by Tait, Gilson, etc. as genuine (Tait, *Chester Cartulary*, pp. 62 ff.).

ALSO: copies: (*a*) Cartulary of St. Werburgh's, Chester, MS. B.M. Harleian 1965 f.6a; (*b*) Two 17th-century transcripts MSS. ibid. 2060 f.67b and 2071 f.112b.

DATE: *c.* 1153.

PRINTED: J. Tait, *Cartulary of St. Werburgh's, Chester* (Chetham Society, 1920), p. 75; J. R. Planché in *British Archaeological Association* (1851), p. 323; translation in the *Journal of the Chester Archaeological Association* (old series), i, 297, with a 'facsimile' of the first four lines opposite p. 283 and a 'sketch' of the whole charter opposite p. 279.

69

Confirmation by Theobald to Chester Abbey of the vills and churches of Eastham and Bromborough (Cheshire) granted to them by Ranulf, earl of Chester (1129–53) and confirmed by Bishop Walter of Coventry (1149–59).

MS. B.M. Harleian 1965 f.10b (Cartulary of St. Werburgh's Chester).

Confirmacio Theobaldi archiepiscopi super ecclesiis Estham et Bromb'.

THEOBALDUS Cantuariensis archiepiscopus confirmavit ecclesie sancte Werburge donacionem Ranulfi comitis Cestr' super villis et ecclesiis de Estham et Brombur' quas antea W[alterus] Coventrensis episcopus confirmaverat. Item idem archiepiscopus dictas ecclesias et omnia bona ecclesie sancte Werburge canonice possessa sub proteccione Cantuariensis ecclesie suscepit, prohibens sub anathemate ne quis in bona ecclesie sancte Werburge manum violentam extendat nec diminucionem eorum faciat.

DATE: 1153-61.

PRINTED: Tait, *Cartulary of St. Werburgh's, Chester* (Chetham Soc.), p. 129.

70

Notification by Theobald of his decision in the case between the dean and chapter of Chichester and John abbot of Séez. The new priory of monks of Séez to be established by Bishop Hilary of Chichester (1147–69) in accordance with a papal mandate in the church of St. Nicholas Arundel (Sussex) has granted to the chapter of Chichester the prebend now held by William archdeacon of London in Singleton, East Dean and West Dean (W. Sussex) free from the jurisdiction of Arundel, but the chapter has renounced all rights in presenting to the other prebends of Arundel.

MS. Chichester Bishop's Archives Liber Y f.94a.

Carta confirmacionis prebende de Sengetona. Carta archiepiscopi Theob'.

T. DEI gratia Cantuariensis archiepiscopus Anglorum primas et apostolice sedis legatus decano et canonicis Cycestrensis ecclesie salutem. Cum venerabilis frater noster Hylarius episcopus vester secutus mandatum sedis apostolice ecclesiam beati Nicholai de

Arundello de monachis Sagiensis monasterii ordinare inten-
deret, visum est vobis quod justicie ecclesie vestre in hoc dero-
garetur, eo quod in donacione prebendarum ipsius ecclesie de
Arundello plurimum juris habere confideretis et idcirco eidem
ordinationi diu contradixistis. Tandem vero utriusque partis
assensu, nostra et interveniente auctoritate inter vos et predictum
monasterium facta est amicalis compositio in hunc modum:
Johannes ejusdem Sagiensis monasterii abbas et totus conventus
concesserunt ecclesie vestre et vobis prebendam quam tenuit
Willelmus Lundoniensis archidiaconus in Sengeltona, Estdena,
Uestdena, cum appendiciis suis perpetuo jure possidendam et
ab omni subjectione ecclesie de Arundello liberam. Vos vero
donationi prebendarum jam dicte omnino renunciastis. Quia
igitur nullus umquam finis litibus inponitur si ea que semel
recte sopita sunt iteratis refragationibus perturbentur, nos
memoratam compositionem ratam habemus et auctoritate
officii quo fungimur confirmamus.

DATE: 1150–52.

Summarised by W. D. Peckham, *Sussex Record Soc.*, 46, no. 160.

71

Notification by Theobald of his decision in the case between Hilary,
bishop of Chichester and Robert de Turneham, the archbishop
being assisted by Bishop Robert II of Lincoln (1148–66) and
William of Ypres. Robert quitclaims to the bishop six knights' fees
in Icklesham and Bexhill (Sussex). The bishop grants Wickham
(near Bexhill) to Robert. Robert will help the bishop recover the
lands belonging to Bexhill, when he will receive half of them and do
homage for them to the bishop, as well as for Wickham.

MS. Chichester Bishop's Archives Liber Y f.94a.

Confirmatio de terra de Bixle.

T. DEI gratia Cantuariensis[1] archiepiscopus Anglorum primas
et apostolice sedis legatus omnibus matris ecclesie filiis ad quos
littere iste pervenerint salutem. Universitati vestre notum esse

volumus quod super controversia que de terris pertinentibus ad manerium de Bixla inter venerabilem fratrem nostrum Hylarium Cycestrensem episcopum et Robertum de Turneham diu agitabatur, per nos et venerabilem virum R[obertum] Lincolniensem episcopum et domini Willelmi de Ipra utriusque assensu taliter facta est amicalis compositio. Idem Robertus dimittit episcopo in pace et quiete sex feoda militum que sunt apud Ichelesham et in ipsa villa de Bixla ita quod inde nullum deinceps servitium nec aliquam omnino consuetudinem requiret, set erunt in illa libertate atque conditione in quibus per regis cartam sunt confirmata. Ipse vero episcopus concessit Roberto terram que dicitur Wicham pro servitio quod inde fieri solet. Ad hec etiam Robertus debet sine omni fictione episcopum studiose juvare ad alias terras recuperandas que noscuntur ad ipsam Bixlam pertinere, ita quod de ipsis recuperatis habebit Robertus medietatem et tam de hiis quam de predicta terra de Wicham faciet homagium et solitum servitium episcopo et ecclesie Cycestrensi. Ambo quidem hanc[2] compositionem in manu nostra firmaverunt et nos eam presentis scripti auctoritate confirmamus.

ALSO: MS. D. and C. Chichester Liber B f.46a. Carta Thome archiepiscopi etc.

VARIATIONS: [1]omits. [2]omits.

Summarised by W. D. Peckham, *Sussex Record Soc.*, 46, no. 161.

DATE: 1150–54.

72

Confirmation by Theobald of the possessions of Clerkenwell Priory (Ben. Nunnery Middx.) in accordance with the charter of Bishop Richard of London (1152–62).

Original MS. B.M. Harleian Charters 83 C26.

TEOBALDUS dei gratia Cantuariensis archiepiscopus tocius Anglie primas apostolice sedis legatus omnibus sancte matris ecclesie fidelibus salutem. Res ecclesiarum sicut sanctorum patrum testatur auctoritas sunt patrimonia pauperum et precia

prec[ato]rum. Et quemadmod[um sacrosancta ecc]lesia nostre
salutis ac fidei perpetua mater est, ita nichilominus ejus patrimonium illesum debet perpetuo conservari et nulla desidia
nulla pravorum hominum perversitate convelli. Hoc nimirum
intuitu noverit universitas vestra nos justis postulationibus
Cristiane priorisse et aliarum sanctimonialium ecclesie beate
Marie de Clerkenewella annuimus et ea que juste et canonice
juxta tenorem carte venerabilis fratris nostri Ricardi Lond'
episcopi inpresentiarum possident aut in futurum justis modis
adipici poterunt presentis scripti munimine confirmamus et
auctoritate qua fungimur corroboramus has videlicet possessiones: terram quoque de Mosewella et terram illam quam
Jordanus dominus illius fundi eis dedit et concessit et quater
viginti acras apud Neutonam de donatione Bertrandi filii
Theodorici, et totam decimationem victus et potus et cande-
larum Henrici de Esexia, ferarum etiam ejus indagine clau-
sarum sicut carte eorum testantur. Prefatas igitur[1] . . . . modis
eis concessis siquis eas infestare temere aut contra rationem
vexare presumpserit [nisi] cito resipuerit indignationem omnipotentis dei et nostram maledictionem se noverit incursurum.
Earum quoque conservatoribus sit vita et pax et letitia sempiterna in secula seculorum. Amen. Valete.

ENDORSEMENT: De confirmacione archiepiscopi Cantuariensis.

SEAL: usual, with counterseal.

SIZE: 9·7 in. × 8·2 in., slightly damaged.

DATE: 1152–59.

PRINTED: *Records of Harringay to 1216*, p. 61, S. J. Madge (facsim.); W. Mc. B.
Marcham and F. Marcham, *Court Rolls of Hornsey*, p. xxix (facsimile);
J. F. Connolly and J. H. Bloom, *An Island of Clerkenwell* (facsimile, no text);
W. O. Hassall, MS. Bodleian, D.Phil. D 395 p. 1005 (typescript); (partly)
J. H. Round, *Archaeologia*, 56, p. 223.

73

Confirmation by Theobald of the possessions and liberties of Colchester Abbey (Ben. Essex) as confirmed by Pope Calixtus II
(1119–24) and Archbishop Ralph (1114–22).

[1] Hole in charter. About six words lost.

MS. Cartulary of Colchester, Earl Cowper (not checked with MS.; folio not given).

Theobaldus Cantuariensis archiepiscopus confirmat ecclesiam sancti Johannis et sua omnia.

THEOBALDUS dei gratia Cantuariensis archiepiscopus et totius Anglie primas omnibus episcopis et universo clero et populo per Angliam constitutis salutem. Paci et utilitati fratrum religiosorum in omnibus secundum rationem pro posse studere ipsa nos injuncta nobis officii episcopalis sollicitudo et cura ortatur et compellit. Sanctorum igitur antecessorum nostrorum exemplo et auctoritate provocati et corroborati, omnia bona et possessiones et elemosinas in terris et in ecclesiis et decimis aliisque rebus omnibus quecunque ecclesia sancti Johannis baptiste de Colecestria et monachi in ea deo servientes, temporibus sanctorum predecessorum nostrorum Radulfi, Willelmi, vel etiam nostro tempore, donatione fidelium seu aliis piis modis, possiderunt, presentis scripti pagina confirmamus, et ut inperpetuum illibata sibi permaneant, censemus et precipimus consuetudines et libertates quas rex Henricus eidem monasterio concessit, quas etiam dompnus papa Kalixtus confirmavit intemeratas conservari precipimus, et sententiam quam in perturbatores ejusdem monasterii vel antecessor noster dompnus Radulfus archiepiscopus vel dompnus papa Kalixtus imposuit, nos etiam corroboramus. Quicunque vero beneficia et elemosinas suas eidem loco impenderint et jura ecclesie manutenuerint orationes ecclesie nostre eis concedimus. Pax et benedictio omnibus benefactoribus suis. Valete.

DATE: probably 1139–54.
PRINTED: S. A. Moore, ed., *Roxburgh Club* (1897), i, 107.

74

Mandate of Theobald, probably to Bishop Robert of London (1141–51) and his archdeacons. They are to support the cause of the monks of Colchester against those levying unjust exactions and to excommunicate offenders without delay.

MS. Cartulary of Colchester, Earl Cowper (not checked with MS.;
folio not given).

Mandatum Theobaldi archiepiscopi episcopo Londoniensi contra transgressores sancti Johannis.

THEOBALDUS dei gratia Cantuariensis archiepiscopus et totius
Anglie primas venerabili fratri R. Londoniensi episcopo et
omnibus Londoniensis ecclesie archidiaconis salutem. Perlata
est ad nos filiorum nostrorum monachorum Colecestrie gravis
super quibusdam parrochianis vestris querimonia quod eorum
tenuras imminuunt exactionibus et consuetudinibus indebitis
gravant, nec anathema quod per illius ecclesie cartas archiepiscoporum et episcoporum auctoritate firmatas et per apostolice sedis litteras eis intorquetur aliquatenus reformidant. Unde
per presentia vobis scripta mandantes precipimus, ut servorum
dei quieti providentes nullis eos contra rationem permittatis
pulsari molestiis, set in eos qui tenuras aut dignitates monasterii prefati violando se implicant anathemate ut predictum est
justitiam ecclesiasticam remota omni frustratoria dilatione
faciatis. Valete.

DATE: 1141–61.
PRINTED: S. A. Moore, ed., *Roxburgh Club* (1897), i, 111.

75

Mandate of Theobald to Aylward archdeacon (of Colchester) and
the rural dean of Colchester. They are to excommunicate the
burgesses of Colchester if they continue to oppress Colchester Abbey
by making the monks responsible for the farm of the town.

MS. Cartulary of Colchester, Earl Cowper (not checked with MS.;
folio not given).

Idem [i.e. Theobaldus] contra burgenses Colecestrenses et sententia ejus in perturbatores.

THEOBALDUS dei gratia Cantuariensis archiepiscopus Anglorum
primas et apostolice sedis legatus Ailwardo archidiacono et

decano Colecestrie salutem. Pervenit ad aures nostras quod burgenses Colecestrenses abbatem et monachos sancti Johannis et eorum homines villam Colecestrie ad firmam tenere compellunt, et multis aliis modis libertatem ecclesie sue multorum regum temporibus habitam inquietant et infringunt. Ea propter precepimus quatinus easdem libertates quas habuit eorum ecclesia tempore felicis memorie illustris Henrici Anglorum regis amodo inconcusse possideat. Ex quo autem prepositi sive burgenses Colecestrenses monachos ad firmam tenendam compulerint vel aliquatinus eorum libertates violaverint, statim excommunicationis in eos et interdicti sententiam in villa Colecestrie proferre non differatis. Valete.

DATE: 1150–61, probably 1151–52 during vacancy in see of London.
PRINTED: S. A. Moore, ed., *Roxburgh Club* (1897), i, 108.

76

Grant by Theobald of twenty days' indulgence to those visiting Earl's Colne Priory (dep. on Abingdon, Essex) on the anniversary of the dedication of the church of St. Mary Colne.

MS. Chelmsford Essex Record Office D/D Pr 149 f.6a (Cartulary of Colne).

> Confirmatio ejusdem [i.e. Theobaldi] de condonatione peccatorum omnium venientium hominum ad dedicationem ecclesie de Colum.

T. DEI gratia Cantuariensis archiepiscopus omnibus sancte ecclesie fidelibus salutem. Notum sit devotioni omnium fidelium me condonasse omnibus ad dedicationem sancte Marie de Colun unoquoque anno venientibus xx^{ti} dies de penitentia peccatorum suorum unde confessi sunt.

ALSO: MS. B.M. Addl. 5860 f.113b (Cole's transcript of the above).
DATE: probably 1148. Colne was dedicated in 1148 (f.10a).
PRINTED: J. L. Fisher, *Cart. Prioratus de Colne*, Essex Arch. Soc. (1946), p. 7.

77

Confirmation by Theobald of the possessions of Colne Priory in Waldingfield (Suffolk). One third of the church and the demesne tithes of Roger de Ver and the tithes of his men as confirmed by Bishop Everard of Norwich (1121–45) and also two-thirds of the demesne tithes of Ralph son of Adam in accordance with his charter.

MS. Chelmsford Essex Record Office D/D Pr 149 f.5b (Cartulary of Colne).

> Confirmatio T. Cantuariensis archiepiscopi de eccle-
> sia de Walding' et aliis rebus.

T. dei gratia Cantuariensis archiepiscopus [to]tius Anglie primas et apostolice sedis legatus omnibus sancte matris ecclesie filiis salutem. Universitati vestre notificamus quod nos auctoritate domini apostolici et nostra qui [vi]cem ejus exequimur confirmamus et scripti nostri testimonio consolidamus mona-[chi]s de Colun terciam partem ecclesie de Waldingefeld cum xx^{ti} acris terre et totam decimam de dominio Rogeri de Ver et de terra hominum suorum in eadem villa et ceteris omnibus beneficiis sicut eis predictus Rogerus de Ver in elemosinam perpetuam concessit et [Ebrar]dus episcopus Norwic' confirmavit. Duas preterea partes decime de dominio Radulfi filii Ade in prenominata villa de Waldingefeld munimine perpetuo confirma[mus sicut] ipsius Radulfi donationis carta testatur, sed et cetera omnia beneficia quecumque in ecclesiis in terris in decimis in redditibus sive in quibuslibet bonis juste possident vel possessuri sunt perpetuo rata esse precipimus. Et ne quis in jus eorum [man]um[?] violentam extendere presumat vel bona eorum diminuendo invadat [sub] anathematis vinculo interdicimus. His testibus: Toma Lond' capellano nostro, W. de Norhala, [magistro W.] medico, W. et Ricardo de Clara monachis et Petro clerico nostro.

Also: MS. B.M. Addl. 5860 f.113a (Cole's transcript of the above).

Date: 1150–54.

Printed: J. L. Fisher, *Cart. Prioratus de Colne*, Essex Arch. Soc. (1946), p. 6.

78

Notification by Theobald to Bishop William of Norwich (1146-74) of the decision in his presence in the case between Ralph son of Adam and Bernard the clerk over his tithes (see No. 77). Ralph gives one mark of silver to Bernard who abandons his claim and surrenders his charter.

MS. Chelmsford Essex Record Office D/D Pr. 149 f.6b (Cartulary of Colne).

Confirmatio T. Cantuariensis archiepiscopi de possessionibus ecclesie de Colum.

T. DEI gratia Cantuariensis archiepiscopus totius Anglie primas apostolice sedis legatus venerabili fratri et amico W[illelmo] eadem gratia Nor' episcopo et omnibus aliis sancte ecclesie fidelibus salutem. Super controversia que inter Radulfum filium Ade et Bernardum clericum de duabus partibus decimationis de Watlingefeld, sub nostra presentia hoc modo sciatis esse transactum, quod ipse Radulfus dat jam dicto Bernardo unam marcam argenti et ipse B[ernardus] illi R[adulfo] decimationem illam liberam et quietam ab omni reclamatione et querela de cetero in manu nostra refutavit et cartam quam inde habebat ei reddidit et fidem interposuit quod nullo modo contra hoc pactum venire presumeret. Istis testibus: Toma Lond' capellano nostro, W[illelmo] de Norhala, magistro W. medico, Rogero Specie, W[illelmo] et Ricardo de Clara monachis, Waltero clerico de Mideltona. Valete.

ALSO: MS. B.M. Addl. 5860 f.113b (Cole's transcript of the above).

DATE: 1150-54.

PRINTED: J. L. Fisher, *Cart. Prioratus de Colne*, Essex Arch. Soc. (1946), p. 8.

79

Confirmation by Theobald of the grant made to Abingdon Abbey (Ben. Berks.) by Aubrey de Ver in the presence of Bishop Maurice of London (1086-1107) and in accordance with the charters of Henry I and Stephen of the church of Kensington (Middx.) with land gelding at two hides.

MS. Chelmsford Essex Record Office D/D Pr 149 f.6a (Cartulary of Colne).

> Confirmatio T. Cantuariensis archiepiscopi de possessionibus ecclesie de Colum.

T. DEI gratia Cantuariensis archiepiscopus Anglorum primas et apostolice sedis legatus sancte matris ecclesie filiis et fidelibus salutem. Que ad honorem et utilitatem ecclesie dei statuta rationabiliter esse noscuntur in sua stabilitate conservare debemus. Inde est quod terram illam quam Albericus de Ver assensu regis Henrici in presentia Mauritii bone memorie Lond' episcopi pro redemptione anime sue cum ecclesia de Kinsuetona ecclesie sancte Marie de Abendona dedit pro duabas hidis defendendam pro omni servitio, eidem ecclesie confirmamus et presentis scripti pagina communimus, dei et domini pape cujus vice fungimur et nostra auctoritate prohibentes ne quis omnino contra predecessorum nostrorum et nostram institutionem et regum Henrici et Steffani sicut eorum carte testantur, confirmationem, donationem istam infirmare aut exactionibus aut indebitis consuetudinibus contra predictorum regum statuta honerare presumat. Valete.

ALSO: MS. B.M. Addl. 5860 f.113b (Cole's transcript of the above).
DATE: probably 1150–54.
PRINTED: J. L. Fisher, *Cart. Prioratus de Colne*, Essex Arch. Soc. (1946), p. 7.

80

Notification by Theobald of his decision at Lincoln in the dispute between the nuns of (Nun) Coton (Ben. Priory Lincs.) and Ralph the priest of Swallow, over half the church of Kelby (Lincs.). Ralph has abandoned his claim.

MS. Bodleian Top. Lincs. D 1.f.14a (Cartulary of Cotham).

> Hec est confirmacio T. Cantuariensis archiepiscopi de medietate ecclesie de Keleby, pace facta inter Radulfum filium Ro[berti] sacerdotis et domum de Cot'.

T. DEI gratia Cantuariensis archiepiscopus Anglorum primas et apostolice sedis legatus universis sancte ecclesie fidelibus salutem. Notum esse volumus universis presentis temporis et futuri quod in causa que agitabatur in presencia nostra apud Linc' inter moniales de Cotun et Radulfum filium Roberti de Swalue sacerdotis super ecclesie medietate de Keleby, pace et concordia interveniente compositum est, ita quod idem Radulfus in manu nostra ecclesiam illam et nominatim porcionem quam juri suo vendicabat ad opus ancillarum Christi monialium de Cotun penitus refutavit et possessioni et juri suo omnino renunciavit. Iccirco eam predictis monialibus auctoritate qua fungimur confirmamus et presentis scripti munimine corroboramus. Valete.

DATE: 1150–60; Theobald was in Lincoln at Christmas in 1157.

81

Confirmation by Theobald of the grant by Walter bishop of Coventry (1149–59) to William the baker and his heirs of a mill. William is to pay 2s. annually and to mill grain freely for the bishop's table at (Bishops) Tachbrook (Warwicks.) in accordance with the bishop's charter.

Original   MS. P.R.O. Exchequer, O.A. Ancient Deeds B 11086 (E 326).

T. DEI gratia Cantuariensis archiepiscopus Anglorum primas universis sancte dei ecclesie fidelibus salutem. Noverint tam presentes quam futuri quoniam molendinum de Lee quod bone memorie Walterius Coventrensis episcopus dedit Willelmo pistori et heredibus suis hereditabiliter tenendum pro servitio suo et per cartam suam confirmavit, nos quoque auctoritatem donationis ejus ratam habentes eidem Willelmo illud molendinum hereditabiliter sibi et heredibus ejus tenendum confirmamus et presentis scripti nostri testimonio corroboramus, reddendo singulis annis duos solidos de censu et molendo quiete annonam Coventrensis episcopi de mensa sua de Tacheslesbroc sicut prenominatus episcopus in carta sua hoc expressit. Precipimus ergo ut idem Willelmus et heredes ejus molendinum illud hereditabiliter teneant. Quicumque ergo illius donationi sive nostre con-

firmationi ausu temerario obviare presumpserit vel aliquam ei
inde injuriam irrogaverit indignationem dei et nostram maledictionem noverit se incursurum. Valete.

ENDORSEMENT: Carta Willelmi pistoris de molendino de Lea pro ii solidis
quieta moletura.

SEAL: usual and counterseal varnished green (or white?).

SIZE: 3·1 in. × 8·3 in.

DATE: 1159–61.

PRINTED: T. Madox, *Formulare Anglicanum* (1702), p. 40. The charter of
Bishop Walter is printed op. cit., p. 177.

82

Grant by Theobald of twenty days' indulgence to those contributing
to the building of St. Bartholomew's Hospital, Buckland (nr. Dover,
Kent).

MS. Bodleian. Rawlinson B 335 f.5b (Cartulary of St. Bart's. Hosp.
Dover).

Indulgencia Theobaldi archiepiscopi de xx^{ti} diebus
et de participacione omnium bonorum que fiunt in
ecclesiis tocius diocesis.

THEOBALDUS dei gratia Cantuariensis archiepiscopus Anglorum primas apostolice sedis legatus omnibus sancte matris
ecclesie fidelibus salutem et benediccionem. Cum omnem intencionem vestram racio boni operis poscat augeri, non est aliquis
vestrum sicut devote confidimus qui spe ad bonum opus non
gaudeat incitari. Quoniam sicut homo potest habere quo recidat, ita elemosinis deo donante potest habere quo crescat.
Proinde per presentia vobis scripta mandamus et in domino
consulimus quatinus aliquam porcionem substancie vobis a deo
collate hospitali domo de Dovorr' quam duo fratres videlicet
Osbernus et Godwynus ad pauperes et peregrinos suscipiendos
nostro assensu et consilio et auxilio, et assensu tocius conventus
eorum diligenter edificant in remissionem peccatorum vestrorum conferre dignemini. Quicumque ergo aliquod beneficium
devota mente predicte domui et fratribus Christi receptis et

x

recipiendis juxta instantem neces- /[f.6a] sitatem contulerit de penitencia injuncta viginti dies in dei misericordia confidentes relaxamus et oracionum et beneficiorum Cantuariensis ecclesie et nostrarum et omnium ecclesiarum nobis subjectarum participem esse concedimus. Predicti ergo fratres sive eorum nuncii propter elemosinas vestras colligendas si ad vos venerint, tam a clericis quam a laicis diligenter recipiantur et pro domino honorentur. Illius enim nuncii sunt qui ait 'Hospes fui et collegistis me' [Matthew, xxvi. 35]. Valete.

DATE: 1150–61.

This hospital was founded by the authority of Theobald in 1141 (*V.C.H. Kent*, ii, 208).

83

Notification by Theobald of his ordinance regulating the status of St. Martin's Priory, Dover which is to be a cell of 'the Church of Canterbury'. The prior must be a monk of Canterbury Cathedral, his appointment and removal being in the hands of the archbishop, and the monks of Dover must make their profession at Canterbury.

Original   MS. D. and C. Canterbury C.A. D72.

T. DEI gratia Cantuariensis archiepiscopus Anglorum primas et apostolice sedis legatus omnibus sancte matris ecclesie fidelibus salutem. Que ad honorem et utilitatem ecclesie dei et religionis pacem et quietem statuta sunt, ut stabilia et inconvulsa permaneant munienda sunt perpetuis firmamentis. Inde est quod nos ecclesiam beati Martini de Dovera in qua auctore deo monasticum ordinem ibidem perpetuo mansurum sub ordine et disciplina Cantuariensis ecclesie instituimus eidem sancte Cantuariensi ecclesie confirmamus, statuentes ut jam dicta beati Martini ecclesia monasticum ordinem sub regimine prioris perpetuo servans sicut cella Cantuariensis ecclesie in dispositione archiepiscoporum successorum nostrorum et ecclesie cui subjecta est omni tempore permaneat, et ut nunquam priorem habeat nisi monachum professum Cantuariensis ecclesie, et ut fratres qui apud Doveram monachicum suscipient habitum suam semper in ecclesia Cantuariensi faciant professionem et

sicut ecclesie professi obedientiam matri Cantuariensi ecclesie
semper usquequaque exhibeant, et ut eadem ecclesia Doverensis Cantuariensem ecclesiam tanquam matrem et dominam
in omnibus veneretur nec unquam a subjectione illius subtrahatur. Institutionem vero et destitutionem prioris Doverensis
successorum nostrorum quibus in nullo prejudicare volumus
nec debemus reservamus arbitrio. Justum enim est ut qui
Cantuariensis ecclesie rector et dispositor est, plenam disponendi in omnibus auctoritatem in Doverensi que se Cantuariensis
ecclesie filiam debet exhibere obtineat. Hec itaque firmiter in
omne tempus precipimus observari sub anathemate inhibentes
ne quis contra hec venire aut hujus nostre constitutionis robur
aliquo modo enervare moliatur vel hanc quocumque modo
solvere unitatem. Si quis autem hoc attemptaverit omnipotentis
dei et beatorum apostolorum ejus et omnium sanctorum et
nostram maledictionem incurrat. His testibus: magistro Bartho-
lomeo Exoniensi archidiacono, Philippo Norwicensi archidiacono, magistro Johanne de Sareb', Ricardo fratre ejus, Hugone
de Gant, Eudone notario, Willelmo de Norhall', Osberto de
Presteton', Ricardo medico, Alveredo elemosinario, et multis
aliis.

ENDORSEMENT: Theobaldi archiepiscopi de subjectione Doverensis ecclesie.

SEAL: none.

SIZE: 4·5 in. × 9·6 in.

DATE: 1157–61.

COPIES: MS. D. and C. Canterbury Reg. I f.83a; B.M. Addl. 6159 f.286a
(Reg. of Christ Church).

84

Variant of No. 83.

Original   MS. D. and C. Canterbury C.A. D83.

T. DEI gratia Cantuariensis archiepiscopus Anglorum primas et
apostolice sedis legatus omnibus sancte matris ecclesie filiis
salutem. Que ad honorem et utilitatem ecclesie dei et religionis
pacem et quietem statuta sunt, ut stabilia et inconvulsa perma-

neant munienda sunt perpetuis firmamentis. Inde est quod nos
ecclesiam beati Martini de Dovera in qua auctore deo monasticum ordinem ibidem perpetuo mansurum sub ordine et
disciplina Cantuariensis ecclesie instituimus eidem sancte Cantuariensi ecclesie confirmamus, statuentes ut jam dicta beati
Martini ecclesia monasticum ordinem sub regimine prioris
perpetuo servans sicut cella Cantuariensis ecclesie in dispositione successorum nostrorum archiepiscoporum et ecclesie cui
subjecta est omni tempore permaneat, et ut nunquam priorem
habeat nisi monachum professum Cantuariensis ecclesie, et ut
fratres qui apud Doveram monachicum suscipient habitum
suam semper in ecclesia Cantuariensi faciant professionem et
sicut ecclesie professi obedientiam matri Cantuariensi ecclesie
semper usquequaque exhibeant, et ut eadem ecclesie Doverensis Cantuariensem ecclesiam quasi matrem et dominam in
omnibus veneretur nec unquam a subjectione illius subtrahatur.
Institutionem vero et destitutionem prioris Doverensis successorum nostrorum quibus in nullo prejudicare volumus nec
debemus reservamus arbitrio. Justum enim est ut qui Cantuariensis ecclesie rector et dispositor est, plenam disponendi in
omnibus auctoritatem in Doverensi que se Cantuariensis ecclesie
filiam debet exhibere obtineat. Hec itaque firmiter in omne
tempus precipimus observari sub anathemate inhibentes ne
quis contra hec venire aut hujus nostre constitutionis robur
enervare aliquo modo moliatur vel hanc quocumque modo
solvere unitatem. Siquis autem hoc attemptaverit omnipotentis
dei et beatorum apostolorum ejus et omnium sanctorum et
nostram maledictionem incurrat. His testibus: magistro Bartho-
lomeo Exoniensi archidiacono, Philippo Norwicensi archidiacono, magistro Johanne de Sareb', Hugone de Gant, Eudone
notario, Willelmo de Norhall', Osberto de Presteton', Ricardo
Exoniensi canonico, Ricardo medico canonico Meriton', Alveredo elemosinario et multis aliis.

ENDORSEMENT: Theobaldi archiepiscopi de subjectione Doverensis ecclesie.
SEAL: none.
SIZE: 4·6 in. × 9·3 in.
DATE: 1157–61.
PRINTED: J. B. Sheppard, *Literae Cantuarienses* (R.S.), iii, 370.

COPIES: MS. D. and C. Canterbury Reg. A f.187b; Reg. E f.62a; C.A. D98
(Inspeximus); C.A. D99 (Inspeximus); Lambeth 241 f.18a (Cartulary of
Dover); Corpus Christi College, Cambridge, 438 (Gervase's Chron.).
PRINTED: Gerv., ii, 288.

85

Confirmation by Theobald to the monks of Dover of the possessions
of the former secular canons of Dover.

MS. Lambeth 1212 p. 118 (Documents of Archbishop of Canterbury).

Nota pro monachis Dovorie: prima institucio monachorum ibidem.

THEOBALDUS Cantuariensis ecclesie dei gratia humilis minister
universis sancte ecclesie filiis salutem. Noverint presentes et
post[1] futuri quod ecclesie beati Martini de Doura[2] monachos
preordinavimus ad servicium dei et sancti Martini et ad hospitalitatem ibidem tenendam pro anima venerabilis memorie
Henrici regis et pro salute anime mee et antecessorum meorum
Lanfranci Ancellmi[3] Radulfi Willelmi concessique illis omnia
ad eandem ecclesiam pertinentia quecumque videlicet aut ego
in dominio meo habebam aut que ad prebendam clericorum
pertinebant. Quod siquis hoc nostrum statutum aut mutare aut
diminuere presumpserit anathematis sentencia feriatur.

ALSO: MS. Bodleian, Tanner 223 f.71a.
VARIATIONS: [1]omits. [2]Dovera. [3]Ancelmi.

In both MSS. followed by an inspeximus of it by Archbishop Hubert Walter.
At the end of the inspeximus in the Lambeth MS. is the following note:
'Originalia predictarum litterarum resident apud monachos predictos.'
Date of this is about the second half of the 13th century.

DATE: 1139-48.

For another instance of Theobald's use of the title 'humilis minister' see
John of Salisbury's Letters, P.L., 199, ep. 43, col. 27.

86

Confirmation by Theobald to the monks of Dover of the possessions
of the former secular canons and grant by Theobald to the monks of
the toll of Dover.

MS. B.M. Cott. Cleopatra E i f.34b. (Canterbury Docs. 12th century).

Carta Theobaldi archiepiscopi de theloneo Dovorie.

THEOBALDUS Cantuariensis ecclesie dei gratia humilis minister universis sancte ecclesie fidelibus salutes.[1] Noverint presentes et post futuri quod ecclesie beati Martini de Doura[2] monachos preordinavimus ad servitium dei et sancti Martini et ad hospitalitem ibidem tenendam pro anima venerabilis memorie Henrici regis et pro salute anime mee et antecessorum meorum Lanfranci Anselmi[3] Rodulfi[4] Willelmi[5], concessique illis omnia ad eandem ecclesiam pertinentia quecunque videlicet aut ego in dominio meo habebam aut que ad prebendas clericorum pertinebant qui veteri ecclesie beati Martini serviende ascripti erant, et nominatim theloneum quantum ad nos pertinebat. Quod siquis hoc nostrum statutum aut mutare aut diminuere presumpserit anathematis sententia feriatur. Testibus[6] Walterio [7]Cant' priore[7], Walterio archidiacono, Willelmo [8]priore Dourensis ecclesie[8], Arnulfo cantore ejusdem ecclesie; monachis Cantuar' Hugone de Cadumo[9] et Ricardo; clericis Alano, Johanne et Radulfo de Luxoviis et Thoma; militibus Odone, Willelmo de Mellinges, Ricardo de Maris[10], [11]Rodulfo Picot, Willelmo de Ainesford[11].

ALSO: in MS. Lambeth 241 f.2b. (Dover Cartulary.)

VARIATIONS: [1]salutem. [2]Dovera. [3]Ancelmi. [4]Radulfi. [5][f.3a]. [6]Teste. [7-7]priore Cantuar'. [8-8]Doffrensis ecclesie priore. [9]Chadamo. [10]Marys. [11-11]omits.

In the Lambeth MS. on f.8a is an inspeximus of this charter by Archbishop Hubert Walter, giving the first two witnesses only. MS. D. and C. Canterbury C.A. D95, a roll of Dover Charters, contains this charter and its inspeximus with similar variations. The inspeximus of Hubert Walter is also in MS. D. and C., Canterbury Reg. D. f.171b.

DATE: 1143–48.

87

Letter of Theobald to the burgesses of Dover thanking them for their grant to Dover Priory of the tithe of fish caught from Michaelmas to St. Andrew's day (30 Nov.). He asks them to give the tithe from fish caught during the rest of the fishing season and grants an indulgence of fifteen days to those dying during the fishing season.

MS. Lambeth 241 f.35a (Cartulary of Dover Priory).

Litera deprecatoria burgensibus Dovorr' pro decima
piscacionis ante festum sancti Michaelis facta per
archiepiscopum.

THEOBALDUS dei gracia Cantuariensis archiepiscopus dilectis
filiis et fidelibus parochianis suis omnibus probis hominibus de
Dovorr' salutem deique benediccionem et suam. Audivimus et
grates vobis scimus quoniam bene et fideliter decimas vestras
de piscatura vestra a festo sancti Michaelis usque ad festum
sancti Andree ecclesie vestre attribuitis. Decimas enim deo
dandas Habraham factis Jacob dictis insinuat. Deinde omnes
sancti commemorant. Unde quoniam ubique et omni tempore
debetis benefacere precamur et precando monemus ut si quandoque dominus dono gratie sue ante festum vel post festum per
piscationem vos ditaverit eidem domino omnium bonorum
largitori et retributori et ecclesie vestre pro salute animarum
vestrarum quamdiu piscacio duraverit decimam diligenter concedatis. Et si quis vestrum infra terminum piscacionis viam uni-
verse carnis ingressus fuerit, quantum sua expetit accusacio et
ad nos pertinet remissio, absolucionem dei et nostram habeat et
relaxacionem quindecim dierum de onere penitencie sue unde
penitens et confessus fuerit et insuper omnium oracionum et
beneficiorum ejusdem ecclesie vestre et nostri conventus et
nostrorum particeps fiat. Valete.

DATE: 1139–50.

88

Letter of Theobald to the burgesses of Dover thanking them for
acceding to his request in No. 87.

MS. Lambeth 241 f.35a (Cartulary of Dover Priory).

Litera supplicatoria ad burgenses Dovorr' pro decima
piscacionis solvenda monachis Dovorr'

THEOBALDUS dei gracia Cantuariensis archiepiscopus Anglorum primas et apostolice sedis legatus karissimis filiis suis
hominibus universis de Dovorr' salutem et benediccionem.

Gratulamur vobis in domino quia bonum de vobis audivimus sermonem. Audivimus quod decimam omnium piscium quos capturi estis deo et matri ecclesie vestre concessistis. Inde est quod magnas deo et vobis reddimus gracias et pro vobis specialiter et successoribus vestris in ecclesia nostra Cantuar' multiplicabimus ad deum oraciones. Rogamus ergo quatinus in bono proposito vestro perseveretis et quod causa dei et animarum vestrarum salute incepistis firmum et diuturnum esse faciatis. Valete.

DATE: 1150–57, before 89 and 90.

Cf. Suppl. C.2.

89

Mandate by Theobald and Canterbury Cathedral Priory to the burgesses of Dover to pay their tithes to Hugh, prior of Dover (1149–57) and in return offering prayers and masses for their and their ancestors' souls.

MS. Lambeth 241 f.39b (Cartulary of Dover Priory).

Concessio beneficiorum ecclesie Christi Cant' burgensibus Dovorr' per Theobaldum archiepiscopum.

THEOBALDUS dei gracia Cantuar' ecclesie archiepiscopus Anglorum primas et apostolice sedis legatus, et conventus ecclesie Christi Cant', dilectis filiis burgensibus Dovorr' salutem et benediccionem cum munere oracionum. Quoniam nostri officii interest lapsos revocare dubios et negligentes hortari bene agentibus perseveranciam persuadere, rogamus liberalitati vestre gracias agentes ut sicut Hugonem dompnum priorem Dovorr' et fratres cum eo habitantes diligitis et elemosinarum ac decimarum vestrarum beneficio fovetis, sic perpetuis liberalitatis vestre subsidiis infatigabiliter sustineatis, scientes quoniam qui parce seminat parce et metet, et qui seminat in benediccionibus de benediccionibus et metet. Dignam igitur meritis vestris recompensacionem referentes, sancte Cantuar' ecclesie communionem tam in missis quam elemosinis et oracionibus publicis et privatis, omnibus jura decimarum deo debita et

monachis beati Martini juste et legittime solventibus, concedimus et ut benevolencie vestre fervorem percipiatis predecessores
ac successores vestros ejusdem participii quantitate donavimus.
Valete.

DATE: 1150–57.

90

Notification by Theobald to Hugh, prior of Dover. The new tithe
of fish or its commutation is to be used for building and maintaining
the monastic church.

MS. Lambeth 241 f.36a (Cartulary of Dover Priory).

> Confirmacio Theobaldi de nova decima piscacionis
> cum sentencia lata in detentores.

THEOBALDUS dei gracia Cantuariensis archiepiscopus tocius
Anglie primas et apostolice sedis legatus Hugoni priori Dovorr-
ensis ecclesie et omnibus subsecutoribus suis et universo conventui ejusdem ecclesie et omnibus probis hominibus Francis
et Anglis de Dovorr' salutem. Sciatis nos concessisse novam decimam tam de piscibus quam de nummis, ecclesie monachorum
construende et edificande et inde imperpetuum conservande.
Quia ergo volumus ut ad hunc usum de cetero illa decima integre permaneat presenti scripto eam illi ecclesie confirmamus et
auctoritate qua fungimur corroboramus. Quicumque ergo
contra hanc nostram concessionem et confirmacionem ausu
temerario venire presumpserit et eam infregerit nisi cito et con-
grue resipuerit indignacionem omnipotentis dei et nostram
maledictionem se noverit in ultimo judicio incursurum. Valete.

DATE: 1150–57.

91

Confirmation by Theobald addressed to Bishop Walter of Rochester
(1148–82) and the clergy and people of Kent of all the fish-tithes
of Dover granted by the burgesses to the monks of Dover Priory.

MS. Lambeth 241 f.36b (Cartulary of Dover Priory).

Confirmacio Theobaldi de decima piscacionis novam mensionem faciens de allecibus.

THEOBALDUS dei gracia Cantuariensis archiepiscopus Anglorum primas et apostolice sedis legatus venerabili fratri et amico Walterio Roffensi episcopo et universo clero et populo tocius Cancie salutem et benediccionem. Que deo auctore semel divinis prestita sunt usibus irrevocabiliter firmare et firmata inviolabiliter conservare debemus. Inde est quod decimam tocius anni de omni genere piscacionis burgencium Dovorr' quam dederunt deo et monasterio beati Martini in usum monachorum et pauperum perpetualiter preter illam communem decimam allecis inter festum beati Michaelis et passionem beati Andree apostoli ab antiquo tempore datam sicut communi assensu pro salute animarum suarum et omnium successorum suorum incolumitate eam dederunt, ita eam ad opus monachorum sancti Martini de Dovorr' confirmamus et ratam hujus elemosine donacionem et a monachis oracionum promissam burgensibus recompensacionem cum monasterii fraternitate firmam esse volumus. Hanc itaque elemosinam a nobis confirmatam conservantes eterne retribucionis gloriam consequantur. Diminuere seu aliquatenus inquietare presumentes dei et nostram incurrant malediccionem. Amen. Valete.

DATE: 1150–61.

92

Grant by Theobald of forty days' indulgence to all those contributing towards the building of Dover Priory church.

MS. Lambeth 241 f.52a (Cartulary of Dover Priory).

Indulgencia Theobaldi archiepiscopi de xl^a diebus.

THEOBALDUS dei gracia Cantuariensis archiepiscopus tocius Anglie primas et apostolice sedis legatus universis sancte ecclesie fidelibus salutem. Equum est ac racionabile ecclesias sanctorum dei venerari votis et muneribus et edificare attencius

in terris quos certum est coronari in celis. Quicumque ergo
aliquas possessiones sive bona sibi a deo collata ecclesie beati
Martini que apud Dovorr' mirifico tabulatu construitur et in
qua deo deservitur ob reverenciam dei et beati Martini contulerit, quoniam proprie facultates illius loci ad illam perficien-
dam non suppetunt, in dei misericordia et beati Martini suffragiis confidentes de penitencia ei injuncta xl dies relaxamus
et oracionum et beneficiorum Cant' ecclesie eum imperpetuum
participem esse concedimus. Valete.

DATE: 1150-59.

93

Grant by Theobald of fifteen days' indulgence to all those contributing gifts at the altar of St. Giles in Dover Priory church, which
the archbishop has dedicated on St. Giles' day (1 September).

MS. Lambeth 241 f.55a (Cartulary of Dover Priory).

> Indulgencia Theobaldi archiepiscopi de quindecim
> diebus ad altare sancti Egidii.

THEOBALDUS dei gracia Cantuariensis archiepiscopus Anglorum primas apostolice sedis legatus universis sancte ecclesie
fidelibus salutem. Equum est ac racionabile fideles dei oracionibus atque dignis beneficiis venerari in terris quos fide deifica
credimus coronari in celis. Quicumque ergo fideli devocione
beatum Egidium in festivitate ejus in ecclesia beati Martini de
Dovorr' in qua quoddam altare in honore ipsius dedicavimus
invocaverit, et eum facultatibus sibi a deo donatis honoraverit
illius suffragiis confidentes, de penitencia sibi injuncta xv dies
relaxamus et oracionum et beneficiorum Cant' ecclesie eum
participem esse concedimus. Valete.

DATE: 1150-61.

94

Grant by Theobald of twenty days' indulgence to all those visiting
and contributing to Dover Priory on the anniversary of its dedication.

MS. Lambeth 241 f.52a (Cartulary of Dover Priory).

Indulgencia Theobaldi archiepiscopi de xx^{ti} diebus tempore dedicacionis.

THEOBALDUS dei gracia Cantuariensis archiepiscopus Anglorum primas et apostolice sedis legatus universis sancte ecclesie dei fidelibus ad quoscumque presentes litere pervenerint salutem. Noverit universitas fidelium ecclesie dei quoniam in honore dei et pro veneracione beatissimi confessoris atque pontificis Martini in cujus honore et nomine dedicatum est monasterium Dovorrense, statuimus indulgenciam fieri viginti dierum singulis annis in anniversario die dedicacionis illius monasterii et in septem diebus sequentibus. Proinde quicumque in anniversario dedicacionis illius die vel in aliquo sequencium septem dierum ecclesiam Dovorensem in honorem dei et beati Martini visitaverint et aliquo beneficio beatum Martinum honoraverint, de divina confisi misericordia eis viginti dierum de penitencia sua concedimus indulgenciam et omnium oracionum ac beneficiorum tam Cant' ecclesie quam fratrum illius monasterii eos perpetuo constituimus participes. Amen. Valete.

DATE: *c.* 1160. The dedication took place on 19 October 1159.

95

Notification by Theobald to all his men French and English of the hundred of Dover of an exchange of land between Hugh of Dover and the Priory of St. Martin's. Hugh gives the monks 10 acres adjoining the Priory and the monks give Hugh 10 acres adjoining Dover Castle and 10 marks. Hugh has solemnly undertaken before the archbishop not to withdraw from the agreement.

MS. Lambeth 241 f.59a (Cartulary of Dover Priory).

Litera testimonialis Theobaldi de x acris ante fores ecclesie pro x acris juxta castellum.

THEOBALDUS dei gracia Cantuariensis archiepiscopus tocius Anglie primas apostolice sedis legatus universis hominibus

Francis et Anglis de hundredo de Dovorr' et ceteris fidelibus
sancte ecclesie salutem. Noverit universitas vestra Hugonem de
Dovorr' sub presencia nostra concesse in perpetuam elemosinam
ecclesie beati Martini de Dovorr' ubi monachi nostri habitant,
x acras que sunt ante faciem ecclesie illius et ei ita necessarie et
competentes quod eis nulla occasione carere posset, et ipsi
monachi ei x acras juxta castellum Dovorr' fere in aquilonali
parte quasi in concambio dederunt inperpetuum et preter illas
acras, x marcas argenti illi dederunt tali pacto quod ipse a
predicta concessione x acrarum de cetero non resiliret et hoc in
manu nostra ipse affidavit et religionem fidei sue quasi obsidem
interposuit coram istis testibus: Willelmo [sic] episcopo Roff',
magistro J[ohanne] Sar', magistro J[ohanne] Tylebriensi,
Waltero Maminoth, Radulfo filio Geroldi, Jordano Picot,
Rogero de Conde, Thoma de sancta Margareta, Reinberto, et
multis aliis. Valete.

The bishop of Rochester at this time was Walter.

DATE: 1150-61.

96

Confirmation by Theobald addressed to Bishop Walter of Rochester
(1148–82), Thomas archdeacon of Canterbury (1154–62) and the
clergy and people of the archbishopric of the grant to the monks of
Dover by Hugh son of Fulbert of Chilham of the church of Hougham
(Kent), saving episcopal rights.

MS. Lambeth 241 f.189a (Cartulary of Dover Priory).

Confirmacio Theobaldi archiepiscopi super donacione Hugonis de Chileham.

THEOBALDUS dei gracia Cantuariensis archiepiscopus Anglorum primas et apostolice sedis legatus venerabili fratri et amico
Walterio Rofensi episcopo et Thome Cantuar' archidiacono et
toti clero et populo Cantuar' archiepiscopatus salutem. Notum
vobis esse volumus quod[1] Hugo filius Fulberti de Chileham per
manum nostram dedit et in perpetuam possessionem concessit
ecclesie sancte Marie et beati Martini de Dovorr' et monachis

ibidem deo servientibus ecclesiam de Hugham cum terris et decimis et omnibus beneficiis ad eam pertinentibus in perpetuam elemosinam possidendam et donacionem illam per cartam suam confirmavit. Nos igitur donacionem ejus ratam habentes, predictam ecclesiam de Hugham cum omnibus pertinenciis suis ecclesie beate Marie et beati Martini et ejusdem ecclesie fratribus concedimus et confirmamus et presentis scripti nostri munimine necnon et auctoritate qua fungimur corroboramus. Salvis in omnibus episcopalibus consuetudinibus, prohibentes sub anathemate ne quis contra hanc donacionem et nostram confirmacionem veniens donatam revocet elemosinam nec pertinencium bonorum faciat diminucionem. Valete.

ALSO: inspeximus of this charter by Hubert Walter on f.189b.

VARIATIONS: [1]quoniam.

DATE: 1154–61.

97

Grant by Theobald notified to the clergy of the chapter of Dover of the church of St. Mary's Dover to Matthew on condition that he pays an annual pension of 20*s*. to Dover Priory.

MS. Lambeth 1212 p.215 (Documents of Archbishop of Canterbury).

Carta Theob' archiepiscopi super ecclesia beate Marie de Dovorria.

THEOB' dei gratia Cantuariensis archiepiscopus Anglorum primas et apostolice sedis legatus omnibus clericis de capitulo Dovorie salutem. Quoniam ea que a nobis rationabiliter facta sunt posteris nostris nota fieri volumus, ne transcursu temporis super his aliquid dubium oriatur, ea scripto reservanda commisimus. Sciant tam posteri quam presentes quod concessimus et dedimus Matheo ecclesiam beate Marie de Doura cum omnibus pertinentiis suis in elemosinam, ita tamen quod jam dictus Matheus monachis beati Martini de ecclesia illa singulis annis pensionis nomine xx solidos reddet. Unde precipimus ut ecclesiam illam libere et quiete teneat et nequis ei aliquam injuriam irrogare presumat quamdiu predictos xx annuos

memoratis monachis in duobus terminis videlicet natalem
domini et pascham persolverit. T. etc. [*sic*].

Date: 1150–61.

98

Confirmation by Theobald to Ely Cathedral Priory of the grant by
Bishop Nigel of Ely (1133–69) of the manor of Hadstock (Essex)
with its church of St. Botulph to be appropriated to the service of
the altar and shrine of St. Audrey.

Original   MS. D. and C. Ely C.A. 83.

Tedbaldus dei gratia Cantuariensis archiepiscopus et totius
Anglię primas venerabili fratri Nigello Elyensi episcopo salutem et paternam benedictionem. Majestas ecclesiastici regiminis hanc propriam obtinet sollicitudinem ut piis fratrum
studiis ubique congaudeat eaque contra omnes impetus constanti auctoritate corroboret. Unde tuam venerabilis frater
Nigelle episcope benivolam largitatem gratanter amplectimur
et dignanter veneramur qua commissam tibi divinitus Elyensem
ecclesiam ad firmandam in perpetuum divinam servitutem
personis possessionibus ornamentis aliisque necessariis beneficiis
studes amplificare tuamque apud deum memoriam per secula
commendare. Statuimus ergo et nostra auctoritate confirmamus
ut rata et inconcussa sit tua devotissima largitio qua monachis
Elyensibus manerium de Hadestoca cum ecclesia beati Botulfi
ibidem constituta omnibusque quas carta tua continet rectitudinibus, sicut antiquam eorum possessionem proprie ac nominatim ad facienda opera altaris et feretri sancte Ætheldrethe
eternaliter restituisti veteremque religionem quam in prefata
sancti Botulfi abbatis ibidem quiescentis ecclesia ex parte renovare statuisti, statuimus et nos inviolabili decreto renovari.
Quicumque igitur successorum tuorum vel quilibet alii hanc
nostram confirmationem intemeratam servaverit divinę et
nostrę benedictionis particeps fiat. Si quis vero eam temerare
presumpserit quecumque persona sit sive ecclesiastica sive

secularis, sine discretione ordinis aut potestatis nisi citius emendaverit eterno anathemati subjaceat. Amen.

ENDORSEMENT: Confirmatio de Hadestoche, and Confirmatio Tebaldi archiepiscopi. Est alia carta ejusdem tenoris.

SEAL: none.

SIZE: 3·7 in. × 11·1 in.

DATE: 1144–50.

COPIES: in Cartularies of Ely, MSS. B.M. Cott. Tib. A vi f.118b; Tit. A i
f.41a and in a transcript Jesus Coll., Oxford, 76 f.162a; and in MSS. of
Liber Eliensis: Ely Cathedral Library, and Cambridge Trinity Coll.
MS. o.2.1. chapter 91.

99

Similar to No. 98 after Theobald had become legate.

Original   MS. D. and C. Ely C.A. 84.

T. DEI gratia Cantuariensis archiepiscopus Anglorum primas et
apostolice sedis legatus venerabili fratri et amico Nigello Elyensi
episcopo salutem et paternam benedictionem. Majestas ecclesiastici regiminis hanc optinet propriam sollicitudinem ut piis
fratrum studiis ubique congaudeat eaque contra omnes teme-
rarios impetus constanti auctoritate corroboret. Unde tuam
venerabilis frater Nigelle episcope benivolam largitatem gratanter amplectimur et merito laudabilem arbitramur qua commissam tibi Elyensem ecclesiam ad firmandam in perpetuum
divinam servitutem personis possessionibus ornamentis aliisque
necessariis beneficiis studes amplificare tuamque apud deum
memoriam per secula commendare. Statuimus ergo piam ac
discretam devotionem tuam commendantes et auctoritate qua
fungimur confirmamus ut rata et firma permaneat largitio tua
qua monachis Elyensibus manerium de Hedestocha cum ecclesia
beati Botulfi ibidem constructa et cum omnibus quas carta
hujus donationis tue continet rectitudinibus sicut antiquam
eorum possessionem proprie ac nominatim ad facienda opera
altaris et feretri sancte Ældrede eternaliter restituisti veteremque
religionem quam in prefata sancti Botulfi ibidem quiescentis
ecclesia ex parte renovare statuisti, statuimus et nos inviolabili

decreto renovari. Quicumque igitur successorum tuorum vel quilibet alii hanc nostram confirmationem intemeratam servaverit divinam optineat semper et nostram consequatur benedictionem. Si quis autem ausu temerario adversus eam venire attemptaverit nisi cito emendaverit divine in districto examine subjaceat ultioni et nostre maledictioni. Valete.

ENDORSEMENT: Confirmatio T. archiepiscopi pro manerio de Hadestoche: est alia carta ejusdem tenoris.

SEAL: usual with counterseal.

SIZE: 6·1 in. × 9·3 in.

DATE: 1150–61.

COPIES: in Cartularies of Ely: B.M. Cott. Tib. A vi f.118b; B.M. Addl. 9822 f.69b; B.M. Egerton 3047 f.17b; ibid. f.33b in an inspeximus of the abbot of St. Augustine's, Canterbury and the prior of Canterbury Cathedral in 1279.

IOO

Notification by Theobald of the decisions in five cases concerning the monks of Ely: (a) William archdeacon (of Cambridge) to pay an annual pension of 10s. for the churches of Hauxton and Newton (Cambs.); (b) Philip de Maisi to pay a mark annually to the monks for the church of Melbourn (Cambs.); (c) Wulfward to pay 5s. annually to the monks for two-thirds of the church of Lakenheath and one-third of the church of Undley (Suff.); (d) Joseph to pay 12d. annually to the monks for the chapel of Stuntney (Cambs.); (e) and the composition between Nicholas chaplain of Wentworth (Cambs.) and the monks in accordance with the charter of Bishop Nigel.

MS. B.M. Cott. Tib. A vi f.119b (Cartulary of Ely).

TEDB'[1] dei gratia Cantuariensis archiepiscopus Anglorum primas et apostolice sedis legatus universis [2]sancte ecclesie[2] fidelibus salutem. Causam que nitebatur inter monachos Elyenses[3] et Willelmum de Lanventona[4] archidiaconum[5] super ecclesiis de Havethestona[6] et Neutona[7] interveniente transactione diffinitam sicut carta monachorum eam diffinitam esse testatur ratam habemus et confirmamus, salvo redditu annuo monachorum quem idem archidiaconus eis solvet singulis annis

Y

videlicet x solidos annuos. Causas quoque aliarum ecclesiarum videlicet de Meldeborna[8] quam Philippus de Maisi tenet qui annuatim eis marcam argenti solvet, et[9] de Lagingaheda[10] et de Undeleia[11] unde Wluuardus reddet annuatim v solidos excepta tercia garba de Lachingaheda[12] et duabus de Undeleia quas monachi retinent in manu sua, interveniente compositione diffinivimus ita quod[13] predicti clerici[14] in vita sua tenebunt nomine monachorum [15]et post eorum decessum redibunt in usus monachorum[15]. De capella etiam de Stunteneia reddet annuatim Joseph xii solidos ad iiii[or] terminos. Post decessum[16] vero[17] ipsius Joseph redibit supradicta capella ad luminaria ecclesiae[18] Elyensis[19]. Hoc namque ante nos similiter diffinitum est. Compositionem quoque factam inter ipsos mona-/[f.120a] chos et Nicholaum [20]de ecclesia[20] de Winthewrda[21] sicut carta fratris nostri Nigelli Elyensis[19] episcopi eam factam esse testatur ratam habemus et confirmamus. Test' [22]Thom' Lund' et Philipp' cancell' et Willelmum de Ver et Petrum scriptorem.[22] Valete. Apud Tenham.

ALSO: MS. B.M. Cott. Tit. A i f.44b (Cartulary of Ely).

VARIATIONS: [1]Tedbaldus. [2-2] ecclesie sancte. [3]Elienses. [4]Laventona. [5]archidiaconem. [6]Havekestuna. [7]Neutuna. [8]Meldeburna. [9]omits [10]Lackingehida. [11]Wdeleia. [12]Lakingehida. [13]ut. [14]omits. [15-15]omits. [16]discessum. [17]omits. [18]ecclesie. [19]Eliensis. [20-20]capellanum. [21]Wintewrtha. [22-22]Thoma de Lund' et Philippus cancellarius et W. de Veir et Petrus scriba.

ALSO: in MSS. of Liber Eliensis, Ely Cathedral and Cambridge Trinity Coll. chapter 106 (not checked); in transcripts (1) MS. B.M. Addl 5819. f.8b; (2) MS. Jesus Coll., Oxford, 76 f.168b.

DATE: 1152; it is preceded by a mandate of Pope Eugenius III of that year delegating jurisdiction (Holtzmann, ii, 236).

101

Notification by Theobald of the decision in the case between William archdeacon of Cambridge and the monks of Ely after receipt of mandates from Pope Eugenius III (1145–53). William is to have the customary payments from the churches of the Isle of Ely due to the mother church (of Ely) paying the monks 10s. annually (see also the decision in No. 100). After William's death all is to go to the monks.

MS. B.M. Cott. Tit. A i f. 44b (Cartulary of Ely).

Carta Teodb' archiepiscopi super ecclesias insule.

TEODB' dei gratia Cantuariensis archiepiscopus et apostolice sedis legatus et Anglorum primas venerabili fratri Nigello Eliensi episcopo et omnibus fidelibus salutem. Causa quę nitebatur inter Elienses et Willelmum archidiaconum Cantebregie, mutato nomine de Ely ex archidiaconatu ex mandatis domini pape Eugenii et interveniente transactione, idem Willelmus tenebit et habebit consuetudines de ecclesiis insule quę ad matricem ecclesiam pertinere noscuntur et nomine monachorum possidebit, reddendo eis annuum canonem x solidos et ex ecclesiis de Hevekestune et de Neutune eodem modo faciet annuam pensionem eis tribuens et post illius decessum omnia ad usus monachorum convertantur. Hoc namque de ceteris ecclesiis suis canonice susceptis hoc modo nostra auctoritate censemus et judicamus. Valete.

ALSO: in MSS. of Liber Eliensis (not checked); in a transcript MS. Jesus Coll., Oxford, 76 f. 169a (Baker: deposited in Bodleian).

DATE: 1152.

102

Mandate of Theobald to Henry the clerk and Ralph, Roger and William de Halstede. They are not to interfere with the church of Stetchworth (Cambs.) from which Henry has been ejected. Theobald has invested the monks of Ely with the church by papal authority.

Original   MS. D. and C. Ely C.A. 82.

T. DEI gratia Cantuariensis archiepiscopus Anglorum primas apostolice sedis legatus H[enrico] clerico et Radulfo et Rogero et Willelmo de Halsteda salutem. Juxta tenorem mandati domini pape quod nuper accepimus monachos Elyensis ecclesię manerio de Stivitheswrđa investimus et in ejus possessionem introducimus et investimus et te Henricum auctoritate apostolicę sedis ab illo manerio et ejus pertinentiis removemus et alios prenominatos viros prohibemus ne de illo manerio decetero se intromittant nec aliquam molestiam illis fratribus inferre presumant. Alioquin in personas vestras anathema proferemus et firmiter observari faciemus. Valete.

ENDORSEMENT: no contemporary end. (14 cent.) Litera Theobaldi archiepiscopi Cantuar' ad investiendos monachos Elyenses in manerio de Steuchewrth'.

SEAL: none.

SIZE: 3·6 in. × 6 in.

DATE: end of 1153; cf. Holtzmann, ii, 253.

COPIES: in MS. B.M. Cott. Tit. A i f.48a. (Cartulary of Ely) and in two transcripts MS. Jesus Coll., Oxford, 76 f.174a (Baker: deposited in Bodleian) and MS. B.M. Addl. 5819 f.134b (abridged: Cole); and in MSS. of Liber Eliensis.

MS. B.M. Cott. Tit. A i f.48a. Stephanus rex Radulfo de Halstede et Rogero et Willelmo fratribus suis et Willelmo filio Baldewini salutem. Precipio vobis quod permittatis esse in pace terram monachorum de Ely de Stevecheuurde nec amplius vos intromittatis ullo modo nec inde quicquam capiatis et nisi feceritis justicia mea Canteb'scire faciat fieri ne super hoc inde clamorem audiam pro penuria justicię. Teste Willelmo Martel.

103

Mandate of Theobald to Bishop Nigel of Ely (1133–69). He must recover alienated or seized possessions of the church of Ely, especially Rettendon (Essex), Marham (Norf.) and Hartest (Suff.). Charters in the contrary sense are invalid and secular judges must be ignored. He has given instructions to all bishops to assist Nigel in his work.

MS. B.M. Cott. Tit. A i f.48b (Cartulary of Ely).

Preceptum Theodb' archiepiscopi de eodem.

THEDBALDUS dei gratia Cantuariensis archiepiscopus et tocius Anglie primas venerabili fratri Nigello eadem gratia Eliensi episcopo salutem. Pervenit ad aures nostras quod violenti quidam et pauperum oppressores ęcclesiam cui presides exactionibus et rapinis infe-/[f.49a] stare non cessant et, quod gravius ferimus, possessiones et villas quasdam beate Ædeldrede oppressionibus et aliis maleficiis a te violenter et contra quod licuit extorserunt. Set quoniam que vi vel timore facta sunt pro infectis habentur et item sacrorum canonum prescribit auctoritas, quod rerum ęcclesiarum venditiones emptiones donationes commutaciones factę sine assensu et conscriptione cleri inutiles et nullius momenti sunt, precipimus ęcclesię tuę bona sua restitui et omnia que a te violenter et ab invito extorta sunt ad prefatam ęcclesiam revocari, et precipue Radenduna, Merham, Herdhest, quę tuę ecclesię ablata esse audivimus. Si quę vero munimenta vel cartas tuas vel capituli tui oppressores ęcclesię tuę extorserunt, eas inutiles esse precipimus quoniam cum res ęcclesię tuę alienare non liceat, multo minus ne a raptoribus teneantur in posterum licuit confirmare. Si quis vero super his secularem adeat judicem ut illius auctoritate prefatę ecclesię bona possideat, licet ab ipso judice in causam voceris ne cujusquam omnino secularium sistas judicio prohibemus. Quoniam res ęcclesię que sunt redemptio peccatorum oblationes fidelium seculari judicio non moventur nisi sacrorum canonum negligatur auctoritas. De cetero ęcclesię tuę possessiones immobilium te volumus amodo conservare quantacumque poteris vigilantia ne distrahantur quia injustum est sustinere illa dispergi quorum te Christus preelegit collectorem atque custodem. Preterea siquis ecclesiam tuam in prediis, possessionibus, libertatibus, debitis, imminuere presumpserit postquam ipsius episcopo semel hoc demonstraveris nisi tibi satisfaciat in eum sentenciam canonicam proferas sive in episcopatu tuo fuerit sive Lundoniensi sive Norwicensi sive Lincollniensi. Fratribus autem nostris coepiscopis precipimus quatenus ecclesie tuę malefactores ex quo excommunicatos denunciaveris eos excommunicent et excommunicatos esse denunciant nec a sentencia posita relaxentur donec condigne satisfaciant. Valete.

ALSO in MSS. of Liber Eliensis (not checked) and in a transcript MS. Jesus Coll., Oxford, 76 f.175b (Baker: deposited in Bodleian).
DATE: 1157; follows mandate of Pope Adrian IV of 17 March 1157.

104

Confirmation by Theobald of the agreement between the church of Exeter and the monks of St. Martin des Champs (Clu. Paris) notified to Robert bishop of Exeter (1138–55) and the chapter. The chapel of St. James Exeter is to be held by the monks from the canons and the tithes are to go to the chapter. Parishioners can neither be made monks of St. Martin nor be buried in the chapel without the consent of the chapter, but the monks may have a cemetery.

Original (not checked with MS.). MS. D. and C. Exeter 2074.

THEOBALDUS dei gratia Cantuariensis archiepiscopus Roberto eadem gratia Exoniensi episcopo et ecclesie beati Petri Exoniensis capitulo salutem. Convencionem que inter vos et monachos sancti Martini de Campis facta est, videlicet quod ecclesia sancti Martini capellam sancti Jacobi a vobis imperpetuum teneat; decimas illius territorii capitulo ecclesie beati Petri Exoniensis reddat annuatim; de parrochianis eorum vel ad monachandum vel ad sepeliendum preter vestrum consensum nullum recipiat; concessum autem cimiterium quod a vobis multis et magnis suis et estimabilium personarum precibus obtinere promeruit, absque refragacione apud eandem capellam in perpetuum possideat, vobis et ecclesie vestre confirmavimus.

SEAL: none.

DATE: Oct. 1143 or a little later.

PRINTED: G. Oliver, *Monasticon Diocesis Exoniensis* (1846), p. 194; the agreement confirmed, ibid., p. 193.

See also H.M.C., *Various Collections*, iv, 45. R. L. Poole, who gives the text of the agreement writes, 'To the parchment strip which once bore the seal is appended a confirmation of the agreement by Archbishop Theobald.'

105

Confirmation by Theobald to the monks of Eye Priory (Ben. Suff. dep. of Bernay) of the parish church of Eye and the church of St. Leonard Dunwich (Suff.) appropriated to their uses and also of the pensions due to them from other churches granted to them by their founder Robert Malet.

MS. Chelmsford Essex Record Office D/D By Q19 f.31b (Register of Eye).

Carta Theobaldi Cantuariensis archiepiscopi.

OMNIBUS Christi fidelibus ad quos presens scriptum pervenerit Theobaldus dei gratia Cantuariensis archiepiscopus Anglorum primas et apostolice sedis legatus salutem in domino. Ad omnium vestrum noticiam volumus pervenire nos auctoritate nostra concessisse et confirmasse deo et ecclesie beati Petri de Eya et monachis ibidem deo servientibus ecclesiam sancti Petri de Eya parrochialem, et ecclesiam sancti Leonardi de Donewic' in proprios usus inperpetuum possidendas et eciam pensiones annuas debitas et antiquas ecclesiarum quas Robertus Malet eorum fundator eis dedit vel adquisivit in archiepiscopatu nostro, scilicet in episcopatu Lincoln' de ecclesia de Bergebi et capella de Steynwat sex marcas argenti, de ecclesia de Seckebroc triginta et quinque solidos, de ecclesia de Weleburn' quinquaginta et tres solidos; et in episcopatu Norwic' de ecclesia de Benseya duas marcas, de ecclesia de Laxfend unam marcam, de ecclesia de Badingeham unam marcam, de ecclesia de Bedefend' viginti solidos, de ecclesia de Jakeleya unam marcam, de ecclesia de Melles iiii solidos, de ecclesia de Thorendon' unam marcam, de ecclesia de Stok' iiii solidos, de ecclesia de Plaiford' quinque solidos, de ecclesia de Thornham quinque solidos, de ecclesia de Pelecoch iiii solidos, de ecclesia de Halegestowe sancte Margarete totam oblacionem candele ad festum sancte Margarete; et de ecclesiis de Donewic' scilicet de ecclesia sancti Petri duas marcas, de ecclesia sancti Johannis decem marcas et medietatem oblacionis candele tam in vigili quam in die sancti Johannis baptiste, de ecclesia sancti Nicholai unam marcam, de ecclesia Omnium Sanctorum quinque solidos, de ecclesia sancti Michaelis v solidos, de ecclesia sancti Bartholomei v solidos, de ecclesia sancti Martini xxx solidos. /[f.32a] Et ut ista concessio et confirmacio nostra firmam optineat stabilitatem presens scriptum sigilli nostri apposicione munivimus; salva apostolice sedis auctoritate et sedis Cant' justicia et episcoporum Linc' et Norwic'.

DATE: 1150–61.
COPY: MS. B.M. Addl. 8177 f.140a.

106

Confirmation probably by Theobald of the possessions of Eye Priory.

MS. Chelmsford Essex Record Office D/D By Q19 f.31a (Register of Eye).

Carta Thome Cantuariensis archiepiscopi prima.

T. DEI gratia Cantuariensis archiepiscopus Anglorum primas et apostolice sedis legatus universis sancte matris ecclesie filiis salutem. Noscat universitas vestra tam presencium quam futurorum quod monasterio beati Petri de Eya et monachis ejusdem loci ecclesias omnes de Donewic' tam factas quam faciendas et de Eya, nec non et ecclesiam de Bergebi et ecclesiam de Seckebroc et ecclesiam de Weleburn' cum capellis, ecclesiam de Benseya, ecclesiam de Laxfend, ecclesiam de Badingeham cum decimis, ecclesiam sancte Margarete de Satesham, ecclesiam de Thorendon', ecclesiam de Stok', ecclesiam de Pelecoch, ecclesiam de Melles, ecclesiam de Bedefend, ecclesiam de Thornham, ecclesiam de Jakesl', ecclesiam de Plaiford', ecclesiam sancti Botulphi de Yca cum appendiciis suis quas dedit eis Willelmus de Rovill' et Beatrix uxor ejus, et omnes quas habent ex donacione antiqua Roberti Maleth fundatoris sui auctoritate bone memorie Herberti quondam Norwic' episcopi et Willelmi successoris sui et omnes alias possessiones suas quas possident concedimus et auctoritate qua fungimur confirmamus. Concedimus vero eis ecclesiam beati Leonardi de Donewic' et ecclesiam beati Petri /[f.31b] que est infra villam habendas et possidendas in proprios usus, et omnes possessiones suas sicut rex H[enricus] eis concessit et carta sua confirmavit; prohibentes sub anathemate ne quis injuriam faciat inde nec in bona eorum violentam manum extendat. Valete.

DATE: 1150–61 or 1166–70.
COPY: MS. B.M. Addl. 8177 f.139b.

107

Confirmation by Theobald to Eye Priory of the churches of Eye and Dunwich and all other possessions in accordance with the charter of Henry I.

Original   MS. B.M. Harleian Charters 43 G 22.

T. DEI gratia Cantuariensis archiepiscopus Anglorum primas et apostolice sedis legatus universis sancte matris ecclesie fidelibus salutem. Noscat universitas tam presentium quam futurorum quoniam monasterio beati Petri de Eia et monachis ejusdem loci ecclesias omnes de Dunewica et de Eia quas habent ex donatione antiqua Roberti Malet auctoritate bone memorie Herberti quondam Norwic' episcopi et omnes alias possessiones suas quas juste et canonice possident concedimus et auctoritate qua fungimur confirmamus sicut rex felicis memorie Henricus eis concessit et carta sua confirmavit, prohibentes sub anathemate ne quis eis inde injuriam faciat nec in bona eorum manum violentam extendat. Valete.

ENDORSEMENT: Confirmatio Th. archiepiscopi Cantuariensis super pensionibus.

SEAL: none.

SIZE: 3·5 in. × 5·4 in.

DATE: 1150–61.

PRINTED: *Monasticon*, iii, 406.

COPIES: Register of Eye f.31b at Chelmsford and in transcript of the Register of Eye, MS. B.M. Harleian 8177 f.140a, which attribute the charter to Becket.

108

Confirmation by Theobald of the possessions of Eynsham Abbey (Ben. Oxon.).

MS. Oxford Christ Church Cart. of Eynsham f.20b (not consulted).

THEOBALDUS dei gratia Cantuariensis archiepiscopus tocius Anglie primas et apostolice sedis legatus universis sancte matris ecclesie filiis salutem. Noverit universitas vestra nos sub protectione sancte Cantuariensis ecclesie ecclesiam de Egnesham suscepisse et universa que ei canonice et rationabiliter a viris religiosis sunt collata perpetuo ei jure confirmasse et nostre consignationis munimine roborasse, ecclesiam videlicet sancte Ebbe in Oxeneford', ecclesiam de Tetteberia, ecclesiam de Stantona Joh[annis] de sancto Johanne, ecclesiam de Leges, ecclesiam de Meritona, ecclesiam de Merstona, ecclesiam de Suleþorna, capellam de Chersintona, capellam de Ærdintona, ecclesiam de Cumba, molendinum de Dailinton' et molendina duo in Circecstra. Has possessiones et universa quę justis modis fratres prefate ecclesie de Egnesham adepti sunt, auctoritate qua fungimur eis in perpetuum confirmamus. Teste Roberto de Cheisnei episcopo Lincolniensi et David archidiacono Bucking' et Roberto archidiacono Oxenef'.

DATE: 1155–61.

PRINTED: H. E. Salter (Oxford Hist. Soc. 1906–7), *Cartulary of Eynsham*, i, 57.

109

Mandate of Theobald to Henry (*c.* 1140–88) abbot of Fécamp (Ben.) to recover the possessions of his monastery lost during the war by revoking wrongful grants of monastic property.

MS. P.R.O. Transcripts Record Commission ii vol. 140a no. 321 (Trans. 8/140a). (1835).

From the Original at Rouen.

TEOBALDUS dei gratia Cantuariensis archiepiscopus Anglorum primas apostolice sedis legatus dilecto filio suo Henrico Fiscannensis monasterii abbati salutem. Querimoniam fratrum Fiscannensis monasterii quod sub protectione sancte Romane ecclesie quadam prerogativa cum omnibus pertinentiis suis esse dinoscitur sepius suscepimus quod possessiones, bona illius monasterii cui attenta sollicitudine preesse deberetis, incongrue distraxistis et dilapidastis in tempore verre quam diu sustinuimus, et eas raptoribus et depredatoribus quod fieri non licet in dampno predictorum fratrum concepistis. Quia igitur debito officii nostri prefato monasterio quod ad jus sancte Romane ecclesie cujus legatione fungimur debita subjectione pertinet attentius suffragari volumus et debemus, apostolica auctoritate et nostra vobis mandantes precipimus quatinus omnes possessiones et bona prefati monasterii que minus rationabiliter aliis concessistis, attenta sollicitudine et cura, quatinus revocare studeatis ne eorum alienatio et dilapidatio in ordinis vestri periculum revocentur. Illis vero qui post mortem illustris regis Henrici sepius dicti monasterii possessiones vestra cessione vel propria usurpatione occupare usque ad hec nostra tempora in quibus sancta ecclesia respirare videtur presumpserint, per presentia scripta mandantes precipimus quatinus ea ubicunque locorum fuerint, ita dicto monasterio omnino relinquant, alioquin de eis justiciam faciemus. Valete.

ENDORSEMENT: De quibusdam rebus alienatis revocandis.
CALENDARED: *C.D.F.*, p. 43.
DATE: 1150–61.

IIO

Letters of protection by Theobald in favour of the canons of Glemsford (Suffolk).

MS. Cambridge U.L. Ff.ii.33 f.141a. (Register of Bury St. Edmund's.)

> Sentencia sancti Thome archiepiscopi   [margin]de Glemisforde.

T. DEI gratia Cantuariensis archiepiscopus Anglorum primas et apostolice sedis legatus universis sancte ecclesie filiis ac fidelibus salutem. Volo ut sciatis quod ego concessi congregacioni clericorum de Glemisford ut teneant bene et libere omnes consuetudines elemosinarum et orationum quas actenus sub pace ecclesie sancte tenuerunt. Et hoc idem hiis meis litteris sub testimonio sancte ecclesie confirmo ne aliquis eis injuriam vel contumeliam inferat. Quare mando vobis et obsecro ut eandem congregationem ad honorem sancte ecclesie et ad salutem animarum vestrarum diligatis atque manuteneatis quatenus deus omnipotens absolucionem et remissionem omnium peccatorum vestrorum in hoc presenti seculo vobis tribuat et in futuro vitam concedat perpetuam. Amen. Si quis autem in illis vel in rebus suis manum injuste extenderit sentencie anathematis subjaceat nisi ad satisfaccionem et emendacionem veniat.

DATE: 1150–61 but the style of the charter in general seems to indicate an earlier date. Possibly the legatine title was interpolated.

PRINTED: D. C. Douglas, *Feudal Documents from Bury St. Edmund's* (British Academy Records of Social and Economic History, vol. viii), p. 161.

III

Confirmation by Theobald of the possessions of Gloucester Abbey (Ben.), in accordance with the charters of Stephen and Bishop Simon of Worcester (1125–50).

MS. P.R.O. Chancery, Cartulary of Gloucester (C. 150) f.37b.

Confirmatio Theobaldi archiepiscopi.

T. DEI gratia Cantuariensis archiepiscopus et totius Anglie primas dilecto filio G[ilberto] abbati Glouc' totique conventui monasterii beati Petri de Glouc' salutem et benedictionem. Injuncti nobis officii sollicitudo nos admonet ut paci et tran-quillitati commissarum nobis ecclesiarum pro modulo parvi-tatis nostre providere studeamus. Eapropter dilecte in Christo fili Gilleberte abbas Glouc' justis peticionibus tuis annuentes monasterium beati Petri cui preesse dinosceris speciali protec-tionis nostre cura amplectimur cum omnibus que de jure ejusdem monasterii sunt possessionibus quas scilicet carte illus-trium regum Angl' confirmant, quas etiam carta dyocesani episcopi domni Wygorn' sigillo impressa cartis et sigillis regum vel episcoporum aliorumque fidelium vobis concessas et donatas esse contestatur, necnon et illas quas in posterum liberalitate regum largitione principum oblatione fidelium vel aliis justis modis adipiscemini, inter que hec propriis duximus exprimenda vocabulis: manerium quod dicitur Berthona, Stanedys, Lecche, Otinton', manerium de Mayesmore cum silva et terris adja-

centibus ex dono Henrici regis, Brocthrop ex dono Aeline de
Hybreio, Culnam sancti Andree et duos rattnichenes, et unam
ecclesiam cum una hyda terre, et unum molendinum ex dono
Rogerii de Gloucestr'; ecclesiam sancti Petri de Hereford' cum
prebendis et terris et decimis et omnibus rebus que ad eam
pertinent ex dono Hugonis de Laceyo, escambium de orto
monachorum in quo turris Glouc' sedet sicut Walterius vicecomes eis liberavit, ecclesiam sancti Cadoci de Lancarvan cum
terra que vocatur Treigof ex dono Roberti filii Hamonis, in
Hamtesyra unam terram que vocatur Luttelton' ex dono
Hugonis de Portu, Lynkeholt' ex dono Ernulfi de Hes-/[f.38a]
dinge, Ledene quam reddidit Walterius de Laceyo, in Deven-
esira Plumtreu ex dono Odonis filii Gamelini quam postea
abbas Serlo excambivit Nicholao de Pola pro terra que dicitur
Alnodestuna, Clehangra ex dono Rogerii de Berkelay, in
Herefordesira unam hidam apud Asperton' ex dono Roberti
Curti, in eadem provincia unam hidam ex dono Willelmi de
Ebroicis, in Herchenefeld' terram de Westwode de dono
Walterii de Glouc', unam terrulam apud Gutinges de dono
Jurici de Logis, molendinum de Framiloda quod Winebaldus
de Badelone reddidit ecclesie, Clifford' de dono Rogerii de
Buseleyo, Rudeford' ex dono Henrici regis, ecclesiam de
Haethrop cum decima ejusdem ville et terra presbiteri, et in
eadem villa unum molendinum cum terra pertinente, ecclesiam
de Kynemereford' cum decima et terra sacerdotis, ecclesiam de
Northon' cum quinque virgatis terre et cum decima et aliis
rebus adjacentibus ex dono Ernulfi de Hesding' et Emeline
uxoris ejus, decimam Certertone de dono Nigelli de Oilli, de
dono Helye Gifford quamdam partem silve cum tribus bor-
dariis, de dono Patricii de Cadurcis unam virgatam terre in
Kinemereford' liberam ab omnibus rebus exceptis geldis meis
[sic], et unam mansuram in Mora nigri fossati similiter liberam,
et domo [sic] Edrici prefecti in Mora illa positas et terram que
ei pertinet et decimam pratorum illius ville, et unum molendinum cum terra ei pertinente et decimam duorum molendinorum ibidem, et unam hydam terre in Omenay de feodo et
concessu Patricii, in eadem villa dimidiam hydam quam Thovi
tenuit in elemosina de rege Henrico, Glasberiam apud Breken-

nio cum terris et silvis et omnibus ed eam pertinentibus, et totam decimam totius dominii de Brekennio scilicet annone pecorum, caseorum, venationum, mellis, insuper etiam ecclesiam de Coura cum tota decima illius parochie et terra ad ipsam ecclesiam pertinente et unam hydam que vocatur Beche ex dono Bernardi de Novo Mercato, ecclesiam sancti Gundlei cum terra et decimis ei pertinentibus ex dono Willelmi regis, molendinum de dono Helye Giffard', ecclesiam de Cerneye cum decima ad eam pertinente, et ecclesiam sancte Helene cum una virgata terre ex dono Walterii vicecomitis, duo essarta cum pratellis adjacentibus illis et silvulam in feodo meo [sic] de Celesworth' /[f.38b] ex dono Willelmi regis, terram de Rugge quam Thomas de sancto Johanne reddidit predicte ecclesie, Duntesburna ex dono Ermeline uxoris Walterii de Laceyo, unum molendinum cum virgulata terre adjacentis liberum et quietum ex dono Willelmi de Auco, terram de Sotthesora quam reddidit Rogerius de Berkelay, aquam que currit per abbatiam ex dono et concessu antecessorum meorum regum [sic] ecclesiam sancti Petri que est in foro de Norwico ex dono Willelmi regis senioris, unam culturam terre de Bulleya apud Hammam et decimam tocius venationis mee [sic] que capte erunt in forestis provincie Glouc' ex dono Henrici regis, ubicumque aliquid sibi vel ecclesie sue necessarium emerint vel transierint absque ulla thelonei vel transitus redditione liceat cum pace remeare ex dono Henrici regis, ubicumque evenerit capi piscem sturionem piscaturis suis sit eorum totus et integer et hoc ex dono Willelmi regis, totam terram ejusdem ecclesie quietam de carruagio et summagio et conducto ex dono Henrici regis, ecclesiam sancti Martini que est super Thamisiam apud London' et totam terram quam presbiter ejusdem ecclesie tenet solutam et quietam ab omnibus consuetudinibus et scotis ex dono Ranulfi Peverel, ecclesiam sancti Guthlaci in Hereford' cum omnibus ad eam pertinentibus ex dono venerabilis fratris nostri Roberti Hereford' episcopi [sic], ecclesiam de Wyrecesbur' et ecclesiam de Laverkestoke ex dono Roberti Gernun et assensu domini A[lexandri] Lincoln' episcopi, ecclesiam sancti Leonardi de Stanleya cum omnibus ad ipsam pertinentibus, capellam sancti Johannis Baptiste in silva que dicitur Basinch cum omnibus ad

eam pertinentibus, ecclesiam de Northona cum omnibus ad
eam pertinentibus, ecclesiam sancti Johannis Baptiste de Glouc',
ecclesiam sancti Paterni cum capell' et terris ad eam pertinentibus de dono Ricardi Gilberti filii, ecclesiam de Teyntona et
capellas de silva cum virgata terre, ecclesiam de Kilpeec cum
terris et decimis et omnibus ad eam pertinentibus, ecclesiam
sancti Michaelis de Ewyas cum omnibus ad ipsam pertinentibus,
insuper et decimas omnium maneriorum Roberti de Ewyas,
[ecclesiam?] sancti Michaelis de Uggemore et sancte Brigide
virginis cum omnibus ad ipsam pertinentibus, totam terram de
manerio de Estlecche quam pro manerio Glasberie de Waltero
de Clifford' escambierunt, ecclesiam etiam de Quenintona cum
virgata terre et decimis totius ville et aliis ad eam pertinentibus,
/[f.39a] parochiam etiam castelli Gloucestr' absque alterius
ecclesie participatione, relique etiam civitatis tam intra quam
extra muros sicut eam tempore Wlstani Wigorn' episcopi et
successoris ejus Sampsonis habuerunt, unam hydam terre in
Cumba ex dono Hugardi de Baskervilla, et ecclesiam de
Dugledi et omnes capellas et decimas ad eam pertinentibus ex
dono Wyzonis et Walterii filii ejus. Hec que ecclesie vestre
cartis et sigillis legittime confirmata dyocesani vestri testimonio
cognovimus, nos quoque eidem tam scripto presenti quam nostri
impressione sigilli confirmamus.

The following letter of Simon, bishop of Worcester (1125–50), on
f.32b follows King Stephen's confirmation of 1138 to Gloucester of
the same possessions.

Original   MS. B.M. Cott. Charters, xvii, 3.

Patri suo et domino Cantuariensi dei gratia archiepiscopo et totius
Anglie primati T., Simon Wigornensis ecclesie minister caritatis et
obedientie famulatum. Quoniam plenum habent firmamentum
apostolica auctoritate confirmante donationes, iccirco peticione
dilecti fratris nostri G[ilberti] abbatis Gloec' et fratrum ejus ecclesie
sancti Petri Gloec' cartas inspeximus et de his que in eis continentur
veritatis testimonium sullimitati vestre conscribimus quatinus hec et
vestra si placet auctoritate confirmetis et de hiis in apostolica testari
presentia non dubitetis. Noverit igitur serenitas vestra singula que in
presenti carta regis Stephani subscripta sunt tam ipsius quam
predecessorum ejus catholicorum regum et episcoporum et virorum

etiam nobilium donatione ecclesie sancti Petri Gloec' concessa esse et eorum cartis simul et sigillis confirmata. Valete.

DATE: *c.* 1139.

PRINTED: *Hist. et Cart. Mon. Gloucestriae* (R.S.), ed. W. H. Hart, i, 226. Simon's letter also in *Monasticon*, i, 551.

112

Confirmation by Theobald to Hamelin abbot of Gloucester (1148–79) and the monks of the action of the canons of Bromfield (Salop.) who have handed their house over to Gloucester Abbey and have become monks there.

MS. B.M. Cott. Domitian A viii f.146a (List of possessions of Gloucester Abbey).

Hic Bromfelda datur et canonicus monachatur.

ANNO domini m°c°lv° canonici de Bromfeld dederunt ecclesiam suam et seipsos sancto Petro Glouc' ibi monachari per manum Gilberti episcopi Hereford', Theobaldo archiepiscopo Cantuar' confirmante, tempore Hamelini abbatis.

DATE: 1155.

PRINTED: *Hist. et Cart. Mon. Gloucestriae* (R.S.), ed. W. H. Hart, i, 66.

ALSO: MS. Queen's Coll., Oxford, 367 (not consulted).

113

Mandate of Theobald to Bishop Uchtred of Llandaff (1139–48). He must forbid the celebration of divine service in chapels lately built in the parish of St. Cadoc Llancarfan (Glam.) to the loss of Gloucester Abbey. This also applies to the churches of St. Michael and St. Bride (Wigmore Heref.).

MS. P.R.O. Chancery, Cartulary of Gloucester (C150) f.115b.

De eodem [i.e. Lancarvan].

[T]HEOBALDUS dei gratia Cantuariensis archiepiscopus Uthredo dilecto fratri eadem gratia Land' episcopo salutem et benedictionem. Mandamus vobis atque mandando precipimus ut in capellis que in parochia sancti Cadoci de Lancarvan absque assensu et voluntate abbatis Glouc' nuper constructe sunt, divinum officium fieri non sinatis nec amplius alias fieri aut in aliquo jus prefate ecclesie minui permittatis et parochianis redditus et decimas persolvere rigore justitie coherceatis. Illam namque et alias quas habent ex dono Mauricii de London' videlicet ecclesiam sancti Michaelis et ecclesiam beate Brigide cum omnibus rebus ad eas pertinentibus in tutelam et protectionem nostram suscipimus et presenti scripto ecclesie Glouces-trensi in perpetuum assignamus. Valete.

DATE: 1139–48.

PRINTED: *Hist. et. Cart. Monast. Gloucestriae* (R.S.), ed. W. H. Hart, ii, 14; G. L. Clark, *Cartae et munimenta de Glamorgan* (1910), i, 98.

114

Grant by Theobald of fifteen days' indulgence to all those visiting and contributing to the church of St. Woollo, Newport (Monmouth).

Original MS. B.M. Cott. Charters, xvi, 38.

T. DEI gratia Cantuariensis archiepiscopus Angl' primas universis sancte ecclesie fidelibus salutem. Penitentibus et peccata confessis et ecclesiam dei devota mente venerantibus pietatis instinctu admonemur misericordie solatium retribuere et indulgentie remedium compensare. Inde est quod omnibus Christianis qui devotionis intuitu ecclesiam sancti Gunlei de Novo Burgo requisierint et in aliquo beneficio pro dei amore et animarum suarum salute eam honoraverint quindecim dierum indulgentiam de penitentia sua facimus et omnium orationum ac beneficiorum Cantuariensis ecclesie eos perpetuo participes constituimus. Valete.

ENDORSEMENT: .... de dono indulg. ....

SEAL: none.

SIZE: 3 in. × 5 in.

DATE: 1139–61.

Z

PRINTED: G. L. Clark, *Cartae et Munimenta de Glamorgan* (1910), i, 92.

COPY: MS. P.R.O. Chancery Cart. of Gloucester, f.133b (C 150/1).

PRINTED: *Hist. et Cart. Monast. Gloucestriae* (R.S.), ed. W. H. Hart, ii. 62.

See also J. E. Lloyd, *History of Wales*, index, s.v. Gwynllyw.

115

Mandate of Theobald to Bishop Nicholas of Llandaff (1148–83) after hearing from him that the church of St. Woollo was restored to Gloucester Abbey by the judgment of a Llandaff synod. The church must be entered even if a new key has to be made and Nicholas must invest the abbot of Gloucester (Hamelin 1148–79) corporally with the church and excommunicate anyone proving recalcitrant.

MS. P.R.O. Chancery, Cartulary of Gloucester (C 150) f.130a.

De [Novo Burgo].

T. DEI gratia Cantuariensis archiepiscopus Anglorum primas et apostolice sedis legatus venerabili fratri et amico N[icholao] Land' episcopo salutem. Accepimus ex tenore litterarum vestrarum quod judicio synodi Land' ecclesie, ecclesia sancti Gundlei de Novo Burgo restituta sit etiam vestra auctoritate abbati et monachis Gloucestrensis monasterii. Nos ergo judicium illud ratum habemus, et quod inde fecistis patrocinari per omnia volumus. Si vero clavem ecclesie quis detineat ut dicitur vos ad ecclesiam illam in persona vestra accedatis et nisi sacrilegus ille detentam clavem reddiderit, vos clavem novam nostra auctoritate faciatis et ecclesiam aperiatis et corporalem investituram abbati Glouc' tam de ecclesia sancti Gundlei quam de domibus et officinis et omnibus ad eam pertinentibus absque dilatione exhibeatis. Et si quis vobis restiterit vel abbati beneficia ecclesie detinuerit vel quamlibet molestiam ei irrogaverit, vos eum ecclesiastica disciplina coherceatis et in omnibus confidenter agatis, quia in hac re pro ecclesia Glouc' per omnia vobis validum prestabimus patrocinium. Valete.

DATE: 1150–56.

PRINTED: *Hist. et Cart. Monast. Gloucestriae* (R.S.), ed. W. H. Hart, ii, 53.

Possibly there was an appeal which would account for Nos. 116 and 117.

116

Notification by Theobald of evidence favourable to Gloucester Abbey in the case of the church of St. Woollo.

MS. P.R.O. Chancery, Cartulary of Gloucester (C 150) f.129b.

De [Novo Burgo].

T. DEI gratia Cantuariensis archiepiscopus Anglorum primas et apostolice sedis legatus universis sancte ecclesie fidelibus salutem. Notum esse volumus omnibus ad quos presens carta pervenerit nos audivisse testes Hamelini abbatis Glouc' super ecclesia sancti Gundlei, tres videlicet sacerdotes, testificantes se audisse et vidisse quod Robertus de Haya assensu Roberti filii Hamonis superioris domini concesserit ecclesie Glouc' et monachis ecclesiam sancti Gundlei et quod Herewaldus tunc Landavensis episcopus a manibus Roberti de Haya receptam abbati Serloni Glouc' tradidit et eum inde canonice investivit. Set et alios duos ejus audivimus testes laycos cum uno sacerdote testificantes se vidisse monachos in possessione ecclesie sancti Gundlei et eosdem monachos fructus percipere et quod sub nostro conspectu testati sunt consequenter juramento confirmaverunt. Ista audivimus et vidimus et hec testamur etc. [*sic*].

DATE: probably early 1156.
PRINTED: *Hist. et Cart. Monast. Gloucestriae* (R.S.), ed. W. H. Hart, ii, 51.

117

Notification by Theobald to Bishop Nicholas of Llandaff of his decision in the case between Gloucester Abbey and William earl of Gloucester (1147–83) over the church of St. Woollo, assisted by Bishops Hilary of Chichester (1147–69) Robert of Bath (1136–66) Jocelin of Salisbury (1142–84) Nigel of Ely (1133–69) and Nicholas of Llandaff (1148–83). By the evidence of charters and witnesses the church is adjudicated to Gloucester Abbey.

MS. P.R.O. Chancery, Cartulary of Gloucester (C 150) f.130a.

De [Novo Burgo].

TEOBALDUS dei gratia Cantuariensis archiepiscopus totius Anglie primas apostolice sedis legatus venerabili fratri et amico Nicholao Land' episcopo et universis aliis sancte ecclesie fidelibus salutem. Visis cartis monasterii beati Petri Glouc' et juramento multorum testium sane opinionis accepto super ecclesia beati Gun-/[f.130b] lei de Novo Burgo ex quibus, cum aliquotiens controversia in nostra presentia inter Willelmum comitem Glouc' et Hamelinum abbatem prefati monasterii super eadem ecclesia agitata fuisset, intellegentes illam ecclesiam ad jus jam dicti monasterii pertinere, consilio venerabilium nostrorum videlicet Hillarii Cycestr' et Roberti Bathon' et Jocelini Sar' et Nigelli Elyensis et Nicholai Land' episcoporum, predictam ecclesiam beati Gundlei abbati et monachis Glouc' adjudicavimus. Deinde inspecta carta prefati comitis, advocati hujus ecclesie qua illam ecclesiam cum omnibus pertinentiis suis predicto monasterio liberam et quietam inperpetuum concessit et dedit et confirmavit, ne lapsu temporum quod vel ante nos vel per nos super eadem ecclesia factum est in irritum posset revocari, auctoritate qua fungimur sepedictam ecclesiam cum omnibus ad eam pertinentibus monasterio Glouc' in elemosinam perpetuam concessimus et presentis scripti munimine confirmamus et eam ita confirmatam inperpetuum esse concedimus. Hec autem confirmatio facta est in anno m⁰ c⁰ lvi ab incarnatione domini et xvii kal. junii. Valete.

DATE: 16 May 1156.
PRINTED: *Hist. et Cart. Monast. Gloucestriae* (R.S.), ed. W. H. Hart, ii, 53.

118

Mandate of Theobald to Bishops Robert of Bath (1136–66) and John of Worcester (1151–57). If William earl of Gloucester still refuses to restore the church of St. Woollo to Gloucester Abbey, they are to excommunicate him and uphold the sentence which (Nicholas) bishop of Llandaff shall have passed on him.

MS. P.R.O. Chancery, Cartulary of Gloucester (C 150) f.129b.

De [Novo Burgo].

T. DEI gratia Cantuariensis archiepiscopus Anglorum primas apostolice sedis legatus venerabilibus fratribus et amicis R[oberto] Bathon' et J[ohanni] Wygorn' episcopis salutem. Quod a nobis super ecclesia beati Gundlei gestum est et qua ratione eam H[amelino] abbati et monachis Gloucestr' restituimus presenti scripto vobis significamus. Quoniam igitur W[illelmus] comes Glouc' ad diem peremptorium ante nostram presentiam omnino apparere contempsit et H[amelino] abbati et monachis Glouc' super ecclesia beati Gundlei respondere qua eos injuste spoliaverat, sentencia canonica dictante ipsi abbati et ejus monachis prefatam ecclesiam canonice restituimus. Quod si prescriptus comes eos contra sentenciam diffinitivam qua illam ecclesiam adepti sunt, et a nobis inde investiti vexare presumpserit, ecclesiastica ultione eum, secundum officium vobis per dyoceses vestras injunctum, coherceatis et compescatis, et sentenciam quam dominus Landav' episcopus in eum horum occasione protulerit et vobis denuntiaverit firmiter per vestras /[f.130a] dyoceses observari precipitis quousque resipiscat et ablata integre eis restituat.

DATE: 1156–57.
PRINTED: *Hist. et Cart. Monast. Gloucestriae* (R.S.), ed. W. H. Hart, ii, 52.

119

Confirmation by Theobald to Gloucester Abbey of the churches of Wraysbury and Langley (Bucks.) in accordance with a royal charter and the charters of Bishops Robert I (1094–1123) and Alexander (1123–48) of Lincoln, and of Bernard of St. David's (1115–47) and the recent decision of a synod presided over by David archdeacon of Buckingham.

MS. P.R.O. Chancery, Cartulary of Gloucester (C150) f.173a.

De [Wirecesburia].

[1]T. DEI gratia Cantuariensis archiepiscopus Anglorum primas et apostolice sedis legatus dilectis sibi in domino omnibus sancte

matris ecclesie filiis[1] salutem in domino et benedictionem. Incolumitati ecclesiarum et paci producentes[2] ea que ecclesiis ipsis bonorum principum largitione vel rationabili quorum-cumque executione adquiruntur pia ipsis benignitate conce-dimus et auctoritate nostra confirmamus. Audientes itaque ecclesiam[3] de Wirecesbur'[4] et ecclesiam de Langeleia ecclesie beati Petri Gloucestr' jam diu donatas rationabiliter et hoc plenius ex carta regia et [5]cartis venerabilium episcoporum Roberti scilicet episcopi quondam Lincoln' et Alexandri suc-cessoris ejusdem et reverendi[5] fratris nostri Bernardi episcopi sancti David cognoscentes, deinde cum quidam[6] se in easdem ecclesias intruserit[7], easdem ecclesias[8], et in pupplica synodo[9] ecclesie beati Petri adjudicatas, ex carta David archidiaconi Bukinghamie[10] et synodi[11] illius attestatione cognoscentes, et[12] plenius rescientes[13], ipsi ecclesie beati Petri Glouc' in earumdem ecclesiarum possessione plenum nostre auctoritatis robur concedimus et prefatas ecclesias ipsi ecclesie Glouc' pre-senti scripto inperpetuum confirmamus.

ALSO: in MS. Reg. A Gloucester Cathedral (not consulted).

VARIATIONS: [1-1]Dilectis sibi in domino omnibus sancte matris ecclesie filiis Theobaldus Cantuariensis archiepiscopus. [2]providentes. [3]ecclesias. [4]Wiresdesbiria. [5-5]scripto venerabilis. [6]quodam. [7]intruserint. [8]*adds* ipsis abjudicatas. [9]sinodo. [10]Blichingehamie. [11]sinodi. [12]*omits*. [13]*adds* plenum.

DATE: 1150–61.

PRINTED: *Hist. et Cart. Monast. Gloucestriae* (R.S.), ed. W. H. Hart, ii, 167, which gives above variations from Gloucester MS.

120

Mandate, probably by Theobald, to Bishop William of Norwich (1146–74). The bishop is to see that Gloucester Abbey obtains the greatest possible benefit from the church of St. Peter in the market of Norwich.

MS. P.R.O. Chancery, Cartulary of Gloucester (C 150) f.123b.

De eodem [i.e. pensione de Norwyco].

T. DEI gratia Cantuariensis archiepiscopus Anglorum primas et apostolice sedis legatus venerabili fratri et amico W[illelmo]

Norwic' episcopo salutem. Noverit dilecta nobis et veneranda fraternitas vestra quod speciali amico nostro H[amelino] abbati et monachis Glouc' speciale indulsimus gratie beneficium, videlicet ut ecclesiam sancti Petri quam habent in foro Norwici ad commodum suum prout melius poterint collocent. Et in hoc et in ceteris negotiis suis vestrum, nostri amore et gratia, impendatis auxilium et consilium necnon et auctoritatem, ne ex defectu vestre auctoritatis aliquid rerum suarum incurrant detrimentum ut vobis gratias referamus et vobis pro illis obnoxiores existamus.

DATE: 1150–61 or 1166–70.

PRINTED: *Hist. et Cart. Monast. Gloucestriae* (R.S.), ed. W. H. Hart, ii, 34.

121

Confirmation, probably by Theobald, of the decision of Bishop Hilary of Chichester (1147–69) in the case between Gloucester Abbey and the Knights Hospitallers over the church of Quennington (Glouc.).

MS. P.R.O. Chancery, Cartulary of Gloucester (C 150) f.145b.

De [Quenintone],

T. DEI gratia Cantuariensis archiepiscopus Anglorum primas et apostolice sedis legatus omnibus sancte matris ecclesie fidelibus ad quos carta ista pervenerit salutem. Quia controversia que inter monasterium beati Petri Glouc' et hospitalem domum Jerosolomitanam super ecclesia Quenintone vertebatur amicabili compositione interveniente sopita est, ne succedente tempore in dubium revocari possit, nos eam scripto nostro in posterorum notitiam deducere decrevimus eam ratam habentes et sigilli nostri munimine confirmantes sicut carta venerabilis fratris nostri episcopi Cycestrensis in presentia ipsius episcopi compositionem illam factam esse testatur. Valete.

DATE: 1160–61 or 1166–69.

PRINTED: *Hist. et Cart. Monast. Gloucestriae* (R.S.), ed. W. H. Hart, ii, 93.

Preceded by the decision of Hilary bishop of Chichester as delegate of Pope Alexander III.

122

Confirmation by Theobald of the possessions of the nuns of Green-field (Cist. Priory Lincs.).

Original   MS. B.M. Harleian Charters 43 G 20.

T. DEI gratia Cantuariensis archiepiscopus Anglorum primas et apostolice sedis legatus universis ecclesię dei fidelibus salutem. Que caritatis intuitu religiosis locis collata esse et in divinos usus conversa noscuntur, sicut diocesani episcopi sunt auctoritate roborata, ita et metropolitani perpetua stabilitate consolidanda. Inde est quod religiosis mulieribus ancillis Christi monialibus de Grenefelda locum ipsum in quo divinis noscuntur mancipate obsequiis cum omnibus possessionibus quas deo auctore in presentiarum rationabiliter noscuntur possidere seu quascumque rationabilibus modis in futurum poterunt adquirere perpetuo possidendum confirmamus et presentis scripti nostri auctoritate corroboramus et eas cum omnibus bonis suis in dei et sancte ecclesie et nostra protectione suscepimus, prohibentes sub anathemate ne quis in bona earum manum violentam extendat nec eis molestiam sive injuriam faciat.Valete.

ENDORSEMENT: [late] Carta Thebaldi Cantuariensis archiepiscopi.
SEAL: usual with counterseal, yellow-brown.
SIZE: 3·5 in. × 7·6 in.
DATE: 1150–61.
PRINTED: F. M. Stenton, *Danelaw Charters* (1920), p. 75.

123

Confirmation by Theobald of the possessions of Greenfield in accordance with the charter of Bishop Robert II of Lincoln (1148–66).

Original   MS. B.M. Harleian Charters 43 G 21.

T. DEI gratia Cantuariensis archiepiscopus Angl' primas universis sancte ecclesie fidelibus ad quoscumque presentes pervenerint littere salutem. Que a venerabilibus fratribus nostris coepiscopis canonice fieri noscuntur, ea nostre auctoritatis munimine merito confirmantur. Inde est quod justis petitionibus sanctimonialium de Grenefeld' adquiescentes ecclesie sancte Marie de Grenefeld' et monialibus in eodem loco divino mancipatis obsequio omnes possessiones et terras sive elemosinas quas Robertus venerabilis frater noster Linc' episcopus eis per cartam suam confirmavit nos quoque auctoritate qua fungimur confirmamus et presentis scripti nostri munimine corroboramus, sicut predicti episcopi carta confirmationis testatur. Que ergo in carta predicti episcopi continentur dignum duximus propriis exprimenda nominibus, scilicet: ecclesiam de Abi ex dono Eudonis de Grenesb' cum omnibus pertinentiis suis et duas culturas in eadem villa cum xii acris prati et totum nemus de Croshage. Preterea ex donatione Hamfridi de Haga xlv acras terre et v acras prati, ex dono Gisleberti de Rigesbi totam partem suam in nemore de Wolurichaga et quicquid pertinet ad dominium suum in nemore Presthage, ex donatione Rocelini filii Ricardi de Riggesb' totam terram quam habuit in Wolurichage, ex concessione Al' de Mundbi totam partem suam de Wolurichage et unam bovatam terre que pertinet at Snauthacroft cum communi pastura, et preterea ex donatione Willelmi filii Otvelis xxxii acras in campis de Toresbi. Hec quoque et alia omnia que juste et canonice in presentiarum possident et que futuris temporibus rationabiliter adquirere poterunt eis similiter confirmamus prohibentes sub anathemate ne quis in bona earum manum violentam extendat nec possessiones earum perturbare sive minuere contra justitiam presumat. Valete.

ENDORSEMENT: Carta Theobaldi Cantuariensis archiepiscopi.
SEAL: none.
SIZE: 9·2 in. × 5·5 in.
DATE: 1150–61.
PRINTED: F. M. Stenton, *Danelaw Charters* (1920), p. 76, and charter of Robert, ibid., p. 77.

124

Grant by Theobald notified to all his men, French and English, of Harrow (Middx) to Edmund son of Osmar, the physician, of the land which his father held in the archbishop's manor of Harrow, 1½ hides with pannage with an annual rent of 5s.

MS. Westminster Abbey Muniments 'Domesday' f.501b.

Carta domini archiepiscopi Cantuariensis de terra de Herges.

T. DEI gratia Cantuariensis archiepiscopus Anglorum primas et apostolice sedis legatus universis hominibus suis Francis et Anglis de Hergis salutem. /[f. 502a] Sciant presentes et post futuri quoniam concessimus et confirmavimus Eadmundo filio Osmari medico terram patris sui quam pater suus tenuit in manerio nostro de Hergis, scilicet hidam unam et dimidiam faciendo servicium quod ad ipsam terram pertinet, scilicet v solidos annuatim pro omni servicio. Iccirco precipimus quod eam honorabiliter et libere tenat [sic] in bosco et plano et prato et pascuis cum pasnagio suo sicut pater suus illud diracionavit. T. N[igello] Eliense episcopo, Ricardo de Belmes et Thoma de London' et Philippo cancellario et Ricardo Castel et Petro scriptore et Rogero Spic[ie] apud Lamhedam.

DATE: 1150–52.

All Westminster Abbey Muniments are printed by permission of the Dean and Chapter.

125

Grant by Theobald notified to his reeves and servants and all his men, French and English, of Harrow, to Alfwin the son of Godmar of Pinner, of his father's land, $1\frac{1}{2}$ hides and 12 acres with pannage at an annual rent of 19s. with $7\frac{1}{2}d$ landgable; with an additional virgate at a rent of 4s. and $7\frac{1}{2}d$ landgable.

MS. P.R.O. Chancery Enrolments Charter Rolls 16 Henry III m.12 (C53/26)

H[enricus] rex etc. salutem. Inspeximus cartam beati Thome martiris quondam Cantuariensis archiepiscopi in hec verba:

TH. DEI gratia Cantuariensis archiepiscopus Anglorum primas et apostolice sedis (legatus) prepositis et ministris suis et universis hominibus suis Francis et Anglis de Hereghes salutem. Sciatis nos concessisse et presenti carta nostra confirmasse Alwino

filio Godmari de Pinnora terram patris sui scilicet hidam et
dimidiam et xii acras pro xix solidis et pro vii denariis et obolo
de gabulo pro omni consuetudine et nominatim pro pasnagio
nutriture sue, et preter hoc concedimus ei unam virgatam terre
super quam mansit Brictiva reddendo singulis annis pro omni
servicio et consuetudine quatuor solidos et septem denarios de
gabulo et unum obolum. Quare volumus et precipimus quod
bene et in pace et hereditabiliter teneat per prenominatum
censum. T. Philippo cancellario et magistro Johanne Sar' et
Johanne de Tyleberia et Petro scriptore et Willemo de Norhal'
et Aluredo elemosinario et Hugone de Gant et Willelmo
Duredent et Roberto Halsard et Ricardo de Hida et Willelmo
sacerdote de Hese apud Hesam.

> Nos igitur hanc concessionem et confirmacionem
> ratam et gratam habentes eam pro nobis et heredibus
> nostris concedimus et sigillo nostro confirmamus.
> [Witnesses: 12 April 1232.]

DATE: 1150–61.
PRINTED: *Calendar of Charter Rolls*, i, 151.

126

Confirmation by Theobald notified to Bishop Walter of Coventry
(1149–59) in accordance with the charter of Bishop Roger of Chester
(1129–48) which he has inspected. The chapels and cemeteries at
Acton (Reynald) and (Great) Withyford belong to the mother
church of Shawbury (Salop.) which served the whole area before
they were built.

MS. B.M. Addl. 33354 f.8ob (transcript of Cartulary of Haughmond, 18th century).

> Confirmacio archiepiscopi dicti testimonii [i.e. of
> Roger of Chester].

T. DEI gratia Cantuariensis archiepiscopus tocius Anglie primas
apostolice sedis legatus venerabili fratri et amico W[altero]
Coventrensi episcopo salutem. Que divinis sunt mancipata serviciis justum est ut ea ipsis locis quibus rationabiliter concessa

sunt auctoritate qua fungimur confirmemus. Quare Actonam et Witheford', super quibus testimonium Rogeri quondam episcopi Cestrensis in litteris suis inspeximus quod antequam cimiteria sive capelle fierent apud Actonam et Withiford' ambe ville predicte fuerunt de parrochia de Sachesburia, juxta cujus testimonium ecclesie de Sachesburia in elemosinam perpetuam concedimus et presentis scripti munimine confirmamus, prohibentes sub anathemate nequis ausu temerario irritare seu infirmare presumat quod tanta est auctoritate roboratum. Valete.

DATE: 1150–59.[1]

The following is the charter of Roger of Chester on ff. 65a and 80b:

Rogerus dei gratia Cestrensis episcopus omnibus filiis sancte ecclesie salutem. Testimonium perhibemus quod antequam fierent cimiteria vel capelle apud Actonam et Withiford' utraque villa parochia fuit matris ecclesie de Scachesburia et quando cimiteria consecravimus terras et adcrementum que domini feudi fecerunt, matri ecclesie de Sachesburia concesserunt et nos ei confirmavimus. Valete.

There is another charter of Roger on f.65a confirming another church and cemetery to the same mother church.

PRINTED: R. W. Eyton, *Antiquities of Shropshire* (1854–60), viii, 147, from Cartulary.

The Haughmond Cartulary is now in the Shrewsbury Public Library.

127

Confirmation by Theobald to the Abbey of St. Benet's Holme (Ben., Norf.) of the two hundreds of Flegg and the hundred of Happing (Norf.) in accordance with the charter of King Stephen.

MS. B.M. Cott. Galba E ii f.44a (Register of St. Benet's Holme).

Theobaldus: confirmacio doni domini S[tephani] regis de hundredis de Fleg et Happinge.

THEOBALDUS[1] dei gratia Cantuariensis archiepiscopus et Anglorum primas omnibus sancte ecclesie filiis tam clericis quam laicis per Angliam constitutis salutem. Noverit universitas vestra quoniam donum et elemosinam quam dominus noster rex Stephanus ecclesie Hulmensi juste sive[2] canonice dedit concedimus et auctoritate dei et nostra confirmamus et sigilli nostri munimine corroboramus, videlicet duo hundreda de Fleg et tercium quod dicitur de Happingge[3] hundr'[4], sicut carta ipsius regis testatur. Precipimus itaque quod ecclesia Holmensis elemosinam hanc cum ceteris bonis ejus canonice adquisitis libere et honorifice et in pace bona teneat et inperpetuum possideat ne aliquis[5] inquietare aut temere perturbare presumat. Valete.

ALSO: MS. D. and C. Norwich Register 8 f.45b.

VARIATIONS: [1]T. [2]seu. [3]Heppinge. [4]hundret. [5]*adds* eam.

DATE: 1148–54.

PRINTED: J. R. West, *Register of St. Benet's Holme* (Norfolk Record Society, 1932), i, 46, and Stephen's charter on p. 28.

128

Confirmation by Theobald of the possessions of Holme. He takes it under his protection and confirms the grants of King Stephen in accordance with his charter.

MS. B.M. Cott. Galba E ii f.44a (Register of St. Benet's Holme).

Theobaldus: litera protectionis domini archiepiscopi.

THEOBALDUS[1] dei gratia Cantuariensis archiepiscopus et tocius Anglie primas episcopis abbatibus archidiaconis et omnibus sancte ecclesie ministris ac fidelibus salutem. Religiosorum virorum quieti in omnibus pro posse juste consulere et eorum utilitatibus in posterum racionabiliter providendo studere a deo nobis commissi episcopalis officii nos cura compellit. Ea propter[2] paci et quieti abbacie de Hulmo cui dilectus ac spiritualis filius noster Hugo abbas preesse et prodesse dinoscitur ac monachorum ibidem deo serviencium paterna solicitudine[3] invigilantes eidem venerabili abbati et abbacie predicte de Hulmo omnes terras et ecclesias et universas possessiones quas hactenus ubicumque [4]possederunt juste[4] vel in posterum deo opitulante canonice possessuri sunt presentis scripti[5] pagina confirmamus et confirmando corroboramus. Predictum igitur abbatem tancquam[6] spiritualem filium cum pretaxata abbacia sibi a deo commissa[7] in nostra custodia et defensione[8] suscipientes auctoritate dei et nostra mandamus et precipimus ut omnia bona que eadem ecclesia de Hulmo canonice possedisse[9] dinoscitur perpetualiter in pace possideat cum omnibus libertatibus et dignitatibus[10] suis quas illustris rex Stephanus ejusdem abbacie miserie pristine et destruccioni[11] pie consulens et succurens eidem loco concessit et dedit quemadmodum ejusdem regis Stephani carta testatur. Nullus igitur deinceps idem monasterium vel bona sua temere turbare vel ausu nephario[12] inquietare presumat, set in pace et quiete perpetua illibata[13] permaneant. Conservantibus eidem monasterio hec omnia pax et benediccio[14] dei ac nostra proveniat. Temere autem et nequiter ipsam[15] violantibus et perturbantibus donec resipiscant[16] ira et malediccio dei et nostra incumbat. Valete.

ALSO: MSS. B.M. Cott. Rolls, iv 57 no. 37 (*A*); Bodleian Norfolk Rolls 82 (oo) (*B*); D. and C. Norwich Reg. 8, f.46a (*C*).

VARIATIONS: [1]*B* Teobaldus, *C* Teob'. [2]*C* Eapropter. [3]*BC* sollicitudine. [4-4]*ABC* juste possederunt. [5]*ABC* adds nostri. [6]*AC* tanquam. [7]*A* comissa. [8]*A* defencione. [9]*A* possidisse. [10]*A* dingnitatibus. [11]*A* distruccioni. [12]*ABC* nefario. [13]*A* illibare, *B* illibate. [14]*A* benedicio. [15]*B* ipsa. [16]*A* recipiscant, *AB add* nichilominus *C adds* nihilominus.

DATE: 1147–49.

PRINTED: J. R. West, *Register of St. Benet's Holme* (Norfolk Record Society, 1932), i, 46.

129

Mandate of Theobald to Bishop William of Norwich (1146–74). He has received the (first) complaint of William abbot of Holme (1153–68) and Roger de Valognes that the church of Ranworth has been bodily removed from their land. The evidence of witnesses should be taken, and if the complaint is justified the bishop must see that the church is restored to its former position. The tithes must be sequestrated in the meanwhile.

MS. Bodleian Norfolk Rolls 81 no. 12 (Roll of St. Benet's Holme).

CONQUERUNTUR nobis dilecti filii nostri abbas sancti Benedicti de Hulmo et Rogerus de Valeines quod Avelina uxor H. de Ri et fautores sui ecclesiam sancte Helene in feudo suo apud

Randewrdam ab antiquo constructam convulserunt et in alio loco et alterius fundo, in eodem tamen cimiterio, abbate et ceteris reclamantibus, bellico confisi tumultu, plantaverunt. Eos etiam ad prestandas decimas suas et cetera quę prius ecclesie competebat a fundo abbatis et R[ogeri] de Valeines in alium translate dare compellunt et quendam Hermerum eis ad ecclesiam de fundo abbatis et R[ogeri] transferendam pro viribus patrocinantem propria auctoritate in ecclesia intru-serunt. De novo etiam postquam deo auctore serenum pacis Anglorum populo illuxit, altare quod in proprio loco translata capella sub divo reliquerant post interminationem vestram ut abbas asserit ipso abbate prohibente, et ne tolleretur auctori-tatem vestram opponente, noctu minuatim [?] asportaverunt. Unde fraternitati vestre mandantes precipimus ut utramque partem ante vestrum examen vocetis et assertione legitimorum testium clericorum et laicorum quibus neutra pars imperare vel interminari possit diligenter cum examinatione et cautione juratoria inquirere studeatis, utrius partis querela veritati innitatur. Porro si ita rem processisse constiterit prout abbatis querimonia astruit sine omni dilatione ecclesiam in priori loco reedificari precipiatis ab his qui eam asportaverunt et nisi sponte voluerint ad agendum debita pena coerceatis et omnia in ejusdem statu quo fuerunt tempore Herberti pie recordationis [pre]decessoris vestri reduci faciatis. Decime vero in ipso loco et feudo abbatis et alterius ubi ecclesia prius fuit congregentur, ipsoque in loco a iiii legitimis clericis vel laicis neutri partium faventibus, integre serventur donec lis ista debito fine termine-tur. Illis vero qui contra auctoritatem nostram et vestram altare fregerunt, ter citatis anathema infligere non differatis. Valete.

DATE: 1155–57.

PRINTED: First sentence, J. R. West, *Register of St. Benet's Holme*, Norfolk Record Society (1932), ii, 254.

130

Mandate of Theobald to Bishop William of Norwich. He has received the (second) complaint of Abbot William about the church of Ranworth. Further enquiries should be made as to whose territory the church originally stood in. Then the question of ownership and who should be the parson can be dealt with.

MS. Bodleian Norfolk Rolls 81 no. 13 (Roll of St. Benet's Holme).

De ecclesia de Randewrthe.

VENIENS ad nos dilectus noster W[illelmus] abbas de Hulmo repetitam querelam auribus nostris deposuit super ecclesia de Randw' de qua sibi nondum exhibitam esse justiciam asserit. Inde est quod fraternitati vestre presentium auctoritate mandamus quatinus convocato vicino capitulo et eo in quo prefata sita fuit ecclesia diligenti studio inquiratis in cujus territorio constructa fuit ecclesia. Et si prenominatus abbas docere vera testium assertione poterit locum illum a quo eruta ecclesia monasterio suo et sibi jure competere, eum et monasterium suum sepedicta ecclesia mediante justicia reinvestiri faciatis et deinceps controversiam seu de proprietate seu de personatu ordine judiciario fine justicie amico terminetis. Abbas enim nisi reinvestiatur prius cum se injuste queritur spoliatum proprietati rei de qua litigatur stare judicio non debet, nec jure potest compelli. Valete.

DATE: c. 1158.

131

Mandate of Theobald to Bishop William of Norwich. He has received the (third) complaint of William abbot of Holme and Roger de Valognes, about the church of Ranworth. The same procedure is to be followed as in Nos. 129 and 130. A royal mandate forbids appeal to the pope in view of the schism (1159–60).

MS. B.M. Cott. Galba E ii f.32a (Register of St. Benet's Holme).

Litera Theobaldi archiepiscopi de ecclesia de Randewrthe.

T. DEI gratia Cantuariensis archiepiscopus et tocius Anglie primas venerabili fratri et amico Willelmo Norwicensi episcopo salutem. Querimoniam dilecti filii nostri Willelmi abbatis de Hulmo et com . . . . sepius repetitam accepimus super ecclesia de Randewrtha de qua sibi nullam adhuc exhibitam fuisse justiciam conqueruntur. Inde est quod fraternitati vestre presencium auctoritate mandamus precipientes, quatinus evocato vicino capitulo et eo in quo prefata ecclesia sita fuit diligenti studio inquiratis in cujus territorio constructa fuerit ecclesia. Quod si prenominatus abbas et jamdictus . . . . vera testium assercione docere poterunt locum illum a quo eruta fuit ecclesia monasterio et abbati Hulmensi et feodo . . . . jure debere competere, eos et monasterium Hulmense sepedicta ecclesia mediante justicia reinvestiri faciatis et deinceps controversiam seu de proprietate seu de personatu, ordine judiciario et fine justicie amico terminare studeatis, nisi enim prius reinvestiantur inde cum se injuste querantur spoliatos de rei proprietate de qua litigatur stare judicio non debent nec de jure poterunt compelli. Preterea mandatum domini regis super hoc specialiter accepimus de exhibenda eis justicia, videlicet quod quid a vestra discrecione jubemus media equitate executioni mancipari, ne tam speciali precepto quam communi a domino rege vobis destinato videamini obviasse, quo precipimur diligencius omnibus conquerentibus justiciam exhibere, ne manente scismate in ecclesia Romana quemquam oporteat regnum egredi nostrum ob secutionem justicie. Decime in ipso loco et feudo abbatis /[f.32b] ubi ecclesia prius fuit congregentur, ipsoque in loco a quatuor legitimis clericis vel laicis neutri partium faventibus integre serventur, donec lis ista debito fine terminetur. Illis vero qui contra auctoritatem nostram et vestram altare fregerunt, ter legitime citatis anathema infligere non differatis. Valete.

DATE: 1159–60.

PRINTED: J. R. West, *Register of St. Benet's Holme,* Norfolk Record Society (1932), i, 16.

132

Mandate of Theobald to Bishop William of Norwich. As William of Oby has taken the Crusader's badge and has proposed to visit the Holy Sepulchre, the bishop must see that the land of Oby (Norf.) which William rented from the monks of Holme is restored to them in the condition in which his father Richard had best held it.

2A

MS. B.M. Cott. Galba E ii f.32b (Register of St. Benet's Holme).

Litera de resignacione manerii de Ouby.

T. DEI gratia Cantuariensis archiepiscopus Angl' primas venerabili fratri et amico W[illelmo] Norwicensi episcopo salutem.
Significavit nobis dilectus filius noster W[illelmus] abbas sancti
Benedicti de Hulmo quod Willelmus de Ouby qui porcionem
monachorum sancti Benedicti de eadem villa de Ouby ad
firmam tenuit, signo dominice crucis assumpto sepulcrum
domini visitare proposuerit. Unde quia regis auctoritate et
mandato feodum ipsum quod de sancto Benedicto ad firmam
tenebat antequam iter propositum arripiat[1] ad manus abbatis
et monachorum in dominio devolvendum est, precipimus
quatinus eundem Willelmum antequam iter arripiat districte
ecclesiastica censura coherceatis ad restituendam monachis
firmam suam preteriti temporis plene in omnibus, et terram
ipsam ita plene restauratam domibus et virgultis et aliis edi-
ficiis et instauramentis sicut Ricardus pater ejus melius instau-
ratam recepit, ne ecclesia sancti Benedicti in aliquo juris sui
detrimentum sustineat per defectum justicie vestre occasione
peregrinacionis illius hominis. Valete.

ALSO: MS. D. and C., Norwich Register 8 f.43a.

VARIATIONS: [1][f.43b].

DATE: probably 1153–61.

PRINTED: J. R. West, *Register of St. Benet's Holme*, Norfolk Record Society
(1932), i, 18, and *Monasticon*, iii, 88.

133

Confirmation by Theobald of the appropriation to Holme of the
churches of Neatishead, Irstead and Bastwick (Norf.) in accordance
with the charter of Bishop William of Norwich.

MS. B.M. Cott. Galba E ii f.44a (Register of St. Benet's Holme).

Theobaldus: Confirmacio ecclesiarum de Neteshirde
et de Bastwic.

THEOBALDUS[1] dei gratia Cantuariensis archiepiscopus Angl'[2]
primas universis sancte ecclesie fidelibus salutem. Quod a

venerabilibus fratribus nostris coepiscopis canonice fieri dinoscitur, id[3] nostre auctoritatis testimonio merito confirmatur.
Inde est quod ecclesias de Netheshirde[4] et de Irsted'[5] et de
Bastwyk[6] monasterio sancti Benedicti Holmensis et fratribus
ibidem [7]deo servientibus[7] ad obsequium altaris sancti Benedicti
et ad reparacionem edificiorum sicut venerabilis frater noster
Willelmus Norwicensis episcopus eis concessit in perpetuam
elemosinam et per cartam suam eis[8] confirmavit, nos quoque
auctoritate qua fungimur confirmamus et presentis scripti
nostri[9] munimine in perpetuum[10] corroboramus, salva in
omnibus diocesani episcopi dignitate[11], prohibentes sub anathemate ne quis contra presentis pagine nostre auctoritatem
temere veniat nec in bona eorum manus violentas extendat.
Valete.

ALSO: MSS. B.M. Cott. Rolls iv. 57, no. 15 (*A*); Bodleian, Norfolk Rolls
   82 (t) (*B*); D. and C., Norwich, Reg. 8 f.2b (*C*).

VARIATIONS: [1]*C* T. [2]*AB* Anglie. [3]*A* ad. [4]*ABC* Neteshirde. [5]*ABC* Irstede.
   [6]*AB* Bastwik, *C* Bastewic'. [7–7]*AB* servientibus deo. [8]*ABC* omit. [9]*AB*
   omit. [10]*AC* inperpetuum. [11]*AB* dingnitate.

DATE: 1153–61.

PRINTED: J. R. West, *Register of St. Benet's Holme*, Norfolk Record Society
   (1932), i, 47.

134

Notification by Theobald of the decision in his presence of the dispute
between William abbot of Holme and Hubert de Munchesney over
Little Melton (Norf.). Hubert has recognised that the vill is in the
fee of the abbey of Holme and that he had seized it during the civil
war. Hubert did homage and fealty to the abbot and received it back
for himself and his heir for an annual payment of 10*s*.

MS. B.M. Cott. Galba E ii f.44a (Register of St. Benet's Holme).

> Theobaldus: Litera de recongnicione Huberti de
> Monte Kanisio de Parva Meltuna.

THEOBALDUS[1] dei gratia Cantuariensis archiepiscopus Anglorum primas et apostolice sedis legatus venerabili fratri et amico
W[illelmo] Norwicensi episcopo et Norwicensis ecclesie conventui et universis sancte ecclesie filiis salutem. Noverint [2]tam

presentes² quam futuri quoniam Hubertus de ³Monte Kanisio³
sub nostra presencia recongnovit⁴ Willelmo abbati de Hulmo
feodum sancti Benedicti, de villa scilicet que dicitur Parva
Medeltona et ibi eidem abbati hominium et fidelitatem de
eodem feodo fecit et de manu abbatis feodum illud recepit, quod
tempore guerre pravorum hominum consilio detinuerat. Ipse
vero abbas consequenter concessit illud Huberto et heredibus
suis hereditabiliter tenendum ita quod ecclesie de Hulmo
singulis annis Hubertus et heres suus post eum reddet decem
solidos. Hanc igitur reddicionem ecclesie de Hulmo factam
vidimus et testamur et ecclesie Holmensi confirmamus. Si vero
Hubertus aliud inde contra racionem fecerit absque /[f.44b]
assensu Holmensis conventus ratum non habemus set inde
justiciam ecclesiasticam faciemus. Valete.

ALSO: MS. D. and C. Norwich Register 8 f.43a.

VARIATIONS: ¹T. ²⁻²universitas vestra (*underlined for deletion*). ³⁻³Monte-
chanesio. ⁴recognovit.

DATE: 1155–57.

PRINTED: J. R. West, *Register of St. Benet's Holme*, Norfolk Record Society
i, 47 (see also p. 106).

135

Mandate of Theobald to Bishop William of Norwich. William abbot
of Holme has complained that Amfrid Butterturte has taken away
from him part of the advowson of four churches of Caister (Yarmouth, Norf.) and is disturbing his possession of St. Andrew's church
in the abbot's own fee. The abbot is to be restored to St. Andrew's,
but if Amfrid objects, the controversy should be decided by the
evidence of witnesses. The question of the churches of Caister should
be decided by the chapter of Flegg, which should apportion the
advowson in proportion to the land held by the parties.

MS. Bodleian Norfolk Rolls 81 no. 11 (Roll of St. Benet's Holme).

QUERITUR nobis dilectus noster W[illelmus] abbas de Hulmo
quod Amfridus Butterturte injuste aufert ei partem advocationis
iiii ecclesiarum de Castre et de quinta ecclesia quam in suo
territorio sitam possidet idem abbas, contra formam justicie et

equitatis vexat. Et quia omnium ecclesiarum pacem desiderare
et ipsarum jure conservare debimus, per presentia vobis scripta
mandantes precipimus quatinus predictum abbatem faciatis
possidere in pace ecclesiam sancti Andree quę in territorio suo
sita esse dinoscitur. Et si Amfridus vel aliquis alius adversus
abbatem de advocatione ejusdem ecclesie experiri voluerit,
per legitimos testes jurantes et secundum formam canonum
diligenter quibus non possit imperare nec cogere examinatos
controversia decidatur. Nichilominus precipimus quatinus cum
omni diligentia inquiras quid juris secundum proportionem
territorii supradictus abbas habere debeat in prenominatis iiii
ecclesiis per legitimos viros clericos capituli de Flegg et laicos,
et illud ei assignare non differas. Valete.

DATE: 1153–61.

PRINTED: J. R. West, *Register of St. Benet's Holme*, Norfolk Record Society
(1932), i, 175.

136

Mandate of Theobald to Bishop William of Norwich. The church of
Thorpe (Norwich) had been adjudged to a priest N. by Bishop
Hilary of Chichester (1147–69) and others, saving an annual pension
of 2s. to his uncle who had to purge himself with 7 compurgators
from the charge of having assaulted his nephew in the porch of the
church. The nephew complained at a council that he had not been
restored nor had his uncle purged himself and the bishop of Norwich
had then promised to set things right. The nephew, however, decided
to appeal to the pope as he still had to overcome the opposition of
Peter but he changed his mind and agreed to abide by Theobald's
ruling. The bishop is to restore him and if Peter or anyone ese
wishes to make his claim, the bishop is to cite them both before
Theobald for his final decision.

MS. Bodleian Norfolk Rolls 81 no. 10 (Roll of St. Benet's Holme).

Norwicensi episcopo

A MEMORIA nostra minime excidit quod presentium latori N.
presbitero, ecclesia de Torp, presente venerabili fratre nostro
Hilario Cic' episcopo aliisque religiosis viris cum integritate

restitui fuerit adjudicata, salvo censu annuo duorum solidorum avunculo ejus N. persolvendo. Eidem etiam avunculo ejus adjudicata est cum septima manu purgatio que in istum violentas manus non insederit nec eum in atrio ecclesie verberaverit. Postmodum autem in concilio conspectui nostro apparuit conquęrens quod nondum fuisset restitutus nec avunculus ejus sicut oportuit purgatus. Ibique in communi fratrum coepiscoporum audientia promisistis sententiam nostram tam circa restitutionem quam circa purgationem effectui mancipare. Quam quia integre ut asserit habere non potuit nisi prius Petro super eadem ecclesia respondisset, ad apostolicam inconsulto calore dicitur appellasse majestatem. Verumtamen in se reversus mavult appellationem illam transferendo tantum declinare laborem et in nostra audientia siquis adversus eum agere voluerit judicio stare. Eapropter per presentia vobis scripta precipiendo mandamus quatinus eum in integrum primum restituatis. Postmodum si Petrus vel alius adversus eum agere voluerit, utramque partem die congruo assignato ante nostram vocate presentiam, et nos deo auctore auditis hinc inde rationibus mediante equitate controversie finem debitum imponemus. Valete.

DATE: 1151–60.

137

Confirmation by Theobald to the Aug. canons of Hornchurch Priory (Essex, dep. on St. Nicholas and St. Bernard Montjoux) of 25 librates of land in the royal manor of Havering (Essex) and 8 librates in Chislehurst (Kent) in accordance with the charter of Henry II, together with their oratory in Havering, saving the rights of the mother church.

Original MS. New Coll., Oxford, Hornchurch Charters no. 530(i).

T. DEI gratia Cantuariensis archiepiscopus Anglorum primas [et] apostolice sedis lega[tus] episcopis abbatibus archidiaconis decanis et univer[sis ecclesie] dei filiis tam clericis quam laicis per Angliam constitutis salutem. Que a princip[ibus viris] tam re[gibus] quam aliis fidelibus religiosis locis [divi]ne pietatis intuitu [col]lata esse noscuntur, [nostrum est] officium [in nostra jurisdicti]one ea confirmare et perpetuis scripti nostri auctoritate stabilire temporibus. Inde est quod religiosis fratribus canonicis regularibus sancti Nicholai et sancti Bernardi de monte Jovis viginti quinque libratas terre in manerio regis de Haveringis et octo libratas terre in Ches[el]herst sicut [rex] Henricus Angl' et dux Norm' [et] Aquit' et comes And' eis dedit et in perpetuam elemosine possessionem per cartam suam confirmavit, nos quoque auctoritate qua fu[ngimur illis easdem] redd[itus] cum oratorio suo quod in Havering' in eadem elemosina eis salvo jure matricis [ecclesie] concessimus presentis scripti nostri testimonio confirmamus et in perpetuum corroboramus, prohibentes sub anathemate ne [quis] contra regie auctoritatis liberam [donatio]nem aliquando temere veniat nec aliquatenus eorum pacem contra justiciam per[turb]et nec a eorum bonorum diminutionem ullatenus aspiret. Pax dei omnibus eis pacem conservantibus. Valete.

ENDORSEMENT: Carta sancti Thome . . . . [rest illegible; late].

SEAL: fragment with Theobald's counterseal on string.

SIZE: 3·8 in. × 9·7 in.

DATE: 1158–61 (see H. E. Salter, *Oxford Charters* (1929), no. 34 n.).

COPIES: MS. ibid. nos. 530 (ii), 531 from which missing parts of text have been recovered.

138

Notification of Theobald to Bishop Henry of Winchester (1129–71). The truth of the agreement between the bishop and the monks of Jumièges (Ben. Abbey) is that the monks promised to pay 100 marks for Hayling (Island) (Hants.) of which the bishop remitted 20 marks. There was no other agreement and that is all the monks owe Henry.

MS. P.R.O. Transcripts Record Commission ii vol. 140a no. 324 (Trans. 8/140a) (1835). From Great Cartulary of Jumièges no. 506.

Carta Theobaldi Cantuariensis archiepiscopi de Hairingia.

THEOBALDUS dei gratia Cantuariensis archiepiscopus et totius Anglie primas venerabili fratri et amico H[enrico] eadem gratia

Wintoniensi episcopo salutem et amorem. Monachi Gemmeti-
censes nos nuper adierunt obnixe postulantes a nobis testifica-
tionem veritatis super conventionem de terra de Haringia que
inter vos nobis assistentibus facta est. Nos igitur salva pace
vestra simpliciter quod inde meminimus fatemur. Recordamur
siquidem quoniam idem monachi pro eadem terra in pace et
quiete possidenda in perpetuum c marcas pacti sunt vobis
persolvere, e quibus xx marcas vestri gratia, vobis si placeat
recordari, condonastis. Aliam super hoc pactionem vobis factam
vel de vivo vel aliunde, aut nos aut alii qui huic negotio nobis-
cum interfuerunt nullatenus reminiscimur. Hoc audivimus hoc
testamur. Ex conventione sane pro hoc nichil aliud vobis
debent, ex gratia vero quicquid libet rationabiliter et quicquid
ipsi possunt. Sit igitur gratum deinceps quod coram tot testibus
actum dinoscitur, et corroboranti quod ante a vobis cautum et
firmatum est beatitudinem eternam vobis deus concedere et
corroborare dignetur. Valete.

DATE: 1143–47. A charter of Henry of Winchester relating to this one is
attested by Hilary dean of Christ Church, who became bishop of Chichester in 1147.

CALENDARED: *C.D.F.*, p. 56.

139

Confirmation by Theobald of the possessions of Kenilworth Priory
(Aug., Warwick) in accordance with various episcopal charters.

MS. B.M. Harleian 3650 f.55b (Register of Kenilworth).

T.—Ratificatio et confirmatio ecclesiarum, terrarum
et tenementorum in diocesibus Coventr', Wygorn' et
Lincoln'.

T.[1] DEI gratia Cantuariensis archiepiscopus Angl'[2] primas et
apostolice sedis legatus universis sancte dei ecclesie fidelibus ad
quoscumque presentes pervenerint apices [3]salutem in domino[3].
Que a venerabilibus fratribus nostris coepiscopis canonice fieri
noscuntur, ea ad nostrum spectat officium confirmare et ut

futuris maneant inconcussa temporibus perpetuo stabilire[4].
Inde est quod ecclesie beate Marie de Kenilt'[5] et religiosis
fratribus canonicis regularibus ejusdem loci omnes ecclesias et
quascumque possessiones in terris et decimis et aliis quibuslibet
redditibus quas bone memorie Rogerus et Walterius Coven-
trenses et Simon et[6] Aluredus Wigornenses et Alexander et
Robertus Lincolienses episcopi eis cartis suis confirmaverunt[7],
presenti[8] scripti pagina communimus et nostre attestationis
auctoritate corroboramus sicut in donatorum cartis continetur.
Ex quibus propriis hec duximus exprimenda vocabulis videlicet
ipsam villam de Kenilt'[5], [9]manerium de Saltford' et manerium
de Utilicota cum duobus pratis sester et Tachesmora, manerium
de Neweham et Hichendenam[10] cum omnibus pertinenciis et
libertatibus suis; in Lillenton'[11] dimidiam hidam terre; ecclesias
de Kinton'[12], de Budiford'[13], de Brailes[14], de Wellesburna[15],
de Cumpton'[16], de Barton', de Stanleia[17], de Wotton'[18] [9],
ecclesiam de Stanes[19], terram que fuit Bresardi[20] et midie-
tatem[21] tocius nemoris, terram que fuit Alani[22] in Waletona[23]
cum essartis[24], [25]terram Aldewini, terram de Newetona[26] et de
Lodbroc[27], et in Wotton'[18] terras quas habent per Odonem de
Turri cum prato et molendino de Kibbecliva[28]; ecclesias de
Wilmelecton'[29] de Radeford' et de Stivelay[30] et de Clinton';[25]
terram que[31] fuit Curteisi[32] in Tysso[33], molendinum in
Wotton'[34] proximum ecclesie: apud Stafford'[35] terram Walterii
filii /[f.56a] Ivete[36], terram Briani filii Cadiou[37], terram de
Frodeswella, medietatem ecclesie de Stokes[38], [39]dimidiam
hidam terre in Herdewica[40] [39], ecclesiam sancti Nicholai in
castro de Stafford'[41], ecclesias de Medelega[42], de Wolwarda[43],
de Tyssou[33] cum virgulto et molendino ecclesie proximo;
[44]terram de Broc cum nemore et exsartis, ecclesias de Etendon',
de Smita, de Cesterton'[45], de Witenasse[46], ecclesias de Lamin-
ton' et de Cobinton' ecclesie de Wotona[18] pertinentes, ecclesiam
de Hichenden'[47], terras et mansuras quas habent in Ware-
wich'[48], pratum de Bathekinton'[49], terram que fuit Miloni in
Chinton'[44]; ecclesiam de Lockeslega[50], [51]manerium de Pakin-
ton'[52], totam Lamintonam, in Woluricheston'[53] unam hidam
terre et unam virgatam[51], terram de Stalinton', [54]ecclesiam de
Herberbir'[55] [54]. Hec ergo et omnia alia quecumque justis ac

rationabilibus modis adquirere poterunt eis similiter confirm-amus. Nulli ergo omnino hominum liceat bona eorum dimin-uere, pacem temere perturbare, nec aliquo modo[56] contra justiciam eorum possessionem inquietare. Pax dei omnibus pacem eis conservantibus; pacis eorum perturbatores dei et nostram habeant maledictionem et in districto examine divine ultionis debite subjaceant pene. Valete.[57]

ALSO: MSS. B.M. Cott. Charters xiii. 6 no. 16 (Stone Roll); (*A*), and B.M. Holkham Hall Cartulary f.88b (*B*).

VARIATIONS: [1]*B* Thomas. [2]*B* Anglie. [3-3]*A* in domino salutem. [4]*B* stabelire. [5]*A* Kinild', *B* Kenell'. [6]*B* omits. [7]*B* con[f.89a]firmaverunt. [8]*AB* presentis. [9-9]*A* et cetera. [10]*B* Hychendon'. [11]*B* Lillintona. [12]*B* Kyntona. [13]*B* Budeford'. [14]*B* Brayles. [15]*B* Wallesburna. [16]*B* Comtona. [17]*B* Stanleya. [18]*B* Wottuna. [19]*A* Stanis. [20]*A* Brisardi. [21]*A* medietatem. [22]*A* adds generi Enisani. [23]*A* Walet'. [24]*A* exartis. [25-25]*A* omits. [26]*B* Newentona. [27]*B* Lodbroc. [28]*B* Kybecliva. [29]*B* Wylmelectona. [30]*B* Stiveley. [31]*B* quam. [32]*A* Curtesii. [33]*A* Thiso, *B* Tyessou. [34]*A* Witona, *B* Wottuna. [35]*A* Stafford. [36]*A* Juthe. [37]*A* Cadiho. [38]*A* Stoces, *B* Stoches. [39-39]*A* omits. [40]*B* Herdwica. [41]*A* Staford, *B* Statford'. [42]*A* Maddel', *B* Medeleya. [43]*A* Wlfuuard'. [44-44]*A* omits. [45]*B* Cestretuna. [46]*B* Wytenes. [47]*B* Hychendona. [48]*B* Warwic. [49]*B* Badechintona. [50]*A* Lochesl', *B* Lockesleya. [51-51]*A* omits. [52]*B* Pecchin-tona. [53]*B* Wolurychestona. [54-54]*A* et cetera. [55]*B* Herburburya. [56]*B* f.89b. [57]*B* omits.

The following extract from a confirmation of Archbishop Richard proves the above charter to be of Theobald and not of Becket:

Ricardus etc. . . . Inde est quod ecclesie beate Marie de Kenilt' etc. . . . omnes ecclesias et quascumque possessiones in terris et decimis et aliis quibuslibet redditibus quas bone memorie Rogerus et Walterus Coventr' et Simon et Aluredus Wigorn' et Alexander et Robertus Lincol' et Robertus Bathon' episcopi eis cartis suis confirmaverunt presentis scripti pagina com-munimus et nostre attestacionis auctoritate corroboramus pie recordacionis Teobaldi predecessoris nostri vestigia sequentes sicut in donatorum cartis continetur. (MS. Har. 3650 f.53b.)

DATE: 1158–61.

140

Notification by Theobald of the decision in his presence in the case between Hugh prior of Kenilworth and John clerk of Barton (Sea-grave) (Northants.) over the church of Barton (Seagrave). The evidence of four witnesses causes the church to be awarded to Hugh.

MS. B.M. Harleian 3650 f.55a (Register of Kenilworth).

De controversia ecclesie de Barton' et racio reddendi ejusdem.

T.[1] DEI gratia Cantuariensis archiepiscopus Anglorum primas apostolice sedis legatus universis sancte ecclesie filiis salutem. Que sub nostra presencia canonice terminata sunt ne transcursu[2] temporis in oblivionem[3] revocentur scripto commendare decrevimus. Noverit ergo universitas vestra quod causa que inter Hugonem[4] de Kenilt'[5] et Johannem clericum de Berton' diu est agitata super ecclesiam de Bertona hoc modo sub nostra presencia ordine canonico terminata est. Testimonio enim et juramento quatuor legitimorum virorum videlicet trium presbiterorum et unius laici[6] sane opinionis et integre fame prefatus prior[7] ante nos probavit[7] illum Johannem clericum reddidisse in manum Radulfi prioris qui predecessor hujus extiterat quicquid administracionis et juris in ecclesia de Bertona habuerat per clavem ejus ecclesie in capitulo apud eandem Barton'[8] celebrato. Hoc autem predicti testes probaverunt eum fecisse sponte propria absque omni choactione et dolo. Suscepto ergo predictorum virorum ex more juramento prefatam ecclesiam /[f.55b] H[ugoni] priori et ecclesie de Kenilt'[5] liberam et quietam decetero ab omni predicti Johannis peticione et administratione [9]racionem canonicam exequentes[9] adjudicavimus. [10]Ne ergo contra hec que ante nos facta sunt alicujus instinctu vel patrocinio fretus deinceps ille Johannes venire presumat veritatem hujus sentencie a nobis date huic scripto nostro commendari precepimus et coram subnotatis testibus confirmari, videlicet Ricardo Lond' et Hylario Cicest' et Johanne Wigor' episcopis, W[illelmo] abbate de Lilleshilla, et Radulfi de Dyci archidiacono, et Rogero de Stanes et Ger' canonico de Dereby, et Gaufrido Abbate milite comitis Legercest', Johanne de Tylebyria. Valete.[10]

ALSO: MS. B.M. Holkham Hall Cartulary f.90a.

VARIATIONS: [1]Thomas. [2]transcurso. [3]oblivione. [4]*adds* priorem. [5]Kenell'. [6]laice. [7-7]ante jus probavit ante nos. [8]Bertonam. [9-9]ratione canonici exequantes. [10-10]etc.

DATE: 1152–57.

141

Mandate of Theobald to Bishop Walter of Coventry (1149-59). The Cistercian monks of Combe and Stoneleigh must pay to the canons of Kenilworth the tithes from their parishes of Stoneleigh and Smite (Warwick). If the monks of Stoneleigh want a cemetery the bishop must see that the canons are indemnified.

MS. B.M. Harleian 3650 f.54b (Register of Kenilworth).

T. de decimis monachorum de Cumba et de Stanleia in parochiis de Smita et Stanleia.

T. DEI gratia Cantuariensis archiepiscopus Anglorum primas apostolice sedis legatus venerabili fratri et amico W[altero] Coventr' episcopo salutem. Sicut vestra novit discretio in rebus secularibus suum cuique jus et proprius ordo servandus est, quanto magis in ecclesiasticis disposicionibus, ubi nulla debet induci confusio, ne ibi discordia locum inveniat, unde pacis bona procedere debent. Quare per presencia scripta fraternitati vestre mandamus quatinus canonicis regularibus de Kenilt' attenta sollicitudine ita provideatis ut monachi Cistercienses infra parochias suas videlicet de Stanleia et de Smita habitantes plenam decimacionem eis persolvant tam de nutrimentis aninalium quam de agricultura et de omnibus de quibus ante eorum ingressum eisdem canonicis et predictis ecclesiis decimaciones reddi solent. Et quando a fraternitate vestra monachi de Stanleia cimiterium sibi benedici picierint eorum postulacioni nequaquam assensum ante prebeatis donec caucione accepta predictos canonicos idem monachi securos efficiant de indempnitate et integritate omnium beneficiorum que ante eorum adventum in eadem parrochia perceperunt. Valete.

DATE: 1155-59. Cf. *V.C.H.*, *Warwick*, ii, 79 and vi, 233.

142

Confirmation by Theobald to Godfrey the priest of the church of Salford Priors with the chapels of Little Salford, Wixford and Exhall (Warwick) with appertaining lands and all demesne tithes including salt, in accordance with the charter of Bishop Simon of Worcester (1125-50).

MS. B.M. Harleian 3650 f.55a (Register of Kenilworth).

Ratificatio confirmacionis ecclesie de Salteford' cum
capellis et ceteris terris suis.

T.[1] DEI gratia Cantuariensis archiepiscopus Anglorum primas
idemque[2] apostolice sedis legatus universis sancte matris ecclesie
fidelibus salutem. Ad nostram spectat dignitatem ex vice nobis
commissa ea que a fratribus nostris et coepiscopis canonice facta
sunt, ut firmiora permaneant, rata habere et auctoritate scripti
nostri suffulcire. Inde est quod ecclesiam de Saltfordia[3] cum
capellis suis de Parva Saltford' et de Witlakesford'[4], Eccleshale[5]
et cum omnibus pertinenciis suis in terris in pratis et nominatim
in prato quod dicitur Litleham[6] cum plenaria decimatione
vivorum et mortuorum dominicarum curiarum ejusdem ville
et nominatim salis qui ad villam pertinet et tocius parochie et
cum omnibus ecclesiasticis beneficiis et nominatim in pascuis in
aquis in bosco in plano et aliis liberalibus[7] consuetudinibus et
nominatim curiam que ipsi ecclesie adjecta est de dominio,
Godefrido presbitero confirmamus, sicut bone memorie Simon
Wigorn' episcopus carta sua confirmavit. Valete.[8]

ALSO: MS. B.M. Holkham Hall Cartulary f.89b.
VARIATIONS: [1]Thomas. [2]idque. [3]Salford'. [4]Witlachesford'. [5]Eccleshala.
[6]Tytleham. [7]libertatibus[f.90a]. [8]omits.
DATE: 1150–61.

143

Confirmation by Theobald of the agreement between the Knights
Templars and the monks of Kirkstead (Cist. Abbey, Lincs.) over the
lands of Nocton and Dunston (Lincs.) in accordance with the charter
of Bishop Robert II of Lincoln (1148–66).

MS. B.M. Cott. Vespasian E xviii f.74a (Cartulary of Kirkstead).

Th. Cantuariensis archiepiscopus hoc ipsum (i.e.
Ricardus de Hastinges quietam clamat terram super
Anehaid).

T. DEI gratia Cantuariensis archiepiscopus Anglorum primas et
apostolice (sedis) legatus universis sancte ecclesie fidelibus salu-

tem. Quod a venerabilibus fratribus nostris coepiscopis canonice statuitur, id merito nostre auctoritatis testimonio confirmatur. Ea igitur ratione concordiam quam venerabilis frater noster Robertus Lincol' episcopus super controversia terrarum de Nochetun' et de Dunestun' inter religiosos fratres monachos Kirkestedienses et milites Templi amicabili transactione conposuit, et carta sua firmavit, nos quoque auctoritate qua fungimur confirmamus et presentis scripti nostri munimine corroboramus sicut prefati episcopi fratris nostri carta factam fuisse atestatur. Valete.

DATE: 1155.

PRINTED: B. A. Lees, *Records of the Templars in England in the 12th Century* (British Academy series, ix), p. 242.

144

Mandate of Theobald to Bishops Simon of Worcester (1125–50), Gilbert of Hereford (1148–63) and David of St. David's (1148–76) ordering them to safeguard the privileges and possessions of Llanthony (Augustinian Canons, Glos.) in accordance with a papal mandate he has received. The bishops are to warn the advocates of Llanthony not to hinder the canons in any way.

MS. P.R.O. Chancery Masters' Documents, Llanthony Cartularies 1 (C115/A1) (unfoliated), section 1, no. cvii.

Carta T. archiepiscopi super libertatibus et privilegiis veteris Lanthonie et nove etc.

T. DEI gratia Cantuariensis archiepiscopus et totius Anglie primas venerabilibus fratribus S[imoni] Wigornensi, G[ilberto] Herefordensi, et D[avid] Menevensi episcopis salutem et dilectionem. Mandata sedis apostolice cum magna sunt sollicitudine a nobis effectui mancipanda et privilegia ejusdem cum omni vigilantia in sua sunt stabilitate conservanda. Nos siquidem apostolica auctoritate jussi sumus jura regularium fratrum de Lanthonia pro debito officii illibata et conservare et precipue bona eorum que privilegio sedis apostolice confirmata sunt ita tueri quod neque super in judicium vocentur neque ab aliquo injuriam vel molestiam sustineant vel inquietentur. Quamo-

brem eadem auctoritate fraternitati vestre precipiendo mandamus, quatinus super eisdem bonis sive possessionibus que
memorato privilegio inserta sunt nullatenus eos infestari vel
inquietari permittatis nec eidem privilegio contraire presumatis.
Nec enim vestrum est testes adversus eos super hiis audire vel
recipere, set tantum eos in libertate et quiete sibi indulta studiose confovere. Ad hoc etiam precipimus quatinus advocatos
ecclesie Lanthon' districte commoneatis ut prefatos fratres non
impediant bona tam veteris Lanthonie quam nove libere
amministrare, set in utraque ecclesia ad libitum suum permit-
tantur eadem in usus et utilitates suas impendere. Quod si contemptores exstiterint ipsos et terras ecclesiastica districtione ita
coerceatis quod ad nos iteratus clamor non debet pervenire.

DATE: *c.* 1149.

145

Notification of Theobald to Bishop Robert II of Lincoln (1148–66)
of settlement in his presence of the dispute between Llanthony and
St. Nicholas of Angers (Ben. abbey) over the church of Henlow
(Beds.). The canons are to hold the church and two-thirds of the
tithes from the monks making an annual payment of 22*s.*

MS. P.R.O. Chancery Masters' Documents, Llanthony Cartularies 1
(C115/A1) (unfoliated), section 10, no. lxxvi.

Testificatio T. Cantuariensis archiepiscopi super
compositione facta inter ecclesiam sancti Nicholai de
Andegavis et ecclesiam de Lanthonia de ecclesia de
Henl'.

T. DEI gratia Cantuariensis archiepiscopus Anglorum primas
apostolice sedis legatus venerabili fratri[1] R[oberto] Lincolniensi episcopo et omnibus aliis sancte matris ecclesie[2] fidelibus
salutem. Controversia inter ecclesiam sancti Nicholai de Andegavis et ecclesiam de Lanthonia[3] super ecclesia de Henlawe[4] diu
agitata hujusmodi compositione in nostra presentia decisa est,
videlicet quod ecclesia de Lanthonia[5] prefatam ecclesiam de
Henl'[6] et duas partes decimacionis de dominio tenebit de predicta ecclesia sancti Nicholai, reddendo ei inde annuatim xx

solidos quos Erfastus[7] vel Nigellus filius ejus reddere solebat.
Et ut inter ipsas ecclesias firma pax de cetero conservetur, duos
solidos apposuit ecclesia de Lanthonia[5] ut summa illius redditus
sit xxii solidi. Et hunc redditum ad pentecosten persolvendo,
ecclesia de Lanthonia ipsam ecclesiam de Henlowe[8] cum
omnibus pertinentiis suis et prefatam decimationem[9] de dominio utraque parte libere concedente inperpetuum[10] possidebit.
[11]Hiis testibus[11]: Ricardo de Belmes Lond' archidiacono et
Rogero[12] [sic] archidiacono de Derebi, [13]Radulfo Dunelmensi,
Alano de Welles, Philippo cancellario et [14]aliis[14]. Valete.[13]

ALSO: MSS. ibid. no. lxxii (A) and Llanthony Cartularies 4, f.71a (C115/A4)
(B).

VARIATIONS: [1]AB et amico. [2]B omits. [3]B Lanthonie. [4]A Henl', B Hanelawe.
[5]B Lant'. [6]B Hanel'. [7]B Herfastus. [8]A Henl', B Hanelawa. [9]B donacionem. [10]B imperpetuum. [11-11]A T. [12]B Frogero De. [13-13]A omits.
[14-14]B Rogero Species.

DATE: 1150–52.

146

Notification of Theobald to Walter archdeacon of Canterbury
(1142–48) and the chapter of Reculver that on the petition and presentation of Ralph Picot and Elias de Crevequer he has granted the
church of St. Giles Sarre (Kent) to Leeds Priory (Aug. Canons,
Kent). He has granted the church to Norman the clerk with the
assent of the canons to hold it from them for life on the annual payment of 2s. After his death the church will be at the free disposal of
the canons.

MS. Maidstone, Kent Archives Office, U/120, Q/13, f4a (Fragment
of Leeds Cartulary).
Inspeximus of Archbishop Kilwardby.

THEOBALDUS[1] dei gratia Cantuariensis archiepiscopus et tocius
Anglie primas Gualterio[2] archidiacono Cantuariensi totique
capitulo de Raculphe[3] salutem et benedictionem. Sciatis quod
peticione et presentacione Radulphi[4] Picoti et [5]Elie de Crevequer[5], dedi et concessi in elemosinam perpetuam ecclesiam
beati Egidii de Serres religiosis canonicis nostris de Ledes cum
omnibus ad eandem ecclesiam juste pertinentibus[6] quecumque
scilicet aliqua personarum ejusdem ecclesie canonice ibidem
possedisse dinoscitur. Eorumdem vero canonicorum assensu et

bona voluntate concessimus eam Normanno clerico in vita sua tenendam et recognoscendam de ipsis canonicis singulis annis per duos[7] solidos in [8]solempnitate paschalis[8] super altare sancti Nicholai de Ledes persolvendos, quos sicut ille canonicis subtrahere non[9] poterit[10], ita nec illi ab eo amplius exigere non poterunt. Post vitam vero predicti Normani[11] ecclesia illa in dominium canonicorum libere redibit. Teste[12] Johanne de Pagham[13], Rogero de Ponte Episcopi, Gilberto de Clara, [14]Gwaltero de Murry[14], Radulpho[15] de Luxoviis, Johanne de Cantuaria, Thoma de London'[16], Alano de Welles[6], Malgerio sacerdote, Guydone de Prissuinaco, Ricardo Castello[17], Radulpho[15] elemosinario et multis aliis.

Also: MS. Cambridge U.L. EE.v.31. f.151b. (Register of Henry of Eastry) (Inspeximus).

Variations: [1]Theob'. [2]Gwaltero. [3]Racolf. [4]Radulfi. [5–5]Elye de Crevecor. [6]*adds* et. [7]ii. [8–8]solempnitatem pasche. [9]*omits.* [10]poterint. [11]Normanni. [12]T. [13]Pageham. [14–14]Waltero de Morry. [15]Radulfo. [16]Lond'. [17]Castell.

Date: 1143–48.

147

Notification by Theobald to Ascelin bishop of Rochester (1142–48) and (Walter) archdeacon of Canterbury that he has invested the canons of Leeds with the church of Easling (diocese of Canterbury, Kent) saving customary episcopal rights. This was done on the petition of Alice of Easling and with the agreement of Gervase the incumbent who is henceforth to hold the church from the canons. On his death they are to have control of the church.

MS. Maidstone, Kent Archives Office, U/120, Q/13, f6b (Fragment of Leeds Cartulary).

Hubertus dei gratia Cantuariensis archiepiscopus tocius Anglie primas omnibus Christi fidelibus ad quos presens scriptum pervenerit salutem in domino. Universitati vestre notum facimus nos scriptum attenticum [*sic*] bone memorie Theobaldi quondam archiepiscopi Cantuariensis predecessoris nostri sub hac verborum continencia inspexisse:

T. dei gratia Cantuariensis archiepiscopus et tocius Brittannye primas venerabili fratri A[scelino] Roffensi episcopo archi-

2B

diacono quoque Cant' totique clero universisque sancte ecclesie filiis tocius archiepiscopatus salutem et benedictionem. Rogavit nos Alicia de Eslinges que fuit uxor Radulphi de Cycestria ut ecclesia de Eslinges que in fundo illius sita est, monasterio et canonicis regularibus de Ledes in perpetuam elemosinam concederemus, nam et illa quantum ad se spectabat in presencia nostra temporalia eis perpetualiter concessit. Gervasius quoque sacerdos qui ecclesiam illam canonice possidebat et personatum ejusdem ecclesie gerebat, ut predicte mulieris postulacio et nostra postmodum hujus rei confirmacio efficacie locum usquequaque optineret, prefatam ecclesiam cum omnibus appendiciis in manu nostra libere refutavit, eo tamen tenore ut quo advixerit ipsam de canonicis, nomine canonicorum non suo, teneat libere et quiete. Eo autem de medio sublato in jus et proprietatem canonicorum perpetuo deinceps redigatur et eorum usibus et disposicionibus ordinanda et possidenda permaneat. Quod quia tam predicti Gervasii spontanea dimissione quam Alicie illius fundi domine prece presentacioneque factum est, ipsos canonicos eadem ecclesia de Eslinges canonice investimus et eam eis inperpetuum /[f.7a] possidendam concessimus et, salvis per omnia episcopalibus consuetudinibus, confirmavimus. Ipsi autem Gervasio canonici eam nostro assensu postmodum concesserunt ut eam quo advixerit nomine eorum libere teneret. Teste Waltero archidiacono et magistro Johanne de Pageham et magistro Johanne [*sic*] de Ponte Episcopi et Thoma de London' et Alano et Malgerio et Johanne de Saresberia et Willelmo Cumin et Hamone filio Rogeri apud Maydstan.

Nos igitur memorati Theobaldi predecessoris nostri vestigiis inherentes et ea que in hac parte ob favorem predictorum canonicorum de Ledes ab eo pro intuitu acta sunt rata habentes et grata, concessionem illam prout rationabiliter facta est ut tanto majorem optineat firmitatem presentis scripti attestacionem et sigilli nostri apposicione confirmari duximus. Hiis testibus [witnesses].

DATE: 1147.

See E. Hasted, *History of Kent* (*1797–1801*), vi, 435.

148

Confirmation by Theobald of the possessions of Leeds Priory.

MS. Maidstone, Kent Archives Office, U/120, Q/13, f.2b (Fragment of Leeds Cartulary).

Confirmacio Theobaldi Cantuariensis archiepiscopi.

TEOBALDUS[1] dei gratia Cantuariensis archiepiscopus Anglorum primas apostolice sedis legatus omnibus sancte matris ecclesie fidelibus salutem. Equum est ac[2] rationabile ea que divinis sunt canonice mancipata serviciis ecclesiastico privilegio confirmari. Ea propter[3] dilecte in domino fili Alexander tuis justis postulacionibus clementer annuimus[4], omnes possessiones quecumque bona ecclesia Ledensis cui te deo disponente preesse cognoscimus in presenciarum juste et canonice possidet aut in futurum justis modis deo propicio adipisci poterit, ipsi ecclesie concedimus et[5] presentis scripti[6] autoritate[7] qua fungimur confirmamus. Hec autem propriis duximus exprimenda vocabulis: ecclesiam sancte Marie de Wodnesberga[8] cum omnibus pertinenciis suis et precipue decimam de Sumerfelda[9] quam in sinodo Cant'[10] ante nostram presenciam judicio predictus preior disraciocinavit[11], et decimam de Hartangra[12], ecclesiam sancti Egidii de Serris[13] et medietatem decime castri Cant'[14], ecclesiam sancte Margarete de Renham, ecclesiam sancte Marie de Chetham, ecclesiam sancte Marie de Lamberhersta[15], [16]et omnes decimas tam majores quam minores de Curtehope[17] et de Guherste[18] [16], ecclesiam Omnium Sanctorum de Farelega[19], ecclesiam sancti Petri de Trestana[20], ecclesiam sancte crucis de Bergesteda[21], ecclesiam[22] de Chert, et quoddam molendinum et unam virgatam terre in villa que /[f.3a] dicitur Bradesteda[23] et in foro ejusdem ville mansionem unam et dimidiam, in mariscis[24] de[25] Grean[26] x x solidos et[25] decimas de Benesteda[27], decimas de[28] Childistuna[29]. Decernimus ergo et omnino exparte[30] dei prohibemus ut[31] nulli homini liceat prefatam ecclesiam temere[32] perturbare aut ejus possessiones auferre vel ablatas retinere, minuere aut[33] aliquibus vexacionibus fatigare, set omnia integra conserventur usibus[34] et utilitati in ipsa ecclesia deo militancium omnimoda[35] profutura[36]. Si quis igitur infuturum contra hanc nostre confirmacionis[37] paginam sciens ausu temerario venire temptaverit[38], nisi congrua satisfactione resipuerit in extremo examine districte ulcioni subjaceat et sit anathema[39] maranatha. Amen.

ALSO: MSS. ibid., f.3a, inspeximus of Hubert Walter (A); ibid. f.5b (B); Cambridge U.L. EE.v.31 f.32b, inspeximus by Henry of Eastry, 1291, (C); ibid. f.153b (D).

VARIATIONS: [1]ABD Theobaldus, C Theob'. [2]B f.6a. [3]C Eapropter. [4]D annuintes. [5]MS adds et. [6]MS scriptis, B scripto. [7]BCD auctoritate. [8]B Wednesbergh, CD Wodnesbergh. [9]A Sumresfelda, B Somerfelda, C Sumerfeld, D Somerfelde. [10]B Cantuar'. [11]A disracionaverit, BD disracionavit. [12]A Herhangara, C Hertangre. [13]BD Serres. [14]A Cantuar', ecclesiam sancte Marie de Aslinges,. [15]A Lamberhursta, CD Lamberherst. [16-16]A omits. [17]B Curthope. [18]CD Guherst. [19]A Farlega, B Farlegha, CD Farlegh. [20]AB Terstana, C Terstane, D Testane. [21]A Barvasteda, B Berghesteda, C Berghestede. [22]A adds sancti Michaelis. [23]CD Bradestede. [24]A adds hic. [25]MS adds de. [26]A Gren, D Grea. [27]B Bentesteda, C Benestede, D Bensteda. [28]MS adds de. [29]AD Childestona, C Childestone, A adds et terram quam Elena uxor Ansfridi de Dovera per manum nostram prefate ecclesie dedit et nos concessimus, que est in villa de Ferlaga. [30]BCD ex parte. [31]B ne. [32]B omits. [33]D vel. [34]BD usui. [35]A omnimodis, B omnimod', CD omnimodo. [36]ACD in futurum, B pro futura. [37]A congregacionis. [38]B temptaverat. [39]A anithema.

DATE: 1150–61.

149

Notification by Theobald of a composition in his presence at a synod of Canterbury between the canons of Leeds and the monks of St. Albans (Ben. Abbey, Herts.) over the tithes of Ringleton (in Woodnesborough, Kent) by the oaths of three old men of the vill. The canons are to have the thirteen men named here and the monks are to have the rest.

Original   MS. Windsor, St. George's Chapel, xv. 24. 35.

T. DEI gratia Cantuariensis archiepiscopus Anglorum primas et apostolice sedis legatus universis sancte ecclesie fidelibus salutem. Noverit universitas tam presentium quam futurorum quoniam controversia inter monachos beati Albani et canonicos regulares de Sledis diutius super decimis de Ringetona agitata [in presentia] nostra in sinodo Cant' trium hominum antiquorum ejusdem ville jurament[o finita est] hoc modo: videlicet

quod predicti canonici habebunt decimas xiii subscriptorum
hominum de illis terris quas tenuerunt die qua idem manerium
de Ringetona in manu Nigelli de Wasto primum devolutum
fuit. Woluricus de Hemwolda tenuit tunc 1 acras; Edwinus
Boddi 1 acras; Brictmarus filius Wolurici 1 acras; Edwinus de
Ringetona xvi acras; Woluricus Merspic ii acras; Alfwinus
sacerdos i acram; Gotselinus ii acras; Aderedus iiii acras et i
virgatam; Eadelmus i acram; Alfwinus fullo i acram; Wolfwinus faber vii acras; Wolfwinus le Blache i curtillagium; Leof-
winus Langeteill' i acram. De his itaque terris prenominatorum
hominum habebunt decimas canonici decetero absque calumpnia et pulsatione monachorum inperpetuum. Monachi vero de
omnibus aliis terris ejusdem ville decimas percipient singulis
annis perpetuo absque [reclam]atione canonicorum. Precipimus itaque ut hujus controversie finis firmus [et validus]
maneat, nostra auctoritate et testimonio confirmatus. Valete.

ENDORSEMENT: T. archiepiscopus super decimis de Ringeltun' *and* Conpo-
   sitio inter nos et monacos de sancto Albano.

SEAL: none.

SIZE: 6·6 in. × 6·2 in (mutilated).

DATE: 1150–61.

PRINTED: by R. L. Poole, *H.M.C.*, *Various Collections*, vii, St. George's
   Chapel, Windsor, p. 36.

150

Confirmation by Theobald to the monks of Lewes (Clu. Priory,
Sussex) of the church of St. Mary Haughley (Suffolk) granted to
them by Gilbert, earl of Lincoln (1147(?)–56) and confirmed by
Bishop William of Norwich (1146–74).

Original   MS. P.R.O. Exchequer T.R. Ancient Deeds A 14107
   (E 40).

T. DEI gratia Cantuariensis archiepiscopus Anglorum primas et
apostolice sedis legatus universis ecclesię dei fidelibus ad quoscumque presentes pervenerint apices salutem. Quę a venerabilibus fratribus nostris coepiscopis canonice fieri noscuntur,
ea tum maxime cum in religiosorum usus transferuntur nostre

auctoritatis robur merito consecuntur. Inde est quod deo et ecclesię beati Pancracii Lewensis et religiosis fratribus ibidem deo militantibus ecclesiam sancte Marie de Hagenet cum omnibus ad eam pertinentibus quam Gislebertus de Gant comes Linc' eis in perpetuam elemosinam concessit et carta sua confirmavit et preter hoc de donatione ejusdem comitis Gisleberti terram quam Petrus sacerdos filius Brunsune tenuit per servitium duorum solidorum et duas summas de brasio quas Adam homo predictę ecclesię reddere solebat comiti pro grava una sicut venerabilis frater noster Willelmus Norwic' episcopus concessit et per cartam suam confirmavit, nos quoque auctoritate qua fungimur confirmamus et presentis scripti nostri munimine corroboramus, prohibentes sub anathemate ne quis decetero predicte ecclesię sive reddituum factam monachis donationem ausu temerario revocare seu bona eorum diminuere presumat. Valete.

ENDORSEMENT: Thedbaldi Cantuariensis de Hagenet.

SEAL: none.

SIZE: 7·6 in. × 5·8 in.

DATE: 1150–56; Gilbert died in 1156.

Request from donor to Theobald to confirm in Cartulary of Lewes printed *Sussex Record Society, Lewes Chartulary Supplement* (1943); Norfolk portion no. 65.

151

Grant by Theobald to the monks of Lewes of the church of his manor of Slindon (Sussex).

Original MS. P.R.O. Exchequer T.R. Ancient Deeds A 14200 (E 40).

T. DEI gratia Cantuariensis archiepiscopus omnibus sanctę dei ęcclesię fidelibus salutem. Notum facimus caritati vestrę dilectissimi filii et fratres me concessisse deo et sancto Pancratio de Lewes et fratribus ibidem deo servientibus ecclesiam manerii nostri de Slindonia cum apendiciis suis in libera elemosina pro salute animę meę et omnium predecessorum meorum. Hujus

concessionis testes sunt Gislebertus de Clara et Henricus monachi, Wlfricus et Johannes clerici, Willelmus de Ainesford' et
Willelmus de Pageh[am] milites. Valete.

ENDORSEMENT: De ecclesia de Slindona   [added]: data a T. archiepiscopo
Cantuariensi priori Lewis.

SEAL: none.

SIZE: 4 in. × 6·7 in.

DATE: 1139–50, probably early.

152

Confirmation by Theobald to the monks of Lewes of the gifts of
Alfred de Benneville and his wife and of an exchange they made with
the monks.

Original MS. P.R.O. Exchequer T.R. Ancient Deeds A 15417
(E 40).

T. DEI gratia Cantuariensis archiepiscopus Anglorum primas et
apostolice sedis legatus universis sancte matris ecclesie filiis ad
quos presens scriptura pervenerit salutem. Pastoralis sollicitudo
officii nos compellit domesticorum fidei precipue quos religionis
nomen commendat quieti per omnia in quibus secundum deum
possumus providere et ipsis ecclesiastice protectionis et confirmationis munimenta conferre. Eapropter universitatem tam
presentis quam futuri temporis fidelium Christi scire volumus
quod donationem et terras ab Alveredo de Bennevilla et Sibilla
ejus uxore monasterio sancti Pancratii de Lewis et monachis
in commutatione terre quam eis dedit in loco que dicitur
Vallis Dei donatas et scripto venerabilis fratris nostri Hilarii
Cicestr' episcopi confirmatas secundum quod in cartis eorum
continetur confirmamus et presentis scripti auctoritate communimus et ad usum fratrum ibidem deo militantium semper
manere censemus. Terrarum autem quas predictus A[lveredus]
et ejus uxor S[ibilla] pro dei amore et salute animarum suarum
eidem monasterio in predicte terre concambium contulisse
dinoscuntur in presentiarum dignum duximus annotare nomina
sicut in carta predicti fratris nostri episcopi annotata esse viden-

tur: videlicet unam hidam in parrochia de Grenesteda et terram de Pleghe et de Hesteshewinde, terram etiam de Buntesgrava et terram de Crotesbrige et de Hiectona et terram de Runctintona et terram de Reda et terram que est juxta pontem de Tonebruggia cum pratis ad ipsam terram pertinentibus

ENDORSEMENT: Tedbaldi Cantuariensis archiepiscopi de dono Alveredi de Bendevilla.

SEAL: none.

SIZE: 6·4 in. × 8·9 in.

DATE: 1150–61.

The charter ends abruptly but it was sealed and there is no room for any more writing. Cf. L. F. Salzman, *Sussex Record Society*, 38, pp. 73 f (Lewes Chartulary) which gives original charter of Alfred and ends 'and for this gift the prior and monks have granted to me to provide two monks, one for me and the other for my wife, on whose death others shall take their place, for our souls'. This seems to be the portion omitted in Theobald's confirmation.

153

Confirmation by Theobald to the monks of Lewes of Monk's Horton Priory (Kent) and its possessions as founded by Robert de Ver and his wife. The priory is to be subject to them.

MS. P.R.O. Exchequer T.R. Ancient Deeds A 15418 (E 40/15418).

Hubertus dei gratia Cantuariensis archiepiscopus totius Anglie primas et apostolice sedis legatus omnibus Christi fidelibus eternam in domino salutem. Ad universitatis vestre noticiam volumus pervenire dilectum filium nostrum priorem de Lewes cartam bone memorie Theobaldi archiepiscopi predecessoris nostri nobis in hec verba presentasse:

THEOBALDUS dei gratia Cantuariensis archiepiscopus Anglorum primas et apostolice sedis legatus omnibus sancte matris ecclesie filiis salutem in domino. Pastoralis sollicitudo officii nos compellit domesticorum fidei, precipue quos religionis nomen commendat quieti per omnia in quibus secundum deum possumus providere et ipsis ecclesiastice protectionis et confirmationis munimenta conferre. Eapropter universitatem tam presentis quam futuri temporis fidelium Christi scire volumus quod deo et sancto Pancracio et monachis de Lewes apud Hortun' deo servientibus et servituris inperpetuum concedimus et episcopali et legationis qua fungimur auctoritate confirmamus monasterium sancti Johannis apostoli et evangeliste de Hortun' cum ecclesiis capellis terris et decimis cum libertatibus et inmunitatibus et omnibus rebus aliis quas Robertus de Ver constabularius regis et Adelina de Munford uxor ejus, ipsius loci fundatores eidem monasterio contulerunt et cartis suis confirmaverunt. Habebit autem prior de sancto Pancracio in perpetuum emendationem et ordinacionem et subjectionem de priore et monachis de Hortuna tanquam de suis propriis in claustro Lewensi commorantibus secundum regulam sancti Benedicti et ordinem Cluniacensem. Reddet autem prior de Hortun' priori et conventui de Lewes singulis annis inperpetuum in festo sancti Pancracii unam marcam argenti. Damus eciam, concedimus et confirmamus predictis monachis de Lewes totam terram de Karesle quam tenuit Alwinus presbiter et filius ejus liberam et quietam ab omni servicio et consuetudine sicut unquam melius et honorabilius et quietius eam tenuerunt cum omnibus pertinenciis suis temporibus antecessorum nostrorum bone memorie Radulfi et Willelmi archiepiscoporum. Concedimus eciam et confirmamus eisdem monachis ecclesiam de Burstowe quam habent ex donacione antecessorum nostrorum et in ea viginti solidos nomine pensionis, ecclesiam quoque de Thangemere quam dedit eis Johannes de Pageham et in ea viginti solidos nomine pensionis, ecclesiam eciam de Slindona et in ea dimidiam marcam nomine pensionis, et decimas Willelmi militis de Westlovington' de omnibus rebus, et totam decimam Osberti de Baillel videlicet de bladis de fenis de animalibus et de omnibus aliis rebus suis in Bivelham unde decime dari solent et debent, decimam quoque totius pannagii sui in denariis et porcis et unam mansuram in Bixla que fuit canabaria patris sui et triginta acras terre in eadem villa juxta mare, et in parrochia de Haselholth decimas Alfredi de Churtun' in omnibus, et apud Stanlach' totam terram cum pertinenciis suis quam dedit illis Radulfus Pichot. Hiis testibus Thoma Cant' archidiacono,

Philippo cancelario, Willelmo de Ainesford, Radulfo Pichot, Pagano de Otteford et Willelmo filio Nigelli et multis aliis.

Quia igitur quod a predecessore nostro rationabiliter ordinatum est firma volumus stabilitate gaudere, concessionem et confirmationem ipsius auctoritatis nostre munimine dignum duximus roborare et eam sicut rationabiliter facta est sigilli nostri apposicione approbare [Witnesses].

DATE: 1154–58; Becket became archdeacon in 1154 and left England in 1158.

154

Admonition of Theobald to Ala countess de Warenne (d. 1174(?)) to pay Lewes priory the tithe of money from her dower lands, if the report of her default is correct.

Original MS. B.M. Cott. Vespasian F xiii p. 12.

T. DEI gratia Cantuariensis archiepiscopus Anglorum primas et apostolice sedis legatus dilecte filie Ale comitisse Warrenne salutem. Pervenit ad aures nostras religiosorum fratrum Lewensis ecclesie monachorum stupenda querimonia quod cum ipsi ex antiqua donatione comitum Warenne videlicet avi et patris Willelmi viri tui et sui ipsius etiam antequam dotem tuam consecuta fuisses de omnibus dominiis comitis decimationem denariorum semper inconcusse tanquam ecclesie sue dotem possederint, tu post perceptam dotis tue investituram eisdem fratribus ipsam decimationem que ad dotem tuam spectabat subtraxeris. Quod si ita est vehementer admiramur cum eorum que deo et ecclesie sue in elemosinam collata esse noscuntur nichil doti tue vendicare debeas nec possis. Crudele enim est et sacrilegio proximum quod super divinum altare semel devote oblatum est iterum repetere et ad secularia transferre. Proinde tibi salubriter consulimus et in domino admonemus quatinus sicut vis jus tuum tibi a deo libere conservari, ita jus suum cum integritate monachis relinquas et nullatenus datam eis denariorum decimationem dotis tue retineas, alioquin eis in justicia deesse non poterimus cujus debitores omnibus existimus. Valete.

ENDORSEMENT: T. archiepiscopus Cantuariensis ad Alam comitissam Warrennie pro decimo denario dotis sue.
SEAL: none.
SIZE: 4 in. × 7 in.
DATE: c. 1150.
PRINTED: *E.Y.C.*, viii, 95. This gives other references to several printed texts. Translated in *Sussex Arch. Coll.*, vi, 107.

155

Notification by Theobald that the nuns of Stratford-by-Bow (Ben. Middlesex) had abandoned all claims to the manor of Lillechurch (Kent) in the presence of himself, Bishop Hilary of Chichester (1147–69) Queen Matilda (d. 1152) Clarembald abbot of Faversham (1148–78) and others. The manor had been brought to the nunnery with Mary daughter of King Stephen. The resignation was on condition that Mary and the nuns of St. Sulpice (Rennes) accompanying her should leave Stratford. This had been fulfilled and Mary and her companions were now settled at Lillechurch.

MS. B.M. Harleian 7048 f.87b (Baker Collectanea).

T. DEI gratia Cantuariensis archiepiscopus Anglorum primas et apostolice sedis legatus universis sancte ecclesie filiis tam presentibus quam futuris ad quos presentes pervenerint litere salutem. Testimonium veritati duximus scripto perhibendum ne quod inter ecclesiam beati Leonardi Stretfordie et ecclesiam Lillecherchie super ipso manerio Lillecherchie immutetur inposterum. Sciant igitur presentes et post futuri quum [*sic*] moniales Stretfordie in presentia nostra et venerabilis fratris nostri Hilarii Cicestr' episcopi et Matildis regine et Clarembaldi abbatis de Faversham et aliarum religiosarum personarum, ea conditione manerium de Lillecherchia quod cum Maria filia regis Stephani ex dono ipsius regis et regine susciperint, reddiderunt et cum appendiciis suis quietum penitus clamaverunt, ut moniales sancti Sulpicii quas cum predicta Maria receptas, propter ordinis difficultatem et morum dissonantiam, ferre non

valebant, ab ipsis prorsus recederent et ecclesiam de Stretford'
a se, omni reclamatione sepulta, penitus liberarent. Hac igitur
facta transactione, collectis sarcinulis et omnibus que ad se
/[f.88a] spectabant comportatis, Maria sepedicta regis filia cum
monialibus suis ecclesiam Stretfordie penitus liberam dereliquit
et in manerio de Lillecherchia se tanquam in proprietate sua
recepit. Hoc vidimus: hoc testamur. Valete.

DATE: 1150–52.

PRINTED: *Monasticon*, iv, 381.

This charter is alleged to have been taken from the original 'sub sigillo' at
St. John's College, Cambridge. It cannot now be traced there, although
there are a number of charters in the muniment room relating to Lillechurch. (Information from the librarian.)

156

Confirmation by Theobald of the gift of Richard de Belmeis, dean
of the collegiate church of St. Alkmund's Shrewsbury (bishop of
London, 1152–62) of his prebend of Lilleshall and Atcham (Salop.)
and of all the other prebends when they should fall vacant, to the
Arroasian canons of Dorchester (Oxon.) to build an abbey at Lilleshall as confirmed by Roger bishop of Chester (1129–48) in accordance with a mandate of Pope Eugenius III (1145–53).

MS. B.M. Harleian 3868 f.24a (Lichfield Register).

THEOB' dei gratia Cantuariensis archiepiscopus et tocius Anglie
primas cunctis sancte ecclesie fidelibus salutem. Devocioni
fidelium assensum prebere eorumque oblaciones quas pietatis
intuitu religiosorum fratrum conventibus canonice impenderent
confirmare, ad episcopalem maxime spectat solicitudinem.
Quocirca donacioni [*sic*] et elemosinam Ricardi de Belmis
decani sancti Alcmundi de Salop', scilicet prebendam suam de
Lilleshull' et de Atingham cum earum pertinenciis et omnes
alias prebendas prefate ecclesie cum vacue fuerint quas predictus Ricardus pro salute anime sue et omnium suorum juste
et canonice fecit canonicis Arroas' de ecclesia sancti Petri in
Dorcacestr' egressis ad abbatiam edificandam in honorem

sancte Marie semper virginis, in bosco de Lilleshull' sicut venerabilis frater noster Rogerus Cestr' episcopus ipsis jussu domini
pape Eusebis [*sic*] confirmavit, et nos concedimus atque presentis scripti munimine confirmantes in perpetuum corroboramus. Valete.

Date: 1145–48.

Printed: *Monasticon*, vi, 263.

According to R. W. Eyton, *Antiquities of Shropshire*, viii (1859), 215, n. 1, 'The
original Deed, with a perfect and probably unique seal of Archbishop
Theobald is among the Duke of Sutherland's muniments at Trentham.'

157

Confirmation by Theobald addressed to the dean and chapter of
Lincoln of the charters of Alexander (1123–48) and Robert II
(1148–66) bishops of Lincoln granting to the office of precentor as
held by Roger de Almaria the churches of the borough of Lincoln
and the song-school.

Original　MS. D. and C. Lincoln Dii/63/1/9.

T. dei gratia Cantuariensis archiepiscopus et totius Britannie
primas decano totique Lincol' ecclesie capitulo omnibus quoque
sancte matris ecclesie fidelibus salutem. Noverit tam presentium
quam futurorum universitas quoniam Rogerio de Almaria
quem venerabilis frater noster bone memorie Alexander Linc'
episcopus consilio Lincoliensis capituli in precentorem Lincoliensis ecclesie constituit omnes ecclesias de burgo Lincol' sive
intra muros sive extra existentes quas prefatus episcopus eidem
Rogerio dedit et concessit et ad precentoris dignitatem testimonio litterarum suarum decetero debere pertinere edocuit et
confirmavit, concedimus et auctoritate scripti nostri confirmamus sicut illius carta necnon et successoris ejus venerabilis
fratris nostri R[oberti] Linc' episcopi testatur. Ipsas autem
ecclesias quas ad prefati precentoris honorem ex tenore litterarum predictorum episcoporum pertinere dinoscitur presenti
paginae assignare et propriis decrevimus eas exprimere nominibus: ecclesiam videlicet sancti Michaelis juxta portam, eccle-

siam sancti Petri in vico pargamenariorum, ecclesiam sancti Georgii, ecclesiam sancte Trinitatis, ecclesiam sancti Eadmundi, ecclesiam sancti Suithuni; et extra muros, ecclesiam sancte Trinitatis, ecclesiam sancti Rumoldi, ecclesiam sancti Bavonis, ecclesiam sancti Augustini, in Estgata, ecclesiam sancti Petri, in Wicheford' juxta pontem, ecclesiam sancti Johannis, ecclesiam sancte Trinitatis, ecclesiam sancti Petri, ecclesiam sancti Michaelis, ecclesiam sancte Margarete, ecclesiam sancti Marci, scolam quoque de Cantu et alias simul dignitates que ad hunc honorem pertinere dinoscuntur eidem Rogerio concedimus et confirmamus, sicut prefati fratres nostri Linc' episcopi concesserunt et cartis confirmaverunt. Valete.

ENDORSEMENT: [13th century] Lincon.

SEAL: none.

SIZE: 5·4 in. × 6·9 in.

DATE: 1148–61.

PRINTED: C. W. Foster, *Registrum Antiquissimum*, Lincoln Record Society, xxvii, 263, with a facsimile whence this is taken. Alexander's charter and its facsimile is on p. 262.

COPY: Registrum Antiquissimum f.185b.

158

Confirmation by Theobald to Robert II bishop of Lincoln and the church of Lincoln of Rannulf earl of Chester's gift of the church of Repton (Derbyshire). (1129–53.)

MS. Lincoln Registrum Antiquissimum f.38b (not checked with MS.).

De ecclesia de Rapendon'

T. DEI gracia Cantuariensis archiepiscopus et Anglorum primas venerabili fratri R[oberto] Linc' episcopo salutem. Que divinis usibus sunt mancipata ecclesiastica debent tuitione muniri. Eapropter dilecte in Christo frater R[oberte] Linc' episcope tuis justis postulationibus annuentes tibi et per te Linc' ecclesie ecclesiam Rappendone cum omnibus suis pertinenciis in perpetuam confirmamus elemosinam possidendam ex munificentia illustris comitis Rannulfi de Cestra collatam in recompensa-

tionem dampnorum ab eodem comite ecclesie Linc' illatorum
sicut sepedicti comitis de Cestra privilegium distinguit.

DATE: 1148–53.

PRINTED: C. W. Foster, *Registrum Antiquissimum*, Lincoln Record Society,
xxviii, 19.

159

Confirmation by Theobald to Robert II bishop of Lincoln of Simon
earl of Northampton's (1136(?)–53) gift of Fordales (near Northampton).

MS. Lincoln Registrum Antiquissimum f.38b (not checked with
MS.).

T. DEI gracia Cantuariensis archiepiscopus et Anglorum primas
venerabili fratri R[oberto] Linc'[1] episcopo salutem. Que divinis
sunt usibus mancipata ecclesiastico debent munimine roborari.
Eapropter dilecte in Christo frater R[oberte] Linc' episcope tuis
justis postulationibus annuentes tibi et per te Linc' ecclesie[2]
pratum juxta Norhamton'[3] quod vocatur Fordales perpetualiter
in elemosinam possidendum confirmamus a nobili viro Symone
comite de Norhamton'[4] concessum in recompensatione ecclesie
de Saltre quam tu frater episcope prefato comiti ad construen-
dam abbatiam liberam dedisti et absolutam.[5]

ALSO: MS. Lincoln, Registrum praeantiquissimum no. 12 (not checked).

VARIATIONS: [1]Lincol'. [2]episcopo. [3]Norhantonam. [4]Norhant'. [5]*adds* Valete.

DATE: 1148–53.

PRINTED: C. W. Foster, *Registrum Antiquissimum*, Lincoln Record Society,
xxviii, 19.

160

Confirmation by Theobald of the possessions of Littlemore (Ben.
Nunnery, Oxon.). Mutilated.

Original   MS. Bodleian Oxon. Charters a 8 f.3.

TEOBALDUS dei gratia Cantuariensis archiepiscopus tocius
Anglie primas apostolice sedis legatus [venerabili] amico

Roberto Linc' episcopo et universis aliis sancte ecclesie fidelibus salutem. Desiderium [quod ad (?) reli]gionem pertinere dinoscitur augmentandam et conservandam pio affectu promovere et confor- / . . . . attentius . . . . Nos itaque justis postulationibus dilecte filie nostre Matildis sanctimonial'- / . . . . famulatum[?] more paterno annuentes omnes possessiones / . . . . si qua in futurum justis modis poterunt / . . . . [perpe?]tuam concedimus et auctoritate qua fungimur / . . . . [confirm?]antur eis concedimus et / . . . . in dominio . . . . de / . . . . ad / . . . . et decem acras quas de / . . . . versus via de Gersundona in capite de Linland' et / . . . . rmat; ex dono . . . . /

ALSO: another fragment containing parts of four lines
         . . . . de domo . . . .
         . . . . sue eis dedit super . . . .
         . . . . filii ejus octo acras sic[ut] . . . .
         . . . . dimidias . . . .

ENDORSEMENT: (mounted).

SEAL: none.

SIZE: 11·2 in. plus × 10 in.

DATE: 1150–61.

PRINTED: first two lines with facsimile of them, C. R. Cheney, *English Bishops' Chanceries* (1950), p. 153.

161

Grant by Theobald to the canons of Holy Trinity priory London of the church of St. Mary's Bexley (Kent) with tithes and the liberty to have ten animals in Theobald's demesne herbage and ten hogs in his wood without paying pannage.

Original MS. P.R.O. Exchequer T.R. Ancient Deeds A 5002 (E 40).

THEOBALDUS dei gratia Cantuariensis archiepiscopus Roffensi episcopo et omnibus amicis et hominibus suis tam clericis quam laicis totius archiepiscopatus salutem et dei benedictionem. Sciatis me concessisse et dedisse in elemosinam ecclesiam sancte Marie de Bix' monasterio sancte Trinitatis Lund' et canonicis ibidem deo famulantibus tam presentibus quam futuris in perpetuum cum omnibus decimis omnium rerum que decimari debent et nominatim de pasnagio de porcis et de denariis et decem animalia in dominico herbagio nostro et decem porcos in bosco nostro sine pasnagio et cum omnibus rectis consuetudinibus ad eandem ecclesiam pertinentibus. Teste Martino abbate de Burh et Anselmo abbate de Holm et Engenulfo et Gisleberto de Clare monachis, et Alveredo priore sancti Gregorii et Fulcone priore canonicis, et Wlfrico et Alano capellanis, et Willelmo de Ainesf' dapifero et Radulfo Picot conestabulario et Gisleberto camerario et multis aliis apud Cant'. Pax benefactoribus.

ENDORSEMENT: Theob' archiepiscopi de ecclesia de Bixle et de x animalibus in dominico herbagio et de x porcis sine pannagio et decima pannagii.

SEAL: usual, fragment.

SIZE: 3·9 in. × 7·3 in.

DATE: 1139–40; Anselm of Holme died in 1140.

COPY: MS. B.M. Lansdowne 448 f.11b (Reg. of Holy Trinity). The church had been previously given to the canons by William, Theobald's predecessor. Fulk was the prior of St. Osyth (Essex).

162

Confirmation by Theobald to the canons of Holy Trinity priory of the gifts by William of Ypres of Eadred's Hythe (Queenhithe) and by Queen Matilda (d. 1152) of the custody of St. Catherine's hospital by the Tower of London, with its mill and land.

Original   MS. P.R.O. Exchequer T.R. Ancient Deeds A 6684 (E 40).

T. DEI gratia Cantuariensis archiepiscopus Anglorum primas et apostolice sedis legatus universis sancte ecclesie fidelibus salutem. Ad pastoris spectat sollicitudinem omnium quieti maxime eorum qui divinis mancipantur obsequiis studiose providere et que eorum rationabiliter provisa noscuntur usibus perpetuo stabilire. Proinde notum esse volumus tam presentibus quam futuris nos concessisse et confirmasse deo et ecclesie sancte Trinitatis Lond' et canonicis regularibus ibidem deo famulantibus donationem quam Willelmus de Ipra eis fecit de Edrede-

2C

shyda cum omnibus pertinentiis suis sicut dominus noster rex Stephanus eis carta sua confirmavit et sicut carta ejusdem Willelmi de Ipra testatur. Preterea confirmamus eis custodiam hospitalis regine Matild' in perpetuum habendam cum molendino juxta turrim London' et cum terra pertinente ad ipsum et cum ceteris ad ipsum hospitale pertinentibus sicut predicta regina eis concessit et carta sua confirmavit et sicut rex ipse testimonio carte sue hoc totum ratum habuit et perpetua stabilitate firmavit. Pax igitur omnibus eis pacem servientibus; obviantes vero perpetue subiciantur ultioni. Valete.

ENDORSEMENT: Confirmacio T. archiepiscopi de hospitali [juxta turrim Lond'] et de Edredeshitha. [Later addition in brackets.]

SEAL: usual, fragment.

SIZE: 4·5 in. × 7·5 in.

DATE: 1150–52.

COPY: Cartulary of Holy Trinity f.172 (Glasgow University Library) whence printed by Ducarel in J. Nichols, *Bibl. Topog. Brit.*, ii, sec. 1, p. 101.

PRINTED: J. H. Round, *Ancient Charters to 1200*, Pipe Roll Society (1888), p. 52.

163

Confirmation by Theobald of the possessions of Holy Trinity priory.

Original MS. P.R.O. Exchequer T.R. Ancient Deeds A 11970 (E 40).

T. DEI gratia Cantuariensis archiepiscopus Anglorum primas et apostolice sedis legatus universis sancte ecclesie fidelibus salutem. Ad pastoris spectat curam subjectorum pacem fovere et maxime quos religionis nomen commendat eorum bona studiosius tueri et ampliori sollicitudine patrocinari. Inde est quod karissimos filios nostros Radulfum priorem et fratres religiosos canonicos regulares sancte Trinitatis Lond' bonę conversationis in domo dei nomen habentes, quadam fraterne caritatis familiaritate arcius amplectimur et omnia eorum bona tam mundana quam ecclesiastica secundum deum et propter deum illis collata, auctoritate qua fungimur eis presentis scripti testimonio confirmamus. Eas itaque possessiones quas in presentiarum possidere noscuntur propriis dignum duximus distinguere nominibus, scilicet de dono regis Stephani c solidatas terre in Bracchinges, item ibidem sex libratas terre in ea portione manerii in qua ecclesia et forum est pro concambio molendini sui et terre in qua regina construxit hospitale juxta turrim Lond', et alias terras quas in eodem manerio habent de dono Huberti camerarii, in Theia de ejusdem Huberti dono xx soli datas, de dono Ricardi de Luci xx solidos annis singulis in Niwetona, de dono Willelmi de Ipra c solidos annuos de Edredeshyda, de dono regis Scottorum ecclesiam de Toteham cum pertinentiis suis. Has itaque possessiones sibi confirmatas et quascumque decetero canonice adipisci poterint volumus ut in pace et libere possideant et in perpetuum habeant sicut carte sue sibi habenda et tenenda testantur, prohibentes ne quis hominum audeat decetero eos inquietare aut in aliquo temere bona sua perturbare. Quod si quis presumpserit anathema sit. Valete.

ENDORSEMENT: Theobaldus archiepiscopus de ecclesia de Totham et terris de Bracchinges et de Teia et xx s. de Niwetona et c s. de Edredshyda. Prima archiepiscoporum de pluribus.

SEAL: none.

SIZE: 4·6 in. × 11·1 in.

DATE: probably 1150–52.

This charter is summarised in *Catalogue of Ancient Deeds*, v, 224.

164

Confirmation by Theobald to the canons of Holy Trinity of the church of Shoreditch (Middlx.) given to them by Bishop Robert of London (1141–51).

Original MS. P.R.O. Exchequer T.R. Ancient Deeds A 13848 (ii) (E 40).

T. DEI gratia Cantuariensis archiepiscopus et totius Angl[ie] primas clero et populo totius episcopatus Lond' salutem. Notum sit presentibus et futuris nos auctoritate episcopali cum presentis scripti munimine confirmasse donum et elemosinam ven-

erabilis fratris nostri R[oberti] Lond' episcopi quam fecit
ecclesie sancte Trinitatis Lond' et canonicis ibidem deo servientibus de ecclesia de Soredich cum terris et decimis et aliis rebus
ad eam pertinentibus. Unde precipimus ut prefati canonici bene
et in pace et honorifice et libere et quiete predictam teneant
ecclesiam cum omnibus appendiciis suis ut nulli hominum
liceat eos inde temere perturbare aut aliquibus inquietudinibus
fatigare. Test' G[ilberto] de Clara, Waltero de Moyri monachis
et capellanis; R[ogero] de Ponteepiscopi, Johanne de Cantuaria clericis; Odone dapifero, R[oberto] pincerna et aliis
multis.

ENDORSEMENT: T. archiepiscopus de ecclesia de Soresdich.

SEAL: none.

SIZE: 2·4 in. × 5·7 in.

DATE: 1141–48; same date as No. 165.

For the loss of Shoreditch Church by the priory shortly after this, cf. L.C.C.,
Survey of London, viii, 91.

165

Confirmation by Theobald to the canons of Holy Trinity of the
church of Walthamstow (Essex) given to them by Alice de Toeni.

MS. P.R.O. Exchequer T.R. Ancient Deeds A 13850 (ii) (E 40).

T. DEI gratia Cantuariensis archiepiscopus et totius Angl[ie]
primas clero et populo totius episcopatus Lond' salutem et benedictionem. Notum sit presentibus et futuris nos auctoritate
episcopali cum presentis scripti munimine confirmasse donum
et elemosinam A[licie] de Toeni quam fecit ecclesie sancte
Trinitatis Lond' et canonicis ibidem deo servientibus de ecclesia
de Welcomestow in terris et decimis et aliis rebus ad eam pertinentibus. Unde precipimus ut prefati canonici bene et in pace
et honorifice et libere et quiete predictam teneant ecclesiam
cum omnibus appendiciis suis ut nulli hominum liceat eos inde
temere perturbare aut aliquibus inquietudinibus fatigare. Test'
G[ilberto] de Clara, Waltero de Moyri monachis et capellanis;

R[ogero] de Ponteepiscopi, Johanne de Cantuaria clericis; Odone dapifero, R[oberto] pincerna et aliis multis.

ENDORSEMENT: T. archiepiscopus de ecclesia de Wulcumestowe.

SEAL: none.

SIZE: 2·7 in. × 4·8 in.

DATE: 1141–48; same date as No. 164.

For litigation over the tithes of Walthamstow see John of Salisbury's Letters, *P.L.*, 199, col. 70, ep. 84.

166

Confirmation by Theobald to the canons of Holy Trinity of the church of Lesnes (Erith, Kent) as granted and confirmed by Bishop Walter of Rochester (1148–82).

MS. Rochester Diocesan Registry, Register of Bishop John Fisher f.95b.

Confirmatio Cantuariensis archiepiscopi.

T. DEI gratia Cantuariensis archiepiscopus et totius Anglie primas universis sancte ecclesie fidelibus salutem. Noverit presens etas et secuta [*sic*] posteritas quod ecclesie sancte Trinitatis London' et priori et canonicis ibidem deo ministrantibus, ecclesiam de Leseness libere habendam et quiete possidendam concessimus et per presencia scripta confirmamus, sicut venerabilis frater noster Walterus Roffensis episcopus eis carta sua concessit et confirmavit, omniaque eidem ecclesie adjacencia et jure pertinencia, illibata tenere eos volumus, prohibentes ut nulli hominum memoratos canonicos temere liceat perturbare aut aliquibus vexacionibus fatigare. Valete.

DATE: 1148–61.

PRINTED: *Reg. Roff.*, p. 327.

167

Decision by Theobald in the dispute between Peter and the canons of St. Paul's London over possession of land pertaining to Theobald's manor of Wimbledon and Barnes (Surrey) after a writ of Henry II had been received by the archbishop. Peter's claim for seisin fails, but the question of right is left open.

MS. D. and C. London St. Paul's Liber A f.16b (not checked with MS.).

T. DEI gratia Cantuariensis archiepiscopus Anglorum primas et apostolice sedis legatus omnibus sancte matris ecclesie fidelibus ad quos presentes littere pervenerint salutem. Noverit universitas vestra controversiam que vertebatur inter canonicos beati Pauli Lond' et Petrum super possessione terre illius que pertinet ad manerium nostrum de Wymmendona et Berna vocatus [*sic*] ex precepto domini nostri regis Henrici judicio curie nostre hoc modo terminatam esse. Nam cum jam dictus Petrus seisinam prefate terre quia eam pater suus ut dicebat die qua rex H[enricus] primus obiit possederat, et postmodum mater ejus eandem possessionem habuerat usque dum violenter ejecta est postularet, nulla tamen habita mentione hereditatis vel feodi, et canonici paternam et maternam ejus possessionem ex qua ei vel alicui successio deberetur inficiarentur, Petrus vero nec instrumenta nec testes produceret nec aliquam omnino probationem presentem haberet aut futuram promitteret, judicavit curia quod saisinam ulterius petere non debebat. Et quia eos jam triennio Petrus fatigaverat et semper in probatione defecerat, a peticione seisine quam ille habiturus erat si probationibus habundaret absoluti sunt canonici, salva tamen questione juris si eam Petrus instituendam crediderit. Hiis testibus et cetera [*sic*].

DATE: 1154–61.
PRINTED: M. Gibbs, *Early Charters of the Cathedral Church of St. Paul, London,* Camden Soc., 3rd Series (1939), 58, p. 126.

168

Mandate of Theobald to Aylward archdeacon (of Colchester). He has received a complaint from Henry bishop of Winchester (1129–1171) and dean of St. Martin's-le-Grand London that the archdeacon is forcing the canons of St. Martin's into litigation over the chapel of Bonhunt which belonged from of old to their church of

Newport (Essex). The bishop as dean cannot be present owing to the civil war and the archdeacon must therefore cease litigation until he can come.

Original   MS. Westminster Abbey Muniments 997.

T. DEI gratia Cantuariensis archiepiscopus et totius Anglie primas venerabili fratri Eilwardo archidiacono salutem. Questus est nobis venerabilis frater noster H[enricus] Wintoniensis episcopus ęcclesię sancti Martini Lond' decanus quod compellas canonicos suos procedere in causam de capella de Banhunt quam asserit ęcclesiam suam de Niweport antiquitus in pace possedisse et precipue tempore predecessorum tuorum archidiaconorum et venerabilis memorię Ricardi videlicet et Gisleberti episcoporum et deinceps usque in presens tempus. Pretendit etiam se ita guerris et tribulationibus occupatum et impeditum quod ad presens cum ipsis nec pro ipsis sicut ratio expostulat, in causa stare potest. Unde tibi mandamus et precipimus quatinus ita in pace et inconcusse canonicos predictos tenere permittatis sicut temporibus prescriptis ipsos et ęcclesiam suam prenominatam tenuisse manifestum est. Videtur enim eis se non esse compellendos in causam de possessionibus [ecc]lesie sine presentia decani sui cujus est et de [rebus] ecclesie disponere et pro ipsis cum canonicis in causa stare. Valete.

ENDORSEMENT: Newport de capella de Barut [*sic*].

SEAL: fragment, yellow.

SIZE: 3·4 in. × 6·7 in.

DATE: *c.* 1144.

COPY: MS. Westminster Abbey Muniments 13167 no. cxviii (Roll of St. Martin's-le-Grand).

PRINTED: (from copy) L. Voss, *Heinrich von Blois* (1932), p. 152, although she claims to have printed it from the original.

169

Notification of Theobald addressed to Bishop Robert of London (1141–51) the justices and the citizens of London of a decision reached in the presence of the legate (Cardinal Ymar) and all the council in the dispute between the monks of Bermondsey and the canons of St. Martin's-le-Grand over land formerly of Rainer the clerk. The monks are to give the canons land worth 12*s.*, or if they prefer they are to keep all the land at issue and pay them annually 14*s.*

MS. Westminster Abbey Muniments 13167 no. cx (Roll of St. Martin's-le-Grand).

Concordia inter priorem de Beremundesheie et capitulum sancti Martini.

T. DEI gratia Cantuariensis archiepiscopus venerabili fratri Roberto eadem gratia Londoniensi episcopo et justiciis et civibus London' amicis suis salutem. Controversia que fuit inter monachos sancti Salvatoris de Bermundeseya et canonicis sancti Martini London' de terra que fuit Raineri clerici, in presencia domini legati totiusque concilii diu ventilata, sic tandem me teste terminata est, scilicet quod monachi illi donabunt ecclesie beati Martini xii solidatas terre, vel de ipsa terra vel de alia que sit ejusdem condicionis et ejusdem libertatis aut ipsi monachi si maluerint tenebunt terram illam de ecclesia sancti Martini reddentes singulis annis xiv solidos de ipsa terra. Valete.

DATE: 1145.

170

Confirmation by Theobald of the gift to St. Martin's-le-Grand by King Stephen and Queen Matilda of the churches of Chrishall and Witham (Essex) to support a tenth canon.

Original MS. Westminster Abbey Muniments 8040.

T. DEI gratia Cantuariensis archiepiscopus et totius Anglię primas venerabilibus fratribus episcopis et abbatibus et universis Christi fidelibus tam clericis quam laicis per Angliam constitutis salutem. Noveritis quod rex Stephanus et Mathildis regina uxor ejus de proprio jure suo, hoc est de hereditate ipsius reginę dederunt ęcclesię sancti Martini Lond' et canonicis ibidem deo famulantibus duas ęcclesias in perpetuam elemosinam ad faciendum decimum canonicum in eadem ęcclesia videlicet ęcclesiam sancte Trinitatis de Cristeshala et ęcclesiam sancti Nicolai de Witham cum omnibus pertinentiis earum. Et quoniam justa poscentium non est differenda petitio, donationem illam concedimus et auctoritate nostra roborando confirmamus. Precipimus quoque ut canonici in pace et cum honore eas teneant cum omnibus eis pertinentibus, prohibentes etiam ne ulli liceat personę eos inde temere perturbare. Valete.

ENDORSEMENT: Confirmatio beati Th[ome] archiepiscopi.

SEAL: usual, fragment.

SIZE: 3·3 in. × 6·7 in.

DATE: 1139–52.

COPY: MS. Westminster Abbey Muniments 13167 no. cxxiv (Roll of St. Martin's-le-Grand).

PRINTED: (from copy) L. Voss, *Heinrich von Blois* (1932), p. 153.

171

Mandate, probably of Theobald, to Richard (Rufus) archdeacon of Essex and his rural deans. The canons of St. Martin's-le-Grand have complained of unjust exactions in respect of their church at Maldon (Essex) by the archdeacon and deans, and the interdiction of the church (of Maldon) and the suspension of a priest. They are ordered to relax these measures and only to exact the normal episcopal dues. As the canons are the parson of the church, they should be allowed to appoint a vicar, who should pay the *episcopalia*.

MS. Westminster Abbey Muniments 13167, no. cxxxiv (Roll of St. Martin's-le-Grand).

T.[1] DEI gratia Cantuariensis archiepiscopus et totius Anglie primas Ricardo archidiacono et decanis suis de Essex' salutem. Conquesti sunt nobis filii nostri canonici sancti Martini de London' quod intollerabilibus exactionibus et angariis ecclesiam eorum de Meldon'[2] gravatis, et propter hoc et ecclesiam eorum interdicitis et sacerdotem eorum suspenditis, quod vobis minime licet. Contra canones enim esse manifestum est quicquid preter episcopalia jura ab hac aut ab aliis ecclesiis exactum est.

Crudele est enim et ab omni ratione alienum ut ecclesias et sacerdotes ita pro hujusmodi temporalibus interdicatis nisi manifestior culpa sacerdotis aut alia ratio expostulaverit. Nunc itaque omnino prohibemus [3]vobis omnem[3] preter episcopalia jura exactioni [sic][4] ab illis exigere et si illis pro exaccionibus divina interdicta sunt aut eorum sacerdos suspensus, relaxetur et in ecclesia divina celebrentur. Cum autem et ipsi canonici persona sint ecclesie sue, non cogantur aliam substituere personam set ydoneum constituant vicarium qui ecclesie deserviat et episcopalia jura persolvat. Valete.

ALSO: MS. Westminster Abbey Muniments, Cartulary of St. Martin's f.25a.

Sanctus Thomas archiepiscopus Cantuariensis inhibet archidiacono Essex' ne a canonicis sancti Martini London' exemptis omnem preter jura episcopalia exaccionem pro ecclesia eorum de Maldon' presumat exigere quovismodo.

VARIATIONS: [1]Thomas. [2]Mealdon'. [3-3]omnem vobis. [4]exaccionem.

DATE: 1143–61 or 1162–70.

172

Mandate, probably of Theobald, to the canons of St. Martin's-le-Grand, in accordance with a papal mandate. The canons are to be subject to (Henry) bishop of Winchester as their dean, and to anyone representing him.

MS. Westminster Abbey Muniments 13167, no. cxlv (Roll of St. Martin's-le-Grand).

T.[1] DEI gratia Cantuariensis archiepiscopus[2] Angl'[3] primas et apostolice sedis legatus toti capitulo sancti Martini London' salutem. Accepimus mandatum domini pape de conservandis omnibus et protegendis que ad jus Wintoniensis ecclesie et venerabilis fratris nostri domini Wintoniensis jure aliquo competere dinoscuntur. Vobis itaque mandamus et presentium auctoritate precipimus quatinus prefato episcopo tanquam decano vestro obediatis et ei cui vicem suam in illa ecclesia commisit, nichilque mutare vel innovare in lesionem vel minoracionem potestatis episcopi presumatis. Valete.

ALSO: MS. Westminster Abbey Muniments, Cartulary of St. Martin's-le-Grand f.25a.

Idem Sanctus Thomas ad mandatum domini pape suscipit in proteccionem et conservacionem in omnia que ad Wyntoniensem ecclesiam et venerabilem fratrem suum domini Wyntoniensis et specialiter ecclesiam sancti Martini London' cujus idem Wyntoniensis episcopus est decanus jure aliquo competere dinoscuntur.

VARIATIONS: ¹Thomas. ²*adds* tocius. ³Anglie.

DATE: probably 1150–61.

173

Confirmation by Theobald of the possessions of the nuns of Malling (Ben. abbey, Kent).

MS. Rochester Diocesan Registry Hamo de Hethe's Register f.15a (not checked with MS.).

Omnibus Christi fidelibus presens scriptum visuris et audituris Ricardus divina miseracione Roffensis ecclesiae minister humilis eternam in domino salutem. Noveritis nos cartam venerabilis patris nostri beati Thome martiris Cantuariensis archiepiscopi inspexisse sub hac forma:

T. DEI gracia Cantuariensis archiepiscopus Anglorum primas et apostolice sedis legatus omnibus sancte ecclesie matris fidelibus salutem. Cum ad omnes nostre jurediccioni subjectos sollicitudinis nostre aciem debeamus extendere, eisque jura sua inviolata conservare, specialiter quasdam tamen diligencia religionis compellimur pauperes Christi in utroque sexu arcioris vite regulam in monasteriis professos conservare ac studiose debemus confovere, et ne pravorum intrusione ullave potestatum secularium vexacione injuste perturbentur vel possessionibus sibi in solatium victus seu regum largicione seu principum et potentum donacione misericordie intuitu juste et canonice collatis destituantur, sedula nos convenit circumspectione providere nostraque auctoritate quatenus poterimus precavere. Tali itaque inducti racione ut monialibus apud Mallinges in ecclesiam beatissime virginis Marie jugem deo famulatum prestantibus in posterum provideatur, donaciones eis a regibus principibus aliisque viris illustribus et fidelibus Christi factas tam in terris quam in decimis aliisque rebus utilibus confirmare decrevimus, et ut inconvulsa et inmutilata in perpetuum perseverent omnia que monasterio et ancillis Christi in eo manentibus collata sunt auctoritatis nostre munimine dignum duximus roborare. Hec autem que eis communimus propriis censuimus exprimenda vocabulis: Mallinges Parvam cum pertinenciis suis cum foro ejusdem ville, ecclesiam sancti Leonardi cum adjacenciis suis, ecclesiam quoque sancte Marie in Mallinges, totam eciam decimam vinearum de Hallynges, decimam de Cuclestane de terris quas episcopus Gunulfus manerio de Cuclestane accreverat, decimam quoque Ranulfi de Bromlegh, totam decimam de Borstalle de frugibus duas partes decime de terra Radulfi de Borstalle, terciam partem decime Radulfi de Wldeham de frugibus de dominico duas partes, Roberti de Wldeham totam decimam de Parva Wldeham, Mallinges que prope monasterium sita est quam beatus Ancellmus archiepiscopus eis concessit, totam decimam de terra Reginaldi de Lodesdona quam tenet de feodo Thalebot, Cornherde cum suis pertinenciis, unam hidam terre et dimidiam partem decime de dominio de Wynbisse, decimam de dominio de Schorham de omnibus unde decime solent dari et unam acram Lactonam cum pertinenciis suis, unam eciam carucatam terre que Thorna vocatur, quam judicio comitatus moniales evicerunt. Hec autem omnia prescripta monasterio et monialibus Mallinges cartis illustrium regum Anglorum Willielmi Henrici primi Stephani Henrici secundi confirmata, cartis eciam venerabilium archiepiscoporum Cant. Anselmi Radulfi Willielmi, cartis eciam fratrum nostrorum episcoporum Roffen. Gundulfi Radulfi Annulfi Johannis Anselmi Walteri roborata et concessa, eorum vestigiis inherentes, presentis scripti pagina et sigilli nostri attestacione communivimus prout carte donatorum quas vidimus et audivimus eis illa donata esse testantur. Cum hiis eciam que in presenciarum possident ea que deo auctore eisdem monialibus confirmata et roborata esse jubemus.

Nos igitur [etc.] . . . . in cujus rei testimonium [etc.]
. . . . (1249).

DATE: 1154–61.

PRINTED: *Reg. Roff.*, p. 481, summarised C. Johnson, *Registrum Hamonis Hethe*, p. 20 (Cant. and York Soc.).

A charter of Gilbert de Glanville bishop of Rochester on the same matter refers to a confirmation of Theobald and not to Thomas. If the charter transcribed above were of Thomas, the archbishop should have mentioned Theobald in addition to Anselm Ralph and William. Printed *Reg. Roff.*, p. 480.

174

Letters of protection of Theobald to the nuns of Malling addressed to Bishops Walter of Rochester (1148–82) William of Norwich (1146–74) Robert II of Lincoln (1148–66) Thomas (Becket) archdeacon of Canterbury (1154–62) and Ralph Picot (sheriff of Kent).

MS. P.R.O. Chancery Enrolments Charter Rolls 21 Ed. III m.11 (C 53/134).

One of many charters inspected. (8 May 1347.)

Inspeximus eciam literas patentes quas T. Cant' archiepiscopus fecit in hec verba:

T. DEI gratia Cantuariensis archiepiscopus Anglorum primas et sedis apostolice legatus venerabilibus fratribus et amicis Walterio Roffensi et Roberto Lincol' et Willelmo Norwic' episcopis et Thome Cant' archidiacono et Radulfo Picot et omnibus sancte ecclesie fidelibus salutem et benedictionem. Noverit universitas vestra quod omnes possessiones et terre et res tam ecclesiastice quam mundane sanctimonialium de Melling' ubicumque sint in Anglia in manu et tutela dei et sancte ecclesie et domini pape, cujus vices gerimus, consistunt et in nostra. Nemo igitur in aliquo presumat eas vel res earum opprimere, minuere vel aliquam injuriam seu molestiam eis inferre, set omnino in pace dei et domini pape et nostra permaneat, absque omnium exactionum gravamine. Quod si quis hoc statutum nostrum ausu temerario violaverit, noverit se sine dubio excommunicacione et maledictione domini pape et nostra tamdiu multandum et innodandum quousque eisdem sanctimonialibus ad victum earum omnia reddiderit et plene satisfecerit. Pax et benedictio

omnibus benefactoribus: earum malefactoribus vero maladictio
[*sic*] dei donec resipiscant eveniat. Amen. Valete.

DATE: 1154–61.

PRINTED: *Calendar of Charter Rolls*, v, 61.

175

Notification by Theobald of the decision in favour of the abbess
Ermelina and the nuns of Malling given in the court of Malling.
They are awarded the seisin of two 'oakdenes' and a wharf wrongly
occupied by the brothers Richard and William.

MS. P.R.O. Chancery Enrolments Charter Rolls 21 Ed. III m.11
(C 53/134).

One of many charters inspected. (8 May 1347.)

> Inspeximus insuper literas patentes quas T. Cant'
> archiepiscopus fecit in hec verba.

T. DEI gratia Cant' archiepiscopus Angl' primas universis
sancte ecclesie fidelibus salutem. Noverint tam presentes quam
futuri quoniam Ermelina abbatissa de Meallinges et moniales
adversus duos fratres Ricardum et Willelmum saisinam duarum
acdennarum cum heittha ad quam naves applicant, quas
quidem acdennas quia sine assensu nostro et sine waranto
occupaverant predicti fratres, predicte inquam abbatissa et
moniales dirationaverunt judicio in curia de Mealling' coram
Pagano de Otteford' et Dinisio clerico et multis aliis, et quod
ibi dirationaverunt nos eis confirmamus prohibentes sub anathemate ne de hoc quod ibi eis judicatum fuerat ulterius inquietentur. Valete.

DATE: 1139–61, probably late.

PRINTED: *Calendar of Charter Rolls*, v, 61.

176

Grant by Theobald of West Malling (Kent) to the nuns of Malling
for an annual rent of £10. He asks that the same terms should be
granted to the nuns by his successors.

MS. Lambeth 1212 p. 78. (Documents of Archbishop of Canterbury.)

Th' archiepiscopi de Parva Malling'.

T. DEI gratia Cantuariensis archiepiscopus Anglorum primas et apostolice sedis legatus amicis et fidelibus suis salutem. Sciatis quod ego concedo ancillis dei sanctimonialibus que deo et beate Marie serviunt apud Meallinges in parochia Roffensis episcopi villam meam que vocatur Parva Mealling'[1] et est juxta eas ad firmam ita ut eam habeant [2]quam diu[2] ego vixero pro decem libris denariorum omni anno et rogo ut hoc ipsum eis concedatur pro elemosina[3] a successoribus meis archiepiscopis. Hujus rei testes sunt: Philippus cancellarius et Johannes de Sar' /[p.81] et Petrus scriptor et Aluredus elemosinarius et Osbertus clericus et Ricardus de Clara et Ricardus de Cant' et Willelmus de Alinton'[4] et Robertus, Rannulfus, Hunfridus[5], capellani de Mealling'[6] et multi alii apud Mealling'[6] in pleno capitulo.

ALSO: MS. Bodleian Tanner 223 f.47a.

VARIATIONS: [1]Mal-[f.47b]linges. [2-2]quamdiu. [3]elimosina. [4]Alingtona. [5]Humfridus. [6]Malling.

DATE: 1150–61.

The original of this charter was found in the Treasury of the archbishop of Canterbury in 1330. (I. J. Churchill: *Camden Miscellany*, xv, sect. iii, p. 14.)

177

Notification by Theobald of the grant by Philip canon of South Malling (Sussex) to Bec (Ben. Abbey) of the church of Glynde (Sussex) with the assent of his brother William and of his nephew Godfrey.

Original   MS. Windsor, St. George's Chapel, xi. G.2.

TEOB' dei gratia Cantuariensis archiepiscopus et totius Anglie primas omnibus sancte æcclesie fidelibus salutem. Noverit universitas vestra quod Philippus canonicus de Melling' se demisit de ecclesia de Glindes et in manum nostram posuit eam et per nos reddidit eam ecclesie Becci, presente et concedente

Willelmo de Melling' fratre suo: ita videlicet, quod quandiu in clericali vita vel habitu vixerit, eam de monachis Becci tenebit, et de recognitione eis duos solidos singulis annis reddet et ipsi monachi reddent pro eo ii solidos ecclesie sancti Michaelis de Melling' quos Philippus reddere solebat. Post mortem vero ejusdem Philippi vel si forte religione aliqua vitam mutaverit, cum omnibus decimis et pertinentiis suis ipsa ecclesia de Glindes in jus et manum predictorum monachorum Beccensium veniet et remanebit. Si quis vero hanc ejusdem Philippi et Willemi fratris ejus donationem et nostram confirmationem infringere seu violare in posterum attemptaverit, deleat eum deus de libro vite nec in terra viventium consortium vel portionem aliquam habeat. Hujus donationis testes sunt: Elinandus monachus Becci quem manu mea de eadem ecclesia investivi vice et loco ecclesie Becci et monachorum aliorum Becci, Gislebertus capellanus et monachus Becci, Ælavus decanus de Melling', Alanus de Well[is], Willelmus de Norum canonicus de Melling', Frogerius de Luxoviis, Gislebertus camerarius, Godefridus camerarius et Gislebertus frater ejus. Hanc etiam donationem Godefridus filius Willelmi concessit nepos scilicet predicti Philippi. Testibus Ricardo de Mares, Radulpho de Bec, Herluino Caritet, Ricardo dispensatore. Apud Mellinges.

ENDORSEMENT: Confirmatio Theob' Cantuariensis archiepiscopi de ecclesia de Glindes.

SEAL: usual, but yellow.

SIZE: 4 in. × 7·4 in.

DATE: 1139–48 (earlier than No. 178).

PRINTED: R. L. Poole: *H.M.C.*, *Various Collections*, vii, St. George's Chapel, Windsor, p. 27, and M. Chibnall, *Documents of Bec.*, p. 1 (Camden Soc., 1951).

COPIES: MS. Windsor xi. G.55. (First of three charters relating to Glynde on a paper, 15th century). MS. ibid. xi.G.11 (Roll of charters, 13th century) (not consulted).

177a

Confirmation by Theobald notified to the hundred of Malling of the grant in No. 177.

MS. Windsor, St. George's Chapel, xi. G.11 (Roll of Bec) (not checked with MS.).

Confirmacio T. archiepiscopi de ecclesia de Glinde.

T. DEI gracia Cantuariensis archiepiscopus Anglorum primas et apostolice sedis legatus universis hominibus suis tam clericis quam laicis tam Francis quam Anglicis de hundreto de Melling' salutem. Noverint tam presentes quam futuri nos concessisse in perpetuam elemosinam ecclesie Beccen' et monachis ecclesiam de Glinda cum terris et decimis et omnibus ad eam pertinentibus quam Philipus canonichus de Melling' post decessum suum eis perpetuo concessit; quamdiu tamen Philipus vixerit solvent ei monachi singulis annis de eadem ecclesia triginta solidos et post ejus decessum cedet ecclesia cum omnibus pertinenciis suis in usus monachorum perpetuos. Nos itaque eandem ecclesiam hoc tenore monachis Becci concedimus et in perpetuam possessionem auctoritate qua fungimur confirmamus salvis episcopalibus consuetudinibus ejusdem dyoecesis in qua ecclesia illa est. Omnes igitur qui hanc donacionem revocare vel perturbare injuste attemptaverint divine ulcioni in districta summi judicis examine subjaceant et dei et nostram maledictionem incurrant. Valete.

DATE: 1150–61.

PRINTED: M. Chibnall, *Documents of Bec*, p. 2 (Camden Soc., 1951).

178

Notification by Theobald of William's grant and assent as in No. 177.

MS. Windsor, St. George's Chapel, xi. G.55.

TEOB' dei gratia Cantuariensis archiepiscopus et tocius Anglie primas omnibus sancte matris ecclesie fidelibus presentibus et futuris salutem. Notum sit universitati vestre Willelmum de Melling' concessisse et dedisse in elemosinam monachis Bec[ci] ecclesiam de Glinde post mortem videlicet Philippi fratris sui vel si forte ipse Philippus vitam suam ali[qua] religione mutaverit, et hanc concessionem sive donacionem in manum meam

2D

posuisse me conceden[te] et [hac] carta mea confirmante. Volo et precipio ut idem monachi Beccenses ipsam ecclesiam cum omn[ibus] decimis et dignitatibus et pertinenciis suis post mortem videlicet prefati Philippi [in pace et] quiete imperpetuum et inconcusse teneant et habeant. Si quis vero hanc Willelmi donacionem et nostram confirmacionem attemptaverit [*sic*], deleat eum deus de libro vite nec in terra vivencium porcionem aliquam habeat. Amen. Hujus donacionis testes sunt: Walterus archidiaconus Eborac' ,Willelmus thesaurarius Exon', Elavus presbiter, Rogerius de Ponte Episcopi, Ricardus Castell, Thomas de Lond', clerici; Gervasius miles Willelmi, Robertus de Apletot, Hugo Rufus, Godefridus camerarius archiepiscopi, Willelmus Durdent. Valete.

The second of three charters relating to Glynde on a paper (15th century).
ALSO: MS. ibid. xi.G.11 (not consulted).
DATE: 1143–48.
PRINTED: M. Chibnall, *Documents of Bec*, p. 7 (Camden Soc., 1951).

179

Grant by Theobald to the canons of S. Malling, on the occasion of his consecration and dedication of the church of St. Michael, S. Malling, of all his demsene tithes of S. Malling. Their corn is to be collected and their hay to be mown in the same way as if it were Theobald's.

MS. Lambeth 1212 p.106 (Documents of Archbishop of Canterbury).

T. DEI gratia Cantuariensis archiepiscopus Anglorum primas apostolice sedis legatus universis ministris et hominibus suis Francis et Anglis de hundreto de Mellinges salutem. Noverint omnes communitas tam presentes quam futuri quoniam in dedicatione ecclesie beati Michaelis de Maellinges quam ipsi consecravimus et dedicavimus, dotavimus ipsam ecclesiam et ei [1]in perpetuam[1] dedimus dotem omnes decimaciones dominii nostri de Malling' in segetibus in fenis et[2] caseis in lana in pullis in vitulis in agnis in porcellis in capris et in omnibus aliis rebus que decimari debent tam de meo dominio quam de membris ad dominium pertinentibus. Precipimus etiam quod bladum eorum et fenum metatur et colligatur quando nostrum proprium et ab illis qui nostrum messuerint. Hanc itaque donacionem et hanc libertatem concedimus et presentis scripti nostri auctoritate ecclesie sancti Michaelis et canonicis ejusdem ecclesie [1]in perpetuam[1] possessionem confirmamus. T. Rogero archidiacono Cant' et Philippo cancellario /[p.107] et Alano de Welles et Petro scriptore et Rogerio Species et Malgerio et Roberto filio Simonis et Willelmo del Bec et Roberto Halsard et Radulfo del[3] Bec et Hugone del Bec et Daniel forestario apud Maelling'.[4]

ALSO: MS. Bodleian Tanner 223 f.63a.

VARIATIONS: [1-1]imperpetuam. [2]adds in. [3]de. [4]Mailling.

There are two transcripts from the Tanner MS. in a volume of Sussex Collectanea, MS. B.M. Addl. 5706 ff. 87a, 88a. Also Court Book of S. Malling, MS. B.M. Addl. 33182 f.7a.

DATE: 1150–54.

180

Grant by Theobald to the canons of South Malling notified to the dean and provost of S. Malling and all his servants there of the tithe of pannage and of the right to keep 24 pigs in the archbishop's forest free from pannage.

MS. Lambeth 1212 p.107 (Documents of Archbishop of Canterbury).

T. DEI gratia Cantuariensis archiepiscopus Anglorum primas[1] et apostolice sedis legatus decano et preposito et universis ministris de Melling' presentis et futuri temporis super villam Melling' constitutis salutem. Noverit presentis temporis etas et futuri posteritas quoniam pro amore dei et salute anime mee et omnium predecessorum meorum dedi et concessi in perpetuam elemosinam[2] ecclesie beati Michaelis de Melling' et ejusdem loci canonicis plenarie, totam decimam pasnagii[3] tam in denariis quam in porcis; et preter hoc concedo ut[4] singulis annis inperpetuum[5] habeant quietos de pasnagio viginti quatuor porcos de dominio suo in foresta mea. Hec illis inperpetuum[5] concedo et presentis scripti mei testimonio confirmo. T. Thoma Lond' et Philippo cancellario et Radulfo Dunelm' et Alano de Welles et Rogerio Species et Petro scriptore et Eilafo decano apud Melling'.

ALSO: MS. Bodleian Tanner 223 f.63a.

VARIATIONS: [1]*omits.* [2]*elimosinam.* [3]*pastragii.* [4]*omits.* [5]*imperpetuum.*

There are two transcripts from the Tanner MS. in a volume of Sussex Collectanea, MS. B.M. Addl. 5706 ff. 87a, 88a. Also Court Book of S. Malling, MS. B.M. Addl. 33182 f. 7a.

Followed in Lambeth and Bodleian MSS. by an inspeximus of it by Archbishop Baldwin.

DATE: 1150–54.

181

Mandate of Theobald to Bishops Henry of Winchester (1129–71), Jocelin of Salisbury (1142–84) and Robert of Exeter (1138–55 or 1155–60). He has taken the English lands of Montebourg Abbey (Ben. Coutances Dioc.) under his protection and orders the bishops to do justice to the monks in the matter of their complaints.

MS. P.R.O. Transcripts Record Commission ii vol. 140b part 2 p.157. From Cartulary of Montebourg f. 101 (Trans. 8/140b/2).

T. DEI gratia Cantuariensis archiepiscopus Anglorum primas et apostolice sedis legatus venerabilibus fratribus et amicis H[enrico] Winton', et Jocelino Sarisbur', et Roberto Exonie episcopis salutem. Noveritis quoniam bona et possessiones ecclesie Montisburgensis quas juste et canonice habent in Anglia, videlicet Lawicam, Lodres, Ovelay et Axemudam in custodia nostra suscipimus. Iccirco precipimus ut quocienscumque super illatis injuriis, monachi ejusdem ecclesie nobis queremoniam deposuerunt, absque dilatione eis justiciam ecclesiasticam exhibeatis ne aliam ad nos debeant reportare queremoniam. Valete.

DATE: 1150–60.

CALENDARED: *C.D.F.*, p. 314.

182

Notification by Theobald to Bishop Nicholas of Llandaff (1148–83) of a composition arrived at in his presence between Job the priest, parson of St. Leonard's, Newcastle (Glam.), and Master Henry Tusard, parson of St. James', Kenfig (Glam.). Henry relinquishes the tithe of Geoffrey Esturmi to the church of Newcastle and 30 acres of land belonging to Kenfig church.

Original (not consulted) MS. Penrice Castle Margam Charters no. 387. (Now at Aberystwyth.)

Cirographum (lower half).

T. dei gratia Cantuariensis archiepiscopus Anglorum primas et apostolice sedis legatus venerabili fratri et amico N[icholao] Landavensi episcopo et universis sancte matris ecclesie filiis ad quoscunque presentes pervenerint littere salutem. Causam inter ecclesiam sancti Leonarti de Novo Castello et ecclesiam beati Jacobi de Chenefeg super parrochianis et decimis per earundem ecclesiarum personas, Job videlicet presbiterum et magistrum Henricum Tusard' contendentes, sub nostra presentia sepius agitatam, desiderio et assensu utriusque inter ipsas ecclesias, interveniente amicabili personarum compositione perpetualiter diffinivimus et litem diremimus hoc modo: videlicet Henricus ecclesie de Novo Castello decimam Gaufridi Esturmi imperpetuum reliquit et triginta acras terre de terra ecclesie de Chenefeg donec eidem ecclesie de Novo Castello tantumdem terre adquirat in loco propinquiori et hoc tenore inter illis ecclesiis [?] perpetuum firmavimus pacem. Testibus R[ogero] Eboracensi electo et Johanne Eboracensi thesaurario et Thoma Londoniensi et J[ohanne] Saresberiensi et Ricardo Castel apud Cantuariam anno ab incarnacione domini mcliiii°.

Endorsement: Testimonium archiepiscopi Cantuariensis de controversia que fuit inter ecclesiam de Kenefec et illam de Novo Castello. (Later) De Stormy.

Seal: none.

Date: 1154.

Printed: Godfrey L. Clark, *Cartae et Munimenta de Glamorgan* (1910), i, 138. Summarised in W. Birch, *Penrice and Margam MSS.* (1893), 1st series, p. 146.

183

Confirmation by Theobald of the possessions of Newhouse Abbey (Prem. canons, Lincs.).

Original MS. B.M. Harleian Charters 43 G 19.

TEOB' dei gratia Cantuariensis archiepiscopus et tocius Angl[ie] primas omnibus sancte ecclesie filiis per diocesim suam constitutis salutem et benedictionem in domino. Ex injuncto nobis cure pastoralis officio ecclesiasticis tenemur studere profectibus et generaliter universis specialiter vero singulis paternam sollicitudinem maternam exhibere pietatem. Illis etiam ampliorem nobis competit impendere benivolentiam qui cum Maria dominicos pedes studiosius amplexati meliorem sibi partem elegerunt qui abjectis mundi sarcinis soli deo militare querunt. Eapropter honestis peticionibus dilectorum filiorum nostrorum abbatis et canonicorum de Neuhusa facilem prebentes assensum ipsos et ecclesiam suam et omnia quecumque aut largitione principum aut oblatione fidelium aut aliis justis modis deo propitio vel adepti sunt vel adipisci poterunt sub nostre protectionis speciali cura complectimur: in primis quicquid habent in villa de Neuhusa ex donatione Petri de Golsa cum ecclesia de Haburch et sexta parte ecclesie de Broclousebi et cum ecclesia de Saxolebi et omnibus que ad illas pertinere noscuntur; ecclesiam sancti Michaelis de Glentewurde cum omnibus appenditiis suis; ecclesiam sancti Petri de Haltona cum hiis que ad eam pertinent ex donatione Radulfi de Haltona et Gervasii fratris ejus; ex donatione Gaufridi de Neuhus et Willelmi filii ejus ecclesiam de Kirningtun cum omnibus ad eam pertinentibus; ecclesiam sancti Michaelis de Hireford et quicquid ad eam pertinet ex donatione Willelmi de Albeni. Hec et alia rationabiliter adquisita vel adquirenda presentis scripti nostri pagina prenominatis abbati et fratribus et ecclesie sue in perpetuam elemosinam confirmamus. Si quis autem contra hoc nostre protectionis et confirmationis scriptum ausu temerario venire temptaverit anathematis vinculis subjaceat donec deo et predicte ecclesie et abbati et fratribus ibidem deo servientibus condigne satis fecerit.

ENDORSEMENT: Confirmatio Theobaldi Cantuariensis archiepiscopi de omnibus ecclesiis de Neuhus.

SEAL: usual seal.

SIZE: 4·1 in. × 11·4 in.

DATE: 1143–61.

PRINTED: F. M. Stenton, *Danelaw Charters*, p.168.

184

Confirmation by Theobald of the possessions of St. Andrew's Priory, Northampton (Clu.).

MS. B.M. Royal 11 B ix f.23b. (Reg. of St. Andrew's Northampton).

T. DEI gratia [1]Cantuariensis archiepiscopus[1] et tocius Anglie primas universis sancte ecclesie filiis tam clericis quam laicis per Angliam constitutis salutem[2] et paternam benediccionem. Noverint tam presentes quam futuri quoniam[3] omnes terras et ecclesias et possessiones et decimas sive quecumque bona ecclesie sancti Andree de Norh't'[4] et fratribus ibidem deo ministrantibus, largicione comitis Simonis senis qui primus fundator eorum ecclesie extitit,[5] sunt collata canonice et ab illustri Anglorum rege bone memorie Henrico in carta sua confirmata in privillegio[6] domini pape E[ugenii] annotata, sive quecumque decetero juste et canonice adipisci potuerunt, prefate ecclesie et fratribus concedimus confirmamus et auctoritate scripti nostri corroboramus, precipientes ut[7] libere quiete et honorifice et in summa pace teneant. Si quis autem quod absit nostre confirmacioni obviando predictorum fratrum bona diminuere libertates eorum infirmare temere attemptaverit, in districti judicis examine divine ulcionis iram incurrat. Eorum vero bona conservantibus et pacem tenentibus omnium bonorum retributorum vitam et eternam pacem retribuat deus. Amen. Valete.

ALSO: in MS. B.M. Cott. Vespasian E xvii f.33a.

Confirmacio reverendi in Christo patris domini Thome Cantuariensis archiepiscopi de omnibus rebus et possessionibus monasterio sancti Andree North' pertinentibus.

VARIATIONS: [1-1]archiepiscopus Cantuariensis. [2]f.33b. [3]quod. [4]North', [5]exstitit. [6]privilegio. [7]quod.

DATE: 1145–53.

185

Mandate of Theobald to Bishop Robert II of Lincoln (1148–66) and to William, archdeacon of Northampton (*c.* 1143–69) to compel Geoffrey de Normanville to pay a mark annually to the monks of Northampton, which he had assigned as a charge on the mill of Helpringham (Lincs.).

MS. B.M. Royal 11 B ix f.23b. (Reg. of St. Andrew's Northampton).

T. DEI gratia Cantuariensis archiepiscopus Anglorum primas et apostolice sedis legatus venerabili fratri et amico R[oberto] Linc' episcopo ac dilecto filio W[illelmo] archidiacono Norh't'[1] salutem. Pervenit ad aures nostras quod G[aufridus] de Normanvilla[2] marcam argenti quam dilectis filiis nostris monachis de Norh't'[1] pro anima fratris sui singulis annis solvendam pepigerat et in molendino de Helpingham[3] assignaverat detinere presumpserit contra cartam suam veniens qua eis memoratam marcam confirmaverat ut dicunt. Inde est quod vestre mandamus discrecioni[4] precipientes[5] quatinus jam dictum G[aufridum], nisi a vobis commonitus marcam restituerit monachis, ecclesiastica disciplina coherceatis et ad solvendam marcam compellatis. Valete.

ALSO: in MS. B.M. Cott. Vespasian E xvii f.33b.

Qualiter Thomas Cantuariensis archiepiscopus scripsit R. Linc' episcopo et W. archidiacono North' quod compellerent G. de Normanvilla reddere monachis sancti Andree i marcam argenti quam injuste detinuerat.

VARIATIONS: [1]North'. [2]Mormanvilla. [3]Helpyngham. [4]discrescioni. [5]*omits*.
DATE: 1150–61.

186

Mandate of Theobald to the men of East Anglia, French and English, inhibiting their project of building a chapel at Yarmouth against the parochial rights of Norwich Cathedral Priory in spite of the prohibition of William of Norwich (1146–74). He has ordered the bishop of Norwich and Hilary of Chichester (1147–69) to excommunicate them if they persist.

MS. D. and C. Norwich Register 1 f.15b.

Temporibus ejusdem Willelmi (episcopi Norwicensis) voluerunt Portenses quandam capellam in prejudicium ecclesie Norwyc' apud Jernemutam construxisse, set bone memorie Theobaldus Cantuariensis archiepiscopus eos a presumptione incepta revocavit per hoc breve:

THEOBALDUS dei gratia Cantuariensis archiepiscopus totius Anglie primas apostolice sedis legatus universis hominibus Francis et Anglis de Hestengles[1] salutem. Relatione quorundam jam frequenter audivimus quod in episcopatu Norwycensi[2] apud Jernemutam[3] intenditis capellam novam contra episcopi Norwycensis[2] prohibitionem construere et dignitatem Norwycensis[2] ecclesie diminuere. Quoniam igitur ad nostre dignitatis officium spectat vos commovere et consulere et a tam iniqua et stulta presumptione revocare, presentium auctoritate vobis mandantes precipimus et super christianitate vestra omnino prohibemus ut in prefato loco neque capellam construere [4]neque /[f.16a] divina celebrare[4] absque prefati episcopi consensu et auctoritate et voluntate ullatenus presumatis.[5] Quod[6] si feceritis venerabilibus fratribus nostris Hylario Cicestrie episcopo nostro et Willelmo Norwyc'[2] episcopo jam in mandatis dedimus ut vos vinculo anathematis innodare non differant et vos sub anathemate esse nostra auctoritate atque precepto permanere constringant quousque domini pape presenciam visitaveritis. Valete.

ALSO: MSS. ibid. Reg. 2. f.11a (A), Reg. 7 f.34a (B).

VARIATIONS: [1]*B* Hestingis. [2]*A* Norwic'. [3]*B* Gernamudam. [4–4]*B* divina neque celebrare. [5]*B* f.34b. [6]*B* erased.

DATE: 1150–61.

PRINTED: Norfolk Record Society, 1939, *First Register of Norwich Cathedral Priory*, ed. H. W. Saunders, p. 80.

187

Confirmation by Theobald to Nuneaton Abbey (Ben. Nunnery, Warw.) as founded by Robert, earl of Leicester (1118–68) of all its possessions, in accordance with the charters of the earl and of Henry II.

Original MS. B.M. Addl. Charters 47390.

T. DEI gratia Cantuariensis archiepiscopus Anglorum primas et apostolice sedis legatus episcopis abbatibus comitibus justiciis baronibus vicecomitibus ministris et omnibus sancte ecclesię dei filiis per Angliam constitutis salutem et benedictionem. Quę largitione principum seu collatione quorumlibet fidelium in usus divinos et religiosorum sustentationes cum precipue religiosarum domorum quilibet princeps prima jecerit fundamenta rationabiliter ac pietatis intuitu transisse noscuntur, ad nostrum spectat officium ea nostre auctoritatis testimonio roborare et litterarum nostrarum auctoritate perpetuo stabilire. Inde est quod omnes terras illas et elemosinas quas Robertus comes Legrecestr' dedit abbatie quam fecit et fundavit apud Ettonam de ordine monialium de Fonte Ebraudi videlicet totam Ettonam cum omnibus pertinentiis suis in qua ipsa abbatia fundata est et in Keneteberia viginti quinque libratas terre; ex dono regis Henrici domini nostri ecclesiam de Chautona cum omnibus pertinentiis suis; ex dono Gervasii Paganelli molendinum de Ingepenna cum omnibus pertinentiis suis; et omnes illas donationes quę eidem abbatie jam facte sunt seu adhuc restant faciende ipsam etiam abbatiam et collatarum sibi elemosinarum regiam concessionem et sigilli sui confirmationem nos ratam habemus et auctoritate qua fungimur confirmamus et presentis carte nostre testimonio stabilem perpetuis temporibus constituimus cum omnibus libertatibus et quietantiis et dignitatibus cum quibus predictus comes Legrec' eam fundavit et dominus noster rex H[enricus] eidem abbatie concessit et per cartam suam confirmavit assensu et concessione Roberti filii comitis Legrec'. Quare volumus et precipimus quatinus eadem abbatia et moniales de ordine Fontis Ebraudi ibidem deo servientes habeant et teneant in perpetuam elemosinam omnia hec predicta cum omnibus pertinentiis suis libere et quiete ab omni seculari exactione et mundana servitute et servitio vel qualibet consuetudine seculari sicut eandem abbatiam dominus noster rex Henricus per cartam suam liberavit et quietam clamavit in perpetuum. Quicumque ergo hujus libertatis collate diminutor seu perturbator contra nostre confirmationis tenorem temerario ausu venire attemptaverit seu quibuslibet injustis modis bona monialium diminuere vel inquietare indignationem omnipotentis dei et nostram maledictionem se noverit incurrisse. Valete.

ENDORSEMENT: Hec est confirmatio archiepiscopi Cantuarie de elemosinis et de pertinentibus Eatone.

SEAL: usual with good counterseal.

SIZE: 9·8 in. × 8·8 in.

DATE: 1154–61.

188

Notification by Theobald to Bishop Everard of Norwich (1121–45) that he has dedicated the church of St. Paul belonging to the hospital [of St. Paul] at Norwich. He confirms the possessions of St. Paul's hospital and grants an annual indulgence of eight days on the anniversary of the dedication of the church of St. Paul.

MS. B.M. Cott. Charters ii 19 no.9 (Norwich Roll).

Carta Tedbaldi archiepiscopi Cantuariensis.

TEDBALDUS dei gracia Cantuariensis archiepiscopus et tocius Anglie primas Eborardo Norwycensi episcopo et omnibus sancte ecclesie filiis salutem deique et suam benediccionem. Notum sit tam presentibus quam futuris Christi fidelibus quod ego Tedbaldus archiepiscopus dedicavi ecclesiam sancti Pauli que pertinet ad hospitale pauperum apud Norwycum. Qua propter confirmo et precipio liberam esse sub pace dei et domini pape et nostra omnia que pertinent eidem prenominate ecclesie, precipue in ecclesiis de Ormesby quas Ricardus archidiaconus ei consessu regis Henrici et postea Stephani regis dono dedit, et in aliis quoque rebus in terris in decimis et in redditibus et in omnibus possessionibus quas habuit vel habitura est dono Cristi et suorum fidelium. Quicumque autem benefecerit eidem hospitali benediccionem dei et domini pape nostramque habeat, et econtra qui res ejusdem domus diripuerit sive diminuerit anathemati subjaceat nisi ad emendacionem et satisfaccionem venerit. Fiat. Fiat. Amen. +Et in anniversario dedicacionis ejusdem basilice sancti Pauli perdonum facio de relaxacione penitencie octo dierum singulis annis.

One of a number of charters confirmed by John Salmon bishop of Norwich in 1301.

DATE: 1139–45.

The following charter (no. 10) is an inspeximus of this charter by Ralph bishop of Norwich in 1292.

189

Confirmation by Theobald to the nuns of Nunappleton (Cist., Yorks.) of the grant made by Alice de St. Quintin and Robert her son and heir in accordance with the charter of Alice which he has inspected.

MS. *Ex ipso autographo penes Thomam dominum Fairfax de Cameron a. 1622.*

T. DEI gratia Cantuariensis archiepiscopus Anglorum primas et apostolicae sedis legatus universis sanctae ecclesiae fidelibus salutem. Quae pietatis intuitu locis religiosis a fidelibus Christi conferuntur ea nostrae authoritatis munimine merito confirmantur. Ea igitur ratione elemosinam quam Adeliz de S. Quintino et Robertus haeres ejus Deo et sancto Johanni et fratri Richardo et ibidem religiose viventibus dederunt concesserunt et carta sua confirmaverunt, nos quoque juxta tenorem cartae suae eidem loco in perpetuam confirmavimus possessionem et praesentis scripti nostri testimonio corroboramus, scilicet in Appiltona duas bovatas terrae quas Juliana tenuit in terra circa locum partim sartatam partim non sartatam ex utraque parte rivi usque ad metas positas ab Hugone et Siwardo et Willielmo, et unam bovatam terrae in Thorp, liberas et quietas ab omni seculari servitio et exactione solutas, sicut carta predictae Adeliz quam oculis nostris conspeximus attestatur. Quicumque hanc igitur elemosinam infirmare vel inquietare attemptaverit, in divini Judicis examine divinam ultionem incurrat. Valete.

DATE: 1150–61 perhaps 1153–54 during vacancies at York.

PRINTED: *Monasticon*, v, 653. This is a confirmation of the charter printed in *E.Y.C.*, i, 419.

190

Confirmation by Theobald of the possessions of Oseney (priory of Augustinian Canons, Oxon.) addressed to Prior Wigot (became abbot 1154).

Original MS. Christ Church, Oxford, Oseney Charters deposited at Bodleian 902.

T. DEI gratia Cantuariensis archiepiscopus et tocius Anglię primas et apostolice sedis legatus fratri Wigodo priori de Oseneia salutem. Justis peticionibus facilem debemus prebere assensum ut fidelium devocio celerem sortiatur effectum. Proinde rationabilibus postulacionibus tuis assensum prebentes, omnes ecclesias et terras et decimas et domorum redditus et omnia que ecclesia beate Marie cui deo auctore prees legitime adepta est vel futuris temporibus justis modis adipisci poterit presenti scripto ei confirmamus et auctoritate officii quo fungimur corroboramus. Pervasores earum et distractores ante tribunal ęterni judicis dampnandos esse denuntiamus et a presenti ęcclesia eos sequestramus, nisi resipuerint et Christi patrimonium humili satisfactione reformare studuerint. Conservantibus autem pax sit a domino nostro Jesu Christo qui cum dives esset, pro nobis pauper factus est ut nos ditaret sua paupertate et sanaret sua infirmitate.

ENDORSEMENT: Confirm' T. arch' omnium rerum nostrarum.

SEAL: Fragment.

SIZE: 4·2 in. × 7·2 in.

DATE: 1151-54.

COPIES: MS. Oxford Christ Church Cart. of Oseney f.19b; MS. B.M. Cott. Vitellius E xv f.170b.

PRINTED: H. E. Salter, Oxford Hist. Soc., 1934. *Cartulary of Oseney Abbey,* iv, 42.

191

Notification by Theobald to Bishops Jocelin of Salisbury (1142–84) Robert II of Lincoln (1148–66) William of Norwich (1146–74) and John of Worcester (1151–57). From the evidence of a charter of Archbishop William (1123–36) he has learnt that Ralph Basset justiciar of Henry I (d. 1127) granted the lordship and advowson of all the churches of his demesne to his son Ralph the clerk. This son has now given 'by the hand of Theobald' all the churches with their lands and tithes to Oseney. The bishops are to confirm the grants and help the canons to secure their possessions.

MS. B.M. Cott. Vitellius E xv f.33a (Register of Oseney).

Confirmatio Teob' archiepiscopi de eisdem (churches given by Basset).

T. DEI gratia Cantuariensis archiepiscopus Anglorum primas et apostolice sedis legatus venerabilibus fratribus et amicis suis Joscelino Saresberiensi, Roberto Lincoln', Willelmo Norwicensi, Johanni Wigorniensi, episcopis salutem. Ex testimonio carte felicis memorie predecessoris nostri Willelmi Cantuariensis archiepiscopi cognovimus quod Radulfus Basset regis Henrici justiciarius Radulfo clerico filio suo per manum ejusdem archiepiscopi dominatum et advocationem omnium ecclesiarum dominii sui donaverit, et earundem ecclesiarum confirmationem ab eodem archiepiscopo predicto filio suo impetraverit. Idem vero filius postmodum succedente tempore per manum nostram omnes illas ecclesias cum terris et decimis et capellis, scilicet ecclesiam de Halruge, ecclesiam de Messewurda cum capella de Tiscecota, ecclesiam de Aclea cum capella de Clopeham, ecclesiam de Missebiri cum capella de Wilanestona, ecclesiam de Treotuna, ecclesiam de Wivelicota, ecclesiam de Pellinges, ecclesiam de Turchendene, ecclesiam de Risendene, ecclesiam de Leecumba, ecclesiam de Quidenham, ecclesiam de Stantona cum pertinentiis suis ecclesie beate Marie de Oseneia, cui se ipsum devoverat in perpetuam donavit elemosinam. Nos itaque hanc donationem ad opus Oseneiensis ecclesie illi eam confirmantes universitatem vestram ob[secramur] quatinus et vos quoque consequenter easdem do[nationes] ecclesie Oseneiensi confirmetis et in quibus potestis fratres ejusdem loci ad tam honestum hujus possessionis ingressum secundum deum juvetis. Valete.

DATE: 1151–57.

PRINTED: H. E. Salter, *Oseney Cartulary*, vi, 130. Archbishop William's charter is on the same page.

192

Confirmation by Theobald to the canons of Oseney of the church of Watlington (Oxon.) granted to them by Robert d'Oilli and Henry his son and afterwards by William de Chesney by the authority of King Stephen and in accordance with the charter of Robert II bishop of Lincoln (1148–66).

MS. B.M. Cott. Vitellius E xv f.22b (Register of Oseney).

> Confirmatio Teob' Cantuariensis archiepiscopi de Watlint'.

[T. DEI] gratia Cantuariensis archiepiscopus Anglorum primas [et apostoli]ce sedis legatus universis sancte ecclesie fide[libus sa]lutem. Ecclesiam de Watlint' quam Robertus de [Oilli et] Henricus filius ejus et postmodum Willelmus de Caisneto [qua]ndo in manu sua regis Stephani au[ctori]tate et donatione devolveretur religi[osis fratri]bus canonicis regularibus de Osen' [in pur]am concesserunt elemosinam sicut venerabilis [frater noster] Robertus Lincoln' episcopus eisdem fratribus concessit [et carta sua] canonice confirmavit, nos quoque [presenti]s scripti auctoritate confirmamus.

ALSO: in a 16th-century transcript MS. B.M. Cott. Vitellius F iv f.314b.
DATE: 1150–54.
PRINTED: H. E. Salter: *Oseney Cartulary*, iv, 407.

193

Confirmation by Theobald to the canons of Oseney of the church of Watlington granted to them by Halinad de Bidun and also of lands granted to them by Henry d'Oilli after the death of his father (Robert) and by Wygan of Wallingford.

MS. Christ Church Oxford Oseney Cartulary f.128a (not checked with MS.).

> Confirmacio Theobaldi archiepiscopi de ecclesia de Watlintona.

THEOBALDUS dei gracia Cantuariensis archiepiscopus Anglorum primas et apostolice sedis legatus universis ecclesie filiis salutem. Facile datur peticioni consensus cui justicie astipulatur assensus. Hac induti racione ea que Henricus de Olleyo post mortem patris sui ecclesie sancte Marie de Oseneya contulit presentis scripti auctoritate confirmamus: in Hokenorthona, Butyrhylle et Prestfeld et xxiiii ^{or} acras prati de dominio et unam acram terre; in Cleydona tres hidas terre; in Westona hidam et dimidiam; apud Etonam insulam que Sperweseya dicitur; et ecclesiam de Watlintona cum pertinenciis suis de dono Halinadi de Bydun et unam virgatam terre et duas acras quas idem adjecit; unam eciam hydam terre quam dedit prefate ecclesie Wyganus de Walingeforde in manerio suo Fulebroke concessu fratris sui Mainfelini. Pervasores igitur (etc. anathema).

DATE: 1154–61.

PRINTED: H. E. Salter, *Oseney Cartulary*, iv, 409.

194

Confirmation by Theobald to the canons of Oseney of St. George's church in the castle of Oxford in accordance with the charter of Robert II bishop of Lincoln (1148–66).

Original MS. Christ Church Oxford Oseney Charters deposited at Bodleian 897a.

T. DEI gratia Cantuariensis archiepiscopus et totius Anglie primas omnibus sancte matris ecclesie fidelibus per Angliam extantibus tam presentibus quam futuris tam clericis quam laicis salutem et benedictionem. Ex commisso nobis admonemur officio peticionibus quas ad religionis incrementum dinoscimus pertinere facilem ac benignum prebere assensum. Quocirca karissimorum filiorum nostrorum canonicorum scilicet sancte Marie de Oseneia piis postulationibus annuentes, concedimus et presenti scripto in perpetuam elemosinam confirmamus ipsis et monasterio in quo divino mancipantur officio ecclesiam sancti Georgii que sita est in castello Oxeneford' cum universis tenaturis et possessionibus et cum omnibus ad eandem ecclesiam pertinentibus in ecclesiis in decimis in terris in hominibus et libertatibus et omnibus aliis redditibus, sicut venerabilis frater noster Robertus Lincol' episcopus illis eam concessit et carta sua quam occulis nostris conspeximus confirmavit et sicut carta ipsa testatur. Hujus igitur nostre confirmationis perturbatoribus dampnationis periculum imminere denunciamus; conservatores autem benedictione dei et nostra potiantur. Valete.

ENDORSEMENT: Carta T. archiepiscopi de sancto Georgio . . . cum suis pertin'. Dup^a.

SEAL: usual.

SIZE: 3·8 in. × 7·0 in.

DATE: *c.* 1149 (see *Cartulary of Oseney* (1929–36), iv, p.43, n.1. ed. H. E. Salter).

PRINTED: with facsimile, H. E. Salter, *Oxford Charters* (1929), no. 62.

195

Same as No. 194 after Theobald had been made legate. The consent of the king and the advocates of St. George's is now added.

Original MS. Christ Church Oxford Oseney Charters deposited at Bodleian 897.

T. DEI gratia Cantuariensis archiepiscopus et totius Anglię primas et apostolicę sedis legatus omnibus sanctę matris ęcclesię fidelibus per Angliam extantibus tam presentibus quam futuris tam clericis quam laicis salutem et benedictionem. Ex commisso nobis admonemur officio petitionibus quas ad religionis incrementum dinoscimus pertinere facilem ac benignum prebere assensum. Quocirca karissimorum filiorum nostrorum canonicorum scilicet sanctę Marię de Oseneia piis postulationibus annuentes, concedimus et presenti scripto in perpetuam elemosinam confirmamus ipsis et monasterio in quo divino mancipantur officio ęcclesiam sancti Georgii que sita est in castello Oxeneford' cum universis tenaturis et possessionibus et cum omnibus ad eandem ęcclesiam pertinentibus in ecclesiis in decimis in terris in hominibus et libertatibus et omnibus aliis redditibus, sicut venerabilis frater noster Robertus Lincol' episcopus illis eam concessit unanimi consensu regis et ejusdem ęcclesię advocatorum et carta sua confirmavit quam oculis nostris perspeximus et sicut carta sua testatur. Hujus igitur

2E

nostrę confirmationis perturbatoribus dampnationis periculum imminere denunciamus, conservatores autem benedictione dei et nostra potiantur. Valete.

ENDORSEMENT: Carta T. Cant' archiepiscopi de conf' Sancti Georg'. Dupª.

SEAL: usual and counterseal.

SIZE: 2·7 in. × 11·3 in.

DATE: 1150–61.

COPIES: MS. Oxford Christ Church Cartulary of Oseney f.19b; B.M. Cott. Vit. E xv f.13a.

PRINTED: H. E. Salter (Oxford Hist. Soc., 1934), *Cartulary of Oseney Abbey,* iv, 42 (cf. p. 37).

196

Mandate of Theobald to all bishops archdeacons and priests in whose areas of administration are tithes belonging to the canons of Oseney. They must compel defaulters to pay.

Original   MS. Christ Church Oxford Oseney Charters deposited at Bodleian 902a.

T. DEI gratia Cantuariensis archiepiscopus totius Anglie primas et apostolice sedis legatus omnibus episcopis archidiaconis presbiteris in quorum potestate et parrochia sunt decimationes ad ecclesiam sancte Marie de Oseneia pertinentes salutem. Questi sunt nobis filii nostri karissimi regulares canonici de Oseneia decimationes quasdam ad jus ecclesie sue spectantes contra justiciam a quibusdam detineri. Eapropter per presentia vobis scripta precipimus quatinus illos qui jura predicte ecclesie detinent districte conveniatis et ut ea ex integro restituant admoneatis. Si autem restitere noluerint eosdem a liminibus sancte ecclesie arceatis. Valete.

ENDORSEMENT: T. Cantuar' archiepiscopi de decimis ad jus nostrum spectantibus.

SEAL: usual archiepiscopal with counterseal.

SIZE: 2·3 in. × 5·6 in.

DATE: 1150–61.

PRINTED: with facsimile, H. E. Salter, *Oxford Charters* (1929), no. 72.

COPY: Oseney Cartulary f.20a (MS Christ Church, Oxford).

PRINTED: H. E. Salter, *Oseney Cartulery,* iv, 43 (Oxford Hist. Soc.).

197

Confirmation by Theobald of the possessions and liberties of Owston (abbey of Augustinian Canons, Leics.).

Original MS. B.M. Cott. Charters xi 4.

T. DEI gratia Cantuariensis archiepiscopus Anglorum primas apostolice sedis legatus universis sancte ecclesie fidelibus salutem. Equum est ac rationabile ea que divinis sunt canonice mancipata servitiis ecclesiastico privilegio confirmari. Inde est quod nos justis postulationibus dilecti filii nostri Odonis abbatis et canonicorum regularium ecclesie de Osolvetona quos religionis nomen commendat attentius annuentes eis omnia que in presentiarum juste et canonice possident et siqua in futurum justis modis adipisci poterunt, juxta tenorem cartarum venerabilis fratris nostri R[oberti] Linc' episcopi, in elemosinam perpetuam concedimus et presentis scripti munimine confirmamus, videlicet: ecclesiam de Osolvestonia cum omnibus pertinentiis suis et totum illud manerium cum omnibus ad illud manerium pertinentibus et viii virgatas terre in Cnossitonia ex dono Walteri de Chevrecurt; et libertatem illam quam predictus episcopus R[obertus] illis canonicis concessit et carta sua confirmavit, videlicet predictam ecclesiam fore liberam et quietam a synodalibus et ab omni episcopali consuetudine absolutam excepto denario beati Petri. Quicumque ergo contra hanc nostram confirmationem ausu temerario venire presumpserit nisi illam presumptionem cum integritate correxerit indignationem omnipotentis dei et nostram maledictionem se noverit incursurum. Amen. Valete.

ENDORSEMENT: Confirmatio T. archiepiscopi Cantuariensis de Osolvestona de libertatibus et synodalibus (13th century).

SIZE: 8 in. × 6·4 in.

SEAL: usual with counterseal.

DATE: 1150–61.

PRINTED: F. M. Stenton, *Danelaw Charters* (1920), p. 316.

198

Notification by Theobald that Osbert of Paxton has, with his companions actual or prospective, with the archbishop's consent become a canon regular in the church of Holy Trinity, (Great) Paxton (Hunts.) and confirmation of Osbert's benefices in churches or other possessions for the maintenance of religious life at (Great) Paxton.

MS. Lincoln Registrum no. 294 (not checked with MS.).

T. DEI gracia Cantuariensis archiepiscopus omnibus sancte dei ecclesie fidelibus tam futuris quam presentibus salutem et dei benediccionem et suam. Noveritis fratres dilectissimi quoniam Osbertus de Paxtuna vitam suam in melius mutare volens cum sociis suis quos secum recepit vel recepturus est, assensu et concessu nostro canonicus regularis in ecclesia sancte Trinitatis de Paxtuna effectus est et omnia beneficia sua in ecclesiis videlicet sive in aliis possessionibus que ad hanc religionem tenendam in ecclesia prefata posuit vel positurus est, hac presenti carta nostra confirmamus et inperpetuum stabilia dei auctoritate et nostra sine aliqua contradiccione fore jubemus. Insuper eciam interdicimus ne quis ad hanc regulam destruendam vel ad beneficia dicte ecclesie minuenda ullatenus sub anathemate huic carte nostre contraire presumat. Valete.

DATE: 1139-50 (probably early).

PRINTED: C. W. Foster, *Registrum Antiquissimum*, Lincoln Record Society, xxix, 152.

199

Confirmation by Theobald of all the customary rights of the abbey of Pershore (Ben., Worcs.) and especially the payments due from the free men and villeins of Westminster abbey i.e. two-thirds of the tithes of all the men of the hundred of Pershore and payments due to the mother church, in accordance with the charter of Gilbert abbot of Westminster (?1085-1117) and the convent, which the archbishop has inspected.

MS. P.R.O. Exchequer O.A. Miscellaneous Books i 61 (E 315/61).
Cartulary of Pershore f.104b.

> Confirmacio sancti Thome Cantuariensis archiepis-
> copi decimarum et consuetudinum et rectitudinum
> ecclesie Persor' pertinentium et specialiter de liberis
> hominibus et colonis sancti Petri Westm'.

T. DEI gratia Cantuariensis archiepiscopus Anglorum primas et
apostolice sedis legatus universis sancte ecclesie fidelibus salutem. Ad pastoris spectat officium omnibus et maxime religionem
professis quietem et pacem providere et que illorum juste et
rationabiliter deputata sunt usibus perpetuo stabilire. Inde est
quod ecclesie sancte Marie de Persor' omnes rectitudines et
consuetudines quas antiquitus habere solebat et de liberis
hominibus et colonis sancti Petri de Westmonasterio scilicet
duas partes decimarum omnium hominum de hundredo Per-
sore et alia omnia beneficia que solvi debent matri ecclesie ubi
corpora defunctorum sepeliuntur, concedimus et in perpetuum
confirmamus sicut venerande memorie Gilbertus Westm' abbas
et ejusdem loci conventus predicte ecclesie de Persora et
monachis ibidem deo militantibus concesserunt et carta sua
quam oculis nostris conspeximus confirmaverunt. Valete.

DATE: 1150–61.

200

Confirmation by Theobald at the petition of Martin abbot of Peterborough (1133–55) and the convent of the subjection of the church
of (East) Carlton to the church of Cottingham (Northants.) in
accordance with the charter of Robert I bishop of Lincoln (1094–
1123).

MS. D. and C. Peterborough Swaffham Cartulary f.90a.

> Theobaldi archiepiscopi super ecclesia de Carletune
> ad ecclesiam de Cotingham.

THEOBALDUS dei gratia Cantuariencis [sic] archiepiscopus
tocius Anglie primas apostolice sedis legatus omnibus sancte

ecclesie fidelibus salutem et benediccionem. Juste postulacio voluntatis effectui prosequente debet compleri. Noverit ergo universitas vestra quod nos justis postulationibus dilecti filii nostri Martini abbatis et conventus monasterii de Burgo inclinati, ecclesiam de Karletona cum omnibus pertinenciis suis juxta tenorem carte R[oberti] quondam Lincolniensis episcopi ecclesie de Cotingham auctoritate qua fungimur confirmamus et presentis scripti munimine roboramus. Valete.

DATE: 1150–55.

The following is the charter of Bishop Robert Bloet alluded to: f.92a.

Robertus Lincolniensis episcopus Roberto archidiacono et Hugoni vicecomiti et Gosfrido Ridel et Michaeli de Hamesclap' et Waltero Ponhar' et omnibus parochianis suis de Norhamtunescire salutem. Sciatis me consecrasse ecclesiam de Carlenton' que fuerat capella subjecta ecclesie de Cotingham et hoc feci requisicione dominorum Carlenton et proborum virorum ejusdem ville; et Osbertus de Cotingham concessit ut predicta ecclesia Carleton' cum suo cimiterio consecraretur, hac videlicet convencione quod Robertus filius Ricardi eidem /[f.92b] ecclesie daret unam bovatam terre et Walterus Ponhar' unam bovatam Radulfus de Pippewelle dimidiam bovatam et villani ejusdem ville quinquedecim [sic] acras exceptis Fordalis cum prato quod ibi pertinet et dederunt ad presbiterum hospitandum unam mansuram terre. Et hoc factum et confirmatum fuit coram me tali condicione quod si ipsi nollent hanc convencionem sequi, rediret predicta capella in subjeccionem priorem ecclesie de Cotingham. Et si hec, ut prenominata sunt, manutenerent, maneret ecclesia mater cum cimiterio suo, ita quod Osbertus inveniret clericum idoneum qui ibi deo et parochianis serviret. Quod etiam habebunt in eadem ecclesia Carlenton omnes successores Osberti qui ecclesiam habebunt de Cotingham.

There are marginal cross-references between these two charters.

201

Confirmation, probably by Theobald to the monks of Pipewell Abbey (Cist., Northants.) of the hermitage in Rockingham Forest and surrounding lands in which they established themselves (from Newminster).

MS. B.M. Cott. Caligula A xii f.9a (Cartulary of Pipewell).

Confirmacio sancti Thome Cantuariensis archiepiscopi.

T. DEI gratia Cantuariensis archiepiscopus tocius Anglie primas universis sancte matris ecclesie filiis salutem et benediccionem.

Noverit caritas vestra quoniam abbacie de Divisis que juxta Rokingam sita est et monachis ibidem deo servientibus vel servituris inperpetuum per presentem cartulam confirmamus heremitorium illud et landas circumjacentes quod una cum illis se regia munificencia juste adeptos carta ipsius regis quam pre manibus habent testatur. Valete.

DATE: 1141–61 or 1162–70.

202

Confirmation by Theobald of the possessions of the monks of Pontefract (Cluniac, Yorks.) and of their dependent priory of Monk Bretton (Yorks.).

MS. Woolley Hall, Cartulary of Pontefract f.13b (not checked with MS., which is deposited at Leeds with the Yorks. Archaeological Society).

THEBBALDUS dei gratia Cantuariensis archiepiscopus Anglorum primas apostolice sedis legatus omnibus sancte ecclesie fidelibus salutem. Res ecclesiarum sicut sanctorum patrum testatur auctoritas sunt patrimonia pauperum et pretia precatorum; et quemadmodum sacrosancta ecclesia nostre salutis ac fidei perpetua mater est, ita nichilominus ejus patrimonium illesum debet perpetuo conservari et nulla desidia, nulla pravorum hominum perversitate, convelli; que enim sine macula et ruga utpote sponsa Christi virtutum circumdata fulgore clarescit, dignum est ut nullum rerum suarum detrimentum vel prejudicium patiatur, sed potius grata in omnibus tranquillitate ac libertate letetur. Noverit ergo universitas vestra quod nos justis postulationibus religiosorum monachorum de Caritate qui in monasterio beati Johannis ewangeliste de Pontefracto deo assidue et devote deserviunt attentius annuentes, omnes possessiones et bona que inpresentiarum juste et canonice possident et siqua justis modis in futurum adipisci poterint, eis in elemosinam perpetuam juxta tenorem cartarum suarum concedimus et presentis scripti munimine confirmamus. Ad majorem ergo evidentiam illa duximus certis exprimenda vocabulis: ex dono Roberti de Laceio tempore Willelmi secundi regis situm ecclesie

ipsorum monachorum in Pontefracto et ibidem vii acras cum
mansuris suis, et in Brakenhil xiii acras, et ecclesiam Omnium
Sanctorum in eadem villa et quicquid ad eam pertinet, et
ecclesiam de Ledesham cum omnibus pertinentiis suis et dimidiam ejusdem ville de Ledesham, et Ledestonam et Witewde et
Doddewrdam et aquam a molendinis Castelforde usque ad
Thornestrem, et custodiam hospitalis sancti Nicholai de Pontefracto; ex dono Willelmi Folioth unam carrucatam terre in
Pontefracto; ex dono Ailsy in Silkestona vi bovatas terre; ex
dono Suani filii Ailrici ecclesiam de Silkestona cum omnibus ad
eam pertinentibus, et ecclesiam de Calthorn cum duabus partibus decimarum totius dominii sui; ex dono Hugonis de Laval
decimam redditus ville de Pontefracto et ecclesiam de Darding-
tona et ecclesiam de Kippeis cum omnibus ad eas pertinentibus,
et in Boolanda ecclesiam de Sleiteburna cum omnibus ad eam
pertinentibus, et in Cestresira ecclesiam de Walleya et quicquid
ad eam pertinet, et capellam castelli de Clitherou cum decimis
omnium rerum dominii sui, et ibidem ecclesiam beate Marie
Magdalene et ecclesiam de Calna et ecclesiam de Brunley et
quecumque ad illas pertinent, et ecclesia beati Clementis de
Pontefracto alii ecclesie non dabitur nisi ecclesie sancti Johannis
de Pontefracto; ex dono Willelmi Maltraver[si] et uxoris sue
Damete unam bovatam terre in Torph; ex dono Henrici de
Laceyo villam de Kellingl[ey] cum omnibus pertinentiis suis, et
piscatoriam unam in Begala, et decimam sue carnis de vena-
tione sua et coriorum; item ex dono ipsius et Radulfi de Capri-
curia villam de Bernesleya cum omnibus pertinentiis suis preter
unum sartum et molendinum quod dedit illis soror ipsius
Radulfi Betrix; ex dono Pagani de Landa et Hugonis de Stiven-
tuna totam terram de Pecchesfeld finaliter pro iiii or solidis per
annum; ex capitulo beati Petri Eboracensis ecclesie dimidium
de Ledeshama in perpetuum pro x marcis per singulos annos
solvendis; ex dono Pagani filii Bucardi xxx acras in Pontefracto: in Sithintuna xii bovatas terre, sex ex dono Hugonis de
Laval, et sex ex dono Willelmi comitis de Warenna; ex dono
Henr' de Campels duas mansuras in Pontefracto cum toftis
earum; ex dono Ascelini de Dai unam mansuram cum tofto in
Pontefracto; ex dono W[illelmi] de Fristona duas bovatas terre

in Fristona et iii acras juxta molendinum, et ex dono Roberti
patris sui ipsum molendinum; ex dono Ailsi Bacun unam bovatam terre in Ravenesfeld; ex dono Symonis de Muhalt ii bovatas
terre in Co'sehist; ex dono Radulfi de Cathewic dimidietatem
ecclesie ejusdem ville, et ex dono Symonis filii ejus unam bovatam terre in eadem villa; ex dono Adam filii Suani duas bovatas
terre in Calthorna; ex dono Gilleberti de Gaunt passagium de
Suthferibi et iii bovatas terre et dimidiam cum xiiii mansuris in
eadem villa; ex dono Rogerii de Molbrai et uxoris sue Aliz unam
carrucatam terre in Ingolvesmeles et quicquid ad illam pertinet; ex dono Aliz de Romeli unam carrucatam terre in Broctona cum omnibus pertinentiis suis; ex dono Adam filii Swani
situm monasterii beate Marie Magdalene de Lunda cum
Brettona et Neuhala et Reinesberga et Lintueit et quicquid in
Bramtona et quicquid habetur inter Hairam et Stainclif usque
Meresbroch, et molendina de Dirna et Lundam patris sui, in
Cumberlanda capellam beate Andree apostoli juxta Culgaid
cum omnibus pertinentiis suis. Nulli ergo hominum fas sit pre-
scriptos fratres super possessionibus suis tam juste adeptis vel
rationabiliter adipiscendis temere perturbare aut aliquam eis
exinde molestiam vel diminutionem vel contrarietatem inferre.
Siquis autem huic nostre confirmationi ausu temerario contraire presumpserit, nisi presumptionem suam congrua satisfactione correxerit, indignationem omnipotentis dei et beati
Johannis evangeliste incurrat et excommunicationi subjaceat.
Conservantes autem hec eorumdem benedictionem et gratiam
consequentur. Amen. Valete.

DATE: 1150–61 but probably 1153–54.

PRINTED: *E.Y.C.*, iii, 168 (text above), Cartulary printed in *Yorks. Archaeological Soc. Record Series*, xxv, no. 57.

203

Confirmation by Theobald to the monks of Quarr (Cist., I.O.W.) of
the chapel of St. Nicholas in Carisbrooke Castle and the land of
Whitefield (in Brading, I.O.W.) with all other possessions in accordance with the charter of Henry II.

Original MS. P.R.O. Exchequer T.R. Ancient Deeds A 14236 (E 40).

T. DEI gratia Cantuariensis archiepiscopus Angl' primas et apostolice sedis legatus universis sancte matris ecclesię filiis salutem. Quecumque bona a principibus viris seu a quibuscumque fidelibus auctoritate diocesani episcopi et principis interveniente assensu in divinos usus transferri noscuntur, ea nostre auctoritatis robore ad inexterminabilem et perpetuam stabilitatem merito deducuntur. Inde est quod religiosis fratribus monachis de insula Wicht in cenobio Quarrarie deo famulantibus capellam sancti Nicolai de castello de Caresbroc cum terris et decimis et oblationibus et omnibus pertinentiis suis et terram de Whitefelda totam cum hominibus, nemore, pratis, pascuis, aquis, molendino et omnes alias possessiones suas tam ecclesiasticas quam mundanas quas in presentiarum canonice adepti sunt vel in futuro adipisci rationabiliter poterunt juxta tenorem cartarum donatorum seu donantibus auctoritatem prestantium salva diocesani episcopi dignitate sicut et dominus noster rex Henricus eis carta sua confirmavit, nos quoque auctoritate qua fungimur confirmamus et presentis scripti nostri munimine corroboramus. Prohibemus ergo sub anathemate ne quis in bona eorum manum violentam extendat nec aliquam eis vel suis molestiam faciat. Valete.

ENDORSEMENT: (Contemporary) Carta de capella sancti Nicholai et de Whitefelda. (Little later) Carta T. archiepiscopi Cantuariensis de capella de Caresbroc et de confirmatione rerum omnium nostrarum.

SEAL: none.

SIZE: 6·8 in. × 5·8 in.

DATE: 1158–61. Later than 204.

204

Notification by Theobald of the grant by Hugo de Witville of Whitefield to the monks of Quarr made in his presence. Hugo had confirmed the grant by charter and had given Theobald security for good faith.

Original MS. P.R.O. Exchequer O.A. Ancient Deeds Madox 84 (E 327/84).

T. DEI gratia Cantuariensis archiepiscopus Angl' primas et apostolice sedis legatus universis ecclesię dei fidelibus salutem. Noverit universitas vestra quoniam Hugo de Witvilla ante nostram presentiam veniens donationem quam fecerat ecclesie sancte Marie de Quarraria in insula de Wict de terra que dicitur Whitefeld' quam eidem ecclesie et monachis ejusdem loci donavit et per cartam suam confirmavit, fide in manibus nostris prestita corroboravit a se et heredibus suis perpetuo pro viribus observandam, ab omni terreno servitio liberam preter orationum suffragia. Nos igitur ejus audita devotione et fidei sue cautione de collato eis beneficio firmando suscepta, auctoritate qua fungimur eis predictam terram confirmamus et presentis scripti nostri testimonio donum corroboratum, perpetuo eis habendum et quiete possidendum statuimus, prohibentes sub anathemate ne quis decetero in terram illam vel bona eorum manum violentam extendat nec eis injuriam faciat. Valete.

ENDORSEMENT: Carta T. archiepiscopi de terra de Witefeld.

SEAL: none.

SIZE: 5·5 in. × 6 in.

DATE: 1158–61. An accompanying Memorandum of the early 14th century says the manor was given in 1158, attributing this charter, however, to Becket.

PRINTED: T. Madox, *Formulare* (1702), p. 46.

205

Confirmation by Theobald of the grant of King Stephen to Ramsey Abbey (Ben., Hunts.) of his manor of (King's) Ripton in free alms.

Original MS. B.M. Addl. Charters 34014.

TEDBALDUS dei gratia Cantuariensis archiepiscopus regi Anglie archiepiscopis episcopis abbatibus comitibus baronibus justiciis vicecomitibus ministris et omnibus sancte ecclesie fidelibus salutem et benedictionem. Sicut sacerdotalis officii est pravorum quorumlibet erroneis conatibus justicie zelo contraire, sic nimirum esse convenit censura ecclesiastica proborum acta omnimodis confirmare. Hoc igitur intuitu donationem piissimi regis nostri Stephani, scilicet manerium suum quod Ripetona vocatur quod pro anima avunculi sui regis Henrici et propria salute et regine et filiorum suorum et pro incolumitate totius regni, ęcclesię sancti Benedicti de Ramiseia et monachis ibidem deo servientibus omnino liberum et quietum sicut ipse possederat jure perpetuo possidendum concessit, presenti paginula in nomine domini laudamus, laudando corroboramus et corroborando auctoritate nobis a deo concessa perpetuo observatumiri [sic] sancimus. Quisquis igitur hanc donationem ex integro servaverit et huic nostrę sanctioni obediens fuerit, benedictione dei omnipotentis et nostra in hac vita bonis omnibus abundare et in futura eterna incelis [sic] perfrui mereatur beatitudine. Siquis vero contra hęc quod absit venire vel quoquam modo hec ipsa mutare vel imminuere temptaverit, a communione corporis et sanguinis domini alienus, nisi citius resipuerit et digna satisfactione sacrilegii culpam deleverit, cum Sathana et angelis ejus ęternis ignibus concremandus perpetuo anathemate feriatur. Amen. Fiat.

ENDORSEMENT: Confirmacio Teodb' archiepiscopi de Riptona. (Later) sentencia Thedbaldi Cantuariensis archiepiscopi pro Riptona.

SEAL: none.

SIZE: 4 in. × 6·8 in.

DATE: 1139–50 probably early.

COPY: MS. Bodleian Rawlinson B 333 f.50b (Ramsey Cartulary).

PRINTED: (from copy) W. D. McCray in *Chronicon Abbatiae Ramesiensis* (R.S., 1886), p. 307.

206

Mandate of Theobald to Robert Foliot, Walter de Wahille and others to cease their depredations on the possessions of Ramsey Abbey.

MS. P.R.O. Exch. K.R. Misc. Books i 28 f.21a (E 164/28) (Cartulary of Ramsey).

(Index only.)

LITERE Theobaldi Cantuariensis archiepiscopi Roberto Foliot, Waltero de Wahill' et quibusdam aliis invasoribus abbatie omnino tunc destructe, quod desistant. ·

DATE: *c.* 1145.

PRINTED: W. H. Hart and P. A. Lyons, *Cartulary of Ramesy* (R.S., 1884–93), i, 106.

207

Notification by Theobald to Bishops Alexander of Lincoln (1123–48) and Nigel of Ely (1133–66) of a decision in his presence and also before Bishops Robert of London (1141–51) Henry of Winchester (1129–71) Jocelin of Salisbury (1142–84) Hilary of Chichester (1147–69) Robert of Hereford (1131–48) and Ascelin of Rochester (1142–48) at Lambeth by papal mandate, whereby Robert Foliot abandoned the manor of Graveley (Cambs.) to the monks of Ramsey by the hand of his brother Elias and of the prior of St. Neot's.

MS. Bodleian Rawlinson B 333 f.50b (Cartulary of Ramsey).

De Graveleia.

T. DEI gratia Cantuariensis archiepiscopus et totius Britannie primas venerabilibus fratribus A[lexandro] Linc' et N[igello] Elyensi episcopis et omnibus sancte ecclesie filiis eorum salutem. Notum sit vobis causam inter abbatem et monachos Ram' et inter Robertum Foliot de manerio Graveleie diu ventilatam, ita per apostolicum mandatum ante nos et fratres nostros coepiscopos Robertum Lond', H[enricum] Wint', Jocelinum Saresberiensem, Hyllarium Cicestr', Robertum Herefordensem, A[scelinum] Roffensem, finitam esse videlicet quod idem Robertus per manum Elye fratris sui et prioris sancti Neoti, videntibus prenominatis fratribus nostris, in manum nostram predictum manerium refutavit libere et inconcusse de cetero monasterio Ramesie possidendum sicut dominium mense monachorum. T. predictis episcopis et multis aliis apud Lamhudam.

DATE: 1147-48.

PRINTED: W. D. McCray, *Chronicon Abbatiae Ramesiensis* (R.S.), p. 306.

The original of this charter was in the Cotton Library under Vitellius A 30, but presumably was lost in the fire of 1731 (MS. B.M. Addl. 38683 f.38a).

208

Mandate of Theobald to Bishops Alexander of Lincoln, (Nigel) of Ely and William of Norwich (1146–74) to compel Robert Foliot and his abettors to restore Graveley to Ramsey Abbey. Theobald complains his previous instructions to the bishops of Ely and Lincoln had not been obeyed.

MS. Bodleian Rawlinson B 333 f.51b (Cartulary of Ramsey).

De pervasione quorundam hominum.

T. DEI gratia Cantuariensis archiepiscopus et tocius Anglie primas venerabilibus fratribus et coepiscopis A[lexandro] Lincol' R. [*sic*] Elyensi et W[illelmo] Norw' salutem. Fatigatis jam sepius ad nos per multos veniendo labores monachis Ramesie super justicie requisicione compacientes, fraternitati vestre per presentes litteras commune mandatum dirigimus, districte vobis precipere coacti, quatinus vel de cetero prefatis monachis debitum et que sui intererit officii de pervasoribus bonorum suorum quisque vestrum studeat exhibere justiciam, juxta quod eorum accepta querimonia, ipsis noverit expedire, nominatim autem R[obertum] Folioth et illos quibus idem R[obertus] terram eorum de Graveleia injuste distribuit, Radulfum etiam de Roleia, reddere eis integre quas per violenciam occupant ecclesie sue possessiones canonice et districte compellatis, quod et vobis domine Lincoln' et domine Elyensis alia nos vice precipisse meminimus, eo magis mirantes quod nondum preceptum nostrum effectui mancipare curastis. Valete.

DATE: *c.* 1147.

PRINTED: W. D. McCray, *Chronicon Abbatiae Ramesiensis* (R.S.), p. 311.

209

Confirmation by Theobald of the grant by Walter abbot of Ramsey (1133–61) to the almonry of Ramsey of the church of Warboys (Hunts.) as assented to and confirmed by Robert II bishop of Lincoln (1148–66). The grant is to become fully operative after the present holders of the church, Nicholas de Sigillo and Richard the clerk of Warboys have ceased to hold it.

Original MS. B.M. Addl. Charters 34174.

T. DEI gratia Cantuariensis archiepiscopus Anglorum primas universis sancte ecclesię fidelibus salutem. Quod a venerabilibus fratribus nostris coepiscopis canonice fieri dinoscitur, id nostri est officii auctoritate nostra conivente roborare et scripti nostri testimonio stabilire. Inde est quod ecclesiam de Wardebois cum omnibus appenditiis suis quam Walterius abbas Ramesiensis assentiente et confirmante venerabili fratre nostro Roberto Linc' episcopo, postquam Nicolaus de Sigillo et Ricardus clericus de Wardeb' qui eandem ecclesiam tenent eam possidere desierint, dedit assensu conventus elemosinarie de Ramesia in perpetuam possessionem ad pauperum sustentationem sicut carta donationis predicti abbatis et carta confirmationis predicti episcopi testatur, nos quoque auctoritate presentis scripti nostri predicte elemosinarie in perpetuam elemosinam confirmamus et in perpetuam possessionem ad sustentandos pauperes post mortem predictorum clericorum perpetuo elemosinarie remanendam corroboramus, salva tamen in omnibus diocesani episcopi dignitate, prohibentes sub anathemate ne quis tam justum tam pium tam religiosum factum aliqua temeritate vel pravo consilio circumventus revocare vel inquietare presumat. Valete.

ENDORSEMENT: Confirmacio T. archiepiscopi Cantuariensis de ecclesia de Wardeboys ad elemosinariam habendam.

SEAL: yellow fragment and Counterseal.

SIZE: 4·6 in. × 9·9 in.

DATE: 1148–61.

COPY: MS. Bodleian Rawlinson B 333 f.49b (Cartulary of Ramsey).

PRINTED: W. D. McCray, *Chronicon Abbatiae Ramesiensis* (R.S.), p. 301.

Copy: MS. P.R.O. Exch. K.R. Misc. Books i 28 (E 164/28) (Cartulary of Ramsey) f.162a.

Printed: W. H. Hart and P. A. Lyons, *Cartulary of Ramsey* (R.S.), ii, 171.

Inspeximus by Archbishop Hubert Walter (Original) in MS. P.R.O. Exch. O.A. Misc. Books 31 no. 45.

210

Notification by Theobald of the grant by Walter abbot of Ramsey and the convent, of the church of Shillington (Beds.) to Roger de Almaria, precentor of Lincoln, for life. Subsequently the church is to be appropriated to the almonry of Ramsey. Done in the presence of Bishops Nigel of Ely, William of Norwich and Robert II of Lincoln.

MS. Bodleian Rawlinson B 333 f.50a (Cartulary of Ramsey).

De ecclesia de Scithlingd'.

T. dei gratia Cantuariensis archiepiscopus Anglorum primas et apostolice sedis legatus universis sancte ecclesie fidelibus salutem. Noverint universi quoniam abbas[2] Walterus[1] et totus conventus Ramesiensis[2] monasterii [3]dederunt et[3] concesserunt ecclesiam de Scithlingdun'[4] Rogero de Almaria [5]Lincol' ecclesie precentori cum omnibus ad eam pertinentibus[5] quamdiu vixerit tenendam reddendo singulis annis quinque[6] solidos elemosinario[7] Ramesie[8] ad pascendos pauperes [9]hoc videlicet tenore[9], ut postquam [10]idem Rogerus[10] decesserit vel forte[11] ad religionem conversus fuerit, ipsa ecclesia in[12] perpetuam [13]Ramesiensis monasterii revocetur possessionem[13] et in dominium elemosinarii ad pauperes sustentandos[14], salvis tamen justis dyocesani episcopi per omnia consuetudinibus et dignitatibus, ita ne [15]ad aliam aliquam ulterius[15] transferatur personam. Hoc factum est assensu abbatis[16] et tocius conventus in presencia venerabilium fratrum nostrorum N[igelli] Elyensis,[17] W[illelmi] Norwicensis et R[oberti] Linc' episcoporum.[18]

Also: MSS., ibid., next charter (*A*), P.R.O., Exch. K.R., Misc. Books i 28 f.162b (*B*).

Variations: [1]*B adds* abbas Rames'. [2]*B omits*. [3-3]*AB* hoc tenore. [4]*A* Schitlingd', *B* Schitlingdon'. [5-5]*A* precentori Linc' ecclesie, *B* precentori ecclesie Linc'. [6]*B* v. [7]*B* f.163a. [8]*B* Rames'. [9-9]*AB omit*. [10-10]*AB omit*.

¹¹*AB omits.* ¹²*B* imperpetuam. ¹³⁻¹³*AB* revocetur possessionem Ramesiensis ecclesie. ¹⁴*A* sustinendos. ¹⁵⁻¹⁵*AB* ulterius ad aliquam aliam. ¹⁶*AB add* Walteri. ¹⁷*B adds* et. ¹⁸*A adds* Valete.

DATE: 1150–61.

PRINTED: (Bodl.) McCray, *Chronicon Abbatiae Ramesiensis* (R.S.), p. 301. (P.R.O.) Hart, *Cartulary of Ramsey* (R.S.), ii, 175.

211

Notification by Theobald to Bishop Alexander of Lincoln (1123–48) of the settlement of a dispute between St. Denys, Southampton (Priory of Aug. Canons) and Reading (Ben. Abbey, Berks.) over the parish of Northmoor (Oxon.). St. Denys is to build a chapel with a cemetery at Northmoor, holding it from Reading and paying one mark annually to the mother church of Stanton (Harcourt). Done before Theobald at Canterbury in the presence of Bishops Robert of Hereford (1131–48) Simon of Worcester (1125–50) Jocelin of Salisbury (1142–48) Robert of Bath (1136–66) Roger of Chester (1129–1148) and others.

MS. B.M. Egerton 3031 f.50a (Cartulary of Reading).

Carta ejusdem (i.e. Theobaldi archiepiscopi) super ecclesia de Mora.

THEODB' dei gratia Cantuariensis archiepiscopus et tocius Anglie primas venerabili fratri A[lexandro] Linc' episcopo et omnibus sancte ecclesie fidelibus salutem. Controversia que inter ecclesiam sancti Dionisii et ecclesiam sancte Marie de Rading' super parrochia de Mora diutius agitata dinoscitur utraque parte in nostram presentiam evocata hoc modo tandem finita ¹ac terminata est¹. Convenit siquidem nobis mediantibus inter utramque ecclesiam quod ecclesia sancti Dionisii construeret in predicta Mora capellam cum cimiterio et teneret et recognosceret eam cum parrochianis ad eandem Moram pertinentibus simul cum decimis de ecclesia sancte Marie de² Rading' annuatim in perpetuum reddendo inde matrici ecclesie sue de Stantune³ in subjectionis recognitionem marcam argenti ·mediatatem ad festum sancti Michaelis et aliam medietatem ad pascha, ita videlicet quod neutra ecclesia de prescripto annuo redditu in perpetuum /[f.50b] aliquid minuere valeat vel

2F

addere vel aliunde super hoc quicquam exigere, salvo jure episcopali quod persolvet capelle ipsius possessor. Hec ut diximus pacis concordia in nostra presentia Cantuarie facta est, assistentibus et cooperantibus nobis atque attestantibus venerabilibus fratribus et coepiscopis nostris Roberto Herford', Simone Wigorn', Jocelino Sar', Roberto Baton', Rogero Cestr' et multis aliis abbatibus et clericis diverse dignitatis et ordinis. Valete.

ALSO: on f.50b.

Item testimonium ejusdem super eodem cum sigillo conventus de sancto Dionisio.

VARIATIONS: ¹⁻¹est ac terminata. ²omits. ³Stantona.

DATE: 1141–48.

PRINTED: F. M. Stenton, *Cambridge Historical Journal*, 1929, p. 3.

MS. Bodleian (Cave) E Mus. 249 f.11a. (Letters of Gilbert Foliot).

Patri suo et domino Cantuariensi dei gratia archiepiscopo et totius Anglie primati T., frater G[ilbertus] Glo' dictus abbas obedientiam humilem et de toto corde dilectionem. Ad agendum quod imperastis quamplures amici nostri jam semel et iterum tertioque convenimus et causam domini abbatis Rading' et fratrum ejus adversus dominum Rericum ceterosque beati Dionisii monacos plenius audiendo discuteremus. Causa itaque deducta in medium ad hunc finem usque perducta est. Conquerebantur Radingenses ecclesiam suam de Stantona parrochia de la Mora que terram quedam est beati Dionisii injuste spoliatam fuisse. Asserebant enim predictam ecclesiam de Stantona in terra / [f.11b] illa de Mora parrochialia jura tam in spiritualibus quam in corporalibus continue et quiete triginta et eo amplius annis habuisse. Hujus rei testes producebant in medium quamplures monachos sacerdotes et clericos multos, honestos etiam laicos non paucos, probationi predicte possessionis si eis adjudicaretur paratissimos. Postulabant Radingeneses probationem suam suscipi seque in possessionem induci. Set dominus Redericus et qui cum eo stabant e contrario perorabant. Aiebant enim super hac re Radingensium nec debere probationem suscipi nec ipsos oportere possessione predicta aliquatenus investiri. Hanc parrochiam in integrum de jure beati Dionisii esse dicebant, et ad ecclesiam suam de Tentona non nova quadam usurpatione set antiqua et longi temporis prescriptione pertinere. Constanter asserebant ecclesiam suam de Tantona a prima fundatione sua plusquam lx annis predictam possessionem continue et quiete possedisse, se etiam adhuc in ipsa actionis die eadem possessione investitos in ipsa tanquam in sua consistere. Assertionis etiam sue testes producebant dominum abbatem de Egnesham et conventus ejus partem non modicam, aliosque sacerdotes clericos et quamplures laicos probationi jam dicte promptissimos. Quoniam igitur in causis hujusmodi melior est affirmantis et possidentis quam solummodo repetentis conditio probationem possessionis sue postulabat dominus Redericus suscipi, seque deinceps inconcussum si justum foret dimitti. Cum itaque de singulis cum domino Hereford', decano Lond', archidiacono Oxenefor', ceterisque aliis viris qui convenerant decerneremus, nulla data sententia prior Rading' se ab archidiacono Oxenefor' et abbate de Egnesham nescimus in quo gravari conquerens, audientiam domini pape appellans injuncte nobis finem imposuit sollicitudini. Unde ne vestram que penes nos acta sunt possint latere prudentiam vobis ista transscripsimus quem munitum per omnia et esse semper incolumem preoptamus. Valete.

DATE: 1143-48.

PRINTED: *P.L.* 190 col. 762.

212

Notification by Theobald of his decision in a case between Roger abbot of Reading (1158-64) and Gilbert, delegated to him by Pope Adrian IV (1154-59). Gilbert's claim to Aston (Herts.) fails, as do his allegations that he was violently deprived of certain documents.

MS. B.M. Harleian 1708 f.97b (Register of Reading).

Carta T. Cantuariensis archiepiscopi de terra quadam in Estona.

T. DEI gratia Cantuariensis archiepiscopus etc. [*sic*] salutem. Ne ea que coram nobis fine canonico terminantur processu temporis queant in dubium revocari ea quidem presentium attestatione litterarum usque ad notitiam vestram transferre curavimus. Universitatem /[f.98a] ¹itaque vestram¹ non lateat controversiam que inter Gil' nepotem Amfr' et dilectum filium nostrum Rogerum abbatem Rading² vertebatur super terra quadam de Eston' et de quibusdam instrumentis que G[il'] sibi violenter ablata fuisse querebatur que mandato venerabilis patris nostri pape Adriani remota omni appellatione nobis audienda et terminanda delegata fuit, interveniente judicii equitate terminatam et omnino fuisse decisam. Auditis namque hinc inde rationibus et sufficienter intellectis et cognitis abbatem a petitione memorati Gil'³ omnino absolvimus. Valete.⁴

ALSO: MS. B.M. Cott. Vespasian E xxv f.49b (Register of Reading).

VARIATIONS: ¹⁻¹vestram itaque. ²Radyng'. ³G. ⁴*omits.*

DATE: 1158-59.

213

Grant of indulgence by Theobald to Reading abbey of forty days on the festival of St. James, 25 July.

Original MS. B.M. Addl. Charters 19589.

TEOBALDUS dei gratia Cantuariensis archiepiscopus totius Anglie primas apostolice sedis legatus universis sancte ecclesie fidelibus salutem. Equum est ac rationabile illos sanctos et maxime dei apostolos devotione precipua venerari in terris de quorum societate certum est angelos gratulari in celis. De quorum utique consortio indubitanter esse credimus beatum Jacobum dei apostolum qui speciali prerogativa omnes ei devotos exaudire dignetur. Quicumque ergo in festivitate illius apostoli que octavo Kal. Augusti celebratur ecclesiam beate Marie matris domini de Redingis in qua gloriosa manus ejusdem apostoli cum multis aliis reliquiis continetur pio affectu visitaverit sive infra octavas illam ecclesiam petierit et ipsum apostolum sibi patronum fecerit, meritis ipsius apostoli et aliorum sanctorum quorum reliquie ibidem gloriose continentur atentius confidentes, de penitentia ei injuncta xl dies relaxamus et orationum et beneficiorum sancte Cant' ecclesie [eum partic]ipem inperpetuum esse concedimus. Valete.

ENDORSEMENT: T. Cantuariensis archiepiscopi de absolucione penitentium in festivitate sancti Jacobi.

SEAL: white fragment.

SIZE: 6·8 in. × 8·9 in.

DATE: 1150–61.

COPY: MS. B.M. Egerton 3031 f.57b. which supplies the part missing.

214

Grant of indulgence by Theobald to Reading abbey of twenty days on the occasions of *inventio* and *exaltatio sancte crucis*, 3 May and 14 September.

MS. B.M. Egerton 3031 f.57b (Cartulary of Reading).

Carta Theodb' Cantuariensis archiepiscopi super absolutione penitentium in festivitate inventionis et exaltationis sancte crucis.

THEODBALDUS dei gratia Cantuariensis archiepiscopus tocius Anglie primas et apostolice sedis legatus omnibus sancte matris fidelibus ecclesie per Angliam constitutis salutem in domino. Nulli Christiane professionis dubium esse credimus Jhesum Christum per lignum vivifice crucis antiquum diaboli abolevisse cyrographum quo hostis antiquus mundum, seducto primo parente in suam redegerat potestatem. Per hanc agnus qui in ea occisus est nos mortis eripuit casibus eterneque restituit saluti. Quanto igitur honore et venerationis reverentia sit digna per quam nobis salus reparatur eterna omnibus liquet. Hujus itaque pretiosum lignum crucis devota mente piaque sollicitudine venerari debetis. Ecclesias equidem in quibus hujus ligni dominici portionem conditam esse noveritis cum elemosinis et orationibus debetis visitare et ad devotionis vestre inditium debitam reverentiam exhibere. Quicumque itaque Radingensem ecclesiam die inventionis vel exaltationis sancte crucis fideli cum devotione visitaverint et lignum crucis quod in ea continetur ut condecet honoraverint, de divina confidentes misericordia de injuncta eis penitentia xx dierum indulgentiam facimus et orationum et beneficiorum Cantuariensis ecclesie eos participes esse concedimus. Valete.

DATE: 1150–61.

215

Confirmation by Theobald of the possessions of Reading abbey.

MS. B.M. Egerton 3031 f.50a (Cartulary of Reading).

> Carta Theodbaldi archiepiscopi de eodem (i.e. de confirmatione fundationis et libertatum ecclesie Rading' et testimonium de escambio ecclesiarum de Chelseia et de Waregrava).

THEODBALDUS dei gratia Cantuariensis archiepiscopus Angl' primas et apostolice sedis legatus universis sancte ecclesie fidelibus ad quoscumque presentes[1] pervenerint apices salutem. Quecumque pietatis intuitu religiosis locis largitione regum seu principum seu quorumcumque fidelium oblatione, interveniente diocesani episcopi coniventia, sub nostra jurisdictione in usus divinos cessisse noscuntur, nostri est officii illa roborare et nostre auctoritatis munimine perpetuo stabilire. Inde est quod

deo et ecclesie beate Marie Rading' et religiosis fratribus ejusdem loci monachis filiis nostris dilectis omnes possessiones et
omnia bona tam ecclesiastica quam mundana que gloriose
memorie Henricus Anglorum rex nobilissimus Rading' ecclesie
primus fundator eidem ecclesie contulit et carta confirmavit
scilicet Rading' in qua [2]eorum constructum est[2] monasterium
cum ecclesiis et capellis ejusdem ville et ceteris omnibus ad
eam pertinentibus et Tacheham[3] et Chelseiam[4] cum ecclesia
sua, quam quidem ecclesiam et ecclesiam de Weregrava[5] predictus H[enricus] rex ab abbate et monachis de Periculo Maris
per concambium optinuit et ecclesie Rading' concessit, sicut
carta donationis predicti regis et carta confirmationis predecessoris nostri venerabilis memorie Willelmi Cantuariensis archiepiscopi testatur, necnon ecclesiam de Stantona et ecclesiam de
Haneberga et ecclesiam de Estona cum omnibus earum pertinentiis, similiter et possessionem que dicitur Wigestana[6] quam
habent in Legrecestrescira[7] sicut venerabilis frater noster
Robertus Linc' episcopus eis per cartam suam[8] confirmavit.
Preterea quicquid in presenti canonice possident seu in[9] futuro
rationabilibus modis adipisci poterunt, nos quoque auctoritate
nostra et scripti nostri testimonio confirmamus et in perpetuum
possidenda corroboramus.[10] Quicumque igitur adversus hujus
nostre confirmationis auctoritatem venire et predictorum
fratrum possessiones perturbare vel temere inquietare presumpserit in districti judicis examine indignationem omnipotentis dei
incurrat et nostre maledictioni perpetuo subjaceat. Amen.
Valete.[11]

ALSO: MS. B.M. Harleian 1708 f.188a. (Cartulary of Reading).
VARIATIONS: [1]omits. [2-2]constructum est eorum. [3]Thacheham. [4]Chals'.
[5]Weregrave. [6]Wiggestan'. [7]Leic'syre. [8]omits. [9]f.188b. [10]roboramus. [11]omits.
DATE: 1150–61.
The following is the charter of Archbishop William referred to by Theobald.
MSS. ibid.

Ego dei gratia Cantuariensis ecclesie archiepiscopus Willelmus concedo
ecclesie Rading' et ejus abbati primo domino Hugoni et monachis in eadem
ecclesia deo et beate dei genetrici virgini Marie in cujus honore ipsa
ecclesia constructa est servientibus, omnia illa que dominus noster Henricus
rex Anglorum eidem dedit ecclesie. Hec sunt: et Radingia in qua ipsa
ecclesia constructa est cum ecclesiis et capellis et ceteris omnibus ad eam
pertinentibus, et Leoministria cum ecclesiis et capellis et omnibus ad eam

pertinentibus, et Thacheham et Chealseia cum ecclesia sua quam scilicet ecclesiam et ecclesiam de Weregrava dominus noster H[enricus] rex ab abbate et monachis de Periculo Maris escambiavit et ecclesie Rading' concessit. Hec predicta sicut dominus noster rex monasterio Rading' libere et quiete dedit ego concedo. Et quia Rading' et Leoministria et Chelseia antiquitus abbatie fuerunt et nostris temporibus pio studio domini nostri H[enrici] regis ad abbatiam Radingensem per Christi gratiam redacte sunt nos concedimus et presenti carta confirmamus et dei benediccione et nostra persequimur.

ALSO: in an inspeximus of Archbishop Baldwin MS. Harleian 1708 f.188b.

216

Confirmation by Theobald to Roger abbot of Reading (1158–64) of the dependent priory of Leominster (Heref.) and its possessions.

MS. B.M. Egerton 3031 f.54a (Cartulary of Reading).

Confirmatio T. Cantuariensis archiepiscopi super donatione ecclesie sancti Petri de Leom' cum omnibus subscriptis pertinentiis.

THEODB'[1] dei gratia Cantuariensis archiepiscopus et tocius Anglie primas omnibus sancte matris ecclesie fidelibus [2]per Angliam constitutis[2] salutem. Que a venerabilibus fratribus nostris episcopis ecclesiis aut locis religiosis canonice conferuntur, ut in firma stabilitate perseverent sunt nostre confirmationis munimine roboranda. Donationem itaque ecclesie Radingensi factam et Hugoni primo loci illius[3] abbati auctoritate qua fungimur confirmamus dilecto filio nostro Rogero ecclesie illius abbati et fratribus ibidem jugem deo famulatum exhibentibus. Que autem eis confirmata esse volumus propriis dignum duximus[4] exprimere vocabulis. Ecclesiam itaque beati[5] Petri de Leom' prenominato abbati et monasterio Rading' confirmamus cum omnibus ad eam pertinentibus; parrochiam /[f.54b] quoque de Bradeforda et de Ach et de Lenhale et de Deliga[6] i[a] et ii[a], que ambe proxime sunt Leom', et de Lentelega[7] et de Kinardeslega[8] et de Wennetona[9] et de utraque Sernesfelda et de Titelega[10], de Hopa quoque et de Wavertona et de Niwetona et de Gatredehope, de Stokes et de utraque Hetfelda[11] et de Risebiria et Humbra et Gedesfenna et Buterlega[12] et Bradefelda et utraque Hamtona et Forda, Henhoura[13], Eatuna, Hentona[14], Stoctuna et Essetuna[15] et Bremesfelda[16] et Uppetuna[17] et Miclatona et Dreituna et Hamenesse[18] et Wlhale[19] et Putlesdona et Brocmantona[20] et Forda, de Lustuna quoque et Eya[21] et Croftona.[22] Hec autem prescripta ad parrochiam ecclesie de Leomin' jure parrochiali pertinere viri antiqui et autentici protestati sunt, sicut carta venerabilis fratris nostri G[ilberti] Herfordensis[23] episcopi testatur ipsum ex tenore carte bone memorie Ricardi predecessoris sui didicisse. Et nos jam dictorum episcoporum cartis[24] fidem habentes universa que ab eis Radingensi ecclesie confirmata sunt Rogerio abbati et dilectis filiis nostris monachis Rading' communimus et auctoritatis nostre robore confirmamus sub anathemate prohibentes ne quisquam super ulla[25] predictarum possessionum aut super parrochia ecclesie de Leomin' eos injuste vexare aut inquietare presumat. Valete.

ALSO: MS. B.M. Cott. Dom. A iii, f.69b. (Reading and Leominster Cartulary) Confirmatio T. archiepiscopi de pertinentiis ecclesie Leom'.

VARIATIONS: [1]T. [2-2]omits. [3]omits. [4](MS.) duximumus. [5]sancti. [6]Diliga. [7]Luntelega. [8]Chinardesl'. [9]Winnet'. [10]Titelleg'. [11]Hethfeld'. [12]Butterl'. [13]Heanoura. [14]Heant'. [15]Esschetun'. [16]Bremefeld'. [17]Upton'. [18]Hamenesche. [19]Whiale. [20]Brocmanet'. [21]Heya. [22]Crofta. [23]Heref'. [24](MS.) carte. [25](MS.) ullam.

DATE: 1158–61.

217

Confirmation by Theobald of the arrangements made by Bishops Robert (1138–48) and Gilbert of Hereford (1148–63) for the cemetery at Hatfield (Heref.) for the benefit of Leominster priory. The oblations for those buried at Hatfield or their own dying bequests are to be paid over to the monks at Leominster as if they were buried there. The chapel at Hatfield is to be treated by the diocesan as a chapel and not as a mother church.

MS. B.M. Egerton 3031 f.54b (Cartulary of Reading).

Confirmatio ejusdem (Theobald) super consecratione cimiterii de Hethfelda.

T. DEI gratia Cantuariensis archiepiscopus [1]et tocius Anglie primas omnibus sancte matris ecclesie fidelibus per Angliam constitutis salutem.[1] Venerabilium fratrum nostrorum G[ilberti], [2]Roberti Herf' episcoporum[2] vestigiis inherentes, que ab eis[3] in consecratione cimiterii de Hethfeld' utilitati monasterii de Leoministria provisa sunt, potestate nobis ab altissimo indulta confirmamus et presentis scripti testimonio corroboramus, mandantes ut quod in augmentum cimiterii de Hethfeld' a jamdictis fratribus dicitur consecratum habeatur augmentum cimiterii de Leom' hac inserta conditione ut oblationes ad sepulturam defunctorum ibidem evenientes vel quod ipsimet in extremis agentes matri ecclesie de Leoministria pro se dandum diviserint totum cum integritate in usus monachorum de Leoministria cedat ac si corpora eorum in cimiterio de Leom' sepulture traderentur. Clericus eciam quicumque in capella de Hetfelda[4] ministraverit monachis debitam faciat securitatem quod eis predictum jus quantum in ipso erit, firmum illibatumque servabit.[5] Capella autem in his[6] que ad episcopum diocesanum pertinent, non sicut mater ecclesia set sicut capella episcopo respondebit. Ne autem quis hanc nostre confirmationis paginam infringere attemptaverit injuste auctoritate qua fungimur inhibemus. Valete.

ALSO: MS. B.M. Cott. Dom. A iii f.69b (Reading and Leominster Cartulary).
Carta ejusdem (Theobald) de cimiterio et sepultura de Hethfeld.

VARIATIONS: [1-1]etc. [2-2]Rodberti episcoporum Heref'. [3]f.70a. [4]Hethfeld'. [5]conservabit. [6]hiis.

DATE: 1150–61.

218

Various charters relating to the churches of the honour of Berkeley.

MS. B.M. Harleian 1708 f.200b (Cartulary of Reading).

Carte iiii antique de ecclesiis de Berkel' prius magistro Serloni concessis videlicet Th. Cantuariensis archiepiscopi, Symonis Wigorn' episcopi, Matildis imperatricis et Aalize regine.

(Whether these charters were actually given in the cartulary is unknown as the next few pages have been cut out.)

MS. B.M. Harleian 1708 f.200b (Cartulary of Reading).

T. DEI gratia Cantuariensi archiepiscopo et totius Anglie primati et apostolice sedis legato et universis sancte ecclesie fidelibus Willelmus comes Cicestr' salutem. Sciatis me concessisse et dedisse per manum Symonis Wigorn' episcopi deo et ecclesie sancte Marie de Rading et monachis ibidem deo servientibus in perpetuam elemosinam ecclesiam de Berkel' cum omnibus ejusdem pertinentiis, cum omnibus ecclesiis de dominio de Berkeleihern[esse], scilicet ecclesiam de Camma cum omnibus pertinentiis suis, et ecclesiam de Erlingham et ecclesiam de Beverstan' et ecclesiam de Wotton' cum omnibus pertinentiis suis et ecclesiam de Almodesbir' cum omnibus pertinentiis suis cum capellis et decimis et omnibus libertatibus eisdem predictis ecclesiis pertinentibus. Quare volo et firmiter precipio ut bene et in pace honorifice et inconcusse ea teneant. T. Francone capellano et magistro Serlone etc. [*sic*].

MS. ibid.

SYMONI dei gratia Wigorn' episcopo magister Serlo salutem. Sciatis me pro dei amore et anime mee salute, assensu domine mee Aalide regine, concessisse deo et sancte Marie et monachis de Rading' in elemosina omnes ecclesias de Berkeleihern' sicut vos mihi illas dedistis et carta vestra confirmastis set precor vos ut inde eos saisiatis. Precor etiam vos quatinus ecclesiam de Camma quam monachi de Gloec' absque vestro assensu super me invaserunt cum omnibus pertinentiis suis mihi ad opus illorum monachorum scilicet de Rading' deliberetis et prebendam ecclesie de Berkel' quam Rogerus de Berkel' dedit Rainero filio Walteri de Camma absque vestro et meo assensu postquam ego inde saisitus fui, *sicut Theobaldus Cantuariensis archiepiscopus vobis viva voce precepit et postea litteris suis mandavit.* Test' Aalid' regina etc. [*sic*].

MS. ibid. f.25a (also MS. B.M. Egerton 3031 f.20a).

VENERABILI patri et amico karissimo T. dei gratia Cantuariensi archiepiscopo et apostolice sedis legato, H[enricus] eadem gratia dux Norm' salutem et dileccionem. Notum sit paternitati vestre

me dedisse et concessisse monachis sancte Marie de Rading'
ecclesiam de Berkel' cum omnibus ad eam /[f.25b] pertinentibus. Set quia hanc donationem audivi displicere Rogero de
Berkel' cuidam meo firmario, paternitati vestre preces porrigo
quod si opus fuerit et monachi petierint, prefatum Rogerum ab
eorum infestatione si forte infestare presumpserit ecclesiastica
animadversione cohibeatis. T[este Willelmo cancellario apud
Falesiam].

For the significance of these documents see above p. 231.

219

Notification by Theobald to Walter archdeacon of Canterbury
(bishop of Rochester 1148). The church of Boxley (Kent) belongs to
the monks of Rochester Cathedral and therefore Theobald's chaplain, holding the church, and his successors must pay the monks an
annual pension of 60s. until Theobald or his successors restore the
church to the monks.

MS. Lambeth, Islip's Register f.203a.

THEOBALDUS gratia dei Cantuariensis archiepiscopus, tocius
Anglie primas dilectis filiis Waltero archidiacono Cant' et universis clericis per Kantiam constitutis salutem. Et infra— [sic]
Similiter et de ecclesia de Boxle de qua nobis constat fide plena
quod eam monachis Roffen' dedit dominus Henricus rex primus
et quam usque ad nostra tempora in suis propriis usibus pacifice
tenuerunt, nos obtentu specialis gratie quam nobis fecerunt
presentandum ad eam Galfridum capellanum nostrum, mandamus quod quamdiu vixerit idem Galfridus solvat eisdem
annuam pensionem lx s. et sic tam ipse quam successores sui de
anno in annum sine difficultate reddant eis predictum numerum
solidorum quousque nostra vel successorum nostrorum auctoritate ecclesiam ipsam rehabeant et eam in usus suos sicut ante
habuerant sunt adepti etc. [sic].

DATE: 1139–48.
PRINTED: Reg. Roff., p. 180.
An inspeximus of Archbishop Islip (1363).

220

Confirmation by Theobald of the possessions of Rochester Cathedral
Priory.

MS. D. and C. Rochester Textus Roffensis f.204b.

TEODBALDUS[1] gratia dei Cantuariensis archiepiscopus et totius
Britannię[2] primas omnibus sancte ęcclesię fidelibus salutem.
Notum vobis esse volo quod omnes donationes et concessiones
omnium maneriorum et omnium terrarum et omnium ęcclesiarum cum omnibus redditibus et rectitudinibus[3] suis et omnium
decimarum quę hactenus concessę et donatę sunt ęcclesię sancti
Andreę apostoli quę sita est in civitate Rovecestra a quibus-
cunque[4] sive regibus sive archiepiscopis vel episcopis seu comitibus seu aliis quibuslibet hujus regni nobilibus concessę sint aut
donatę, ego Teodbaldus[1] gratia dei Cantuariensis archiepiscopus
et totius Britannię primas auctoritate mihi a deo collata omnimodo ratas et [5]in perpetuum[5] stabiles esse confirmo, et eas
nominatim quas Gundulfus illius ęcclesię episcopus ut ad usum
monachorum illorum qui in [6]eadem ęcclesia domino Christo et
prędicto apostolo devote famulantur permaneant ordinavit, ego
eidem ęcclesię et eisdem monachis jure ęternę hereditatis
habendas et libere atque quiete confirmo possidendas, et sicut
ipse pręnominatus episcopus qui ęcclesiam illam fundavit et
monachos illos illic /[f.205a] congregavit et ipsa maneria et
terras quas in suo dominico habebat, ipsis monachis a suo proprio victu discrevit discretas dedit, videlicet Wldeham cum
omnibus appenditiis suis, Frendesberiam cum omnibus appenditiis suis, Stokes cum omnibus appenditiis suis, Suthfletam
cum omnibus appenditiis suis, Danitunam[7] cum omnibus
appenditiis suis, Lamhetham[8] cum omnibus appenditiis suis,
Hedenham cum manerio quod appendet Cudintuna nomine et
cum omnibus xl hidis terrę quę appendent, et omnes alias
minutas terras et omnes redditus omnium terrarum quas suo
tempore adquisivit et illis dedit, ita firmiter et stabiliter in
omnibus, omnia ista monachis illis confirmo et corroboro; et
sicut beatę memorię Anselmus Cantuariensis archiepiscopus et

Gundulfus[9] supradictę ecclesię episcopus ista omnia a rege Henrico confirmata[10] confirmaverunt et eidem ęcclesię et monachis prędictis atque post illos in perpetuum victuris firmiter stabilia et stabiliter firma et illibata permanere sanxerunt et auctoritate dei omnipotentis /[f.205b] patris et filii et spiritus sancti et omnium sanctorum ejus, omnes illos qui aliquid de regia concessione et illorum institutione vel confirmatione infringerent excommunicaverunt, ita et ego tantorum virorum exempla secutus institutiones concessiones et confirmationes et omnia prędicta ipsis monachis [5]in perpetuum[5] habenda firmiter stabilio et stabiliter firmo et illibata permanere sancio,[11] et sub eadem interminatione omnes qui hanc eorum et nostram confirmationem infirmare vel absque communi fratrum ęcclesię illius vel consilio vel consensu immutare pręsumperint, a liminibus sanctę matris ęcclesię donec ad satisfactionem congruam veniant, ex omnipotentis dei patris et filii et spiritus sancti omniumque sanctorum auctoritate sequestro.

PRINTED: T. Hearne, *Textus Roffensis* (1720), p. 205.

ALSO: MS. B.M. Cott. Dom. A x f.111a.

VARIATIONS: [1]Theobaldus. [2]*omits tailed* e *throughout.* [3](MS.) rectitudibus. [4]quibuscumque. [5-5]inperpetuum. [6]f.111b. [7]Danintunam. [8]Lamtheham. [9]Gunduifus. [10]f.112a. [11]sanctio.

This version concludes with a confirmation of Theobald's charter by Ascelin then bishop of Rochester: 'Et ego Ascelinus', etc.

DATE: 1142–48.

PRINTED: *Reg. Roff.*, p. 38, and J. Nichols, *Bibl. Topog. Brit.*, ii, sect. 5, p. 12.

221

Confirmation by Theobald of the possessions and rights of Rochester Cathedral Priory.

MS. B.M. Cott. Faustina B v f.70a (Rochester Register 1315–50). One of many charters inspected by Richard prior of Christ Church Canterbury in 1332.

THEOBALDUS gracia dei Cantuariensis archiepiscopus tocius Anglie primas et apostolice sedis legatus omnibus sancte ecclesie fidelibus salutem. Notum vobis esse volo quod omnes donaciones concessiones et restituciones omnium maneriorum et omnium terrarum et omnium ecclesiarum cum omnibus redditibus consuetudinibus et rectitudinibus suis et omnium decimarum que hactenus concesse et donate sunt ecclesie sancti Andree apostoli que est sita in civitate Rovcestr' a quibuscumque sive regibus sive archiepiscopis vel episcopis se[u] comitibus seu aliis quibuslibet hujus regni nobilibus et Christi fidelibus concesse sunt aut donate necnon omnimoda jura episcopalia in maneriis nostris ac in manerio de Frekenham et Iselham que de episcopatu Rovcestr' esse dinoscuntur, sicut carte celebris memorie predecessorum nostrorum Lamfranci et Anselmi patenter manifestant et possessio continuata ipsorum omnium per episcopos Roffenses hucusque est testificata—ego Theobaldus dei gracia Cantuariensis archiepiscopus et tocius Anglie primas et auctoritate mihi a deo collata omnimodo rata et firma et imperpetuum stabilia esse concedo et illa nominatim que beate memorie Anselmus predecessor noster in carta sua autentica testatur Lamfrancum predecessorem suum ecclesie Roffensi /[f.70b] concessisse et sursum reddidisse per cartam suam quam oculis conspexi, sub interminacione dei et omnium sanctorum ac predecessorum nostrorum precipio ut nullus contra confirmaciones eorum et nostram venire audeat nec presumat, et si qui fecerint, a liminibus sancte matris ecclesie donec ad satisfaccionem congruam veniant ex omnipotentis dei patris et filii et spiritus sancti auctoritate sequestrentur. Test' Ascelino episcopo et multis aliis.

DATE: 1142–48.

PRINTED: *Reg. Roff.*, p. 443.

The ascription to Theobald of a legatine title is erroneous.

222

Inspeximus by Theobald of a charter of Gundulf bishop of Rochester (1077–1108) confirming the possessions of Rochester Cathedral Priory.

MS. D. and C. Canterbury C.A. R 50.

Universis sancte matris ecclesie filiis presens scriptum inspecturis Th[omas] permissione divina prior ecclesie Christi Cant' et ejusdem loci capitulum salutem in domino sempiternam. Noverit universitas vestra nos litteras confirmacionis felicis recordacionis Teobaldi Cantuariensis archiepiscopi tocius Anglie primatis super carta quondam Gundulfi Roffensis episcopi quam fecit priori et conventui Roffensi non abolitas non cancellatas nec in aliqua sui parte viciatas sub hac forma inspexisse:

Teobaldus dei gracia Cantuariensis archiepiscopus et tocius Anglie primas omnibus sancte Christi ecclesie filiis salutem. Ad omnium noticiam volumus pervenire nos in plena synodo nostra apud Cant' vidisse, legisse et propriis manibus attrectasse litteras bone memorie Gundulfi Roffensis episcopi in qualibet sui parte sanas et illesas quam cum post diligentiam investigacionem et examinacionem tam in scriptura quam in sigillo, omni carentes macula et vicio repperissemus, eas in presentis scripti seriem de verbo ad verbum redigi fecimus in hunc modum:

Gundulfus Roffensis episcopus omnibus sancte ecclesie fidelibus salutem. Noscat vestra universitas quod cognita et intellecta caritate Christi fidelium domini videlicet Henrici regis et quorundam procerum nobilium ad monachos ecclesie beati Andree apostoli cui deo auctore etsi indignus deservio, ego in eorum bona intencione laudans deum et gratias agens domino Jesu Christo devociones eorum ad ipsos religiosos approbo et ratas habeo et eis [episcop]alem autoritatem attribuo et consensum conferens ipsis et concedens decimas intra parochias diversarum ecclesiarum nostre diocesis constitutas, decimas videlicet in Strodes et in Chealk' de dominico ejusdem domini regis ex ejus liberalitate, decimas de tenemento Wlwardi cognomento Henri in parochia sancte Marie de Hou et in Cobeham, decimas magnas et minutas de Delce Majori et Minori ex devocione Ansgoti et Godrici, decimas de Nessenden', Borstall' ex benivolencia Rodberti de Sancto Amando Ernulfi et Godrici, decimas de Henherst ex liberalitate Goscelini, decimas de Rundale et de Thange ex liberalitate Smalemanni de Schornes, decimas de Ocle ex devocione Willelmi de Clovile, decimas in Chelesfeld' et Farbergh' ex benivolencia Alolch et Ernulfi de eorum dominicis, decimas de Modingeham ex benivolencia Ansgoti de Chiselherst, decimas de Bertreye ex largicione Haymonis Maminot, decimas de Crongebur' ex beneficio Willelmi filii Willelmi de Horsburden', decimas de dominico ville de Erdinton' ex largicione Willelmi de Gurnay, decimas de Westbrok' in parrochia de Culing' ex gracia Radulphi pincerne; decimas etiam de feudis episcopatus mei, videlicet de Wicham et decimas de tenemento Hugonis de Stok' et Gaufridi de Sunderesse in Cukelstan' et Ricardi de Beresse in Sufflete, ego dictis monachis meis do et concedo in perpetuum. Volo insuper et mando quod ipsi monachi decimas provenientes tam de nutrimentis animalium suorum quam de agriculturis suis in maneriis eorum infra diocesim nostram constitutis, videlicet in Frendesbur', Denintona et in Sufflete et in aliis habeant semper et retineant in omni pace. Has vero decimas omnes superius expressas tam eas que ex devocione fidelium adquisite sunt quam eas quas de feudis meis et de maneriis eorum ipsis assigno auctoritate episcopali qua fungor mando et constituo quod monachi Roffenses eas habeant et teneant in usus victualium suorum sempiternis temporibus convertendas. Hec autem omnia feci ad honorem dei et pro amore beati Andree sanctorum mitissimi, ministris ejusdem sancti pro anima mea et successorum meorum qui hoc meum factum approbabunt, ita quod in die anniversarii singulorum episcoporum qui post me sedebunt in episcopali sede ipsius ecclesie una missa de defunctis in conventu monachorum pro eisdem futuris temporibus decantetur. Amatores autem et observatores istorum que digne per me facta sunt dextera dei protegat et benedicat, eos vero qui aliquid ex hiis preter consensum monachorum infirmare temptaverint apponat et preponderet dominus illam eorum sacrilegii iniquitatem super omnes alias iniquitates eorum et nisi ad satisfaccionem venerint in die juste retribucionis cum in sinistra parte positis subeant sentenciam districte ulcionis. Amen. Istas concessiones et ordinaciones pro amore sancti Andree in ejus ecclesia feci assensu domini Anselmi archiepiscopi et istorum testimonio, Radulphi abbatis de Sagio, Ordwyni prioris, Willelmi archidiaconi Cant', Asketilli archidiaconi Roffensis, Ansfridi clerici, Godardi clerici, Haymonis vicecomitis, Willelmi de Eynesford' et aliorum. Act' anno ab incarnacione domini nostri Jesu Christi millesimo nonagesimo primo. Valete.

Igitur que per predictum episcopum prudenter facta cognovimus in premissis rata habentes et firma decimas omnes prenotatas de quibus nobis constat fide plena quod eis ipsi monachi a tempore quo [hujusmodi] collacionem ipsis fecerat memoratus episcopus usque modo pacifice possederunt, nos auctoritate Cantuariensis ecclesie cui divina miseracione presidemus ipsis monachis perpetuo possidendas ex certa sciencia confirmamus, mandantes et providentes quod quandocumque ex vetustate vel casu aliquo contigerit litteras ipsius episcopi deperire hoc nostri testimonii scriptum semper sufficiat ac si ipsum originale in medium proferretur. Interminaciones autem quas predictus episcopus in violatores premissorum proposuit, nos auctoritate nobis a deo collata ore et toto corde confirmamus et nichilominus auctoritate dei omnipotentis, patris et filii et spiritus sancti excomunicamus omnes illos qui aliquid premissorum a monachis predictis auferre temptaverint vel ablatum cognita veritate retinuerint, seu auctoritatem dederint retinendi donec ad satisfactionem venerint competentem. Hujus facti nostri testes sunt: Hugo abbas sancti Augustini, Walterus prior Cant', Brienus prior Roffensis, Willelmus prior Dovrensis; Clemens, Reynaldus, Hugo, monachi Cant'; Felix, Herveus, Malgerus, clerici nostri. Act. Cant' anno ab incarnacione domini millesimo c°xlv kal. Septembr'.

Nos autem supradicti Gundulfi Roffensis episcopi donaciones et concessiones necnon venerabilis patris nostri Teobaldi Cantuariensis archiepiscopi confirmacionem ratas habentes et firmas, quantum in nobis est predictis monachis Roffensibus auctoritate capituli nostri confirmamus. In cujus rei testimonium pre-

2G

senti transcripto sigillum nostrum duximus appo-
nendum. Dat' Cant' in capitulo nostro terciodecimo
kal' Februarii anno domini m ºcc ºlxx ºsexto.

DATE: (Theobald's charter) 1 September 1145. Gundulf's charter is not
above suspicion.

PRINTED: C. R. Cheney: *English Bishops' Chanceries*, p. 150 (omitting most
of Gundulf's charter).

COPY: in John Fisher's Register (Rochester).

PRINTED: *Reg. Roff.*, p. 87.

223

Notification by Theobald that the manors of Lambeth (Surrey) and
Haddenham (Bucks.) were adjudicated to the monks of Rochester
Cathedral before the legate Ymar and his council at London. Bishop
Ascelin of Rochester (1142–48) has resigned all claims to the manors
in consideration of a payment of 100 marks.

MS. B.M. Cott. Dom. A x f.125a (Rochester Register).

Item testimonium pro monachis.

THEOBALDUS Cantuariensis archiepiscopus et totius Anglie
primas omnibus Christi fidelibus salutem. Notum sit universitati
vestre quod Imarus Tusculanus episcopus sancte sedis Romane
legatus Angliam ingressus, Rof' monachorum querimoniam
super episcopo suo Ascelino susceperit. Evocatis itaque utrisque
partibus London' ante suam presentiam et nostram, assiden-
tibus nobis venerabilibus fratribus Rodberto Lond', Henrico
Winton', Alexandro Lincolniensi, Ebrado Norwicensi, Seifredo
Cicestrensi, episcopis; Eaduuardo de Radinges, Gervasio West-
monast', Petro Scireburnie, Waltero Ramesie, abbatibus;
Aimaro priore sancti Pancratii, Clarenbaldo priore Bermundeseie, et aliis quampluribus religiosis et honestis personis—
conquerebantur monachi episcopum suum Ascelinum ex prava
quadam usurpatione predecessoris sui Johannis manerium
Lamhetham nomine sibi penitus injuste abtulisse, et ex alio suo
manerio Hedenham nomine sive Cudintuna decem libras
annuatim injuste violenter exigere. Asserebant autem memorata

maneria sibi ad victum proprium a rege Anglorum Willelmo
juniore et Lanfranco pie recor-/[f.125b]dationis Cantuariensi
archiepiscopo et Gundulfo Rofensi episcopo concessa rationabiliter et donata, et ad ejusdem rei evidentiorem probationem,
eorundem cartas et confirmationes et sequentium regum
Anglorum Henrici et Stephani, et Anselmi Cantuariensis
archiepiscopi, in medium proferebant. Contraque cum prefatus
Ascelinus Rof' episcopus nil firmum nichil validum responderet,
nec se in pretaxatis maneriis jus habere probare posset, predictas possessiones de jure monachorum esse cognovimus et eas
judiciario ordine ipsorum esse decrevimus. Evolutis autem
postea diebus paucis, revocato a Romana curia predicto Imaro,
cepit Rofensis episcopus conqueri quod eorundem monachorum
factione, tum in itinere Romano tum in Rodbertum Pullanum,
plurimos labores ac gravamina sustinuerat. Rursus itaque evocatis utrisque partibus in nostram presentiam Cantuarie, predicti monachi nostro usi consilio, nullam aliam ob causam nisi
ad reconpensationem laborum et gravaminum suorum atque
ob ejus gratiam firmiter obtinendam, pacti sunt ei dare centum
marcas, l eodem persolvendas anno, tribus vero subsequentibus
annis unoquoque anno xv marcas, quinque autem marcas que
supersunt quarto persolventur anno. Episcopus vero ipsos
monachos /[f.126a] in osculo pacis suscepit et eis omnium
ecclesiarum tam de maneriis que eis ad proprium usum concessione et confirmatione Henrici regis et patris Anselmi Cantuariensis archiepiscopi et Gundulfi Roffensis episcopi ordinata
sunt, quam omnium illarum que eis a quibuscumque sive regibus sive archiepiscopis sive episcopis sive aliis quibuslibet dei
fidelibus rationabiliter concesse et donate sunt, liberam dis-
positionem et presentationem vicariorum cum omnibus possessionibus et rectitudinibus et libertatibus illis hactenus indultis
nostro assensu et consilio concessit et confirmavit. Hiis testibus
presentibus etc.

DATE: 1145.

PRINTED: *Reg. Roff.*, p. 41; J. Nichols, *Bibl. Topog. Brit.* (1780–1800), 2,
sect. 5, appendix p. 15.

In Ymar's account of the case Geoffrey, abbot of St. Albans and Master
Hilary are also mentioned as being present (Holtzmann, ii, 193).

224

Confirmation by Theobald of the grant by Fulco de Niwenham to the monks of Rochester Cathedral of the church of Norton (Kent) after the death of Nicholas the priest, perpetual vicar there; meanwhile Nicholas is to pay the monks 10s. annually; saving the rights of the archbishop and archdeacon of Canterbury.

MS. B.M. Cott. Dom. A x f.131b (Rochester Register).

Confirmatio de ecclesia de Nortune.

THEOBALDUS dei gratia Cantuariensis archiepiscopus Anglorum primas universis sancte matris ecclesie filiis tam clericis quam laicis ad quoscumque presentes pervenerint apices salutem. Notum universitati vestre esse volumus nos concedere et ratam habere donationem quam Fulco de Niwenham fecit monasterio sancti Andree Rofensis et monachis ejusdem loci, videlicet de ecclesia de Nortune cum omnibus ad eam pertinentibus quam idem Fulco eis inperpetuam concessit elemosinam, /[f.132a] ita tamen quod quamdiu vixerit Nicholaus presbiter, qui in eadem ministrat ecclesia perpetuus vicarius, solvet predictis monachis nomine ecclesie predicte de Nortune decem solidos singulis annis. Postquam autem idem Nicholaus decesserit, cedet ecclesia ipsa cum bonis suis in usus monachorum Roffensium. Salva dispositione successoris nostri Cantuariensis archiepiscopi et Cantuariensis archidiaconi. Valete.

DATE: 1139–61.

The charter of Fulco is on f.131a:

Fulco de Niwenham omnibus sancte matris ecclesie fidelibus tam presentibus quam futuris salutem. Sciatis quoniam ego dedi et concessi in elemosinam perpetuam deo et sancto Andree apostolo et ecclesie sue et monachis Rofensibus ecclesiam de Nortune cum omnibus pertinentiis suis, et assensu meo, auctoritate etiam archiepiscopi Cantuariensis, reddet eis Nicholaus capellanus meus singulis annis nomine ecclesie de Nortuna x solidos annue pensionis; et postquam ipse Nicholaus decesserit cedet tota ecclesia de Nortuna in perpetuos usus monachorum cum omnibus bonis suis libera et quieta ab omnibus heredibus meis pro dei amore et salute anime mee et uxoris mee et omnium propinquorum meorum. Test' his etc.

PRINTED: *Reg. Roff.*, p. 507.

225

Notification by Theobald to the clergy of Rochester diocese that whereas Paris archdeacon of Rochester had formerly enjoyed a moiety of the proceeds of ecclesiastical causes, he has now, in the presence of the archbishop restricted himself to a third of the proceeds, the rest going to Bishop Walter of Rochester (1148–82).

MS. Rochester Diocesan Registry, Registrum Temporalium Ep. Roff. f.138a.

> Litera Thome archiepiscopi de jurisdictione archidiaconi.

T. DEI gratia Cantuariensis archiepiscopus Anglorum primas et apostolice sedis legatus omnibus clericis per episcopatum Roffensem constitutis salutem. Noverit universitas vestra Paridem archidiaconem Roffensem cum prius haberet medietatem eorum que ex causis ecclesiasticis proveniebant in presencia nostra domino Waltero Roffensi episcopo duas partes integre concessisse et reddidisse ut tercia dumtaxat parte velit esse contentus. Quia ergo peticioni vestre et voluntati domini Roffensis satisfecit, firma pax et vera concordia inter eos reformata est, tam sopitis omnibus querelis quam salvis archidiaconi possessionibus universis. Hec autem sub presencia testium subscriptorum facta sunt: magistri Radulfi Bixon', magistri J[ohannis] a Tilleburia; Alani de Welles, Radulfi de Wyngeham, Eudonis, clericorum; Ricardi de Hwytstaple, R[icardi] de Clara, Walteri Glouc', monachorum nostrorum; Henrici monachi ecclesie Roffensis; laicorum vero, Radulfi Pycot vicecomitis, Henrici dapiferi episcopi Roffensis, Hugonis de Tirrevilla camerarii. Valete.

DATE: 1150–61.
PRINTED: *Reg. Roff.*, p. 58.

226

Notification by Theobald to Thomas archdeacon of Canterbury (1154–62) that he has instituted William Turco as parson of Stourmouth (Kent) on the presentation of the monks of Rochester, the advocates. He is to hold the church subject to an annual payment of 10*s*. to the monks and saving the rights of the (mother) church of Reculver (Kent).

MS. B.M. Cott. Dom. A x f.133a (Rochester Register).

De presentatione ecclesie de Sturem'.

THEOBALDUS dei gratia Cantuariensis archiepiscopus et totius Anglie primas dilectis filiis Thome archidiacono Cant' et universis clericis per Cantiam constitutis salutem. Noscat universitas vestra quod nos Willelmum Turconem constituimus personam in ecclesia de Sturmutha, presentantibus eum nobis dilectis filiis nostris monachis Rofensibus qui jamdicte ecclesie advocationem habent. Eapropter mandamus et precipimus ut /[f.133b] ut [*sic*] jam dictam ecclesiam cum omnibus ad eam pertinentibus juste libere et quiete teneat, salva pensione decem solidorum annuatim monachis Rofensibus solvendorum, salvo etiam jure ecclesie de Raculfo, prescriptam ecclesiam cum omnibus juste et canonice ad eam pertinentibus ei confirmatam et corroboratam esse jubemus. Valete.

DATE: 1154–61.

227

Confirmation by Theobald of the grant by Henry II to Hugh, archbishop of Rouen (1130–64) of the moiety of the manor of Kilham (Yorks.).

MS. D. and C. Canterbury C.A. R.53.

T. DEI gratia Cantuariensis archiepiscopus Anglorum primas et apostolice sedis legatus omnibus sancte matris ecclesie fidelibus ad quos presens carta pervenerit salutem. Que regum largicione seu principum concessione ecclesiis aliisve locis religiosis conferuntur, ut inconvulsa permaneant auctoritatis nostre munimine roborare debemus, et ne locis quibus caritatis intuitu sunt collata subtrahantur vel in alios usus cedant sedula circumspectione providere. Ea igitur ratione confirmamus medietatem manerii de Killun venerabili fratri nostro et amico Hugoni archiepiscopo Rothomagensi et post eam [*sic*] canonice substituendis archiepiscopis et auctoritate qua fungimur communimus prout carta serenissimi regis Anglorum Henrici, scilicet medietatem prefati fundi in usus Rothomagensis archiepiscopi concessam et donatam esse testatur. Dei igitur auctoritate et nostra inhibemus ne quis contra regis cartam archiepiscopum super tenura illa vel libertatibus ei de terra illa concessis vexare ullatenus ne inquietare presumat. Quod si quis injuste atteptaverit [sic] dei omnipotentis indignationem et nostram se noverit incursurum.

Universis Christi fidelibus presentem paginam inspecturis, Ricardus dei gratia Ebroicensis episcopus et R. dei gratia abbas sancti Audoeni Rothomagensis salutem in domino. Noverit universitas vestra nos cartam bone memorie T. Cantuariensis archiepiscopus Angl' diligenter et fideliter sigillo predicti archiepiscopi consignatam sub prescripta forma verborum inspexisse et ad petitionem capituli Rothomagensis presenti pagine sigilla nostra in testimonium appendisse. Data vi⁰ idus Aprilis anno domini M⁰ CC⁰ xx⁰ septimo.

DATE: 1155–61.

228

Confirmation by Theobald of the grant by Henry II to the canons of Rouen of the (other) moiety of the manor of Kilham (Yorks.).

MS. P.R.O. Transcripts Record Commission II vol. 140a no. 326 (Trans. 8/140A) (1835)

From a Vidimus of 1275 in archives of Seine Inferieure, G 4053.

Carta Teobaldi Cantuariensis archiepiscopi de Killon manerio.

T. DEI gratia Cantuariensis archiepiscopus Anglorum primas et apostolice sedis legatus omnibus sancte matris ecclesie fidelibus ad quos presens carta pervenerit salutem. Que regum largitione seu principum concessione ecclesiis aliisve locis religiosis conferuntur, ut inconvulsa remaneant auctoritatis nostre munimine roborare debemus, et ne locis quibus caritatis intuitu sunt collata subtrahantur vel in alios usus cedant cedula circumspectione providere. Ea igitur ratione confirmamus medietatem manerii de Kilum ecclesie beatissime dei genetricis et virginis Marie Rothomag' et canonicis in eadem ecclesia manentibus et auctoritate qua fungimur communimus prout carta serenissimi regis Anglorum Henrici secundi, scilicet medietatem prefati fundi in usus memoratorum canonicorum concessam et donatam esse testatur. Dei igitur auctoritate et nostra inhibemus ne quis contra regis cartam canonicos super tenura illa vel libertatibus eis de terra illa concessis vexare ullatenus ne presumat inquietare. Quod si quis attemptaverit injuste dei omnipotentis indignationem et nostram se noverit incursurum.

ALSO: in Cartulary of Rouen MS. Rouen Y 44 f.26b (not consulted).
DATE: 1155–61.
PRINTED: *E.Y.C.*, i, 339 (also *C.D.F.*, p. 5).

229

Confirmation by Theobald of the grant to St. Albans Abbey (Ben., Herts.) by William earl of Gloucester (1147–83) of the churches of Luton and Houghton (Beds.) as confirmed by his charter; also the land held by William Chamberlain from the Gloucester fee in the soke of Luton, in Hertwell (Bucks.), Battlesden and Potsgrove (Beds.) for the service of half a knight as confirmed by the earl's charter.

MS. B.M. Cott. Otho D iii f.117b. col. 1 (Register of St. Albans).

Confirmacio T. Cantuariensis archiepiscopi de ecclesiis de Luiton' et Houghton' cum pertinentiis sicut comes Glouc' W[illelmus] eas dedit et tota terra quam W. camerarius tenuit in feodo ejusdem comitis in soka de Luiton', Hertewelle, Badelesdon' et Potesgrave.

T. DEI gratia Cantuariensis archiepiscopus Anglorum primas et apostolice sedis legatus universis sancte ecclesie fide[libus salutem]. Que a principibus . . . . viris[?] et fidelibus in loca religiosa deo auctore conferuntur, nostri est officii illa stabilire et perpetuis firmare monimentis. Inde est quod monasterio beati Albani et fratribus religiosis monachis ejusdem loci in perpetuam confirmavimus possessionem ecclesiam de Luitona et ecclesiam de Houghtona cum terris et decimis et omnibus pertinenciis suis sicut comes Gloucest' Willelmus eis illas dedit et carta sua confirmavit. Preterea confirmamus eis perpetuo jure possidendam totam terram quam Willelmus camerarius de feodo ejusdem comitis tenuit videlicet quicquid tenuit in soca Luitone et in Hertewella et in Badelesdona et in Potesgrava sicut predictus comes eis dedit et carta sua confirmavit pro servicio dimidii mi-[litis] quod prefatus Willelmus camerarius Roberto comiti Gloucestrie facere solebat. Quicumque igitur /[c.2] dece[tero] .... possessionem .... / jus .... / inquietaverit .... / diminuere aut .... [nisi· res-]/ipuerit divine ult[ionis in extremo]/ examine subjaceat .... / nostram malediccionem .... / Valete.

DATE: 1150–61.

See also *Gesta Abbatum Monast. S. Albani* (R.S.), i, 114–17, ed. H. T. Riley.

230

Confirmation by Theobald of the grant to St. Albans by Hamo son of Mainfeninus Brito of land at Chalfont (Bucks.) in accordance with his charter and that of Robert II bishop of Lincoln (1148–66).

MS. B.M. Cott. Julius D iii f.82a (Register of St. Albans).

Confirmacio Teob' archiepiscopi Cantuariensis atque sedis apostolice legati de terra de Chalfhunta.

T. DEI gratia Cantuarie archiepiscopus Anglie primas et apostolice sedis legatus omnibus tam presentibus quam futuris sancte ecclesie fidelibus salutem. Ex officii nostri debito religiosa nos loca diligere convenit et eorum utilitati ac quieti in posterum providere. Iccirco universitatem vestram nosse volumus nos ratam habere donacionem quam Hamo filius Mainfenini Britonis fecit deo et ecclesie sancti Albani et monachis ejusdem loci in liberam et sempiternam elemosinam de una virgata terre et dimidia et uno assarto in villa que Chalfhunta dicitur /[f.82b] cum pastura et libera pascua porcorum in eadem villa et cum omnibus libertatibus et liberis consuetudinibus quas eidem ecclesie juxta tenorem carte sue dedit et concessit; et sicut venerabilis frater noster Rodbertus Lincolniensis episcopus hanc donacionem scripto suo confirmavit, sic quoque nos confirmamus et concessa nobis auctoritate firmam atque inviolatam cunctis diebus manere precipimus.

DATE: 1150–61.

231

Notification by Theobald addressed to Henry archdeacon of Huntingdon (?1110–57) of a decision reached in his presence over the tithes of Kingsfeld at (Great) Gransden (Hunts.). Gerinus the parson of Gt. Gransden through his procurator abandoned his claim and the tithe was accordingly adjudged to St. Neot's (dependent priory of Bec, Hunts.).

MS. B.M. Cott. Faustina A iv f.43a (Cartulary of St. Neot's).

T. DEI gratia Cantuariensis archiepiscopus et tocius Anglie primas dilecto filio Henrico archidiacono Hunt' et omnibus sancte matris ecclesie fidelibus per Huntendenesiram constitutis salutem. Provide litteris commendantur que firmam debent et stabilem habere memoriam. Ad vestram itaque curavimus transferre notitiam controversiam que vertebatur inter ecclesiam sancti Neoti et ecclesiam de Grantendena super decimationibus de Kingesfeld juxta Offordeshawa coram nobis sopitam esse hoc modo: Gerinus qui decimatione illa [sic] sibi vendicabat per procuratorem suum jamdictam decimam in integrum et solidum cessit ecclesie et monachis sancti Neoti. Nos itaque prenominatam decimam ecclesie sancti Neoti adjudicatam ecclesie et fratribus confirmamus pleno jure perpetuo possidendam et presentis scripti testimonio communivimus, sub anathemate prohibentes ne quis decetero eis super predicta decima vexare et inquietare presumat. Valete.

DATE: 1139–57.
See *V.C.H. Hunts.*, ii, 301.

232

Confirmation by Theobald of the grant to St. Neot's by Gilbert earl of Pembroke (1138–48) of the church of Everton (Hunts.).

MS. B.M. Cott. Faustina A iv f.38b (Cartulary of St. Neot's).

T. DEI gratia Cantuariensis archiepiscopus Anglorum primas et apostolice sedis legatus omnibus ecclesie dei fidelibus salutem et benedictionem. Universitati vestre notum fieri volumus donationem quam Gislebertus comes de Penbroc deo et ecclesie sancti Neoti monachisque in ea deo servientibus de ecclesia Evertome cum omnibus ejusdem ecclesie pertinentiis tam in terris /[f.39a] quam in decimis et pratis et ceteris redditibus per manum nostram in Londoniensi concilio fecit nos ratam habere. Quam quidem ut firma inperpetuum et inconcussa permaneat memoratis fratribus confirmamus et presentis sigilli nostri testimonio communimus. Siquis autem post hoc nostre confirmationis munimentum prefatam donationem temerare vel in aliquo minorare presumpserit dei et nostra autoritate a cetu fidelium exterminatus perpetue maledictionis nisi recipuerit sententia feriatur.

DATE: probably 1143–48 in which case the legatine title would be an interpolation.

A confirmation of this gift by Alexander bishop of Lincoln (d. 1148) mentions 'et [sicut] Tedbaldus archiepiscopus carta sua confirmavit'. This is on f.38b. of the cartulary. The Council of London referred to was that of 1143 as Gilbert was dead by the time of the next one in 1151. It is preferred to make this charter the one confirmed by Alexander, as the other charter of Theobald in the Cartulary confirming the gift omits the phrase 'per manum nostram in Londoniensi concilio' which suggests a remoter date.

233

Later confirmation by Theobald of the previous grant in No. 232.

MS. B.M. Cott. Faustina A iv f.39a (Cartulary of St. Neot's).

T. DEI gratia Cantuariensis archiepiscopus Anglorum primas et apostolice sedis legatus omnibus ecclesie dei fidelibus salutem et benedictionem. Universitati vestre notum fieri volumus donationem quam comes Gislebertus de Penbroc deo et sancto Neoto et monachis in ecclesia sancti Neoti deo servientibus de ecclesia de Evertone cum omnibus ejusdem ecclesie pertinentiis tam in terris quam in decimis et pratis et ceteris redditibus fecit nos ratam habere. Quam quidem ut firma et illibata permaneat memoratis fratribus nostris confirmamus et sigilli nostri testimonio communimus. Valete.

DATE: 1150-61.

234

Confirmation by Theobald to the monks of St. Neot's of the church of Tempsford (Beds.) and of the concord thereon between the monks and Nicholas archdeacon of Bedford in accordance with the charter of Bishop Robert II of Lincoln.

MS. B.M. Cott. Faustina A iv f.39b (Cartulary of St. Neot's).

TEOB' dei gratia Cantuariensis archiepiscopus et tocius Anglie primas omnibus sancte ecclesie fidelibus salutem. Universitati vestre notum esse volumus nos confirmasse ecclesie sancti Neoti et monachis ibidem deo servientibus in perpetuum ecclesiam de Tamiseford et concordiam que inde facta est inter monachos sancti Neoti et Nicholaum archidiaconum Bedeford' per easdem conventiones que inter eos firmate et concesse sunt, sicut Robertus Lincolniencis episcopus id ipsum carta sua confirmavit et testatur.

DATE: 1148-61.

The concord as set out in the previous charter was that Nicholas was to hold the church from the monks for life or for as long as he remained a secular, paying them an annual pension of 5s. Should Goisbert the dean survive Nicholas he could hold the church on the same terms. Afterwards the monks were to be in absolute possession.

235

Notification by Theobald of the grant by Reginald Brito agreed to by John his son and heir to St. Neot's of a hide at Wintringham (near St. Neot's). In return the monks in Theobald's presence have agreed

to accept them as monks if required, and as long as Reginald remains
a layman he is to receive his food from the monks like any lay
brother.

MS. B.M. Cott. Faustina A iv f.38a (Cartulary of St. Neot's).

TEOB' dei gratia Cantuariensis archiepiscopus Anglorum primas et apostolice sedis legatus omnibus sancte matris ecclesie
filiis ad quos littere presentes pervenerint salutem. Ad posterorum notitiam litterarum memorie que coram nobis gesta sunt
comendamus. Itaque universitati vestre notificetur quod Regin-
aldus Brito concessione Johannis filii et heredis sui per manum
meam dedit secum ecclesie et monachis de sancto Neoto unam
hidam terre in Wintringeham quam tenebat de feudo ecclesie
ut habeant et teneant eam in dominio ipsius ecclesie in perpetuam et liberam elemosinam. Cujus beneficii gratia monachi
eis in nostri presentia concesserunt quod utrumque ex quo
peterent ad habitum monachatus susciperent, et ipsi Reginaldo
victualia sicut aliis fratribus conversis et ecclesie deditis in sua
curia invenirent quamdiu ipse in habitu seculari consisteret.
Test'.

DATE: 1150–61.

236

Confirmation by Theobald of the grant by Henry II to the monks of
Bec and St. Neot's of the church of Holy Trinity, Huntingdon.

MS. B.M. Cott. Faustina A iv f.41b (Cartulary of St. Neot's).

T. DEI gratia Cantuariensis archiepiscopus Anglorum primas et
apostolice sedis legatus omnibus sancte matris ecclesie dei
fidelibus salutem et benedictionem. Universitati vestre notum
fieri volumus nos ratam habere donationem et confirmationem
quam Henricus rex Angl' fecit deo et ecclesie sancte Marie
Becci et ecclesie sancti Neoti monachisque in ea deo servientibus
de ecclesia sancte Trinitatis in Hunt' cum omnibus ejusdem
ecclesie pertinenciis tam in terris quam in decimis quam ceteris
redditibus. Quod quidem ut firmum in perpetuum et inconcussum permaneat memoratis fratribus nostris monachis con-

firmavimus et presentis sigilli nostri testimonio communivimus. Si quis autem post hoc nostre confirmationis munimentum prefatam donationem et confirmationem temerare vel in aliquo minorare presumpserit dei et nostra auctoritate a cetu fidelium exterminatus perpetue maledictionis nisi resipuerit sententia feriatur. Hiis testibus.

DATE: 1154–61.

237

Confirmation by Theobald of gifts made to St. Frideswide's Oxford (Aug. Canons) by Roger bishop of Salisbury (1107–39).

MS. B.M. Cott. Vitellius E xv f.16b (Cartulary of Oseney).

Confirmatio Teob' archiepiscopi data canonicis sancte Fr[ideswide].

T. DEI gratia Cantuariensis archiepiscopus episcopis abbatibus et ceteris sanctis ordinibus per Angliam constitutis salutem et benedictionem. Sollicitudo ministerii nostri nos admonet ecclesiarum necessitudinibus providere ac adversariorum incursibus resistere, quatinus in ea pro voluntate dei pax conformetur tranquillitatis ope fideles ad omne opus bonum obnixius excitentur. Hoc quidem intuitu ne ecclesia sancte Frideswide virginis nunc vel futuris temporibus possessionum suarum dampna paciatur, quecunque a venerabili fratre nostro Rogero episcopo Saresberiensi eidem ecclesie donata sunt et juxta tenorem carte ipsius reddita, inperpetuum confirmamus, auctoritate nobis a deo concessa, prohibentes ne quis ea minuere sive in jus aliud abducere presumat. Siquis vero ausu temerario hanc nostre confirmationis formulam sciens violare temptaverit et predictam donationem sive redditionem diminuere et in jus alienum abducere, cupiditatis diabolici illectus obstinacia, perpetuo anathematis vinculo constringatur et a corpore et sanguine domini nostri Jhesu Christi separetur, quousque ad condignam satisfactionem venerit et prefate ecclesie sua pro posse restituerit.

DATE: 1139.
PRINTED: H. E. Salter (Oxford Hist. Soc.) *Cartulary of Oseney*, ii, 231.

238

Mandate of Theobald in accordance with a papal mandate to Bishops Robert II of Lincoln (1148–66) and Jocelin of Salisbury to compel the earl of Leicester (Robert 1118–68) to restore Edington (Oxon.) to the canons of St. Frideswide's Oxford.

MS. Corpus Christi Coll. Oxford 160 p. 313 (Cartulary of St. Frideswide's: deposited in Bodleian).

Littera exortatoria sancti Thome Cantuar' directa R[oberto] Lincolniensi et J[ocelino] Saresberiensi episcopis, mandato domini pape pro restitucione ville de Edinetona facienda quam comes Legr' invasit etc. [*sic*]. (Christ Church Rubric.)

T. DEI gratia Cantuariensis archiepiscopus Anglorum primas et apostolice sedis legatus venerabilibus fratribus R[oberto] Lincol' et J[ocelino] Sar' episcopis salutem. Accepimus mandatum domini pape nobis et vobis super conveniendo comite Legr' directum ut villam de Edinetona quam ad jus ecclesie sancte Frideswide de Oxon' pertinentes [*sic*] postquam prior ejusdem ecclesie iter ad dominum papam arripuit, violenter invasit ecclesie sancte Frideswide restitueret, et nisi commonitus prefate ecclesie de restitucione pretaxate ville satisfecerit infra xxx dies post nostram commonicionem in personam ejus anathematis et in totam terram ejus interdicti sentenciam promulgaremus. Inde est quod fraternitati vestre mandamus ut vice /[p. 314] nostra et vestra predictum comitem districte conveniatis super facienda restitucione illius manerii jam dicte ecclesie eique diligenter insinuetis quod nisi commonicioni vestre obtemperaverit, quoniam in personam ejus anathematis sentenciam et in totam terram ejus interdictum pariter proferamus sine lesione apostolice majestatis differre nec dissimulare poterimus. Valete.

ALSO: MS. Christ Church, Oxford, f.269b (not checked).

DATE: *c.* 1150.

PRINTED: *Cartulary of St. Frideswide's* (ed. S. R. Wigram, Oxford Hist. Soc., 1896), ii, 328.

Followed by charter of Robert, earl of Leicester, renouncing all his rights and mentioning Archbishop Theobald.

239

Confirmation by Theobald notified to Roger archdeacon of Canterbury (1148-54) of the grant to the monks of St. Bertin (St. Omer) of the church of Throwley (Kent) by William of Ypres, saving the rights of the see of Canterbury.

MS. P.R.O. Transcripts Record Commission ii vol. 144 p. 68 (Trans. 8/144).

From the original at St. Omer.

THEOBALDUS dei gratia Cantuariensis archiepiscopus Anglorum primas et apostolice sedis legatus Rogberto Cantuariensi archidiacono et toti clero Cantuariensis diocesis salutem. Noverit tam presens etas quam futura posteritas quoniam ex presentatione et postulatione Willelmi de Ipra tunc advocati dedimus et concessimus in perpetuam elemosinam monasterio beati Bertini et ejusdem loci fratribus ecclesiam de Trullega cum terris et decimis et capellis et omnibus de jure ad illam pertinentibus, salvis tamen per omnia episcopalibus ad ecclesiam Cantuariensem pertinentibus consuetudinibus. Unde volumus et precipimus ut predicti loci monachis ecclesia ipsa in jus et possessionem perpetuam cedat et ut ipsi monachi eam perpetuo possideant. Testibus Ricardo Londoniensi episcopo et Waltero Roffensi episcopo et Rogberto Cantuariensi archidiacono et Philippo cancellario apud Cantuariam.

ALSO: in the Cartulary of St. Omer (St. Bertin).

DATE: 1152-53 (confirmed by Pope Anastasius IV).

CALENDARED: C.D.F., p. 484.

PRINTED: Société des Antiquaires de la Morinie—Cartulaire de St. Bertin, ed. Abbé Haignéré, i, 97.

The transcript has 'Philippo cantore'. The original has a seal.

240

Confirmation by Theobald of the grant to the monks of St. Bertin of the church of Chilham (Kent) by Hugo son of Fulbert.

MS. P.R.O. Transcripts Record Commission, ii vol. 144, p. 83 (Trans. 8/144).

From Grand Cartulary of St. Omer.

THEOBALDUS dei gratia Cantuariensis archiepiscopus Anglorum primas et apostolice sedis legatus omnibus sancte matris ecclesie fidelibus salutem. Notum fieri volumus tam presentibus quam futuris quod Hugo filius Fulberti dedit et concessit ecclesiam de Chilleham cum omnibus ad eam pertinentibus per manum nostram monasterio sancti Bertini in perpetuam elemosinam. Nos quoque jam dictam ecclesiam eis ab advocato et domino fundi datam et concessam nobis coram auctoritate qua fungimur et presentis scripti pagina communimus ita tamen quod quicumque de cetero predictam possederit ecclesiam, nomine ecclesie beati Bertini et monachorum eam possidebit et annuam persolvet abbati et monachis pensionem. Hujus donationis testes sunt: Silvester abbas sancti Augustini, W[illelmus] prior sancti Augustini, Philippus cancellarius, Johannes de Saresburia, Hugo de Raculf, Helias de Chilleham, Sigerus monachus de Favresham et multi alii. Valete.

DATE: 1154–61.

CALENDARED: *C.D.F.*, p. 483.

PRINTED: Société des Antiquaires de la Morinie—*Cartulaire de St. Bertin*—ed. Abbé Haignéré, i, 97.

In the last line MS. reads Kuesham for Favresham.

241

Notification by Theobald of the quitclaim by Jocelin bishop of Salisbury (1142–84) of Devizes castle (Wilts.) to Henry II in his presence and also before Roger archbishop of York (1154–89) and Bishops Robert II of Lincoln (1148–66) and Hilary of Chichester (1147–69). In return the king has granted to the bishop thirty librates of land and will help the bishop to recover the possessions of the bishopric lost since 1135 and has meanwhile restored to the bishop the churches of Westbury and Figheldean (Wilts.), Odiham (Hants.), Godalming (Surrey) and the prebend of Bedminster (Bristol).

2H

Original MS. D. and C. Salisbury Muniment Room Box C 3.

T. DEI gratia Cantuariensis archiepiscopus Anglorum primas et apostolice sedis legatus omnibus ad quos presens carta pervenerit salutem. Noverit universitas vestra venerabilem fratrem nostrum Jocelinum Saresberiensem episcopum et ecclesiam suam in nostra et venerabilium fratrum nostrorum R[ogeri] Eboracensis archiepiscopi, R[oberti] Lincolniensis, H[ilarii] Cicestrensis episcoporum presencia, quietum clamasse domino nostro regi H[enrico] castrum de Divisis cum duobus parcis et burgum de Divisis sicut fossata ea dividunt et claudunt, et preter hec nichil aliud. Propter que rex dedit episcopo Saresbiriensi et ecclesie sue triginta libratas terre ad eleccionem ipsius episcopi de dominica terra corone regis, que omnino sit absque calumpnia et que sit in episcopatu Saresbiriensi. Et per hoc gratiam suam et amorem suum reddidit rex episcopo, ita quod de cetero eum diliget et manutenebit. Dedit etiam rex episcopo potestatem revocandi distracta et redintegrandi episcopatum, sicut fuit tempore Osmundi episcopi, et die qua rex Henricus fuit vivus et mortuus. Et in his revocandis dominus rex non impediet episcopum set juvabit et manutenebit. Preterea reddidit dominus rex ecclesie Sarisbiriensi ecclesiam de Westbiria cum pertinenciis suis, ecclesiam de Fikeldena cum pertinenciis suis, ecclesiam de Odiham cum pertinenciis suis, ecclesiam de Godelminges cum pertinenciis suis, prebendam de Bedmenistre quam tenuit Wido et Johannes post eum et post Johannem Josep. Hoc autem factum est anno M°C°l° vii^{mo} crastina die post festum sancti Luce ewangeliste. Valete. Et nos predicti episcopi idem sigillorum nostrorum impressione attestamur.

ENDORSEMENT: De castro Divisarum et collatio ecclesie de Hodiam et de Godelming et aliarum ecclesiarum (14th century).

SEAL: none; incisions for four seals.

SIZE: 6.9 in. × 9.9 in.

DATE: 19 October 1157.

COPIES: Reg. B, Reg. C, Reg. Rubr. (Diocesan Registry).

PRINTED: *Sarum*, p. 29.

242

Grant by Theobald of an indulgence of forty days to those visiting the church of Heytesbury (Wilts.) on the day of *inventio beate crucis* (3 May).

MS. Salisbury Diocesan Registry, Register of St. Osmund's.

T. DEI gratia Cantuariensis archiepiscopus omnibus sancte ecclesie fidelibus salutem et benedictionem. Pauperibus ecclesiis subvenire et eis suas elemosinas impendere opus bonum est deoque acceptissimum. Quicumque igitur ecclesiam beati Petri de Hegtred' et reliquias sanctorum que ibi sunt devote requisierint, et elemosinas suas ibi deo optulerint, xl dies de peccatis suis unde penitentiam acceperint, sibi in nomine domini condonamus et hoc in inventione beate crucis. Interdicimus autem et anathematizamus omnes quicunque venientes ad predictam ecclesiam vel inde redeuntes in pretaxata festivitate aliquo modo disturbare vel impedire presumpserint.

DATE: 1139-50, probably early.

PRINTED: W. H. R. Jones, *Register of St. Osmund's* (R.S., 1883-4), p. 343.

243

Grant by Theobald of an indulgence of forty days to those visiting Salisbury Cathedral on the feast of relics. The date of the feast, having been found inconvenient, is changed to 17 September.

MS. Salisbury Diocesan Registry, Register of St. Osmund's.

T. DEI gratia Cantuariensis archiepiscopus Anglorum primas et apostolice sedis legatus venerabilibus filiis suis decano et archidiaconis et toti clero Saresberiensis ecclesie universisque fidelibus per Saresberiensem episcopatum constitutis salutem. Quoniam festum reliquiarum ecclesie Saresberiensis non satis opportuno tempore prius celebrabatur, eo quod temporis difficultatem nec populus illuc convenire nec reliquias sicut deceret venerari poterant, venerabilis frater noster Joscelinus Saresberiensis episcopus ideo festum tempore magis congruo, id est xv⁰ Kal. Octobris, celebrari instituit. Nos itaque ejus institutionem ratam habentes, universitati vestre mandamus quatinus predicto die festum illud celebretis. Omnibus itaque qui ad celebrationem hujus festi vel infra octavas ad venerationem illarum reliquiarum illuc convenerint, nos de divina confisi misericordia xl dies de penitentia sibi injuncta singulis annis relaxamus. Valete.

DATE: 1150–61.
PRINTED: W. H. R. Jones, *Register of St. Osmund's* (R.S., 1883–4), p. 277.

244

Confirmation by Theobald of the grant to the Templars, of Merton (Oxon.) by Simon earl of Northampton (?1136–53).

MS. Bodleian Wood Empt. 10 f.102b (Sandford Cartulary).

T. DEI gratia Cantuariensis archiepiscopus Anglorum primas et apostolice sedis legatus universis etc. [*sic*] salutem. Ad nostram spectat solicitudinem religiosorum virorum quieti providere et que suis sunt usibus a regibus sive a principibus rationabiliter collata nostra auctoritate firmare. Idcirco fratribus religiosis de Templo domini militibus terram de Meriton' quam comes de Norhampton' Simon eis in perpetuam dedit elemosinam confirmamus et scripti nostri munimine corroboramus sicut regis Stephani carta quam habent testatur. Valete.

DATE: 1152–53.
PRINTED: A. M. Leys, *Sandford Cartulary*, ii, 282 (Oxford Rec. Soc.) and B. A. Lees, *Records of the Templars in England in the 12th Cent.*, p. 186.

245

Confirmation by Theobald of the possessions of Sele Priory (dep. on St. Florence Saumur, Sussex) in accordance with the charter of Bishop Hilary of Chichester (1147–69).

MS. Magdalen Coll., Oxford, Cartulary of Sele f.7a (by permission of the President and Fellows).

Confirmacio et testificacio carte Theobaldi Cantuariensis archiepiscopi super decimis et possessionibus. Universis sancte matris ecclesie filiis presens scriptum visuris vel audituris Galfridus permissione divina decanus, et capitulum Cycestr' salutem in domino. Noverit universitas vestra nos cartam bone memorie Theobaldi Cantuariensis archiepiscopi et apostolice sedis legati in nulla sui parte viciatam inspexisse in hec verba:

THEOBALDUS dei gratia Cantuariensis archiepiscopus Anglorum primas et apostolice sedis legatus universis sancte matris ecclesie filiis salutem. Que a fratribus nostris coepiscopis auctoritatis sue et litterarum sunt canonice firmata testimoniis ea, adjecto nostre auctoritatis testimonio, rata et firmissima perpetuis decrevimus et volumus manere temporibus. Inde est quod ecclesias et terras et decimas et omnia alia beneficia tam mundana quam ecclesiastica que ecclesia beati Petri de Sela et monachi in ea regulariter viventes ad monasterium sancti Florencii de Salmur pertinentes juste et /[f.7b] canonice possident, eisdem fratribus inperpetuum concedimus et auctoritate qua fungimur confirmamus sicut venerabilis frater noster Hyllarius Cycestr' episcopus carta sua quam oculis nostris conspeximus eis illa confirmavit, scilicet ipsam ecclesiam sancti Petri de Sela cum omnibus pertinenciis suis, ecclesiam sancti Nicholai de Brembria, ecclesiam sancti Nicholai de Soreham, ecclesiam sancte Marie de Portu, ecclesiam sancti Petri de Veteri Ponte, ecclesiam de Wassingetona, decimas de dominio Willelmi de Breuse apud Findonam et Dentonam, decimam de Roberti Salvagii apud Durington' duas mansiones apud portum de Sorham ex dono Willelmi de Breuse, liberas ab omni tallagio et consuetudine cum quarta parte nundinarum ejusdem loci, quinque mansiones apud Brambriam ex dono comitis Simonis et patris ejus. Hec itaque et omnia alia bona que inposterum justis et racionabilibus modis poterint adipisci presentis scripti nostri auctoritate confirmamus sub periculo anathematis prohibentes ne aliquis supradictis fratribus hec auffere vel imminuere presumat. Facta est hec confirmacio anno incarnacionis dominice M oC o quinquagesimo primo, apud Pageham.

Nos igitur etc. In rei geste testimonium etc.

DATE: 1151.

PRINTED: (translation, partly) L. F. Salzman, *Chartulary of Sele Priory* (1923), p. 10.

246

Confirmation by Theobald of agreement between Sherborne Abbey (Ben., Dorset) and the bishop and chapter of Salisbury. The bishop (Jocelin 1142–84) has quitclaimed to Clement abbot of Sherborne the land of Kington (Dorset) and the parish church of Sherborne in return for the service of one vicar-choral in Salisbury Cathedral and the payment of ten marks in silver to the canons on the death of an abbot of Sherborne, the monastery to be a canon of Salisbury.

MS. B.M. Addl. 46487 f.24b (Cartulary of Sherborne).

T. DEI gratia Cantuariensis archiepiscopus Anglorum primas et apostolice sedis legatus omnibus sancte matris ecclesie fidelibus ad quos presentes littere pervenerint salutem. Ad officii nostri sollicitudinem spectat que a fratribus nostris canonice gesta sunt rata habere et ne futuris temporibus convelli possint aut concuti auctoritate qua fungimur confirmare. Inde est quod dilecto filio nostro Clementi abbati Scireburnie et per ipsum ecclesie Scireburnie confirmamus terram de Kingestuna quam ei Saresberiensis ecclesia quietam reddidit, et ecclesiam Scireburnie parrochialem cum capellis, terris, decimis et omnibus pertinentiis suis, cum omnibus dignitatibus et libertatibus quas aliquis antecessorum suorum plenius et melius habuit in prebendam perpetuo possidendam, per servitium unius vicarii quod abbas Scireburnie qui pro tempore fuerit assidue faciet in Saresberiensi ecclesia sicut alii concanonici sui, statuentes ut cum abbas obierit, ecclesia Scireburnensis infra annum decem marcas argenti canonicorum communioni persolvet, eoque contenti erunt canonici, nec umquam in communionem eorum jam dicta prebenda devocabitur. Si quis vero ausu temerario adversus hanc confirmationem nostram venire temptaverit, indignationem omnipotentis dei et nostram se proculdubio noverit incursurum. Valete.

DATE: 1150–61.

247

Confirmation by Theobald notified to Bishops Roger of Chester (1129–48) and Robert of Hereford (1131–48) of the possessions of Shrewsbury Abbey confirmed by them and of the payments due to the monks from the parish priests of their churches and of the payments due from chapels to their mother churches.

MS. Nat. Lib. of Wales, Aberystwyth, Cartulary of Shrewsbury f.53a.

Confirmatio sancti Thome martiris de bonis in episcopatu Herford' et Cest'.

T. DEI gratia Cantuariensis archiepiscopus et tocius Anglie primas venerabilibus fratribus Rogerio[1] Cestrensi[2] et Roberto Herefordensi episcopis salutem. Noverint tam presentes quam futuri nos ecclesias vel decimas sive possessiones monachis Salop' a fidelibus vestri episcopatus [sic] datas et ad vestrum usque tempus inconcusse ab illis possessas quas auctoritate litterarum[3] vestrarum canonice illis confirmastis, predictis monachis auctoritate nostra confirmasse et sigilli nostri munimine corroborasse[4] precipientes ut que ab ipsis[5] sacerdotibus qui ecclesias tenent predictis[6] monachis annuatim reddi nostra dispositione constituta sunt, simul et de subjectione capellarum sue matri ecclesie et de consuetudinibus quas mater ecclesia de capella tanquam de filia reclamare habet que vestra consideratione diffinita sunt et in ipsis cartulis prenotata, rata absque ulla refragatione[7] sive controversia et inconcussa remaneant. Valete.

ALSO: in MS. B.M. Harleian 3868 f.8a (Lichfield Register).

VARIATIONS: [1]Rogero, [2]Cestrenci. [3]literarum. [4]f.8b. [5]episcopis. [6]predictas. [7]refractione(?).

DATE: 1139–48.

COPY: in transcript of Shrewsbury Cartulary, MS. B.M. Addl. 30311 f.50b.

The charter of Roger of Chester mentioned by Theobald is on f.7b of the Harleian MS. The following is an abstract:

Rogerus . . . . archidiaconis et decanis . . . . salutem . . . . Ecclesias et omnes decimas que fratribus . . . . date sunt, ut ex eis monachis necessaria administrentur nostra auctoritate . . . . confirmamus . . . . Clerici vero qui constitucione eorundem fratrum ipsis ecclesiis prefuerunt, de ipsis ecclesiis omni anno debitam eis persolvant pensionem secundum modum a nobis sibi concessam. Omnes vero decimas quas actenus sine calumpnia possederunt tam ex suis quam ex aliorum divinis volumus ut amodo inconcusse teneant. Et quoniam necessitate cogente in quibusdam eorum parochiis cimiteria benediccimus et capellas dedicavimus, precipimus . . . . ut capelle ipse matricibus ecclesiis sicut filie subjecte sint ita ut in diebus solempnibus non ad eas set ad matrem ecclesiam populus omnis conveniat et corpora defunctorum que voluerit presbiter matris ecclesie ad ipsius cimiterium deportari faciat . . . . [there follows a list of nineteen churches, eleven of which have one or more chapels. The total amount of the pensions is £17 14s. 0d.]. . . . Quoniam volumus, etc. . . .

248

Confirmation by Theobald of the grant of Henry I to the monks of Shrewsbury and especially of Aston (under the Wrekin) (Salop.) and as renewed by the Empress Matilda.

MS. Nat. Lib. of Wales, Aberystwyth, Cartulary of Shrewsbury f.53a.

Confirmatio dicti sancti Thome.

T. DEI gratia Cantuariensis archiepiscopus et totius Anglie primas omnibus sancte ecclesie fidelibus salutem. Religiosorum desideriis justis facilem prebere assensum ad episcopalem proculdubio spectat sollicitudinem. Ea nimirum consideratione peticioni monachorum sancti Petri de Salop' condescendentes confirmamus et hac carta nostra eis corroboramus terras et omnia que Henricus illustris rex Angl' eis in elemosinam concessit vel dedit juste et canonice et maxime villam de Estona et omnia escangia que M[atildis] imperatrix ejusdem H[enrici] regis filia eisdem monachis concessit et carta sua confirmavit. Similiter quoque eis concessimus et confirmamus quicquid inposter-/[f.53b]um justis modis adipisci potuerint, statuentes ut quicumque ea ausu temerario auferre vel imminuere presumpserint donec resipuerint et digne satisfecerint, anathematis sentencie subjaceant. Amen.

DATE: 1139–54.

See R. W. Eyton, *Antiquities of Shropshire* (1854–60), ix, 58.

COPY: in transcript of Shrewsbury Cartulary, MS. B.M. Addl. 30311 f.50b.

249

Mandate of Theobald to Walter bishop of Coventry (1149–59). Ranulf, formerly abbot of Shrewsbury (before 1155) had alienated two-thirds of the tithes of Emstrey (Salop.) to the church of Atcham now belonging to Lilleshall Abbey (Salop.) without the consent of the convent. He has given permission to abbot Robert to revoke the concession (1155–67). Walter is to maintain the cause of the abbey of Shrewsbury.

MS. Nat. Lib. of Wales, Aberystwyth, Cartulary of Shrewsbury f.338b.

> Carta sancti T. Cantuariensis archiepiscopi de revocatione decimarum duarum porcionum decime de Eministr' quas concessit abbas Ranulfus ecclesie de Atingham sine consensu sui conventus.

T. DEI gratia Cantuariensis archiepiscopus Anglorum primas et apostolice sedis legatus venerabili fratri et amico W[altero] Conventrensi episcopo et archidiaconis suis salutem. Discrescio vestra ignorare non debet quod bone memorie Rannulfus abbas Salop' preter conscientiam et consensum conventus sui, ecclesie sue conditionem deteriorem facere non potuit nec debuit. Unde si ut accepimus duas portiones decime dominii de Eministr' preter conscientiam et consensum conventus sui diminuit et inde ab ecclesia sua aliquam portionunculam alienando sine concessione conventus sui ecclesie de Etingeham que nunc est in bonis Lilleshillensis abbatie assignata concessit liceat nichilominus Roberto abbati Salop' eandem decime portionunculam justicia dictante in pristinum statum revocare /[f.339a] et in usus monachorum sicut antiquitus erat reducere. In hoc quoque vobis precipimus quatinus justiciam Salopesberiensis monasterii summopere manuteneatis. Valete.

DATE: 1155–59.

COPY: in transcript of Shrewsbury Cartulary, MS. B.M. Addl. 30311 f.312a.

PRINTED: H. Owen and J. B. Blakeway, *History of Shropshire* (1825), ii, 108, n. 3.

250

Grant by Theobald of a courtyard worth eightpence to the church of Slindon (Sussex) on the occasion of his dedication of the church.

Original MS. P.R.O. Exchequer T.R. Ancient Deeds A 15775 (E 40).

T. DEI gratia Cantuariensis archiepiscopus Anglorum primas et apostolice sedis legatus universis hominibus suis de Slindona Francis et Anglicis salutem. Sciant tam presentes quam futuri quoniam quando dedicavimus ecclesiam beate Marie de Slindona dedimus eidem ecclesie in perpetuam elemosinam curtillagium quod fuerat Schirwaldi quod reddere solebat annuatim octo denarios, et volumus et precipimus quod quietum et liberum remaneat eidem ecclesie perpetuo possidendum. T. Thoma Lond' et Philippo cancellario et Alano de Wellis et Radulfo Dunelm' et Hugone de Holingeb[urna] et Petro scriptore apud Lovintonam.

ENDORSEMENT: Thedbaldi Cantuariensis de curttilagio in Slindona.
SEAL: none.
SIZE: 2·9 in. × 6·9 in.
DATE: 1150–54.

251

Confirmation by Theobald to Adelard the prior and the Aug. Canons of St. Denys', Southampton of Northam (Southampton) granted to them by William son of Audoen and confirmed by Bishop Henry of Winchester (1129–71).

MS. B.M. Addl. 15314 f.95a (Register of St. Denys', Southampton).

Confirmacio Thome archiepiscopi Cantuariensis de manerio de Northam.

T. DEI gratia Cantuariensis archiepiscopus Anglorum primas et apostolice sedis legatus universis sancte ecclesie ministerialibus et fidelibus salutem. Que a fratribus nostris coepiscopis statuuntur et firmantur quatenus ratio et justicia permiserit debemus et nos auctoritate nostra corroborare et perpetua stabilire.

Hoc ergo rationis intuitu terram de Norham cum omnibus rebus et libertatibus ad eam pertinentibus quam Willelmus filius Audoeni Aelardo priori et canonicis regularibus sancti Dion' juxta Hamtonam in perpetuam concessit et dedit elemosinam sicut venerabilis frater noster H[enricus] Wint' episcopus eis concessit et carta sua confirmavit, nos consequenter confirmamus et ipsam elemosinam predictis fratribus nostra auctoritate perpetuo stabilimus. Valete.

DATE: *c.* 1151.

That the charter is of Theobald can be stated fairly confidently as the first charter on the same page states the gift to have been made in 1151. Thomas was not legate until 1166.

252

Confirmation by Theobald to the Aug. canons of St. Mary Overy, Southwark, of the church of All Saints Graveney (Kent) (previously granted by Lanfranc).

Original MS. B.M. Cott. Nero C iii f.188 (Various Collections).

T. DEI gratia Cantuariensis archiepiscopus Gualtero archidiacono totique capitulo de Tenham salutem. Concedimus et presentis cartę pagina confirmamus ęcclesiam Omnium Sanctorum de Gravene canonicis regularibus Sanctę Marię de Suthwerca in elemosinam cum omnibus ad eandem ęcclesiam pertinentibus sive in terris sive in decimis vel aliis quibuslibet beneficiis. Testibus: Rogero de Ponteepiscopi, Wlurico de Wrateham, Alano de Wellis, Johanne de Cantuaria, Toma de Lund', clericis; Ricardo de Gravenel, Hugone Paisforiere, Johanne converso, (laicis).

ENDORSEMENT: Confirmacio T. archiepiscopi de ecclesia Omnium Sanctorum de Gravenel.

SIZE: 1·9 in. × 7 in. Cut down at top and bottom.

SEAL: none.

DATE: 1143–48.

COPY: MS. ibid. Additional Charters 44694 (15th century).

PRINTED: (partly) C. R. Cheney, *English Bishops' Chanceries* (1950), p. 71, n. 1.

253

Confirmation by Theobald to Southwark of the church of **Stoke** (Poges) (Bucks.) in accordance with the charter of Bishop Robert II of Lincoln (1148–66).

MS. B.M. Addl. 38683 f.38a. (This is H. E. Salter's transcript of Smith's Manuscript Catalogue of the Cottonian Library, now MS. Bodleian Smith 90 (S.Cat. 15695).)

Part of a section dealing with the Cotton Charters. They were kept in drawers under the various effigies.

Vitellius A.16.

CONFIRMATIO donationis ecclesiae de Stokes et terrarum olim ecclesiae sanctae Mariae de Sudwerka et ejusdem canonicis concessarum per T. archiepiscopum Cantuariensem et R[obertum] episcopum Lincolniensem.

DATE: probably 1148–61.

This charter presumably perished in the fire of 1731.

254

Confirmation by Theobald notified to Bishop Simon of Worcester (1125–50) of the possessions of **Stanley Priory** (Glos., dep. priory of Gloucester Abbey) in the honour of Berkeley, granted originally to Sabricht the prior and the canons of Stanley.

MS. *Ex ipso autographo in Bibl. Cottoniana.*

THEOBALDUS Dei gratia Cantuariensis archiepiscopus Anglorum primas et apostolicae sedis legatus venerabili fratri et amico S. Wigorn. episcopo et dilectis sibi in Domino omnibus sanctae matris ecclesiae filiis salutem et benedictionem. Incolumitati ecclesiae et paci providentes ea quae ecclesiis ipsis bonorum principum largitione vel rationabili quorumcunque executione adquiruntur, pia ipsis benignitate concedimus, et auctoritate nostra confirmamus. Audientes itaque ecclesiam de Estona et ecclesiam de Comberleia et ecclesiam de Osleworda et ecclesiam de Camma et ecclesiam de Erlingeham cum omnibus pertinentiis earum, et unam praebendam quae fuit Bernardi capellani in Berchelai et omnes elemosinas quas habuit idem Bernardus in Berchelai Hernesse, ecclesiae S. Leonardi et Sabrieto priori et canonicis de Stanleia jamdiu rationabiliter donatas et hoc plenius ex cartis regiis et cartis dilecti filii nostri Rogerii de Berchelai ejusdem ecclesiae advocati, attestatione cognoscentes, ipsi ecclesiae beati Leonardi de Stanleia in earundem ecclesiarum possessionem plenum nostrae auctoritatis robur concedimus et praefatas ecclesias ipsi ecclesiae de Stanleia praesenti scripto imperpetuum confirmamus. Valete.

DATE: 1149–50.

PRINTED: *Monasticon*, iv, 470; translations: S. Rudder, *New History of Gloucs.* (1779), App. 24; R. Atkyns, *Hist. of Gloucs.* (1712), p. 683.

255

Confirmation by Theobald of the possessions of Stoke-by-Clare (Suffolk, dep. priory of Bec).

MS. B.M. Cott. Appendix xxi f.63a (Cartulary of Stoke-by-Clare).

Confirmaciones T. Cantuariensis archiepiscopi de omnibus decimis redditibus ecclesiis in archiepiscopatu ut in ea continetur.

T. DEI gratia Cantuariensis archiepiscopus Anglorum primas et apostolice sedis legatus episcopis et universo clero et populo per Angliam constitutis salutem. Paci et utilitati fratrum religiosorum in omnibus secundum racionem pro posse studere et providere, ipsa nos injucti [*sic*] nobis officii episcopalis sollicitudo et cura hortatur et compellit. Sanctorum igitur antecessorum nostrorum exemplo et auctoritate provocati et corroborati donaciones et elemosinas que presenti scripto notantur, ecclesie sancti Johannis baptiste de Stok' et monachis ibi deo servientibus pertinentes, in manu et protectione nostra suscipimus et sigillo nostro munimus et ut inperpetuum illibata sibi permaneant censemus et precipimus. Anno ab incarnacione domini millesimo nonagesimo Gilbertus de Clara filius Ricardi filii

Gilberti comitis Brionie dedit ecclesie sancte Marie Beccensi et monachis in ea deo servientibus ecclesiam sancti Johannis de Clara cum omnibus que ad eam pertinent, in prebendis in decimis in silvis in vineis in terris in aquis, jure perpetuo possidendam in subjeccionem abbatum qui in Beccensi ecclesia preerunt. Dedit eciam eis septem prebendas a bone memorie Elurico filio Wihtgari temporibus Eadwardi regis institutas, scilicet prebendam Alfwini que continet terram de Brochol' et totam decimam de dominico de Hunedena; et prebendam Willelmi filii Alboldi que continet ecclesiam de Gaisleia et capellam de Kenteford et totam decimam de Deseinge et totam decimam de molendinis de Cavenham et unum miliarium et dimidium anguillarum apud Lachingehedam et terram de Boctune; et prebendam Rengerii de Lundoniis que continet ecclesiam de Tastede et totam decimam de dominico Clare; et prebendam Walterii de sancto Germano que continet ecclesiam sancti Pauli de Clara et terram de Haverhelle et decimam de Cavenedis et decimam de Saham et decimam de Benecleia et decimam de Alesford et decimam de Neilingeherst; et prebendam Sawini que continet ecclesiam de Pebenersc et terram, et terram de Polheia et terram de Suberia et terram de Bulileia; et prebendam Bernardi /[f.63b] que continet ecclesiam de Hunedena et decimam de Gestingetorp et decimam de Halstede et decimam de Buris; et prebendam Oggerii que continet ecclesiam de Stok' et terram de eadem villa et decimam de Cornerth' et decimam de Herefeld'. Constituit eciam et confirmavit predictus Gilbertus quatinus monachi sine aliqua contradictione vel dilatione omnes prebendas suas ex quo a persona vacarent in manus suas proprias secundum voluntatem suam disponendas acciperent, et cum omni libertate et pace inperpetuum obtinerent. Dedit eciam eis culturam que appellatur Waltune et holmum juxta eam et quatuor bubulcos in villa que vocatur Stok' cum omnibus terris suis et boscum de Clara qui [sic] est juxta villam que vocatur Trillawa, et illum villanum qui ibidem manet cum omni terra sua et Aluricum piscatorem cum omni terra sua et Sturemaram et piscacionem tocius fluminis ab ipsa Sturemara usque ad castellum de Clara concedentibus fratribus suis Roberto et Rogero et l acras terre apud Huneden' juxta boscum de Trillawa. Dedit eis eciam ad luminaria ecclesie molendinum de Smalebruge quod ei per singulos annos xx solidos reddere solebat et ecclesiam de Bradefeld cum omnibus pertinenciis suis et ecclesiam de Gelham cum pertinenciis suis et ecclesiam de Essa cum pertinenciis suis et ecclesiam de Wothingis cum pertinenciis suis et ecclesiam de Cremplesham cum pertinenciis suis et in eadem villa Goche fabrum cum omni tenemento suo. Dedit eciam eis integre decimas omnium rerum de quibus decima dari debet de toto dominio omnium maneriorum suorum in Nortfolc, videlicet totam decimam de Cremplesham, totam decimam de Wiram, totam decimam de Welles, totam decimam de Bertona et ecclesias omnium istorum maneriorum cum vacaverint, et redditum x solidorum scilicet v solidorum in Fincham et v solidorum in Buchetuna et duo milia anguillarum cum piscatura apud Fordham et quatuor milia anguillarum apud Lachingeh' et singulis annis licenciam picandi [*sic*] per unum diem et duas noctes in vivario de Caveham ante festum sancti Johannis et unam damam in parco de Hunedena et ibidem unam quercum ad natale domini ad calefaciendum monachos infirmos et duas quadrigas in nemore de Bradefeld ad portanda lingna ad quoquinam suam et in eodem nemore merenum quantum opus est ad tres carucas per annum et quietudinem lx porcorum de pasnagio cum porcis suis ubi- /[f.64a]cumque voluerunt in nemoribus suis. Confirmamus eciam eis donaciones omnes quas fecit eis Ricardus filius predicti Gilberti et commutaciones terrarum que inter eos facte sunt sicut hic notantur. Anno ab incarnacione domini millesimo c°.xx°iiii°. Ricardus filius Gilberti transtulit monachos de castello Clare ad ecclesiam sancti Augustini de Stok' et dedit eis molendinum de Stok' in escambium molendini de Clara et terram Rogerii carpentarii liberam et quietam a geldo et scoto et omnibus consuetudinibus in escambium terrarum que monachi habebant in Clara, culture scilicet que vocatur Horscroft et vinee que est juxta eandem culturam et culture que vocatur Waltune et vinee quam Goisfridus filius Hamonis dederat eisdem monachis et horti eorum et molendini eorum de Clara et xii mansurarum quas habebant in villa Clare, masure [*sic*] videlicet Sauuini, Willelmi filii Alboldi, Bernardi, Leofuuini,

Alfwini, Rengerii, canonicorum; Leofirici Longi, Canevaz, Heudonis hostiarii, Ernaldi de Nazandes, Godwini stotarii, Godwini Galilee. Preterea constituit ipse dominus Ricardus quod geldum et scotum et omnes consuetudines que jacebant super Lintonam Roais et terram quam Rogerus carpentarius ad tempus tenuerat debent dari de dominica cultura Clare que vocatur Horscroft. Istas etenim terras fecit predictus Ricardus monachis liberas solutas et quietas a geldo et omnibus consuetudinibus in predicta commutacione perpetuo possidendas. Hac siquidem convencione factum est istud escambium quod monachi auxiliante domino Clare construerent apud Stok' ecclesiam sancti Johannis baptiste ad habitandum in ea cum omnibus redditibus et libertatibus et privilegiis et auctoritatibus suis et cum prebendis quas habuerat ecclesia beati Johannis baptiste sita in castello Clare. Dedit eciam eis quoddam nemusculum quod vocatur Stokeho et aliud prope ecclesiam sancti Augustini. Dedit eciam eis ecclesiam de Caveham cum omnibus pertinenciis suis pro ecclesia de Denham que erat monachorum quam Alberico de Ver dedit concedentibus monachis eidem ecclesie de Denham medietatem decime. Gilbertus vero comes filius istius Ricardi dedit eis ecclesiam de Bures cum omnibus pertinenciis suis. Omnes etiam elemosinas quas barones predictorum dominorum seu quilibet alii fideles predictis monachis dederunt confirmamus et corroboramus: ex dono Ernaldi /[f.64b] de Nazanda duas partes decime de Hamstedia omnium rerum de quibus decima dari debet et unum hospitem in villa Clare; ex dono Roberti Psalterium xv acras terre apud Hunedena [sic]; ex dono Ricardi de Reda xxxᵃ acras terre in eadem villa; ex dono Roberti de Neiela decimam de Denarnestune, decimam de Stanesfelda de omnibus unde decima dari debet; ex dono Hunfridi cognomento Burnardi terram de Geldham de feudo domini Gilberti de Clara; ex dono Elinandi vicecomitis totam decimam suam de Finchingefelda et decimam de Fornham et ibidem x acras terre et molendinum de Waldingefeld cum Adam filio suo leproso quem monachum fecit et terram ad molendinum pertinentem; ex dono Galfridi filii ejus totam terram suam de Forenham et terram suam de Reda et terram Wlgari de Tya et terram Huctredi de Mora et tres mansuras in

Clara; ex dono Gaufridi filii Haymonis et Ansgoti de Buchehala
duas partes decimacionis de Bucheshala; ex dono Herluini
filii Goismeri x solidatas terre de terra Wlurici Smukel apud
Finstede; ex dono Radulfi de la Cressunera duas partes decimacionis sue de Haukeduna et de Chemesingas; ex dono
Rogeri de Carlevilla duas partes decimacionis sue de Alveredes-
feld et de Hertsterst; ex dono Canevaz duas partes decimacionis
sue de Herningewella; ex dono Galfridi filii Hamonis duas
partes decimacionis sue de Samford et totam minutam decimam; ex dono Ricardi filii Hugonis duas partes decimacionis
sue de Meleford et de Culinges et de Nedham et totam terram
suam de Brochola; ex dono Rogeri de sancto Germano decimam de Cavenedis; ex dono Rogeri de Gisnei duas partes decimacionis sue in Haveringelande et Witewella et de terra sua
apud Norwicum et ecclesiam beati Clementis martiris cum pertinenciis suis in eadem villa; ex dono Gaufridi de Favarches
duas partes decimacionis de Walsingeham; ex dono Osulphi
Maskerel duas partes decimacionis sue de Cavenedis; ex dono
Gaufridi duas partes decimacionis sue de Badeleia; ex dono
Goismeri duas partes decimacionis sue de Cipeleia; ex dono
Elye coci duas partes decimacionis sue de Poselingeworthe; ex
dono Roberti pincerne et Mabilie uxoris sue ecclesiam de
Trillawia cum pertinenciis suis et v sol' terre in eadem villa; ex
dono Symonis filii Arnaldi terram Ingenulphi de Bradeleia; ex
dono Albrici de Ca-/[f.65a]pell' totam moram suam de Stok';
ex dono Baldewini filii Galfridi totam terram quam Willelmus
claviger de eo tenuit apud Claram ; ex dono Adam filii Warini
terram de Heni; ex dono Roberti de Cloptune decimam suam
de eadem villa; ex dono Galfridi de Blavenni xii acras terre in
Bridebroc; ex dono Roberti de Blaveni et Ricardi filii ejus xii
acras terre ibidem; ex dono Ingeranni de Abernun ecclesiam de
Frisentune cum pertinenciis suis et totam decimam suam de
Barue et illam de Labisse; ex dono Roberti de Pressinni et
Mabilie uxoris ejus et Helie filii ejus decimam suam de Boctune; ex dono Tebaldi de Stamburna iii acras terre in eadem
villa; ex dono Danielis de Crevequer x acras terre apud Gaislea;
ex dono Rogeri de Dalham v acras terre in eadem villa; ex dono
Osberti parcarii ii acras terre apud Heham; ex dono Alexandri

21

de la Cressunere ii acras terre apud Nedham; ex donu Algeri filii Goismeri decimam de terra sua de Bellocampo: ex dono Walteri cum barba terciam partem decime quam habet in Stok' et totam decimam de terra sua apud Priditune et ii acras terre in villa de Stok'; ex dono Ernaldi Buzecalla et uxoris ejus et Roberti filii ejus totam decimam suam de Topesfeldia et de Holeneheia; ex dono Willelmi Capra Robertum de Bolileia reddendo annuatim vi solidos, duas etiam partes decimacionis Roberti Flandrensis in Bumstedia et duas partes decimacionis Ricardi filii Guberti in eadem villa et duas partes decimacionis Fulconis de Blendac in Stamburna et totam decimam Ade filii Warini in Binnisleia et duas partes decimacionis Hugonis de Wicham in eadem villa et totam decimam Willelmi de la Landa in Essa et dimidiam decimacionem Salomonis in Tilleberi et duas partes decimacionis Rainaldi de Codeham in Mucheleia. Hec omnia predicte ecclesie beati Johannis baptiste de Stok' confirmamus et sigilli nostri apposicione corroboramus et auctoritate beati Petri apostoli et ecclesie Cantuariencis cui auctore deo presidemus et nostra, interdicimus et sentencia excommunicacionis percellimus siquis ex predictis donacionibus ante nominate ecclesie beati Johannis baptiste aliquid violenter auferre presumpserit. Test' Rogerus archidiaconus Cant' ecclesie, Thomas clericus de Lond', magister Johannes Saleb', Johannes de Cantuar', Philippus de Sal', magister Guido de Pressenni, magister Johannes de Tyleberia, magister Rogerus Species et multi alii.

[Underneath in a later hand:]

Osebertus clericus crucifer, Willelmus, Gilbertus, Rogerus, Lechardus, nepotes domini archiepiscopi, Thomas clericus Ebroisensis magister eorum, Elinandus cancellarius, Ricardus de Clare, [Walterus] de Gloucestre monachi et capellani archiepiscopi, Robertus pincerna, Ricardus dispensarius, Gilbertus camerarius, Odo senescallus, Willelmus magister cocus, Laurencius ostiarius, Willelmus filius Pagani portarius, Baylehache marescallus et multi alii.

DATE: 1150–53. John of Canterbury became Treasurer of York in 1153.
PRINTED: *Monasticon*, vi, 1659.

256

Confirmation by Theobald of the possessions of Stoke-by-Clare giving the witnesses to the grantors' charters.

MS. B.M. Cott Appendix xxi f.65b (Cartulary of Stoke-by-Clare).

> Confirmacio T. Cantuariensis archiepiscopi de omnibus hominibus decimis redditibus et ecclesiis.

T. DEI gratia Cantuariensis archiepiscopus Anglorum primas et sedis apostolice legatus episcopis et universo clero et populo per Angliam constitutis salutem. Paci et utilitati fratrum religiosorum in omnibus secundum racionem pro posse studere et providere, ipsa nos injucti [*sic*] nobis officii episcopalis sollicitudo et cura hortatur et compellit. Sanctorum igitur antecessorum nostrorum exemplo et auctoritate provocati et corroborati donaciones et elemosinas que presenti scripto notantur, ecclesie sancti Johannis baptiste de Stok' et monachis ibi deo servientibus pertinentes, in manu et proteccione nostra suscipimus et sigillo nostro munimus et ut inperpetuum illibata sibi permaneant censemus et precipimus. Anno ab incarnacione domini MIC Gilbertus de Clara filius Ricardi filii Gilberti comitis dedit ecclesie sancte Marie Beccensi et monachis in ea deo servientibus ecclesiam sancti Johannis de Clara cum illis omnibus que ad eam pertinent, in prebendis in decimis in silvis in vineis in terris in aquis jure perpetuo possidendam in subjeccionem abbatum qui in Beccensi ecclesia preerunt. Hanc donacionem fecit ipse Gilbertus pro anima sua et pro animabus patris et matris sue et maxime pro anima fratris sui Godefridi qui in cimeterio sancti Johannis de Clara sepultus requiescit. Pro cujus anima exceptis prebendis et aliis ipsius ecclesie redditibus ex suo dominio victum quatuor monachorum ibi constituit et ad luminaria ecclesie quoddam molendinum quod ei per singulos annos xx solidos reddebat, concessit. Hec donacio facta est apud castrum quod vocatur Clara eratque tunc dies anniversarius patris sui. Dedit eciam ipse Gilbertus deo et eidem ecclesie sancti Johannis baptiste apud Claram ad victum supradictorum quatuor monachorum ibidem deo serviencium de rebus suis ista: culturam que appellatur Horscrofst et aliam culturam que appellatur Waltuna et quatuor bubulcos in villa que vocatur Stok' cum omnibus terris suis et boscum Clere qui [*sic*] est juxta villam que vocatur Trillavia et illum villanum qui ibidem manet cum omni terra sua et alios duos villanos in supradicta cultura Horscrofto manentes et prata que sunt juxta culturam sicut cursus fluminis veteris molendini fluxerit et molendinum de Clara et ecclesiam de Bradevelda cum omnibus que ad eam pertinent et duas carucas boum et unum caballum et Alricum piscatorem cum omni /[f.66a] terra sua et l acras terre apud Hunedenam juxta predictum boscum et singulis annis ducentos caseos et quatuor milia anguillarum de piscatura Lacchingeth' et v milia allecium apud Deseninges' et ortum et virgultum suum apud Claram quod est juxta molendinum. Hec omnia de suo dominio dedit ipse Gilbertus et posuit super altare sancti Johannis baptiste per quoddam candelabrum ejusdem ecclesie. Deinde obsecrando precepit baronibus suis ut eidem ecclesie de terris suis ecclesiis vel decimis quantum vellent absque exheriditacione successorum suorum donarent, quod omnes de se suisque hominibus libentissime concesserunt. Horum omnium qui affuerunt predictorum testes fuerunt isti, Girulfus capellanus, Gotfridus filius Hamonis, Elinandus vicecomes, Razo dapifer, Oilardus de Algo, Goifridus de Burg', Arnulfus de Bria, Ernaldus de Nazanda, Willelmus Hurant, Adam filius Uuarini, Hubondus cubicularius, Robertus pincerna, Radulfus de la Cressunere, Willelmus de Curtuna, Robertus Folet, Robertus de Suuna, Willelmus filius Tezonis, Canevaz Makerel. Dedit idem Gilbertus deo et sancto Johanni de Clara quicquid Girulfus capellanus suus habebat in Norfolc in terris, scilicet, ecclesiis decimis atque villanis, testantibus et credentibus Adel' uxore ejus et filio ejus Ricardo. Testibus eciam Elinando vicecomite, Ricardo filio Hugonis, Radulfo presbitero filio Germundi. Adhuc eciam dedit ipse Gilbertus quendam holmum juxta pratum suum de Waltuna. Testes Gilbertus filius ejus et Walterus Dabernun. Dedit eciam singulis annis piscacionem unius diei in vivario suo apud Cavenham. Testes Hunfridus filius Goismeri, Adam filius Warini, Galfridus filius Hamonis, Radulfus de la Cressunere, Albericus de Capell', Gilbertus filius

Rainaldi; et Edmarum villanum de Hunedena cum tota terra
quam tenebat de feodo domini, quem villanum primus dederat
Robertus Psalterium sancto Johanni de Clara quod singulis
annis quendam stocum in bosco apud Hunedenam ante natale
domini ad calefaciendum monachos. Testes Helin' vicecom' et
Hug' presbitero [*sic*] de Stratesele. Ricardus filius predicti
Gilberti dedit deo et sancto Johanni de Clare nemusculum
quod vocatur Stokeho. T. Gilbertus frater ejus, Walterus capellanus, Mauricius de Cassel, Hugo de Ovintuna, Galfridus filius
Elinaldi, Robertus filius Ernaldi, Willelmus claviger, de hominibus monachorum Eliet, Sigar, Willelmus. /[f.66b] Concessit
eciam idem Ricardus quod Salomon teneret totam terram
quam dominus Gilbertus dederat eidem Salomoni de sancto
Johanne et monachis Clare ita bene et honorifice sicut melius et
honorabilius tenuerat eam de patre suo Gilberto et pro hac
concessione dedit ei Salomon unum palefridum. Testibus Waltero et Roberto filio Ricardi, Alberico de Ver, Hunfrido filio
Goismeri, Alveredo de Bennewilla, Adam fil' Uuarini, Albericus [*sic*] de Capell'; pepigitque sibi dominus Ricardus coram
idem [*sic*] testibus quod numquam amplius intraret Salomon in
placitum contra aliquem pro hac eadem terra. Dedit idem
Ricardus deo et sancto Johanni de Clara ecclesiam de Denham
cum omnibus que ad eam pertinent. T. Robertus capellanus,
Adam filius Warini, Galfridus filius Elinandi, Albertus Franci-
gena, Willelmus de Bascetvilla. Dedit eciam idem Ricardus
eidem sancto Johanni de Clara unoquoque anno unum [*sic*]
dammam in parco de Hunedena. T. Adam filius Uuarini,
Robertus de Wanceio, Rogerus de Carlevilla, Godefridus filius
Elinandi, Robertus filius Gaufridi. Precepit idem Ricardus
omnibus baronibus suis et hominibus quatinus monachis suis de
Clara de decimis suis facere permitterent quicquid ipsi monachi
vellent et eas ad hostia grangiarum colligerent, quod preceptum
constituit ipse inperpetuum servari et nullus unquam temeritate quassari. Concessit iterum ipse Ricardus predictis monachis
ut cum prebente [*sic*] ecclesie sancti Johannis deliberare forent,
ipsi eas sicut suas statim saississent neque inde alium saisiatorem
requirerent. Hee sunt donaciones que date sunt predictorum
dominorum temporibus ipsis eisdem testimonium istis rebus

adhibentibus et suo testimonio eas confirmantibus:—Alestanus presbiter de Huneden' et filius ejus Eduuardus dederunt ecclesiam sancti Petri de Hunedena sancte Marie Becci sanctoque Johanni de Clara et omnia que ad ipsam ecclesiam pertinent, totam scilicet terram quam habebat in Hunedena et omnes decimas ad eandem ecclesiam pertinentes. T. Robertus Psalterium, Arnulfus de Bria, Elinandus vicecomes, Girulfus capellanus. Robertus Psalterium dedit sancto Johanni de Clara xv acras terre apud ipsam Hunedenam. Testis Elinandus vicecomes. Ricardus de Reda dedit sancto Johanni de Clara xxx acras terre in ipsa villa. T. Ansuuidus presbiter et Robertus de Neiela. Robertus de Neiela dedit decimam suam de Denardestune et illam de Stanesfelda de omnibus de quibus /[f.67a] decima dari debet. T. Ansuuinus [sic] sacerdos, Ricardus de Reda. Hunfridus cognominato Burnardus postea monachis [sic] sancte Marie Becci dedit sancto Johanni de Clara terram quam tenebat apud Geldham de feudo domini Gilberti de Clara. T. Willelmus filius ejus cognominato Paganus, Willelmus Hurandus, Walterus de Poselingeuuorda, Norioldus de eadem villa, Herveus, Robertus, Benedictus, Radulfus filius Hurandi, Osbernus, Ricerius. Rogerus carpentarius dedit sancto Johanni de Clara decimam de terra sua de Stok' omnium rerum de quibus decima debet dari. T. Ansehetillo, Alurico, Osberto de Gellam, Gilberto coco. Rogerus de Carlewille dedit sancto Johanni de Clara decimam de Aluredesfelda et de Hertsterste, duas scilicet partes omnium rerum de quibus decima debet dari. Testantibus atque concedentibus uxore sua et filio suo Galfrido et Radulfo de la Cressunere, Elrico presbitero, Baldeuuino, Watemanno, Hugone, Ricardo, Gilberto, Wlmero, Anschitillo, Aluuino de Totinges, Benedicto de Beluaco. Ingerannus Dabernun dedit sancto Johanni de Clara ecclesiam de Frinsentune cum omnibus que ad eam pertinent et totam decimam suam de Berue et decimam de Labysse et ecclesiam de Wochinges cum omnibus que ad eam pertinent. Testantibus atque concedentibus fratribus suis Jordano atque Waltero et Willelmo Dabernun cognato eorum et Baldewino presbitero. Herlewinus filius Goismeri dedit sancto Johanni de Clara omni anno x solidos de terra Uulurici Smucle apud Finstede perpetuo possidendos pro anima filii sui Gilberti concedente domino nostro [*sic*] Gilberto et filio ejus Ricardo. T. Ricardus filius Hermeri, Radulfus de la Cressunere, Willelmus de Uuatevilla, Gunzel' filius Goismeri, Hunfridus frater ejus, Radulfus filius Hurandi, Ricardus filius Algeri, Elinandus vicecomes, Robertus de Sethune, Robertus filius Hugonis. Radulfus de la Cresunere dedit sancto Johanni de Clara decimam suam de Havechedune et decimam de Chemesinge de omnibus de quibus decima debet dari. T. Gilbertus et Gaufridus filii ejus, Rogerus de Carleville, Willelmus famulus, Gilbertus cocus, Wlmerus. Canevaz dedit sancto Johanni de Clara decimam suam de Herningewelle et hospitem unum quem habebat in Clara. T. Ricardus, Walterus Dabernun, Osbernus de Gellam, Heldeuuinus, Gilbertus cocus, Wlmerus Allehalegen, Ailwinus Catus. Willelmus de sancto Germano et Emma mater ejus dederunt sancto Johanni /[f.67b] de Clara totam decimam suam de Cavenedis et illam de Saiham et illam de Beneclee et illam de Nailingeherst de omnibus de quibus debet decima dari pro animabus suis et pro anima domini sui Rogeri sicut Walterus de sancto Germano frater Rogeri eas unquam melius habuerat. T. Albericus de Ver, Robertus de la Cresunere, Elinandus vicecomes, Ansfredus, Gilbertus cocus, Wlmerus, Willelmus, Azo, Terri, Moberd. Ricardus filius Hugonis dedit sancto Johanni de Clara decimas suas de Denham et de Culinges et de Meleford de omnibus de quibus debet decima dari et totam terram suam de Brochole concedente domino nostro [*sic*] Gilberto et uxore ejus Adel'. T. Elinandus vicecomes, Wlmarus et frater ejus Gilbertus cocus, Willelmus Israel et Elieth. Postea vero idem Ricardus quando suscepit habitum monachi, iterum concessit et confirmavit totum quod antea dederat et totam terram illam quam antea dederat, liberam et quietam, concedentibus filiis suis et uxore sua, quorum hec sunt nomina, Hugo et Bartholomeus et Gaufridus filii ejus et Matildis. T. Alvinus de Gulinges et Adelardus gener ejus, Gosleus et Robertus fratris [*sic*] ejusdem uxoris Ricardi, Hugo, Alem, Manasses filius Burnench', de hominibus monachorum Rogerus clericus et Osebernus et Herbertus. Galfridus filius Hamonis et Ansgotus de Bucheshale dederunt deo et sancto Johanni de Clara duas partes tocius decime terre quam tenebat idem Ansgotus de eodem Gaufrido domino apud Bucheshale, ita quod in die nativitatis sancti Johannis ambo venerunt et ante videntibus multis per candelabrum posuerunt. Inde testes multi Sauuinus canonicus et Leuuinus prepositus et Gilbertus cocus et Wlmarus pistor frater ejus. Walterus de Aluredesvilla cum uxore sua et filiis suis concesserunt deo et sancto Johanni de Clara quicquid habebant in alveo fluminis molendini de Waldingefelde et in ripa ejusdem fluminis, et ita ut si aliquo eventui fregerit ripa in toto feudo suo sine causacione et eciam licencia restaurabitur ab his qui tenebunt molendinum de monachis Clare et quicquid in ibi calumpniabant ante totum quietum dimiserunt. T. Robertus de Carlevilla, Norman et alii plures. Wluuina moriens dedit deo et sancto Johanni de Clara unam acram terre apud Stok'. T. Wluuinus presbiter. Alexander miles dedit deo et sancto Johanni de Clara tres acras terre ex altera parte molendini monachorum juxta viam. T. Robertus de Blavinn' et alii. Godefridus filius Elinandi et uxor ejus reddiderunt deo /[f.68a] et sancto Johanni decimam de Bucheshale quod concesserunt et confirmaverunt filii sui. T. Gervasius et Rogerus capellanus ejus. Idem vero Godefridus moriens dedit redditum xii denariorum apud Stok' de quodam rustico nomine Uhtred. T. Hunfridus filius Goismeri, Albericus de Capell'. Godefridus filius Elinandi concessit sancto Johanni de Clara molendinum de Walsingefeld et acram et dimidiam terre quam pater suus Elinandus dederat pro Adam filio suo. T. Willelmus frater ejus, Mauricius de Brochole. Elinandus vicecomes dedit sancto Johanni de Clara totam decimam suam de Finchingefeld et illam de Forneham et quoddam molendinum apud Waldingefelde et acram et dimidiam terre pertinentem ad molendinum et x acras apud Fornham concedentibus filiis suis Bernardo et Willelmo. T. Gilbertus filius Ran', Teodericus presbiter. Ernaldus de Nazanda dedit deo et sancto Johanni de Clara duas partes decime de Hamestede rerum quarum decima debet dari et unum hospitem Clare concedentibus uxore sua et filiis. T. Adam filius Warini, Rogerus de Carleville. Willelmus claviger dedit sancto Johanni de Clara decimam de terris quas habet et adquirere poterit. T. Hutredus cementarius, Gilbertus cocus. Ricardus de Halstede dedit sancto

Johanni de Clara duas partes decime tocius terre quam habebat
in Halstede. T. Willelmus filius Goismeri, Algerius frater ejus.
Algerius filius Goismeri dedit sancto Johanni de Clara decimam
terre sue de Bellocampo. T. et concedentibus Ricardo filio ejus
et Willelmo fratre ejus. Siuuardus venator dedit sancto Johanni
de Clara decimam suam et tres acras terre concedente filio suo
et fratribus ejus. Herveus Dabelgar et uxor ejus dederunt sancto
Johanni de Clara unam acram prati et duas acras terre arabiles.
T. Walterus cum barba, Sigarus. Godricus Grance dedit sancto
Johanni de Clara tres rodas terre. T. Sigarus, Ailmerus. Wilde-
lardus de Bailol et Ida uxor ejus dederunt sancto Johanni in
villa de Stok' viii acras terre et i de prato pro quo dono habuerunt xx solidos. T. Gaufridus nepos Oilardi, Salio presbiter.
Willelmus Peccatum dedit sancto Johanni de Clara totam decimam de Gestingethrorp perpetuo de omnibus unde decima
debet dari. T. Hunfredus filius Goismeri, Robertus de Uuan-
ceio et alii multi. Robertus filius Ricardi dedit deo et sancto
Johanni et monachis de Clara totam partem suam aque de
Sturemere pro anima sua et omnium antecessorum suorum et
pro amore Gi-/[f.68b]rardi Giphardi prioris cognati sui inperpetuum possidendam. T. Willelmus Capra, Matheus constabu-
lator, Robertus filius Walteri, Sigarus, Willelmus Cusin, Mabun.
Hugo de Berneres et uxor sua dederunt sancto Johanni baptiste
de Clara quoddam pratum quod est situm juxta Witechesho.
T. Willelmus filius Goismeri, Rogerus filius Walteri. Gaufridus
de Blavineio miles Rogerii filii Ricardi veniens ad conversionem
monachatus dedit deo et sancto Johanni de Clara duodecim
acras terre apud Bridebroc eodem domino suo Rogero et uxore
ejusdem Gaufridi et Roberto filio ejus et ceteris filiis concedentibus. Predictus eciam Robertus filius et heres ejus addidit predicte donacioni post mortem patris sui sex acras terre arabiles et
duas et dimidiam prati. T. Gaufridus filius Elinandi, Robertus
pincerna. Ricardus filius Gilberti dominus Clare dedit sancto
Johanni et monachis de Clara ecclesiam de Caveham cum
omnibus ad eam pertinentibus pro ecclesia de Denham que erat
monachorum quam dedit Alberico de Ver concedentibus
monachis eidem ecclesie de Denham medietatem decime. T.
Gaufridus filius Elinandi, Adam filius Wazonis, Alveredus de

Benn[evilla]. Ricardus filius Gilberti dedit monachis Clare ecclesiam sancti Augustini de Stok' et totam terram quam Martinus capellanus habebat in eadem villa et illam que fuit Rogerii carpentarii solutam et quietam a geldo et scoto et omnibus consuetudinibus et molendinum suum quod ipse dominus habebat in eadem villa dedit in escambium ecclesie sancti Pauli et terrarum et pratorum que monachi habebant in Clara et molendini eorum de Clara et mansurarum xii quas habebant in Clara. Hac siquidem convencione factum est istud escambium, quod monachi constituerent apud Stok' ecclesiam sancti Johannis baptiste ad habitandum in ea cum omnibus privilegiis et auctoritatibus et libertatibus et redditibus quos habuerat ecclesia sancti Johannis sita in castello Clare. Geldum autem et omnes consuetudines que jacebant super Lintune Rohais et super terram que fuit Rogerii carpentarii dabunt de dominica cultura domini. T. Baldevinus filius Gilberti, Albericus de Ver, Baldevinus filius Gaufridi. Gilbertus dominus Clare comes Hertford' filius predicti Ricardi dedit sancto Johanni de Stok' ecclesiam de Bures cum omnibus ad eam pertinentibus jure perpetuo possidendam. T. comes Albericus et Willelmus frater ejus, Gaufridus filius Elinandi, Adam filius Warini. Robertus pincerna concedentibus Matil' uxore sua et filiis suis dedit mo-/[f.69a]nachis de Stok' ecclesiam de Trillawa cum omnibus que ad eam pertinent et insuper in predicta villa dedit terram que reddebat quinque solidos. T. Johannes presbiter, Willelmus de Landa.

The charter as it stands seems to be incomplete.

DATE: 1150–61.

PRINTED: *Monasticon*, vi, 1660.

257

Mandate of Theobald to the rural deans of Gestingthorpe, Hedingham (Essex) and Denham (Suffolk) to compel defaulters to pay their tithes to the priory of Stoke-by-Clare.

MS. B.M. Cott. Appendix xxi f.61a (Register of Stoke-by-Clare).

Nullius utilitatis.

[T]HEOBALDUS dei gratia Cantuariensis archiepiscopus et tocius Anglie primas Eadmundo decano de Gestingetorp et W[altero] decano de Haingeham et R. decano de Deneham salutem. Mandamus vobis et precipimus ut de quibuscumque clamorem prioris et monachorum de Clara audieritis pro decimis suis quas non recte vel more ecclesiastico dare volunt vel quod pejus est detinent, talem eis justiciam ecclesiasticam faciatis ut ipsi corrigantur et ceteri timorem habebant [*sic*] et ne opus sit ut pigricia vestra nos manum apponere oporteat quia et vobis non expedit. Valete.

DATE: 1139–61.

For Walter the dean of Hedingham and his chapter see *Cartulary of Colne Priory*, ed. J. L. Fisher, p. 14 (Essex Arch. Soc., 1946), date 1152–62.

258

Mandate of Theobald to Richard de Belmeis archdeacon (of Middlesex 1138–52). The monks of Stoke-by-Clare have complained that their tithes from Pentlow, Toppesfield and Halstead (Essex) have been withheld and that they have been unjustly involved in litigation over the church of Ash (Suffolk). The archdeacon is to restore the monks in all cases but to reserve the question of right to the archbishop.

MS. B.M. Cott. Appendix xxi f.62a (Register of Stoke-by-Clare).

Litere misse archidiacono pro monachis de Stok' ne super decimis inquietentur.

T. DEI gratia Cantuariensis archiepiscopus et tocius Anglie primas Ricardo de Belmers archidiacono salutem. Conquesti sunt nobis proprii filii et fratres nostri monachi de Stok' quod in archidiaconatu tuo quedam decime sibi injuste detinentur, videlicet de Pentelau de Toppesfield de Halstede et quod de ecclesia de Esse injuste ducuntur in causa, quamquam ea omnia ut asserunt xl annis inconcusse usque ad hec tua tempora possederunt. De quibus omnibus jam tibi alia vice scripsimus miramurque plurimum quod nec prece nostra nec precepto aliquod juris sui a te emolumentum obtinere potuerunt. Quia qui se in hiis nimium gravari et injuste asserunt et jure suo quadragenaria injuste destitui precipientes tibi per presencia scripta precipimus ut eos in hiis nullatenus gravari paciaris, set si eos tandiu investitas [sic] predictis decimis et ecclesia constiterit omnino rem vestiri et in pace tenere precipias usque ad redditum nostrum. Tunc vero si quis super hiis adversus eos agere voluit nostre presencie assistat et deo favente /[f.62b] sibi justicia non deerit. Valete.

DATE: 1139–52.

259

Confirmation by Theobald notified to Walter (?1155–?68) abbot of Tavistock (Ben., Devon) of the church of Milton (Abbot) (Devon) appropriated to the sacristy and almonry in accordance with the charter of Bishop Robert (Warelwast) of Exeter (1155–60).

MS. Woburn Abbey, Duke of Bedford Cartulary of Tavistock f.10a. (not checked with MS.).

Confirmatio Theobaldi Cantuariensis archiepiscopi de ecclesia de Middelton'.

THEOBALDUS dei gratia Cantuariensis archiepiscopus Anglorum primas et apostolice sedis legatus Waltero abbati et conventui Tavistoch' salutem. Que a venerabilibus fratribus nostris episcopis rationabiliter circa statum ecclesie fieri novimus, merito ea rata habere debemus et auctoritate nostra corroborare. Ea igitur ratione ecclesiam de Middeltune cum omnibus /[f.10b] pertinentiis suis sacristarie de Tavistoch' et elemosinarie auctoritate qua fungimur confirmamus sicut venerabilis frater noster Robertus Exoniensis episcopus eis ecclesiam illam confirmavit et carta sua communivit et nos presentis scripti pagina communimus. Valete.

DATE: 1155–61.

PRINTED: H. P. R. Finberg, *E.H.R.* (1947), p. 358. (Description of MS. p. 353.)

260

Mandate of Theobald to Walter, abbot of Tavistock to recover lands alienated to laymen by his predecessor (Robert Postel ?1147–?55) and to declare void all charters in a contrary sense in accordance with the writ of Henry II.

MS. Woburn Abbey, Duke of Bedford Cartulary of Tavistock f.14b (not checked with MS.).

Confirmatio Theobaldi Cantuariensis archiepiscopi.

THEOBALDUS dei gratia Cantuariensis archiepiscopus Anglorum primas et apostolice sedis legatus dilecto filio Waltero abbati Tavist' salutem. Tue ut credimus discretioni satis innotuit possessiones in sustentationem pauperum Christi domibus ac locis religiosis collatas minime debere distrahi aut preter assensum et coniventiam fratrum loci quibus conferuntur in usus laicorum transferri. Quod si a quoquo illorum qui domibus custodiendis ac negociis ecclesiarum gerendis preficiuntur aliter actum esse constaverit, ad ejus poterit dejectionem sufficere, nisi quod presumptum est ab eo cum festinatione studuerit revocare. A predecessore quidem tuo quasdam terras inconsulto conventu cui prefuit distractas esse, alias laicis datas esse /[f.15a] et cartis confirmatas audivimus . . . . opera quedam esse remissa . . . . obediencie precipientes quatinus ea que distracta vel minus consulte data et alienata sunt per predecessorem tuum contra assensum conventus satagas studiosius revocare et cartas surrepticias super illicitis donationibus impetratas evacuare et infirmare cures, ne occasione cartarum hujusmodi regium mandatum de revocandis dispersis tibi destinatum pretermittas. Valete.

DATE: 1155–61.
PRINTED: H. P. R. Finberg, *E.H.R.* (1947), p. 359.

261

Grant by Theobald of an indulgence of twenty days to those visiting the church of St. Mary (Old Temple, Holborn) on the anniversary of its dedication at Whitsun.

MS. B.M. Cott. Nero E vi f.24a (Templar Cartulary).

De viginti diebus indulgencie concesse in festo dedicacionis dicte ecclesie.

T. DEI gratia Cantuariensis archiepiscopus Anglorum primas et
apostolice sedis legatus universis sancte ecclesie fidelibus salutem. Ad pastoris spectat solicitudinem omnibus maxime religionis cultum professis in sua providere necessitate. Proinde
universitati vestre pro religiosis fratribus militibus de Templo
preces porrigimus et in domino obsecramus quatinus ecclesiam
eorum que dicitur dominicum Templum extra London' in
honore beate Marie dedicatum in ebdomada pentecostes singulis annis cum devocione visitetis et elemosinas vestras eidem
loco pro dei amore et in remissionem peccatorum vestrorum
inpendatis. Quicumque ergo singulis annis predicto tempore
ecclesiam illam devote visitaverint eis viginti dies de penitencia
sibi injuncta relaxamus et oracionum et beneficiorum Cantuariensis ecclesie participium concedimus. Valete.

DATE: 1150–61.

PRINTED: B. A. Lees, *Records of the Templars in England in the 12th Century,*
p. 162.

262

Confirmation by Theobald of the grant of the church of Sompting
(Sussex) to the Templars as confirmed by bishop Hilary of Chichester
(1147–69) and of the manor of Bisham (Berks.) granted to them by
Robert earl of Derby (1139–?60) in accordance with the charter of
Bishop Jocelin of Salisbury (1142–84).

MS. B.M. Cott. Nero E vi f.155a (Templar Cartulary).

Confirmacio Cantuariensis archiepiscopi de eadem
ecclesia (i.e. de Suntynges) et manerio de Bustelesham.

THEOBALDUS dei gratia Cantuariensis archiepiscopus Angl'
primas apostolice sedis legatus universis sancte ecclesie fidelibus
salutem. Ea que pietatis intuitu in religiosas personas canonice
collata esse noscuntur bona, nostrum est teneri et stabilire. Inde
est quod religiosis militibus Templi qui fidei inimicis pro

orientalis ecclesie defencione nituntur obsistere ecclesiam de
Suntynges cum omnibus appediciis [*sic*] quam venerabilis frater
noster Hillarius Cicestrensis episcopus ejus [*sic*] carta sua confirmavit et manerium de Bustelesham quod ex donacione comitis
de Ferrariis adepti sunt /[f.155b] juxta tenorem carte venerabilis
fratris nostri Jocelini Sar' episcopi confirmamus et auctoritate
qua fungimur eis imperpetuum sicut carte predictorum coepiscoporum nostrorum testantur corroboravimus. Quicumque
ergo contra hanc nostram confirmacionem ausu temerario
venire et eos super hujus [*sic*] inquietare vel vexare presumpserit, nisi cito resipuerit et dampna cum integritate resarcierit,
indignationem omnipotentis dei et nostra[m] malediccione[m]
in extremo examine se noverit incursurum. Valete.

DATE: 1150–61.

PRINTED: B. A. Lees, *Records of the Templars in England in the 12th Century*,
p. 236.

263

Notification by Theobald to bishop Hilary of Chichester of the
settlement in his presence of the dispute between the Templars represented by (their provincial Master) Richard of Hastings and Pain clerk
of Findon (Sussex) over the chapel of Sompting. Pain has resigned his
rights over the chapel in return for an annual payment of 20*s*.

MS. B.M. Cott. Nero E vi f.156b (Templar Cartulary).

Confirmacio composicionis inter Templarios etc. de
capellaria de Sumptinges.

T. DEI gratia Cantuariensis archiepiscopus Angl' primas et
apostolice sedis legatus venerabili et dilecto fratri H[ilario]
Cicestr' episcopo et omnibus fidelibus per episcopatum Cices-
trensem constitutis salutem. Universitati vestre notum fieri
volumus qualiter in nostra presencia super controversia que diu
agitata est inter religiosos milites fratres Templi et Paganum
clericum de Findona super capellaria de Suntynges transactum
sit. Paganus juri capellarie quod sibi competere dicebat renunciavit et capellariam cum possessionibus et omnibus ad eam
pertinentibus in manu nostra omnino refutavit. Fratres vero de

Templo ei annuatim in festo sancti Michaelis xx solidos se daturos pepigerunt et in manu nostra per R[icardum] de Hastynges qui tunc temporis rerum suarum in terra ista curam gerebat, id se facturos posuerunt quoad usque Paganus predictus in habitu seculari viveret. Pensionis autem pretaxate solucio in ecclesia de Suntynges a fratribus Templi celebrabitur. Hanc vero transaccionem ut imposterum inconvulsa permaneat auctoritate qua fungimur corroboravimus precipientes ne quis eam temere infringere presumat. Si vero milites predicti ab hac transaccione resilire voluerint, per ecclesiam suam de Suntynges composicioni stare compellentur. Hii autem testes sunt: Paris archidiaconus Roffensis, magistri—Vacarius, Johannes Sar', Rogerus Species, Willelmus de Norhall', Osbertus de Prestona, Eudo Manefer', clerici archiepiscopi; Nicholaus Atilleburia, Fabianus de London' et multi alii.

DATE: 1150–61.

PRINTED: B. A. Lees, *Records of the Templars in England in the 12th Century*, p. 237.

264

Confirmation by Theobald notified to Robert (Chichester), bishop of Exeter (1138–55) of the bishop's confirmation of the grant by Roger de Nunant to Totnes Priory (Devon, dep. on Ben. Abbey of Angers) of the churches of Brixham and Clyst (Devon) with their chapels.

Original MS. W. G. Hole's collection, Totnes Priory Deeds xvii.

T. DEI gratia Cantuarie archiepiscopus et tocius Anglie primas venerabili fratri et amico R[oberto] Exoniensi episcopo salutem. Noverit dilecta fraternitas vestra quoniam ecclesias de Brixeham et de Clist Rogerii de Nunant cum capellis et omnibus rebus ad eas pertinentibus quas monachis sancti Sergii Andegavis in ecclesia sancte Marie de Toteneis deo ministrantibus concessistis et carta vestra confirmastis, illis concedimus et confirmamus et auctoritate literarum nostrarum vestram confirmationem corroboramus et ratam habemus. Precipientes ut in perpetua pace et quiete teneant ne quis eis sub anathemate molestiam aut injuriam aut possessionum earundem diminutionem irrogare presumat.

SEAL: usual.

SIZE: 6·5 in. × 7 in.

DATE: *c.* 1149. Confirms charter of Bishop Robert of 1149.

FACSIMILE and TRANSLATION: H. R. Watkin, *History of Totnes*, ii, plate vii, and i, 52.

COPY: Inspeximus by Wm. de Beaumont, bishop of Angers (1224–39), translation ibid.; i, 136 (Totnes Priory Deeds lxxv).

265

Mandate of Theobald to Bishops Robert II of Lincoln (1148–66), Walter of Coventry (1149–59), Jocelin of Salisbury (1142–84), John of Worcester (1151–57) and their archdeacons to compel defaulters to pay their tithes to Tutbury (Ben. Priory, Staffs.).

MS. College of Arms, Arundel 59 f.19a (Cartulary of Tutbury).

Carta T. archiepiscopi contra detentores decimarum.

T. DEI gratia Cantuariensis archiepiscopus Anglorum primas apostolice sedis legatus venerabilibus fratribus et amicis R[oberto] Lincolniensi W[altero] Coventrensi Jocelino Saresberiensi Johanni Wigornensi episcopis et eorum archidiaconis salutem. Circa utilitates ecclesiarum que nostre sollicitudini sunt comisse, nos ita oportet esse sollicitos ut que justis modis possident ejus [*sic*] immutilata conserventur. Quo circa per presencia scripta vobis mandamus quatinus si dilecti filii nostri videlicet monachi de Tuttesbur' a quibuscumque et ubicumque terre ille sint culte et per testes sane opinionis et per cartas suas monstraverint decimaciones ex illis terris sibi esse solvendas, eas decimas eis cum integritate reddi faciatis. Quod si aliquis ausu temerario post eorum probacionem illas retinere vel eos super hiis vexare presumpserit, ecclesiastica ulcione eum compellatis ut quod sui juris esse constiterit eis solvere celeritate adhibita non contempnat. De terris quoque baronum decimaciones, si predictis modis ostenderint sibi esse solvendas nichilominus eis reddi faciatis. Nolumus enim predictos fratres

2K

aliquibus possessionibus vel bonis injuste defraudari que eis in ele-/[f.19b]mosinam perpetuam canonice noscuntur esse concessa. Valete.

DATE: 1151–57.
COPY: in an 18th-century transcript MS. B.M. Addl. 6714, p. 3.

266

Grant by Theobald of fifteen days' indulgence to those visiting Walden (Ben. Priory, Essex) on the anniversary of St. James (25 July) and contributing to St. James' church being built there.

MS. B.M. Harleian 3697 f.42a (Register of Walden).

Carta Theobaldi Cantuariensis archiepiscopi de relaxacione penitencie.

THEOBALDUS dei gracia Cantuariensis archiepiscopus tocius Anglie primas apostolice sedis legatus omnibus sancte ecclesie fidelibus salutem. Ad nostrum spectat officium vos comovere, quoniam non est aliquis vestrum sicut de vobis confidimus qui se ad bonum opus non gaudeat incitari, ut in precipuis festivitatibus ecclesias vestras votis et muneribus honoretis et in illis deum attencius studeatis venerari. Nos ergo ob reverenciam beati Jacobi apostoli vobis omnibus qui ad ecclesiam ejus que apud Waledenam edificanda est in ipsius festivitate corde contrito conveneritis et oracionibus vestris et aliqua porcione substancie vobis a deo collate illud opus beati apostoli edificandum adjuveritis in dei misericordia confidentes de penitencia vobis injuncta quindecim dies relaxamus et oracionum et beneficiorum Cantuariensis ecclesie participes vos esse concedimus. Valete.

DATE: 1150–61.

267

Notification by Theobald (probably) of a settlement in his court of the dispute between the monks of Stoke-by-Clare (Suff.) and Warin the priest over two-thirds of the tithes of the demesne of Walsingham (Norf.). Warin has abandoned his claims. The prior of Walsingham

(Aug.) holds the aforesaid tithes from the monks paying them 20*s.* annually.

MS. B.M. Cott. Nero E vii f.12b (Cartulary of Walsingham).

Carta Thome archiepiscopi Cantuariensis de xx solidis de Stokes.

T. DEI gratia Cantuariensis archiepiscopus et tocius Anglie primas omnibus sancte matris ecclesie fidelibus ad quos presentes littere pervenerint salutem. Provide litteris commendantur que firmam futuris temporibus sunt habitura memoriam ne adversus veritatem malignancium calliditas quandoque possit prevalere. Sciant itaque tam presentes quam futuri quod controversia que inter priorem et monachos de Stokes et Warinum presbiterum super duabus partibus decimarum dominii de Walsingham vertebatur hoc modo in curia nostra terminata est. Predictus itaque Warinus dum causa nobis coram actitaretur, exploratis juribus partis sui postquam juramentum de calumpnia prestiterat, liti et controversie renunciavit et decimam de qua litigium vertebatur, videlicet duas porciones prefate decimacionis de dominio jam dicti fundi monachis cessit et tactis sacrosanctis evangeliis juravit quod nec per propriam personam nec per alios jam dictum priorem aut monachos de Stokes diucius vexabit. Set prior de Walsingham qui decimam predictam nomine monachorum possidet et xx solidos annuatim illis de prefatis decimacionibus solvere debet, quo presente et concedente ista composicio facta fuit, decimam in integrum percipere debet de rebus omnibus terris et pascuis et aliis quecumque ad dominium de Walsingham pertinebant die quo rex Henricus primus decessit, et ita omnia controversia que inter jam dictum priorem de Stokes et monachos suos et Warinum presbiterum super prescriptis decimis extiterat sopita est. Valete.

DATE: 1154–61 or 1162–70.

268

Notification by Theobald and Walter Prior of Canterbury Cathedral (1143–49) that they have granted the manor of Walworth (Kent) to Gervase de Cornhill for life at an annual rent of £6. After his death

his son (Henry) may hold the manor for life at an annual rent of
£6 10s. If not the manor is to return to the monks.

Original MS. P.R.O. Duchy of Lancaster Ancient Deeds LS 48
(DL 27/48).

T. DEI gratia Cantuariensis archiepiscopus et Walterius prior
totusque conventus ecclesie Christi Cantuarie omnibus fidelibus
salutem. Scire volumus universitatem vestram nos concessisse
Gervasio de Cornhulle tenere de nobis omni vita sua manerium
de Walewrthe pro vi libris per annum. Quod si, eo defucto
[*sic*], filius ejus voluerit ipsum manerium tenere, super hunc
numerum x solidos addat et sine feudo et hereditate quam diu
vixerit teneat. Si autem ipsos x solidos ad vi libras addere
noluerit, ipsum manerium quiete et libere in dominio monachorum remanebit cum omni instauramento quod idem
G[ervasius] ibidem faciet. Valete.

ENDORSEMENT: Carta de Waleworth' facta Henrico de Cornhull'.

SEAL: First seal of Christ Church on strip on left side; strip cut out at the
bottom.

SIZE: 2·9 in. × 8·1 in.

DATE: 1144–49.

269

Confirmation by Theobald of the endowment of Warwick College
(Collegiate church of St. Mary Warwick) as completed by Roger
earl of Warwick (1123–53).

MS. P.R.O. Exchequer K.R. Miscellaneous Books 22 f.15a (E
164/22). (Cartulary of Warwick College).

Scriptum confirmacionis sancti Thome martiris
[*Theobaldi* written above in a later hand] Cantuariensis archiepiscopi super libertatibus et possessionibus
concessis et datis per Rogerum comitem ecclesie beate
Marie Warr'.

T. DEI gracia Cantuariensis archiepiscopus episcopis abbatibus
archidiaconis necnon Ro[gero] comiti de Warewic' et baronibus
suis et universis fidelibus sancte matris ecclesie in domino salutem. Sciat karissimi dileccio vestra nos firmiter concessisse et

archiepiscopali auctoritate confirmasse donum libertatis quam prefatus Rogerus comes Warewic ecclesie sancte Marie apud Warrewic et clericis ejusdem ecclesie pro anima patris sui et antecessorum suorum et sua, dedit et concessit scilicet ut canonico more et concessa sibi libertate deo et sancte Marie serviant ibi sicut melius et liberius idem comes Rogerus concessit et sicut carta donacionis ejus testatur. Monemus igitur, et archiepiscopaliter canonicis omnibus precipimus, ut secundum libertatem istam digne et canonice /[f.15b] serviant ibi et sub anathemate prohibemus nequis donacionem libertatis hujus diabolico instinctu violare presumat. Omnibus autem libertatem istam conservantibus et sicut premonuimus in eadem ecclesia canonice et digne deo et sancte Marie servientibus benediccionem dei concedimus et nostram. Valete.

DATE: 1139–50 probably early.

270

Mandate of Theobald to William Cumin archdeacon of Worcester. The archbishop has inspected the charter of Bishop Simon of Worcester (1125–50) who consecrated a cemetery for the use of the Aug. canons of St. Sepulchre (Warwick) only, the mother churches of All Saints and St. Mary to suffer no loss thereby. But Ralph, Prior of St. Sepulchre has usurped the parishioners and parochial rights of the mother churches. The archdeacon is to restore the rights usurped by Ralph and the contumacious parishioners.

MS. P.R.O. Exch. K.R. Misc. Books 22 f.16b (E 164/22) (Cartulary of Warwick College).

> Littera sancti Thome martiris Cantuariensis archiepiscopi directa archidiacono Wigorn' ad restituenda jura parochialia subtracta per priorem Sancti Sepulcri.

T. DEI gracia Cantuariensis archiepiscopus Angl' primas et apostolice sedis legatus dilecto filio W[illelmo] Cumin Wigorn' archidiacono salutem. Inspeximus cartam bone memorie Simonis Wig' episcopi qui sicut ipsa ejus carta testatur, altare in ecclesia Sancti Sepulcri consecravit et cimiterium ad sepeliendos ibi tantummodo regulares canonicos, et canonicum habitum habentes, ea condicione benedixit, ut mater ecclesia Omnium Sanctorum et eciam ecclesia sancte Marie de Warwic' neque in decimis neque in sepulturis neque in oblacionibus neque in confessionibus neque in visitacionibus infirmorum neque in aliquibus consuetudinariis beneficiis ad predictas matres ecclesias pertinentibus detrimentum aliquod sentirent vel diminucionem. Omnem quoque hujus convencionis violatorem anathema denuciavit. Contra quam cartam audivimus Radulfum priorem Sancti Sepulcri inpudenter venisse et parochianos et omnia alia parochialia jura sibi et ecclesie Sancte Sepulcure usurpasse. Quod si ita est, per presencia tibi precipimus scripta quatinus juxta formam carte predicti episcopi parochianos et decimas et cetera parochialia beneficia matricibus ecclesiis prenominatis assignes et in debitum statum juxta episcopale statutum reformes, et parochianos qui se et beneficia sua contra statutum sepedicti episcopi subtraxerunt et propria auctoritate contra jus ecclesiasticum et episcopale mandatum ad aliam quam ad matricem ecclesiam suam se transtulerunt, in eandem quam predictus episcopus formavit nisi resipuerint anathematis retrudas sentenciam. Valete.

DATE: 1157 probably during vacancy of see; in response to a papal mandate of November 1156 (Holtzmann, i, 306).

271

Mandate of Theobald to Bishop Simon of Worcester. William priest of Haselor (Warw.) has complained of lay violence trying to detach the chapel of Upton (nr. Alcester, Warw.) from the mother church of Haselor. If this is correct the bishop must restore the chapel to its former subjection.

MS. P.R.O. Exchequer K.R. Misc. Books 22 f.123a (E 164/22) (Cartulary of Warwick College).

Litera sancti Thome martiris Cantuariensis archiepiscopi pro ecclesia de Haselore.

T. DEI gracia Cantuariensis archiepiscopus et tocius Anglie primas venerabili fratri et amico S[imoni] Wig' episcopo salutem. Querimoniam deposuit in auribus nostris Willelmus sacerdos de Haseloura quod quidam laica violencia querit alienare a matre ecclesia de Haseloura capellam de Uptona et rectitudines in preteritis temporibus habitas ei de novo subripere et subjeccionem auferre. Unde per presencia vobis scripta precipiendo mandamus quatinus si ejus querimonia veritate innititur laicum illum quicumque fuerit ecclesiastica severitate coherceatis et matri ecclesie predicte subjeccionem et rectitudinem quam a predicta capella habere in preteritis temporibus consuevit plenissime habere faciatis. Valete.

DATE: 1139-50.

272

Confirmation by Theobald to the canons of Wells of the grant by King Stephen of the churches of North Curry and Petherton (Som.) to make prebends in the church of Wells.

MS. D. and C. Wells Liber Albus I f.11a.

Confirmacio Theobaldi archiepiscopi de dono predicto (i.e. de ecclesiis de Northcuri et de Perretona).

THEOBALDUS[1] dei gratia Cantuariensis archiepiscopus Anglorum primas et apostolice sedis legatus universis sancte ecclesie filiis in domino salutem. Noverit fraternitatis vestre dilectio quod ecclesiam de Northcuri[2] et ecclesiam de Perretona[3] assensu et concessione Stephani regis Angl'[4] ecclesie sancti Andree apostoli de Well' ad faciendum ibi[5] prebendas auctoritate dei et nostra presenti scripto nostro confirmamus. Valeat in domino fraternitas vestra.

ALSO: MS. ibid. Liber Albus II f.26a.
VARIATIONS: [1]T. [2]Northcury. [3]Peretona. [4]Anglie. [5]ibidem.
DATE: 1150-54.

273

Confirmation by Theobald to the canons of Wells of the grant by Bishop Robert of Bath (1136-66) of the land of Huish (Episcopi) (Som.) to be constituted as a perpetual prebend.

MS. D. and C. Wells Liber Albus I f.26b.

Firmatio Th. archiepiscopi.

T. DEI gratia Cantuariensis archiepiscopus et[1] totius Anglie primas omnibus sancte matris ecclesie fidelibus salutem. Que donatione regum vel principum venerabilium ve fratrum nostrorum episcoporum aut illustrium virorum ad aliquam ecclesiam canonice devoluntur, ut [2]in perpetuum[2] firma stabilitate inconvulsa[3] perseverent utique nostre confirmationis firmitate sunt roboranda. Inde est quod donationem venerabilis fratris nostri Roberti[4] Bathoniensis[5] episcopi ratam habentes de terra quadam que vocatur Hywis[6] quam ecclesie beati Andree apostoli de Well'[7] in perpetuum[8] prebendam consilio et assensu cleri sui canonice contulit et carta sua confirmavit eandem terram memorate ecclesie sicut a jam dicto episcopo ecclesie donata est et confirmata per cartam suam confirmamus et auctoritate qua fungimur communimus et presenti scripto et sigilli nostri attestatione corroboramus, sub anathemate prohibentes ne quis contra hanc nostre confirmationis paginam memoratam ecclesiam vel canonicos in ea manentes temere inquietare aut vexare super prescripta terra ullatenus presumat. Valete.

ALSO: MS. ibid. Liber Albus II f.366b.
    Thomas archiepiscopus de Hiwis.

VARIATIONS: [1]*omits.* [2-2]inperpetuum. [3]in commissa. [4]Rodberti. [5]Battoniensis. [6]Hiwis. [7]Wellis. [8]perpetuam.

DATE: 1159–61, as can be seen from accompanying charter of Robert of Bath. (H.M.C., D. and C. of Wells, i, 27).

274

Mandate of Theobald to Bishop Robert of Bath. Seeing that the bishop has maintained the rights of Wells, supported by charters, against Philip de Furnell', he must put his decision into effect and compel the restoration of the goods of Wells. He should tell Bishop Robert of Exeter (Chichester 1138–55 or Warelwast 1155–60) to take similar action.

MS. D. and C. Wells Liber Albus I f.50b.

Littere T. archiepiscopi ad Reginaldum [sic] episcopum.

T. DEI gratia Cantuariensis archiepiscopus Anglorum primas et apostolice sedis legatus venerabili fratri et amico R[oberto] Bathoniensi episcopo salutem. Significatum est nobis quod post plurimarum querimoniarum iteraciones, tadem [sic] productis cartis et munimentis ecclesie et canonicorum de Well' jus et diuturna [sic] eorum possessionem attestantibus, Philippo quoque de Furnell' canonicorum adversario ad multas vocaciones vestras deficiente et se ipsum a causa absentante, ipsis canonicis jus suum ex tenore munimentorum suorum liquido recognitum reddidistis. Quod si ita est per presentia fraternitati vestre scripta precipiendo mandamus quatinus hoc ipsum quod ratione monente fecistis effectui mancipetis et detentatores bonorum predicte ecclesie a tanta temeritate ecclesiastica dictante sententia coerceatis et ut a venerabili fratre nostro R[oberto] Exoniensi episcopo similiter coerceantur ei ex parte tua significetis. Valete.

DATE: 1150–60. The see of Exeter was vacant between 28 March and 5 June 1155.

275

Confirmation by Theobald to Westminster Abbey of King Stephen's quitclaim from geld of the manor of Westminister (6½ hides) and also of 44 hides of the manor of Battersea (Surrey) the remaining 28 hides still to geld, and also one virgate belonging to the church of Hanwell (Middx.) in accordance with the charters of King Stephen which the archbishop has inspected.

Original   MS. B.M. Campbell Charters xvi 1.

TEODBALDUS dei gratia Cantuariensis archiepiscopus Anglorum primas et apostolice sedis legatus universis sanctę ęcclesię fidelibus salutem. Noverit universitas tam presentium quam futurorum quoniam dominus noster rex illustris Stephanus pro dei amore et salute animę suę et predecessorum suorum necnon et pro incolumitate liberorum suorum manerium de West-monasterio in quo regia aula et alię regię domus edificate sunt quietum clamavit inperpetuum de geldatione vi hidarum et dimidię in omnibus rebus que sive ad coronam regis sive ad-ministrorum suorum spectant consuetudinem. Clamavit etiam quietum manerium beati Petri et monachorum ejusdem loci quod dicitur Patricheseia de geldatione xliiii hidarum de omni-bus rebus similiter que dicuntur ad coronam regis sive adminis-trorum ejus consuetudines spectare ut ille xliiii hide ulterius non geldent nec aliquid secularibus potestatibus debeant, set residue xxviii hide ejusdem manerii geldabunt et omnia ad regem perti-nentia persolvent. Preterea clamavit quietam unam virgatam terrę pertinentem ad ęcclesiam de Hanewella de omnibus ad coronam regis pertinentibus sive administros suos. Hujus itaque quietationis sive nove libertatis donationem beato Petro de Westmonasterio et monachis ejusdem loci ab ipso rege perpetuo factam sicut carte ipsius regis quas oculis nostris conspeximus testantur ratam habemus et auctoritate qua preminemus confir-mamus precipientes ut ęcclesia sancti Petri et monachi cum hac libertate teneant et perpetuo possideant, ne quis hanc libertatis donationem infringere vel inquietare vel aliqua temeritate per-turbare presumat. Siquis autem eam infringere vel temere perturbare aliquando attemptaverit anathema sit.

ENDORSED: Confirmacio Theobaldi archiepiscopi Cantuariensis super ii cartis Stephani et de omnibus libertatibus in maneriis de Batriccheseye, Westm' et Hanewell'.

SEAL: none.

SIZE: 6·5 in. × 9·9 in.

DATE: 1150–54.

Also referred to by Professor V. H. Galbraith in *Antiquaries Journal* (1932), p. 278, n. 2.

COPIES: MS. Westminster Abbey Muniments, 'Domesday' f.56b and f.162a.

PRINTED: (with facsimile) G. F. Warner and H. J. Ellis, *Facsimiles of Charters in B.M.* (1903), i, no. 28; also *Monasticon*, i, 309.

276

Notification by Theobald of his decision in the case between William of Ockendon (Essex) and Abbot Gervase of Westminster (?1137–?58) over the advowson of the church of Ockendon. It was awarded to Gervase.

Original MS. Westminster Abbey Muniments LI.

T. DEI gratia Cantuariensis archiepiscopus Anglorum primas et apostolice sedis legatus universis sancte ecclesie filiis salutem. Noverit tam modernorum universitas quam futurorum posteritas quoniam controversia, quam Willelmus de Wochendona super ecclesia de Wochendona adversus monasterium de Westm' et ejusdem loci abbatem Gervasium sepius moverat, hoc modo interveniente assensu nostro et auctoritate finem accepit. Willelmus siquidem prefatus post multas utriusque partis inductas allegationes liti et possessioni ejusdem ecclesie absolute renuntiavit et eandem ecclesiam monasterio de Westmost' perpetuo possidendam concessit ita quod de cetero licebit abbati Gervasio et omnibus successoribus suis predicte ecclesie de Wochendona personas preordinare cui voluerit salva tamen diocesani episcopi dignitate donare. Hanc itaque concessionem ratam habemus, confirmamus et auctoritate qua preminemus perpetuo permanendam decernimus. Valete.

ENDORSEMENT: Controversia de ecclesia de Wokendona terminata. (Later) super patronatu ejusdem ecclesie.

SEAL: none.

SIZE: 4 in. × 7·3 in.

DATE: 1150–58.

COPY: Westminster Abbey Muniments. 'Domesday' f.506a.

277

Mandate of Theobald to Bishop Robert II of Lincoln (1148–66), to compel A. de Condeio, Robert Foliot and John de Stutville to restore the revenues and possessions of Westminster Abbey. John has taken the land of Uppingham (Rutland) and Robert the land of Sulby (Northants.).

MS. Westminster Abbey Muniments 'Domesday' f.649b.

Litera T. archiepiscopi Cantuariensis super censu ad vestitum monachorum pertinente.

T. DEI gratia Cantuariensis archiepiscopus et Anglorum primas venerabili fratri R[oberto] Lincolniensi episcopo salutem. Crebras de A. de Condeio querimonias accipimus maxime a monachis beati Petri Westmonasterii quorum censum ad vestitum eorum pertinentem violenter detinet. Nichilominus de J[ohanne] de Stutehilla et R[oberto] Foliot quorum alter scilicet Johannes terram eorum de Yppingham, R[obertus] manerium de Solebi eis auferunt graviter conqueruntur. Super hiis autem tam eis quam vobis nos scripsisse recordamur. Ideoque per repetita vobis scripta mandamus et precipimus ut severius in eos animadvertatis prout dictaverit canonice rigor censure. Valete.

DATE: 1148–54.

278

Mandate of Theobald to Geoffrey Bataille and Richard de Fracheville to restore the manor of Kelvedon (Essex) to Abbot Gervase and the monks of Westminster Abbey.

MS. Westminster Abbey Muniments 'Domesday' f.650a.

Litera T. archiepiscopi Cantuariensis super terra de Chollintona.

T. DEI gratia Cantuariensis archiepiscopus Anglorum primas apostolice sedis legatus Gaufrido Batailla et Ricardo de Frachevilla salutem. Ex parte G[ervasii] abbatis et monachorum Westmonasterii gravem querimoniam adversus vos accepimus quod violenter et ipsis omnino contradicentibus ingressi estis manerium de Chelindona quod a tempore Edwardi regis predicta ecclesia possedisse dicitur et illud ad usum vestrum et ad eorum dampnum retinetis. Quoniam vero nostre sollicitudinis est ecclesias et earum possessiones in quantum racio exposcit defendere et manutenere per presentia vobis scripta mandamus quatinus predictam terram ipsi ecclesie libere et quiete quantum ad vos pertinet infra xv dies relinquatis, alioquin in vos anathematis sentenciam proferemus et latam per totam Angliam observari faciemus. Valete.

DATE: 1150–58.

PRINTED: (partly) J. A. Robinson, *Gilbert Crispin* (1911), p. 47.

279

Grant by Theobald of forty days' indulgence to those visiting West-minster Abbey on Christmas, Easter, Ascension day, Whitsun and the feast of relics.

MS. Westminster Abbey Muniments 'Domesday' f.390b.

> Indulgencia Theobardi Cantuariensis archiepiscopi de xl diebus injuncte penitencie concessis veneranti-bus ecclesiam Westmonasterii elemosinis suis in festis subscriptis.

TEOBARDUS dei gratia Cantuariensis archiepiscopus Anglorum primas apostolice sedis legatus universis sancte ecclesie fidelibus salutem. Condignum est et deo amabile sicut novit vestra dis-cretio ut illis qui sanctam ecclesiam fideli devocione venerantur et bonis sibi a deo prestitis eam sustentant spiritualia remedia benigne conferamus. Noverit ergo universitas vestra nos pro dei et beate Marie matris ejus et beati Petri apostolorum principis veneracione, omnibus fidelibus qui ecclesiam beati Petri de Westmonasterio in natali domini et in pascha et in domini ascensione et in pentecosten et in festivitate sanctarum reli-quiarum que in illa ecclesia gloriose continentur et in omnibus festivitatibus beati Petri votive adierint et elemosinis suis illam ecclesiam honoraverint, de penitenciis eis injunctis suffragiis Jhesu Christi et beati Petri confisi xl dies relaxamus et orationum et beneficiorum Cantuariensis ecclesie eos participes esse con-cedimus. Amen. Valete.

DATE: 1150–61.

280

Confirmation by Theobald of the possessions of the nuns of Wintney (Cist., Hants.) in accordance with the charter of Bishop Henry of Winchester (1129–71).

MS. P.R.O. Chancery Enrolments Charter Rolls 11 Ed. III m.30 (C 53/124).

One of many charters inspected (18 March 1337).

THEOBALDUS dei gratia Cantuariensis archiepiscopus Anglorum primas apostolice sedis legatus universis sancte ecclesie fidelibus salutem. Ad nostram spectat solicitudinem ecclesiasticis personis et maxime ancillis Christi de Wintineia quas religionis nomen commendat, que eis concessa sunt et in elemosinam perpetuam donata ita confirmare ut decetero ea eis inmutilata conserventur. Nos ergo justis postulacionibus predictarum sanctimonialium inclinati, omnia que inpresentiarum juste et canonice possident aut si quid in futuro justis modis adipisci poterunt juxta tenorem carte venerabilis fratris nostri H[enrici] Wyntoniensis episcopi in elemosinam perpetuam concedimus et presentis scripti munimine confirmamus.Quicumque ergo contra hanc nostram confirmacionem ausu temerario venire presumpserit et ea que eis donata sunt et in carta prefati episcopi confirmata injuste abstulerit, nisi cito resipuerit et eis cum integritate ablata reddiderit, indignacionem omnipotentis dei et nostram maledictionem in extremo examine se noverit incursurum. Amen. Valete.

DATE: 1150–61.
PRINTED: *Calendar of Charter Rolls*, iv, 395.

281

Confirmation by Theobald of the possessions of the nuns of Wix (Ben. Priory, Essex).

Original MS. P.R.O. Exchequer T.R. Ancient Deeds A.S. 356(i) (E 42/356).

TEOB' dei gratia Cantuariensis archiepiscopus Anglorum primas et apostolice sedis legatus universis sancte matris ecclesie fidelibus salutem gratiam et benedictionem. Notum sit universitati vestre nos divine pietatis intuitu sicut nostrum exigit officium confirmasse sanctimonialibus de Wikes dilectis filiabus

nostris omnes donationes et elemosinas que eis in archiepiscopatu nostro a fidelibus date sunt et collate, scilicet de dono
Maurici de Windesor' et Alexandri de Waham insulam de
Siricheseie et omnes decimas de dominio de Purle exceptis
duabus acris et uno agno et uno vellere, et de dono Radulfi de
Lodnes omnes decimas de dominio suo in Prestuna exceptis
duabus acris, et omnes alias possessiones suas ubicumque eis
infuturo pro dei amore collate fuerint, divina vero autoritate
prohibemus nequis filiabus nostris sanctimonialibus prefatis de
possessionibus suis calumniam vel molestiam facere presumat.
Hiis testibus: Anselmo abbate sancti Eadmundi, priori Cantuar',
Willelmo capellano, Osberto capellano, Rogero capellano,
Ricardo de Hastinges milite, Willelmo filio Roberti, magistro
Henrico, magistro Ricardo, magistro David.

ENDORSEMENT: Confirmatio Theobaldi archiepiscopi de insula de Sehy-
    rycchesseye et de decimis de Purlee et de decimis de Prestona [later] et
    omnium terrarum et possessionum.

SEAL: none.

SIZE: 1·9 in. × 8·6 in.

DATE: 1144–48. Anselm of Bury, a witness, died in 1148.

COPY: in a transcript MS. ibid. E 40/14542.

The ascription of the legatine title to Theobald at such an early date and in
what purports to be an original charter raises a serious problem, but it is
possible to discredit the charter and reduce its value for this purpose. The
following charter was written by the same scribe:

Omnibus sancte matris ecclesie filiis, R. dei misericordia Lond' episcopus
salutem. Ecclesie catholice dilationi et sancte religionis propagationi pia
fidelium debet devotio congaudere et loca religiosa amplicare [sic], protegere et fovere. Inde est quod religionem sanctimonialium in monasterio
beate Marie de Wikes constitutam auctoritate episcopali confirmamus et
futuris inperpetuum temporibus immotam et ratam permanere volumus.
Nos vero petitione Mauricii de Windesor et Alexandri de Waham insulam
de Siricheseie et omnes decimas de dominio suo de Purle preter duas acras
et unum agnum et unum vellus, possessiones quoque omnimodas monasterio illi in elemosinam collatas, bona etiam omnia quecumque loco prefato
a fidelibus dei conferentur, rata ei et illibata esse volumus et ea presenti
pagina communimus et in nostram protectionem et tutelam suscipimus.
Imprecamur quoque et sententiam anathematis in eos proferimus quicumque de cetero violenter monasterium predictum inquietare vel possessiones ejus ausu temerario pervadere vel amovere attemtaverint. Testibus:
Galfrido dapifero, Rogero Bruno, Roberto capellano, Ricardo capellano,
magistro Willelmo, magistro Ernulfo. (P.R.O. Exchequer T.R. Ancient
Deeds E 40/14042).

Apart from the handwriting, the charters have in common a rather singular witness list. Theobald's charter contains three chaplains and three masters and the charter of the bishop of London has two of each. The masters occupy the last place in both charters, which is again peculiar. This would appear to be one of the rare cases where a charter can be shown almost certainly to have been composed by the beneficiaries. In view of this, all the evidence in favour of assigning a later date to Theobald's assumption of the title of legate cannot be invalidated by this charter of Theobald. As to the identity of 'R., bishop of London' in the charter transcribed above, there is a charter of Robert de Sigillo, bishop of London, confirming the possessions of Wix in much the same terms and mentioning Theobald's charter (E 40/5271). Most probably, therefore, the charter above is an earlier confirmation of the same bishop issued at the same time as Theobald's.

282

Confirmation by Theobald to the prior and monks of Worcester Cathedral of the church of (West) Bromwich (Staffs.) granted to them by Wido de Offeni and his son Richard and confirmed by the charter of Bishop Roger of Chester (1129–48). As established at the synod held at Lichfield by Bishop Roger the church of (West) Bromwich is a mother church in its own right and owes no subjection to the church of Handsworth. The monks have the right of appointing and removing vicars to the church at will.

MS. Cambridge U.L. EE.v.31 f.140b. (Register of Henry of Eastry).

Confirmacio capituli Cantuariensis de ecclesiis appropriatis priori et conventui Wygornensi.

[Theobald's is the first charter inspected.]

T. DEI gracia Cantuariensis archiepiscopus et tocius Anglie primas omnibus sancte ecclesie fidelibus salutem. Inspectis literis confirmacionis venerabilis fratris nostri Rogerii Cestrensis episcopi quam fecit priori et monachis de Wyrecestre super ecclesia videlicet de Bramwik quam Guydo de Offeni et Ricardus filius ejus in elemosinam canonice dedit libere et quiete cum omnibus pertinenciis suis inperpetuum possidendam cum vicaria ad libitum prioris et monachorum Wigornensium statuenda canonice et subtrahenda, et nos auctoritate nobis a deo collata eandem ecclesiam ipsis monachis cum pertinenciis suis canonice confirmamus et presentis scripti pagina inperpetuum corroboramus. Volumus igitur et precipimus ut sicut presencia predicti Censtrensis episcopi et sinodi ejus apud Lycef[eldam] idoneis tam laicorum quam clericorum testimoniis comprobatum est, ipsam ecclesiam de Bramwik nullam subjeccionem debere ecclesie de Hunesworka set ipsam esse liberam antiquitus et matrem ecclesiam ita et maneat et predicti monachi eam liberam et quietam sicut in predicta sinodo statutum est, ab omni calumpnia possideant. Valete.

ALSO: MS. Worcester Liber Pensionum no. 124 (not checked).

DATE: 1139–48.

CALENDARED: *Worcester Hist. Soc.*, 1924, p. 39.

283

Confirmation by Theobald, to Hugh, son of Gervase, of the lands and tithes of Saltmarsh (Westbury-on-Trym) previously held by his father in accordance with the charter of Bishop Simon of Worcester (1125–50).

MS. Worcester, Bishop Giffard's Register f.278b.

T. DEI gratia Cantuariensis archiepiscopus et totius Anglie primas universis filiis et fidelibus Wygorn' ecclesie salutem. Noveritis nos hac carta confirmasse Hugoni filio Gervasii terras et decimas de Saltemers quas tenuit ibi predictus Gervasius, sicut venerabilis frater noster S[imon] Wygorn' episcopus sibi canonice dedit et carte sue privilegio confirmavit. Valete.

DATE: 1139–50.

PRINTED: (with facsimile and translation) H. J. Wilkins, *Westbury College* (1917), p. 14.

284

Beginning of a letter from Theobald to Bishop Simon of Worcester.

MS. B.M. Royal 6 C vii f.216b (from Worcester cathedral).

T. DEI gratia Cantuariensis archiepiscopus et tocius Anglie primas venerabili fratri et amico Symoni Wig' episcopo salutem. Non turbetur cor vestrum dilectissime fili nec vestra modestia confundatur, set potius gaudeat

DATE: 1139–50.

2L

285

Confirmation by Theobald to Robert, master of St. Peter's hospital, York, of the possessions of the hospital.

MS. B.M. Cott. Nero D iii f.39a (Cartulary of St. Leonard's, York).

Teobaldus Cantuariensis archiepiscopus et apostolice sedis legatus confirmat auctoritate sua possessiones hospitalis sancti Petri de Ebor'.

TEOBALDUS dei gratia Cantuariensis archiepiscopus Anglorum primas apostolice sedis legatus omnibus sancte ecclesie fidelibus salutem. Equum est ac rationabile ea que divinis sunt justis modis mancipata serviciis unde pauperes Christi sustentantur ecclesiastico privilegio confirmari. Nos ergo justis postulacionibus dilecti filii nostri Roberti, custodis hospitalis domus Ebor' civitatis ubi pauperes Christi humano auxilio fere in omnibus sicut vestra noverit discrecio destituti humanitus reficiuntur, attencius annuentes omnia bona et possessiones que inpresenciarum prefata domus juste et canonice possidet juxta tenorem cartarum suarum et si qua in futurum justa acquisicione adipisci poterit, in elemosinam perpetuam ei concedimus et auctoritate qua fungimur confirmamus. Ad majorem ergo evidenciam congruum duximus illa propriis exprimenda esse vocabulis: ex dono domini regis Steffani xl solidos de redditibus suis civitatis Ebor', ex dono comitis Conani xx solidos, ex dono Eustacii filii Johannis x solidos, ex dono Ricardi de Camvilla v solidos, ex dono Rollandi Hacet iii solidos, ex dono Roberti Basset unam bovatam terre, ex dono Roberti de Occhet unam bovatam terre cum tofto uno de quinque solidis annuatim solvendis, ex dono Folconis de Quirquesle xii denarios, ex dono Mauricii tinctoris redditum xxviii numorum, ex dono Roberti filii Godrici toftum unum sexdecim numorum, ex dono Petri de Tresc xii denarios, ex dono Aschetilli ostiarii xii denarios, de dono Edwardi et uxoris ejus viii denarios, ex dono Wilardi in vita sua vi denarios et xii in morte, ex dono Sturst' iiii denarios et xii in morte. Hec quoque beneficia in dedicacione ecclesie beati Leonardi prefate domui ad usum pauperum annuatim reddenda sub nostra presencia promissa sunt. Ante hanc quoque dedicacionem totam terram de Brungareflet cum omnibus pertinenciis suis sicut Rogerus de Molbrai carta sua testante illam predicte domui concessit et dedit cum omnibus libertatibus et consuetudinibus et tenuris, et quicquid est inter Brungareflet et illam terram quam fratres de Templo tenent de ipso Rogero sicut idem Rogerus dedit prefate domui Alicia uxore sua concedente sicut carta ejus /[f.39b] testatur, et Unam [sic] cum omni conquestura sua, et cum mansura terre quam de illo tenet in Cava, et insuper omnes illas terras quas homines sui illi hospitali dederunt sive daturi sunt quas de feodo suo tenent, et ex dono ejusdem v carrucatas terre in Heslinget', ex dono Budi matris ejus iiii bovatas terre in Baggebi, item ex dono ipsius Rogeri de Molbrai ecclesiam de Briganhala et tres bovatas terre in eadem villa, ex dono comitis Steffani et Alani filii ejus juxta tenorem cartarum ipsorum ecclesiam de Bogas et dimidiam carrucatam terre in eadem villa. Nulli ergo homini fas sit prefatam domum super istis possessionibus temere perturbare aut aliquam ei exinde diminucionem vel contrarietatem inferre. Si quis autem huic nostre confirmacioni ausu temerario contraire presumpserit nisi presumpcionem suam congrua satisfactione correxerit, indignacionem omnipotentis dei et beate Marie virginis et beati Leonardi incurrat, conservantes autem hec eorundem benedictionem et graciam consequantur. Amen. Amen. Amen.

DATE: 1150–54.
PRINTED: *E.Y.C.*, i, 155.

286

Grant by Theobald of twenty days' indulgence to benefactors of St. Peter's hospital, York, which has suffered great devastation.

MS. B.M. Cott. Nero D iii f.9a (Cartulary of St. Leonard's, York).

Exhortacio Thome Cantuariensis archiepiscopi ad benefactores et relaxacio xx^{ti} dierum.

T. DEI gratia Cantuariensis archiepiscopus Anglorum primas et apostolice sedis legatus universis sancte ecclesie fidelibus ad quoscumque presentes pervenerint litere salutem. Ad nostrum spectat officium religiosa loca tueri et viros religione et sanctitate probatos sub nostre protectionis munimine retinere et auctoritate qua fungimur adversus pravorum studia fovere. Ea igitur ratione dilectum in Christo filium Robertum, virum religione et honestate probatum, et hospitale sancti Petri Ebor' cui preest cum terris redditibus et omnibus rebus ad ipsum pertinentibus in dei et sancte ecclesie et domini pape cujus vices ex officio nostro gerimus et nostra suscipimus protectione, prohibentes sub anathemate ne quis manum violentam in bona sua extendat nec molestiam irroget. Et quoniam hec domus tam caritativa tam utilis tam necessaria est in suscipiendis hospitibus in Christi pauperibus et infirmis refovendis, dum ex se sufficiat ad tanta beneficia impendenda tum propter ipsius domus destructionem et animalium suorum depredacionem et villarum suarum exustionem et ipsius provincie devastacionem, ad sinum pietatis vestre confugientes pro ipsa postulamus et in domino obsecramus et in remissionem peccatórum vestrorum vobis injungimus quatinus de bonis vestris vobis a deo collatis, prout vobis deus inspiraverit eis subveniatis et ad hospitalitatem sustentandam et edificia reparanda vestras illuc elemosinas per manus fratrum ejusdem domus transmittatis. Nos ergo de divina confisi misericordia omnes qui predicte domui aliquod pro dei amore contulerint beneficium omnium oracionum ac beneficiorum Cant' ecclesie eos participes perpetuo constituimus et insuper de injuncta sibi penitencia xx^{ti} dies ex parte dei et beati Petri et nostra eis relaxamus.

DATE: 1150–61.
PRINTED: *E.T.C.*, i, 153.

287

Grant by Theobald of forty days' indulgence to visitors and benefactors of St. Leonard's hospital, York, and of eight days' indulgence to those visiting the hospital church on the anniversary of its dedication, and also of the right to celebrate divine service there during an interdict of York.

MS. B.M. Cott. Nero D iii f.9a (Cartulary of St. Leonard's, York).

Theobaldi Cantuariensis archiepiscopi et legati indulgencia xl dierum benefactoribus hospitalis, et viii
dies illis qui in anniversario die dedicacionis ecclesie
sancti Leonardi veniunt.

THEOBALDUS dei gratia Cantuariensis archiepiscopus Anglorum primas apostolice sedis legatus omnibus sancte ecclesie
fidelibus salutem. Qui ad celestem patriam pervenire desiderant,
utile est eis misericordie operibus insistere et precipue sanctam
ecclesiam devote venerari. Quicumque ergo ecclesiam beati
Leonardi hospitalis domus Ebor' civitatis benigna mente visitaverit et aliquam porcionem substancie sibi a deo collate ad
sustentacionem pauperum prefate domus contulerit seu destin-
averit, in dei misericordia confisi de penitencia ei injuncta
quadraginta dies relaxamus et oracionum et beneficiorum
Cantuariensis ecclesie eum participem esse concedimus. Ob
reverenciam quoque illius loci omnibus in anniversario dedicacionis prescripte ecclesie locum illum visitantibus octo dierum
indulgenciam concedimus. Preter has autem indulgencias predicte ecclesie hujusmodi prerogativam concedimus ut si aliqua
occasione in jam dicta civitate divina celebrari prohibeantur in
prefata ecclesia, ejectis inde nominatim excommunicatis et
clausis januis, divinum officium celebretur condigne.

DATE: 1150–61.
PRINTED: *E.Y.C.*, i, 154.

288

Grant probably by Theobald of fifteen days' indulgence to visitors
and benefactors of St. Peter's hospital, York.

MS. B.M. Cott. Nero D iii f.10a (Cartulary of St. Leonard's, York).

Th. Arch' Cant'.

T. DEI gratia Cantuariensis ecclesie minister humilis universis
sancte matris ecclesie filiis salutem. Opus pietatis esse nemo
ambigit pauperum Christi inopias sublevare, eorum maxime
quibus solum relictum est mendicandi suffragium. Inde est

quod universitatem vestram monemus et exhortamur in domino ut ad hospitalem domum sancti Petri de Ebor' sustentandam de facultatibus vestris opem exhibeatis. Omnibus autem qui pietatis et caritatis obtentu eidem domui subvenerint, de injuncta sibi penitencia xv dies relaxamus et communionem omnium bonorum que in sancta fiunt Cant' ecclesia concedimus; eosque qui hanc opem emendicando circueunt per omnem jurisdictionem nostram ad verbum dei predicandum recipi sicut moris est precipimus.

DATE: 1139–61 or 1162–70.
PRINTED: *E.Y.C.*, i, 151.

289

Confirmation by Theobald of the grant (1112–22) made to St. Mary's Abbey, York, by Guy de Balliol of the church of Stokesley (Yorks.) with one carucate and tithes of the demesne, the church of Gainford (Yorks.) with two bovates and the church of Stainton (Yorks.) with two bovates.

MS. D. and C. York Cartulary of St. Mary's, York f.305a (not consulted).

Confirmatio Thome Cantuariensis archiepiscopi de
ecclesiis de Gaynesford et Steynton et Stokesley etc.

THOMAS dei gratia Cantuariensis archiepiscopus Anglorum primas et apostolice sedis legatus universis sancte ecclesie fidelibus salutem. In amplificationem honoris ecclesie dei studium et diligentiam adhibere et in usus divinos pie collata fovere et firmare pium et sanctum est et ad nostram precipue spectat sollicitudinem. Inde est quod donationem ecclesiarum et decimarum terrarum quam Guido de Baillol dedit et concessit in perpetuam elemosinam ecclesie beate Marie Eboracensis et monachis ejusdem loci, scilicet ecclesiam de Stokesley et unam carrucatam terre in eadem villa et decimam dominii ejusdem ville, et ecclesiam de Gaynesford et duas bovatas terre et decimam dominii ejusdem manerii, et ecclesiam de Steynton et duas bovatas terre et decimam dominii ejusdem ville, nos concedimus et auctoritate qua fungimur eis imperpetuum confirmamus, prohibentes sub anathemate ne quis in bona illa manum violentam extendat, nec fratribus predictis injuriam inferre vel inquietationem movere attemptet. Valete.

DATE: probably 1150–61.

PRINTED: *E.Y.C.*, i, 439; *Monasticon*, iii, 565; John Stevens, *Continuation to Monasticon* (1722–3), ii, app. 82.

290

Confirmation by Theobald of grants made to Gloucester Abbey by Harold lord of Ewyas.

MS. B.M. Cott. Dom. A viii f.149a (List of possessions of Gloucester Abbey).

ANNO domini M°c° Haraldus dominus de Ewyas dedit ecclesie sancti Petri Glouc' ecclesiam sancti Michaelis, [Diveles] cum capella sancti Nicholai de Castro, capellam sancti Jacobi de Ewyas, capellam sancte Kaene cum capella de Caneros in puram et perpetuam elemosinam, ita quod apud Ewyas sit in perpetuum conventus serviens deo. Insuper concessit decimam annone sue venacionis sue et mellis et omnium de quibus Christianus decimare debet. Insuper ecclesiam de Foy cum una carucata terre et decimis gurgitis sui de Foy, molendinum . . . . dedit ecclesiam de Lidred cum omnibus pertinentiis, ecclesiam de Alyngeton' et ecclesiam de Burnham. Insuper [decimas] dominii sui per totas terras suas [in] proprios usus concessit et decimam molendinorum suorum et anguillarum, Theobaldo Cantuar' archiepiscopo confirmante tempore Hamelini abbatis.

ALSO: MS. Queen's Coll. Oxford 367 (not checked) which supplies 'Diveles' in line 2.

DATE: 1148–61.

PRINTED: *Hist. et Cart. Mon. Glouc.* (R.S.) ed. W. H. Hart, i, 76.

291

Confirmation by Theobald of grants made to Gloucester Abbey by Robert son of Harold lord of Ewyas.

MS. B.M. Cott. Dom. A viii ff .147b and 150a (List of possessions of Gloucester Abbey).

Robertus confirmat donum Haraldi patris sui. Insuper dedit ecclesiam de Burnham prioratui de Ewyas ut conventus ibidem inveniatur, quod concessum est [sed] non prosecutum. Insuper dedit eisdem decimas omnium maneriorum suorum de quibus Christiani decimare debent, Theobaldo archiepiscopo Cantuar' confirmante. Johannes episcopus [Wigorn'] confirmat [tempore Hamelini abbatis].

MS. makes John bishop of Salisbury.
Also: MS. Queen's Coll. Oxford 367.
Date: probably 1151–57.
Printed: *Hist. et Cart. Mon. Glouc.* (R.S.) ed. W. H. Hart, i, 76.

292

Confirmation by Theobald of the decision in his presence and also of Robert II bishop of Lincoln (1148–66) in the case between the canons of Dunstable (Aug. Priory, Beds.) and the canons of Merton (Aug. Priory, Surrey).

MS. B.M. Harleian 1885 f.25b (Register of Dunstable).

Hec est conventio inter canonicos de Dunst' et canonicos de Meritone coram Teobaldo Cantuariensi archiepiscopo et R[oberto] Lincoln' episcopo facta et eorum auctoritate confirmata. Canonici de Dunst' dabunt annuatim canonicis de Meritone ii solidos scilicet xii denarios ad festum sancti Michaelis et xii denarios ad pascha, pro tota decima terre de Sortegrave que eis tempore B[ernardi] prioris in elemosinam data est, que pertinet ad parochiam ecclesie de Eytone, tam frugum quam pecorum et hominum, si qui in prefata terra ad Eytonam pertinente forte residue fuerint.

Date: 1148–61.
Calendared: *Beds. Hist. Rec. Soc.* 1926, p. 63., ed. G. H. Fowler.

293

Grant by Theobald of fifteen days' indulgence to Glastonbury Abbey (Ben., Somerset).

MS. Trinity Coll., Cambridge, R. 5.33 (Glastonbury Documents) (not checked with MS.).

List of charters compiled under abbot John of Taunton 1274–91.

[f.78a.]

DIES indulgenciarum Glastoniae unde cartas non habemus licet habuerimus: [the fourth to be mentioned] De Theobaldo archiepiscopo xv dies.

[Similarly on f.80a:]

Tebertus [*sic*] Cantuariensis archiepiscopus xv dies.

PRINTED: T. Hearne, *John of Glastonbury* (1726) pp. 378, 383.

294

Confirmation by Theobald to Osbert de Caduna of the parish church of Faversham with certain tithes except those of the royal demesne, as granted to him by Hugh abbot of St. Augustine's.

MS. B.M. Cott. Claud. D x f.33b (Red Book of St. Augustine's).

EUGENIUS episcopus . . . . Osberto de Caduna salutem . . . . Ecclesiam sancte Marie de Favresham cum capella beati Jacobi cum terris et decimis totius parochie scilicet omnium hominum regis pertinentium ad manerium de Favresham et hominum Heltonis filii Ricardi, excepta decima de dominio regis, quemadmodum per dilectum filium nostrum Hugonem secundum abbatem sancti Augustini tibi concessa scripto quoque venerabilis fratris nostri Theobaldi Cantuariensis archiepiscopi tibi juste et canonice confirmata est presentis scripti pagina roboramus.

Cf. No. 57.

295

Confirmation by Theobald of the decision in the presence of Abbot Hugh of St. Augustine's in the dispute between the incumbents of Faversham and Selling (Kent) over the parochial allegiance of the men of the king belonging to the manor of Faversham. (Decided in favour of Faversham.)

(Continuation of the above confirmation of Pope Eugenius.)

STATUIMUS etiam ut terminatio cause que fuit inter Reinaldum Apostolicum quondam personam sancte Marie de Favresham et Algarum sacerdotem de Sellinges et deinde inter te et Matheum sacerdotem de Sellinges de hominibus videlicet regis pertinentibus ad manerium de Favresham ita rata permaneat, sicut primum terminata in presentia prefati Hugonis abbatis et postmodum confirmata a predicto venerabili Theobaldo Cantuariensi archiepiscopo et sicut in ipsorum cartis continetur. . . . .

DATE: The bull is dated 3 June at Perugia. As Eugenius is not otherwise recorded to have visited Perugia, Holtzmann emends to Paris which would make the date 3 June 1147. Theobald's charters can therefore be dated 1139-47 and probably c. 1146.

PRINTED: Holtzmann, i, 272. Cf. *Elmham*, p. 406; Jaffé 10122 (Adrian IV).

Holtzmann appears to query the unusual name Reinaldus Apostolicus, but it is also found in No. 10 and No. 58.

296

Confirmation by Stephen Langton to the nuns of St. Radegund, Cambridge, of their possessions, after inspection of the charters of Archbishops Theobald and Thomas and of Bishop Nigel of Ely (1213-28).

MS. Jesus Coll., Cambridge, A 5.

PRINTED: K. Major, *Stephen Langton* (Canterbury and York Soc. 1950) p. 152.

297

Confirmation by Theobald to Bec Abbey (Normandy) of the church of Saltwood (Kent) with all its appurtenances given by Robert de Montford, in accordance with the charter of Ralph, archbishop of Canterbury (1114–22).

MS. Windsor, St. George's Chapel, xi. G.29 n.3 (Roll of Bec).

T. DEI gratia Cantuariensis archiepiscopus Anglorum primas et appostolice sedis legatus omnibus sancte matris ecclesie fidelibus salutem. Cum ea que a venerabilibus fratribus nostris episcopis circa statum ecclesie rationabiliter ordinantur rata inmutilataque confirmare debeamus, majori diligencia et studio ea que a predecessoribus nostris Cantuar' ecclesie archiepiscopis statuta esse et de ecclesiis canonice ordinata noverimus ut inperpetuum durent confirmare et auctoritatis nostre munimine roborare debeamus. Ea igitur ratione dilectis filiis nostris monachis Beccensibus et monasterio sancti Philiberti quod prope Montem Fortis situm est et monachis ibidem deo servientibus ecclesiam sancti Petri de Saltwod' cum omnibus a[d] eam pertinentibus in capellis et decimis et aliis possessionibus sicut carta predecessoris nostri bone recordacionis Radulphi Cantuar' archiepiscopi prefatam ecclesiam cum pertinenciis suis eisdem monachis datam et concessam esse testatur a nobili viro R[oberto] de Monte Forti presenti quoque pag[ina e]andem ecclesiam cum decimis de Cupperland' memoratis monachis et sigilli nostri auctoritate communimus dei ac nostra auctoritate pro-[hibentes] ne quis eos super prescripta ecclesia temere inquietare vel eis ullam inferre presumat molestiam. Quodsi quis attemptaverit dei omnipotentis indignacionem et nostram se noverit incursurum. Valete.

DATE: 1150–61.

Cf. M. Morgan, *English Lands of the Abbey of Bec* (1946), p. 143.

298

Grant by Theobald to the Knights Templars of the manor of (Temple) Waltham (Kent).

MS. P.R.O. Exchequer K.R. Misc. Books i 16 (E 164/16) f.10b
(Inquest of the Templars of 1185).

DE elemosina Theodbaldi archiepiscopi est quod Hamo de
Chilham tenet. Tenura de Waltham singulorum hominum et
servientium.

DATE: 1139–61.
PRINTED: B. A. Lees, *Records of the Templars in England*, p. 25, cf. E. Hasted,
History of Kent (1797), ix, 320.

299

Confirmation by Theobald to Ralph prior of Worcester Cathedral
and his successors of the possessions of Worcester Cathedral Priory,
in accordance with the charter of Bishop Simon of Worcester
(1125–50) which he has inspected.

MS. D. and C. Worcester Register I f.11a (no. 74).

T. DEI gratia Cantuariensis archiepiscopus et totius Anglie primas venerabilibus fratribus episcopis abbatibus archidiaconis
decanis universisque sancte matris ecclesie fidelibus tam clericis
quam laicis tam presentibus quam futuris salutem et benedictionem. Notum facimus universitati vestre quoniam deo et
ecclesie sancte Marie Wigornie omnes possessiones quas inpresentiarum possidet, in ecclesiis in terris in decimis in hominibus
in molendinis in redditibus sive in quibuscumque tenuris, aut in
futurum canonice adipisci poterit seu donatione regum sive largitione principum, seu quorumcumque fidelium oblatione ipsi
ecclesie et fratri Radulfo priori et omnibus successoribus suis
canonice substituendis, monachisque in ea deo ministrantibus
concedimus et presentis scripti nostri munimine confirmamus
et auctoritate nostri testimonii corroboramus sicut venerabilis
frater noster Symon Wigorn' episcopus eis illa concessit et testimonio carte sue quam oculis nostris conspeximus confirmavit.
Possessiones autem ejus propriis in hac cartula decrevimus annotare nominibus videlicet Croppethorn, Netherton, Cherleton,
Segesberga, Onerberia cum Penedoc etc. [*sic*]. Siquis autem has
eorum possessiones minuere aut indeterius permutare temere

presumpserit, anathematis vinculo donec condigne satisfecerit obligatus teneatur. Si vero contra quis eas augmentaverit, adaugeat ei deus et presentium bonorum copiam et infuturo vitam eternam. Amen.

DATE: 1149 (see Supp. H.2).

300

Confirmation by Theobald of the possessions of Thorney Abbey (Ben., Cambs.) under Abbot Robert (1113–51).

MS. Cambridge U.L. Additional 3020 f.170b (Red Book of Thorney).

> Confirmatio domini Tedbaldi dei gratia Cantuariensis archiepiscopi omnium maneriorum et possessionum ecclesie Thorn' tempore predicti Roberti abbatis. c.xvii.

TEDBALDUS dei gratia Cantuariensis archiepiscopus Anglorum primas et apostolice sedis legatus venerabilibus fratribus episcopis abbatibus archidiaconis decanis universis quoque fidelibus tam clericis quam laicis per Angliam existentibus salutem. Pastoralis sollicitudo officii nos compellit domesticorum fidei quieti maxime eorum quos religionis nomen commendat per omnia in quibus secundum deum possumus providere et ipsis tum protectionis tum confirmacionis nostre munimenta confirmare. Ea propter fili dilecte in domino Rodberte abbas de Thorneya justis postulationibus tuis annuentes deo et beate Marie et sancto Botulfo locum Ancraeie que nunc Thorn' vocatur in quo eadem ecclesia constructa est et omnes res eidem loco pertinentes omnesque alias possessiones quas juste et canonice ecclesia tua possidere dinoscitur concedimus et confirmamus. Earum autem nomina possessionum quas inpresentiarum possidet in presenti pagina dignum duximus annotare. In comitatu Cantebrig': Witeleseyam et omnes illas consuetudines et causas seculares quas habebat Eliensis ecclesia in hundredis suis de Witheford de terra et de hominibus Thornensis ecclesie de Witleseia exceptis propriis regalibus consue-

tudinibus que super terram illam evenerint quas Herveus
primus Eliensis episcopus concessit et dedit in elemosinam
Thornensi ecclesie in die dedicationis ejusdem ecclesie concessu
totius conventus Eliensis ecclesie his testibus Gileberto Lundon'
episcopo, Johanne Roffensi episcopo; in /[f.171a] comitatu
Huntend': Neutonam, Wdestonam, Jakeleiam et mercatum
ejusdem ville cum saka et soca et tol et tem et infangenethef et
omnibus consuetudinibus eidem pertinentibus, ad hec medietatem stagni quod Witlesmere dicitur, Stangrund, Farreshefed,
Haddune, Sibestune duas hidas et dimidiam, et in Stibinctune
quinque virgatas pertinentes ad Sibestonam et decimam unius
caruce in Sibestona, in Stibinctona decimam Rogerii, in prato
de Stantune xxviii acras de diversis hominibus, in Coppede-
thorn xiv acras terre et pratum eidem terre pertinens, item de
dono Simonis comitis de Hampt' terciam partem molendini
Huntend' reddentem singulis annis xl s. et in eadem villa duas
domos et terras in quibus ipse domus sunt et medietatem ecclesie
Omnium Sanctorum de mercato ejusdem ville, decimam
Widonis filii Gocelini de Cestretune, in Folkeword' duas virgatas terre et dimidiam et aliam terciam in eadem villa viii s.
annuatim reddentem, de dono Andree Revelli in predicta villa
xv acras quas dedit in elemosinam pro se et omnibus parentibus
suis vivis et mortuis; in comitatu Hamptonie: Twiwelle, duas
hidas et molendinum terram in Luffewik, item dimidiam virgatam terre et x acras de inland in predicta villa, unam hidam
in Rand' cum redditu ejus scilicet xii sol., Cherwoltune, in
Stokes unam carucatam terre de dominio Willelmi Britonis de
Albeni cum tofta et prato et tota communitate in bosco et plano
et pascuis, de dono Alberici de Twiwell' duas garbas decimarum v carucarum trium villarum scilicet Islepe Draitune
Edentune; in comitatu de Warewik: Salubrigge, virgatam unam
terre in Flekenho et molendinum de Rugentune, servitium
Edrici de Flekenho cum terra sua scilicet v jugera in campo et
in villa tres toftas et dimidiam; in comitatu Bedefordie: ecclesiam de Guieldena cum una hida terre et decimis ejusdem ville
et omnibus oblationibus, duas hidas et dimidiam in Bolleherst
et ecclesiam ejusdem ville, in Wildena duas virgatas terre cum
hominibus qui illas tenent, in Bedeford' unam domum et

terram ei pertinentem; item in Norfolk': in villa que dicitur
Tuameres unam terrulam reddentem v s., item medietatem
tocius ville que dicitur Wenga et molendinum ejusdem ville,
insuper villanum unum nomine Normannum cum terra sua
scilicet unam virgatam in predicta villa, item x sol. de redditu
molendini de Teseburga cum dimidio augmentacionis quantum
creverit, piscacionem de Welle de Helm de Tillinga et de
Trillinga, item duas ecclesias de Deping' cum terris et omnibus
ad eas pertinentibus, item ecclesiam sancti Georgii de Thed-
ford', item terram de Stamford', item heremitorium de Troken-
holt, et libertatem quam beatus Adelwoldus episcopus fundator
predicti cenobii loco eidem favente rege Eadgaro et sancto
Dunstano Dorobernensi archiepiscopo et Oswaldo Eboracensi
archiepiscopo et omnibus aliis episcopis abbatibus et baronibus
tocius Anglie concessit et privilegium ejus testatur. Precipimus
itaque ut prefata ecclesia supradictas possessiones tam in
ecclesiis quam aliis beneficiis ecclesiasticis et mundanis /[f.171b]
redditibus libere et in summa pace teneat et inperpetuum possideat, salvis per omnia diocesani episcopi dignitatibus. Conservantibus igitur predicte ecclesie pacem et bona illius augentibus
sit salus et pax et vita eterna: adversantibus autem et ejus jura
diminuentibus pena sempiterna. Amen. Valete.

DATE: 1150–51.

The following letter to Theobald refers to the church of Whittlesey as confirmed above:

[f.172b.]

Reverentissimo domino suo et patri T. dei gratia Cantuariensi archiepiscopo et tocius Anglie primati Willelmus qui fuit archidiaconus nepos
Hervei Eliensis episcopi defuncti salutem et dilectionem in domino. Sciat
revera paternitas vestra nunquam sive in tempore Hervei episcopi avunculi
mei sive sui successoris Nigelli domini episcopi Rogerum clericum nec in
capitulo nec in senatu [sic], de ecclesia de Witles' personam factum fuisse
nec breve nec testimonium de datione abbatis et conventus de Thorn'
unquam aliam personam preter abbatem et conventum Torneye habuisse
set abbatem in manu propria ad Thornensis ecclesie luminaria et orna-
menta emendanda semper illam tenuisse. Nos vero consuetudines episco-
pales ad ecclesiam illam pertinentes ab abbate et conventu Thorneye omni
tempore exegimus. Valete.

301

Confirmation by Theobald to Thorney Abbey of the market held every Thursday at Yaxley (Hunts.).

MS. Cambridge U.L. Additional 3020 f.409b. (Red Book of Thorney.)

> Confirmacio domini Theobaldi dei gratia Cantuariensis de mercato de Jakele.

T. DEI gratia Cantuariensis ecclesie archiepiscopus A[lexandro] episcopo Lincolniensi et Pagano vicecomiti et omnibus fidelibus Francis et Anglis de Huntadunasire salutem. Sciatis me confirmasse Tornensi ecclesie mercatum ad manerium suum de Jaceslaia ita tranquillum et quietum cum soca et saca et theloneo et omnibus aliis consuetudinibus per diem Jovis uniuscujusque ebdomade sicut tres reges concesserunt et cartis suis confirmaverunt, scilicet Willelmus rex junior et Henricus rex frater ejus et rex Stephanus nepos eorum. Sitque anathema et extra communionem fidelium quicumque hoc perturbare vel adnichilare temptaverit. Valete.

DATE: 1139–48.

302

Letters of protection of Theobald in favour of Thorney Abbey.

MS. Cambridge U.L. Additional 3020 f.409b (Red Book of Thorney).

> Item scriptum prefati T. archiepiscopi, predicto Pagano vicecomiti Hunt' et aliis infra contentis directum, de abbatia Thorn' et rebus ipsius protegendis et manutenendis.

T. DEI gratia Cantuariensis archiepiscopus Anglorum primas et apostolice sedis legatus dilectis filiis suis in Christo Simoni filio Petri et Pagano de Hemingeforde vicecomiti et Fulconi de Lusoris salutem. Noveritis quoniam abbatia sancti Botulfi de Turneia in custodia nostra est, iccirco vobis preces porrigimus rogantes quatinus nostri amore abbatiam illam et homines et terras et omnes alias res ad abbatiam illam pertinentes vice nostra custodiatis et manuteneatis et nullam eis violentiam vel injuriam inferri susteneatis, et tantam diligentiam in protegendis rebus suis inpendatis quatinus preces nostras sibi non modicum profuisse deprehendant et nobis gratiam referre debeant. Valete.

DATE: 1150–61.

303

Mandate of Theobald to the clerks of the archbishop of York in the diocese of Worcester. They are to obey Bishop Alfred of Worcester (1158–60) and receive chrism and oil from him as had been the practice under his predecessors, and under William archbishop of Canterbury (1123–36).

MS. Worcester Liber Albus (called 'Liber Ruber') f.58a.

T. DEI gratia Cantuariensis archiepiscopus Anglorum primas et apostolice sedis legatus universis clericis venerabilis Eboracensis archiepiscopi in Wigornensi diocesi existentibus et precipue clericis sancti Oswaldi de Gloec' salutem. Mandamus vobis et in virtute obedientie precipimus quatinus a venerabili fratre nostro Aluredo Wigornensi episcopo et ejus ministris crisma et oleum singulis annis suscipiatis, sicut suscipere consuevistis a predecessoribus suis episcopis Theold', Simon', Johanne; et ei similiter canonicam obedientiam et subjectionem absque contradictione exhibeatis quam predictis predecessoribus suis exhibuistis, sicut fecistis tempore predecessoris nostri bone memorie W[illelmi] Cantuariensis archiepiscopi et nostro postea, usque in presentem diem.

DATE: 1158–60.

304

Confirmation by Theobald to Spalding Priory (Lincs.; dep. on St. Nicholas Angers) of its possessions and in particular the churches of Sibsey, Stickney and Alkborough (Lincs.), in accordance with the charter of Robert II, bishop of Lincoln (1148–66).

MS. B.M. Addl. 35296 f.372a (Register of Spalding).

Archiepiscopi de ecclesiis Cibeseia, Stiken', Hautebarg'.

THEOBALDUS dei gratia Cantuariensis archiepiscopo [*sic*] Anglorum primas apostolice sedis legatus omnibus sancte matris ecclesie fidelibus salutem. Sollicitudinis nostre debito convenit viros religiosos diligere et eorum possessiones et bona pia proteccione munire et ea a pravorum hominum nequicia tueri et nostro patrocinio refovere. Eapropter dilecte in domino fili Herberte prior et monachi ecclesie de Spald' vestris justis postulacionibus clementer annuimus quecumque bona et possessiones juxta tenorem carte venerabilis fratris nostri R[oberti] Lincolniensis episcopi in presenciarum juste et canonice possidetis vobis vestrisque successoribus in elemosinam perpetuo concedimus et vobis illibata permaneant, in quibus hec propriis duximus exprimenda vocabulis: ecclesiam de Cibeseie et ecclesiam de Stikeneia, ecclesiam de Hautebarge cum omnibus earundem appendiciis. Decernimus ergo ut nulli omnino hominum liceat prefatam ecclesiam temere aut ejus possessiones auferre vel ablatas retinere, minuere vel aliquibus vexacionibus fatigare set omnia integra conservent predictorum fratrum usibus profutura salva diocesani episcopi canonica obediencia. Siqua igitur in futurum ecclesiastica secularisve persona hanc nostre confirmacionis paginam sciens contra eam temere venire temptaverit, si non satisfaccione congrua emendaverit in extremo districte ulcioni subjaceat et a sanctorum consorcio aliena fiat. Amen. Amen. Amen.

DATE: 1150–61.
COPY: MS. B.M. Addl. 5844 f.211b (Cole's transcript).

305

Confirmation by Theobald of the agreement between the monks of Castle Acre Priory (Clu., Norf.) and the canons of Rudham over the tithes of East Rudham (Norf.).

MS. B.M. Addl. 47784 f.78a (Cartulary of Coxford).

THEOB' dei gratia Cantuariensis archiepiscopus et tocius Anglie primas omnibus sancte ecclesie fidelibus salutem. Notum sit omnibus tam presentibus quam futuris quod concordiam et convencionem decimarum de Rudham que facta est inter monachos de Acra et canonicos de Rudham, ego confirmo et hoc sigillo meo inperpetuum corroboro, ita inposterum nulli omni eam liceat violare vel immutare. Valete.

DATE: probably 1139–50.
Cf. J. C. Dickinson, *The Origins of the Austin Canons* (1950), p. 149.

306

Confirmation by Theobald of the possessions of St. Mary's Abbey, York, especially of its possessions in the province of Canterbury including the dependent priory of Rumburgh (Suff.).

MS.   *Ex rotulo quodam vetusto in Bibliotheca Cottoniana.*

T. DEI gratia Cantuariensis archiepiscopus Anglorum primas et apostolicae sedis legatus universis sanctae ecclesiae fidelibus salutem. Ad officium nostrum spectat religiosorum nostrorum utilitati providere et eorum bona augere et fovere: ea propter notum vobis facimus nos Savarico abbati et successoribus ejus et monachis sanctae Mariae Eboraci confirmasse cellam de Romburg cum omnibus pertinentiis ejus et beneficiis quae possidebat antequam praefatis monachis in elemosinam data erat; similiter confirmamus eis ecclesiam de Banham et de Wilgehebi cum pertinentiis suis et ecclesiam de Heselingfeld et ecclesiam sancti Petri in Lincolnia et ecclesiam sancti Botulfi in Hoyland et ecclesiam sanctae Mariae de Binebroc et ecclesiam de Belton et ecclesiam de Boswrth cum omnibus quae ad eas pertinent; necnon et omnia ecclesiastica beneficia quae prefatum monasterium in diocesi Cantuariensi donatione fidelium juste possidet, eidem monasterio confirmamus. Prohibentes sub anathemate ne quis in bona illa manum violentam mittat nec praedictis fratribus injuriam faciat vel inquietudinem moveat. Testibus Thoma archidiacono, Ricardo monacho, magistro R[ogero] Spe[cie].

DATE: 1154–58.

PRINTED: *Monasticon*, iii, 612.

307

Confirmation by Theobald of the possessions of Southwick priory (Aug. canons, Hants.) granted by William de Pont l'Arche and confirmed by Henry, bishop of Winchester.

MS. B.M. deposited Cartulary of Southwick vol.i f.1b.

> Karta seu privilegium Theob' Cant' archiepiscopi de loco de Suw' et de bonis eidem a Willelmo de P. Arch' collatis et ab H. episcopo . . . .

THEOBAL' dei gracia Cantuariensis archiepiscopus Anglorum primas et apostolice sedis legatus universis sancte ecclesie fidelibus salutem. Ad pastoris spectat sollicitudinem loca religiosa protegere et confirmacionis be[ne]ficio communire. Ea propter religiosis fratribus integre opinionis viris canonicis regularibus de Sudwi[ca lo]cum ipsum de Sudwica et cetera bona sua juste et canonice a Willelmo de Pontearch' eis collata et a[b episcopo?] suo fratre nostro venerabili Henrico Wint' confirmata confirmamus et presentis scripti nostri munimine [et auc]toritate vicis apostolice qua fungimur in perpetuum corroboramus prohibentes sub anathemate ne quis eundem locum vel fratres ibidem in dei servicio devotos infestare vel eorum bona aliquatenus ausu temerario inquietare seu diminuere presumat. Quod si quis presumpserit iram et indignationem dei omnipotentis incurrat. Valete.

DATE: 1150–61.

308

Grant by Theobald of thirty days' indulgence to those assisting the canons of Porchester to build their new house (Southwick).

MS. B.M. deposited Cartulary of Southwick vol.iii f.233a.

Confirmacio Teobaldi Cant' archiepiscopi de muta-
cione loci nostri et de indulgencia.

[T]EOBALDUS dei gratia Cantuariensis archiepiscopus et tocius
Anglie primas universis sancte ecclesie fidelibus salutem. Religiosorum fratrum quieti providere ad episcopale specialiter pertinet officium. Eo nimirum intuitu religiosis fratribus canonicis
videlicet de Porcestria providentes qui de castro ubi in arto
positi erant exterius amplitudinis gratia edificandi locum ampliorem elegerunt et ob hoc ad nova omnia instruenda fidelium
omnium auxilio indigent, universitati vestre mandantes obsecramus ut de copiis vestris eorum inopie subveniatis xxx dies
penitencie sue cunctis qui beneficia sua ipsi loco impenderint
relaxantes. Valete.

DATE: probably 1145–50 (*V.C.H., Hants.*, iii, 159, n. 131).

309

Notification by Theobald to his suffragans that he will ratify any
indulgences which they may proclaim in favour of the canons of
Southwick.

MS. B.M. deposited Cartulary of Southwick vol.iii f.233a.

Exhortacio T. Cantuar' archiepiscopi ad suffraganeos
suos pro ecclesia Sudwicensi.

T. DEI gratia Cantuariensis archiepiscopus tocius Anglie primas venerabilibus fratribus suis coepiscopis per Angliam constitutis salutem et benedictionem. Necessitatem fratrum canonicorum videlicet regularium in ecclesia beate Marie de Soth
Wike juxta Porcestr' deo jugiter serviencium plerosque vestrum
audisse arbitramur. Si quis itaque vestrum compaciens inopie
benefactoribus ipsorum de injunctis penitenciis aliquam fecerit
indulgenciam nos eam confirmantes ratam habebimus. Pax
omnibus benefactoribus eorum.

DATE: probably 1145–50.

310

Grant by Theobald to Harbledown Hospital (Kent) of the tithes of his manor of Westgate (Canterbury).

MS. Bodleian Top. Kent c 2 f.2b (Transcript of Reg. of Eastbridge Hospital, Canterbury).

THEOBALDUS dei gratia Cant' archiepiscopus totius Anglie primas et apostolice sedis legatus toti hundredo de Westgate salutem. Sciatis quod ego concessi sancti Nicholai de Harbaldowna[1] et presbiteris eidem servientibus decimam omnium fructuum tam minorum quam majorum manerii de Westgate. Teste Waltero priore, et Felice et Milone et Waltero monachis et capellanis archiepiscopi; Alano et Johanne clericis; Nigello filio Godfridi et Gaufrido de Cromillo militibus.

[1] The transcriber must have omitted 'hospitali'.

DATE: 1150–52.

311

Notification by Theobald to the monks of Pershore that he has restored their abbot Thomas, having forgiven both abbot and monks for their offences.

MS. Emmanuel Coll., Cambridge, no. 38, flyleaves, f.2b.

T. DEI gratia Cantuariensis archiepiscopus et totius Anglie primas conventui de Persora salutem. Sciatis quoniam consilio fratrum nostrorum coepiscoporum remisimus culpam Thome abbati vestro restituimusque eum in gradu suo precipientes ut ei tamquam abbati vestro debitam obedientie reverentiam exibeatis. Vobis quoque, quod subticuistis que de illo vos nosse profiteri preceperamus, ignoscimus. Valete.

DATE: probably 1139–1150.

Followed by a letter of the monks of Pershore to Bishop Simon of Worcester complaining of his oppression and pointing out that, in Simon's presence, they had put themselves under the protection of the archbishop.

III

Supplementary Documents

A

Chirograph between Canterbury Cathedral Priory and Godfrey of (S.) Malling embodying the agreement reached between the parties before Theobald. Godfrey is to hold Patching (Sussex) for life from the monks at an annual farm of £18, but he has abandoned his claim to Wootton (Sussex). (With the seals of Theobald and of the convent.)

Original MS. D. and C. Canterbury C.A., W 50 a.

C Y R O G R A PHU M:

ANNO ab incarnatione domini millesimo c. lv. fer. ii post diem pascalem id est quinto kl. April. facta est hęc conventio inter Wibertum priorem et conventum ęcclesię Christi Cantuar' et inter Godefridum filium Willelmi de Mealling' in presentia domini Teob' archiepiscopi in camera sua Cantuarię. Godefridus itaque filius Willelmi de Mealling' clamabat se debere tenere de conventu ęcclesię Christi Cantuar' Pecching' manerium eorum cum Wudetona in feudo firma. Prior autem et conventus contradicentes hoc nequaquam esse debere responderunt. Et quia denique predictus Godefridus nec jure nec ratione procedere potuit liti renunciavit et omnem hereditatem et feudum quod se in maneriis illis Pecching' scilicet et Wudetona debere habere dixerat coram domino Teob' archiepiscopo et multis aliis quod et antea pater suus Willelmus coram Waltero Duredent priore et multis aliis per fidem suam et sacramentum fecerat imperpetuum monachis omnimodo quietum clamavit. Prior autem et conventus tandem precibus quorundam condescendentes Pecching' tantummodo absque Wudetona quam prior et conventus in manu sua retinuerunt sine omni feudo et hereditate predicto Godefrido solummodo ad firmam de ipsis tenendum concesserunt propter decem et octo libras singulis annis quam diu ipse firmam decem et octo librarum ad terminos constitutos bene et plenarie monachis inde reddiderit. Et dum ipse hoc fecerit non auferetur ab eo manerium. Hanc autem conventionem secundum tenorem hujus cyrographi ipse Godefridus se servaturum in presentia domni Teob' archiepiscopi in camera sua Cantuarię eodem die quo hęc conventio facta est super quattuor evangelia juravit Radulfo Picot vicecomite jusjurandum ei escariante. Hujus autem conventionis testes sunt: Willelmus supprior, Felix, Ærnaldus, Symon, Herveus monachi; Phylippus cancellarius, Johannes Salesb'[1], Randulfus de Sancto Albano, Petrus scriptor, clerici archiepiscopi; Radulfus Picot, Phylippus de Tanghes, Robertus Halsardus, Willelmus decanus, Tomas de Bochtona, Bartholomeus dapifer, Willelmus et Rogerius portarii, Henricus aurifaber et Humfridus gener ejus; de coquina: Walterus, Johannes, Saefughel[2] et Willelmus filius ejus; de pistrino: Colemannus; de bracino Smalman[3], Wulri, Walterus, Raginaldus, Edmerus; et preter istos: Willelmus camerarius, Robertus marescal, Drogo, Humfridus Scottus, Aschetillus, Godwinus, Symon, Robertus, Paganus, Ricardus, Eilsi, Johannes, Osbertus, et multi alii.

+ Signum Wiberti prioris +

VARIATIONS: [1]Saleb'. [2]Saewughel. [3]Smeleman.

DATE: 28 March 1155.

PRINTED: T. Madox, *Formulare* (1702), p. 74.

W 50 b is the top half of the cyrograph and ends:
Signum Godefridi de Mealling' + (a most feeble cross—probably in his own hand).

The two halves are sealed on the left side with Theobald's usual seal above and the first seal of Christ Church below.

B

Account of how Theobald obtained Deepham (Norf.) for the Cathedral Priory from Henry de Rye.

MS. D. and C. Canterbury Reg. B f.213b.

Qualiter ecclesia Christi Cantuar' tenet manerium de Deepeham.

HUBERTUS de Rye dedit ecclesie Christi Cant' manerium suum quoddam quod dicitur Mucheberdesham[1] et illud tenuit Goldwinus[2] ejusdem ecclesie monachus post mortem Huberti donec per violenciam deseita [sic] fuit ecclesia de illo manerio. Postea[3] tempore Radulfi archiepiscopi missi fuerunt ab eodem archiepiscopo Hugo monachus qui post factus est abbas sancti Augustini et Ricardus de Beanfulk atque abbas sancti Albani ad calumpniandum prefatum manerium ad opus monachorum ecclesie Christi, verum per plurimum tempus interim sic remansit. Deinde tempore regis Stephani dominus Theobaldus archiepiscopus et tocius Anglie primas audito quod sic donatum fuit predictum manerium ecclesie sue et violenter ablatum, misit ad Henricum filium videlicet Huberti de Ryes rogans ut ablatum manerium ecclesie sue restitueret aut justiciam inde faceret set nihil horum idem Henricus facere voluit. Dehinc iterum atque iterum de hoc requisitus Henricus ab archiepiscopo ut faceret omnino contempsit, more itaque canonico idem non semel set sepius ad justiciam faciendam vocatus nichilominus venire supersedit, unde dictante justicia a domino archiepiscopo excommunicatus est et in eadem excommunicacione per aliquod tempus perduravit donec remordente se propria conscientia de culpa ductus penitencie, venit ad dominum archiepiscopum Theobaldum in festo sancti Magni martiri[4] Cant' ibique in camera archiepiscopi habitis hinc inde multis sermonibus de negotio asseruit tandem sepenominatum manerium ita a se alienatum ut nullo modo posset illud ad opus ecclesie revocare. Rogavit tamen ut sibi liceret loco illius manerii dare terram de sua hereditate liberam que valeret singulis annis annis decem marcis argenti ad ecclesiam Christi, cujus postulacioni dominus archiepiscopus et Walterus prior cum nonnullis monachis qui ibi affuerunt consensit. Quod cum factum est juravit idem Henricus de Ryes super iiiior evangelia quod ad diem sibi constitutam ab archiepiscopo terram illam x marc' monachis ecclesie Christi traderet imperpetuum possidendam. Hiis itaque peractis mox ad ecclesiam perrexit et altare Christi presente archiepiscopo et multis aliis de predicta terra seisivit per quemdam cultellum, ibique accepit pleniter fraternitatem ejusdem ecclesie ab archiepiscopo eo scilicet modo ut si velit circa finem vite sue monachus ibi fiat. Eadem quoque die coram conventu in capitulo renovavit donacionem quam pro anima patris sui et matris sue atque salute anime sue fecerat, pre magna iterum devocione accepta plenaria societate, osculatis pro more omnibus per ordinem monachis letus dimid' [*sic*] discessit. Postea vero tradidit eis manerium de Deepeham[5] quod est in Norf' imperpetuum. Huic devocioni[6] presentes fuerunt: Walterus prior, Wybertus monachus, Hugo celerarus, Felix monachus, Dunstanus monachus, clerici, Walterus archidiaconus Cant', Johannes de Pageham, Rogerus de Ponte Episcopi, Thomas de Lond', Alanus de Welles, Willelmus Cumin et Jordanus Fantasma; laici, Goffridus de Ros, Robertus filius Goffridi, Bernerius dapifer, Willelmus portarius, Rogerus portarius, Willelmus portarius ecclesie, et multis aliis. Hec acta sunt anno ab incarnacione m⁰c. xlvi⁰.

ALSO: MS. ibid., Reg. E f.395a.

VARIATIONS: [1]Mucheberdecham. [2]Goldwynus. [3]*adds* vero; *MS. leaves gap equal to one word.* [4]Martini. [5]Deepham. [6]donacioni.

Both MSS. have corrupt readings in the witness list—Rogerus de Pente Episcopi, Alanus de Pelles, Willelmus et Jordanus Fant' Cumin.

ALSO: in a shorter account MS. ibid. C.A., C 156.

DATE: 1146. (Soon after 19 August.)

C

1. Mandate of Thomas (Becket) chancellor of the king and archdeacon of Canterbury to the burgesses of Dover. They are to pay their tithes due to Dover Priory.

2. Letter of Faramus, castellan of Dover, to Theobald, informing him of the decision of the burgesses of Dover to grant to the monks of Dover Priory the tithe of all their fishing the whole year round, and exemplifying the letter of the burgesses to Theobald announcing this grant. The burgesses are prepared to pay in cash or in kind. The monks are also freed from their obligations in respect of repairing the wall of the borough. In return they have granted the burgesses the right of burial in their cemetery.

3. Writ of Henry II to his men of Dover ordering them to pay their tithes. Witnessed by Theobald at Canterbury.

4. Grant by Henry of Essex, constable of the King to Dover Priory, on the advice of Theobald, of a strip of land in 'King's Furlong', 21 perches by 10, which was inside the precincts of the Priory. Witnessed by Theobald and members of his household.

5. Extracts from the Annals of Dover.

MS. Lambeth 241 (Cartulary of Dover Priory).

1. f.35a.

Monicio sancti Thome tunc cancellari regis et archidiaconi Cantuar' pro decima piscacionis.

THOMAS regis cancellarius et Cant' archidiaconus burgensibus Dovorr' salutem. Mando vobis et consulo ut priori et ecclesie Dovorrensi decimam vestram ita plenarie reddatis sicut in privilegio domini pape et in carta regis et in cirographo vestro continetur. Quod si facere nolueritis justicia regis meo adjutorio et fortasse /[f.35b] non sine vestro dampno faciet fieri. Insuper et ego ecclesie et monachis in justicia ecclesiastica deesse non potero. Valete.

DATE: 1154–62.

2. f.35b.

Litera Pharani castellani de Dovorria exemplificans et testificans donacionem burgencium Dovorr' de decima piscacionis et remissionem reparacionis muragii.

SANCTISSIMO patri dei gracia Cant' archiepiscopo Theobaldo ac tocius Britannie primati et apostolice sedis legato, Pharamus castellanus de Dovor' salutem et obedienciam. Quoniam de ovium vestro regimini commissarum spirituali fructu vos gaudere certissime scio, ut hoc gaudium vestrum crescat in domino annuncio vobis filios vestros scilicet burgenses de Dovorr' omnem omnino et plenam decimam tocius piscacionis sue per annum preter eam quam antiquitus dare solebant de allece a festo sancti Michaelis usque ad festum sancti Andree tam in piscibus quam in denariis de piscibus venditis, scilicet decimum piscem sicut capiuntur vel decimum denarium sicut venduntur, in omni loco deo et sancte Marie et beato Martino dedisse ad victum monachorum Dovorr' degencium et ad hospicium pauperum omnino sicut in presenti suo scripto continetur. Quod quoniam in nostro tempore et in nostra presencia factum est, hanc illorum donacionem et nostram concessionem literarum vestrarum auctoritate petimus premuniri et confirmari. Valete. Sanctissimo patri dei gracia Cant' archiepiscopo T. ac tocius Britannie primati et apostolice sedis legato burgenses de Dovorr' salutem et obedienciam. Notum sit paternitati vestre quod ex quo placuit juste vestre disposicioni ut in ecclesiam sancti Martini que apud nos est monachos introduceretis non modice letati sumus. Unde et bona illorum conversacione animati, statuimus illis imperpetuum dare ad honorem dei et sancte Marie et beati Martini tocius piscacionis nostre plenam decimam per annum preter eam quam antiquitus dare solebamus de allece a festo sancti Michaelis usque ad festum sancti Andree tam in piscibus quam in denariis de piscibus venditis, scilicet decimum piscem sicut capiuntur vel decimum denarium sicut venduntur, ubicumque facta fuerit piscacio, nulli videlicet ante datam vel alicui concessam aut ab aliquo calumpniatam libere et in liberam ac perpetuam elemosinam in usum illorum et ad hospitalitem tenendam. Ita quidem quod si presentes fuerint monachi vel monachorum legati in omni loco quod magis placuerit illis pisces aut denarios sine omni contradiccione libenter dabimus. Si vero non affuerint nos ipsi eos reportabimus. Et ut modum hujus nostre oblacionis agnoscatis primum, in hundredo simul congregati una cum devocione et auctoritate cum graciarum accione manibus singulorum super textum euuangeliorum positis deo eam obtulimus, statimque eadem die seniores nostros ad monasterium sancti Martini ut hoc idem facerent et saisinam super altare ponerent communi assensu misimus, et ne unquam ab aliquo hujus donacionis fieret ablacio vel diminucio quod libere et in liberam ac perpetuam elemosinam data est, seniorum nostrorum juramento confirmavimus, promittentes quod siquis eos super hac re inquietare voluerit, omni tempore ad hanc donacionem diraciocinandam et contra omnes defen-/[f.36a]dendam monachis presto erimus. Adjudicavimus eciam quod si quis ex nobis aliquid de hac decima defraudaverit excommunicetur et a nostro consorcio separetur.

In cujus beneficii recompensacione idem monachi concesserunt nobis et nostris antecessoribus atque successoribus plenam beneficiorum suorum participacionem in missis scilicet in oracionibus et elemosinis et pro voto petencium in obitu liberam in suum cimiterium suscepcionem. Sciat eciam universitas fidelium quod quicquid prior et monachi de opere muri vel claustura ville nobis petentibus faciendum promiserunt, ad votum nostrum bene compleverunt ita quod quicquid inde amplius evenerit nichil ab eis ultra repetemus vel queremus set imperpetuum quietos dimittemus. Et quoniam beneficia ecclesiis collata tunc rata sunt apud homines et apud deum accepta, si cum benediccione prelatorum fiant et auctoritate firmentur petimus nostre elemosine donacionem literarum vestrarum auctoritate premuniri et confirmari. Valete.

DATE: 1150–57. Cf. No. 88.

3. f.36a.

> Carta regis Henrici precipiens Dovorensibus ut solvant novam decimam piscacionis super forisfacturam.

HENRICUS rex Anglie et dux Normann' et Aquitan' et comes Andeg' omnibus hominibus suis de Dovorr' Francis et Anglis salutem. Precipio vobis quod reddatis monachis sancti Martini de Dovorr' decimam novam piscium ita bene et plenarie et juste sicut eam ecclesie beati Martini dedistis et concessistis et sicut dandam eam juravistis et super ipsum altare eam optulistis. Et super hoc nullus vestrum eam injuste retineat super forisfacturam meam. Test' T. archiepiscopo Cant' apud Cantuar'.

DATE: 1156–63.

4. f.58b.

> Carta Henrici de Essexia de omni terra sua in Kyngesforlang libere et sine firma vel redditu.

HENRICUS de Essexia constabularius regis Angl' omnibus episcopis ceterisque sancte dei ecclesie ministris per Angliam constitutis salutem. Notum facio tam presentibus quam post futuris fidelibus me concessisse et in puram elemosinam donasse deo et monachis sancti Martini de Dovorr' quicquid de terra mea de

Kyngesforlang muri ambitu curie eorumdem monachorum continetur, videlicet perticas in longitudine xxi in latitudine x, in remissione peccatorum meorum et pro animabus antecessorum meorum patris et matris mee et domine Adeline matertere mee et omnium propinquorum meorum. Test' domino Cant' archiepiscopo Theobaldo cujus sancta ammonicione et doctrina has et alias elemosinas facere instituimus; test' quoque Walterio Rofensi episcopo, Hugone priore de Dovorr', Rogerio Cant' archidiacono; monachis, Herveo tunc archiepiscopi capellano, Ricardo de Bex, Simone de Dovorr'; clericis, Thoma de Londonia, Johanne filio Marie, Rogerio Specie; militibus, Radulfo Picot tunc vicecomite, Simone de Cruil, Stephano de Polton', Mauricio de Essexia, Reginaldo de O[springe?], Hugone Corbeile, Ricardo de Dovorr' et Elnoth et aliis.

DATE: 1149–54. Becket became archdeacon of Canterbury in 1154.

5. Extracts from the Annals of Dover (MS. B.M. Cott. Jul. D v).

f.23b.

1140

MONACHI introducti sunt in ecclesiam Dovor' a Theobaldo archiepiscopo. Anselmus factus est prior Dovor' primus.

1143

ANSELMUS prior Dovor' factus est episcopus Rofen'. Successit in prioratum Willelmus prior secundus.

f.24a.

1149

INTERDICTUM tocius Anglie. Hugo de Cadomo factus est prior Dovor' tercius. [Later hand] Iste fuit monachus Dovor' de proprio conventu quem Theobaldus prefecit in priorem Dovor' tempore dissensionis inter ipsum et monachos Cant'.

1157

RICARDUS capellanus archiepiscopi Theobaldi factus est prior Dovor' quartus.

1160

ECCLESIA beati Martini Dovor' dedicatur per Ricardum priorem a duobus episcopis.

D

Writ of Henry II to Theobald and the clergy subject to him, inhibiting appeals to Rome during the schism of 1159.

MS. Bodleian Rawlinson Q. f.8 f.11a (Becket correspondence etc.).

HENRICUS rex Anglorum et dux Normannorum et comes Andegavorum Theobaldo Cantuariensi archiepiscopo episcopis abbatibus et toti clero sibi subjecto salutem. Sicut ad vestram potest pervenisse noticiam cardi-/[f.11b]nales sancte Romane ecclesie post obitum Adriani pape felicis memorie inter se divisi duos, Roll' scilicet cancellarium et Octovianum, in summum pontificem elegerunt. Et quia similis scissura fidei contraria tempore avi mei H[enrici] regis in apostolica sede accidisse dinoscitur, et ipse sicut catholicus princeps et sapiens neutri electo sine sano et salubri consilio assensum prebere festinavit, mando vobis et precipio quatinus nautri [sic] de supradictis electis assentiatis vel obediatis neque occasione hujus negotii sive appellacionis Angliam exeatis, donec ex maturo sicut decet consilio, divina disponente gratia, quid mihi et vobis super hac re agendum sit certius intelligamus et vobis notificemus. Erit igitur discretionis vestre et studium ita jurisdictionem vestram moderare in justicia omnibus exhibenda sive conservanda ut nullus de vobis juste conqueri debeat neque detrimentum paciatur, ex hoc quod sibi non liceat ad sedem apostolicam appellare. T. Phillippo [sic] Bajocensi et Rotroco Ebroicensi episcopis apud Phalesiam.

DATE: probably Christmas 1159.
PRINTED: A. Saltman, *Bulletin of the Institute of Historical Research*, 1949, p. 154.
COPY: MS. Bodleian Bodley 278 f.110a (Baker's transcript of above MS.).

E

Charter of Bishop Everard of Norwich (1121–45) with a subscription by Theobald.

MS. D. and C. Norwich Reg. 5 f.7 (not consulted).

CHARTER of bishop Everard of Norwich making provision for the building and maintenance of the Cathedral. 'Done in the chapter of the Holy Trinity before me and the whole convent in the presence of the archdeacon of our church William (I), the other William (II) and Roger and of many others.'

'I, Theobald archbishop of Canterbury, primate of all England subscribed and with apostolic authority I denounce etc.'

DATE: 1139–45.

PRINTED: L. Landon *Proceedings of the Suffolk Institute of Archaeology and Natural History*, 1930, p. 18.

The archbishop is not mentioned as being present at the chapter and his sanction must have been obtained later.

F

Grant by William of St. Clare to Colchester Abbey, in the presence of Theobald and witnessed by members of the archbishop's household.

MS. Cartulary of Colchester, Earl Cowper (folio not given) (not consulted).

WILLELMUS de Sancto Claro omnibus qui audierint aut viderint has litteras salutem. Sciatis me concessisse ac donasse monasterio sancti Johannis de Colecestria in perhennem et liberam elemosinam totam meam tenuram de Grenestede ut monachi teneant eam ita bene et ita libere sicut ego melius et liberius concedere potui et ita plene in terra et in aqua et silvis et pratis et pascuis et omnibus rebus sicut ego eam umquam plenius tenui vel ante me dominus meus Eudo dapifer; et hoc feci pro salute anime mee et fratrum meorum qui jacent ad illud monasterium et pro salute fratris mei Hamonis de Sancto Claro ac filii sui Huberti, quorum consensu feci hanc elemosinam et pro salute omnium ad nos pertinentium. Hanc elemosinam posui super altare sancti Johannes baptiste in presentia dompni Teobaldi archiepiscopi Cantuariensis. Testes hujus elemosine sunt Robertus episcopus Lundoniensis; Rogerus, Thomas et

Johannes et Ricardus Castel clerici archiepiscopi. Feci autem hoc de Grenestede cum consilio Hamonis fratris mei quia monachi Colecestrie saisiti fuerant inde antea per donationem Eudonis dapiferi, sed postea et contra eandem donationem et contra regis Henrici confirmationem dissaisiti fuerant per ministros Eudonis et regis, quam ministrorum culpam placuit nobis emendare pro salute animarum nostrarum tradendo ecclesie quod antea possederat.

DATE: 1143–48.

PRINTED: *Roxburgh Club* (1897), ed. S. A. Moore, i, 155.

A grant on the previous page has the following witnesses of Theobald's household in addition: 'Gillebertus et Walterus monachi archiepiscopi'.

G

Account of relations between Theobald, Ralph prior of Holy Trinity, Aldgate, and the royal family.

MS. London Guildhall Library 122 (Transcript of Cartulary of Holy Trinity).

/[p.19] (Radulfus prior) qui curam confessionum dicte regine Matildis ab archiepiscopo Theobaldo suscepit . . . . /[p.20] vocatus specialiter ab ea triduo ante suum obitum quia pater extitit suarum confessionum ex licencia et commissione Theobaldi archiepiscopi . . . . Archiepiscopus vero /[p.21] Theobaldus eundem priorem Radulfum magno honore favoreque non modico proveniebat et huic ecclesie de suis largens, numquam gravaminis aliquid intulit, aut abstulit quicquam quod noceret: qui anno incarnacionis dominice m⁰c⁰lv⁰ filium regis Henrici de regina Alienora natum in ista ecclesia baptizavit qui nominabatur Henricus, ac anno sequenti ejusdem regis filiam natam de dicta regina idem pontifex hic eciam baptizavit que Matildis vocabatur.

H

1. Letter of Simon bishop of Worcester (1125–50) to Theobald, begging him to see that the church of St. Mary, Strand, London, is

restored to Worcester Cathedral Priory. Simon had wrongfully granted it away.

MS. D. and C. Worcester Reg. f.10b (not consulted).

DOMINO et patri suo karissimo T. dei gratia Cantuariensi archiepiscopo et totius Anglie primati Symon Wigornensis dictus episcopus subjectionem. In extremo vite mee positus revocavi ad memoriam erratum meum, in quo multum excessi erga Wigornensem ecclesiam de ecclesia sancte Marie de Strande apud London' quam temere mea culpa dedi Hugoni fratri Bertranni clerici; de excessu illo cum essem in presentia dompni Herefordensis episcopi inter alios excessus meos confessus sum, assidente et audiente priore meo et archidiacono Godefrido et magistro Bernardo Gloec' monacho, et Osberto capellano meo. Quare humillime supplico sancte paternitati vestre quatinus pro amore dei et alleviatione anime mee sitis in auxilium, ut prefata ecclesia in possessionem sancte Wigornensis ecclesie reducatur. Vale pater sancte et domine.

DATE: *c.* 1149.
PRINTED: Wm. Thomas, *Account of the bishops of Worcester* (1725), Appendix, p. 11.

2. Confirmation by Simon bishop of Worcester to his Cathedral Priory, done in the presence of Theobald and witnessed by members of the archbishop's household.

MS. ibid.

(End of general confirmation of Simon bishop of Worcester to the Cathedral Priory.)

FACTA est ista nostra confirmatio coram domino Tedbaldo Cantuarie archiepiscopo in capitulo Wigornensi et coram hiis testibus: Gilberto Herefordensi episcopo, Rogero archidiacono Cantuarie, Godefrido et Gervasio archidiaconis, Laurentio priore Coventrensi, Gilberto priore de Estlee; Thoma, Radulfo filio Randulfi Dunhalmensis episcopi, et Rogero Specie, Petro scriptore, clericis domini archiepiscopi etc. (Dated 26 Jan. 1149).

PRINTED: ibid., p. 10.

I

Canons of Theobald's Legatine Council of 1151.

MS. Paris Bibliothèque Nationale Latin 6042 f.121a (Henry of Huntingdon).

> [1]Anno dominice incarnationis m°c°l°i°, papatus domini Eugenii iii incipiente vii°, Anglorum rege Stephano regnante anno xvi°, presidente Tebbaldo Cantuariensi archiepiscopo totius Britannie primate et sedis apostolice legato anno xiii°, celebratum est Londonie concilium mense Martio in quo statuta hec fuerunt que subter annexa sunt. [1]

MULTORUM experimenta morborum novas nos cogunt medicinas querere, ut tribulationibus que invenerunt nos nimis possimus remediis salubribus obviare. Sancimus igitur ut ecclesie et possessiones[2] ecclesiastice ab operationibus et exactionibus quas vulgo tenserias sive tallagias[3] vocant omnino libere permaneant, nec super his eas aliqui de cetero inquietare presumant. Qui vero contra hoc decretum venire tentaverint[4], divino in terris eorum cessante officio, tandem, donec condigne satisfaciant, anathematis sententia percellantur. Sane operationes regi debitas fieri non prohibemus, regio tamen precedente mandato.

Cap. ii.[5] Quia vero ecclesie per Angliam constitute occasione placitorum corone regis pertinentium attenuantur [6]supra modum[6] et destruuntur, nolumus eas sicut hactenus[7] super eisdem placitis baronibus respondere. Ideoque precipimus quatinus[8] hujus nostre institutionis transgressoribus et terris eorum, episcopi in quorum parrochiis fuerint justiciam satagant ecclesiasticam exercere. Qua in re si episcopi neglegentes extiterint, ab eisdem damna[9] ecclesiis[10] [illata] requirantur.

Cap. iii.[5] Preterea statuimus ut qui pro invasione seu pro[11] rapina rei ecclesiastice anathematis vinculo innodantur, absolvi nullatenus mereantur donec ablata integre restituant, vel ecclesie que damnum[12] passa est sufficienter caveant quod universum debitum infra tempus quadrimenstre persolvant. Verumtamen si de rebus mobilibus eorum qui dampna inferunt eadem resarciri non poterunt[13], supportandos[14] eos esse putamus, ut fidejussoriam prestantes cautionem, vel ea deficiente ¡uratoriam, ad annue prestationis solutionem secundum suas facultates episcopi taxatione teneantur. Si quis autem eos aliter absolvere presumpserit, eadem damna[15] resarcire compellatur.

Cap. iiii.[5] Illud quoque adicientes decernimus, ne liceat de cetero alicui ecclesiastice persone post invasoris seu raptoris excommunicationem de damno[16] ecclesie illato ultra vicesimam partem debiti aliquid remittere. Qui vero remiserit, si episcopus est, per sex menses, si alia ecclesiastica persona, per annum integrum [17]ab officio[17] suspendatur.

Cap. v.[5] Sanctorum patrum vestigia secuti precipimus ut hi[18] qui anathematis sententia condemnantur[19], si per annum integrum in ea pertinaciter perseverent [20]infames et destabiles[20] habeantur, ut neque in testimoniis neque in causis audiantur, et in principis sit potestate ipsos exheredare.

Cap. vi.[5] Prava nimis et[21] statutis canonum[22] contraria inolevit consuetudo ut in ecclesiis Anglie clerici passim et sine delectu recipiantur. Quod ne de cetero fiat modis omnibus prohibemus.

Cap. vii.[5] Nichilominus etiam[23] presentis scripti auctoritate statuendum esse censemus ut quotiens sacerdotibus innotuerit predam sive rapinam rerum ecclesiasticarum ad loca in quibus degunt devenisse, divina[24] ibidem officia celebrare non presumant donec episcopi vel archidiaconi super hoc mandatum suscipiant, vel ipsa rapina restituatur. Cessantibus autem matricibus ecclesiis capelle que intra munitiones[25] constructe sunt, non expectata cessandi jussione ab administratione[26] divinorum cessent. Sacerdotes vero qui hujus sanctionis contemptores extiterint per annum integrum officio proprio careant. Quod si sepius in hac re neglegentes[27] reperti fuerint, pro arbitrio episcopi sui majori severitati[28] subiciantur.

Cap. viii.[5] Hoc quoque presentis sanctionis pagina firmandum esse credimus[29], [30]ne quis[30] in civitate vel portu neque in vico neque in castro neque omnino alicubi locorum nova vectigalia que vulgo pedagia[31] dicuntur, instituere vel institutionibus[32] consentire audeat. Hujus autem statuti[33] temeratores, quia rem exemplo perniciosam inducunt, anathemati subiciendos non dubitamus.

ALSO: MS. B.M. Royal 10 C iv f.145a (Gratian, etc.).

VARIATIONS: [1-1] *omits.* [2]f.145b. [3]taillagias. [4]temptaverint. [5]*omits.* [6-6]*omits.* [7]actenus. [8]*adds* de. [9]dampna. [10](MS.) ecclesie. [11]*omits.* [12]dampnum. [13]poterint. [14]subportandos. [15]*omits.* [16]dampno. [17-17]*omits.* [18]hii. [19]condampnantur. [20-20]detestabiles et infames. [21]*adds* sanctorum patrum. [22]*omits.* [23]et. [24](MS.) diurna. [25]*adds* earum. [26]amministracione. [27]negligentes. [28]*omits.* [29]credidimus. [30-30]nequis. [31]padagia. [32]instituentibus. [33]instituti.

PRINTED: *Mansi*, xxi, col. 750.

The recension of Huntingdon's chronicle ends with the entry for the year 1147. The MS. then continues with the above text.

J

Two unprinted professions of obedience to Theobald.

MS. B.M. Cott. Cleopatra E i f.35b (Ecclesiastical Collections).

Professio Alexandri prioris de Lhedes.

EGO frater Alexander prior de Lhedes promitto obedientiam domino Theob' archiepiscopo ecclesie Christi Cantuarie et successoribus ejus juxta canonicam institutionem.

Professio Lamberti abbatis de Boxeleia.

EGO Lambertus ecclesie de Boxeleia electus abbas, profiteor sancte Dorobernensi ecclesie ejusque vicariis canonicam subjectionem.

ALSO: MS. D. and C. Canterbury Reg. A f.328a.

Manuscripts

ABERYSTWYTH: *National Library of Wales*
Shrewsbury Cartulary.
Penrice Charter 387 Newcastle (Glam.).

BELVOIR CASTLE (Duke of Rutland)
Belvoir Cartulary.

BRISTOL LIBRARY
Charter 173.

CAMBRIDGE
Corpus Christi College
MS. 111 Bath Cartulary
438 Gervase.
Emmanuel College
MS. 38 Pershore.
Jesus College
MS. A.5. St. Radegund's.
Trinity College
MS. o.2.1. Lib. Eliensis.
University Library
MS. Ee.v.31 Canterbury Register.
Ff.ii.33 Bury St. Edmund's
Ll.i.10 Cerne
Ll.ii.15 Canterbury St. Gregory's
Mm.iv.19 Bury St. Edmund's
Additional 3020 Thorney.

CANTERBURY: *Chapter Library*
Cartae Antiquae

A 3, 4	D 72, 83, 95, 98, 99
C 15, 71, 156, 163, 196, 204, 218, 579a, 1099, 1109, 1258, 1292	E 167
	F 81, 87
	H 88, 122, 123

L 71   S 315
M 223   W 49, 50a, 50b, 224.
R 1, 2, 50, 53
Registers A, B, C, D, E, H, I, O.
Fragment of St. Gregory's.

CHELMSFORD: *Essex County Record Office*
  MS. D/D Pr 149 Earl's Colne
    D/D By Q/19 Eye.

CHICHESTER
  Bishop of Chichester
    Liber Y.

  Dean and Chapter
    Liber B.

COLCHESTER: *Town Clerk*
  Colchester Cartulary.

ELY
  Cathedral Library
    Liber Eliensis.

  Diocesan Registry
    Cartae Antiquae 82, 83, 84.

EXETER: *Dean and Chapter*
  MS. 2074 Charter.

GLASGOW: *University Library*
  Cartulary of Holy Trinity, Aldgate.

GLOUCESTER: *Cathedral Library*
  Register A.

LEEDS: *Yorks. Archaeological Society*
  Cartulary of Pontefract.

LONDON
  British Museum
    Cotton MSS.
      Julius   D.ii. Canterbury St. Augustine's
                   D.iii. St. Albans
                   D.v. Dover
      Tiberius   A.vi Ely

Caligula   A.xii Pipewell
Claudius   D.x Canterbury St. Augustine's
              D.xiii Binham
Nero   C.iii Various
              D.iii York St. Leonard's
              E.vi Templars
              E.vii Walsingham
Galba   E.ii Holme
              E.iv Canterbury
Otho   D.iii St. Albans
Vitellius   E.xv Oseney
              F.iv Oseney
Vespasian   E.xvii Northampton
              E.xviii Kirkstead
              E.xx Bardney
              E.xxv Reading
              F.xiii Letters
Titus   A.i Ely
Domitian   A.iii Reading
              A.viii Gloucester
              A.x Rochester
Cleopatra   E.i Canterbury
Faustina   A.iv St. Neot's
              B.v Rochester
Appendix   xxi Stoke-by-Clare.

Cotton Charters and Rolls
    ii.19 Norwich   xiii.6 Stone
    iv.57 Holme   xvi.38 Gloucester
    xi.4 Owston   xvii.3 Gloucester.

Harleian MSS.
    231   Bermondsey   3601 Barnwell
    1708 Reading   3650 Kenilworth
    1885 Dunstable   3697 Walden
    1965 Chester   3868 Lichfield
    2060 Chester   7048 Baker Coll.
    2071 Chester

Harleian Charters
    43.G.19 Newhouse   43.G.22 Eye
    43.G.20 Greenfield   83.C.26 Clerkenwell
    43.G.21 Greenfield   84.C.41 Bittlesden.

Egerton MSS.
  3031 Reading
  3047 Ely.

Lansdowne MSS. 448 Holy Trinity, Aldgate.

Royal MSS.
  6.C.vii Worcester
  10.C.iv Gratian
  11.B.ix Northampton.

Campbell Charters xvi.1 Westminster.

Additional and Sloane MSS.

4526 Madox	15314 Southampton
5706 Sussex Colls.	30311 Shrewsbury
5819 Ely (Cole)	33182 S. Malling
5844 Spalding (Cole)	33354 Haughmond
5860 Earl's Colne (Cole)	35296 Spalding
6159 Canterbury	38683 Cotton Library
6714 Tutbury	46487 Sherborne.
8177 Eye	47784 Coxford
9822 Ely	

Additional Charters

19589 Reading	44694 Southwark
34014 Ramsey	47390 Nuneaton.
34174 Ramsey	

Deposited MSS.
  Burton Cartulary
  Southwick Cartularies (1 and 3).
  Kenilworth, Holkham Hall.

College of Arms: MS. Arundel 59 Tutbury.

Guildhall Library: MS. 122 Holy Trinity Aldgate.

Lambeth Palace
  MS. 241 Dover
  MS. 1212 Canterbury
  Islip's Register.

Lincoln's Inn: MS. Hale 87 Battle.

St. Paul's Cathedral: Liber A.

Public Record Office
  Chancery
    Cartulary of Gloucester
    Charter Rolls 16 Henry III m.12 Harrow
                  11 Edw. III m.30 Wintney
                  21 Edw. III m.11 Malling.

  Chancery Masters' Exhibits: Lanthony Cartularies (1 and 4).

  Duchy of Lancaster: Ancient Deeds LS 48 Walworth.

  Exchequer

    K.R. Ecclesiastical Documents 15/4 Battle
          Miscellaneous Books i.16 Templars
                               i.22 Warwick
                               i.27 Canterbury St. Augustine's
                               i.28 Ramsey.
    O.A. Ancient Deeds B 11086
                 Madox 84
          Miscellaneous Books 31 no. 45
                           i 61 Pershore.
    T.R. Ancient Deeds A 5002, 6684, 11970, 13848, 13850,
                  14042, 14107, 14200, 14236, 15417,
                  15418, 15775
          A.S. 356.

  Transcripts II (French Houses) 140a, 140b/2, 140b/3, 144.

Westminster Abbey Muniments
  Domesday
  33, 51
  997
  8040
  13167 Roll of St. Martin's-le-Grand
  Cartulary of St. Martin's-le-Grand.

MAIDSTONE: *Kent County Archives Office*
  Fragment of Leeds Cartulary. (U/120, Q/13.)

NORWICH: *Diocesan Registry*
  Registers 1, 2, 5, 7, 8.

OXFORD
  Bodleian Library
    MSS.
      Dodsworth 76 Alcester

E Mus 249 Gilbert Foliot
Norfolk Rolls 81, 82. Holme
Oxon Charters a.8 Littlemore
Rawlinson B 333 Ramsey
         B 335 Dover, St. Bartholomew's
         Q. f.8. Becket correspondence.
Tanner 223 Canterbury
Top. Kent c.2. Eastbridge Hospital
Top. Lincs. D.i. Cotham
Wood empt. 10 Sandford.
Deposited MSS.
    Christ Church Oseney Charters 897, 897a, 902, 902a
    Corpus Christi College MS. 160 St. Frideswide's
    Jesus College MSS. 75, 76.

Christ Church
    Eynsham Cartulary
    Oseney Cartulary
    St. Frideswide's Cartulary.

Magdalen College: Sele Cartulary.

New College: Hornchurch Charters 530, 531.

PARIS: *Bibliothèque Nationale*
  MS. Latin 6042 Henry of Huntington
            2342 Bec
          12884 Bec
          13905 Bec.

PETERBOROUGH: *Dean and Chapter*
  Swaffham Register.

ROCHESTER
Cathedral Library
  Textus Roffensis.

Diocesan Registry
  Registers Temporalium
          Hamo de Hethe
          Fisher.

ROUEN: *Departmental Archives*
  Originals of P.R.O. Transcripts.

ST. OMER: *Archives*
  Originals of P.R.O. Transcripts.

SALISBURY
Cathedral Library
   Charter in Box C 3.

Diocesan Registry
   Registers B, C, Rubrum, St. Osmund's.

SHREWSBURY: *Public Library*
   Cartulary of Haughmond.

WELLS: *Dean and Chapter*
   Liber Albus i, ii.

WINCHESTER: *Winchester College Library*
   Charter in Andwell drawer no. 2.

WINDSOR: *St. George's Chapel*
   MSS. xv.24.35. Leeds
         xi.G.2 S. Malling
         xi.G.29 S. Malling
         xi.G.55 S. Malling.

WOBURN ABBEY (Duke of Bedford)
   'Russell' Cartulary Tavistock.

WORCESTER
Bishop
   Giffard's Register.

Dean and Chapter
   Liber Albus
   Register i
   Liber Pensionum.

YORK: *Dean and Chapter*
   Cartulary of St. Mary's, York.

Index

P